Honeyball & Bowers'

Textbook on

Employment Law

···

Eleventh edition

Simon Honeyball, LLB, PhD,
FRSA, FHEA, ARCM, Barrister

OXFORD
UNIVERSITY PRESS

OXFORD
UNIVERSITY PRESS

Great Clarendon Street, Oxford OX2 6DP

Oxford University Press is a department of the University of Oxford.
It furthers the University's objective of excellence in research, scholarship,
and education by publishing worldwide in

Oxford New York

Auckland Cape Town Dar es Salaam Hong Kong Karachi
Kuala Lumpur Madrid Melbourne Mexico City Nairobi
New Delhi Shanghai Taipei Toronto

With offices in

Argentina Austria Brazil Chile Czech Republic France Greece
Guatemala Hungary Italy Japan Poland Portugal Singapore
South Korea Switzerland Thailand Turkey Ukraine Vietnam

Oxford is a registered trade mark of Oxford University Press
in the UK and in certain other countries

Published in the United States
by Oxford University Press Inc., New York

First published by Blackstone Press 1990

Crown Copyright material reproduced with the permission of the Controller,
HMSO (under the terms of the Click Use licence)

Database right Oxford University Press (maker)

First published 1990	Sixth edition 2000
Second edition 1992	Seventh edition 2002
Third edition 1993	Eighth edition 2004
Fourth edition 1996	Ninth edition 2006
Fifth edition 1998	Tenth edition 2008
	Eleventh edition 2010

British Library Cataloguing in Publication Data

Data Available

Library of Congress Cataloging in Publication Data

Honeyball, Simon.
Honeyball & Bowers' textbook on employment law / Simon Honeyball. – 11th ed.
p. cm.
Includes bibliographical references and index.
ISBN 978–0–19–958215–0 (pbk.)
1. Labor laws and legislation–Great Britain. I. Title. II. Title: Honeyball and Bowers'
textbook on employment law. III. Title: Textbook on employment law.
KD3009.B68 2010
344.4101–dc22   2010018304

Typeset by Newgen Imaging Systems (P) Ltd, Chennai, India
Printed in Great Britain
on acid-free paper by
Ashford Colour Press Ltd, Gosport, Hampshire

ISBN 978–0–19–958215–0

1 3 5 7 9 10 8 6 4 2

To the memories of Lewis Bolton (1919–1990)
And Josephine Honeyball (1942–1988)

OUTLINE CONTENTS

DETAILED CONTENTS

1 History and institutions of employment law   1

2 The concept of employment   21

7 Statutory employment protection on dismissal 122

8 Unfair dismissal 148

9 Statutory redundancy payments and consultation procedures 202

10 Discrimination

231

11 Equal pay and family rights

276

12 Statutory rights regulating the employment relationship 305

13 Trade unions 329

14 Collective bargaining 371

15 Industrial action 395

16 Human rights in employment   444

PREFACE

It seems just a short while ago that, as young men, the brilliant up-and-coming barrister called John Bowers and I teamed up to write a textbook on employment law. Now John is a long-standing QC and judge, rightly rated as one of the leading intellects in the field. I too have now grown some grey hairs. This befits, of course, the author of a book which, somehow, has reached its eleventh edition. I can only wonder at the image students hold of the author of their textbook that has such an obviously long history. Several editions ago John decided that he did not have the time to continue to co-author the book, but it still contains enough of his material to more than justify his name continuing to appear, if not in the bye-line, in the title. It is still a work which, in this sense, is both mine and his.

Certainly we could not have envisaged in 1990 that it would be possible to have an 'online resource centre' to accompany the book. When this edition appears there is every likelihood (but at the time of writing no certainty) that discrimination law will be in an entirely different form. Fortunately the ORC will come to the aid of all of us, to ensure that a completely up-to-date account of the law in that area is available to the readers of this book. There can be no better illustration of the topicality of employment law, and the speed with which it can change. This is what makes it such a challenging, but also exciting, subject to study.

I would like to express my gratitude to several people for the support I have received in preparing this edition. First, to my wife and daughter, Helen and Rachel, for allowing me the time to be shut away in my study to do this, although I suspect that they may have looked forward to the opportunities it presented to them. Also, to the students on my Employment Law module at Exeter, who somehow always seem to be the nicest bunch of the year. Finally, to the editorial team at OUP and elsewhere, whose attention to detail is a wonder to behold.

I have attempted to state the law as it appeared to me on New Year's Day 2010.

Simon Honeyball
University of Exeter

TABLE OF CASES

TABLE OF STATUTES

TABLE OF STATUTORY INSTRUMENTS

LIST OF ABBREVIATIONS

AC	Appeal Cases
ACAS	Advisory, Conciliation and Arbitration Service
ACTT	Association of Cinematograph Television and Allied Technicians
All ER	All England Law Reports
AML	additional maternity leave
AUEW	Amalgamated Union of Engineering Workers
BIS	Department for Business, Innovation and Skills
BLJ	Bracton Law Journal
CA	Court of Appeal
CAC	Central Arbitration Committee
CEHR	Commission for Equality and Human Rights
Ch	Chancery
ChD	Chancery Division
CLJ	Cambridge Law Journal
CLP	Current Legal Problems
CML	compulsory maternity leave
CMLR	Common Market Law Reports
CO	Certification Officer
CRE	Commission for Racial Equality
DC	Divisional Court of Queen's Bench Division
DDA 1995	Disability Discrimination Act 1995
DRA	default retirement age
EA 2002	Employment Act 2002
EAT	Employment Appeal Tribunal
ECJ	European Court of Justice
EEC	European Economic Community
EHRR	European Human Rights Reports
ELR	European Law Review
EOC	Equal Opportunities Commission
EPA 1975	Employment Protection Act 1975
EPCA 1978	Employment Protection (Consolidation) Act 1978
ERA 1996	Employment Rights Act 1996
ET	Employment Tribunal
EWC	expected week of childbirth
GCHQ	Government Communications Headquarters
HC	High Court
HMSO	Her Majesty's Stationery Office
HRA 1998	Human Rights Act 1998
ICA	Information and Consultation Agreement
ICR	Industrial Cases Reports
ILEA	Inner London Education Authority
ILJ	Industrial Law Journal
ILO	International Labour Organisation
IRC	Independent Review Committee of TUC

IRLR	Industrial Relations Law Reports
ITR	Industrial Tribunal Reports
KB	King's Bench
KIR	Knight's Industrial Reports
KLR	Kingston Law Review
LQR	Law Quarterly Review
LTR	Law Times Reports
LSG	Law Society Gazette
MLR	Modern Law Review
NALGO	National Association of Local Government Officers
NATSOPA	National Society of Operative Printers, Graphical and Media Personnel
NCB	National Coal Board
NEC	National Executive Council
NIRC	National Industrial Relations Court
NLJ	New Law Journal
NUJ	National Union of Journalists
NUM	National Union of Mineworkers
NUS	National Union of Seamen
NUT	National Union of Teachers
OJLS	Oxford Journal of Legal Studies
OML	ordinary maternity leave
QB	Queen's Bench
QBD	Queen's Bench Division
RPC	Restrictive Practices Court
RRA 1976	Race Relations Act 1976
SDA 1975	Sex Discrimination Act 1975
SJ	Solicitors Journal
SNB	Special Negotiating Body
SPC	service provision change
TASS	Technical, Administrative and Supervisory Staffs
TFEU	Treaty on the Functioning of the European Union
TGWU	Transport and General Workers Union
TINALEA	this is not a legally enforceable agreement
TLR	Times Law Reports
TUC	Trades Union Congress
TULRA 1974	Trade Union and Labour Relations Act 1974
TULR(C)A 1992	Trade Union and Labour Relations (Consolidation) Act 1992
TURERA 1993	Trade Union Reform and Employment Rights Act 1993
TUPE	Transfer of Undertakings (Protection of Employment) Regulations 2006
UCTA 1977	Unfair Contract Terms Act 1977
WebJCLI	Web Journal of Current Legal Issues
WLR	Weekly Law Reports
WU	Waterman's Union

1

History and institutions of
employment law

SUMMARY

This chapter traces the history of employment law from its origins in the 14th century until the present day. Most of the early part of that period is fallow in terms of law, but from the early 19th century until now the picture is painted of an ever-increasing speed of change and innovation giving more and more legal protection to workers.

This chapter also looks at modern institutions of employment law, particularly the important tribunal system of employment tribunals (ETs) and the Employment Appeal Tribunal (EAT). In addition other important bodies are briefly considered, namely the Commission for Equality and Human Rights (CEHR), the Advisory, Conciliation and Arbitration Service (ACAS) and the Central Arbitration Committee (CAC).

1.1 History

1.1.1 Early legislation

The first recognisable labour legislation, the Ordinance of Labourers, was passed in 1349 following the Black Death which caused labour to be in great demand. It maintained wages at rates to be fixed from time to time by justices of the peace. To support that this ordinance, and later the Statute of Artificers 1562, prohibited conspiracies to raise wages. Prosecutions for criminal conspiracy at common law also became more frequent as the first workers' associations were formed. These normally grew out of workmates meeting at public houses. Their main activity was the provision of friendly society benefits such as sick and funeral money and a tramping grant to unemployed workers willing to move. They also sought to limit the number of apprentices entering their trades because of the inevitable consequence of depressing wage rates. This has remained a feature of some craft unions to this day.

1.1.2 Combination Acts

The next recognisable labour legislation occurred much later. The dominant laissez-faire economics of the 18th and early 19th centuries saw interference in wage levels (whether by Government or groups of workers) as anathema. Accordingly Parliament supplemented the common law by banning groupings of workers in particular industries (e.g. wool, silk, and leather). The Combination Act 1799 made this into a general ban. This was an immediate reaction to a widespread strike by millwrights, but passed against the background of fear of radicalism as embodied in the French Revolution. It was, however, soon amended by the 1800 statute known by the same name. This enacted two further specific offences, one of entering into contracts for the purposes of improving conditions of employment or calling or attending a meeting for such a purpose, and another of attempting to persuade another person not to work or to refuse to work with another worker. Jurisdiction was given to justices of the peace, who could pass sentence of up to three months' imprisonment. The similar prohibition on masters combining was enforced with much less enthusiasm.

1.1.3 Master and Servant Act 1823

The Master and Servant Act 1823 was another powerful weapon in the hands of the employers, since thereby an employee who was absent from service before his contract expired was punishable by up to three months' hard labour. There were some 10,000 prosecutions per year between 1858 and 1875 under this provision. (See A. H. Manchester, *Modern English Legal History* (London: Butterworths, 1980), p. 328.)

1.1.4 Repeal of the combination laws and reinstatement

A campaign masterminded by such articulate exponents of the unions' liberties as Francis Place and Joseph Hume led to the Combination Laws Repeal Act 1824. This removed 35 prohibitions on combinations in various sectors of the economy, and repealed most of the 1800 Act. Moreover, union combination ceased to be *per se* criminal at common law. The immediate aftermath was a series of violent and damaging strikes. This caused Parliament to think again the next year and the Combination Act 1825 revived the common law offence, save where the only object of the union collectivity was the determination of wages and hours. It also strengthened the law on the specific crimes of intimidation, violence, molestation and obstruction, which the courts soon applied to persuading a fellow worker to join a strike (*R v Rowlands* (1851)) and inducing a worker to leave in breach of contract (*R v Druitt* (1867)). The former decision was, however, modified by ss 4 and 5 of the Combination of Workmen Act 1859 which rendered it lawful to attempt, with the aim of securing changes in wages or hours, 'peaceably and in a reasonable manner, and without threat or intimidation to persuade others to cease or abstain from work'.

1.1.5 Other legislation

Other less obvious provisions were pressed into service against the early trade unions. The famous prosecution of Dorset farm labourers, known to history as the 'Tolpuddle Martyrs', still lives on in union folklore. Their crime was that they used an oath as a sign of allegiance to their new society because they could not read or write. For this they were sentenced to transportation to Australia under the provisions of the Unlawful Societies Act 1799 and Unlawful Oaths Act 1797 (the latter apparently passed to quell naval mutinies).

1.1.6 **The new model unions and the Trade Union Act 1871**

The most ambitious 19th-century union, Robert Owen's Grand National Consolidated Trade Union, collapsed in 1834, barely a year after its foundation, but the mid-19th century saw the first great expansion of trade unionism with the creation of federations of previously local organisations. The new model unions, as they were later to be called, consisted primarily of skilled craftsmen, and combined efficient internal organisation and a sound financial base with a cautious approach to industrial action. Typified by the Amalgamated Society of Engineers, they began to build a nascent structure of collective bargaining with the masters, some of whom were keen to talk to spokesmen rather than numerous individuals. An agreed list of wage rates was thus determined in the brushmaking trade, for example, as early as 1805.

Soon the courts turned their attention to the new unions' legal status. The first blow came in *Hornby* v *Close* (1867) when the court held them illegal as a restraint of trade. In a pattern often to be repeated in later years, this judgment adverse to the workers' interests was soon redressed by legislation. Gladstone's Trade Union Act 1871 adopted the liberalising minority recommendations of the recent Royal Commission on Trade Unions under Chief Justice Erle, rather than the majority views which sought yet more restrictions of workers' rights. The Act thus accorded the unions the power to enforce certain contracts and to hold property as well as providing for their voluntary registration with the Registrar of Friendly Societies.

1.1.7 **Retreat of the criminal law**

Soon the Criminal Law Amendment Act 1871 cut down somewhat the scope of the offences of intimidation, molestation, and obstruction, but its effect was limited by the continued extent of the common law crime of conspiracy as revealed by the conviction of striking gas stokers in *R* v *Bunn* (1872).

Effective trade union pressure led to the Conspiracy and Protection of Property Act 1875, and it is significant that the Government chose to heed the views of the workers at this time since many urban workers had just been given the franchise in the Representation of the People Act 1867. Their political potential was seen in the first meeting in 1871 of the Parliamentary Committee of the Trades Union Congress, itself established by 34 delegates in Manchester in 1868. One of the proffered explanations for the course which labour law has taken in Britain in contrast to the Continent, where more workers' rights are guaranteed by statute, is that the Industrial Revolution and the birth of trade unionism preceded the advent of democracy for the industrial worker. The unions thus grew accustomed to look to industrial rather than parliamentary strength to achieve their ends.

Statute, however, was useful in some areas. The 1875 Act gave immunity from criminal conspiracy where the defendant was acting in furtherance of a trade dispute, and the act would not have been criminal if done by one person alone. It also recognised some forms of picketing as legitimate by providing that mere attendance at a place for the purpose of peacefully communicating information would not amount to the crime of 'watching and besetting'. Such immunities became characteristic of the English approach to strikes and picketing.

With the repeal also of the Master and Servant Act 1867 (which had replaced the 1823 statute), the criminal law was largely withdrawn from the regulation of labour relations. The next decades saw the widespread organisation into general unions of low-paid and unskilled workers. This trend was sparked off by the famous strike of match girls at Bryant & Mays' London factory, fortified by the formation of the Gasworkers and General Labourers Union, and achieved its greatest success in the securing by the Port of London dockers of their 'tanner' a week after a long and bitter strike in 1889. These new organisations were not usually concerned with the provision of friendly society benefits, which had been a hallmark of the older craft unions. Instead they injected a new spirit of militancy into the movement and were less restrictive in their membership policy; as a result membership increased from 1,576,000 in 1892 to 2,022,000 eight years later.

1.1.8 Civil law and the Trade Disputes Act 1906

With the criminal law largely excluded, the attention of the employers turned to restraining strikes by means of the civil law, especially by the use of injunctions. The law of tort was pressed into service, in particular the tort of inducing a breach of contract (see *Lumley* v *Gye* (1853)), applied to unions' collective action in *Temperton* v *Russell* (1893). Although the House of Lords in *Allen* v *Flood* (1898) rejected any extension to the tort to include action in which no contract was breached, this victory for the unions was shortlived because, three years later in *Quinn* v *Leathem* (1901), the same body held that there was a tortious conspiracy where two or more persons combined without justification to injure another. This threat to the freedom to strike might have been withstood on the generally-held assumption that only individuals, and not the unions themselves, could be sued. Soon, however, the famous case, *Taff Vale Railway Co.* v *Amalgamated Society of Railway Servants* (1901), directly threatened unions with bankruptcy, for the House of Lords held that they could not shelter behind their unincorporated status because the Trade Union Act 1871 had enabled them to be sued in their own name. The Amalgamated Society of Railway Servants thus had to pay damages of £23,000 to the Taff Vale Railway Company for striking, together with costs of £19,000.

The unions reacted by redoubling their support for the newly-formed Labour Party, which appeared to be the institution which could relieve them from this threat to their freedom to strike. Under the prompting of increased Labour representation, the new Liberal Government's Trade Disputes Act 1906 was passed. The statute made union funds themselves altogether immune from any action in tort. It also relieved individual members of liability for conspiracy and inducing breach of contract, whether of employment or commercial agreements, but only if they were acting in contemplation or furtherance of a trade dispute as defined. Other provisions substantially liberalised the law on picketing and, in many respects, this Act did for civil law what the 1875 Act had done for criminal law.

The next judicial onslaught on the unions was not long in coming, however, and this time challenged their new-found political strength. The House of Lords' decision in *Amalgamated Society of Railway Servants* v *Osborne* (1910) held that a union could not spend its funds on political purposes since they were *ultra vires* (outside

the powers of) the purposes laid down in the Trade Union Act 1871. This was, however, soon reversed by the Trade Union Act 1913, which regulated expenditure on
political purposes by the unions.

1.1.9 First World War and the inter-war years

The pre-First World War period saw several bitter disputes and stoppages in manufacturing industry, partly encouraged by the appearance of shop stewards. Unrest
continued into the war years themselves, notwithstanding the prohibition of
strikes in the Munitions of War Act 1915. The Government reacted by setting up a
committee under J. H. Whitley, then Deputy Speaker of the House of Commons. Its
report in 1917 recommended the strengthening of collective bargaining and the
establishment of joint industrial councils to act as a forum for annual discussions.
Several were soon set up and are still known as Whitley Councils. The Industrial
Courts Act 1919 was another consequence. It established (despite its rather misleading name) a permanent government arbitration service for industrial disputes
to operate with the assent of parties.

The ensuing period saw little judicial intervention. The failure of the General
Strike in 1926 demoralised the unions, and the Government reacted with the Trade
Disputes and Trade Union Act 1927. This Act made illegal strikes which had any
object other than the furtherance of a purely trade dispute, especially if it was
a sympathy strike by workers in a different industry, or designed to coerce the
Government by inflicting harm on the wider community. The closed shop was
outlawed in local and public employment, and public employees were restricted in
the unions they could join. These measures had little effect, due to the relative qui-
escence of the unions in the subsequent 20 years. More important was the accompanying requirement that union members had to actively 'contract in' to pay the
union political levy, and this considerably reduced union funds available to the
Labour Party. Not surprisingly the newly elected 1945 Labour Government proceeded to reverse this provision in the Trade Disputes and Trade Union Act 1946.

Another significant feature of the inter-war years was the process of mergers of
unions to produce the giants of today; the Transport and General Workers Union
(soon to merge with amicus to become Unite), Iron and Steel Trades Confederation,
and General and Municipal Workers Union (the forerunner of today's GMB) were
formed in this period. Moreover the range of unionised workers grew markedly,
taking in teachers and civil servants, and expanding for the first time among other
white collar workers, although the boom in their membership came in the 1960s.
The Second World War Government resorted to similar measures to those adopted
in the First World War to prevent industrial disruption; strikes were outlawed with
the *quid pro quo* for the unions of binding dispute arbitration.

1.1.10 The 1960s and the Donovan Report

It was in the 1960s that for the first time employment protection legislation was
passed on a large scale to improve the lot of individual workers. The Contracts of
Employment Act 1963 decreed the provision by the employer to each employee of
a written statement of contractual terms; the Industrial Training Act 1964 sought
better training provisions and set up industrial tribunals to adjudicate on its levy

provisions; and the Redundancy Payments Act 1965 for the first time provided statutory compensation on dismissal.

The main focus of union fears was on the collective side with the unexpected decision in *Rookes* v *Barnard* (1964). The House of Lords applied the tort of intimidation away from its traditional ground of threats of assault to include intimidating for the purpose of inducing breaches of contract. This threatened a return to the law contended for by the employers in *Allen* v *Flood* (1898), rendering virtually every strike illegal, and there was no trade dispute immunity covering it. This latter feature was quickly redressed by the Trade Disputes Act 1965 but the furore surrounding this *cause célèbre* was one of the reasons for the appointment in 1965 of the Royal Commission on Trade Unions and Employers' Associations under the chairmanship of Lord Donovan, a law lord. It was 'to consider relations between management and employees and the role of trade unions and employers' associations in promoting the interests of their members and in accelerating the social and economic advance of the nation...'. From the beginning it was expected that the main focus would be on the role of the unions, especially because of the widely held view that Britain's continuing industrial decline could be ascribed at least in part to their maintenance of restrictive practices and the large number of unofficial 'wildcat' strikes.

The report of this high-powered investigation was published in 1968, and detected a major industrial problem in the 'irreversible shift' from formal industry-wide collective bargaining to informal and often chaotic arrangements led by increasingly powerful shop stewards. It thus prescribed formal written agreements at plant level and called for union rules to indicate clearly the powers and duties of shop stewards. While it was not wholly opposed to legal enactment (and indeed one dissentient member thought there was no other way) it generally favoured machinery based on consensus. It thought that 'the shortcomings of our existing industrial relations are...primarily due to widespread ignorance about the most sensible and effective methods of conducting industrial relations'.

The detailed analysis contained in the Donovan Report provided the background to the subsequent feverish legislative activity. But the immediate response of the Labour Government, which received the report, did not reach the statute book. Its controversial White Paper, *In Place of Strife*, published in January 1969, split the Labour and trade union movements, especially because of its 'penal clauses' which, in aiming to stamp out unofficial strikes by criminal sanctions, went beyond the Donovan recommendations. The proposed legislation was withdrawn in return for rather nebulous undertakings by the Trades Union Congress (TUC) which led to some changes to its Bridlington Rules for inter-union disputes. The Government did, however, set up a Commission on Industrial Relations—the voluntary body recommended in the report.

1.1.11 **The Industrial Relations Act 1971 and industrial strife**

The new Conservative Government elected in 1970 had no qualms about reform, nor internal dissension. The Industrial Relations Act 1971 was more radical than the Donovan Report and sought to translate several concepts from Continental and American labour law. The Act put the law at the centre stage in collective bargaining. It outlawed any obligation of trade union membership as a condition for job applicants (the so-called pre-entry closed shop) and allowed other forms of total unionisation only with the approval of the Commission on Industrial Relations and a ballot of affected workers. Employees were given rights not to be excluded or expelled from their union by arbitrary or unreasonable discrimination or to be subjected to unreasonable disciplinary action. Nor were members to be penalised for refusing to take part in unlawful industrial action. The Act also set up the National Industrial Relations Court (NIRC) as a specialist court to hear both individual and collective labour law cases. The NIRC could order a cooling off period, and a ballot, for those strikes that would be gravely injurious to the national economy, create risk of disorder or endanger lives, a provision used only once, in the 1972 railway dispute. For the first time, collective bargains were to be legally enforceable unless both parties wished otherwise, as in fact proved generally to be the case. One of the most important innovations in the Act was the introduction of unfair dismissal protection in its largely present form. Trade union immunity was removed for sympathy and secondary action except in certain circumstances where, for example, the dispute was about wages and conditions. It also became illegal for any person other than an official of a registered trade union to call a strike without proper notice. This sought to prevent unofficial disputes, and of most concern to trade union leaders was the provision in s. 96 that unregistered unions would be liable to have their funds sequestered if sued for such 'unfair industrial practices'. This effectively re-enacted the House of Lords' decision in *Taff Vale* (1901). Because of their bitter opposition to this and other provisions of the Act, which was shown in mass demonstrations and a one-day general strike called by the Amalgamated Union of Engineering Workers, few unions registered under its provisions. They were thus denied most of the benefits open to them, and were liable to have their funds seized. The most threatening event was the imprisonment of docker shop stewards who became known as the 'Pentonville Five' after the prison where they were sent for failing to obey an order prohibiting a strike over containerisation. A planned general strike in their support was called off only after the intervention of the Official Solicitor. Moreover, the scope of s. 96 was apparently widened by the decision of the Court of Appeal in *Heatons Transport Ltd* v *TGWU* (1973), which held the unions vicariously liable for the actions of their shop stewards even when they were engaged on unofficial action not authorised by the union leadership. This was overturned by the House of Lords in due course, but the bitterness it engendered continued, and in the last year of the Government the Act was virtually a dead letter.

1.1.12 The 'social contract': the Trade Union and Labour Relations Act 1974 and the Employment Protection Act 1975

The Labour Government was returned to power in 1974, following a damaging national miners' strike; it proceeded to dismantle the edifice of the Industrial Relations Act, which had proved unable to control mounting unrest. Thus s. 1 of the quickly-enacted Trade Union and Labour Relations Act 1974 wholly repealed the Industrial Relations Act 1971, although the rest of the statute proceeded to re-enact many of its features, albeit with modifications. The unfair dismissal provisions were strengthened, and listing of unions continued, although no longer providing the gateway to any significant union rights. The immunity of trade unions and individuals in trade dispute cases broadly returned to the position in 1906, although there was a new restriction on the use by employers of injunctions, and the efficacy of no-strike agreements was limited. The minority Government did not quite get the statute it sought through Parliament, so that, on the re-election of the administration with a larger majority, the Trade Union and Labour Relations (Amendment) Act 1976 proceeded to abolish the right to refuse to join a closed shop union on conscientious grounds, which was inserted by the Conservative opposition, and also broadened the protection for trade disputes.

This legislation was part of the Labour Government's 'social contract' with the unions, its *quid pro quo* for wage restraint. This agreement was advanced by the many new employment protection rights accorded by the Employment Protection Act 1975 (EPA 1975). On the collective level the Act gave statutory powers to the new ACAS, which had already taken over from the Commission on Industrial Relations, and transferred the jurisdiction of the Industrial Court (renamed the Industrial Arbitration Board in 1971) to the CAC. Industrial tribunals were given several new jurisdictions, and a new appeal body was created—the EAT, which differed from the NIRC in that on the whole it had neither a primary jurisdiction, nor dealt with collective disputes.

The Act also introduced guarantee payments for lay-off and short time, strengthened provisions for extension of collectively-agreed or general level terms and conditions, enacted the right to maternity pay and the right to return after maternity leave. Where the employer became insolvent, wages and other payments were protected. Employees also became entitled to a regular itemised pay statement. On the collective side, a new procedure for trade union recognition was introduced whereby unions were entitled to be provided with information for collective bargaining purposes and to be consulted about redundancies if they were recognised. And, furthermore, shop stewards and trade union members were given the right to time off for trade union duties and activities respectively.

The Equal Pay Act, actually passed in 1970, was brought into force in 1975 along with the Sex Discrimination Act, which sought to supplement it by prohibiting discrimination against job applicants and employees on the grounds of sex and/or marital status. A new Race Relations Act 1976 widened the scope of the similar enactments of 1965 and 1968, in particular giving the individual employee the right to complain to industrial tribunals. The late 1960s and the 1970s also experienced a major growth in trade unionism, especially in local government and the health service among white collar and professional employees.

1.1.13 Conservative legislation 1980–96

The next three years saw mounting criticism by employers and various pressure groups of the 1974–76 legislation. It was claimed that it greatly increased wage costs at a time of recession, and discouraged employers from taking on more employees, thus defeating their own ostensible objects. Many people reacted sharply against the actions of the unions in the so called 'winter of discontent' of 1978–79, when a series of strikes (especially in the public sector) paralysed the nation, and were accompanied by widespread secondary picketing—that is against employers not directly involved in the relevant dispute.

1.1.14 **The Thatcher years**

Employment Acts 1980 and 1982

After the election of a new Conservative Government, the Employment Act 1980 sought to restrict the powers of the unions and the ambit of individual rights but without mounting the headlong assault on the unions seen in the 1971 legislation. The 1980 Act enabled the Secretary of State for Employment to give public funds to unions for the holding of secret ballots, but the unions viewed this with the gravest suspicion, preferring to finance ballots themselves. The Act further limited the effectiveness of the closed shop by an extension of the remedies against unreasonable exclusion or expulsion. On the one hand it limited employees' rights in relation to unfair dismissal, and on the other introduced a new right to time off work for ante-natal care. Further restrictions were placed upon industrial action directed at employers not in dispute with the union. The statutory recognition procedures in the EPA 1975 were finally laid to rest, although few on any side—government, employers, or unions—were sorry to see their passing. Despite these far-ranging measures, many considered that the Employment Act 1980 did not go far enough to restrain the unions and redress the industrial balance which they thought had been tilted in the unions' favour between 1974 and 1979. Following a Green Paper on Trade Union Immunities in 1980, the Government announced its intention to introduce further measures of industrial law reform. Its stated aim was to 'improve the operation of the labour market by providing a fairer and more balanced framework of industrial relations law and to curb a number of continuing abuses of trade union power'.

The main features of the Employment Act 1982 concerned the tortious liability of unions for acts of their bodies and officials as well as a further tightening of the restrictions placed upon the operation of closed shops by subjecting them to periodic review, prohibiting union-membership-only clauses in contracts and tender documents, and increasing compensation for employees unfairly dismissed in consequence of a closed shop.

Trade Union Act 1984

The Trade Union Act 1984 was intended by the Government to 'give unions back to their members'. The statute provided for ballots for the election of the principal executive committee, before industrial action, and to maintain the union's political fund. The effect has been to take the courts further into the internal affairs of trade unions.

TUPE Regulations

The Thatcher Government was impelled by European Directives to implement two pieces of legislation which were not to its liking. Both were introduced by statutory instrument. They were the Transfer of Undertakings (Protection of Employment) Regulations 1981 (SI 1981 No. 1794), which gave employees various rights on takeovers, and the Equal Pay (Amendment) Regulations 1983 (SI 1983 No. 1794), which gave women the right to claim equal pay when their work is of equal value to a man's instead of merely when he and she perform like work or when it has been rated as equivalent in a job evaluation study. The Government

Minister introducing the former measure to the House of Commons said that he did so without any enthusiasm.

Wages legislation

More in keeping with the Government's overall strategy was the revoking of the Fair Wages Resolution in 1983; and the Wages Act 1986, which repealed the Truck Acts, abolished the Wages Council protection for those over 21, and removed redundancy rebates save for employers of less than ten employees (also abolished by the Employment Act 1989).

The pace of legislation did not thereafter abate; indeed, it may be said to have increased with the Employment Acts of 1988, 1989, and 1990, the Trade Union and Labour Relations (Consolidation) Act 1992 (TULR(C)A 1992), and the Trade Union Reform and Employment Rights Act 1993 (TURERA 1993). This was perhaps partly because of the extent to which unions were able to adapt to the new legislative environment rather than despite it (see Fosh *et al.*, (1993) 22 ILJ 14).

Employment Acts 1988 and 1989

The 1988 Act placed further requirements on unions regarding a number of important union matters, including elections, ballots before striking, and the day-to-day running of internal union affairs. Most notably, perhaps, it created the Commissioner for the Rights of Trade Union Members to help trade unionists bring actions against unions. There were those, even among traditional Conservative Government supporters, who felt that this Act went too far, but the 1989 Act followed. This was far less radical, but contained new important measures relating to sex discrimination, written statements, time off work for union duties, and dissolved the Training Commission set up only a year earlier under the 1988 Act.

Employment Act 1990

The Employment Act 1990 introduced further reforms in collective labour law. It took away the remaining vestiges of legal support for the closed shop which, while not rendering the closed shop unlawful, made it virtually impossible to operate. It did this by making it unlawful for employers and training agencies to refuse to offer employment on the ground of trade union non-membership. To show even-handedness, refusal of employment on the ground of union membership was also made unlawful, but in practice this is of significantly lesser impact. The 1990 Act outlawed secondary industrial action other than secondary picketing. The provisions relating to balloting of union members introduced by the Trade Union Act 1984 and the Employment Act 1988 were also extended to cover independent contractors as well as employees. The liability of trade unions was also extended to cover the acts of their committees and officials, including shop stewards, unless disowned by the union, and employees lost the right to claim unfair dismissal if at the time they are engaged in unofficial industrial action.

1.1.15 The Major years

A further item of legislation, which unusually received cross-party support, was the TULR(C)A 1992 consolidating statutory collective labour law. This Act later partnered the Employment Rights Act 1996 (ERA 1996) which consolidated the law on individual employment rights, notably with regard to unfair dismissal and redundancy.

The next piece of industrial legislation was clearly controversial and constituted a return by the Major Government to the attack on trade unionism which had characterised the Thatcher years. The TURERA 1993 placed further restrictions on the rights of employees to strike and strictly regulated the financial affairs of trade unions. Although it contained some provisions to extend workers' rights, these derived almost entirely from the impulse of European Directives. Indeed this was the first general piece of primary industrial legislation which derived a majority of its provisions from European Community law, in particular on maternity rights, transfer of undertakings, and proof of employment relationship. (For full details see Bowers, Brown, and Gibbons, *A Guide to the Trade Union Reform and Employment Rights Act 1993* (Harlow: Longman, 1993).)

The last years of the Major Government saw the appetite for trade union legislation diminish, marked as they were by two important statutes in the sphere of individual rights. The very last Major act was to consolidate the various legislation on employment rights regarding unfair dismissal, redundancy, and claims of lesser importance. But some would see it as ironic that the long period of Conservative legislative innovation from 1979 should end with a piece of primarily social legislation in the shape of the Disability Discrimination Act 1995. This was a significant addition to the statute book not just because it introduced important measures protecting the disabled from discrimination in the workplace, but also because it perhaps heralded the widening of anti-discrimination law.

1.1.16 The New Labour Government reforms

When the Labour Party won the General Election of May 1997, it was widely expected that the next two or three years would witness a plethora of legislative reform in employment law. This would be normal with any new Labour Government, particularly after having been out of power for so long, but it was all the more likely with a Prime Minister and Lord Chancellor who had specialised in employment law in their careers at the Bar. Those who hoped for this were not disappointed. The next three years saw, amongst other legislative changes, the introduction of a national minimum wage, protection against 'whistleblowing' at work, regulations capping hours of work for many employees, the reduction of employment protection legislation qualifying periods, the establishment of the Disability Rights Commission, parental leave, a major reform and simplification of maternity rights, entitlement to take time off work to care for family and other dependants, added protection for part-time workers, the huge increase in unfair dismissal compensation limits, reform of the law on industrial action ballots and dismissals during industrial action, and greater trade union recognition rights. But, more important and far-reaching than any of this, the Human Rights Act 1998 was passed incorporating the European Convention on Human Rights into domestic law. This proved to be a very far-reaching and importantly influential piece of legislation over the next few years. But the Government was not content with that, and produced yet another Employment Act in 2002 (EA 2002) introducing changes to the law on family rights including a new right to paid paternity leave, reform to aspects of ETs including the possibility for the first time of widespread costs orders, and enabling provisions relating to fixed-term contracts and flexible working. Then 2003 saw new legislation on flexible working time, the national minimum wage, equal pay, religious belief discrimination, race, sex and disability discrimination, and sexual orientation.

The period since 2003 has also seen the now-expected steady stream of legislation in employment. The Employment Relations Act 2004 was passed, following the Secretary of State for Trade and Industry's review into the operation of the Employment Relations Act 1999. It contains a wide variety of changes to the law on, for example, trade union recognition, industrial action, collective bargaining, and trade union membership rights. However, it might be thought surprising that it took New Labour quite so long to do anything substantial in the field of collective labour law, and indeed the tale of the entire period since the 1997 General Election has been one of abstentionism in terms of legislation on trade unions. (See Fredman 'The Ideology of New Labour Law', in Barnard, Deakin, and Morris (eds), *The Future of Labour Law* (Oxford: Hart Publishing, 2004), but *cf.* Bogg, (2009) 20 KLJ 403.) 2004 also saw the meat on the bones of the EA 2002's new procedures for dispute resolution. Greater protection has been created for those bullied at work. A significant move was the creation of a single CEHR to replace the existing commissions covering sex, race, and disability as well as extending coverage to human rights issues. This period has also seen the completion of the obligations imposed under the EU Equal Treatment Framework Directive, Council Directive (EC) 2000/78, regarding anti-discrimination legislation with the introduction of the Regulations on age discrimination, the possibility of future domestic legislation to simplify discrimination by way of a Single Equality Act, and the simplification of EU law in this field. Consequently, there has been the attempt to collate and refine the plethora of anti-discrimination legislation in the Equality Bill which, at the time of writing, is wending its way through the House of Lords, although it is not certain if it will reach the Statute Book before the 2010 General Election and be lost in the mists of time. In the same area, the Treaty of Lisbon, which came into force at the end of 2009, signified the intention of EU member states, through the Charter of Fundamental Rights, to widen the scope of employment protection rights, particularly in the field of discrimination, to cover social origin, genetic features, political and other opinions, property, and birth. (See further, Syrpsis, (2008) 37 ILJ 219.) And then, in early 2009, there was the much-welcomed and little-mourned demise of the statutory dispute resolution procedures mentioned earlier. (The repeal has been subject to some criticism, however—see Sanders, (2009) 38 ILJ 30.) This was proof, much-doubted, that governments do occasionally admit to have got something wrong, without obfuscation, denial, or wriggling. This is unusually refreshing.

1.2 Institutions of employment law

1.2.1 Employment tribunals

If, to use Kahn-Freund's famous phrase, the contract of employment can be considered to be the cornerstone of employment law, then ETs can be considered to be its foundations. Since being set up in 1964 as industrial tribunals, their jurisdiction has grown enormously, and now covers not just statutory claims such as unfair dismissal, discrimination and unlawful deductions from wages, but also breach of contract claims at common law. Over 150,000 claims were lodged with ETs in the year to March 2009, compared to some 189,000 applications in 2007–08. (The overall tendency for growth in the number of claims is mirrored elsewhere—see e.g. for a comparison of the UK and German experiences, Schneider, 22 Comp. Lab. L. & Pol'y J (2001), at p. 261.) For most employment claims, the ET is thus the first port of call.

Tribunals have come a long way since their inception, not only in scope but also in philosophy. The idea that they should hear claims in an atmosphere far removed from the courtroom, accessibly, informally, speedily, and cheaply, no longer pertains as much as it once did. There are a number of reasons for this. Most particularly, the technical aspects of the law with which they have to deal have grown out of all recognition. Lawyers are not kept out of the process, as was originally intended, with many parties preferring to watch lawyers formally doing their work for them rather than representing themselves in what, for all its claims to informality, can nevertheless be a very intimidating atmosphere for the ordinary person. (See Latreille, Latreille, and Knight, (2005) 34 ILJ 308.) On the whole, however, cases are dealt with reasonably speedily, with an average wait of between 12 and 14 weeks from the point a claim is received to hearing, which compares very favourably with the ordinary courts. Cheapness is maintained at one level, in that costs (expenses in Scotland) on the whole do not follow the action, with each party paying their own, win or lose. (Costs may be awarded in some circumstances, but rarely are.) But even this does not deter a growing number of parties, particularly employers, from hiring lawyers or having some form of representation, perhaps from their trade union, the local Citizens' Advice Bureau or a *pro bono* organisation, such as the Free Representation Unit. The use of contingency fees, which are suited to the situation where costs are not awarded, may be of more benefit to employees than to employers—see Johnson and Hammersley, (2005) 14 Nott LJ 19.

Membership

The membership of an ET is made up of, normally, three persons. In order to maintain confidence in the system, which trade unions in particular historically have not had, they represent different aspects of law and industry. There is a chairman (who, since December 2007, may be called an employment judge), who is a lawyer, and sits either full-time or part-time. He or she is flanked by two wing members, one from a list consisting of employers and the other from a list representing workers. The idea is that the wing members bring to the case (which almost always turns on matters of fact rather than law) their particular expertise and experience of everyday industrial and employment practices. Each member of the tribunal is of equal status and voting is by a majority. It is surprising, perhaps, given the differing backgrounds of the tribunal members that in the great majority of cases the decision is unanimous. An interesting feature is that, although the judge is a lawyer, he or she is also involved in the decision even if that is one based purely on findings of fact.

In some cases the employment judge may sit alone, or with only one lay member, for example in breach of contract proceedings, but may also do so if the parties agree—Employment Tribunals Act 1996, s. 4. In such circumstances the parties are entitled to know from which panel the lay member is drawn—see *Rabahallah* v *BT Group plc* (2005). The decision to sit alone is a judicial, not an administrative, decision according to the EAT in *Sterling Developments (London) Ltd* v *Pagano* (2007).

Status

The tribunal is just that—it is not a court of law. Despite the advantages of this for the reasons just considered, it also has disadvantages. For example, not being a court means that the tribunal does not have the power to enforce its own orders, although this may change following the Tribunals, Courts and Enforcement Act 2007. Even where, for example in an unfair dismissal case, the ET makes an order that the employee be re-employed by the employer in one way or another, if the employer fails to do so there is no contempt of court. The order is merely commuted to a money payment, although this may be enhanced as we shall see below. As with any court to some extent, but more so with tribunals, it is one matter to win a case and have an order made in your favour, but it is another matter actually receiving what is owed to you. In the final resort recourse has to be made to the county court to enforce the order made by the tribunal, but that can be the start of a lengthy, expensive, and possibly fruitless exercise.

Structure

Since April 2006 all tribunals have come within a unified service, called the Tribunals Service. Although ETs and the EAT come within the service, they are treated differently from other tribunals. This is because of the differences between the needs of ETs which deal with disputes between parties, and administrative tribunals which deal with disputes between parties and the State. Therefore the new description of tribunals as First Tier Tribunals or Upper Tribunals does not apply in the employment sphere, but they are treated similarly. Responsibility for administering ETs and the EAT now rests with the Ministry of Justice, according to the Tribunals, Courts and Enforcement Act 2007. However, the Department for Business, Innovation and Skills has responsibility for, among other things, Rules of Procedure for ETs, whereas the Lord Chancellor retains responsibility for making the Rules of Procedure for the EAT. Employment judges and lay members continue to be appointed by the Lord Chancellor.

The 2007 Act also reforms the law on enforcement of ET awards and for the first time makes it possible for settlements brokered by ACAS to be enforced in the same way as tribunal awards.

Procedure

One of the aspects of the formalising of ET claims over the years has been the ever-growing detail relating to rules of procedure. These are presently governed principally by the Employment Tribunals (Constitution and Rules of Procedure) Regulations 2004 (SI 2004 No. 1861) as amended by the Employment Tribunals (Constitution and Rules of Procedure) (Amendment) Regulations 2008 (SI 2008 No. 3240). It will be possible to give only an outline here.

A claim is begun in an ET by the claimant making out a claim form, known as an ET1, within the required time limit—usually three months. The ET1 asks for details such as the name and address of the claimant, the details of the person against whom relief is sought, and the grounds of the claim, which need not go into more than basic detail identifying it as within the jurisdiction of the ET—see *Grimmer* v *KLM Cityhopper Ltd* (2005). This must be sent to the tribunal office for the area in which the employee worked.

The employer will then respond on form ET3, and this must be done within 28 days. The response will give the employer's details, and whether or not it intends to defend the claim. The employer may also counter-claim.

An issue which is of fundamental importance here is the imposition of time limits, which we shall consider in some detail as it also goes to the question of eligibility and serves as a good example of the attitude adopted with regard to procedure generally.

A claim is presented when it is delivered (*Hammond* v *Haigh Castle & Co. Ltd* (1973), *Post Office* v *Moore* (1981)). This is deemed to have occurred, unless the contrary is proved, at the time when the letter would be delivered in the ordinary course of post. In the case of first class mail, this is on the second working day after posting, and in the case of second class mail, on the fourth working day after posting, according to the EAT in *St Basil's Centre Ltd* v *McCrossan* (1991). (Interestingly, the Royal Mail claimed to deliver 90.7 per cent of its first class mail on the next working day—figures for the second quarter of 2009–10. It should be borne in mind, however, that this figure will have been distorted by industrial action in London.) Whether the claim is presented in time goes to the jurisdiction of the tribunal to hear the claim. As Lord Denning MR said in *Dedman* v *British Building & Engineering Appliances Ltd* (1974), 'If [an application] arrives a minute after midnight on the last day the clerks must throw it out; the tribunal is not competent to hear it'. A letter requesting a claim form does not count as an application for this purpose (*Alex Munro (Butchers) Ltd* v *Nicol* (1988)).

The ERA 1996, s. 111(3) and (4), however, permits a premature claim, so that where a dismissal takes place with notice the employee may make a claim during that notice period. Although the former time limit has been increased from the original 28 days it often proves inadequate and the ET may allow a reasonable further period 'in a case where it is satisfied that it was not reasonably practicable for the complaint to be presented before the end of the period of three months' (ERA 1996, s. 111(2)(b)). The Court of Appeal in *Palmer* v *Southend-on-Sea BC* (1984) considered that this statutory phrase was 'not really apt in the particular context'. The best approach was to read the word 'practicable' as the equivalent of feasible '… and to ask colloquially and untramelled by too much legal logic—was it reasonably feasible to present the complaint to the industrial tribunal within the relevant three months?'. 'Reasonably practicable' meant more than what is reasonably capable physically of being done. The early cases tended to view this as a general equitable principle, to be 'considered in the light of general standards of ordinary people in industry'. More guidance, however, was given in the important statement of Lord Denning MR in *Dedman* v *British Building & Engineering Appliances Ltd* (1974), then construing the 28-day period for unfair dismissal:

If in the circumstances the man knew or was put on inquiry as to his rights, and as to the time limit then it was practicable for him to have presented his complaint within the four weeks, and he ought to have done so. But if he did not know and there was nothing to put him on inquiry, then it was not practicable and he should be excused.

The working out of this principle did not prove to be particularly liberal primarily because the Master of the Rolls went on to say that mistakes by skilled advisers in this regard did not provide an excuse, and any remedy must be against them in negligence. However, it is arguably unrealistic to suppose that this is a practical option open to applicants, and the Court of Appeal took the more sensible view in *Harber* v *North London Polytechnic* (1990) when it said that a review may be granted in such circumstances when it would be in the interests of justice so to do. The time limit may indeed be extended on the basis that the employee was given erroneous legal advice (*Hawkins* v *Ball and Barclays Bank plc* (1996) and *Chohan* v *Derby Law Centre* (2004)). See too *London International College Ltd* v *Sen* (1993) for a similar view.

There are, however, two reasons why the view taken by the courts on this issue should be strict. First, when Lord Denning MR confirmed the *Dedman* approach in *Walls Meat Co. Ltd* v *Khan* (1979) he added the rider that now the longer three-month time limit applies 'there is less reason for granting an indulgence to a complainant', and that 'tribunals can and should be strict in enforcing [it]'. Secondly, as public consciousness of unfair dismissal provisions grows, mainly through reports in the daily press and Government leaflets, there is less likelihood that an applicant can realistically claim complete ignorance.

Some principles have been established for the more common types of valid excuse for delay. One frequently encountered is that internal proceedings arising out of the dismissal were pending at the same time, and that it was reasonable to delay the application to the ET in order not to prejudice them. The EAT said in *Crown Agents* v *Lawal* (1979):

Merely as a statement of general principle, it would seem to us that in cases where a person is going through a conciliation process, or is taking up a domestic appeal procedure, whether it be on discipline, or whether it be for medical reasons, that common sense would indicate that while he is going through something which involves him and his employer directly, he should be able to say, 'It is not reasonably practicable for me to lodge my application within the three months'.

This dictum was, however, disapproved of as a general principle in *Bodha* v *Hampshire AHA* (1982) (see also *Croydon Health Authority* v *Jaufurally* (1986)). In *Walls Meat Co. Ltd* v *Khan* (1979) Shaw and Brandon LJJ gave as examples of valid excuses physical impediment, absence abroad or a postal strike, while in *Dedman* Scarman LJ spoke of 'some untoward and unexpected turn of events'. In *Porter* v *Brandridge* (1978) Stephenson LJ thought that the tribunal should consider whether the employee 'was discouraged or impeded or misled or deceived'. In *Churchill* v *A. Yeates & Sons Ltd* (1983) the employee excused his delay by reason of the discovery outside the three-month period that his old job declared redundant had in fact been filled. Although this was only one of the five grounds on which he challenged the fairness of his dismissal, the EAT decided that it was not reasonably practicable to bring a complaint until the applicant knew of a fundamental fact which rendered the dismissal unfair (see too *Machine Tool Industry Research Association* v *Simpson* (1988); cf. *Belling & Lee* v *Burford* (1982)). In *James W. Cook & Co. (Wivenhoe) Ltd* v *Tipper* (1990) the Court of Appeal held that it was not reasonably practicable to present applications for redundancy where the employees thought that work would pick up again. The time should run from the moment the business closed down and the dismissals were recognised as irrevocable. This decision seems remarkably favourable to applicants in the light of the Court of Appeal's traditional strictness in this regard.

The following have, however, been held not to be good reasons to present applications out of time:

(a) the holding of union negotiations (*Times Newspapers Ltd* v *O'Regan* (1977));

(b) that criminal proceedings were on foot at the same time (*Norgett* v *Luton Industrial Co-operative Society Ltd* (1976); *Union Cartage Co. Ltd* v *Blunden* (1977));

(c) the claiming of unemployment benefit with a case pending before the National Insurance local tribunal (*Walls Meat* v *Khan* (1979); *House of Clydesdale Ltd* v *Foy* (1976));

(d) misleading advice from the Free Representation Unit (*Croydon Health Authority* v *Jaufurally* (1986)).

The Court of Appeal held in *Marley (UK) Ltd* v *Anderson* (1994) that, in considering whether the employee is reasonable to present a claim out of time, each ground must be considered separately, even if he or she had other grounds for believing that he or she may have been dismissed unfairly. Rubenstein has criticised this decision on the basis that there is only one dismissal per employee but his criticism is unconvincing as the reasonableness or otherwise of not bringing a claim in time may vary with each ground (see [1994] IRLR 150). The fact that an employee has entered into a commission arrangement with his employer may make it a matter of commercial convenience and interest that he should not issue proceedings against his former employer, but it does not render it 'not reasonably practicable' to do so (see *Birmingham Optical plc* v *Johnson* (1995)).

Tribunals in future will have to develop rules with regard to electronic means of making claims. In *Initial Electronic Security Systems Ltd* v *Avdic* (2005) the EAT held that a claim submitted by email eight hours ahead of the deadline but not received in time was acceptable when the sender was given no indication by that time that it had not been received. (See too *Tyne and Wear Autistic Society* v *Smith* (2005).)

Once the response has been made, ACAS is informed, and a representative will try and get the parties to reach a settlement. His function is not to work on behalf of either party, or even to reach the fairest result, but to keep the case from going to a hearing. It is at this stage that a number of cases are settled, but many also go up to the date of the hearing before a compromise is reached, or a claim withdrawn. The latest figures show that just under three-quarters of tribunal applications were either settled or withdrawn before hearing (see *ACAS Annual Report & Accounts 2008/09* (London: The Stationery Office, 2009), at p. 42).

The gathering of evidence might be an important part of the pre-hearing process, and the ET has the power to order the discovery of documents which are relevant and necessary to the proceedings. The parties will receive what is known as a 'directions letter' informing them what has to be revealed. This will not cover documents that are privileged, such as legal advice to one of the parties from a solicitor. The tribunal may also order a party to prepare a written witness statement, stating what the evidence will be to be given by a party he intends to call at the hearing. A witness may be ordered to attend the hearing, but that is not done as a matter of course.

It is possible for the tribunal of itself, or on application of one of the parties, to hold a case management discussion or a pre-hearing review, which may be heard by the employment judge sitting alone. The purpose of this is, in the light of the originating application and the notice of appearance as well as other documents or arguments, to examine whether the claim has no reasonable prospect of success. In such circumstances the tribunal may order the relevant party to make a deposit of up to £500 and warn that, should they lose at the hearing, they may have an order of costs made against them as well as losing their deposit. In addition, the tribunal may strike out an originating application or the notice of appearance if it considers that it, or the manner in which the case is presented, is scandalous, misconceived, or vexatious.

At the hearing itself, which normally lasts for a day or less, the tribunal is free to conduct proceedings as it considers most appropriate. Usually this means the normal court practice of the party with the burden of proof putting their case and calling witnesses (not usually but possibly in an order determined by the tribunal) who are then cross-examined, with the process repeated for the other side, followed by closing addresses. There are no opening addresses. Although the tribunal is addressed formally, the case is heard throughout with everyone seated. If a party does not appear, the tribunal can adjourn proceedings, dispose of the case in their absence or dismiss the application.

At the end of the hearing, which should normally be open to the public (even where the case involves national security issues a judgment whether to hear the matter in private needs to be made according to the EAT in *AB* v *Secretary of State for Defence* (2010)), the employment judge will give a summary of the tribunal's decision. He may alternatively give extended reasons of his own volition, and must do so if requested by one of the parties. If the decision is given immediately with supporting reasons, either summary or extended, these are tape-recorded and later sent to the parties. In some circumstances, for example where there has been a default judgment, a review hearing may be held. It is possible for the ET to reach a decision without a hearing if the parties agree in writing or, if a party defaults, to issue a judgment without the consent of the parties—see Employment Tribunals Act 1996, s. 7.

1.2.2 Employment Appeal Tribunal

The EAT, the successor to the NIRC, hears appeals from ETs numbering about a thousand every year. It does so only on points of law. Like ETs, it too usually has three members but of different status. The Chairman is a High Court judge or circuit judge (but not part-time judges who also appear as counsel there as, according to the House of Lords in *Lawal* v *Northern Spirit Ltd* (2003), this would undermine public confidence in the system) and the wing members are likewise taken from the ranks of employers and workers and can be very senior figures. It may seem a peculiar feature, as appeals are on points of law only (except in appeals from decisions of the Certification Officer, and in some trade union matters) that lay persons sit on the EAT, particularly as they may outvote the chairman, and have done so.

As a tribunal, it is not necessary for representation of the parties to be by lawyers. However, as questions of fact are not reviewed it is much more common for lawyers to appear. This is facilitated by the fact that, unlike ETs, it is possible to be awarded legal aid for an EAT hearing.

The EAT, which sits in London, is headed by a President, a High Court judge, or circuit judge. The atmosphere, whilst relatively informal compared to the High Court, which is its equivalent in many respects, is nevertheless more formal than ETs. (See Burton, (2005) 34 ILJ 273.) Like ETs, the EAT must be open to the public. Appeals lie from the EAT to the Court of Appeal and the EAT has decided that it has no power to review its own decisions, unlike the Court of Appeal— *Asda Stores Ltd* v *Thompson (No. 2)* (2004) (and on the Court of Appeal's position see *Taylor* v *Lawrence* (2002)). From the Court of Appeal, of course, appeal then lies to the Supreme Court in the usual way—see Honeyball, (2005) 24 *Civil Justice Quarterly* 364.

1.2.3 Commission for Equality and Human Rights

There were a number of commissions that dealt with specific areas of discrimination. The Equal Opportunities Commission dealt with sex discrimination, sitting alongside the Commission for Racial Equality and the Disability Rights Commission. The Equality Act 2006 merged these into a new body, formally called the Commission for Equality and Human Rights (CEHR) but which prefers itself to be known as the Equality and Human Rights Commission. (See generally O'Cinneide, (2007) 36 ILJ 141.)

The CEHR has the general duty to encourage and support the development of a society in relation to various aspects of discrimination and human rights, not just law (Equality Act 2006, s. 3). It also has general powers in respect of advice, issuing Codes of Practice and instigating enquiries into its duties—ss 13–16. In addition it has certain enforcement powers—see ss 20–32. It may undertake an investigation, for example, to see if someone has committed an unlawful act, issue Unlawful Act Notices where the Commission believes an unlawful act has occurred and require that person to take remedial action either through the preparation of an action plan or to follow specific recommendations of its own. It may enter into agreements with such persons to prevent future unlawful acts and, if it thinks that a repetition is likely, make an application to a county court for an order. It also has powers of conciliation and to give legal assistance, including arranging legal representation.

1.2.4 Advisory, Conciliation and Arbitration Service

ACAS was set up under the EPA 1975, and has many functions (TULR(C)A 1992, ss 209–214). Its overarching duty is to promote the improvement of industrial relations (s. 209). As we have seen, it has a conciliation function through its conciliation officers with regard to cases brought in ETs and, from 2007, to EAT cases, but also seeks to conciliate in trade disputes. It may do this of its own accord or at the request of one of the parties (s. 210). It may also, with the consent of all the parties to a dispute, refer all or any matter for arbitration. The Service also has an important role in this area, and others, by issuing Codes of Practice (s. 199) which, along with those introduced by the Secretary of State, may be used in evidence in court as to good industrial practice. Inquiries may be held into industrial relations generally (s. 214), but it has done this only rarely, and it may give advice regarding such matters (s. 213). (See further, Chapter 14 below.)

1.2.5 **The Central Arbitration Committee**

The CAC is a body which, although working as part of government, acts independently of ministerial direction (TULR(C)A 1992, s. 259). Its function is to provide services as an industrial relations arbitration body. It does so particularly in the area of failures to disclose information for collective bargaining purposes and with regard to recognition disputes. (See Simpson, (2007) 36 ILJ 287; and Chapter 14 below.)

SELECTED READING

Barnard, C., Deakin S., and Morris, G. (eds) (2004), *The Future of Labour Law: Liber Amicorum Sir Bob Hepple QC*, Oxford: Hart Publishing

Bowers, J., Brown, D., Mead, G., and Ackerman, N. B. (2001), *Employment Tribunal Practice and Procedure,* London: Sweet & Maxwell

Brodie, D. (2003), *A History of British Labour Law, 1867–1945,* Oxford: Hart Publishing

Burton, M. (2005), 'The Employment Appeal Tribunal: October 2002–July 2005', (2005) 34 ILJ 273

Honeyball, S. (2005), 'Employment Law and the Appellate Committee of the House of Lords', (2005) 24 *Civil Justice Quarterly* 364

Latreille, P., Latreille J., and Knight, K. (2005), 'Making a Difference? Legal Representation in Employment Tribunal Cases: Evidence from a Survey of Representatives', (2005) 34 ILJ 308

O'Cinneide, C. (2007), 'The Commission for Equality and Human Rights: A New Institution for New and Uncertain Times', (2007) 36 ILJ 141

Painter, R. W. and Holmes, A. E. (2010), *Cases and Materials on Employment Law,* 8th edn, Oxford: Oxford University Press, ch. 1

Steinfeld, R. (1991), *The Invention of Free Labor: The Employment Relation in English and American Law and Culture, 1350–1870*, Chapel Hill, NC: University of North Carolina Press

2

The concept of employment

SUMMARY

This chapter concentrates on the meaning of 'employment', what is required in law for a worker to be considered to be an employee and what types of workers are not. It begins by examining the tests that have been developed at common law in order to determine this, and the extent to which they are, and should be, driven by policy considerations. Other categories of work relationships are then considered and examined particularly in order to see whether they are mutually exclusive with employment or whether they overlap. In addition, particular types of employees are explored and their legal employment status explained. The chapter ends by critically addressing the question as to whether employment status is considered by the courts to be a question of law or one of fact.

2.1 The purpose of defining employment

Most working people have a contract of employment and are employees or, in the old-fashioned word still very occasionally used by some members of the judiciary, servants. A builder building an extension to a house, a watchmaker repairing a watch, or a plumber mending a tap are, however, more likely to be engaged on contracts for services, that is to say, to be independent contractors.

2.1.1 The importance of employment status

It is fundamental to employment law to identify who is an employee and who is an independent contractor in that, although some rights now extend to the wider category of worker (see Freedland, (2006) 35 ILJ 1; Davidov, (2005) 34 ILJ 57; *cf.* Brodie (2005) 34 ILJ 253) most still require employment status. Yet statute provides only an outline distinction between the modes in which a person may sell labour. The ERA 1996, s. 230(1) defines an 'employee' as 'an individual who has entered into or works under (or, where the employment has ceased, worked under) a contract of employment' but other Acts contain different definitions. For example, Sex Discrimination Act 1975, s. 82(1) refers to 'employment under a contract of service or of apprenticeship or a contract personally to execute any work or labour'. The Act therefore covers many workers who would be considered independent contractors under the 1996 Act. The correct category largely depends on conflicting tests established at common law over several decades. They were first formulated to decide on vicarious liability, that is, when an employer is liable to a third party for the torts of employees, a subject which is still troubling the courts today—see *Lister* v *Hesley Hall Ltd* (2001); *Balfron Computer Industries Ltd* v *Peterson* (2001); *Dubai Aluminium Co. Ltd* v *Salaam* (2003). The distinction is now vital more generally since, for example, only employees qualify for benefits, employment protection rights, protection of wages on their employer's insolvency, the benefit of their employer's common law duty of care, and protection under the health and safety legislation. The distinction is most important on a day-to-day basis for taxation, since employees are taxed differently from the self-employed.

2.1.2 The role of policy

The common law tests are the same for this multiplicity of purposes. Yet the policy considerations behind a decision under each heading differ. Thus, in determining vicarious liability, control by the employer of the employee causing the injury might be considered most relevant, in that policy would seem to dictate that the employer is in fact the real tortfeasor. By contrast, in respect of National Insurance contributions and tax, avoidance by the employee might be uppermost in the court's mind. But it would clearly be unrealistic to expect the courts to take a totally policy-oriented approach, differing in each case. As Hugh Collins has pointed out, it is tempting to urge such a course on the courts, but an attempt to introduce this in the United States proved to be brief. The courts do require (and perhaps ought to have) a firm set of criteria to guide them. Collins himself suggests a rule that a contract of employment may be said to exist for the purposes of employment protection law if the worker performs services for another, referable to an agreement, unless that contract satisfies two conditions, namely that it is for the performance of tasks (not determined by duration) and that no 'badges of membership' of the firm's organisation apply, such as adherence to a dress code (Collins, (1990) 10 OJLS 353 at p. 378).

It may be unrealistic for the courts to have different tests in the light of differing policy issues, but it is altogether another matter not to confuse the policy considerations in one context with those in another, and therefore to clearly delineate and constrict the apposite case law in any given instance. (See further Honeyball, [2005] *Cambrian Law Review* 1.) But this is not so clear a distinction in practice as it might appear. This can be illustrated by the decision of the EAT in *Hilton International Hotels (UK) Ltd* v *Protopapa* (1990). The employee was claiming unfair dismissal. She needed to show that her resignation amounted to a dismissal by the employer because she was entitled to resign by reason of the employer's breach of contract—a constructive dismissal. But the relevant conduct was that of her immediate superior only. The EAT held that the tests for vicarious liability in tort were correct here, although clearly within the context of a statutory claim.

2.1.3 Policy and definition

The existence of differing definitions and approaches shows that the issue is not a simple definitional one. The courts are not, and should not be, engaged on a voyage of lexicographical discovery for the correct definition of 'employment'. Indeed, they never have been, despite appearances to the contrary. As Clark and Wedderburn point out, Victorian judges were able to reaffirm the master's right to control his servant because the notion of control had been inherent in the idea of 'service' from medieval times (see Wedderburn, Lewis, and Clark, *Labour Law and Industrial Relations* (Oxford: Clarendon Press, 1983), p. 147). The courts were intent on bolstering the employer's control since this was in accord with their social and political principles. The position is similar today under statute. Definitions of 'employment' change, not because of differing conceptions, but because the term is used merely as shorthand to signify who in policy terms should be entitled or obligated, as the case may be, in the particular context in question. As the policy changes from Act to Act and context to context, it would seem that any attempt to provide a general definition or working test is doomed to failure. Indeed, Collins recognises this by restricting his definition to employment protection legislation. Since the term 'employment' is used in this functional way, the courts should be vigilant not to imagine that it is employment in the everyday sense with which they are concerned, or indeed, in the senses used in other legal contexts, but it is not clear that they are so vigilant.

2.1.4 Employer status

It is interesting to note that the focus is on the employee, or would-be employee, in all these approaches, with little attention paid to the employer. (See further, Deakin, (2001) 30 ILJ 72.) Indeed, Freedland has described the concept of 'employer' in employment law as in a 'ramshackle' condition—see Freedland, (2005) 58 *Current Legal Problems* 517. This emphasis on the employee can lead to a caricaturing of the employer which is at odds with small employers—see e.g. Fredman, (2004) 33 ILJ 299, who argues that duties fall on employers 'because of the civic responsibility which attaches to those with power'.

   With these observations in mind, let us now examine the various tests that have been constructed by the courts in determining who is an employee.

2.2 The tests of employment

2.2.1 Control

Since it was in the context of vicarious liability that the courts first considered who was an employee, it was natural, as we have seen, that they saw its touchstone as control. They examined whether the master controlled or had the right to control not only what the worker did but also the manner in which he did it (*Yewens* v *Noakes* (1880); *Performing Right Society* v *Mitchell and Booker (Palais de Danse) Ltd* (1924)). The control test was taken to its logical conclusion when a court held that nurses were not employees of a hospital when carrying out duties in the operating theatre as they took their orders from the operating surgeon and not from the hospital authorities (*Hillyer* v *Governors of St Bartholomew's Hospital* (1909)). This rigidity led to criticism (e.g. in *Lindsey County Council* v *Mary Marshall* (1937)). As the pace of technological change hastened, it became obviously unrealistic to conceive of the employer having the knowledge to control many of his increasingly highly skilled employees. One only has to consider as examples a surgeon, a research chemist or an airline pilot, since all will have know-how far beyond that of their employers. The breakthrough towards a more realistic approach came in a series of cases in the late 1940s and early 1950s in which hospitals were held vicariously liable for the acts of surgeons, radiographers, and other specialists (e.g. *Cassidy* v *Ministry of Health* (1951)). It would be a mistake to think that this was a change brought about entirely by technological and other forms of advance, because, as Wedderburn, Lewis, and Clark point out (*supra*, p. 150), very early cases were often concerned with employees who were more skilled than their employer.

However, in the middle of the last century the courts were reluctant to let go the element of control, and the result was that it became one of a number of factors, although sometimes still the determining one—see *Montgomery* v *Johnson Underwood Ltd* (2001). Thus Lord Thankerton in *Short* v *J. & W. Henderson Ltd* (1946) looked at whether the putative master had the power of selection of his servant, the right to control the method of doing the work, and the right of suspension and dismissal. Only if these questions were answered in the affirmative, and the worker received wages or other remuneration, would a contract of employment exist. As this notion developed two general criteria of 'integration' and 'economic reality' came into use.

2.2.2 Integration

In 1952 Denning LJ considered that the decisive question was whether the person under consideration was fully integrated into the employer's organisation (*Stevenson, Jordan and Harrison Ltd* v *Macdonald and Evans* (1952)). A ship's master, a chauffeur, and a reporter on the staff of a newspaper were thus all employed under a contract *of* service and therefore employees, but a ship's pilot, a taxidriver, and a newspaper contributor were hired under a contract *for* services and therefore independent contractors. He detected that: 'one feature which seems to run through the instances is that, under a contract of service a man is employed as part of the business and his work is done as an integral part of the business but under a contract for services his work, although done for the business is not integrated into it but only accessory to it'. In a later case (*Bank voor Handel en Scheepvaart NV* v *Slatford* (1953) reversed by the House of Lords (1954)), Denning LJ reformulated the question as to whether the worker was 'part and parcel' of the employer's organisation (see also *Beloff* v *Pressdram Ltd* (1973)). The great drawback of this approach lies in its failure to define exactly what is meant by 'integration' and 'organisation'. Indeed, it has been doubted whether Denning intended to lay down such a test at all (see Winder, (1964) 80 LQR 160). That doubt would seem to rest more on a desire to retain the control test than on a correct interpretation of the judgment in *Stevenson* itself.

2.2.3 Economic reality and the multiple test

More recently the courts have recognised that no one test or set of criteria can be decisive. Instead they have adopted something like the American notion of an 'economic reality' composite test (see *United States of America* v *Silk* (1946)) and the clearest illustration is the very full judgment in *Ready Mixed Concrete (South East) Ltd* v *Minister of Pensions & National Insurance* (1968). The case concerned the appellant company's liability for social security contributions of their workers which arose only if they had contracts of service. The workers drove ready mixed concrete lorries they were buying on hire purchase agreement from the appellant company, which required in a detailed contract of 30 pages that they must, *inter alia*, use the lorry only on company business, maintain it in accordance with the company's instructions and obey all reasonable orders. Although this suggested a measure of close control, there were no requirements about hours of work and the times at which the drivers took holidays. Moreover, they could generally hire out the driving of their vehicle to another and were paid, subject to a yearly minimum, according to the amount of concrete they transported. McKenna J identified three conditions for a contract of service. First, the employee agrees that in consideration of a wage or other remuneration he will provide his own work and skill in performing some service for the employer. Secondly, the employee agrees expressly or impliedly that in performance of that service he will be subject to the employer's control to a sufficient degree, and thirdly that the other provisions of the contract are consistent with it being a contract of service. The first condition seems unsatisfactory in that the reference to 'other remuneration' clearly does not serve to provide the distinction between employees and others in that it merely sets the requirement of consideration without which there can be no contract of any kind. But it is the third condition which has caused most difficulty in the subsequent case law. In *Market Investigations Ltd* v *Minister of Social Security* (1969) Cooke J paraphrased the fundamental test as whether the person performing services was in business on his own account. If the answer was yes, the contract was for services; but it was not so in the instant case where the respondents engaged interviewers for a short time during which they were free to work when they wished and were permitted to perform tasks for other companies. The judge felt that no exhaustive list of considerations which were relevant to determining the question could be compiled, nor could strict rules be laid down as to the relative weight which various considerations could carry in particular cases. Indeed, in some cases it has been recognised that the only sure test is to ask whether an ordinary person would think there was a contract of service (see *Withers* v *Flackwell Heath Football Supporters' Club* (1981)). This appears to be an abdication of the responsibility to decide, and ignores the fact that it is not the commonly-held conception of 'employment' that is being sought here. The 'shorthand' nature of the term, discussed above, and the policy issues that underlie the need to determine whether the worker is an employee, mean that such a common sense approach is inappropriate here. In *WHPT Housing Association Ltd* v *Secretary of State for Social Services* (1981) Webster J saw the essence of the distinction as the fact that the employee provides himself to serve, while the independent contractor provides only his services. This adds very little to finding a solution in that it merely begs the question. It is precisely because it is problematic to determine when an employee provides himself to serve, or to provide services, that the issue arises.

These sorts of instinctive jury-based approaches which derive initially from Somervell J in *Cassidy* v *Ministry of Health* (1951) may easily devolve into casuistry (see e.g. *Thames TV Ltd* v *Wallis* (1979); *Challinor* v *Taylor* (1972); *Argent* v *Minister of Social Services* (1968); *Warner Holidays Ltd* v *Secretary of State for Social Services* (1983)) and are inappropriate in the context of a judge sitting alone, or even for the guidance of ETs. Certainly the Court of Appeal did not find the approach especially helpful in *Nethermere (St Neots) Ltd* v *Taverna & Gardiner* (1984), although the Privy Council in *Lee* v *Chung* (1990) felt that the matter had never been better put than in *Market Investigations*. In *Nethermere* the court emphasised that a contract of service required an irreducible minimum of obligation on each side of the bargain to do work, or provide work, as the case may be. This is an approach that has been adopted on numerous occasions (see e.g. *Clark* v *Oxfordshire Health Authority* (1998)). (See too *Express and Echo Publications Ltd* v *Tanton* (1999), where the Court of Appeal placed great emphasis on the fact that there was no obligation to perform the contract personally although this does not necessarily mean the contract is not one of service—see *Byrne Brothers (Formwork) Ltd* v *Baird* (2002); *MacFarlane* v *Glasgow City Council* (2001).) However, as Jean Warburton has pointed out (see (1984) 13 ILJ 251), it is difficult in strict contract law to see how there can be any form of contract at all without an irreducible minimum of obligation (a point now taken up by the EAT—see *Cotswold Developments Construction Ltd* v *Williams* (2006)) and this factor alone therefore would not seem to draw the necessary distinction. In addition, of course, the extent of the obligation can arise from the fact of employment. The implication of terms occurs because of the existence of employment status and not vice versa. The test therefore seems to put the cart before the horse.

McNeill J in *Warner Holidays Ltd* v *Secretary of State for Social Services* (1983) was not persuaded that a checklist of criteria was the proper guide or that the court ought to be required to tick off or negate point by point the items on such a list (see also *Hall (HM Inspector of Taxes)* v *Lorimer* (1994)). Essentially, all the relevant facts have to be looked at in the aggregate to determine, in the absence of an unambiguous or unequivocal written contract, what it was that the parties intended. However, some indication of the factors considered by the courts as attributes of employees and independent contractors is possible.

This question was considered by the House of Lords in *Carmichael* v *National Power plc* (2000)—see Clarke, (2000) 63 MLR 757. The Court of Appeal had decided the case in favour of casual workers who were paid on an 'as required' basis. They did this placing greater importance on the term which they found to be implied, that the employers would provide the workers with the work that became available but without the guarantee than any would be available, than on the absence of mutuality of obligation. This signalled a change in direction by the Court of Appeal, but on appeal it was reversed by the House of Lords. This was on a matter of construction of the relevant documentary evidence of the contract, but their Lordships did place emphasis again on mutuality of obligation. The decision prompted an interesting analysis by Collins (see (2000) 29 ILJ 73), which draws a very useful analogy between types of commercial contracts and employment contracts. Collins's view is that the real problem that casual workers should have is not that they are not employed on contracts of employment, because they are. Rather, the difficulty is that these periods of employment are of insufficient continuous duration to allow these workers to satisfy the requirements of continuous employment to make them eligible to bring statutory employment protection claims. As such, the courts should explore the possibilities of establishing continuity for these workers under provisions in the relevant legislation that allow breaks between contracts to be disregarded. (See further *Stevedoring and Haulage Services* v *Fuller* (2001); and Leighton's analysis at (2002) 31 ILJ 71.)

Independence

Clearly, ownership of tools and instruments by the worker points in the direction of self-employment, in that it suggests a degree of independence. However, payment of wages and sick pay indicates that the person under consideration is an employee, since the independent contractor usually receives a lump sum for the job and bears any risk himself. As Lord Widgery put it in *Global Plant Ltd* v *Secretary of State for Social Services* (1972):

> If a man agrees to perform an operation for a fixed sum and thus stands to lose if the work is delayed, and to profit if it is done quickly, that is the man who on the face of it appears to be an independent contractor working under a contract for services.

This factor was of some importance in the case of *Hitchcock* v *Post Office* (1980), where a sub-postmaster who provided the shop for his sub-post office was held to be self-employed even though he had to carry out Post Office instructions and had to advise the head postmaster if he were absent for three days or more. The decision was supported by the facts that he could delegate his duties to others, and bore the risk of profit or loss (see the same result in *Tanna* v *Post Office* (1981)).

Residual control

The presence or absence of residual control (that is to say, potential rather than actual day-to-day control) is still an important factor but it is not the only one. In *Addison* v *London Philharmonic Orchestra Ltd* (1981) orchestral musicians were held to be independent contractors since the obligations imposed on them were the very minimum to ensure that the work was done. Personal attendance at rehearsals and self-discipline were simply prerequisites of a concert artist's work and did not decisively point to a contract of service. (See also *Midland Sinfonia Concert Society Ltd* v *Secretary of State for Social Services* (1981); *Lane* v *Shire Roofing Co. (Oxford) Ltd* (1995).) Indeed, the example of orchestral musicians, who are clearly under actual control in the way they perform their work (namely, of the conductor), shows how relatively unimportant the concept of control may be in determining the nature of the relationship. As Cooke J said in *Market Investigations Ltd* v *Minister of Social Security* (1969): 'The most that can be said is that control will no doubt always have to be considered, although it can no longer be regarded as the sole decisive factor.' Other factors can be highly important. For example, the more discretion a worker has as to *when* his work will be performed, the more likely it is that the worker is under a contract for services. (See e.g. *Narich Pty Ltd* v *Commissioner of Pay-roll Tax* (1984).)

Tax

Deduction of tax and National Insurance contributions point to employment, but this is not decisive *(Davis* v *New England College of Arundel* (1977); *Airfix Footwear Ltd* v *Cope* (1978)) as that is best viewed as a consequence rather than as a determinant of an employment relationship. However, a casual and short-term engagement suggests the status of independent contractor, especially when the worker retains the right to, or actually does, work elsewhere *(Argent* v *Minister of Social Security* (1968)), as does the fact that an individual works at his own premises.

Self-description

Often the parties to a contract describe themselves as hirer and independent contractor or employer and employee. This is not decisive in determining the true characterisation in law, since the courts consider the substance of the relationship and not its form (*Davis* v *New England College of Arundel* (1977); *Autoclenz Ltd* v *Belcher* (2010)). This seems to be especially true where there are public obligations involved, such as social security contributions. The description may, however, have persuasive value. In *Warner Holidays Ltd* v *Secretary of State for Social Services* (1983) McNeill J made it clear that parties to a contract should not, by private arrangement, exclude public or community obligations, but different considerations would seem to apply where the parties have not colluded for this purpose. The issue most commonly comes before the courts where the parties have chosen a self-employed relationship for reasons of tax or National Insurance, but the worker later seeks the benefits of employee status in order to gain statutory employment protection rights. This often happens in the teaching profession and in the building trade where the self-employed 'lump' is a well developed institution. The cases are by no means easy to reconcile.

In *Ferguson* v *John Dawson and Partners (Contractors) Ltd* (1976) the worker was told on his very informal hiring as a 'general labourer' that he would become part of a 'lump' labour force. There were no 'cards' and no deductions were to be made for tax and National Insurance. He nevertheless had to obey the company's instructions concerning what to do and when to do it. When he was seriously injured in the course of his work, the success of his claim for industrial injuries benefit, and damages for breach of statutory duty, depended solely on whether he was an employee, all other criteria being fulfilled. Megaw and Browne LJJ decided that he was so entitled, notwithstanding the arrangements voluntarily entered into. The self-description of the parties was only one factor to be taken into account. Lawton LJ dissented and took a more stringent view. It was, he thought, open to anyone to decide how he was to sell his labour and 'contrary to public policy to allow a man to say that he was self-employed for the purposes of avoiding the incidence of tax, then a servant for the purpose of claiming compensation'. He thought that the parties were estopped from reneging on the agreement made.

At least two later EAT cases followed the majority approach rather than that adopted by Lawton LJ—*Davis* v *New England College of Arundel* (1977); *Tyne and Clyde Warehouses Ltd* v *Hamerton* (1978)—and this was consistent with the academic opinion expressed at the time (see e.g. the views of Russell in (1977) 40 MLR 479 who argues very strongly that the economic realities should be the dominant consideration, making it harder for the parties to conceal the true nature of the relationship). The Court of Appeal has, however, since drawn a distinction between the *Ferguson* case and situations where there is an actual and considered, albeit agreed, change in status. In *Massey* v *Crown Life Insurance Company* (1978) the applicant had been employed for two years by the respondents as a branch manager. He then entered into a new arrangement with them whereby he registered himself as John L. Massey and Associates with the Registry of Business Names and his one-man business was appointed manager. The main effect was that the respondents no longer made tax or other deductions from fees paid to Mr Massey. The Inland Revenue agreed to treat him as self-employed, notwithstanding that his duties largely remained the same. When he was removed with one month's notice, he was held not entitled to bring a claim for unfair dismissal since he was self-employed. Lord Denning MR distinguished *Ferguson* on its facts because:

there is a perfectly genuine agreement entered into at the instance of Mr Massey on the footing that he is 'self-employed'. He gets the benefit of it by avoiding tax deductions and getting his pension contributions returned. I do not see that he can come along afterwards and say it is something else in order to claim that has been unfairly dismissed. Having made his bed as being 'self-employed' he must lie on it.

The written contract here 'becomes the best material from which to gather the true relationship between the parties'. On the other hand, 'the parties cannot alter the truth of [the] relationship by putting a different label on it and use it as a dishonest device to deceive the Revenue'.

However, the Court of Appeal's decision in *Young and Woods Ltd* v *West* (1980) suggests that *Massey* should be confined to its facts. The respondent, a skilled sheet metal worker, chose self-employment, again for tax reasons, but since he was paid on an hourly rate, had normal working hours and had use of the respondent's equipment, he was classified as an employee by the Court of Appeal and was thus eligible to claim unfair dismissal. The important feature for Stephenson LJ was that the applicant was not 'in business on his own account'. He distinguished *Massey* on two grounds; first, that the applicant in that case had two contracts, one of service as manager of the branch office and the other for services under a general agency agreement, and secondly that the self-employment resulted from a deliberate change of relationship. It therefore seems that it is important to distinguish two important policy considerations here. The first concerns the ability of the parties to determine the status of their own relationship. Generally, question of fact or not, that should not be done because to allow the parties to do so would be to give them the capacity to contract out of employment protection provisions by the back door, which is contrary to ERA 1996, s. 203. The courts have not spelt it out in terms, but it is implicit in what Stephenson LJ in particular had to say in *Young and Woods* that estoppel was inapplicable in this area so that the parties should be bound to a position they have deliberately and openly chosen. For no other reason (and the argument considered below that the question is really one of law and not fact is just such another reason) this would seem to be right in principle. That is not to say that the views of the parties are always irrelevant. Indeed, *Massey* and *Ferguson* can be reconciled on the basis that in *Massey* the status of the relationship was ambiguous, as Thompson suggests (see (1979) 95 LQR 190).

The second policy consideration is that it should not be permissible to have one's cake and eat it. It should not be possible to argue a change of status when it suits a person to do so. One way to prevent this would be to apply the doctrine of estoppel, but that has the effect of enabling the parties to contract out of the Act, as we have seen, which is also contrary to policy. But there is an alternative route, and that is to determine the correct position of the parties and then to remedy any advantage taken of an earlier misdescription—hence the statement of Stephenson LJ in *Young and Woods* that the Revenue had a duty to retrieve the balance of tax not paid in the past by virtue of a more favourable tax assessment based upon non-employed status. On the other hand, in *Hewlett Packard Ltd* v *O'Murphy* (2002) the EAT held that an applicant was not an employee for unfair dismissal purposes, even though he was classed as such for tax purposes. In this case, he neither had his cake nor ate it.

The analogy was slightly different in the Court of Appeal's decision in *Protectacoat Firthglow Ltd* v *Szilagyi* (2009)—there it was that the employer 'wanted the ha'penny of treating their installers as employees when it came to attendance and control and also wanted the bun of not having to give them the rights they would enjoy as employees'—but the same issue was still troubling them. The Court of Appeal had previously decided in *Consistent Group Ltd* v *Kalwak* (2008) (reversing Elias J in the EAT below) that for the court to go behind the parties' self-description on the basis that it was a sham, it was necessary for both of them to intend it to be so. In *Protectacoat* the court reverted to the idea that it is simply necessary for the position in reality to be identified, however the parties might describe it. In any event, the status of the relationship may have changed over time since the description was made in the original contract. This therefore places less emphasis on the written terms of the contract and requires the ET to establish what the 'true' relationship is. As Anne Davies has written, this is a 'challenging task'—see Davies, (2009) 38 ILJ 318.

2.3 Other work relationships

2.3.1 Office-holders

The most widely cited general definition of an office is that formulated by Rowlatt J in *Great Western Railway* v *Bater* (1920) (a taxation case), that it is 'a subsisting, permanent, substantive position which has its existence independently from the person who fills it, which continues and is filled in succession by successive holders'. Clearest examples are:

(a) trustees (e.g. *Attorney-General for NSW* v *Perpetual Trustee Co. Ltd* (1955));

(b) bailiffs;

(c) trade union officers (*Stevenson* v *URTU* (1977));

(d) officers of the Salvation Army (*Rogers* v *Booth* (1935));

(e) company directors (*Ellis* v *Lucas* (1967));

(f) police officers (*Fisher* v *Oldham Corporation* (1930));

(g) prison officers (*Home Office* v *Robinson* (1982));

(h) and company registrars (*IRC* v *Brander & Cruickshank* (1971)).

Clergy

An interesting question was raised in two cases relating to the employment status of clergy. In *President of the Methodist Conference* v *Parfitt* (1984) the Court of Appeal held that a Methodist minister did not have a contract of service because there was no contract at all. The House of Lords found the same in *Davies* v *Presbyterian Church of Wales* (1986) although it did allow (but not on the facts here) that it was possible for duties to be owed to God and Man. It would therefore seem, as there was no contract at all, and even if there were one not one of service, that the clergy involved did not hold offices. As Woolman points out ((1986) 102 LQR 356) this presumably meant that a minister could not sue in respect of his emoluments, nor have rights in respect of superannuation. Likewise there could be no vicarious liability on the part of the church. The common sense position seems to be that, at the very least, clergy are either officer-holders or employees—indeed, the lay members of the tribunals in both *Parfitt* and *Davies* came to the conclusion that they were employees. To say, as Lord Templeman did in *Davies*, that neither party *intended* the relationship to be legally binding surely begs the question. Howarth argues convincingly that the decision undermines the traditional analysis, at least in respect of the non-conformist churches (see (1986) 45 CLJ 404). Brodin has argued, at length and convincingly, that to take a broad brush to these categories is to misunderstand their diversity (see Brodin, (1996) 25 ILJ 211). The position of the clergy does not seem satisfactory. Their union, amicus, found in a survey at the end of 2003 that 82 per cent of clergy knew of a fellow minister who had been treated unacceptably by the church.

There are now signs that the courts themselves are adopting a more realistic approach to the issue, opening the door to employment claims. The House of Lords held in *Percy* v *Church of Scotland Board of National Mission* (2006) that the essential difference is between employment and self-employment, not employment and office-holding. It is possible to be both an office-holder and an employee. (See too *New Testament Church of God* v *Stewart* (2008)).

The Church of England has recently stated that it remains committed to giving rights to its clergy 'analogous' to those of employees.

Magistrates

The courts have decided that JPs and rent officers fall within the definition of office-holder (*Knight* v *AG* (1979); *Department of the Environment* v *Fox* (1979)); but not a civil engineer who conducted public inquiries on behalf of what was then the Department of the Environment because of the lack of continuity and permanence of his position (*Edwards* v *Clinch* (1981)). In *R* v *Hertfordshire County Council ex parte National Union of Public Employees* (1985), Sir John Donaldson MR rejected the decision of the judge below that each local authority employee was an 'officer' within Local Government Act 1972, s. 112. It was at least arguable, he said, that only a person who filled a position which had an existence independent of the person who for the time being occupied it merited such description, but this is clearly a distinction easier to state than to identify. The decision has been called 'somewhat cavalier' by one writer (see Stokes, (1985) 14 ILJ 117).

Formality of appointment

The High Court held in *McMenamin (Inspector of Taxes)* v *Diggles* (1991) that the absence of an instrument creating and defining an office of senior barristers' clerk, and the lack of formal appointment, meant that a finding that the appellant was not the holder of an office could not be disturbed. This seems to raise a novel hurdle, and is hardly applicable as a general test.

2.3.2 Directors

A director is an officer of the company but may also have a contract of service, whether an express service agreement or one implied at law. In *Albert J. Parsons & Sons Ltd* v *Parsons* (1979) the Court of Appeal held that there was no contract of employment in the case of a full-time working director who was paid director's fees only and had not been treated as employed for National Insurance purposes. While a director may be removed from office by a simple majority at a general meeting of the company, this is without prejudice to any rights under contract. The decision is essentially one of fact for the tribunal according to the EAT in *Eaton* v *Robert Eaton Ltd* (1988).

The Companies Act 1985 contains two provisions of particular importance in relation to directors' service agreements. First, by s. 318, a company must keep a copy of every written service agreement and a written memorandum of every oral contract. Secondly, under s. 319, a company may not give its directors a contract of employment for more than five years unless the company approves it by resolution in general meeting. If no such resolution is passed, any contract must be terminable on notice by the company.

There is nothing in law to prevent a controlling shareholder from being an employee, and therefore a majority shareholding should be just one factor to be taken into account in determining employment status, according to the Court of Appeal in *Secretary of State for Trade and Industry* v *Bottrill* (1999) and *Sellars Arenascene Ltd* v *Connolly* (2001), and reinforced in *Secretary of State for Business, Enterprise and Regulatory Reform* v *Neufeld* (2009). If in any circumstances a person were to use the corporate veil to obtain advantage by claiming employment status (such as failing to pay himself wages in order for them to be claimed against the Secretary of State in the event of impending insolvency) no doubt this would be an important if not overriding factor. But in other circumstances where no sham is involved, there would appear to be no reason to disallow employment status. (See too the EAT's decisions in *Nesbitt* v *Secretary of State for Trade and Industry* (2007), and *Gladwell* v *Secretary of State for Trade and Industry* (2007).)

2.3.3 Training and learning

Apprenticeship is not only a relationship of employment, for the apprentice agrees to serve the employer for the purpose also of learning and the employer agrees to teach the apprentice. Many old rules, such as the master's duty to provide medical care and right to chastise, apply to the institution which is rarely adopted now. Apprentices are now included in most statutory definitions of employment (see e.g. ERA 1996, s. 230(1)). In 2009 the Government steered through the Apprenticeships, Skills, Children and Learning Act which placed its own apprenticeships programme on a statutory footing, and aims to guarantee that all suitably qualified young people will be entitled to an apprenticeship place. The Act also entitles young people in schools to receive proper information, advice and guidance about vocational training opportunities, and to request of their employer time for training.

Some people provide services only to a limited degree ancillary to their main role of learning and are distinct from apprentices. Thus a university student's essays for a tutor are not services however hard he or she labours on them, and even though there is some sort of contract with the university it is not one of service. The same applies to a research student engaged on a specific project (*Hugh-Jones* v *St John's College, Cambridge* (1979)).

In *Daley* v *Allied Suppliers* (1983) it was held that a person taking part in a work experience scheme as part of the Youth Opportunities Programme was not a person employed within the meaning of the Race Relations Act 1976. There was no contract binding the applicants and respondents together notwithstanding that they owed some obligations towards each other. If there were a contract it was one of training, enabling the applicant to acquire certain skills and experience (see to the same effect *Hawley* v *Fieldcastle & Co. Ltd* (1982)). It is not clear from the reasoning of the EAT, however, why there was no contract in law. If there are obligations existing between the parties, it would seem that the element of a legally binding contract that is missing is the necessary intention to enter a legal relationship. But the EAT did not state on what basis this conclusion was reached, whether it was to be determined by the facts of the instant case alone, or whether a general rule of law could be extrapolated.

A Modern Apprentice may have a contract of employment but is not an apprentice in the traditional sense as, *inter alia*, it is not for a fixed term according to the Court of Appeal in *Flett* v *Matheson* (2006). It all depends upon whether the trainee satisfies the ordinary tests of employment.

An articled clerk in a solicitor's office (equivalent to a present-day trainee solicitor) was held to be employed by the firm and not merely by the partner to whom she was articled in *Oliver* v *J. P. Malnick & Co.* (1983). The normal arrangement for trainee solicitors is for a dual system involving a training contract with the solicitor with whom he or she is placed, with a contract of employment with the firm. It is difficult to see how there is a difference in principle or policy between such trainees and those training in other contexts.

2.3.4 Labour-only sub-contractors

Especially common in the building industry is the practice of the 'lump', whereby an individual contractor supplies his labour to complete a job and is paid in a lump sum. Such workers often move on and off the 'cards' (that is, from employment to this form of self-employment and back again), with regularity, performing the same work in both capacities. This is done with the acquiescence of the 'hirers', the main contractors, who thereby have less paperwork, and there are particular advantages in respect of National Insurance contributions. One drawback is that it retards effective trade unions in the building industry due to the mobility of the workforce (see further the Report of the Phelps Brown Committee of Inquiry into Labour in Building and Civil Engineering (Cmnd 3714) (London: HMSO, 1968)). Moreover, such labourers cannot claim employment protection rights. There has been no legislative intervention on this score, but the widespread avoidance of tax has received specific attention in that such independent lump contractors are treated similarly, but by no means identically, to employees under the Income and Corporation Taxes Act 1988, ss 559–567. Payments made by a main contractor to a sub-contractor accordingly must have tax deducted at source, save where the sub-contractor has obtained a certificate that he is running a *bona fide* business covered by adequate insurance, and that he has complied with tax requirements over a three-year period. Further, the contractor is responsible for Class 1 National Insurance contributions.

2.3.5 Outworkers

Those who work at home (a practice especially common in the garment industry), generally suffer low pay (frequently being paid less than the national minimum wage) and if, as is often the case, the outworker can refuse to do work if asked, it is more likely that the relationship is that of independent contractor. On the other hand, in *Nethermere (St Neots) Ltd* v *Taverna & Gardiner* (1984) the two applicants were found to be employees notwithstanding that they had no fixed hours for doing work brought to their homes by the company and for a number of weeks did no work at all. There was an irreducible minimum of obligation required for the contract to be one of service, and there was 'a picture of the applicants doing the same work for the same rate as the employees in the factory but in their own homes—and in their own time—for the convenience of the worker and the company', per Stephenson LJ (see also *Airfix Footwear Ltd* v *Cope* (1978)). One difficulty with this test is that the irreducible minimum of obligation would seem to go more to the point as to whether there is a contract at all, and not to whether it is one of service. There can, after all, be no contract of any description without an irreducible minimum of obligation.

2.3.6 Casual workers

The most detailed discussion of the position of casual workers is found in the Court of Appeal's judgment in *O'Kelly* v *Trusthouse Forte plc* (1983). The appellants worked as wine butlers at the Grosvenor House Hotel. They were known as 'regular casuals' and were given preference in the work rotas over other casual staff. They had no other employment. The tribunal found that many factors were consistent with a contract of service but one was missing—mutuality of obligation. The respondent had no obligation to provide work, and if the workers could obtain alternative work, they were free to take it. The preferential rota position was not a contractual promise. The court was not attracted by the proposition that there was in fact a series of short contracts of service, instead holding that the workers were self-employed. There are some obvious problems with the court's reasoning here. One is that the fact that the respondent had no obligation to provide work should have been irrelevant in this context, for it has long been established that there is normally (unless the employee's reputation or remuneration depends upon it) no duty on an employer to provide work where there is a contract of service. As one judge put it, so long as a cook is paid her wages, she cannot complain if her employer takes any or all of his meals out (see *Collier* v *Sunday Referee Publishing Co. Ltd* (1940); *Wilson* v *Circular Distributors Ltd* (2006)). Where no wages are due when no work is done, it would seem self-evident that there is no contract of employment, but this was reiterated by the Court of Appeal in *Clark* v *Oxfordshire Health Authority* (1998). Leighton has argued that, although the court in *O'Kelly* notionally applied the economic reality test, it was in fact all but ignored ((1984) 13 ILJ 62). The workers provided no capital or equipment, there was no share in the profits, the hotel provided the uniforms, there was no use of agents and no evidence of multiple employment. The way would therefore, at the very least, have seemed open to the Court of Appeal to have provided some protection for a highly vulnerable sector of the workforce, but it failed to do so.

2.3.7 Agency workers

A growing sector of the economy is manned by agency workers. Until recently they were unlikely to be employees of the agency especially when they work on a temporary basis. In *Wickens* v *Champion Employment* (1984) the main considerations militating against employee status of agency workers were that the agency was held to have no obligation to find work for its workers and the contracts did not create a relationship with the necessary elements of continuity and care, even though the workers were described as employees in the business's documentation. Leighton argued that the EAT in this case failed to understand how most agency contracts work ((1985) 14 ILJ 54). The courts came round to this point of view and in *Consistent Group Ltd* v *Kalwak* (2007) the EAT held that, if there were a sufficient degree of control, there may be an employment relationship between the worker and the agency. However, this might prevent a finding of an employment relationship with the end-user—see *Cairns* v *Visteon UK Ltd* (2007).

Following a suggestion to this effect in *Franks* v *Reuters Ltd* (2003), the Court of Appeal held in *Dacas* v *Brook Street Bureau (UK) Ltd* (2004) that temporary agency workers may be characterised as employees of the end-user—see Reynolds, (2005) 34 ILJ 270. This would be the case if there were an obligation for the end user to provide work and for the worker to perform it, as well as a sufficient degree of control. However, the further point made by the Court of Appeal that an employment relationship would be more likely to be found if it were longstanding did not find favour with the Court of Appeal in the later decision in *James* v *London Borough of Greenwich* (2008). It applied the somewhat restrictive test of whether it was necessary to imply a contract of service between the worker and the end-user to explain the nature of the relationship. This will, of course, be the case only in a very limited range of cases. (See too the Court of Appeal's decision in *Cable & Wireless plc* v *Muscat* (2006), but this case turned on its particular facts. See also Wynn and Leighton, (2006) 35 ILJ 301; Reynolds, (2006) 35 ILJ 320.)

Council Directive (EC) 2008/104 on Temporary Agency Work will require the Government to implement a number of new protections for agency workers. However, these will cover only those who work on temporary contracts, and not all do. Temporary agency workers will be entitled to treatment equal to that of permanent workers from the beginning of their contracts with regard to basic working and employment conditions, as well as collective facilities such as child-care arrangements. Such workers will also be entitled to be informed of permanent employment prospects with the end-user. At the time of writing, the Government has not produced final draft Regulations to put before Parliament. This will need to be put into law by the end of 2011 to accord with the requirements of the Directive. The Regulations are unlikely, however, to change the present position on the employment status of agency workers. (See further, Countouris and Horton, (2009) 38 ILJ 329.)

2.3.8 Workers' co-operatives

The EAT in *Drym Fabricators Ltd* v *Johnson* (1981) considered that workers involved in a co-operative which is registered as a limited company are likely to be employees.

A different result was, however, reached in the case of an orchestra which functioned as a musical co-operative since the musicians were entitled to do other work and effectively provided services in business on their own account. They were subjecting themselves to self-discipline in the orchestra rather than control in the recognised sense of employer direction (*Addison* v *London Philharmonic Orchestra Ltd* (1981)).

2.3.9 Public employees

History

It has not often in practice been necessary in the past to distinguish those who work in the public sector from those in the private. Largely this was because the occasions on which public employees, in particular Crown servants, desired to take their employer to court were relatively rare. Governments traditionally saw their role as being good employers setting an example to employers elsewhere. In reality, therefore, if not in theory, Crown employees had security of tenure, and the peculiarity of their position was not one which they wished to test, or which often concerned them. But Crown service has been considered distinct historically because of the royal prerogative. Because the Crown, it has been thought, must have the capacity to dismiss at pleasure (unless otherwise expressly provided for to the contrary by statute—see *Gould* v *Stuart* (1896)), courts have often held that Crown employees are not employees, not because they do not work under a contract of service, but because they do not work under a contract at all (see e.g. *Malins* v *Post Office* (1975)). This raises the question of how far Crown service can give rise to rights and obligations. The answer given in the past has been that, at least in the case of the civil service (which is a narrower category than Crown employment according to the court in *Wood* v *Leeds AHA* (1974)) appointment is to a public office (see e.g. *IRC* v *Hambrook* (1956)). The courts, however, have frequently been troubled by this, not least because appointment to an office does not seem to preclude a contractual relationship, even if that relationship were not one of service. On occasions, this view has been of limited scope, such as Lord Atkin's statement in *Reilly* v *R* (1934) that he could see no reason why the Crown could not be bound if it expressly contracted for a fixed period.

Most authorities suggested that at least some sort of contract exists (see *Kodeeswaren* v *Attorney-General for Ceylon* (1970); *Attorney-General for Guyana* v *Nobrega* (1969); *R* v *Secretary of State for Foreign and Commonwealth Affairs ex parte Council of Civil Service Unions* (1985)). According to the policy considerations behind the early decisions there seems to be little reason to deny a contractual relationship because the duty to pay damages on a breach of contract on dismissal at common law did not cut across the Crown's ability to dismiss at pleasure. It merely meant that it had to pay a financial price for doing so, namely pay during any notice which had not been given.

The modern position

However, times have changed and the policy considerations are now different. In some respects, even regarding employment protection, most Crown servants are not disadvantaged when compared with other employees as they are included within many statutory provisions (see e.g. ERA 1996, ss 191–192). While not according Crown employees employment status, the legislation at least treats them *as if* they were employees. Other legislation takes a similar approach, such as TULR(C)A 1992, s. 62(7), which is concerned with identifying employees for the purposes of industrial action liabilities. However, in other respects, the issue is more important than ever before. As Fredman and Morris point out (see (1990) 19 ILJ 142) factors such as the growth of judicial review (dependent upon a public/private distinction) and the applicability of EC Directives such as the Equal Pay Directive, Council Directive (EC) 75/117, (which are applicable only against organs of the State) are more recent areas of law giving rise to new considerations. Another example is the public service exemption to art. 45 of the Treaty on the Functioning of the European Union (art. 45 TFEU) (ex art. 39) of the Treaty of Rome (ex art. 39 EC) which attempts to secure free movement of workers within the Community (see Morris, Fredman, and Hayes, (1990) 19 ILJ 20). Fredman and Morris argue that the State as employer cannot function as a private employer, largely because of the State's source of revenue, and that it does not. Witness, for example, the manner in which some employees in the public sector, such as teachers, have their conditions determined by statute, and the way in which the political activities of public employees are curtailed (see too Fredman and Morris, (1991) 107 LQR 298, and *The State as Employer* (London: Mansell, 1989)).

However, the movement of the recent domestic case law has continued to be towards not just treating Crown employees as engaged in a contractual relationship but moving all public employees as closely as possible to those in the private sector. So, in *McLaren* v *Home Office* (1990) the Court of Appeal decided that a claim by a prison officer with regard to his employment was not a matter of public law but private law. The point was specifically made that the power of the Crown to dismiss at pleasure did not mean that the relationship was not contractual. Woolf LJ suggested that there were four principles relevant in determining whether an employee of a public body may, or must, bring proceedings by way of judicial review. These were:

(a) In relation to personal claims against an employer, an employee of a public body is normally in exactly the same position as other employees.

(b) If there is a disciplinary or other body established under the prerogative or by statute, judicial review may be appropriate.

(c) If the public body makes a flawed decision of general application, judicial review may be the proper remedy.

(d) Even if the decisions arising from a disciplinary procedure affect the public, if they are of a purely domestic nature, judicial review will not be appropriate.

Very often, of course, it will be more advantageous for the employee to be treated as an employee in the private sector, not least because of the decision of the Court of Appeal in *R* v *Chief Constable of the Thames Valley Police ex parte Cotton* (1990) to the effect that a real injustice or unfairness must occur for there to be a breach of natural justice and the requirement that leave be given for judicial review proceedings.

This clear trend towards treating public employees as employees has been underlined by three further decisions. In *R* v *Lord Chancellor's Department ex parte Nangle* (1991) the Divisional Court declined to follow its previous decision in *R* v *Civil Service Appeal Board ex parte Bruce* (1989) and ruled that civil servants work under contracts of employment, not under the royal prerogative. Employment of its nature must create legal relations, unless this is expressly excluded. As Emily Jackson has pointed out, it now stretches the bounds of credulity to maintain that civil servants are part of the Sovereign's household, with domestic mutual love and affection rebutting the assumption of contractual intention (see Jackson, (1992) 21 ILJ 64).

In *Bradford City Metropolitan Council* v *Arora* (1991) the Court of Appeal decided that a local authority did not exercise a public function when it entered into, or did not enter into, an employment relationship. It had previously decided that a local authority terminating a contract of employment was not performing a public function (see *R* v *Derbyshire County Council ex parte Noble* (1990)).

2.4 Question of law or fact?

There was for a considerable period controversy as to whether the question of employment status was one of fact or law. The issue is an important one in practical terms because it is only, in general, on a question of law that an appeal can be made from an ET to the EAT (see ERA 1996, s. 37; TULR(C)A 1992, s. 291). Browne LJ in *Ferguson* v *John Dawson & Partners (Contractors) Ltd* (1976) was firmly of the view that it was an issue of fact and thus not open to challenge on appeal. More recent Court of Appeal authority suggests that the question is one of law but that it involves matters of degree and fact which are essentially for the ET to determine (*O'Kelly* v *Trusthouse Forte plc* (1983)). In *Nethermere (St Neots) Ltd* v *Taverna & Gardiner* (1984) the Court of Appeal applied the administrative law authority of *Edwards* v *Bairstow* (1956) to the effect that the EAT could not interfere with a tribunal's decision unless it had misdirected itself in law or its decision was one which no tribunal properly directing itself on the relevant facts could have reached (see also *Warner Holidays Ltd* v *Secretary of State for Social Services* (1983)).

The House of Lords in *Davies* v *Presbyterian Church of Wales* (1986) considered that the *Edwards* v *Bairstow* principle was irrelevant. Lord Templeman said that 'If the industrial tribunal erred in deciding that question (whether the applicant was an employee), the decision must be reversed and it matters not that other industrial tribunals might have reached a similar erroneous conclusion in the absence of an authoritative decision by a higher court'. This seems to make sense in principle, in that the policy behind non-interference with first instance decisions is based on the idea that matters which are peculiar to a particular case (such as facts which are personal to a particular party, or an event) are best assessed in that forum. But matters of fact which are relevant not just to the instant case, but are of wider application, seem in principle to be subject matter properly reviewable by a higher court in order to achieve a desirable uniformity and for this purpose should therefore be deemed questions of law, regardless of the meaning of that word in other contexts.

This, it is argued, sensible conclusion was later compromised by the questionable reasoning of the Privy Council in *Lee* v *Chung* (1990). It was held that *Davies* was exceptional in that it was concerned *only* with the situation where the relationship is dependent solely upon the construction of a written document. Where the relationship has to be determined by the investigation and evaluation of the factual circumstances in which the work is performed, the question is one of fact and degree. But it does not follow that adherence to the latter statement involves restricting *Davies* to the situation where there is a written document.

A construction of a written document can be a question of fact within the meaning assigned to those terms in *Davies*, as it may involve evaluating matters relating to just the parties in the case and not applicable generally. Support for this view can now be found in the decision of the House of Lords in *Carmichael* v *National Power plc* (2000), particularly in the speech by Lord Hoffmann.

Furthermore, as Pitt has pointed out, treating the question as one of fact means that different tribunals may come to different conclusions on the same set of facts (see (1985) 101 LQR 217; (1990) 19 ILJ 252). So a nationwide company may dismiss all its workers in a particular grade, doing the same work, with the possibility that only some of them may claim statutory employment protection as different tribunals may legitimately come to opposite conclusions as to employment status. It is surely not correct to argue that there has been no mistake by at least one tribunal, which it is within the competence of an appellate tribunal to correct. There are policy considerations here, as the approach adopted in *Lee* allows the burden on appeal tribunals and courts to be lightened, but it seems wrong that individual rights should be determined or denied by considerations of administrative efficiency. As McLean points out, it can only be hoped that a braver Supreme Court emerges to overturn these authorities (see [1990] CLJ 410), but the wait continues.

SELECTED READING

Collins, H. (1990), 'Independent Contractors and the Challenge of Vertical Disintegration to Employment Protection Laws', (1990) 10 OJLS 353

Davidov, G. (2005), 'Who is a Worker?', (2005) 34 ILJ 57

Freedland, M. (2003), *The Personal Employment Contract*, Oxford: Oxford University Press

Freedland, M. (2005), 'Rethinking the Personal Work Contract', (2005) 58 *Current Legal Problems* 517

Freedland, M. (2006), 'From the Contract of Employment to the Personal Work Nexus', (2006) 35 ILJ 1

Honeyball, S. (2005), 'The Conceptual Integrity of Employment', [2005] *Cambrian Law Review* 1

Honeyball, S. and Pearce, D. (2006), 'Contract, Employment and the Contract of Employment', (2006) 35 ILJ 30

Wedderburn, W., Lewis, R., and Clark, J. (1983), *Labour Law and Industrial Relations* Oxford: Clarendon Press

3

The contract of employment

SUMMARY

This chapter begins by considering the emergence of contract within the past 200 years as the favoured legal analysis at common law of the employment relationship, and critically analyses why this should be so. The courts' historical interaction with statute along the way is also examined. This is followed by a consideration of the various types of express terms that are commonly to be found in a contract of employment. Then the variety of implied terms is explored and particularly the way the courts have used these to develop the legal foundation of the employment relationship. Then the notion of imposition of terms is looked at by which express terms are imposed upon the parties by way of the contract of employment. The chapter closes with an examination of the legal issues thrown up when a contract of employment is varied.

3.1 Introduction

When the basis on which most work was performed moved away from status, inherent in such ideas as serfdom, a new legal theory of work relationships had to emerge. The new analysis had to take into account rapidly changing social and industrial conditions, particularly in the 18th and 19th centuries. These conditions marked a move to ostensibly freer circumstances, in which workers were at liberty to sell their labour to whom they pleased in return for financial reward, with rights and obligations determined by agreement. The new analysis was a task which had to be brought about by the judiciary, for in the period under discussion there was little by way of a statutory framework regulating employment and laissez-faire ideas predominated.

3.1.1 The attraction of contract

It was hardly surprising that the judges turned to tried and trusted common law concepts to assist them in the analysis and, almost inevitably, it was contract to which they turned. In contract there was a model which the employment relationship seemed to fit, and indeed continues to fit, although in the modern world at times most uncomfortably. The basic elements of a legally enforceable contract are discernible in the way in which employment comes about even if, during its subsistence, the contract frequently has to give way in the light of modern-day policy requirements. There is an offer which is accepted. There is consideration moving from both parties (and so volunteers do not have contracts of employment—*Melhuish* v *Redbridge Citizens Advice Bureau* (2005)), and this all occurs with the firm intention residing in both parties that legal rights and obligations should result. The offer in the vast majority of circumstances comes from the employer and is accepted by the employee orally at an interview, or perhaps in writing, or sometimes even by just turning up for work. The consideration is the financial reward provided by the employer on the one hand, and the work (or the willingness to work—see Napier, [1984] CLJ 337) provided by the employee on the other.

It is true that these contract law ideas best fit the situation where a bargain is struck after negotiations or bartering has taken place, which is not the hallmark of most instances today where an employment relationship is entered into. For various reasons—historical, social, economic, and personal—the power residing in the employer means little bargaining in fact takes place, but there may be some. This inequality of bargaining power has led some writers to suggest that the contractual nature of employment is changing, perhaps back once again to a status relationship. Of itself, the lack of bargaining would not seem to indicate this, as the process which leads to an offer being accepted is not, on the whole, the concern of even classical contract doctrine. It is the fact of an agreement that primarily determines the legal analysis, not the procedure by which it comes about nor its substance. Hence the traditional approach that the law requires consideration to be adequate but not necessarily sufficient. Consideration must be present, but the value of the bargain is of no import to the law. Indeed, if an agreement in the modern world were to be considered contractual only if it followed a process of real bargaining between roughly equal parties, there would be very few contracts. Most contracts entered into on a daily basis, such as the purchasing of drinks, newspapers and groceries, involve even fewer elements of barter than the genesis of an employment relationship, and the existence of power and subservience is often as great if not greater than that which exists in a typical employment relationship. Take the example of a customer buying a pen from W. H. Smith—there is very little equality of bargaining power there and no bargaining at all.

An alternative to status is to see the contract law that applies to employment relationships as an autonomous body of law, rather than the application in a specific context of general principles of classical contract doctrine—see e.g. the important work by Freedland, *The Personal Employment Contract* (2003).

Unless there has been some vitiating element arising from an inequality of bargaining power (such as undue influence), the courts tend to rely on the principle of freedom of contract to justify non-interference (see e.g. *National Westminster Bank plc* v *Morgan* (1985)). However, some writers, such as Thal, have argued very strongly that the courts have gone too far, and the unfairness caused by inequality of bargaining power justifies a limitation in the freedom of contract doctrine (see (1988) 8 OJLS 17). However, as Kessler has pointed out, the doctrine is 'the inevitable counterpart' of a free enterprise system ((1943) 43 Columbia LR 629. See further Beale, (1986) 6 OJLS 123.)

Similar arguments apply with regard to the terms of the agreement. The existence of implied and imposed terms, and statutory regulation, over and above the rather meagre terms expressly agreed by the parties in an employment relationship, paints a picture very little different to the situation that exists when entering into many commercial contracts for consumer goods, for example. All that these factors show is that the background world, for which the traditional rules of contract and the elements of a contract developed, has changed markedly, but it does not show that the employment contract is in any respect different in this regard from any other contractual relationship.

This is not to deny that there are areas of contract law which are more suitable to relationships other than employment. The general unavailability of injunctive relief in respect of contracts of employment indicates this, as such remedies are usually available with regard to other contracts. But this is largely due to the executory nature, or indeterminacy in terms of duration, of employment contracts which makes supervision of such orders difficult, rather than anything to do with the nature of the employment contract itself. For example, the idea that injunctive relief is not available because it would in effect convert a contract of employment into a contract of slavery is clearly not tenable. (See e.g. *De Francesco* v *Barnum* (1890).)

It is possible to argue that contract plays a much more significant part in the employment relationship than is often realised, for example in statutory law conceived to deal with the shortcomings of contract law in the light of modern policy requirements. To take an instance, the law of unfair dismissal is clearly designed in part to give employees protection against poor reasons for dismissal, whereas the common law can give protection only in relation to the formal features of dismissal. However, the limitation of a legal remedy to damages for insufficient notice do not satisfy modern-day views of the obligations an employer should owe to an employee, and so a completely different, statutory scheme is created, not based directly on contract. But then contractual ideas creep in, such as the requirement, not initially conceived, that in a constructive dismissal (where an employee resigns because of the employer's conduct and claims this should be construed as a dismissal) an employer must have committed a repudiatory breach of contract, and not have behaved merely unreasonably. There are many more examples of this infiltration of contract law into areas of employment not of the traditional type (see further Honeyball, (1989) 18 ILJ 97 and, for a more recent treatment of the same theme, Anderman, (2000) 29 ILJ 223).

3.1.2 Judicial use of common law concepts

A different, but related, phenomenon is the way in which the courts seem to undermine statutory intervention in employment by the continued use of common law concepts. John McMullen has given the example of frustration to illustrate this (see (1986) 49 MLR 785). As he pointed out (before tribunals were given jurisdiction in contract), to rule that an employment contract may be terminated by frustration, and therefore by operation of law, limits the jurisdiction of ETs because, in order to claim either unfair dismissal or redundancy, it is necessary to establish that there has been a dismissal. Termination by operation of law does not constitute dismissal even within the necessarily very wide definition of that concept in ERA 1996, s. 95. It is true, as we shall later see, that the practical effect of this difficulty has been somewhat vitiated, largely by attempts by the EAT to restrict the circumstances in which frustration may be said to occur, but the Court of Appeal has been less realistic (see *Notcutt* v *Universal Equipment Co. (London) Ltd* (1986)).

A further example of the type considered by McMullen is illegality. Mogridge has argued that the doctrine that illegal contracts are void as applied to employment contracts results in an employee suffering a double loss as he loses not only contractual rights but statutory rights as well. This need not occur because statutory rights need not be dependent upon contractual entitlements. As such, Mogridge says that the preferred solution to this problem is to allow employees to enforce their statutory rights irrespective of illegality, but she also recognises that such an approach is unlikely to gain judicial approval (see (1981) 10 ILJ 23). In the absence of such a recognition there is little scope for any allowance to be made for disparity of bargaining power in relation to the formation of a contract of employment tainted by illegality. The recent trend has been rigorously to apply the defence of illegality so as to prevent a party to a contract tainted by illegality relying on that contract where that party is aware of the facts giving rise to the illegality irrespective of whether that party thought he was acting lawfully (*Salvesen* v *Simons* (1994)) and irrespective of the relative culpability of the parties (*Tinsley* v *Milligan* (1993)). In *Tinsley* the House of Lords, albeit *obiter*, emphasised that the consequence of being a party to an illegal transaction cannot depend upon such imponderables as whether the public conscience would be affronted by recognising rights created by illegal transactions. One response when faced by these difficulties may be for a tribunal to be more wary of finding that a contract of employment has been performed in such a way as to be tainted by illegality at all (see *Annandale Engineering* v *Samson* (1994)). However, more recently, the courts have been willing to be more flexible and allow claims where the illegality is not bound up with the reason for the claim itself—see *Hall* v *Woolston Hall Leisure Ltd* (2000), and *Colen* v *Celerian (UK) Ltd* (2004)—and to require an element of misrepresentation or lack of good faith. (See the EAT's decision in *Enfield Technical Services Ltd* v *Payne* (2007).)

3.2 Express terms

3.2.1 Written statement of terms

Since a contract of employment is formed at the point when an offer is accepted, often very few items upon which the parties need to agree will have been written down. A contract of employment need not be in writing, but it is clearly of value, with regard to such an important contract, that its terms be reduced to writing, or evidenced in writing. In this way disputes can be averted more easily, and evidence will be easier to obtain in the event of disputes. It is therefore a sensible step for the parties (or at least the employer, who has the facilities) to be charged with the task of reducing the agreement to writing. The duty so to do, and the details relating to this, are to be found in ERA 1996, ss 1–12. The document produced is known as the written statement of terms. The provisions remained substantially unchanged between their original introduction in the Contracts of Employment Act 1963 and TURERA 1993, which made substantial revisions to accommodate the terms of the EC Directive on proof of employment terms, Council Directive (EC) 91/533. The provisions are now reconsolidated in the ERA 1996.

Content of the written statement

The statement must be given to an employee (who has at least a month's continuous employment) within two months after he or she started work (ERA 1996, s. 1(2)), and must contain the identity of the parties, and specify the date on which employment began and when the employee's period of continuous employment began (as there may have been a period of employment with a previous employer which may count in such a calculation (ERA 1996, s. 1(3)). There must also be details, correct as at one week before giving the statement, of remuneration, the intervals at which it will be paid, sick pay, pensions, notice, and a brief description of the work for which the employee is employed. In addition, if there are any terms and conditions on hours of work and holidays, these must be stated. The terms must be 'sufficient to enable the employee's entitlement, including any entitlement to accrued holiday pay, on the termination of employment to be precisely calculated' (see further *Morley* v *Heritage plc* (1993)).

The statement must also include:

(a) in the case of non-permanent employment, 'the period for which it is expected to continue' (ERA 1996, s. 1(4)(g));

(b) 'either the place of work or, where the employee is required or permitted to work at various places, an indication of that fact and the address of the employer' (ERA 1996, s. 1(4)(h));

(c) 'any collective agreements which directly affect the terms and conditions of the employment including, where the employer is not a party, the persons by whom they were made' (ERA 1996, s. 1(4)(j));

(d) in the case of an 'employee... required to work outside the UK for a period of more than one month', the period of such work, the currency of remuneration, any additional remuneration or benefit by reason of the requirement to work outside the UK and 'any terms and conditions relating to his return to the UK' (ERA 1996, s. 1(4)(k)).

Matters relating to sickness and most pension schemes may be contained in 'some other document which the employee has reasonable opportunities of reading in the course of his employment or is made reasonably accessible to him in some other way'. For the length of the period of his or her notice, the employee may be referred to 'the law [that is, in the case of minimum periods of notice] or to the provisions of any collective agreement which directly affects the terms and conditions of the employment' (ERA 1996, s. 2(3)).

Where before the end of two months after the start of employment, the employee 'is to begin work outside the UK for a period of more than one month' the statement must be given to him before he leaves the UK to begin so to work (ERA 1996, s. 2(5)).

Even where there are no terms on holidays, sick pay, pensions, and working outside the UK, there is a duty to state that fact (ERA 1996, s. 2(1)).

The statement must contain a note specifying any disciplinary rules, and now procedures (see Employment Act 2002 (EA 2002), s. 35), applicable to the employee or refer him to a reasonably accessible document setting them out (ERA 1996, s. 3). The employee must also be notified of a person to whom he can apply if he is dissatisfied with any disciplinary decision, and how such application should be made

(ERA 1996, s. 3(1)(b)). Any further steps are to be specified, and the employer should include as much detail as possible as a protection against unfair dismissal claims.

ERA 1996 s. 7A (inserted by EA 2002, s. 37) states that a written statement need not be given where all the information required by ERA 1996, s. 1 is contained in another document given to the employee. Very often in larger enterprises, this could be a document given to the employee on starting work or it may, for example, be the letter of appointment itself.

The statement must be given notwithstanding that the employment ends before the period in which the statement was to be given (ERA 1996, s. 2(6)). This means that the employee will be entitled to a statement even after the employment has ended, which will be useful in any claim he may have.

Changes in terms

The employer's duty is to give notice of changes in terms at the earliest opportunity and, in any event, not later than:

(a) one month after the change, or

(b) where the change arises from the requirement to work outside the UK for more than a month, the time when he leaves the UK (ERA 1996, s. 4(3)).

A total failure to notify does not, however, render any changes ineffective, and where the employer changes in name only, or where the employer's identity changes but continuity is preserved by statute, this may be stated as a change in particulars, rather than necessitating a whole new statement (ERA 1996, s. 4(6)). New particulars need not be given when an employee is re-employed within six months of ending an earlier employment if he comes back on the same terms and conditions and has already been given particulars (ERA 1996, s. 4(5)).

Failure to comply

The remedies for failing to comply with the duty in s. 1(1) to provide a suitable written statement or alternative document, or to properly notify changes, are detailed in EA 2002, s. 38. This applies where the failure is apparent when the employee is bringing a different claim under other provisions. The tribunal must make an award of two weeks' pay in addition to any award already made, and may award four weeks' pay if it considers it just and equitable in all the circumstances.

A difficulty arises in the situation where, although it is mandatory for the employer to include a term in the written particulars, he does not do so. The tribunal then must include a term where there was express agreement between the parties, or it is possible to do so by implication after examining the evidence. If a term cannot be inserted by either of these methods, the tribunal should not invent terms merely because they ought to have been included or referred to, according to the Court of Appeal in *Eagland* v *British Telecommunications plc* (1992). This is not to say that the tribunal will not identify a term by reference to the conduct of the parties, but it will not insert a term where there is no agreement at all on the term, either express or inferred.

The statement and the contract

The general aim of the provisions is to encourage the development of explicit and clear terms about the most important elements of the employee's contract. It is intended to be a mirror of that agreement but it is not the contract itself. This is reflected in the right of both employer and employee to complain to an ET in case of dispute as to whether the correct particulars together with any changes have been communicated. Lord Parker CJ said in *Turriff Construction Ltd* v *Bryant* (1967): 'It is of course quite clear that the statement...is not the contract; it is not even conclusive evidence of the contract.' However, since very often there will be precious little other information, especially in writing, about the agreement, it is quite natural that the statement is frequently treated as the contract itself. This is particularly so where the employee has signed a receipt for the document. In *Gascol Conversions Ltd* v *Mercer* (1974), Lord Denning went so far as to state that, by reason of the parol evidence rule, the statutory statement being reduced to writing is the sole evidence that is permissible of the contract and its terms. It is not, however, clear from the report of the case whether the document in question was just a written statement or purported to be the contract itself. If the former, it is submitted that the decision is wrong.

The most widely cited statement of the effect of the written statement is found in *System Floors (UK) Ltd* v *Daniel* (1982) where Browne-Wilkinson J said that it:

> provides very strong *prima facie* evidence of what were the terms of the contract between the parties but does not constitute a written contract between the parties. Nor are the statements of the terms finally conclusive; at most they place a heavy burden on the employer to show that the actual terms of the contract are different from those which he has set out in the statutory statement.

So, a failure to object to erroneous statements of terms is not to be taken as acceptance, at least where they are of no immediate practical importance (*Jones* v *Associated Tunnelling Co. Ltd* (1981)).

It was thought at one time that the written statement had legal effect in giving rise to an estoppel if an employee relied on it to his detriment. For example, in *Evenden* v *Guildford City Association Football Club* (1975) the employer stated that employment with a previous employer counted towards continuous service and he was not permitted to renege on that assurance. This case was, however, overruled in the House of Lords in *Secretary of State for Employment* v *Globe Elastic Thread Co. Ltd* (1979), a case with similar facts, on the grounds that estoppel could not confer on a statutory tribunal a jurisdiction beyond that given by the empowering Act in respect of continuity of employment. The facts of the case concerned the giving of a redundancy rebate under statute by the Secretary of State who was not privy to the contract, and it may still be argued that an estoppel may arise between employer and employee when there is no third party involved. This is because the decision was that, in the words of Lord Wilberforce, 'a personal estoppel between employer and employee which is the most that this could be, could not bind the Secretary of State'.

3.2.2 Restrictive covenants

Many employers, especially in the professions, protect themselves against damaging competition and misuse of confidential information by an express restrictive covenant. This comes into effect after the termination of employment and restricts the work an ex-employee does in the near future, and where it is done. As such it gives rise to the theoretical difficulty as to how, given that employment is generally thought to be defined by reference to contracts of employment, obligations arising under the contract of employment can survive its termination, indeed only operate then—see Honeyball and Pearce, (2006) 35 ILJ 30, and generally Cabrelli, (2004) 33 ILJ 167.

A typical example of a restrictive covenant would be an accountancy practice which included a contractual clause that assistant accountants shall not work for another practice within five miles during the first two years after leaving. The common law rule against restraint of trade operates in this area just as it does in contracts between the vendor and purchaser of a business (*Esso Petroleum Co. Ltd* v *Harper's Garage (Stourport) Ltd* (1968)). In employment cases, the court attempts essentially to hold the ring between the interest of the employee to be employed in the future as he wishes, and the employer's interest to preserve its business from disclosures by an ex-employee. Thus restrictive clauses must go no further than is reasonable for the protection of the employer's business interests (see *Jack Allen (Sales and Service) Ltd* v *Smith* (1999)) and must serve the public interest. Otherwise, as the House of Lords put it, 'the employee is entitled to use to the full any personal skill or experience even if this has been acquired in the service of his employer...' (*Stenhouse Australia Ltd* v *Phillips* (1974); see too *Cantor Fitzgerald (UK) Ltd* v *Wallace* (1992)). The courts are therefore very restrictive in their interpretation of such restrictive covenants, and do not see it as part of their function to correct errors or omissions in them, but rather to give effect to them specifically as drafted. So where, in *WAC Ltd* v *Whillock* (1990), there was a clause in the employee's contract prohibiting him from carrying on any business in competition with the company, this did not prevent him from acting as a director or employee of a competing company.

Where an employee is wrongfully dismissed (which is to say, in breach of contract) this will render the restrictive covenant unenforceable even though it is reasonable, according to the High Court in *Briggs* v *Oates* (1990); see also *D* v *M* (1996). A restrictive covenant which purports to operate even where the termination has been brought about by the employer's own breach is not necessarily void from the beginning as an unreasonable restraint. The sole issue is whether the contract of employment has been repudiated by the employer in the particular case (*Rock Refrigeration Ltd* v *Jones* (1996)).

Different considerations may apply depending on the nature of the covenant. For example, as Sales points out, a covenant to prevent an ex-employee from recruiting his ex-employer's present employees has less effect upon the ex-employee's ability to trade than a covenant not to compete (see (1988) 104 LQR 600). Nevertheless in *Hanover Insurance Brokers Ltd* v *Schapiro* (1994) the Court of Appeal held that a clause preventing employees (including the plaintiff's chairman) from 'poaching' the plaintiff's employees was unenforceable. The court noted that the clause applied irrespective of the experience and juniority of the employee concerned and could apply on its terms even to those who became employees after the defendants left the plaintiff's employment. However, it was noted in more general terms that such a non-poaching clause faced the difficulty that the employee has the right to work for the employer he wants to work for if the employer is willing to employ him. It has since been recognised by the Court of Appeal that an employer has an interest in maintaining a stable workforce (*Dawnay, Day & Co. Ltd* v *De Braconier d'Alphen* (1997); see also *Alliance Paper Group plc* v *Prestwich* (1996)).

To be upheld by the courts a reasonable restrictive covenant will normally prevent the employee only from actually soliciting former customers, rather than stopping the employee from working at all, unless there are good reasons for so doing. Most generally Stephenson LJ concluded in *Spafax Ltd* v *Harrison* (1980):

An employer is entitled to take and enforce promises from an employee which the employer can prove are reasonably necessary to protect him, the employer, his trade connection, trade interests and goodwill, not from competition by the employee if he leaves his employment, or from his then using the skill and knowledge with which his employment had equipped him to compete, but from his then using his personal knowledge of his employer's customers or his personal influence over them, or his knowledge of his employer's trade secrets, or advantages acquired from his employment, to his employer's disadvantage.

It was, however, held not to be unreasonable in *Dentmaster (UK) Ltd* v *Kent* (1997) to prevent solicitation of customers with whom the employee had no recent connection.

Area of restraint

If the employee is to be restricted from operating within a particular geographical area, the area of restraint placed on the employee must be reasonable; a world-wide restraint may be valid only where the employer's business was of a similar extent, as in the leading case of *Nordenfelt* v *Maxim Nordenfelt Guns and Ammunition Ltd* (1894). Whether covenants against taking employment in a particular area are valid depends on the size of the area and its relationship to the employer's trade or professional connections (*Gledhow Autoparts Ltd* v *Delaney* (1965); *T. Lucas & Co.* v *Mitchell* (1972)).

This can be illustrated by contrasting the Court of Appeal decisions in *Greer* v *Sketchley Ltd* (1979), and *Littlewoods Organisation Ltd* v *Harris* (1977). In *Greer* the plaintiff had been employed for 20 years by the defendants whose branches covered the Midlands and London areas, rising ultimately to become a director of their dry cleaning business with special responsibility for the Midlands. His contract provided that he must not within 12 months of its termination directly or indirectly engage in the UK in any similar business but this was held to be too wide since he had had responsibility for only a part of that area. On the other hand, in the *Littlewoods* case, a nationwide restrictive covenant was held to be reasonable since it was the only way to protect the respondent's mail order business when the ex-employee went to work for their direct national competitor. (See *Marley Tile Co. Ltd* v *Johnson* (1982), electrician; *G. W. Plowman & Son Ltd* v *Ash* (1964), sales representative; *S. W. Strange Ltd* v *Mann* (1965), credit bookmaker.) A restrictive covenant of two miles on a doctor was upheld by the Court of Appeal in *Kerr* v *Morris* (1986). However, an area of restraint of just 1.2 miles for six months was held to be invalid by the Court of Appeal in *Office Angels Ltd* v *Rainer-Thomas and O'Connor* (1991) as it was neither necessary nor appropriate for the protection of the plaintiff's connection with their clients who dealt by telephone with the plaintiff employer's agency.

If a restraint clause is reasonable in concept, the courts will construe it in a reasonable manner (see *Marion White Ltd* v *Francis* (1972)). However, the court should refuse to whittle down covenants which are too wide merely so as to make them enforceable (see *J. A. Mont (UK) Ltd* v *Mills* (1993); *Hanover Insurance Brokers* v *Schapiro* (1994)).

The courts may sever a part of the restraint and uphold the rest of it, however, but only if 'the severed parts are independent of one another and can be severed without the severance affecting the meaning of the part remaining' (Lord Sterndale in *Attwood* v *Lamont* (1920); see also *Putsman* v *Taylor* (1927)).

It is irrelevant that the detriment to the employee imposed by the covenant is out of all proportion to the benefit to the employer as the idea that the doctrine of proportionality applies here was described by the High Court in *Allied Dunbar (Frank Weisinger) Ltd* v *Weisinger* (1988) as a 'novel and dangerous doctrine'. The court would be required, if the doctrine applied, to perform a balancing exercise which it was incapable of doing and which was best left to the parties to resolve by negotiation. This makes sense when one bears in mind that the unenforceability of a restrictive covenant is dependent upon its not being in the public interest, and not to protect the employee (*Spencer* v *Marchington* (1988)).

Restraint in the public interest

The restraint must generally be in the public interest to be enforceable, which effectively depends on the exercise of the judge's discretion in each case. Slade J in *Greig* v *Insole* (1978) held that a ban by the Test and County Cricket Board on cricketers who played in a rival series organised in Australia by Kerry Packer could not be enforced because its benefits at most were speculative and would deprive the public of watching first class cricket players. It was also on this ground that in *Wyatt* v *Kreglinger and Fernau* (1933) the Court of Appeal decided that a pension agreement was void because of a condition that the defendant should not again take a job in the wool trade.

Where the clause is held to be unenforceable on the grounds of public policy, it may be that the employee remains entitled to rely upon the contract as long as the unenforceable provision does not, through removal, necessitate modification to what remains, which is supported by adequate consideration and so long as its removal does not alter the character of the contract (*Sadler* v *Imperial Life Assurance Co. of Canada* (1988) approved by the Court of Appeal in *Beckett Investment Management Group Ltd* v *Hall* (2007); see too *Rex Stewart Jeffries Parker Ginsberg Ltd* v *Parker* (1988); *Marshall* v *NM Financial Management Ltd* (1996)).

Injunctions

Restrictive covenants are normally enforced by injunction, but it has long been the case that a court will not grant an injunction where the effect is to compel the employee to go back to work for the employer (*Whitwood Chemical Co.* v *Hardman* (1891)).

Where an interim injunction is sought, the principles laid down in the leading case of *American Cyanamid* v *Ethicon Ltd* (1975) apply equally to cases where there is a restraint of trade clause as elsewhere. To obtain the injunction the claimant will have to show that there is an arguable case (in other words, that there is a serious issue to be tried) and that damages would not be an adequate remedy. This was held to apply to restrictive covenant cases by the Court of Appeal in *Lawrence David Ltd* v *Ashton* (1989), but the Court of Appeal somewhat modified this position, which appears to considerably favour employers, in *Lansing Linde Ltd* v *Kerr* (1991). Because such covenants frequently apply for a limited period, justice requires that some consideration should be had as to whether the claimant would be likely to succeed at the trial, which may take place after a substantial period of the covenant has elapsed. A reconciliation of the two approaches turns largely on whether the interim decision will effectively decide the matter because of the delay before the matter comes on for trial (see *Hanover Insurance Brokers Ltd* v *Schapiro* (1994) per Nolan LJ).

3.2.3 Garden leave

Increasing use has been made by employers, especially in the financial sector, of the possibility of continuing to pay employees but not requiring them to work out their notice—garden leave. A garden leave injunction to enforce this is not, however, available unless the employer has a contractual right to send the worker home without providing him work to do (*William Hill Organisation Ltd* v *Tucker* (1998)). This is capable of abuse, and the courts will not countenance an injunction which keeps an employee out of his profession for a period which is unreasonably long, or where the employee seeks to take up a post which is not directly competitive with his employer—see e.g. the Court of Appeal's decision in *Symbian Ltd* v *Christensen* (2001). It is not necessary for the employer to offer continuing employment in order to gain an injunction but he must provide all salary and benefits as if the employee were still employed (*Evening Standard Co. Ltd* v *Henderson* (1987); *Euro Brokers* v *Rabey* (1995)). There are, however, limits to the relief which the courts are prepared to grant. Even in a case where the balance of convenience is in favour of granting an injunction because there is a real prospect of the employer suffering loss which will not readily be quantifiable, the relief granted should not go beyond that absolutely necessary to protect the employer's situation. In *GFI Group Inc.* v *Eaglestone* (1994), for example, an injunction was granted enforcing a 13-week garden leave period notwithstanding that the notice period was 20 weeks. Nevertheless the decision reflected the importance that would ordinarily be attached to the contractually agreed period even at the level of remedy rather than rights. Holland J indicated that ordinarily he would have been inclined to hold the employee to the contractual period but he was swayed by the fact that two other employees had already been poached by the competitor in question and that therefore to a large extent the damage had already been done. In exercising his discretion as to the length of the restraint no account appears to have been taken of issues such as whether the employee's skills would atrophy or whether there was a general right to work.

3.2.4 Mobility clauses

In some cases the description of job and place of work does not tell anything like the whole contractual story because of express or implied terms for flexibility. It is not unusual to find a works rule book containing a provision for the working of 40 hours per week or such time as may be communicated to employees by notice from time to time. The employee who works in Land's End may be surprised to find a clause in small print that he is expected to work anywhere in Great Britain, but he may still be expected to transfer to John O'Groats. However, where there is any doubt in the language the courts, in construing such provisions, adopt a test of reasonableness, so that in *Briggs* v *ICI* (1968) a provision that 'you will accept the right of management to transfer you to another job with a higher or lower rate of pay whether day work, night work or shift work', was held by Lord Parker CJ to 'only entitle management to transfer the process worker to another job within the Billingham factory and only as a process worker'. In *Bass Leisure Ltd* v *Thomas* (1994) the EAT held that the place of work for purposes of deciding whether there was a redundancy situation did not include the place where the employee could be contractually required to work but rather where he did work. A mobility clause should therefore not be taken into account in determining the place of work for redundancy purposes. The place is to be determined by a consideration of the factual circumstances which obtained until the dismissal, and there is no warrant for determining that this place always extends to every place where the employee may by reason of his contract be required to work. If the work of the employee has involved a change of location, such as where the nature of the work required the employee to go from place to place, the contract may be helpful to determine the extent of the place where he worked (*High Table Ltd* v *Horst* (1997)).

It may still be important to determine where an employee can be contractually obliged to work, for example in order to determine whether an employee has refused to obey a lawful order or whether an insistence on a transfer constitutes a constructive dismissal (see *Aparau* v *Iceland Frozen Foods plc* (1996)).

Where the term providing for mobility is clear and unambiguous, the courts will not imply an element of reasonableness into the term, according to the EAT in *Rank Xerox* v *Churchill* (1988). However, the appeal tribunal appeared to hold that it was right to imply a requirement of reasonableness despite the literal terms of the contract in *United Bank Ltd* v *Akhtar* (1989) on the basis that, without so doing, the employee would have found the obligation impossible to perform. Faced with these conflicting decisions, the EAT in *White* v *Reflecting Roadstuds Ltd* (1991) attempted to reconcile them. It did this on the basis that *Akhtar* did not decide that there was an implied term that the employer should act reasonably, because to do so would introduce a test of reasonableness into constructive dismissal which had been specifically rejected by the Court of Appeal in *Western Excavating (ECC) Ltd* v *Sharp* (1978). Rather, *Akhtar* is authority that an employer when dealing with a mobility clause in a contract of employment should not exercise his discretion in such a way as to prevent his employee from being able to carry out his part of the contract. The EAT called this 'a very different consideration'. However, as Rubenstein has pointed out (at [1991] IRLR 321) it may not be so different if, as the EAT went on to state, where there are no reasonable or sufficient grounds for requiring the employee to move, there would be a breach of contract which, being fundamental, would satisfy the *Western Excavating* test. This is an idea which can be traced through a number of the authorities in this area (see further Foster, (1989) 52 MLR 251).

3.2.5 Collective bargains

The most important terms in the employee's contract for many workers derive not from an individual bargain with his employer but from a collective agreement entered into by a union recognised for this purpose at his place of work. Very often an individual's statement of terms will do no more than refer him to the relevant collective agreement which is likely to deal with, in particular, wages, hours, holidays and the guaranteed week, as its most important substantive rules. This is the legislative or normative function of the collective agreement, but it also has another side concerning relations between the union and the employer, including negotiating rights, grievance procedures and also a means for renegotiating the agreement at fixed intervals. Its industrial relations implications will be considered below, since we are here concerned only with its effect on the employee's contractual terms.

The effect of the collective bargain on the contract of employment

Unions and employers cannot sue each other on the collective bargain save in the rare cases in which the parties agree that the terms are enforceable at law (TULR(C)A 1992, s. 179). The terms may still be legally binding between employer and employee on an individual basis through the contract of employment, although the law is somewhat pragmatic as to how and why such incorporation is achieved. There must be some sort of bridge between the collective bargain and the individual contract for its incorporation and this is often by way of express reference in the actual contract or in the written statement of terms. Thus in *NCB* v *Galley* (1958) the individual contract fairly typically provided 'wages shall be regulated by such national agreement and the county wages agreement for the time being in force and this agreement shall be subject to these agreements and to any other agreements relating to or in connection with or subsidiary to the wages agreement'. This also means that the contract need not be amended every time negotiations take place.

Incorporation will be readily implied from the universal observance of the collective bargain in the employee's workplace, even though the individual employee may neither know of the pact nor be a member of the union which negotiates it (see *Gray Dunn & Co. Ltd* v *Edwards* (1980)). However, the Court of Session held, in *Hamilton* v *Futura Floors Ltd* (1990), that an employer's membership of an employers' association which is a party to a collective agreement is not of itself sufficient to justify incorporation of that collective agreement into employees' contracts. There will frequently be no other basis for the incorporation, but regular observance by itself is not always decisive.

Knowledge of the terms is usually not necessary for incorporation. However, once there has been incorporation, the terms will become enforceable. In *Marley* v *Forward Trust Ltd* (1986) it was held by the Court of Appeal that the usual clause to the effect that the collective agreement is not enforceable—known as a TINALEA clause as the words used are that 'this is not a legally enforceable agreement'—does not affect the issue of incorporation into the employee's contract of employment. As Hazel McLean has stated, if the decision had gone the other way, trade unions would have had to consider removing TINALEA clauses from collective agreements (see (1987) 16 ILJ 59).

Collective agreements do not require the same precision of language as would be apt for commercial contracts, nor need there be an intention to create legal relations for incorporation to occur (*Burke* v *Royal Liverpool University Hospital NHS Trust* (1997)).

Where the terms of a contract of employment change to the employee's advantage because of a collective agreement, there is an obligation on the employer to inform the employee, according to the House of Lords in *Scally* v *Southern Health and Social Services Board* (1991) or, at least, to take reasonable steps to do so—see *Ibekwe* v *London General Transport Services* (2003). (It should be noted that in *Scally* the employees could not have easily discovered the information which was vital to the amount of pension payments they would receive, whereas the employer could easily have disclosed it at little expense.) It would appear, *a fortiori*, that this should also be the case when there is a change to the employee's detriment. It may be however that the obligation to bring rights to the employee's notice applies only where the right is contingent on action being taken by the employee to avail himself of it and where the employee could not reasonably be expected to be aware of the right if it is not specifically drawn to his attention (see *Griffiths* v *Buckinghamshire CC* (1994)).

The basis of incorporation

The general legal explanation for incorporation has, in fact, been rarely considered by the courts. While it is *prima facie* attractive to view the bargaining union as an agent for its members, the problem is that this would restrict the union to acting only on behalf of employees for the time being, implying that a later hired worker was not so bound. There would also be a serious difficulty if a union member as a principal purported to withdraw his authority from the union to act as his agent (see generally *Heatons Transport Ltd* v *TGWU* (1972); *Singh* v *British Steel Corporation* (1974)). The courts have thus been reluctant to find an agency relationship except when the numbers involved are small. In *Holland* v *London Society of Compositors* (1924) Lush J held that the union acts as a principal and not its members' agent in bargaining. But Arnold J voiced the most widespread view when he said in *Burton Group Ltd* v *Smith* (1977):

> There is no reason at all why, in a particular case, union representatives should not be the agent of an employee to make a contract, or to receive a notice, or otherwise effect a binding transaction on his behalf. But that agency does not stem from the mere fact that they are union representatives and that he is a member of the union; it must be supported in the particular case by the creation of some specific agency.

It is generally recognised that non-unionists as well as union members may be covered by an effective collective bargain. The most pragmatic approach is that collective bargains are implied into individual contracts by way of conduct (*Hill* v *Levey* (1858)), or as Kahn-Freund puts it, they become 'crystallised custom'. In the case of factory gate hiring, there may be no other possible terms.

Termination of collective agreements

Where a collectively bargained term has been incorporated into the individual contract of employment, the employer cannot unilaterally terminate it (*Robertson* v *British Gas Corporation* (1983)). Neither can termination of a collective agreement have an effect on terms of remuneration incorporated into an individual's contract of employment (see *Whent* v *T. Cartledge Ltd* (1997)). An individual contract of employment may, however, be varied without specific consent to the precise change if it includes a provision directly or by the incorporation of other agreements for unilateral variation of its terms (*Airlie* v *City of Edinburgh DC* (1996)). Tribunals are, however, likely to construe any such terms strictly to prevent abuse.

A case which has caused some difficulties is *Cadoux* v *Central Regional Council* (1986). Here, the Court of Session decided that, although the employee did have a right to a life assurance scheme, albeit introduced into the employee's contract unilaterally by the employer, the employer also had the right to terminate it. This was because the relevant document to which the contract referred stated that the employer had this right. The employee therefore had the right to the life assurance scheme, but only so long as the employer allowed it to exist. The decision was heavily criticised, particularly by Napier, on the basis that it is a strange type of contractual obligation under which a party remains free to alter or cancel any indebtedness to the other party (see (1986) 15 ILJ 52). This argument is, however, misconceived. There is nothing illogical, or indeed unusual, in placing oneself under obligations one is at some stage free to terminate. The employment contract itself is a good example of this, as either party can terminate its obligations at will (with proper notice). The mistake lies in not noticing that the obligation survives until it is terminated, and the termination applies only to the future, and not past or present obligations.

On a transfer of a commercial undertaking, whether by sale or some other disposition or by operation of law, the transferee company is obliged to observe the terms of any collective bargain negotiated by the transferor (Transfer of Undertakings (Protection of Employment) Regulations 2006 (SI 2006 No. 246), reg. 5).

Inappropriate terms for incorporation

Some terms of the collective bargain are not susceptible to 'translation' into the individual contract because they relate to obligations entered into by the union collectively, such as union recognition (*Gallagher* v *Post Office* (1970)), or redundancy procedures. Thus in *British Leyland UK Ltd* v *McQuilken* (1978) the appellant company agreed with the union representing the majority of its workers on a phased discontinuance of its experimental department in Glasgow. Skilled employees would have a choice of retraining or redundancy. Some workers who had chosen the latter later changed their minds, and the employees claimed that the employers were breaking their contracts by infringing the collective bargain. Lord McDonald held, however, that the collective agreement 'was a long-term plan dealing with policy rather than the rights of individual employees under their contract of employment'. The court looked for authority to a 1930s Privy Council decision that an agreement between a Canadian railway company and a trade union providing, in a redundancy situation, for staff with the shortest service to be dismissed first was not part of the individual contract (*Young* v *Canadian Northern Railway Co.* (1931)), since '[this agreement] does not appear to be a document adapted for conversion into or incorporation with a service agreement'. Further, a term of a bargain conferring rights or imposing duties on a person other than employer and employee cannot, in the absence of express agreement of the parties (see Contracts (Rights of Third Parties) Act 1999), be incorporated into an individual contract of employment because of the constraints of the doctrine of privity. Ultimately whether a term is appropriate for incorporation turns on construction of the clause in context. If the clause is set out in the context of other primarily procedural matters this may make it more likely that the term will also be regarded as inappropriate for incorporation (see *Griffiths* v *Buckinghamshire CC* (1994)), as would a 'last in first out' agreement according to which employees were to be selected for redundancy (*Alexander* v *STC* (1990) which might now, in any event, be considered to fall foul of age discrimination law). It will, however, be easy to infer that terms of a collective agreement relating to employees' entitlement to severance pay would be incorporated (*Lee* v *GEC Plessey Telecommunications Ltd* (1993)).

Incorporation of non-strike clauses

There is a statutory modification of the rules of incorporation in TULR(C)A 1992, s. 180 which severely restricts the binding inclusion in a collective agreement of clauses which inhibit the taking of industrial action, or have the effect of doing so. Such a provision may be incorporated in the individual contract only if the collective agreement is in writing, expressly states that it is incorporated into the individual contract, is reasonably accessible at the workplace and available during working hours and the contract of employment expressly or impliedly incorporates such a term. This is the case only where the union is defined in law as 'independent' (see Chapter 13 below).

Levels of bargaining

Where there are different levels of collective bargaining the courts have tended to look at the national agreement for incorporation into the individual contract. The courts take this view probably because the national agreement is the more legal-appearing document. Thus in *Loman and Henderson* v *Merseyside Transport Services Ltd* (1967) the road haulage national agreement provided guaranteed weekly pay on the foundation of a 40-hour week, yet at the Barking depot of the respondent warehousing company a local agreement offered 68 hours. The Divisional Court, however, held that the latter was 'in the nature of gentleman's agreement for ironing out local difficulties and providing an incentive for cooperation...'. This was notwithstanding that the local agreement was much more directly effective, on the ground that employees who refused overtime would have been removed (but *cf. Barrett* v *NCB* (1978) and *Saxton* v *NCB* (1970)). The logical approach is to treat a local agreement, insofar as it varies from a national agreement, as an indication of the intention of the parties to depart from the nationally-agreed terms. In that, as we have seen, the legal enforceability of the collective agreement itself is irrelevant to incorporation into the employees' contracts, the decision in *Loman* would now appear to be wrong.

3.2.6 Awards

Some employees' terms derive from an award of an arbitration panel or some other third party. Thus the CAC, in claims under TULR(C)A 1992, ss 183–185 for breach of the duty to disclose information to trade unions, determine fair terms which are thereby automatically incorporated into the individual contracts of employment of affected workers. A similar process of implication arises where an *ad hoc* arbitrator or the CAC itself acts under a voluntary reference of a dispute made by ACAS under TULR(C)A 1992, s. 212.

3.2.7 Works rules

Many employers lay down detailed 'works rules' which include disciplinary provisions but may also take in matters relating to sickness, safety provisions, employee sports facilities, and holidays. They may be given contractual effect by way of express or implied incorporation and may be communicated by notice board, special handbook, sheet of paper, electronically, or even word of mouth. A typical format is where the employee signs a declaration that he accepts the conditions of employment as set out in the works rules, and such acceptance may be implied if the employee has reasonable notice of them.

Works rules are not, however, all contractual terms—some, because they are uncertain and ambiguous like the collective bargain, are not appropriate for incorporation; others are inherently variable, and solely within the prerogative of the employer. In the leading case, *Secretary of State for Employment* v *ASLEF (No. 2)* (1972), the Court of Appeal had to determine whether the respondent union's 'work to rule' was in breach of contract. In disputing this, the union claimed it was merely following the employer's rule book to the letter. The Court of Appeal held, however, that the rules of British Rail, which contained a mass of detailed instructions in 239 rules on 280 pages, were not all contractually binding. Some were clearly out of date, others trivial. Generally, Lord Denning MR stated that, although each employee signed a form saying that he would abide by the rules, this did not mean that they became terms of the contract. They were only instructions as to how the work should be done. The employer might thus alter the rules at will and the boundaries of his prerogative are thereby increased.

If the employee refuses to obey a changed rule he might be lawfully locked out at common law (*Ticehurst* v *British Telecommunications plc* (1992)) and (depending on all the circumstances) probably fairly dismissed under statute. The employee must obey lawful and reasonable orders. This aspect of the employment relationship, perhaps more than any other, shows how uneasily the contractual analysis can be applied to it. Whatever the ostensible equality of the parties, this inherent power in the employer means that the employee will almost always play a subservient role within a bureaucratic hierarchy. (See Collins, (1986) 15 ILJ 1.)

It may confidently be assumed, however, that those sections of work rule books which deal with particulars required in the statutory statement of terms will be part of the contract. Otherwise the test is what the parties intend to be contractual terms. In *Petrie* v *MacFisheries Ltd* (1940) a notice about sick pay posted on the factory notice board was held to have contractual effect, even though the employees had never had their attention specifically drawn to it. In *Dal* v *A. S. Orr* (1980) the EAT determined that a statement in the employees' handbook that 'the Company reserves the right to alter the shift system together with the hours of work to meet production requirements' was contractual. Much will turn upon the nature of the clause in question, and a clause such as a mobility clause, which does not have immediate practical effect, may have to be brought more clearly to the employee's attention. In *Anglia Regional Co-operative Society* v *O'Donnell* (1994) the EAT held that a new mobility clause had not been incorporated into the contract of employment where a document containing the clause had been sent to the employee but she did not know why it had been sent. The employers had not discussed the new terms with the employee and the EAT held that the tribunal should not readily infer an employee's acquiescence to a unilateral variation in contractual terms which does not have immediate practical effect. Indeed (albeit *obiter* and contrary to contractual orthodoxy) the EAT considered that even a signature on a document may not be sufficient to indicate assent to a unilateral variation of contract.

3.2.8 **Unfair terms**

Where contracts of employment have unfair terms, the traditional view has been that the common law basis of laissez-faire applies—the parties should be free, in contract, to agree to what terms they please. We have already seen how the employment relationship is not one in which the parties have equal bargaining power, but we have also examined the notion that this does not affect the contractual nature of the relationship. Most contracts entered into in everyday life are the product of little or no negotiation at all. The person who buys a cup of coffee from a vending machine will have little success in trying to beat down the price. For this reason, where one party (A) is dealing as a business and the other (B) deals as a consumer, not holding himself out as dealing in the course of a business, statute intervenes in order to provide the consumer with protection. This occurs by way of the Unfair Contract Terms Act 1977 (UCTA 1977). If this is the case then protection is provided by s. 3(2) against A claiming exclusion from liability for breach of contract, or attempting to restrict his liability. It also protects B if A claims to be entitled to perform the contract in a substantially different way from what is reasonable, or not to perform it at all if that is not reasonable. This provision has been held by the High Court, in *Brigden* v *American Express Bank Ltd* (2000), to apply to employment contracts but the Court of Appeal pointed out in *Commerzbank AG* v *Keen* (2007) that the employee does not deal as a consumer, and UCTA 1977 should not apply. (See Wynn-Evans, (2007) 36 ILJ 207.)

(See further, Brodie, (2007) 27 *Legal Studies* 95.)

3.3 **Implied terms**

Having considered the express terms of a contract of employment we shall now consider implied terms. Before we consider specific implied terms we shall consider how terms can become implied into a contract of employment.

3.3.1 **Methods of implication**

Officious bystander test

The classic exposition of the process of implication of contractual terms was given by MacKinnon LJ in *Shirlaw* v *Southern Foundries (1926) Ltd* (1939):

Prima facie that which in any contract is left to be implied and need not be expressed is something so obvious that it goes without saying; so that, if, while the parties were making their bargain, an officious bystander were to suggest some express provision for it in their agreement, they would testily suppress him with a common 'Oh, of course!'.

This is in line with Bowen LJ's oft-quoted *dictum* in *The Moorcock* (1889) that an implied term must be 'founded on presumed intention and upon reason'. However, it would now seem that intention and reason do not both have to be present. In *Courtaulds Northern Spinning Ltd* v *Sibson* (1988) Slade LJ said that the courts do not have to be satisfied that the parties to the contract would have agreed to a term only if they were being reasonable. It would thus seem that intention and reason are now alternative methods of implication (see also *Howman & Son* v *Blyth* (1983)). As Holland and Chandler have pointed out, this conclusion means that the courts may come to the conclusion that the parties, as reasonable people, would have agreed to an unreasonable term, although in fact they did not. (See (1988) 17 ILJ 253.) This is a strange result, not least because, as Foster has indicated, it seems to ignore the duty existing in both parties of mutual trust and confidence—see (1989) 52 MLR 251.

Business efficacy

An alternative test provides for implication of terms which are 'necessary in the business sense to give efficacy to the contract' (*Reigate* v *Union Manufacturing Co. Ltd* (1918) per Scrutton LJ). Thus, the employee's implied duties of care, fidelity, and co-operation may not, in fact, be expressly desired at all, or even implicitly intended, but they are nonetheless considered necessary by the courts. Lord Steyn described such general implied terms as 'default rules' in *Malik* v *BCCI* (1997). The existence of such terms will clearly depend upon the facts in each particular case.

The courts have rejected the following suggested terms as inappropriate for implication:

(a) that if employment were terminated without the employee having taken any part of holiday entitlement, the company would pay money in lieu of those holidays (*Morley* v *Heritage plc* (1993));

(b) that by the time of commencement of training, a trainee solicitor would have passed final examinations or be awaiting the results thereof (*Stubbes* v *Trower, Still & Keeling* (1987));

(c) that all the rules of natural justice applied; but the court did imply that the right to suspend an employee must not be exercised on unreasonable grounds (*McLory* v *Post Office* (1992));

(d) in the case of an employee on annualised hours, if an employee left early he would be entitled to the standard rate of pay for any hours he had worked in excess of a 40-hour week (*Ali* v *Christian Salvensen Ltd* (1995)).

On the other hand, these terms have been implied:

(a) to take reasonable steps to bring to the attention of employees the existence of a right to enhance their pension entitlements by the purchase of added years, where the employees could not reasonably be expected to be aware of the term unless it were drawn to their notice; this was especially so since the employees were not involved in negotiating the contract (*Scally* v *Southern Health and Social Services Board* (1991));

(b) that the employer would reasonably and promptly afford a reasonable opportunity to obtain redress of grievances (*Goold Ltd* v *McConnell* (1995));

(c) that the employer will provide and monitor for employees, so far as is reasonably practicable, a working environment which is reasonably suitable for performance by them of their contractual duties. It may thus be a breach of an implied term to require an employee to work in an environment which is affected by the smoking habits of fellow employees. It is not necessary to demonstrate for this purpose that the requirement is directly concerned with health, nor that it is a risk to health (*Waltons & Morse* v *Dorrington* (1997)).

Custom and practice

Day-to-day features of employment may be governed by long-held custom and practice. Indeed, in the 19th century, before collective bargaining took over, most terms were reached in this way. One reason for its continued extent is that some collective agreements are too remote and vague for application in the realities of particular workplaces. To be legally recognised by the courts, however, a custom must be 'reasonable, certain and notorious'. In the leading case of *Sagar* v *Ridehalgh & Son Ltd* (1931) the Court of Appeal decided that customary deductions from a weaver's wages which had been made in the same way for 30 years were contractual terms. The process of incorporation, according to Romer LJ, was that the employee '[e]ntering the appellant's service upon the same terms as the other weavers employed by them…must be deemed to have subjected himself to those terms whatever those terms might turn out to be'. Knowledge of the practice by each worker was not necessary. However, in *Meek* v *Port of London Authority* (1918) the long-established deduction of income tax was held not to be incorporated into the employee's contract because employees did not know of it. The latter would appear to be the better approach as it seems unjust to impose terms on employees of which they are wholly ignorant. The trend to view custom and practice as rooted in the intention of the parties would seem to support this view. (See Brodie, (2004) 33 ILJ 159.)

Custom and practice may also be the basis for the incorporation of a collective agreement. Indeed, many collective agreements, particularly at local level, are simply a distillation of established custom and practice.

There is frequently argument over whether an enhanced redundancy policy has been incorporated into the contract by way of regular grant of its terms. There may be a term of the contract 'if a policy has been drawn to the attention of the employees or has been followed without exception for a substantial period' (per Browne-Wilkinson J in *Duke* v *Reliance Systems* (1982); see also *Mears* v *Safecar Security* (1982)), but this is not merely a mechanistic exercise of counting up how many times enhancements have been made. In *Quinn* v *Calder Industrial Materials Ltd* (1996) the EAT emphasised that the proper question is whether the circumstances in which the policy was made or has become known support the inference that the employers intended to become contractually bound by it.

Employees should be aware that their co-operation with employers in performing more than their contracts require may result in fresh contractual obligations arising on the basis that they have become custom and practice. A common example is music and drama teachers in schools who give up lunch breaks or work after school hours on productions and concerts. These have been argued by employers to have become contractually-required activities. The courts should, however, usually strain against finding that there is a disincentive on employees to co-operate with their employers for fear of attracting new contractual liabilities.

3.3.2 Relationship to express terms

The general common law rule is that an implied term is subject to any express term to the contrary, but the limitations on the application of this were spelt out by the Court of Appeal in *Johnstone* v *Bloomsbury Health Authority* (1991). In that case a hospital doctor was under an obligation to work a certain number of hours and possibly some more hours if called upon by the hospital so to do. In consequence, the doctor became ill. Stuart-Smith LJ said that the express obligation to work the additional hours was subject to the implied term that the employer had an obligation to take care of its employees. This was because such an implied term was necessary in order to give efficacy to the contract. However, the other judge in the majority, Sir Nicolas Browne-Wilkinson V-C, thought that the implied term took effect as to the additional hours because there was no absolute obligation to work the overtime. Therefore there was no conflict between the express and the implied term. However, this does not seem to be a consistent meaning of 'absolute' here. It was not that there was no absolute obligation to work, for whether the doctor did so or not was at the hospital's option and therefore when it required him to work he had an absolute obligation to do so. It was, however, not *absolutely* clear that the hospital would call upon him to work the extra hours. It is hard to see how that fact can be linked to the precedence of the implied term over the express.

3.3.3 Common implied terms

Co-operation and mutual trust and confidence

The courts have frequently implied a duty of co-operation between employer and employee, notwithstanding the potential for conflict between their interests. Most of the authorities deal with the obligation this imposes on an employee. A general statement is to be found in *Secretary of State for Employment* v *ASLEF (No. 2)* (1972). Under the Industrial Relations Act 1971 the Secretary of State for Employment could order a cooling off period for a strike where, *inter alia*, employees were acting 'in breach of contract'. The union claimed that their work to rule was not a breach but instead entailed meticulous observance of British Rail's own rule book. They claimed that they were following their agreement to the letter. Lord Denning, however, identified a breach. '[I]f the employee, with others, takes steps wilfully to disrupt the undertaking, to produce chaos so that it will not run as it should, then each one who is a party to those steps is guilty of a breach of contract.' He gave 'a homely instance' of what he had in mind as a breach:

Suppose I employ a man to drive me to the station. I know there is sufficient time, so that I do not tell him to hurry. He drives me at a slower speed than he need, with the deliberate object of making me lose the train, and I do lose it. He may say that he has performed to the letter of the contract; he has driven me to the station; but he has wilfully made me lose the train, and that is a breach of contract beyond all doubt.

However, Lord Denning disapproved of the term suggested by Donaldson P at first instance that the employee should actively assist the employer to operate his organisation. It was going too far to suggest 'a duty to behave fairly to his employer and do a fair day's work'. Although far-reaching, Lord Denning's was not a positive doctrine: 'A man is not bound positively to do more for his employer than his contract requires. He can withdraw his goodwill if he pleases.' Buckley LJ implied a term that 'an employee must serve the employer faithfully with a view to promoting those commercial interests for which he is employed'. However, it is doubtful whether the duty to obey lawful orders (see below) can be seen as anything other than a positive duty to co-operate, in that the courts look at lawfulness in a way which is wider than a mere contractual entitlement.

More recent authorities, primarily under the impulse of finding a breach of contract for constructive dismissal, have emphasised the mirror-image obligation of the employer to co-operate with the employee, and not to make his task in any way more difficult. It is in this context that the implied duty of co-operation is generally referred to as the duty of mutual trust and confidence, which may be a form of fiduciary duty—see Clarke, (1999) 28 ILJ 348; *Neary v Dean of Westminster* (1999); *cf.* the views of Elias J in *Nottingham University v Fishel* (2000)—see Sims, (2001) 30 ILJ 101, and generally Cabrelli, (2005) 34 ILJ 284. The House of Lords endorsed the duty in *Malik v Bank of Credit and Commerce International* (1997) in holding that employees were entitled to so-called 'stigma damages' because of having been employed by a failed bank and consequently suffering in terms of reputation and career prospects through the criminal actions of senior figures who were engaged in corrupt and dishonest practices. (See generally Lindsay, (2001) 30 ILJ 1; Brodie, (2001) 30 ILJ 84.) Thus, a breach has been identified when employers have criticised managers in front of subordinates (*Associated Tyre Specialists (Eastern) Ltd v Waterhouse* (1976)), used foul language (*Palmanor Ltd v Cedron* (1978)), made groundless accusations of theft (*Robinson v Crompton Parkinson Ltd* (1978)), and failed to show proper respect for a senior employee (*Garner v Grange Furnishings Ltd* (1977)). As Phillips J stated in *BAC Ltd v Austin* (1978):

It must ordinarily be an implied term of the contract of employment that employers do not behave in a way which is intolerable or in a way which employees cannot be expected to put up with any longer.

Another aspect of this rubric of co-operation is that the employer must not put it out of his power to comply with a contract of employment he has entered into. Thus, in *Shindler v Northern Raincoat Co. Ltd* (1960) the plaintiff was managing director of the respondents until their capital was acquired by another company which removed him as a director. His employment as managing director was thus automatically terminated, and notwithstanding that the articles of association of the company clearly permitted this, Diplock J thought they were in breach of an implied term that they would not deprive themselves of the opportunity of using the employee's services. A similar duty rests on the employee.

Not every action undermining trust and confidence will amount to a breach, but where it does so because it is sufficiently serious, this will amount to a repudiatory breach and therefore a constructive dismissal if the employee resigns, according to the EAT in *Morrow v Safeway Stores* (2002). The duty of trust and confidence is thus somewhat different from the duty merely to act reasonably, which the courts have long had an aversion to finding exists as a free-standing implied term in contracts of employment. Nevertheless, it is sometimes referred to in those terms (see e.g. Davies, (2009) 38 ILJ 278), probably erroneously,

In *Johnson v Unisys Ltd* (2001) the House of Lords held that the implied term of mutual trust and confidence does not apply to the manner of the dismissal, which means that an employee cannot rely on this if he is denied a fair hearing. An implied term cannot contradict an express term at common law allowing the employer to dismiss with due notice. Also, the term is concerned with the relationship during its existence, and therefore does not apply where that is being terminated (at least in relation to the employer's acts that form part of the dismissal process—see a further decision of the House of Lords in *Eastwood* v *Magnox Electric plc* (2004); Barnard, [2006] CLJ 27). This seems logical. However, their Lordships in *Johnson* also held that the term could not operate on dismissal because Parliament had put a cap on unfair dismissal compensation, and therefore to have a contractual remedy without limit would run counter to that. (For an example of the application of this principle, see the High Court's decision in *Gibb* v *Maidstone and Tunbridge Wells NHS Trust* (2009).) It would also be unnecessary given the existence of the statutory remedy. This reasoning seems less sustainable, particularly given the fact that not every employee is eligible to bring an unfair dismissal claim. In any event, there is nothing illogical in capping compensation in a claim based on fairness and not capping one based on other grounds even if both are concerned with the manner of dismissal. (See further Bell, (2001) 10 Nott LJ 75; Sims, (2001) 60 CLJ 462; and Barmes, (2004) 67 MLR 435.)

Care and safety

In addition to a variety of duties under health and safety legislation, every employer must take reasonable care for the safety of his employees—but not for their economic well-being (*Crossley* v *Faithful & Gould Holdings Ltd* (2004); Wynn-Evans, (2004) 33 ILJ 355). This is a specialised application of the law of negligence set out generally in *Donoghue* v *Stevenson* (1932), but also takes effect as an implied term of the contract of employment. The courts should, in fact, not be ready to find a tortious duty where a contractual duty to the same effect exists, according to the House of Lords in *Tai Hing Cotton Mill Ltd* v *Lin Chong Hing Bank Ltd* (1986). The consequence of finding a contractual duty may be a different measure of damages (*Wright* v *Dunlop Rubber Co. Ltd* (1971)). The House of Lords in *Wilsons and Clyde Coal Co.* v *English* (1938) categorised three aspects of the generalised duty. The employer must select proper staff, provide adequate materials and provide a safe system of working. As we have already seen, the duty is not absolute, being an implied term, but may on occasions counter-weigh an express term which is inconsistent with it (*Johnstone* v *Bloomsbury Health Authority* (1991); see Barratt, (1991) 20 ILJ 137). However, there is a duty to take positive thought for the safety of workers in the light of what the employer knows, or ought to know, according to the House of Lords in *Barber* v *Somerset County Council* (2004)—see Njoya, (2005) 121 LQR 33; Brodie, (2004) 33 ILJ 261.

There is, however, no specific implied term that an employee should not be transferred to work involving a serious risk to her health in addition to the general contractual duties already discussed (*Jagdeo* v *Smiths Industries Ltd* (1982)). Neither is there a duty on the employer to take reasonable care to protect an employee from economic loss arising from physical injury, such as that occurring because of a lack of, or insufficient, insurance cover (*Reid* v *Rush and Tomkins Group plc* (1989)).

In return, generally the employee must exercise reasonable care in carrying out duties but the court seeks 'the standards of men and not those of angels' (*Jupiter General Insurance Co.* v *Shroff* (1937)). If the employee is sued in tort and the employer is vicariously liable they are treated as joint tortfeasors and the court may thus award such contribution between them as it finds just and equitable having regard to the extent of their responsibility for the damage. The consequence of the contractual duty of care of the employee was controversially demonstrated in the House of Lords case of *Lister* v *Romford Ice and Cold Storage Co.* (1957). The appellant, a driver with the respondent company, ran over a co-employee, who happened to be his father. The company was vicariously liable to the father for the actions of his son but successfully recouped the damages they had to pay by suing the appellant son under his contract of employment. The employee's defensive attempt to imply a term of indemnity, i.e. that he would be covered by the employer's insurance, failed by a three to two majority. Viscount Simonds urged that any such indemnity would 'tend to create a feeling of irresponsibility in a class of persons from whom, perhaps more than any other, constant vigilance is owed to the community'. This might have led to hardship if employers and insurance companies standing behind them regularly used this right to sue their employees, even though later cases held that it did not apply to driving on a special occasion involving unusual tasks (*Harvey* v *O'Dell Ltd* (1958)), nor if the employer was at all at fault (*Jones* v *Manchester Corporation* (1952)). The point is now practically unimportant since the fears raised were soon obviated by an informal agreement among insurance companies not to enforce their rights of subrogation in this respect in the absence of fraud. This was reached in the face of the threat of legislation on the subject and is now adhered to by members of the Association of British Insurers and Lloyd's.

Competence

It has long been thought that the employee impliedly represents that he is reasonably competent to do his job (*Harmer* v *Cornelius* (1858)). He can thus be lawfully dismissed instantly if in serious breach. This harsh common law position is, however, mitigated by the statutory unfair dismissal protection which affords various procedural safeguards to an incompetent employee as well as to others, and is now of much more consequence for the majority of employees.

As far as the employer is concerned, the duty to be competent takes the form of a duty to exercise due care and skill in his relationship with his employees. An increasingly important area as far as this aspect of the duty is concerned is where the employer is asked to provide a reference for an existing or past employee. The House of Lords held in *Spring* v *Guardian Assurance plc* (1994) that an employer has an implied duty of skill and care to the employee in writing a reference for him, and the EAT confirmed in *TSB Bank plc* v *Harris* (2000) that this is a duty that applies in contract as well as in tort. As such, it may form the foundation not just for a claim for damages in contract but also of the fundamental breach necessary for a constructive dismissal claim in unfair dismissal—in constructive dismissal, the employee resigns because of a fundamental breach of the employment contract by his employer, but this is construed by statute as the employer dismissing the employee, enabling him to claim unfair dismissal. The importance of this duty can be seen by the decision of the Court of Appeal in *Bartholomew* v *London Borough of Hackney* (1999) that employers have, in writing references, a duty not only to be honest, but to give a fair and accurate account. In other words, referees cannot rely on ambiguous statements—such as 'I cannot praise this woman highly enough'— nor misleading comments which are strictly capable of being read either as true or as beliefs honestly held. Neither can they rely on partial knowledge if they should reasonably have had more information. Note also that the duty is to provide a reference that is both accurate and fair. It is not enough that what is said is true if this gives a misleading impression. For example, if the employer were to state that, at the time of the dismissal the employee was involved in disciplinary proceedings, the employer would be in breach if the reference omitted to say that the employee was subsequently exonerated. This does not mean that the reference needs to be comprehensive. Neither is there any duty on the employer to provide a reference should he not wish to do so. (See generally, Middlemiss, (2004) 33 ILJ 59.)

Obedience to instructions

At common law the employee is, in general, under an obligation to obey all lawful instructions of the employer, and this was indeed described as 'a condition essential to the contract of service' in *Laws* v *London Chronicle (Indicator Newspapers) Ltd* (1959). That the employee might be summarily dismissed if he does not comply is a great bulwark of the managerial prerogative. In the modern law, the unfair dismissal jurisdiction has established procedural safeguards for the employee who has the requisite eligibility for protection, and even at common law some of the harshest early decisions (e.g. in *Turner* v *Mason* (1845)) would not be reached today, since they reflect a very different view of the extent of the rights of employers. Now instructions must be tempered by reasonableness. *Ottoman Bank Ltd* v *Chakarian* (1930) was a particularly strong case since the employers ordered the plaintiff, an Armenian, to stay in Constantinople where he had previously been sentenced to death and it was held that he was within his rights in refusing. On the other hand, in *Bouzourou* v *Ottoman Bank* (1930) a Christian employee was under an obligation to obey an order to work at a branch in Asia Minor, notwithstanding the well-known hostility of the Turkish Government to his religion. It is suggested this would not be decided the same way today. It has also been held a breach of contract to refuse an order to visit Ireland because of general fear of IRA activity (*Walmsley* v *Udec Refrigeration Ltd* (1972)). An employee is also under an obligation to adapt reasonably to new work methods (*Cresswell* v *Board of Inland Revenue* (1984)) at least in so far as this does not alter the nature of the work itself, but merely the method of performing the work, according to the Court of Appeal in *Bull* v *Nottinghamshire and City of Nottingham Fire and Rescue Authority* (2007).

By contrast, a dismissal for failure to obey an illegal order is always wrongful, so that in *Morrish* v *Henlys (Folkestone) Ltd* (1973), where an employee was ordered to falsify the account books at the garage where he worked, his refusal was not in breach of contract. The same result was reached in *Gregory* v *Ford* (1951) where the employee said he would not take on the road a vehicle not covered by third party insurance.

Fidelity

Several duties owed by the employee are comprised under the rather vague rubric of fidelity. The duties are owed not only to the contractual employer but also to any employer to whom the employee is seconded for a period (*Macmillan Inc.* v *Bishopsgate Investment Trust (No. 2)* (1993)). What the duties have in common is that, without them, the employee's use to the employer would be limited, but their precise character differs according to the status and position of the employee, and is influenced by principles of equity. Moreover, the basic implied obligations are often taken further by express agreement. If there is a fundamental rule, it is that there is a requirement of honesty in the service of the employer. First, the employee must account to his employer for all money and property received during the course of the employment, and can be disciplined in the event of any dishonesty. A blatant example is illicit borrowing from the till (*Sinclair* v *Neighbour* (1967)). In *Boston Deep Sea Fishing & Ice Co.* v *Ansell* (1888) the principle had been taken somewhat further, however. The defendant, who was managing director of the plaintiff company A, also owned shares in company B, which supplied ice to A, and received a bonus on these shares for all sales gained. Such secret profits were in breach of his duty to account to the plaintiffs and he was held to have been lawfully dismissed. The case might, however, be narrowly distinguished since Ansell was a director and under strict fiduciary duties, as well as an employee (see also *Reading* v *AG* (1951); *Nottingham University* v *Fishel* (2000)).

Secondly, there is a duty to disclose misdeeds. The duty to disclose misconduct was considered in *Sybron Corporation* v *Rochem Ltd* (1983). At issue was the occupational pension of the chief manager who was discovered after his retirement to have been involved in a directly competing company while still employed. The plaintiff claimed that the pension had been given as a result of a mistake of fact and sought restitution. The Court of Appeal decided that the company was entitled to recover the money. Stephenson LJ distinguished the House of Lords decision in *Bell* v *Lever Brothers* (1932) on the grounds that, while there might be no duty on the employee to disclose his own misconduct (as *Bell* had held, but *cf. Item Software (UK) Ltd* v *Fassihi* (2004); Berg, (2005) 121 LQR 213; Wynn-Evans, (2005) 34 ILJ 148), he had a duty to report the misdeeds of others particularly where he was senior enough to realise that what they were doing was wrong and he was responsible for reporting on their activities each month. However, there are serious faults in his reasoning and his reading of *Bell* v *Lever Brothers* (see Honeyball, (1983) 42 CLJ 218, and generally Freedland, (1984) 13 ILJ 25; see MacMillan, (2003) 119 LQR 625 for an interesting account of *Bell* v *Lever Brothers*).

The case can be usefully contrasted with *Horcal Ltd* v *Gatland* (1983). The defendant, the managing director of the plaintiff building contractors, was negotiating to purchase the shares of the company when a customer telephoned him asking that work be done on her home. He gave an estimate on the company's notepaper but kept the proceeds of the contract for himself. The company did not find out until after the termination of his contract and the activation of a termination agreement. Although the Court of Appeal found that he had committed a repudiatory breach, due to the breach not being discovered before termination, it held that there was no failure of consideration and no basis on which the money could be recovered. But it would seem the time of discovery of breach should be considered irrelevant as to whether or not there has been a breach (see Honeyball, (1984) 13 ILJ 257).

The courts are vigilant to protect an employer whose employee acts part-time in competition with him, but on the other hand they will not prohibit the individual's legitimate spare time activities. Lord Greene MR indicated how far the courts would intervene to protect this delicate balance in *Hivac Ltd* v *Park Royal Scientific Instruments Ltd* (1946) when he said that it would be deplorable if an employee could consistently, knowingly, deliberately, and secretly inflict great harm on his employer's business. In that case, two weekday employees of the plaintiff company spent their Sundays working on highly specialised tasks for the defendant firm which were in direct competition with the plaintiff. An injunction was granted against continuing this arrangement, notwithstanding that there was no evidence of actual misuse of confidential information, because their actions infringed the general duty of fidelity. Lord Greene MR and Morton LJ referred to the danger of future transfer of information and emphasised the secret nature of their work.

In *Sanders* v *Parry* (1967), a solicitor employed as an assistant by another made an agreement with an important client of the latter to work for the latter, and Havers J restrained this as a breach of the employee's duty of fidelity. There are, however, some contracts of a routine nature in which there is no question of exclusive services being required. Many employees moonlight, that is work for one employer by day as well as for another by night, with the full acquiescence of the employers. In *Nova Plastics Ltd* v *Froggatt* (1982) an odd-job man was held not to be in breach of contract when he worked for a competitor of his employer in his spare time without any evidence of definite harm. (See also *Lancashire Fires Ltd* v *SA Lyons & Co. Ltd* (1997) on the extent to which an employee may engage in preparations for competitive activity while still employed.)

The duty of fidelity is broken where an employee leaves a job and then uses his ex-employer's resources or confidential information to assist him to set up in competition with him. Thus in *Wessex Dairies Ltd* v *Smith* (1935) a milk roundsman who canvassed his employer's customers on his last day to give their business to him thereafter was held to have broken his contract. To copy out a list of customers may be a breach. Where a managing director, while still employed, approached his company's main customer to obtain their views as to whether he and senior colleagues should set up a rival business to the company, the EAT held that that was a breach of contract (*Marshall* v *Industrial Systems and Control Ltd* (1992)). Building up goodwill with customers which may incidentally be valuable if the employee were to set up a business himself on his own account is, on the other hand, quite lawful. In order to prevent even the possibility of such occurring, many employers insert express restrictive clauses but these will be very strictly construed by the courts, as we have seen.

There are indications that the courts are prepared to see employees who are not formally directors of a company having more onerous duties in this regard as fiduciaries—see *Shepherds Investments Ltd* v *Walters* (2007); *Helmet Integrated Systems Ltd* v *Tunnard* (2007).

Confidential information

The Public Interest Disclosure Act 1998 contains statutory protection for 'whistleblowing' employees who disclose information in the public interest. For details, see Chapter 12 below. Here we consider the implied terms in the contract of employment at common law.

If an employee uses information confidential to his employer, both he and the recipients of the details may be liable in damages, and restrained by an injunction. This is a head of implied term that the Court of Appeal specifically distinguished from the duty of fidelity, of which it might have been thought a part, in *Faccenda Chicken Ltd* v *Fowler* (1986) (see below). The main problem lies in identifying the perimeter of confidential information and distinguishing it from the employee's 'individual skill and experience', acquired in the course of employment, which he may legitimately put to use in future for a different employer or for his own use in a self-employed capacity or in partnership. In *Printers and Finishers Ltd* v *Holloway*

(1965) Cross J stated that an injunction would be appropriate 'if the information in question can fairly be regarded as a separate part of the employee's stock of knowledge which a man of ordinary honesty and intelligence would recognise to be the property of his old employer and not his own to do as he liked with' (see also *Fraser* v *Thames TV Ltd* (1983)). However, his former employer's solvency, and the reason why the employee resigned, are not covered by the implied term, according to the Court of Appeal in *Brooks* v *Olyslager* (1998).

In *Thomas Marshall (Export) Ltd* v *Guinlé* (1978) Megarry V-C developed criteria for determining what information was confidential including whether the owner reasonably believes the release of the information will be injurious to him or advantageous to his rivals and whether the owner reasonably believes that the information is not already public. The information must be judged in the light of the usage and practices of the industry involved. The secret need not in any way be unique or complicated, and it is no defence for an employee to contend that a third party has already made it public. The judge held that prices paid, details of manufacturers and suppliers, customer requirements, contract negotiations, and details of fast moving lines were all matters that were confidential.

The leading case is *Faccenda Chicken Ltd* v *Fowler* (1986). Mr Fowler had been employed by Faccenda Chicken Ltd as its sales manager until he resigned along with several other employees and set up a business competing with the plaintiff selling fresh chickens from refrigerated vehicles. The employees who left had no express restrictive clauses in their contracts, but the plaintiff claimed that they had broken the duty of confidentiality by using sales information to its disadvantage. The Court of Appeal held it was necessary to consider all the circumstances in the case, and in particular the nature of the employment and the nature of the information, which could be protected only if it could be classed as a trade secret or as material which was of such a highly confidential nature as to require some protection as a trade secret, although there is some difficulty as to what this covers (see Miller, (1986) 102 LQR 359 at p. 363). It was also important whether the employer had impressed upon the employee the confidentiality of the information and whether the information could be easily isolated from other information which the employee was free to use or disclose. It should be noted that the decision in *Faccenda Chicken* has been heavily criticised, not least because the Court of Appeal did not distance itself from a number of doubtful statements of Goulding J at first instance, and Rideout has remarked that the concept of confidentiality in employment as laid out in the case bears little relation to the equitable or contractual duty applied elsewhere ((1986) 15 ILJ 183; see also *Lancashire Fires Ltd* v *SA Lyons & Co. Ltd* (1997)).

Information, whether confidential or not, may always be revealed by the employee if it discloses misconduct on the part of his employer. Thus in *Initial Services Ltd* v *Putterill* (1968), a sales manager was held entitled to disclose an agreement to maintain prices which was contrary to the Restrictive Trade Practices Act 1965. Ungoed-Thomas J has more broadly defined the circumstances when public interest demands disclosure as 'matters carried out or contemplated in breach of the country's security or in breach of law, including statutory duty, fraud or otherwise destructive of the country or its people, including matters medically dangerous to the public' (*Beloff* v *Pressdram Ltd* (1973); see also *Speed Seal Products Ltd* v *Paddington* (1985); *Roger Bullivant Ltd* v *Ellis* (1987)).

The duty does not extend to bar disclosures to a regulatory body, such as the Inland Revenue, according to the High Court in *Re A Company's Application* (1989), nor to information which has become public knowledge. However, in *Attorney-General* v *Guardian Newspapers Ltd (No. 2)* (1988) the House of Lords stated that there was a duty not to profit from a breach of confidence. This may mean, by implication, that the duty of confidence after public disclosure is merely limited, and does not disappear altogether (see Birks, (1989) 105 LQR 501 at p. 507).

The employer may be granted an injunction if a breach of the duty is established. However, the principles which should apply in so deciding, and the relative weight that should be attached to these principles depending upon whether an interim or final injunction is being sought, is open to debate (see further Lomnicka, (1990) 106 LQR 42). In *Camelot* v *Centaur Communications Ltd* (1998) the Court of Appeal upheld an order that publishers should return to the National Lottery operators confidential documents which would enable them to identify an employee responsible for leaking information. An employer has a legitimate and continuing interest in enforcing an obligation of loyalty and confidentiality against an employee who has made an unauthorised disclosure and use of documents acquired by him in the course of employment. It was for the court in each case to weigh this need against the public interest and the press being able to protect the anonymity of its sources.

That the duty not to disclose confidential information extends to employers as well as to employees is shown by the Scottish case of *Dalgleish* v *Lothian and Borders Police Board* (1991), where the employers were held under a duty not to disclose details such as the contents of staff records to the local authority in respect of community charge payments. Further, the Data Protection Act 1998 provides some regulation of the disclosure of information which is collected and held in an automatically processed form, but this is beyond the scope of this book.

Pay

Generally, remuneration is negotiated expressly by way of collective or individual bargain on a yearly or biennial basis, but so essential is it to the contract, that in the absence of express agreement there is still a right to reasonable remuneration. The court will assess what the employee's labours are reasonably worth by way of a quasi-contractual action for *quantum meruit*. In *Way* v *Latilla* (1937) the statement of the defendants that they 'would look after his interests' was enough to support such an action. The implied term is, however, excluded if there is any contractual term on the subject, even if it is merely an article of association of a company giving entitlement to 'such amount as the directors may determine' (*Re Richmond Gate Property Co. Ltd* (1965)).

3.4 Imposed terms

Terms may also be implied into a contract by statute. These are better viewed as imposed terms because the parties cannot override them by express agreement. Examples of such imposed terms include the equality clause imposed by Equal Pay Act 1970, s. 1, the minimum notice period terms imposed by the ERA 1996 and terms derived from the minimum wages legislation. These are considered elsewhere in this book.

3.5 Tortious and criminal liability

Although the liability incurred for breaches of the employment contract will generally lie in contract, it should not be forgotten that liability may arise in tort and criminal law (on the latter see Harrison, (1992) 21 ILJ 31). In *Spring* v *Guardian Assurance plc* (1994), for example, an ex-employer was held liable for a negligently prepared reference in both contract and tort.

3.6 Variation

The contract of employment is a very dynamic agreement, changing as circumstances alter. Even so, any variation in contractual terms still requires the assent, express or tacit, of both parties and should be supported by consideration. However, in *Lee* v *GEC Plessey Telecommunications* (1993) it was held that where a contract expressly incorporates the terms of collective agreements there is no need for fresh consideration with regard to each variation of the contract of employment. By contrast employers could not rely on other external documents incorporated into the contract of employment to unilaterally vary those contracts unless there was a right to vary terms clearly specified in the contract itself. Paradoxically, considerations may be supplied by the employee simply carrying on working under the altered conditions, although this may be less likely where the clause in question does not have immediate practical effect (see *Anglia Regional Co-operative Society* v *O'Donnell* (1994)). If, however, the employer unilaterally enforces a variation, he repudiates the contract of employment and the employee is put to his election whether to accept the fundamental breach, and resign, or to carry on working and seek damages (*Burdett-Coutts* v *Hertfordshire County Council* (1984)). However, if the employee elects to continue working, it is important that he does so under the new terms, whilst expressing his lack of agreement to the variation. If he were to attempt to continue to work under the old terms that would amount to misconduct for failing to follow a lawful order, according to the EAT in *Robinson* v *Tescom Corporation* (2008). Although this might seem logical in a practical sense, in that it might be very disruptive to the employer's business to have just one employee working in a certain way when others may not be, the idea is predicated on the idea that the old terms have been replaced by new ones through the very act of the employer's fundamental breach of contract. However, traditional analysis would indicate that there is no power to unilaterally vary terms of contracts, particularly by way of a breach. Many contracts contain wide flexibility clauses so that a change of actual duties performed (even a radical variation) may lie within the four corners of the contractual job description—for example that the employee will perform such duties as are from time to time assigned to him by the board of directors or managing director. If not, it is important to have in mind Donaldson LJ's remark in *Janata Bank Ltd* v *Ahmed* (1981) that 'the continuously changing contract is unknown to law' (see also *Parry* v *Holst & Co. Ltd* (1968); *Dal* v *A. S. Orr* (1980)).

It is sometimes necessary to distinguish between a mere variation and a wholly new contract by reason of breach of the old one. A unilateral deduction by the management from the employee's pay and/or hours may amount to a fundamental breach of contract and its termination, while on an agreed variation the contract continues. Often the employee proceeds to work oblivious of the breach or under undue influence to ignore it. Judges have, however, been vigilant not to spell out agreements to apparent new terms in these circumstances. For example, in *Horrigan* v *Lewisham London Borough Council* (1978) Arnold J commented:

It is fairly difficult, in the ordinary way, to imply a variation of contract, and it is very necessary, if one is to do so, to have very solid facts which demonstrate that it was necessary to give business efficacy to the contract, that the contract should come to contain a new term implied by way of variation.

This is a particularly live issue in changes of job duties, the contractual scope of which is vital to decisions on redundancy payments. In *Marriott* v *Oxford and District Co-operative Society Ltd (No. 2)* (1970) the appellant had been employed by the respondents as an electrical supervisor for two years when they found that there was insufficient work for him. They were prepared to offer him another post at £3 less per week and he took this under protest, worked for three or four weeks but then terminated his contract by notice. In defence to his claim for a redundancy payment, the respondents claimed that they had not terminated the agreement by insisting on his taking the new job (as was necessary for him to claim his statutory rights), but had merely varied it. Lord Denning was insistent that:

He never agreed to the dictated terms. He protested against them. He submitted to them because he did not want to be out of employment. By insisting on new terms to which he never agreed, the employer did, I think, terminate the old contract of employment.

In *Shields Furniture Ltd* v *Goff* (1973) the National Industrial Relations Court (the predecessor of the EAT) reiterated that work under an alternative offer for a trial period does not constitute acceptance, and in *Sheet Metal Components Ltd* v *Plumridge* (1974), Sir John Donaldson said: 'the courts have rightly been slow to find that there has been a consensual variation where an employee has been faced with the alternative of dismissal and where the variation has been adverse to his interests' (see also *Norwest Holst Group Administration Ltd* v *Harrison* (1985)). The issue is also important in relation to the introduction of new technology and the extent to which employees can be expected to adapt to new techniques within their contractual terms. In *Cresswell* v *Board of Inland Revenue* (1984), the defendant employer's introduction of computers did not change the nature of the job. The Revenue was entitled to withhold pay for employees who refused to co-operate with the new system. Walton J thought that employees had no right to preserve their working conditions unchanged throughout the course of their employment. They could reasonably be expected, after proper training, to adapt to new techniques especially where, as here, there was no evidence of real difficulty. He thought that the jobs would remain 'recognisably the same job but done in a different way'.

Employers frequently seek to vary terms unilaterally by giving the employee the notice to which he is entitled under his contract. Case law suggests that the employer must make it clear that he is terminating one contract and offering another. In *Burdett-Coutts* v *Hertfordshire County Council* (1984) the employers sought to change the hours of six dinner ladies by means of a circular letter. The plaintiffs, who were entitled to 12 weeks' notice of termination, sought a declaration that the purported variation was invalid and a repudiatory breach, to which the defendants responded that the letter should be read as a termination of the employment coupled with an offer of new terms. Kenneth Jones J could not so read the letter which referred to 'detailed notice of variations in your contract of service'. The employees had elected not to accept the repudiation and could now claim the total wages to which they were entitled under the contract. However, as Fredman has pointed out, the result in *Burdett-Coutts* normally will only be repeated fortuitously, as employers will be able to circumvent it by using a different form of words (see (1984) 13 ILJ 177; also *Aparau* v *Iceland Frozen Foods plc* (1996)).

3.7 **Jurisdiction**

For many years jurisdiction to hear contract claims lay in the courts alone. This led to some illogicalities and the courts often expressed disagreement with this being so. After a number of false starts, contractual jurisdiction was eventually extended to ETs by the Employment Tribunals Extension of Jurisdiction (England and Wales) Order 1994 (SI 1994 No. 1623).

SELECTED READING

Brodie, D. (2005), *The Employment Contract*, Oxford: Oxford University Press

Cabrelli, D. (2005), 'The Implied Duty of Mutual Trust and Confidence: An Emerging Overarching Principle?', (2005) 34 ILJ 284

Davies A. C. L. (2009), 'Judicial Self-Restraint in Labour Law', (2009) 38 ILJ 318

Deakin S. (1998), 'The Evolution of the Contract of Employment 1900–1950: the influence of the Welfare State', in N. Whiteside and R. Salais (eds.) *Governance, Industry and Labour Markets in Britain and France*, London: Routledge

Deakin S. (2001), 'The Changing Concept of the Employer in Labour Law', (2001) 30 ILJ 72

Freedland, M. (2003), *The Personal Employment Contract*, Oxford: Oxford University Press

Honeyball, S. and Pearce, D. (2006), 'Contract, Employment and the Contract of Employment', (2006) 35 ILJ 30

Painter, R. W. and Holmes, A. E. (2008), *Cases and Materials on Employment Law*, 7th edn, Oxford: Oxford University Press, chs 2 and 3

(2007) 36 ILJ 1–140 (Special Issue on Reconstructing Employment Contracts)

4

Termination of contract

SUMMARY

This chapter considers various legal issues associated with the termination of a contract of employment. It examines the several ways by which an employment contract can be brought to an end in law, both by the employer and the employee, and considers the remedies that may be available to the parties for the termination of contract in some cases.

4.1 Termination by notice

4.1.1 Common law notice

Although it used to be presumed that employment was on the basis of a yearly hiring, the modern approach is that a person is employed for an indefinite period subject to termination after a reasonable period of notice. The length of notice is usually expressly agreed and if so it must now be stated in the written particulars of employment. Otherwise the common law will imply a period of reasonable notice depending on the circumstances. In many cases this is taken to be the same length as the period of payment (e.g. monthly or weekly). It also has regard to differences of worker status. Thus, to take examples from the period before statute intervened in this area, a year was held to be reasonable notice for a steamer's chief officer and a newspaper editor (*Grundy* v *Sun Printing and Publishing Association* (1916)), and six months for a manager of 120 cinemas (*Adams* v *Union Cinemas Ltd* (1939)) and a journalist (*Bauman* v *Hulton Press Ltd* (1952)). An airline pilot was held to be entitled to three months in *Nicoll* v *Falcon Airways Ltd* (1962).

4.1.2 Statutory notice

The common law was modified by minima first introduced in the Contracts of Employment Act 1963, later amended and now to be found in ERA 1996, ss 86 and 87. The statutory rule is that the employer must give at least one week's notice to an employee who has worked for him for between one month and two years and thereafter one week for each year served up to a maximum of 12 weeks for 12 years. The employee in return must give at least one week's notice of resignation if employed for more than one month (s. 86(2)). Further, the statute does not prevent either party from waiving the right to notice. Neither does it affect the rights of either party to terminate the contract as a result of the conduct of the other nor prevent a party from accepting a payment in lieu of notice (s. 86(3)). Employers often take the realistic view that an employee under notice is unlikely to be a hard or willing worker and give him money instead, essentially as settlement of damages for breach of contract. According to the EAT in *Cerberus Software Ltd* v *Rowley* (1999), this was not subject to mitigation of loss if there was a pay-in-lieu clause. Thus, higher-paid employment obtained by the employee during what would have been the notice period did not reduce his entitlement. However, the Court of Appeal later reversed this. The claim was not for a sum due under a contract, but damages for wrongful dismissal. As Sedley LJ, dissenting, said: 'If this is the law, there is something wrong with it'. It gave the employer the benefit of the employee finding another job quickly. (For further criticism, see Fodder and Freer, (2001) 30 ILJ 215; Pearce, (2001) 60 CLJ 261.)

The Court of Appeal held in *Trotter* v *Forth Ports Authority* (1991) that, where the right to waive notice is exercised, the right to payment in lieu of notice is lost. Despite the fact that there is nothing in s. 86(3) to this effect, this would appear to be consistent with viewing payments in lieu as damages for breach of contract, for where notice is waived there is no breach of contract, according to the Court of Appeal in *Rex Stewart Jeffries Parker Ginsberg Ltd* v *Parker* (1988) (see Napier, [1989] CLJ 31). The rule that where there has been an unlawful termination payments in lieu are damages for breach of contract rather than wages was reiterated by the House of Lords in *Delaney* v *Staples* (1992) when it said that the essential characteristic of wages was that they were consideration for work done or to be done under a contract of employment. Where the employment is terminated by the employer, it therefore follows that any payment made is not wages but, as the term 'payment in lieu' suggests, a payment made instead of wages. There may or may not be a breach of contract in such circumstances, depending upon whether or not the employer terminated the employment in accordance with the terms of the contract. The most common situation is where the employer summarily (i.e. without notice) dismisses an employee and payment is made to cover the lost notice period. In that event, there is a breach of contract unless there is a contractual right to make a payment in lieu. It is not at all clear that the House of Lords was inexorably drawn to this conclusion, in that the consideration moving from employees on a contract of employment is the *willingness* to work, as we have already seen. In that an employee has generally no right to be given work while the contract subsists, it may be thought that the payment in lieu is merely the consideration (wages) moving from the employer, who does not require the employee to work, or indeed to be willing to work. That the employer does not require the employee to work is not inconsistent with the subsistence of that contract. Furthermore, it seems difficult to see how the employer can terminate the contract unilaterally when he does not have the power to do so if the function of notice is, as it arguably is, to remove that capability from employers. (For further difficulties with the reasoning in the House of Lords decision, see McColgan, (1992) 21 ILJ 219.)

Where there is a payment made in lieu of notice *under the contract*, it is lawful, and thus not damages for breach of contract. It therefore follows that the payment is taxable as an emolument arising from employment—see the Court of Appeal's decision in *EMI Group Electronics Ltd* v *Coldicott (HM Inspector of Taxes)* (1999). In *Marshall (Cambridge) Ltd* v *Hamblin* (1994), a majority of the EAT held that a similar analysis can be applied where the notice is given by the employee. Until the notice expires the employment relationship continues and therefore the employer can take advantage of any contractual right to make a payment in lieu of notice—a PILON. The employee had sought to work out his notice in order to claim discretionary commission payments but the EAT held that if these had been denied in breach of contract a claim for damages could be brought. However, the EAT did not consider whether the employee would have been entitled to work out his notice had there not been an express provision for payment in lieu of notice.

Where an employee does waive the right to notice, or accepts pay in lieu of notice, the contract of employment is brought to an end on that date. This may be important in relation to claims for which there is a minimum qualifying period of continuous employment (see *Secretary of State for Employment* v *Staffordshire County Council* and *Secretary of State for Employment* v *Cameron Iron Works* (1989)).

The ERA 1996 also lays down the rate of pay during notice (ss 88–91). The employer must provide a normal week's pay even though his employee does not work if the latter:

(a) is ready and willing to work but the employer has no work for him;

(b) is incapable of work through sickness or injury; or

(c) is away on holiday; or

(d) is absent because of pregnancy or childbirth.

Any sickness or industrial injury benefit paid during such period may be deducted from what the employee is entitled to under this provision. There is no right to payment where:

(a) the employee takes time off (s. 91(1));

(b) the employee breaks his contract during notice (s. 91(4)); or

(c) the employee has given notice and then goes on strike during the notice period (s. 91(2)).

Fringe benefits like holiday stamps are not included (*Secretary of State for Employment* v *Haynes* (1980)). However, the courts may construe any reference to payment in lieu of notice as meaning gross pay rather than pay net of tax (see *Gothard* v *Mirror Group Newspapers Ltd* (1988)). Indeed, it is arguable that payment net of tax should be considered an unlawful deduction of wages contrary to ERA 1996, s. 13(1).

The legislation has a curious effect which it is hard to imagine was intended by Parliament. Under s. 87(4), if the employee in the circumstances set out in s. 86(1) is entitled to contractual notice at least one week greater than his statutory minimum notice, he becomes disentitled to pay during the statutory period. It is difficult to see either what this provision was seeking to achieve or how it is fair to employees—see *Scotts Company (UK) Ltd* v *Budd* (2003).

4.2 Termination by breach

A party to a contract of employment may be discharged by a fundamental breach. A breach may be considered fundamental if it is one the parties regard as vital (*The Mihalis Angelos* (1971)), or which is so serious in its consequences as effectively to deprive the other party of what he had contracted for (*Hong Kong Fir Shipping* v *Kawasaki Kisen Kaisha* (1962)), or shows that the other party no longer intends to be bound by one or more of the essential terms of the contract (*Western Excavating Ltd* v *Sharp* (1978)). MacCardie J put it thus in *Re Rubel Bronze & Metal Co. Ltd* (1918):

In every case the question of repudiation must depend on the character of the contract, the number and weight of the wrongful acts or assertions, the intentions indicated by such acts and words, the deliberation or otherwise with which they are committed or uttered and on the general circumstances of the case.

The fundamental breach may be made up of a series of small breaches, the last providing the straw which breaks the camel's back (*Pepper* v *Webb* (1969); *Garner* v *Grange Furnishing Ltd* (1977)). In determining whether a breach is repudiatory, regard should be had to the intention of the guilty party. For example, a deliberate refusal to pay the employee's remuneration is to be distinguished from a failure to pay which is not deliberate, according to the Court of Appeal in *Cantor Fitzgerald International* v *Callaghan* (1999).

4.2.1 Must a breach be accepted by the innocent party?

An important theoretical (and sometimes practical) question is whether or not a repudiation of a contract of employment needs to be accepted by the innocent party in order to terminate the contract. This apparently academic question is practically important when deciding the date when termination took place and whether, for example, strikers by the very act of striking, i.e. acting in fundamental breach of contract, put an end to their contract. It is also important in deciding whether a termination/repudiation comes within the definition of constructive dismissal (i.e. where an employee resigns in circumstances where he is entitled to do so by reason of the employer's conduct) for purposes of unfair dismissal and redundancy.

The general contract doctrine

The normal contractual doctrine is that 'an unaccepted repudiation is a thing writ in water', and this was restated by the House of Lords in *Photo Production Ltd* v *Securicor Transport Ltd* (1980). Many cases have determined that this holds true for contracts of employment also. There are, however, special difficulties in this area since an order of specific performance cannot be made in respect of contracts of employment, either at the suit of the employer or the employee, so that, even if a breach is not accepted, the court has no mechanism to force the parties to continue in harmony. The employment relationship depends more than most contracts on the existence of mutual trust and co-operation between the parties.

History of the doctrine

The courts sometimes took the view that a repudiation operates automatically to determine the contract. For example, in *Sanders* v *Ernest A. Neale Ltd* (1974), a group of employees went on strike but after an ultimatum presented themselves for work the next day. The question for the National Industrial Relations Court (NIRC) (the forerunner of the EAT) was whether, by their action, the employees could claim that they had refused to accept the employers' repudiation in the ultimatum. Donaldson P thought not, as the repudiation of a contract of employment was an exception to the general rule. It thus terminated the contract without necessity for acceptance by the injured party.

Megarry V-C reviewed an extensive array of cases in *Thomas Marshall (Exports) Ltd* v *Guinlé* (1978), where the employers were suing the employees. The defendant had been employed as managing director of the plaintiff company under a ten-year service contract, but he resigned and the company discovered that during his contract he had been soliciting business for himself away from the employers in breach of his implied duties of good faith to them. In response to the company's application for an interlocutory injunction to prevent the defendant from so acting, the defendant claimed that, with effect from the date of his resignation, the contract had automatically terminated, so that he was no longer bound by its conditions. Megarry V-C rejected this on three grounds. The first was concerned with policy. He said:

Why should a person who makes a contract of service have the right at any moment to put an end to his contractual obligations? No doubt the court will not decree specific performance of the contract, nor will it grant an injunction which will have the effect of an order for specific performance: but why should the limitation of the range of remedies for the breach invade the substance of the contract?

Secondly, he felt that any other decision would be difficult to reconcile with authority. Finally, he thought that: 'the courts must be astute to prevent a wrong-doer from profiting too greatly from his wrong' and this is supported by the discussion of the House of Lords on the general law of contract in *Photo Production Ltd* v *Securicor Transport Ltd* (1980).

It was thought possible to find a *via media* differentiating between the two extremes of *Sanders* and *Guinlé*. Shaw LJ attempted this in *Gunton* v *Richmond-upon-Thames London Borough Council* (1980). The employee, a college registrar, was dismissed for misconduct on one month's notice without adherence to the contractual disciplinary procedure. Automatic termination was raised as an issue since it was necessary to decide the correct amount of damages for wrongful dismissal—that is, whether this should run from the dismissal or its acceptance. The realism (if not the language) of Shaw LJ's approach may be seen in this passage:

The servant who is wrongfully dismissed cannot claim his wage for services he is not given the opportunity of rendering; and the master whose servant refuses to serve him cannot compel that servant to perform his contractual duties.

Thus a total repudiation was at once destructive of the contractual relationship and a straightforward dismissal would not need to be accepted. But he went on to suggest that there conceivably may be a different legal result where the repudiation is oblique and arises indirectly as, for example, where the employer sought to change the nature of the work required to be done or the times of employment.

These questions were canvassed before the Court of Appeal in *London Transport Executive* v *Clarke* (1981). Mr Clarke was a bus mechanic with London Transport, and when his employers refused him leave to visit his native Jamaica, he just 'took off'. He remained in the sun for seven weeks, sending to London a sick note to cover the exact period of his absence, but was met on his return by the announcement that he was no longer employed by London Transport; he had, they said, dismissed himself. On his complaint of unfair dismissal, the proffered doctrine of 'constructive resignation' was rejected alike by the tribunal, the EAT, and a majority of the Court of Appeal. Dunn and Templeman LJJ sought to lay at rest the heresy of automatic termination, seeing it as 'contrary to principle, unsupported by authority binding on this court and undesirable in practice'. It was manifestly unjust to allow a wrongdoer to terminate a contract if the innocent party wished to affirm the contract for good reason. Thus if a worker walked out of his job (and did not thereafter claim to be entitled to resume work, as did Mr Clarke) it was nevertheless the employer who terminated it by accepting the repudiation. Lord Denning MR, dissenting, thought this weighted the scales too heavily against the employer. He stuck to his guns, first trained in his 1929 edition of *Smith's Leading Cases* and still apparently blazing despite the decision of the House of Lords in *Photo Production Ltd* v *Securicor Transport Ltd* (1980). For him a fundamental breach or breach going to the root of the contract led to the discharge of the contract without any need for acceptance. This happens when the misconduct of the employee is such that it is completely inconsistent with continuance of the contract so that the ordinary member of the ET would say of the employee 'he sacked himself'. The Master of the Rolls exemplified cases when an employee leaves and gets another job, or absconds with the money from the till or goes off indefinitely without a word to his employer.

Self-dismissal

This discussion is closely related to the converse concept of 'self-dismissal'. (See further, Honeyball, (1998) 30 BLJ 7.) The courts at one time threatened to exclude a whole range of terminations from the statutory definition of dismissal, and thus from examination on their merits, by concluding that the employee himself brought the contract to an end when he committed acts of misconduct. The NIRC in *Jones* v *Liverpool Corporation* (1974) described the concept as a 'mere novelty'.

Although the orthodox contractual theory is now preferred in self-dismissal cases one detects in the majority in *Clarke* some concern about its effect on situations posited by Lord Denning. This goes back to the problem of remedies, for it is trite law, now confirmed by statute, that a court will not specifically enforce a contract of service. Yet if the employee repudiates and the employer does not accept it, and instead seeks to affirm the contract, what can the courts do? In the converse case of employer repudiation in *Gunton* v *Richmond-upon-Thames LBC* (1980), the Court of Appeal unusually issued a declaration that the contract remained in being.

The present position

The House of Lords in *Rigby* v *Ferodo* (1988) stated the present generally-accepted position. Although declining to consider whether or not as a general principle acceptance was always required to bring a contract which was the subject of a repudiatory breach to an end, it held that the circumstances in which it would not be necessary were limited to extreme cases where there was an outright wrongful dismissal by the employer or a walk-out by the employee. Otherwise, in the words of Lord Oliver, with whom the other Lords agreed, there is no principle of law that any breach which the innocent party is entitled to treat as repudiatory brings the contract to an end automatically. He said:

I entirely fail to see how the continuance of the primary contractual obligation can be made to depend upon the subjective desire of the contract-breaker and I do not understand what is meant by the injured party having no alternative but to accept the breach. If this means that, if the contract-breaker persists, the injured party may have to put up with the fact that he will not be able to enforce the primary obligation of performance, that is, of course, true of every contract which is not susceptible to a decree of specific performance. If it means that he has no alternative to accepting the breach as a repudiation and thus terminating the contract, it begs the question.

So it is not open to any court below the House of Lords to find that unlawful repudiation without acceptance terminates the contract of employment. In *Boyo* v *Lambeth LBC* (1994) the Court of Appeal therefore accepted that it was bound to hold that an unlawful repudiation was of no effect until accepted. The majority of the court stated however that, free from authority, they would have reached the opposite conclusion.

4.3 Termination by employer

The most important effect now of the termination of the contract of employment by the employer is that it constitutes a dismissal for the purposes of unfair dismissal and redundancy protection under ERA 1996. This will be considered below in Chapters 8 and 9. However, we shall examine here the position at common law.

4.3.1 Summary dismissal

The common law views a dismissal with proper notice as lawful, except in the rare event that procedural provisions for termination are built into the contract (e.g. *Tomlinson* v *LM & S Railway* (1944)).

There are some cases in which a dismissal without notice may be lawful at common law. The general test of whether summary dismissal (i.e. without notice) is justifiable was stated in *Laws* v *London Chronicle (Indicator Newspapers) Ltd* (1959) as 'whether the conduct complained of is such as to show the servant to have disregarded the essential conditions of the contract of service'. Such conduct may be found in just one action by the employee (*Blyth* v *The Scottish Liberal Club* (1983)). According to the EAT in *Hamilton* v *Argyll and Clyde Health Board* (1993) (an unfair dismissal case), the fact that the employer offers the employee further, different, employment does not prevent a finding of gross misconduct. The important factor is that the employee's acts are sufficiently serious so as to render the employee unsuitable for the particular employment from which there has been a dismissal, and not any other employment.

Summary dismissal has been held justified in cases of:

(a) a strike (*Simmons* v *Hoover Ltd* (1977)) and probably a work to rule (*Secretary of State for Employment* v *ASLEF (No. 2)* (1972));

(b) dishonesty, e.g. where a betting shop manager took money from the till for his own purposes (*Sinclair* v *Neighbour* (1967));

(c) a series of incidents of intoxication (*Clouston & Co. Ltd* v *Corry* (1906));

(d) the taking of a secret commission in breach of the employee's duty of fidelity (*Boston Deep Sea Fishing & Ice Co.* v *Ansell* (1888));

(e) gross negligence, e.g. where the manager of the life insurance department of an insurance company negligently recommended the insurance of a life which a few days earlier the managing director had refused to insure (*Jupiter General Insurance Co. Ltd* v *Shroff* (1937));

(f) and wilful disobedience to orders such as refusal to attend meetings (*Blyth* v *The Scottish Liberal Club* (1983)).

In *Laws* v *London Chronicle (Indicator Newspapers) Ltd* (1959), however, the fact that a female employee defied the managing director's orders not to leave the room with her superior following a row between the two men, was insufficiently serious since one act of disobedience or insubordination or misconduct can justify dismissal only if it is of a nature which goes to show in effect that the servant is repudiating the contract or one of its essential conditions. The lawfulness of the dismissal depends, *inter alia*, on the position of the employee, his past record and the social conditions of the time. Many old cases are thus unreliable as precedents today, since as Edmund Davies LJ said in *Wilson* v *Racher* (1974) they:

date from the last century and may be wholly out of accord with current social conditions. What would today be regarded as almost an attitude of Czar-serf, which is to be found in some of the older cases where a dismissed employee failed to recover damages would, I venture to think, be decided differently today.

In the *Wilson* case, the employee, a gardener, was dismissed by the defendant following a heated argument about his early departure the previous Friday. This culminated in his saying: 'Get stuffed'. There was no background of inefficiency or insolence as in *Pepper* v *Webb* (1969), an earlier case with otherwise similar facts. The test the Court of Appeal applied was 'whether the plaintiff's conduct was insulting and insubordinate to such a degree as to be incompatible with the continuance of the relation of master and servant'. Here it was not so serious and the dismissal was therefore wrongful.

In the absence of gross misconduct the employee dismissed without notice may claim for wrongful dismissal and this exists today alongside statutory unfair dismissal. One of the greatest reforms wrought by the introduction of the latter was the new importance of procedure in dismissal, and consequent lessening of the power of summary dismissal. This does not, however, mean that summary dismissal is not still valid in some cases. The ACAS Code of Practice for Disciplinary Practice and Procedures in Employment and the courts have isolated very serious cases of misconduct and incapability which merit dismissal without any pretence of natural justice for the employee.

4.3.2 Remedies for wrongful dismissal

Wrongful dismissal is the term used at common law to denote the situation where an employee is dismissed by an employer in breach of contract. A variety of remedies may be available in this regard. Wrongful dismissal should not be confused with unfair dismissal, which is a statutory claim for which there are very different conditions to be satisfied in order to bring a successful claim.

Specific performance and injunctions

A central difficulty with the common law of wrongful dismissal is that the courts will not enforce a broken contract by specific performance, so that if an employee has been unlawfully sacked there is no way he can regain his job. Moreover, the courts have in general refused to countenance his regaining his old position by injunction preventing the dismissal taking effect. A number of reasons have been advanced for this conclusion.

Perhaps the main reason is that the nature of an employment contract is such that it would be very difficult for the court to supervise performance (although not impossible, particularly with regard to short fixed-term contracts or contracts for a particular purpose), and that in most circumstances damages are an adequate remedy. However, the traditional reason given is that to order specific performance would be tantamount to forced labour. As Fry LJ said in *De Francesco* v *Barnum* (1890), the courts are:

> very unwilling to extend decisions the effect of which is to compel persons who are not desirous of maintaining personal relations with one another to continue those personal relations…I think the courts are bound to be jealous lest they should turn contracts of service into contracts of slavery.

Other reasons proffered have been that it would be inconsistent with the trust and confidence which must exist between employer and employee, and that it offends against the doctrine of mutuality, since to force an employer to reinstate cannot be balanced by forcing an employee to work. TULR(C)A 1992, s. 236 enacts part of this long-established common law principle, providing that 'no court shall issue an order compelling an employee to do any work or attend at any place for the doing of any work'. (See Brodie, (1998) 27 ILJ 37, where the author argues that specific performance should be available.)

The courts have held that these rules do not prevent the court enforcing an agreement by way of restrictive covenants not to compete with the employer whether during or after employment, even where this may have the indirect effect of putting pressure on the employee to carry on working in that employment. Thus in *Warner Bros Pictures Inc.* v *Nelson* (1937) Bette Davis the actress broke her agreement to work solely for the plaintiffs and Branson J granted them an injunction by adopting the negative provision that she should work for no other motion picture or stage producer. She could work in other fields of endeavour and the judge was not impressed by the argument that: 'The difference between what [she] can earn as a film artiste and what she might expect to earn by any other form of activity is so great that she will in effect be driven to perform her contract.' The court will not, however, enforce a provision not to take any employment at all for a period after termination of the contract of service for this would constitute a thinly disguised form of compelling service. (See *Page One Records Ltd* v *Britton* (1967); *Lumley* v *Wagner* (1852).)

Inroads have developed into this general rule. The Court of Appeal in *Hill* v *C. A. Parsons and Co. Ltd* (1972) went considerably further than precedent to grant an injunction which had the effect of specific performance although only in very particular circumstances. The plaintiff was dismissed after 35 years working for the defendant company as a chartered engineer because he would not join the union DATA with which the employers had just signed a closed shop agreement. The Court of Appeal, with Stamp LJ dissenting, granted an interlocutory (now interim) injunction preventing them from implementing the dismissal. Lord Denning MR and Sachs LJ thought that in this case the normal arguments against enforcement did not apply, since there was continued confidence between employer and employee, as it was the union and not the company who sought to remove him and damages would not here be an adequate remedy. (See too, *Lakshmi* v *Mid Cheshire Hospitals NHS Trust* (2008).) It may also have been significant that at the time of the decision the unfair dismissal provisions were due to take effect in two months' time when the remedy of reinstatement would become available. The case was distinguished in *GKN (Cwmbran) Ltd* v *Lloyd* (1972), *Sanders* v *Ernest A. Neale Ltd* (1974), and *Chappell* v *Times Newspapers Ltd* (1975). However, it was followed in *Jones* v *Lee* (1980), where the Court of Appeal issued an injunction to prevent managers of a Roman Catholic primary school from dismissing its headmaster without the consent of the local council and without affording him the opportunity to be heard, both of which were required in his contract. In *Irani* v *Southampton and South West Hampshire Health Authority* (1985) an ophthalmologist was dismissed by the authority without the procedural protection afforded by the Whitley Council. Warner J considered it important that, just as in *Parsons*, damages would not be an adequate remedy since Mr Irani would become virtually unemployable throughout the National Health Service and would lose the right to use NHS facilities to treat his private patients. There was also trust and confidence remaining between the parties, a factor which the courts now consider to be the most important consideration of all. The leading case is *Powell* v *London Borough of Brent* (1987) in which the Court of Appeal decided that trust and confidence remained in the employee (who had been demoted from a post to which she had recently been promoted, following a complaint from an unsuccessful candidate), despite the employer's assertion to the contrary. It weighed heavily with the court that damages would be an insufficient remedy for the employee in that she would be denied the satisfaction and the challenge of the job which she was selected to do. The same test, whether trust and confidence still remains between the parties, has been applied in a number of other more recent cases, most notably by the Court of Appeal again in *Wishart* v *National Association of Citizens Advice Bureaux Ltd* (1990) and by the Outer House of the Court of Session in Scotland in *Anderson* v *Pringle of Scotland Ltd* (1998) where an interim interdict was awarded preventing the employer from sacking the employee for redundancy on principles different to those in the redundancy selection procedure, as trust and confidence remained. (See also *Hughes* v *London Borough of Southwark* (1988); *Ali* v *London Borough of Southwark* (1988); *Alexander* v *Standard Telephones and Cables plc* (1990).)

However, in *Wadcock* v *London Borough of Brent* (1990) the High Court granted an injunction to the employee even though it was impossible to say that trust and confidence remained. Nevertheless, the judge felt that the employee was competent and would be well able to work in the post to which he had been assigned if he were minded to obey his superiors. This non-doctrinal approach was sensible in the instant case, but it will be very rare for the courts to award injunctions where the parties do not agree that mutual trust and confidence remains. One such circumstance is where the employee seeks an injunction, not to remain in his job, but to treat the original dismissal as void in order to recover pay until the proper procedures are gone through. In this event, as the High Court pointed out in *Robb* v *London Borough of Hammersmith and Fulham* (1991), the retention of trust and confidence is not so material. This move away from viewing trust and confidence as essential is to be welcomed. As Ewing pointed out following *Powell*, it is not clear why the employer's lack of confidence should operate as an impediment to employees seeking relief for repudiatory conduct (see Ewing, [1989] CLJ 28). It is an impediment which is unnecessary, for if there is genuinely no confidence in the employee, the employer may dismiss without fear from either common law or statute, as long as the proper procedures are followed.

A possible synthesis of the recent trends, involving a threefold categorisation, has been posited by Ewing (see [1993] CLJ 405). First, there are cases where there has been no attempt to terminate the relationship but merely a unilateral variation amounting to a breach of contract. In such circumstances, such as in *Powell* and *Hughes*, the courts have shown some willingness to find that there has been no loss of confidence and therefore to restrain the breach. Secondly, there are cases where there is a dismissal but it is said that this was in breach of a contractual provision of the contract. Here there is some support for the view that an injunction can be granted even if trust and confidence has been lost (*Robb* v *London Borough of Hammersmith and Fulham* (1991)). Lastly, there are cases where the contract specifically restricts the grounds upon which, or the circumstances in which, an employer can dismiss. In *Jones* v *Gwent CC* (1992), where the contract limited the permissible grounds for dismissal, the court was prepared, pending trial, to grant an injunction preventing a dismissal other than for proper grounds and after following a proper procedure. However, while this merely involves enforcing the terms of the bargain made by the employer, such relief on substantive grounds remains exceptional (see e.g. *Alexander* v *Standard Telephones & Cables plc* (1990)).

In any event, as Ewing notes, the conditions which must be met in order to obtain injunctive relief are shaped by the act that such relief is invariably sought at an interim stage due to the need to obtain a remedy before the employment relationship has been irretrievably destroyed. On the ordinary *American Cyanamid* test (see p. 428) in order to obtain an interim injunction the claimant must first establish an arguable case. As such, it will be necessary to show only that it is arguable that the employer is acting in breach of contract, that an unaccepted repudiation is ineffective to terminate the contract and (if such a requirement is needed) that there is continuing confidence between the parties. If an arguable case is shown it will next be necessary to consider the adequacy of damages. The limits of the scope of damages recoverable at common law (see below) can be cited in support of this (see *Hughes* v *London Borough of Southwark* (1988); *Robb* v *London Borough of Hammersmith and Fulham* (1991)). The final criterion to be applied is whether the balance of convenience lies with the granting of injunctive relief. One important factor in the employee's favour is that if interim relief is not granted then it may well be impossible for the judge to grant a final injunction (see *Irani* v *Southampton and South West Hampshire Health Authority* (1985)). In any event Ewing notes that once the claimants have reached the final balance of convenience stage some kind of relief has invariably been granted. Where the court considers that the interim proceedings will effectively decide the action the court will have regard to the likelihood of the claimant succeeding at trial as one of the relevant and important factors in the balance of convenience (*NWL* v *Woods* (1979); *Hughes* v *London Borough of Southwark* (1988)).

As Brown points out (139 *Solicitors Journal* 152), it may be important to distinguish between interim and final injunctions in this area. Most of the cases in which injunctive relief has been sought to enforce the terms of a contract of employment concern interim injunctions. However, an alternative has been provided by Civil

Procedure Rules 1998 (SI 1998 No. 3132), Part 24. These allow both claimants and defendants to apply for summary judgment where the other side has no real prospect of success in their claim or defence.

Declaration

The declaration is of increasing importance in the area of dismissals. This has been for some time used as a remedy in cases involving statutory status and offices, declaring void the dismissal of a dockworker under the now abolished National Dock Labour Scheme (*Vine* v *National Dock Labour Board* (1956)) and of a trade union official (*Stevenson* v *United Road Transport Union* (1977)), but in the past declarations have been refused in the case of ordinary employees (*Francis* v *Municipal Councillors of Kuala Lumpur* (1962)).

However, the Court of Appeal in *Gunton* v *Richmond-upon-Thames LBC* (1980) countenanced an extension in the use of the declaration to declare that the employee's contract remained in being. They indicated that it was not issued because of any special statutory status of the applicant; it may be particularly appropriate for declaring that a contract still exists and a repudiation has not been accepted by the other party. Alternatively it is open to the court, as said in *Jones* v *Gwent CC* (1992), to declare that a letter of dismissal was not a valid and effective dismissal.

Public law remedies

Office-holders and occupants of statutory positions have greater security at common law than other employees because the law implies a right to natural justice so that each party has a right to be heard in proceedings, and no party acting in a judicial capacity should do so in his own cause (see e.g. *R* v *Chief Constable of Merseyside Police ex parte Bennion* (2000)). In *Ridge* v *Baldwin* (1964) the dismissal of the Chief Constable of ~~Brighton~~ was declared void because he had not been given an opportunity to give his explanation for alleged misconduct. *Malloch* v *Aberdeen Corporation* (1971) was an analogous case, the appellant being a Scottish teacher whose terms were set out mainly in statute, and here Lord Wilberforce sought to clarify the relevant distinctions:

One may accept that if there are relationships in which all requirements of the observance of rules of natural justice are excluded (and I do not wish to assume that this is necessarily so) these must be confined to what have been called 'pure master and servant cases', which I take to mean cases in which there is no element of public employment or service, no support by statute, nothing in the nature of an office or a status which is capable of protection. If any of these elements exist, then in my opinion, whatever the terminology used and even though in some *inter partes* aspects the relationship may be called that of master and servant, there may be essential procedural requirements to be observed, and failure to observe them may result in a dismissal being declared to be void.

(See also *Chief Constable of North Wales* v *Evans* (1982); John McMullen, (1984) 47 MLR 234.)

The rules of natural justice 'must depend on the circumstances of the case, the nature of the inquiry, the rules under which the tribunal is acting, the subject matter that is being dealt with and so forth' (*Russell* v *Duke of Norfolk* (1949)). In employment cases, the essentials are the rights to be heard by an unbiased tribunal, to have proper notice of charges of misconduct, to be heard in answer to the charges, and to appeal from the initial decision.

The Court of Appeal in *Stevenson* v *United Road Transport Union* (1977) held that the plaintiff (a union official) was entitled to be given reports about his dismissal in that, without them, he was unable to explain satisfactorily his conduct or put his case. The Court of Appeal has also held that the graver the charges put in internal proceedings, the greater is the burden of proof (see *R* v *Hampshire County Council ex parte Ellerton* (1985) following *R* v *Secretary of State for the Home Department ex parte Khawaja* (1984)). Neither should an appeal be heard by persons who have been involved in the decision to dismiss where there is a hearing procedure laid down by statute or under statutory regulation (*Re John Snaith* (1982)).

In *R* v *BBC ex parte Lavelle* (1982) Woolf J went further and indicated, albeit *obiter*, that when there is a procedure for dismissal in an employment not covered by statute at all, employers must comply with that procedure for the dismissal to be valid. If the contractual procedure was infringed, an injunction should issue to prevent the dismissal. This view was based partly on the notion that employment protection legislation had substantially changed the position at common law, so that 'the ordinary contract between master and servant now has many of the attributes of an office'. Judicial review was not the appropriate remedy but an injunction could issue in an appropriate case.

Hodgson J, in *R* v *East Berkshire Health Authority ex parte Walsh* (1984), thought that judicial review was appropriate to quash a breach of a health authority's procedure since 'the applicant is an officer of a profession recognised as a profession by Parliament'. Judicial review was not available to review activities 'of a purely private or domestic kind'. This was a heretical notion to the Court of Appeal which reversed the judge's decision. Employment by a public authority did not *per se* inject any element of public law. The relationship, which incorporated the Whitley Council terms, fell into the category of 'pure master and servant', and the rules of natural justice could not be implied. (See further Collins, (1984) 13 ILJ 174.) The decision was narrowly distinguished in *R* v *Secretary of State for the Home Department ex parte Benwell* (1985). The applicant, a prison officer, was charged with disobedience to orders. After an inquiry had recommended a severe reprimand, the Home Office dismissed him after considering notes on his disciplinary file of which he was unaware, and which he had obviously had no opportunity to answer. Hodgson J decided that, if the case were considered on the proper material, no reasonable Home Secretary would have dismissed. Accordingly *certiorari* would issue to quash the decision to dismiss. *Walsh* was distinguished on the ground that, unlike the situation there, the employee would have no other remedy in that he was a constable and thereby excluded from the employment protection legislation. However, the effect of the decision in *Benwell* is very limited in that it is only in very rare cases that an employee has no private rights, as Woolf LJ pointed out in *McLaren* v *Home Office* (1990) echoing a contemporary criticism of *Benwell* by Stokes in 1985 (see (1985) 14 ILJ 117). *McLaren* also concerned a prison officer. The decision in *R* v *Civil Service Appeal Board ex parte Bruce* (1989) to the effect that the Crown is entitled to employ civil servants on contracts of employment, suggests that the relationship gives rise to private rights. In any event under ERA 1996, s. 191, most Crown servants are included within employment protection legislation, whether or not they have contractual status. What is now of crucial importance is the subject-matter of the decision. Even if the employment is in the public sphere, in relation to personal claims relating to private rights, the employee is in the same position as any other employee. With regard to other rights, public law remedies may be pursued (see too *R* v *Derbyshire CC ex parte Noble* (1990)). (For an excellent analysis of this area, particularly the implications of the decision in *Walsh*, see Ewing and Grubb, (1987) 16 ILJ 145. See also Carty, (1989) 52 MLR 449, especially pp. 459–464; Sedley, (1994) 23 ILJ 201; Poole, (2000) 29 ILJ 61.)

It does not follow from the fact that rights have to be pursued in private law that the range of remedies will be reduced, especially if the trend is to be more amenable to enforcement of procedural obligations by way of injunctive relief (see above). Indeed the formalistic public/private procedural divide has been widely criticised. Sedley, for example, observed ((1994) 23 ILJ 201) that the willingness to interfere in public law relationships is founded upon the control of abuse of power and that this reasoning could equally infuse private law relationships. Nevertheless there remains a reluctance to supplement contractual rights by implying principles of natural justice, at least where the contract is wholly silent as to procedural protection (*McLory* v *Post Office* (1992)).

Damages

Damages are the normal remedy for breach of contract and the usual measure is the wages the employee would have earned (and pension rights he would have accrued—see *Silvey* v *Pendragon plc* (2001)) if due notice had been given (*Radford* v *De Froberville* (1977); *Shove* v *Downs Surgical plc* (1984)) for that is the only period when he is entitled by contract to continue in employment (see also *FOCSA Services (UK) Ltd* v *Birkett* (1996)). If his contract can be determined by three weeks' notice he cannot claim his loss over the next three years even though he is unemployed for that length of time, for within that period at any time he might have been dismissed with three weeks' notice unless there is (as there rarely is) an express procedural protection in the contract of employment. Any increase in wages that would have occurred during the notice period will not be taken into account (*Lavarack* v *Woods of Colchester Ltd* (1967)) unless this involves an element of capriciousness or bad faith on behalf of the employer, according to the High Court in *Clark* v *BET plc* (1997). In the latter case a term of the employee's service agreement to the effect that his salary would be reviewed annually at the board's absolute discretion was, after comparing other similar companies, held to amount to an obligation to raise his salary each year. So, the loss to the employee occurring due to the lack of a disciplinary procedure, which may have found that the employee should not be dismissed, will not be taken into account. Such an idea is a 'heresy' according to the EAT in *Janciuk* v *Winerite Ltd* (1998). Although the decision has been criticised on the basis that breach of contract damages seek to put the wronged party in the position he would have been in had the breach not occurred (see Rubenstein, [1998] IRLR 53), it is in line with the traditional approach which prevents a windfall payment to the employee. The effective date of termination for unfair dismissal is extended only so far as the statutory, not the contractual, minimum according to the Court of Appeal in *Harper* v *Virgin Net Ltd* (2004) and so damages for loss of protection caused by not being given the full contractual entitlement are not recoverable.

The amount is also limited in that no damages are recoverable for:

(a) bonuses within the discretion of the employer (*Lavarack* v *Woods of Colchester Ltd* (1967)) unless the employer is contractually obliged to exercise his discretion rationally and in good faith in so exercising that discretion, which may be implied (*Horkulak* v *Cantor Fitzgerald International* (2004)); or

(b) any amount awarded by way of unfair dismissal compensation. However, where the employee's loss exceeds that actually awarded by an ET for unfair dismissal, no set-off should normally be made, because it will not be possible to say that the sum actually awarded falls under any head for which wrongful dismissal damages may be awarded, according to the Court of Appeal in *O'Laoire* v *Jackel International Ltd* (1991);

(c) (if the claim is brought in an ET—where the maximum awardable is £25,000— and the loss is found to be greater) the excess by way of a claim in the High Court for that amount—*Fraser* v *HLMAD Ltd* (2006). It is difficult to see why this ceiling exists in ETs now that unfair dismissal compensation ceilings are so much higher. Furthermore, it encourages litigants to make claims in the High Court when they could be satisfactorily disposed of in a tribunal if it should assess the actual loss as up to £25,000.

It used to be the case (see *Addis* v *Gramophone Co. Ltd* (1909)) that damages were not awarded for the loss the employee suffers due to the fact that he has been dismissed, so-called 'stigma' damages. However, the House of Lords was thought to have reversed that in a case arising out of the collapse of BCCI, *Malik* v *Bank of Credit and Commerce International* (1997). There was no reason why there should be any difference between employment contracts and other contracts in this regard. This applies only to financial loss and not to any injury to feelings that may have been caused. As John McMullen has written, this is perhaps unfortunate (see (1997) 26 ILJ 245). Lord Steyn said in *Malik* that there was no necessity in establishing a breach for the employer's conduct to be directed at individual employees. It was held by the Court of Appeal in *BCCI* v *Ali* (2002) that the stigma must be a real or substantial cause of the employee's failure to obtain employment.

However, the waters are muddied somewhat by the decisions of the Court of Appeal and the House of Lords in *Johnson* v *Unisys Ltd* in 1999 and 2001 respectively, not considered in *BCCI* v *Ali*. The Court of Appeal thought that the House of Lords in *Malik* did not in fact overturn *Addis* where there is an express dismissal, but merely distinguished it. The House of Lords, however, were unclear as to the status of *Addis*, and made no firm decision on that point either way. (See further, Collins, (2001) 30 ILJ 305, but note that *Johnson* was not an unfair dismissal case, and Lord Steyn did not dissent, as the writer states. See too Brodie, (2009) 38 ILJ 228.)

Extra damages may be available in that limited range of cases where the parties envisage from the outset a greater return from the contract of employment than simply pay for hours worked. Thus, an American actress wishing to establish her name in London who contracted to play a part for the defendant was held to have done so in return not only for money but also for full publicity and her damages were thus enhanced (*Marbe* v *George Edwardes (Daly's Theatres) Ltd* (1928)). In *Robert Cort & Son Ltd* v *Charman* (1981), Browne-Wilkinson J suggested *obiter* that damages might include a sum for the loss of the right to compensation for unfair dismissal which the employee would have successfully claimed had the correct notice been given (see also *Stapp* v *The Shaftesbury Society* (1982)). However, the Inner House of the Court of Session in Scotland suggested in *Morran* v *Glasgow Council of Tenants Associations* (1998) that this may be restricted to those cases where there is no right for the employer to make payments in lieu of notice.

If the amount of damages payable is 'unjustifiable' it will be unenforceable as a penalty. However, this will only be the case if the amount is 'extravagant or unconscionable' according to the Court of Appeal in *Murray* v *Leisureplay plc* (2005).

Very large measures of damages are available only where the contract is for a fixed term and cannot otherwise be terminated by notice. This is most usually the case in high status occupations like company directors, football club managers, and accountants. The measure of damages is then the amount which would have been earned in the unexpired part of the fixed term, subject to mitigation and deduction for accelerated payment.

As in every contract, the employee claimant must mitigate his loss as a result of its breach. He cannot sit back at home and mount up his losses in the confident expectation that he will be able to claim them from his former employers. In particular he must take reasonable steps to obtain another job, and if he succeeds in doing so any wages earned in the new position will be deducted from wages due over the period of notice. If, on the other hand, he does not try to find another post, a sum is taken away to represent his lack of effort. Each case depends on its own facts but the dismissed employee does not normally have to take the first job which comes along. He may also act reasonably in refusing to take another position in the company which has just dismissed him. He is entitled to preserve a skilled job, so that a painter is not necessarily expected to take work as a general labourer (*Edwards* v *SOGAT* (1970)) nor a managing director as an assistant manager (*Yetton* v *Eastwoods Froy Ltd* (1967)). A similar approach is taken to that of suitable alternative employment offers after redundancy. There is no duty to mitigate, however, in a case where the contract of employment provides for a specific period of payment on termination which may be thus recovered as a debt (*Abrahams* v *Performing Rights Society Ltd* (1995)).

The employee must also give credit for any opportunities gained as a result of his dismissal, but not where these arise indirectly. Thus in *Lavarack* v *Woods of Colchester Ltd* (1967) the plaintiff after dismissal was able to take shares in a competing company which was profitable, but this was too indirect a benefit to be brought into account in reducing damages to which he was otherwise entitled. In exceptional circumstances, however, the employee may have to account for profits arising from his breach of contract, according to the House of Lords in *Attorney-General* v *Blake* (2001), where normal remedies are not adequate compensation. (But see Simpson, (2009) 125 LQR 433, who argues that this case was decided *per incuriam*.)

Since the relevant damages are based on lost wages, the court deducts from them the amount of tax the employee would have paid if he had received the money week by week or month by month rather than in a lump sum. This is the same rule as applies to damages in tort (*BTC* v *Gourley* (1956)) and is based on the assumption that damages are not taxable in the hands of the claimant, but this is not always the case in all damages claims for wrongful dismissal. HM Revenue and Customs has intervened in respect of termination of employment contracts to prevent 'golden handshakes' being used as tax avoidance devices so that payments of over £30,000 are subject to tax in the claimant's hands. The rule in the *Gourley* case therefore applies only to the first £30,000 (Income Tax (Earnings and Pensions) Act 2003, s. 403) and only where the payment is agreed following a dismissal in breach of contract and not before, when it is better construed as a taxable emolument from employment, according to the High Court in *Richardson (Inspector of Taxes)* v *Delaney* (2001). In *Shove* v *Downs Surgical plc* (1984) Sheen J decided that the assessment of the plaintiff's loss should be increased by such amount as was necessary to leave him after deduction of tax with the net compensation due to him, so as properly to put him in the same position as if the contract had been properly performed.

There are other, often more immediately beneficial, sources of assistance during unemployment besides recourse to the courts for damages. These must be balanced against damages so that the dismissed employee does not recover twice: jobseekers' allowance and income support received during the period of notice for which damages can be gained are deducted (*Parsons* v *BNM Laboratories Ltd* (1964)). The correct figure to deduct is the net sum (*Westwood* v *Secretary of State for Employment* (1984)). This has the effect that it may be cheaper for an employer to dismiss an employee wrongfully than to continue to employ him on full wages during notice as John McMullen has pointed out (see (1984) 13 ILJ 259). However, redundancy payment is not deducted since it is not a substitute for wages but a lump sum recognition of past employment (*Yorkshire Engineering & Welding Ltd* v *Burnham* (1974); *Wilson* v *National Coal Board* (1980)). The sum of social security contributions which the employee has not had to pay while unemployed is deducted (*Cooper* v *Firth Brown Ltd* (1963)). Unfair dismissal compensation is deducted—at least the amount awarded for loss of earnings (*Berry* v *Aynsley Trust Ltd* (1976) but not pension payments, according to the High Court in *Hopkins* v *Norcross plc* (1992)). The reason for this is that pension benefits are not deductible against damages in personal injury cases, and there is no good reason to treat the two types of cases differently. It would therefore be wise for employers to make provision in contracts of employment, or in the rules of the pension scheme itself, to the effect that a pension is not payable in such cases.

Debt

It is not possible to claim in debt for wages on the basis that repudiation of a contract of employment has not been accepted. In *Boyo* v *Lambeth LBC* (1994) the Court of Appeal, applying *Gunton* v *Richmond-upon-Thames LBC* (1980), held that there could be no claim in debt for wages under an employment contract. Since the claim could only proceed in damages, therefore, the claim could only be made up to the date when the employer could lawfully terminate the contract (i.e. after notice). A majority of the court stated that they would also have reached this decision if free from authority. This decision was explained on the basis that to allow recovery in debt would in effect allow specific performance through the back door without the obligation of having to provide the service. However, this appears to rest on the questionable premise that wages are paid in consideration for services actually provided rather than in return for the employee being permitted to provide work (see Peyton, (1994) 23 ILJ 37).

4.4 **Termination by agreement**

If there is a genuine agreement between employer and employee that a contract of employment shall terminate there is no dismissal, either at common law or by statute (*Strange Ltd* v *Mann* (1965)). The same is true where there is a 'pure' resignation, rather than one in response to a repudiatory breach of the employer amounting to a constructive dismissal. The main problem lies in identifying and construing any purported agreement, and assessing when it is reached under employer pressure, in which case it will constitute a dismissal. A statement that it was in the mutual interest of both parties to part company after the employers had given notice may not, however, be enough to amount to an agreed termination (*Harman* v *Flexible Lamps Ltd* (1980)). Moreover, tribunals have been astute not to recognise a consensus where the initiative to terminate has clearly been taken by the employer. (See the EAT's decision in *Optare Group* v *TGWU* (2007) and the Court of Appeal's decision in *Sandhu* v *Jan de Rijk Transport Ltd* (2007).) In *McAlwane* v *Boughton Estates Ltd* (1973) Donaldson J said that tribunals 'should not find an agreement to terminate employment unless it is proved that the employee really did agree with full knowledge of the implications it had for him'.

4.4.1 **Leaving early after dismissal**

The claim that the employee agreed to leave has been made in several cases where the applicant was dismissed but wanted to go early to take another job. Donaldson J thought it would 'be a very rare case' where such agreement overrode the dismissal 'when one realises the financial consequences to the employee of such an agreement'. Indeed he thought 'the possibility might appeal to a lawyer more than to a personnel manager'. However, in *Scott* v *Coalite Fuels and Chemicals Ltd* (1988) the EAT held that there was termination by agreement where the employees took voluntary early retirement while under notice in order to take a lump sum under a pension scheme rather than a redundancy payment.

4.4.2 **Agreed automatic termination**

In *Brown* v *Knowsley Borough Council* (1986) the EAT held that the appellant was not dismissed when her employment as a temporary lecturer came to an end because the course she was teaching did not receive further funding. Her contract of employment stated that 'the appointment will last only as long as sufficient funds are provided either by the Manpower Services Commission or by other firms/sponsors to fund it'. The contract thus terminated automatically on the non-happening of the event specified. (See further, Leighton and Painter, (1986) 15 ILJ 127.)

4.4.3 **Threats**

The courts are understandably reluctant to hold that there has been an agreement where an employee is prevailed upon to resign under threat that if he does not do so he will be dismissed (*Scott* v *Formica Ltd* (1975); *East Sussex CC* v *Walker* (1972)). However, the fact that disciplinary proceedings are in train may not in itself amount to sufficient pressure to avoid an agreed termination (*Staffordshire County Council* v *Donovan* (1981)).

4.4.4 Causation

In *Sheffield* v *Oxford Controls Co. Ltd* (1979) the EAT sought to lay down some principle by means of a rule of causation. The applicant had been a director and employee of the respondent company until a boardroom row when he was threatened that, if he did not resign, he would be dismissed. After negotiations he signed an agreement to leave in return for certain financial benefits, including £10,000, but then claimed to have been unfairly dismissed. The EAT began from the premise that an employee who resigns as a result of a threat is dismissed, but there was in this case an intervening cause: 'He resigns because he is willing to resign as the result of being offered terms which are to him satisfactory terms on which to resign.' It is suggested that not only is this a rather technical view of causation, but it also appears to run counter to ERA 1996, s. 203, which renders void 'any provision in an agreement...so far as it purports to exclude or limit the operation of any provision' of the Act. However, the EAT took the opposite view in *Logan Salton* v *Durham County Council* (1989) on the basis that the courts should, so far as possible, give effect to agreements freely entered into. If the element of freedom is missing, or the opportunity for real reflection on an offer does not exist, the decision may be different—see *Sandhu* v *Jan de Rijk Transport Ltd* (2007).

The courts look for unambiguous, unequivocal words to amount to a resignation (*Hughes* v *Gwynedd Area Health Authority* (1978)) and did not so find where the employer knew that the employee was a mental defective and that he uttered the words in the heat of the moment after an argument (*Barclay* v *City of Glasgow District Council* (1983)). An employer may not rely on a letter of resignation which the employee is induced by the employer to sign on the basis of a misrepresentation (*Makin* v *Greens Motor (Bridgport) Ltd* (1986)).

4.4.5 Applications to retire

In *Birch and Humber* v *University of Liverpool* (1985) the applicants wrote to the university making formal application to retire under a premature retirement compensation scheme and received a reply that, 'The University hereby confirms that it is in the managerial interests for you to retire...and requests you to do so...'. The EAT overturned the tribunal's decision that, since the offer of retirement was subject to the university's approval, it was the giving of that approval which terminated their employments. Instead, both in form and in substance, this was a termination by agreement. The Court of Appeal turned down the appeal. Mark Freedland has suggested that this decision betrays the Court of Appeal's adherence more to laissez-faire ideals in the common law than to issues such as the policy behind legislation. He argues that the facts in *Birch and Humber* are hard to distinguish from other cases in this area where dismissals have been found. But it was the freedom to agree to extricate themselves from the employment contracts which weighed with the Court of Appeal, something from which the redundancy legislation was designed to provide special statutory protection (see Freedland, (1985) 14 ILJ 243).

4.4.6 Ultimatums

Where an employee signs an undertaking that he will return to work on a stated date in order to gain extended leave, and he fails to come back at the agreed time, the trend of authority has ebbed and flowed between accepting the undertaking as an agreed termination and viewing it as a dismissal. In *British Leyland UK Ltd* v *Ashraf* (1978) the applicant sought five weeks' unpaid leave of absence to visit his native Pakistan and this was granted subject to the condition that there be no further holiday. He signed a form stating: 'You have agreed to return to work on 21/2/77. If you fail to do this, your contract of employment will terminate on that date.' The EAT took this at face value as a subsidiary contract and agreed termination, stressing the employee's full knowledge of its terms and open acceptance. It had in mind the fact that these were conditions attached to a privilege, since the applicant had no contractual right to leave of absence; they also pointed out that such failure to return was becoming a widespread problem in British industry. The danger of this approach is that it could be extended to an agreement that the contract would end if the employee was late even once. These draconian implications, which would mean that in such circumstances the employee could not test the fairness of the employer's action since there would be an agreed termination and therefore no dismissal, were indeed spelt out by Phillips J who commented that the employer's argument would prevail even if the return flight 'had been hijacked or diverted because of fog'. The case was, however, distinguished in *Midland Electric Manufacturing Co. Ltd* v *Kanji* (1980), on somewhat narrow grounds. Mrs Kanji's leave of absence was conditional on the 'warning that if you fail to return…for whatever reason the company will consider that you have terminated your employment'. She failed to return on the specified date because of illness, but the EAT found the letter a mere statement of intention by the employer as to what would happen in the event of failure to return, i.e. she would be dismissed. Referring to the more ambiguous wording here than in *Ashraf*, Talbot J was generally mindful 'not to defeat the objects of the employment protection legislation or in particular to fly in the face of the intent of [ERA 1996, s. 203]'.

A return to the *Ashraf* line was signalled by the EAT in *Igbo* v *Johnson Matthey Chemicals Ltd* (1985). Mrs Igbo was given leave of absence after signing a 'contractual letter for the provision of extended holiday absence'. It stated, *inter alia*, that 'if you fail [to return on 28 September 1983] your contract of employment will automatically terminate on that date'. She did not report to work on that day but instead sent a medical certificate. The EAT thought that this was an agreed termination, but the Court of Appeal disagreed, holding that such agreements fell foul of what is now ERA 1996, s. 203, and were void, in that they purport to limit the operation of the employment protection legislation. The whole of the operation of the Act could be defeated by the inclusion of a term in a contract that if the employee is late for work any day, the contract would terminate. Although this decision is to be welcomed (see Upex, (1987) 16 ILJ 63), the conceptual grounds on which the decision rests are not altogether satisfactory. A distinction must be made between an agreement which disallows the employee from claiming despite the fact that there has been a dismissal, and the situation where an agreement is made which has the effect of barring a claim because there has been no dismissal. The facts in *Igbo* would point to the latter. It is altogether a different issue that difficult practical issues thereby arise because it is easy for the employer to engineer a termination which is not a dismissal, but there is a case for making certain forms of consensual termination dismissals within the technical meaning assigned to that term in ERA 1996, s. 95 (see below).

4.4.7 The right approach?

It can be seen that the tribunals and courts have found it difficult to provide any clear guidance as to when a termination of contract is to be taken to be by the employer and when it is to be taken to be agreed. No one test can be determinative, but it seems that matters have been made unnecessarily confusing by the failure to focus on the fact that a dismissal is dependent upon a state of affairs, not on states of mind. For example, the definition of employer termination in ERA 1996, s. 95(1)(a)—constituting one form of dismissal—is that it occurs when the employer terminates the contract with or without notice. This concentrates on *what* happens and not on the state of mind of the parties. There is no suggestion that the employee must oppose the termination for it to amount to a dismissal. It therefore would seem to follow that acceptance of the termination does not negate the dismissal. But note that this is mere acceptance of a state of affairs. In other words, acceptance here means acquiescence. On the other hand, where mutual termination occurs this is because one party (normally the employer) makes an offer to the other which he accepts. This is a different form of acceptance, and one without which there would be no termination. It would thus seem quite possible to have a concept of consensual dismissal, in the sense that the employee acquiesces in the state of affairs. But this idea was disapproved by the Court of Appeal in *Burton, Allton and Johnson Ltd* v *Peck* (1975) on the basis that the idea blurred the distinction between dismissal and mutual termination. But, of course, it does not, because consensus where there is a dismissal refers to acquiescence-type acceptance, not acceptance in the sense of converting an offer into an agreement. As without acceptance in the latter context there would not be a termination, the employee can be taken to have contributed to the termination, but as acquiescence is not an element in the termination in the former case, the employer may be treated as terminating the contract. Duress or other pressure placed on the employee may be relevant to whether there has been true acceptance of an offer, but it is not relevant to acquiescence. It is for this reason that lack of duress is not the only feature which can prevent an employee's voluntary act from amounting to agreement, for two different forms of acceptance are in issue. The Court of Appeal in *Hellyer Bros Ltd* v *Atkinson* (1992) failed to accept this distinction, while noticing it.

4.5 Frustration

A further way by which termination can occur without there being a dismissal is where the contract of employment is frustrated. The general contractual test is that frustration occurs whenever the law recognises that without default of either party a contractual obligation has become incapable of being performed because the circumstances in which performance is called for would render it a thing radically different from that which was undertaken by the contract (per Lord Radcliffe in *Davis Contractors Ltd* v *Fareham UDC* (1956)). When a contract is frustrated the contract is at an end, and there is therefore, in employment cases, no entitlement either to notice or to pay in lieu of notice, according to the EAT in *G. F. Sharp & Co. Ltd* v *McMillan* (1998).

Donaldson P formulated the appropriate test in employment cases in *Marshall* v *Harland & Wolff* (1972), primarily with cases of long sickness or injury in mind, when he asked: Was the employee's incapacity to work of such a nature that further performance of his obligations in the future would be either impossible or be something radically different from that which he undertook under the contract? (See Mogridge, (1982) 132 NLJ 795.) Donaldson P went on to counsel tribunals to take account of:

(a) The terms of contract including provisions as to sickness pay. The whole basis of weekly employment may be destroyed more quickly than that of monthly employment and that in turn more quickly than annual employment. When the contract provides for sickness pay, it is plain that the contract cannot be frustrated so long as the employee returns to work, or appears likely to return to work within the period during which such sick pay is payable. But the converse is not necessarily true. The right to sick pay may expire before the incapacity has gone on for so long as to make a return to work impossible or radically different from the obligations undertaken under the contract of employment.

(b) How long the employment was likely to last in the absence of sickness. The relationship is less likely to survive if the employment was inherently temporary or for the duration of a particular job, than if it was expected to be long-term or even life long.

(c) The nature of the employment. Where the employee is one of many in the same category the relationship is more likely to survive the period of incapacity than if he occupies a key post which must be filled and filled on a permanent basis if his absence is prolonged.

(d) The nature of the illness or injury and how long it has already continued and the prospects of recovery. The greater the degree of incapability and the longer the period over which it has persisted and is likely to persist, the more likely it is that the relationship has been destroyed. (However, this is not determinative—see *Gryf-Lowczouski* v *Hinchingbrooke* (2006).)

(e) The period of past employment. A relationship which is of long standing is not as easily destroyed as one which has but a short history.

He said that 'these factors are interrelated and cumulative, but are not necessarily exhaustive of those which have to be taken into account'. In particular they are hardly appropriate to short-term periodic contracts where the more likely event anyway is dismissal on short notice (*Harman* v *Flexible Lamps Ltd* (1980); *cf. Notcutt* v *Universal Equipment Co. (London) Ltd* (1986); see John McMullen, (1986) 45 CLJ 785).

In *Egg Stores (Stamford Hill) Ltd* v *Leibovici* (1976) Phillips J added four extra considerations in this context:

(a) the need of the employer for the work to be done, and the need for a replacement to do it;

(b) the risk to the employer of acquiring obligations in respect of redundancy payments or compensation for unfair dismissal to the replacement employee;

(c) whether wages have continued to be paid;

(d) the acts and the statements of the employer in relation to the employment, including the dismissal of, or failure to dismiss, the employee.

He asked as a matter of common sense: 'Has the time arrived when the employer can no longer be expected to keep the absent employee's place open?' and this was a similar conclusion to that which had to be reached in determining whether a dismissal for sickness was fair.

4.5.1 Frustration and dismissal

It is instructive to distinguish two cases on either side of the thin frustration/dismissal line. In *Hart* v *Marshall* (1977) the employee was a night service fitter, and described by his employer as a 'key worker'. In 1974 he contracted industrial dermatitis which continued for about 20 months, and during this time regularly sent to his employers medical certificates of his unfitness to work, which were received without comment. On his recovery, he was told that he had been permanently replaced. The EAT decided that, because he was such an important employee, 'this is one of the comparatively rare cases where it can be said that a short-term period contract of employment has been frustrated'. On the other side of the line stands *Hebden* v *Forsey and Son* (1973). The respondents ran a small factory employing two sawyers—Mr Forsey's son, and the applicant—who had worked for the business for many years when he had to undergo an operation on one of his eyes. Since the necessary equipment was not available at the local hospital it would be two years before he could work again. Mr Forsey, with whom the applicant maintained frequent contact, agreed with him that it would be better if he waited on the sick list, drawing state benefits until his eye was fully recovered. There was insufficient work for him to do when he was completely fit, so that he could not return. On these facts it was held that the employer had not discharged the burden resting on him to prove frustration but had in fact dismissed him.

4.5.2 Illness

Although illness is the most common frustrating event, contracts have also been frustrated when the employee was called up to the army (*Morgan* v *Manser* (1948)); interned as an enemy alien (*Unger* v *Preston Corporation* (1942)); suspended from medical practice for 12 months and his name temporarily removed from the register (*Tarnesby* v *Kensington, Chelsea and Westminster AHA* (1981)).

4.5.3 Imprisonment

There have been differing views of the effect of imprisonment. In *Chakki* v *United Yeast Co. Ltd* (1982) the EAT declared that in order to determine whether an

11-month prison sentence frustrated the contract, it was essential to determine precisely when it had become commercially necessary for the employer to decide whether or not to employ a replacement, to have regard to what, at that time, a reasonable employer would have considered the probable duration of the employee's absence to be and to consider whether the employers had acted reasonably in employing a permanent rather than a temporary replacement. In *Hare* v *Murphy Brothers Ltd* (1974) and *Harrington* v *Kent County Council* (1980), the contract was held to be frustrated even though the latter sentence was quashed on appeal. In *Norris* v *Southampton City Council* (1982) the EAT held that imprisonment was a self-induced event, while in *F. C. Shepherd & Co. Ltd* v *Jerrom* (1986) a four-year apprenticeship was held not to be frustrated by a Borstal sentence of six months. The EAT decided that a prison sentence is no more than a potentially frustrating event. The applicant's employment was subject to an agreed and detailed termination procedure and so the courts should be slow to hold that a particular set of circumstances lies outside its scope so as to frustrate the contract. This would seem to make sense where the alternative to frustration is a claim for unfair dismissal (see further Fentiman, (1986) 15 ILJ 54), but there would not seem to be a justification for the approach in *Shepherd* where this was not the case. Having said that, there seems to be a good deal to be said for John McMullen's argument for a statutory provision to negative the application of frustration. The employer's response to the frustrating event (and there normally is a response) could be taken to constitute a dismissal which could, for purposes of unfair dismissal legislation, be tested for fairness. There is, after all, scope within that legislation (under ERA 1996, s. 98) to find the reasons usually leading to frustration (ill-health, imprisonment) as constituting fair reasons for dismissal (see John McMullen, (1986) 45 CLJ 785).

4.6 Termination by performance

A further way by which a contract of employment may be terminated is by the performance of that contract. The EAT in *Ironmonger* v *Movefield Ltd t/a Deering Appointments* (1988) confirmed the approach taken in *Wiltshire County Council* v *NATFHE* (1980), that in such circumstances there will not be a dismissal for the purposes of the statutory remedies, there not being a contract for a limited term.

4.7 Automatic termination

The contract of employment is automatically terminated by operation of law without action by employer or employee in various circumstances. These are, for example, where there is a fundamental change in partners of firms where the contract of employment is fundamental to them (*Brace* v *Calder* (1895); *Tunstall* v *Condon* (1980)), where there is a compulsory winding up of a company (*Fox Bros (Clothes) Ltd* v *Bryant* (1978)), or where a receiver is appointed (*Hopley-Dodd* v *Highfield Motors (Derby) Ltd* (1969); and see Davies and Freedland, (1980) 9 ILJ 95); on the permanent closure of the employees' place of employment or the death of a personal employer (*Glenboig Union Fireclay Co. Ltd* v *Stewart* (1971); *Farrow* v *Wilson* (1869), respectively). However, if any of these events were to take place in the context of a transfer of business or undertaking, the position at common law may be altered by statutory provisions (see Chapters 5 and 6 below).

SELECTED READING

Barmes, L. (2004), 'The Continuing Conceptual Crisis in the Common Law in the Contract of Employment', (2004) 67 MLR 435

Brodie, D. (1998), 'Beyond Exchange: the New Contract of Employment', (1998) 27 ILJ 79

Brodie, D. (1998), 'Specific Performance and Employment Contracts', (1998) 27 ILJ 37

Freedland, M. (2003), *The Personal Employment Contract*, Oxford: Oxford University Press, 2003, chs 6–8

Jacobi. S. (1982), 'The Duration of Indefinite Employment Contracts in the United States and England: an Historical Analysis', [1982] *Comparative Labour Law* 85

Painter, R. W. and Holmes, A. E. (2010), *Cases and Materials on Employment Law*, 8th edn, Oxford: Oxford University Press, ch. 7

5

Continuity of employment

SUMMARY

This chapter marks the beginning of a series of chapters examining the impact of statutory claims that may be made in the context of employment. One fundamental in many such claims for employees is that of continuity of employment. The various reasons why it may be necessary to show that, in law, a period of working in a particular employment can be considered unbroken is examined in detail.

5.1 Introduction

Statutory continuity of employment is centrally important to most statutory employment protection rights including redundancy pay, maternity pay, and unfair dismissal. It is vital in determining whether the employee has served the minimum qualifying period to bring a claim, and if so, what is the appropriate amount of award or payment due. Continuity is extensively defined in ERA 1996, ss 210–219. The aim of the statute is to overcome the common law rule that every fundamental change of terms was a new contract, which doctrine would artificially restrict employee rights if statutory protection were limited to contracts of employment rather than employment itself. The statutory concept of continuity thus means there can be continuity of employment even though that employment consists of a number of different contracts.

We shall consider here only the scheme detailed in the ERA 1996. In addition there are important rights derived from EU law, applying to English law by virtue of the Transfer of Undertakings (Protection of Employment) Regulations 2006 (SI 2006 No. 246). These exist independently of the scheme in the ERA 1996 and will thus be considered separately in the following chapter.

5.2 The method of calculation

Where an employee works for one employer, there is a statutory presumption of continuity and the onus is on the employer to disprove it (ERA 1996, s. 210(5)). In the case of a transfer of business under ERA 1996, s. 218(2), the burden passes to the employee. The presumption does not, however, span the bridge of two employments, in which case continuity is preserved only in special circumstances, discussed below. Continuity is preserved even though, during an employee's service, the duties required by his contract and other incidental terms vary greatly. The employee may thus rise in status from cleaner to managing director and fall all the way back again, but continuity is retained. In *Wood* v *York City Council* (1978), for example, the employee worked for York City Council for three years in various capacities, finishing up in the Treasurer's Department. He resigned from this post in order to take up a position with the Council's York Festival office and, on being made redundant a year later, he qualified to receive redundancy payment since his employment in both capacities was continuous, notwithstanding the change of his duties and intermediate resignation.

The length of continuous service must be stated in the written statement of terms provided under ERA 1996, s. 1(3). The period of service must, however, be lawful employment so that in *Hyland* v *J. H. Barker (North-West) Ltd* (1985) the employee was not able to count a vital month in which he received an illegal lodging allowance.

These provisions have effect whatever the reason for the prior period of employment coming to an end. Therefore, an earlier contract being terminated by frustration will not necessarily mean that continuity has been broken (*Tipper* v *Roofdec Ltd* (1989)).

The units for continuity are calendar months and years. The period of continuity begins on the day on which the employee 'starts work'. This phrase is not free from difficulty as was shown in *General of the Salvation Army* v *Dewsbury* (1984). The EAT decided that it referred to the beginning of contractual employment rather than necessarily the date when the full range of the employee's responsibilities began. Thus, an employee whose post commenced on 1 May, a Saturday, but who did not begin working until 4 May because of the intervening bank holiday, would be held to have started work on 1 May. The end of continuous service depends on the employment protection right in question. In unfair dismissal cases it is known as the effective date of termination and in redundancy cases as the relevant date.

In each case the start date and the final day of working are to be taken into account, so the relevant final day is one day before the start date on the calendar where this is calculated in years. So, if a start date is 1 May, a year's continuity is achieved on 30 April the following year—see *Pacitti Jones* v *O'Brien* (2005).

5.2.1 Hours of work

Until 1995 employees were required to work for 16 hours or more in order to count a week of service, unless they had worked for more than five years when eight hours only would be required. However, the House of Lords held in *R* v *Secretary of State for Employment ex parte EOC* (1994) that this was in breach of art. 157 of the Treaty on the Functioning of the European Union (art. 157 TFEU) (ex art. 141) of the Treaty of Rome (ex art. 141 (EC)) and the EEC Equal Treatment Directive, Council Directive (EEC) 76/207 in that it was discriminatory against women, the majority of whom worked part-time. It may have been possible for employers to justify discrimination against part-timers if men and women were treated equally in this respect, but the Government decided to abolish the requirement altogether. This was achieved by the Employment Protection (Part-Time Employees) Regulations 1995 (SI 1995 No. 31). From then on, it was no longer necessary to work a minimum number of hours per week to be entitled under the unfair dismissal and redundancy legislation.

Nevertheless there appears to be a certain fundamental logic in a requirement of minimum hours for certain statutory employment protection rights. Not only does it appear justifiable to keep small claims out of the busy ET system but, in addition, the scheme of statutory protection reflects the special interest a person has in his or her job, which is less when that job takes up only a small part of a person's life. Likewise, there is an initial attraction in differentiating between part-time and full-time work. It may be questioned why a person who works 40 hours a week has to wait for one year to receive statutory protection when someone who has worked for as long, but for only a proportion of the hours, gets the protection at the same time.

However, on closer examination, this logic is questionable, not least because it appears indirectly to discriminate against women. Women are much more likely than men to be working part-time, and most part-time work in the UK is done by women. Therefore, any legislation which affects part-timers adversely when compared with full-time workers potentially adversely affects women. This is in addition to the other numerous disadvantages which are associated with part-time work (see generally Honeyball, *Sex, Employment and the Law* (Oxford: Blackwell, 1991), ch. 1). For this reason, the European Court of Justice cast doubt on the legality of the requirement of minimum hours, in *Rinner-Kühn* v *FWW Spezial-Gebäudereinigung GmbH* (1989), as contrary to art. 157 TFEU (ex art. 141 EC).

5.2.2 Weeks in which there is no contract of employment

Generally, if a week is not one of employment, continuity is broken, so that the employee has to start again to begin continuous employment. Therefore, for reasons not altogether clear, aggregated service is not considered to be a justifiable gateway to protection, however much it may amount to. There are, however, exceptions to this principle, especially where the employee is not working for reasons not of his own making, yet the layman would consider him to be still 'on the books'. Unfortunately, the legislation has been read by the tribunals in a technical and somewhat restrictive manner.

It should be stressed that in the following cases the employee is treated as retaining continuous employment notwithstanding that the contract of employment has ceased. By ERA 1996, s. 212(3) the provisions protect the continuity of an employee who is absent from work in consequence of sickness or injury, on account of a temporary cessation of work, by arrangement or custom, or on maternity leave. This is so, however, only as long as the parties regard the employee as continuing in employment for some purposes according to the EAT in *Curr* v *Marks & Spencer plc* (2003).

'Absent from work' in all these subparagraphs means 'not only that the employee is not doing any actual work for the employer but that there is no contract of employment subsisting between him and his employer that would entitle the latter to require him to do any work' (*Ford* v *Warwickshire County Council* (1983)).

Sickness or injury

Where the employee is absent from work due to being incapable of work, continuity is preserved so long as the period of absence is not beyond 26 weeks. 'Incapable of work' does not require that the employee should be incapable of work of any kind, according to the EAT in *Donnelly* v *Kelvin International Services* (1992). Although ERA 1996, s. 212(3) does not state this in terms, this would seem to be correct. It would be a wholly artificial argument, except in very rare circumstances, that an employee should be incapable of work of any description, and irrelevant to the purpose of the provision which is concerned with the reason why the employee is away from his or her own work.

In *Pearson* v *Kent County Council* (1993) the Court of Appeal had to consider the situation where an employee was absent from work and then returned to a new position. In such circumstances the test in *Donnelly* v *Kelvin International Services* is more complicated. The Court of Appeal held that the correct approach was not just to consider whether the absence from work was due to sickness or injury in the light of the first position, but also with regard to the new job. If the employee is absent from work even though his illness does not prevent him from undertaking work of the type in the second job, then the tribunal is free to determine that the absence is not due to that illness.

Temporary cessation of work

A temporary cessation of work usually signifies a short-term closure of a factory due to, say, lack of orders, a fire or explosion, or a strike at suppliers (although a dispute at the employee's plant would not fall within this rubric; see *Hanson* v *Fashion Industries (Hartlepool) Ltd* (1980)). Another typical sequence occurred in *Hunter* v *Smith's Dock Co. Ltd* (1968). During the applicant's 40 years of working for the respondents, he was accustomed to being laid off for a week or two at various times until trade picked up. These were treated as temporary cessations of work and his continuity was maintained.

It is sufficient that the employer's work has ceased for the particular employee even if the other aspects of the business run as normal. The issue is whether the work the employee has ceased and not merely whether he is no longer given that work to do (*Byrne* v *City of Birmingham District Council* (1987)). There must be a 'quantum of work' that has ceased. The whole matter received elaborate attention by the House of Lords in *Fitzgerald* v *Hall, Russell & Co. Ltd* (1970). There, although the applicant welder was laid off for an extended period, many of his colleague welders were not, and the employers argued that there had been, from their viewpoint, no cessation of welding work. The House of Lords, however, decided the relevant consideration was that there 'was no longer work available for him [the employee] personally' and Lord Upjohn continued: 'The question whether at the same time the whole works would close down or a department was closed down or a large number of other employees were laid off at the same time would seem to be irrelevant in a computation essentially personal to the particular workman.'

Three questions may be isolated, and must be posed in each case. First, was there a cessation of the employee's work; secondly, did it cause the employee's absence; and thirdly, was it temporary?

The question as to what is temporary has received most attention in respect of schoolteachers. In *Rashid* v *ILEA* (1977) the EAT held that the school holidays were not a temporary 'cessation of work' for the applicant, a supply teacher, who was not paid during them since 'at the end of each term that job finished; at the beginning of the next term he started another one'. This was, however, overruled in the important House of Lords' decision in *Ford* v *Warwickshire County Council* (1983) (see also *Hellyer Brothers Ltd* v *McLeod* (1986)). The employee had been engaged on eight successive contracts for one academic year each. The House of Lords did not consider that it made any difference that the absences for the holidays were foreseeable, predictable, and regular; nor were they attracted by the 'job by job' argument. While it would not be so in every case, here it was conceded that having regard to the length of the total period of employment the holiday absences were temporary. Lord Diplock had in mind also seasonal absences in agriculture and the hotel and catering trade. Furthermore, absence because an employer is short of funds to pay the worker is absence on account of a temporary cessation of work since work in this context means *paid* work, according to the EAT in *University of Aston in Birmingham* v *Malik* (1984).

'Temporary' means in this context transient, i.e. lasting only for a relatively short time in relation to the periods of normal working (the *Ford* case). The temporary nature of the cessation of work is reviewed *ex post facto* and what the parties intended at its inception is only marginally relevant (*Sillars* v *Charrington Fuels Ltd* (1989)). A projected temporary closure may prove permanent because, say, a drop in orders lasts longer than anyone expected. This is a question of fact in each case, and Phillips J stated in *Bentley Engineering Co. Ltd* v *Crown* (1976) that 'The tribunal is enjoined to look at the matter as the historian of a completed chapter of events and not as a journalist describing events as they occur from day to day'. An employee may indeed during the temporary cessation take a job elsewhere (*Thompson* v *Bristol Channel Ship Repairers* (1969)). In *Bentley Engineering Co. Ltd* v *Crown* (1976), a two-year gap was held to be temporary in the circumstances, and Phillips J indicated some factors to be taken into consideration: the nature of the employment; the length of prior and subsequent service; the duration of the breach; what happened during the breach; and what was said on re-engagement. It did not matter in the instant case that re-employment was with a successor employer which was an associated employer by statute.

A strictly mathematical approach, however, is to be avoided. In *Flack* v *Kodak Ltd* (1985) the EAT said that in determining this issue in relation to persons who had worked intermittently over a period of years, the tribunal must have regard to all the circumstances and should not confine itself to taking the percentage that the gap in work bore to the periods of work immediately adjoining it. However, in *Berwick Salmon Fisheries Co. Ltd* v *Rutherford and others* (1991), the EAT held that it would scarcely be possible to describe a period as relatively short in relation to another when it is longer than that other. The Court of Appeal also stated that the whole period of intermittent employment should be considered, not only those weeks in the two-year period which formed the qualifying time. This is not in fact consistent with the House of Lords decision in *Ford v Warwickshire County Council* (1983) in that it was held there that the period to be looked at is the interval between one contract and the contract that next preceded it. This is clearly a poor test (see further Honeyball, (1986) 45 CLJ 402) and has not, it seems, since been followed. In any event, there are further difficulties with that decision, not least because the House of Lords failed to distinguish between a cessation of work, which must be temporary for the provision to apply, and the resulting absence from work, which need not (see further Honeyball, (1984) 47 MLR 228).

It should not be assumed that if a cessation is not permanent it is temporary, or vice versa. In *Sillars*, the Court of Appeal held that cessations of seasonal employment may not be intended to be permanent, but that did not mean that they were, or were not, temporary.

Arrangement or custom

In order to maintain continuity by reason of arrangement or custom there must be an agreement or understanding at the time of departure that the employee will be so absent. The lack of such mutuality was fatal to this claim in *Murphy* v *A. Birrell & Sons Ltd* (1978). The applicant had worked for the respondents for 19 years before taking another job (although not officially resigning) because of an argument with the manager. When things had smoothed over she returned, and the newly appointed managing director told her that 'her old contract stood'. This could not, however, *ex post facto* convert the absence into one by arrangement. Any such understanding must predate the absence.

Secondment is the best example under this rubric. In *Wishart* v *National Coal Board* (1974), for example, the applicant was employed by the National Coal Board (NCB) from 1946 to 1973 except for one year when he worked for a company which carried out development work for the NCB. Since he remained a member of the miners' pension scheme and the two organisations worked closely together, the EAT considered that he was working for the company by arrangement with the NCB. Continuing to pay an employee during a break normally points to such an arrangement.

The EAT somewhat widened the provision in the case of *Lloyds Bank Ltd* v *Secretary of State for Employment* (1979), where the employee, who worked one week on, one week off, was held to be absent from work on her off weeks by arrangement or custom. The case was indeed distinguished in *Corton House Ltd* v *Skipper* (1981), and its authority must be considered very doubtful in the light of *Ford* v *Warwickshire County Council* (1983). In that case, the House of Lords decided that 'absent from work' meant more than merely not at work; rather it was when there was no contract which could require the employee to work.

An 'arrangement' would seem to require that in advance of the break there must have been some discussion or agreement to the effect that the parties regard the employment relationship as continuing despite the termination of the contract of employment. This was so held in *Booth* v *USA* (1999), irrespective of the fact that the employer may purposely have introduced breaks in employment to defeat the application of the legislation. The EAT said that this was not the case in *London Probation Board* v *Kirkpatrick* (2005). However, in so doing, it did not consider the earlier comments in *Booth*.

Strikes

Special rules in ERA 1996, s. 216(1) apply to strikes. Their effect on continuity is hybrid in that, while a week during which for any part the employee is engaged in a strike does not breach continuity, it is not counted as a week of employment (see *Hanson* v *Fashion Industries (Hartlepool) Ltd* (1980)). Nice questions may arise in this regard as to when a strike begins and when it ends. Moreover, even if an employee is not under an obligation to be at work at the particular time, he may be deemed to be taking part in the industrial action if he manifests an intention not to arrive for work when he is next required to present himself (*Winnett* v *Seamarks Brothers Ltd* (1978)).

The weeks of a lock-out are deducted in a similar manner under ERA 1996, s. 216(3). It does not matter that an employee took work elsewhere during the strike or lock-out.

Reinstatement and re-engagement

Where an employee successfully claims to have been unfairly dismissed and is reinstated or re-engaged by his employer, a successor employer, or associated employer, his continuity is preserved and he can include the time in between dismissal and reinstatement or re-engagement. This applies where the re-employment is as a result of an ET order, an agreement made through the good offices of an ACAS conciliation officer or under an approved dismissal procedure agreement or an approved compromise agreement (Employment Protection (Continuity of Employment) Regulations 1996 (SI 1996 No. 3147)). A similar preservation applies to voluntary reinstatement outside the ACAS or tribunals systems according to the EAT in *Ingram* v *Foxon* (1984), but this was not followed by a different division of the same tribunal in *Morris* v *Walsh Western UK* (1997). Continuity, it was said, is a creature of statute, and therefore not to be subject to the agreement of the parties. This does not, however, apply to a redundant employee when the weeks of the interval count only for the purpose of redundancy payment qualification.

Miscellaneous

In the case of redundancy payments, a week does not count if the employee works outside Great Britain during the whole or part thereof and no employer's Class 1 National Insurance contributions are payable by the employer (ERA 1996, s. 215).

Periods spent in the armed forces do not break continuity but do not count as periods of employment (ERA 1996, s. 217).

5.3 Change of employer

The common law took the view that every contract of employment was discrete, and for the good reason that if employees might be transferred at will they would, in the words of Lord Atkin in *Nokes* v *Doncaster Amalgamated Collieries Ltd* (1940), be 'serfs and not servants'. However, this can act as a boomerang against the interests of employees in the modern circumstances of a statutory floor of employment protection rights. Thus, there are five important rules under ERA 1996, s. 218 for maintaining continuity when an employee works in sequence for different employers. The periods are considered continuous where:

(a) 'a trade or business, or an undertaking...is transferred from one person to another...' (s. 218(2));

(b) one body corporate is substituted for another body corporate as the employer by or under an Act of Parliament (s. 218(3));

(c) the employer dies and his personal representatives or trustees keep on the employee (s. 218(4)), even where the employee is also the personal representative (*Rowley, Holmes and Co.* v *Barber* (1977));

(d) there is a change in the partners, personal representatives or trustees who employ him (s. 218(5)). This is necessary since the employees of a partnership are employed by the individual partners jointly, so that each time there is a change of partners continuity would be lost if it were not for this provision;

(e) 'an employee of an employer is taken into the employment of another employer who, at the time when the employee enters the second employer's employment, is an associated employer of the first-employer...' (s. 218(6)).

In applying these rules the capacity in which the worker is employed with the second company is irrelevant. The House of Lords established this important principle in *Lord Advocate* v *De Rosa* (1974). The majority thought that all that was required was employment continuously first by one employer, and then by another to whom the business had been transferred. It was irrelevant that the first employer had terminated the contract and the second had not continued the employment by a suitable alternative offer. The same rule applied both to initial entitlement to rights and assessment of the value of the rights where this depended on length of service.

5.3.1 Transfer of business

The ERA 1996, s. 218 applies to the transfer of a 'trade or business, or an undertaking' and the only further definition is that 'business' includes a trade or business or any activity carried on by a body of persons whether corporate or unincorporate.

Transfer

In *Melon* v *Hector Powe Ltd* (1981) Lord Fraser declared that there was an:

essential distinction between the transfer of a business, or part of a business and a transfer of physical assets...in the former case the business is transferred as a going concern so that the business remains the same but it is in different hands...whereas in the latter the assets are transferred to the new owner to be used in whatever business he chooses.

The Court of Appeal decision in *Woodhouse* v *Peter Brotherhood Ltd* (1972) was a landmark on the path to this decision. Crossleys Ltd had for many years manufactured diesel engines at their Sandiacre factory. They removed this part of their operation to Manchester and sold to Peter Brotherhood Ltd the factory and much of the plant and machinery within it. The latter company ultimately turned it to the production of spinning machines, compressors, and steam turbines. They first completed four large engines on which Crossleys were engaged at the time of the sale. The two employees who claimed redundancy payments had been engaged for the last six months of their service on the same engines as before. The test pronounced by the National Industrial Relations Court for transfer was whether the 'working environment' had changed, and they decided it had not done so. Thus continuity was preserved. They were particularly impressed by the fact that, with the entire workforce taken over, most employees were unlikely to realise that they should at this point claim redundancy payments if continuity was indeed broken. The Court of Appeal, however, rejected this straightforward approach, and decided that 'the new owner did not take over the business as a going concern, but only the physical assets, using them in a different business'. Although 'the same men are employed using the same tools, the business is different'. The EAT was again overruled by the higher courts in *Melon* v *Hector Powe Ltd* (1981). The respondents were multiple tailors who owned a factory at Blantyre where they had, for many years, manufactured men's suits made to measure. In 1977, due to a fall in demand, Executex Manufacturing Ltd took over the factory, including work in progress which they undertook to complete. One hundred and twenty employees sought redundancy payments on the takeover. Hector Powe Ltd defended these claims on the ground that there was a transfer of business and pointed in particular to the continuation of work in progress. Lord Fraser dismissed this factor as 'merely a temporary expedient to help Executex through the initial stages'. In a laissez-faire judgment the House of Lords decided that the issue was one of fact for the tribunal. They also rejected the contention that this was at least a transfer of part of a business since such a change 'will . . . seldom occur except when that part is to some extent separable and severable from the rest of the business either geographically or by reference to products or in some other way'.

The distinctions which have to be drawn on this principle are often narrow. In *Crompton* v *Truly Fair (International) Ltd* (1975), for example, the EAT decided that since the new employer was manufacturing children's clothing rather than men's trousers, the business was different and had not been transferred (see also *Port Talbot Engineering Co. Ltd* v *Passmore* (1975); *Dhami* v *Top Spot Night Club* (1977); *cf. Umar* v *Pliastar Ltd* (1981)).

The essence of a transfer is goodwill and the concept embraces the transfer of goodwill alone of a professional practice where no other assets were sold (*Ward* v *Haines Watts* (1983)). There may be a transfer between partners (*Jeetle* v *Elster* (1985)) but there must be an actual transfer of some sort, and it is insufficient that another company may have assumed *de facto* control while negotiations for purchase of a business took place (*SI (Systems and Instrumentation) Ltd* v *Grist and Riley* (1983)). However, it is not necessary that a transfer be complete, in the sense that if negotiations break down, and there is a re-transfer, continuity is still preserved (*Dabell* v *Vale Industrial Services (Nottingham) Ltd* (1988)). There is also no need for a written agreement in such circumstances where it is clear that everything at the relevant date has been transferred.

The 'transfer of business' as construed by the appeal courts serves to exclude the transfer of a franchise (an increasingly important aspect of modern economic organisation; *McKinney* v *McCaig, Paisley & Melville* (1966)) and a right to sell petrol (*Bumstead* v *John Cars Ltd* (1967)). It also failed the groundsman in *Evenden* v *Guildford City AFC* (1975) who had worked from 1955 to 1968 for the football supporters club and thereafter for the football club itself. Notwithstanding the close interconnection between the two bodies, he was in no sense carrying on a business and so did not qualify when transferred.

Although ERA 1996, s. 218 makes no express reference to the transfer of only part of a business, it is clear that tribunals will include that within its ambit (see e.g. *Gibson* v *Motortune Ltd* (1990)).

Employment 'at the time of transfer'

There are two possible interpretations of the statutory phrase. The first is that the relationship of employer and employee must subsist at that time and the second that the period of employment accumulated counts. Both require that the concept of 'transfer' has a starting and end point. The most searching, but ultimately unsatisfactory, discussion of the concept is found in the Court of Appeal decision in *Teesside Times Ltd* v *Drury* (1980). The applicant had been employed by Champion Publications Ltd for six years, when the company ran into financial difficulties and negotiations were opened with the appellants with a view to a takeover. These reached fruition in a general agreement at about 3 p.m. on Friday 17 November 1975. A few hours later Champion's receiver dismissed all its employees, but this was still some time before the formal contract was signed. Although the appellant's management assured the staff that they would be re-engaged, the applicant was dismissed three days after takeover. He had to establish that there was a transfer of business to claim unfair dismissal. The appellants argued that he was not employed at the 'time of transfer', since he had been dismissed before the formalities of the sale had been completed. All three Lord justices found for the respondent on the ground that he was, under the provisions of what was then Employment Protection (Consolidation) Act 1978 (EPCA 1978), Sch. 13, to be taken to have been employed the whole of the week, and therefore his continuity was preserved until the following Monday.

On the conceptual issue, Eveleigh LJ adopted the first view set out above so that there was continuity 'so long as the dismissal was a step towards the re-engagement'. Stephenson LJ on the other hand considered that a contract must be in effect during the transfer. This was, however, 'a complex of operations which are part of a continuous process through different stages, including dismissal and re-engagement of staff'. The full extent of the transfer was 'a question of fact and degree in the light of common sense'. Goff LJ defined it more narrowly as 'the moment when the transaction of transferring the business is effected'. However, the EAT has reiterated the wider view in *Clark & Tokeley* v *Oakes* (1997) by saying that if the employment survives the transfer it is not necessary to show that the employee was employed at the precise moment of transfer. In this case there was a gap of seven days, during which the transfer took place. The 'time of the transfer' can refer to the whole period of the transfer process.

5.3.2 Associated employer

Continuity of employment is maintained where an employee of one employer enters into the employment of an associated employer of that employer. The ERA 1996, s. 231, gives 'associated employer' a technical and rather limited meaning: '...any two employers shall be treated as associated employers if one is a company of which the other (directly or indirectly) has control or if both are companies of which a third person (directly or indirectly) has control...'. Until 1975 it was akin to the definition of subsidiary company within the Companies Act. The vital question for determination was whether the subsection (then EPCA 1978, s. 153(4)) was exhaustive or had merely illustrative status. The Court of Appeal determined in *Gardiner* v *London Borough of Merton* (1980) that the former was the correct view. The appellant's local government career began in 1965 and he worked for four different authorities before his dismissal in 1977. He sought to count all 12 years in assessing compensation. The Court of Appeal restricted the definition to limited companies and in any event doubted whether anyone had sufficient control of the various councils to fall within the subsection. Griffiths LJ pointed to the problems which might arise if the section were not construed as exhaustive. It would then be necessary to give some other meaning to 'associated'. There was a myriad of possibilities including 'associated in a common purpose, associated through a common element of control or associated through a common interest or associated through common negotiation with a trade union'. This would necessitate 'far-ranging and complex inquiries into the activities of a complainant's present and previous employers'. To predict the outcome of such litigation would prove hazardous. In his Lordship's view, the change from 'company' to employer was merely intended to include the case of the sole trader who became a limited company. Further, if the section was not intended to be exhaustive, it would not be appropriate to conclude with the phrase 'and the expression "associated employer" shall be construed accordingly'. (See too the EAT's decision in *Da Silva* v *Composite Mouldings & Design Ltd* (2009).)

In the normal case, for continuity to be preserved the second employer must be an associated employer at the time when the employee enters his employment with the second employer.

Control by one company of another was at first flexibly construed. It had regard to the direction of operations, not merely the ownership of shares (*Zarb and Samuels* v *British & Brazilian Produce Co. (Sales) Ltd* (1978)). This liberal approach was limited by the EAT in *Secretary of State for Employment* v *Newbold and Joint Liquidators of David Armstrong (Catering Services) Ltd* (1981) and the Court of Appeal declined to follow *Zarb* without expressly overruling it in *South West Launderettes Ltd* v *Laidler* (1986), saying that voting rather than *de facto* control was of more importance. Having said that, the Court of Appeal had second thoughts in *Payne* v *Secretary of State for Employment* (1989), and decided that circumstances other than voting control may be taken into account in certain circumstances, albeit exceptional ones.

In *Washington Arts Association Ltd* v *Forster* (1983) a transfer between the appellants, a guarantee company, and an arts centre which they in effect ran, was not between associated employers. Further, in *Hair Colour Consultants Ltd* v *Mena* (1984), a claim for continuity failed where the applicant had started work as a hair stylist at a salon run by Interhair Ltd which was owned jointly by two brothers, each of whom held 50 per cent of the shares. She then went to the respondents in which one brother owned 85 per cent of the shares, but the other had none. Negative control of just 50 per cent of the shareholding was not enough to satisfy the stringent conditions of the statute. The *Zarb* case is, however, still good authority for the proposition that the persons who control two companies may be a group acting in concert. They must be the same group of individuals in each company (*Poparm Ltd* v *Weekes* (1984)).

In *Pinkney* v *Sandpiper Drilling Ltd* (1989) the Court of Appeal held that an employee cannot be deprived of continuity by the device of one employer being a partnership of limited companies, rather than a limited company, to which the definition of 'associated employer' was restricted in *Gardiner* v *London Borough of Merton* (1980). However, this does not mean that analogous overseas companies are not included within the definition (*Hancill* v *Marcon Engineering Ltd* (1990)).

5.3.3 **Change of partners**

Where there is a change of partners continuity is preserved. In *Harold Fielding Ltd* v *Mansi* (1974) it was held that this did not apply where employment by a partnership is followed by work for one of the former partners on his own account. It can hardly be supposed that such a technical limitation was intended by Parliament and the case was narrowly distinguished in *Allen & Son* v *Coventry* (1979) as applying only when different businesses were involved. Moreover, in *Jeetle* v *Elster* (1985), the transfer from four doctors to one was held to fall within the paragraph (then EPCA 1978, Sch. 13, para. 17). This has now been approved by the Court of Appeal in *Stevens* v *Bower* (2004).

5.3.4 **Estoppel**

Continuity is a purely statutory concept (*Collison* v *BBC* (1998)). So a second employer who told an employee that he would recognise 50 years' previous employment with another employer as continuous with the new job could not be held to his statement under statutory remedies, although he might possibly by contract enforceable in the civil courts. Certainly the Department for Business, Innovation and Skills would not have to pay a rebate for such period, as it would not be privy to the arrangement.

In *Evenden* v *Guildford AFC* (1975) the Court of Appeal suggested that a statement by the respondent football club that the appellant could carry forward his previous service with the Guildford Supporters Club (which was not associated with the Football Club within the meaning of the Act) operated by way of proprietary estoppel, so that the club could not go back on it. Lord Denning MR further thought that the statutory presumption of continuity of employment applied to employment by successive employers. The doctrine *of Evenden* was overruled in *Secretary of State for Employment* v *Globe Elastic Thread Co. Ltd* (1979). The Department of Employment refused to give a redundancy rebate to the respondents in respect of the dismissal of the employee. This was calculated to include not only the five years' work for Globe but also 22 years for Heathcotes which was not an associated company. Further, no business had been transferred from one to the other. There had, however, been a statement, on which the employee relied, that the service would be treated as continuous. The *ratio* of the decision was that the redundancy payment had not been 'made under the Act' so that the Department of Employment was not obliged by statute to pay a rebate, and could not be estopped from denying continuity. The House of Lords stated that any arrangement worked not by estoppel but by contract between Globe and the employee, and went on:

Any employer is perfectly entitled to make his own arrangement with his employees, and no doubt many employers do so, departing in various ways from the terms of the Act. Such arrangements may have the force of a contract, and be enforceable as such, but they cannot commit the Minister to make a rebate. The Minister is only liable to do so in respect of payments made strictly under the Act.

Although this leaves open the possibility of a contractually binding statement by the second employer, it might be difficult to prove the employee had provided consideration.

The 'two way' case of *Smith* v *Blandford Gee Cementation Co. Ltd* (1970) remains good law. The applicant thought he was employed by the respondents as an underground waller on repairs for the NCB. By a Task Work Agreement between the respondents and the NCB, Blandford Gee were agents for the NCB for employment purposes. Since it was Gee which behaved as his employers and gave him his written statement of terms they could not deny they were his employers for the purposes of a redundancy payment.

SELECTED READING

Freedland, M. (2003), *The Personal Employment Contract*, Oxford: Oxford University Press, 2003, ch. 2

Painter, R. W. and Holmes, A. E. (2010), *Cases and Materials on Employment Law*, 8th edn, Oxford: Oxford University Press, ch. 2, section 3

6

Transfer of undertakings

SUMMARY

This chapter considers the increasingly important area of law that deals with the position where businesses and other undertakings are transferred from one employer to another. It considers the modest genesis of legal protection to employees in this area to the modern law which is of huge importance. The extensive Regulations governing the situation are explored in detail beginning with a consideration of what types of transfer are covered and what employees have to satisfy in order to obtain the protection of the Regulations. This is followed by a consideration of the legal effect such a transfer has. Then particular issues are considered such as the position where only part of an undertaking is transferred and where there are group companies involved. The right of employees not to be transferred, the effect on their pensions and their contracts of employment are also examined. Finally, the law on trade union and employee representative involvement in the process is explored.

6.1 Introduction

Council Directive (EEC) 77/187 on acquired rights placed upon member states the obligation to safeguard employees' rights where businesses were transferred from one employer to another. The Government introduced the Transfer of Undertakings (Protection of Employment) Regulations 1981 (SI 1981 No. 1794), to put it into effect, now replaced by the Transfer of Undertakings (Protection of Employment) Regulations 2006 (SI 2006 No. 246). These are normally known as the TUPE Regs. The Regulations contain a scheme of rights which exist alongside the existing legislation in the ERA 1996. The important regulation for continuity purposes is reg. 4 which, on a transfer of an undertaking, automatically transfers the contract of employment from the transferor employer to the transferee. (For detailed commentary on the Regulations see Bowers *et al.*, *Transfer of Undertakings* (London: Sweet & Maxwell), updated service. See too McMullen, (2006) 35 ILJ 113.)

6.2 Relevant transfer

The TUPE apply where there is a relevant transfer of an undertaking, business or part thereof situated in the UK. Regulation 3(1)(a) provides that the Regulations apply where there is a transfer of 'an economic entity which retains its identity'.

'Economic entity' is defined in reg. 3(2) as 'an organised grouping of resources which has the objective of pursuing an economic activity, whether or not that activity is central or ancillary'.

It is necessary for the employer to retain its identity. Therefore, where there has been a transfer of shares only this will not amount to a transfer as in that event identity is retained unless the purchaser assumes subsequent control of the company, according to the Court of Appeal in *Millam* v *Print Factory (London) 1991 Ltd* (2007). However, as Rubenstein points out (at [2007] IRLR 467), whether there is a TUPE transfer should not be dependent upon the state of affairs in the weeks and months following the transaction as TUPE imposes rights and obligations before and after the transfer. The European Court of Justice (ECJ) has held that, in a decision on the identical wording in the Acquired Rights directive, it is not necessary to retain organisational autonomy in order to retain identity after a transfer. (See *Klarenberg* v *Ferrotron Technologies GmbH* (2009).) Indeed, if that were so, many of the privatisations, mergers and acquisitions thought to come under TUPE in the UK would not have done so.

The Regulations also now apply where there is a 'service provision change' (an SPC). This is defined in reg. 3(1)(b) as a situation in which:

(i) activities cease to be carried out by a person ('a client') on his own behalf and are carried out instead by another person on the client's behalf ('a contractor');

(ii) activities cease to be carried out by a contractor on a client's behalf (whether or not those activities had previously been carried out by the client on his own behalf) and are carried out instead by another person ('a subsequent contractor') on the client's behalf; or

(iii) activities cease to be carried out by a contractor or a subsequent contractor on a client's behalf (whether or not those activities had previously been carried out by the client on his own behalf) and are carried out instead by the client on his own behalf.

In addition it is necessary to show that, immediately before the transfer, there is 'an organised grouping of employees' situated in Great Britain which has as its principal purpose the carrying out of the activities concerned on behalf of the client. This is because it would otherwise be unclear which employees would transfer on a change of contractor. There would seem to be no reason why a grouping should not include just one employee. The client must also intend that the activities will, following the SPC, be carried out by the transferee other than in connection with a single specific event or task of short duration. Buying in services on a 'one-off' basis will not therefore be included. There will not, however, be an SPC where the activities consist wholly or mainly in the supply of goods for the client's use—reg. 3(3)(b). The essential question to ask, according to the EAT in *Metropolitan Resources Ltd* v *Churchill Dulwich Ltd* (2009) is whether the activities carried on by the alleged transferor and transferee are fundamentally or essentially the same.

These alternative methods of amounting to a relevant transfer are not mutually exclusive. For example, outsourcing of a service may well amount to both an SPC and a transfer of part of a business.

It is not a requirement for the Regulations to apply that undertakings are operating for gain, so long as they re-engaged in economic activities. They also apply
to both public and private undertakings—reg. 3(4)(a). However, an administrative
reorganisation of a public administrative authority or transfer of such functions
between such bodies is not a relevant transfer—reg. 3(5). The Regulations also
apply even though the transfer, SPC or employment of those employed are governed by foreign law—reg. 3(4)(b). This is also the case where the employees work
outside the UK—reg. 3(4)(c).

The lack of a transfer of tangible assets is not a bar on there being a transfer
within the Directive, according to the ECJ in *Schmidt v Spar und Leihkasse der
Früheren Ämter Bordesholm, Kiel und Cronshagen* (1994). (See further John McMullen,
(1994) 23 ILJ 230.) However, where there is a labour-intensive undertaking which
is being transferred it has been argued that the transferee is in the surprising position of being able to choose whether or not the Regulations apply. This is because
of the Court of Appeal's decision in *Betts v Brintel Helicopters Ltd and KLM ERA
Helicopters (UK) Ltd* (1997), which followed hard on the heels of the decision of the
ECJ in *Süzen v Zehnaker Gebäudereinigung GmbH Krankenhausservice* (1997). It was
stated that whether a labour-intensive undertaking is transferred is determined
by considering whether the staff are combined to engage in a particular activity
which continues or is resumed with substantially the same staff after the transfer
retaining its identity in the hands of the transferee. If the identity is not retained,
as with the loss of a service contract to a competitor when the work is still done
by the same employees, as in *Süzen*, the Regulations do not apply. It is only if the
transferee takes on the bulk (at least) of the tranferor's employees that they will
apply. This is most unsatisfactory. Whether the Regulations apply should not be
dependent upon whether or not the employees are retained. Rather, the rights of
the employees to be retained should depend upon whether or not the Regulations
apply. This also has the effect that it is only *after* the transfer takes place that the
parties will know whether the Regulations apply, whereas they need to know in
advance. (See further, Davies, (1997) 26 ILJ 193; Shrubsall, (1998) 61 MLR 85; and
the decision of the ECJ in *Oy Liikenne AB v Liskojärvi and Juntunen* (2001) when
great emphasis was placed on the importance of a transfer of assets. (See commentary by Davies, (2001) 30 ILJ 231.) See too the ECJ's decision in *Abler v Sodexho MM
Catering Gesellschaft* (2004).)

However, in *ECM (Vehicle Delivery Service) Ltd v Cox* (1999) the Court of Appeal
stated that the importance of this had been overstated. The ECJ in *Süzen* had not
overturned but expressly approved the approach taken in its earlier decisions in
Spjjkers and *Schmidt*. These cases had made clear that national courts should take
into account 'all the facts characterising the transaction in question', in order to
determine whether the undertaking has continued and retained its identity in different hands. *Süzen* simply set limits on the application of the Directive by indicating that the mere fact that the service provided continues to be similar will not be
enough to show that an economic entity has been transferred. Other factors need
to be taken into account. The question of whether the majority of the employees
are taken on by the transferee is just one of these factors, as are the similarity of
the pre- and post-transfer activities and the type of undertaking concerned (e.g. in
labour-intensive sectors). In these circumstances, the Court of Appeal was prepared
to uphold the ET's decision that a transfer of an undertaking had occurred when a

vehicle delivery contract was switched from one contractor to another without any significant transfer of assets or employees. The Court also held that the tribunal was entitled to take into account the reason why, in the present case, the transferee had refused to take on the transferor's employees, which was that it wished to avoid possible unfair dismissal claims (see John McMullen, (1999) 28 ILJ 360, and the later Court of Appeal decision in *ADI (UK) Ltd* v *Willer* (2001) which followed, by a majority, *ECM*. See commentary by John McMullen, (2001) 30 ILJ 396). See also *Ledernes Hovedoeganisation acting on behalf of Ole Rygaard* v *Dansk Arbejdsgiverforening acting on behalf of Stro Molle Akustik A/S* (1996); *Allen* v *Amalgamated Construction Co. Ltd* (2000); *Cheesman* v *R. Brewer Contracts Ltd* (2001).

6.3 The process of transfer

The purchaser need not run the business as a going concern but instead may lease it or sell it on (*Premier Motors (Medway) Ltd* v *Total Oil (GB) Ltd* (1984); *P. Bork International A/S* v *Foreningen af Arbejdsledere i Danmark* (1989)). The transfer may be by operation of law, and a series of two or more transactions between the same parties may constitute one transfer.

It is not necessary that the transfer be formally completed. Where an employee begins work for the intended transferee, to whom assets have been transferred, that may be adequate even if there is a re-transfer and the transaction ultimately does not take place (*Dabell* v *Vale Industrial Services (Nottingham) Ltd* (1988)).

A particular date must be determinable for the transfer to take place. It cannot be deemed to be a period of time, according to the ECJ in *Celtec Ltd* v *Astley* (2005).

Any agreement to contract out of the Regulations is void (reg. 18).

6.4 Effect of transfer on employment

The effect of the transfer is in the nature of a statutory novation of the contract of employment so that the purchaser stands in the shoes of the vendor as far as the vendor's contractual employment responsibilities are concerned. This happens automatically: the transferee need do nothing. More specifically, the transferee of the undertaking takes over all 'rights, powers, duties and liabilities under or in connection with any such contract' (reg. 4(2)). It is only in relation to the contract that these rights are transferred. So non-contractual occupational pension schemes are not transferred and neither is the transferee employer under any obligation to provide them (see the Court of Appeal's decision in *Adams* v *Lancashire CC and BET Catering Services Ltd* (1997)). However, contractual entitlements arising from a collective agreement made by the transferor will also bind the transferee employer, even if that transferee is not a party to the collective bargain, according to the EAT in *Whent* v *T. Cartledge Ltd* (1997). However, the position is different in EU Law with regard to agreements made *after* the transfer, according to the ECJ in *Werhof* v *Freeway Traffic System* (2006), although this does not to apply to TUPE, according to the EAT in *Alemo-Herron* v *Parkwood Leisure Ltd* (2009). This was *because* the ECJ's decision was on a preliminary reference. As Michael Rubenstein has pointed out (see [2009] IRLR 320) even if this is the right result the EAT's argument is a somewhat bold assertion as to the status of ECJ judgments on preliminary references with several well-known examples to the contrary.

In *Wilson* v *St Helens Borough Council* (1996) the House of Lords held that transfer-related changes to the terms and conditions of employment were void, even if for good consideration and with employee consent. However, the EAT has stated that the employee may take advantage of favourable changes effected by the transferee even though the transferee has no such equivalent right—see *Power* v *Regent Security Services Ltd* (2007). It is difficult to see how this can be reconciled with *Wilson* or, indeed, with the earlier decision of the ECJ in *Foreningen af Arbejdsledere i Danmark* v *Daddy's Dance Hall* (1988) from which *Wilson* was derived. (See further, Wynn-Evans, (2007) 36 ILJ 480.)

It might seem clear that the transferor cannot take advantage of any wider application of the terminology in an employee's original contract of employment where the extension is attributable to the transfer itself. An example would be where a mobility clause in the contract with the transferor refers by implication to a smaller geographical area than it would do with regard to the transferee. However, the EAT has underlined this in *Tapere* v *South London and Maudsley NHS Trust* (2009).

The continuity of employment of employees transferred is not broken by the transfer. This is one of TUPE's most important consequences for employees. However, the House of Lords have held in *Preston* v *Wolverhampton Healthcare NHS Trust (No. 3)* (2006), for the purposes of Equal Pay Act 1970, s. 2(4) (which stated at the relevant time there that the time limit for making a claim ran from the end of 'the employment') that, where there was a transfer of an undertaking, employment with the transferee ceased on the transfer and did not continue with the transferee. The reasoning of the House of Lords in the light of the purpose of TUPE is difficult to maintain, and difficult to see how that could be applied consistently to issues of continuity, although it does make sense perhaps when considered in the light of what s. 2(4) was seeking to achieve.

The transferor is discharged from all obligations, whether or not the employees so consent, according to the ECJ in *Berg and Busschers* v *Besselsen* (1989).

This ostensibly simple idea—that all the contractual rights transfer—can cause problems in practice. Take, for example, the situation (as in *Sodexo Ltd* v *Gutridge* (2008)), where an employee who has transferred on the transfer of an undertaking to the transferee employer, makes an equal pay claim and wishes her comparator to be an employee who has not transferred. As Michael Rubenstein has pointed out (see [2008] IRLR 750) the transferee might then need to adduce evidence and reasons relating to employment with the transferor who may have no interest in the proceedings, and this might concern circumstances several years before the transfer.

6.5 Insolvent transferors

Where a transferor is insolvent on the transfer, and rescue proceedings are under way to save the business, unless the purpose of insolvency proceedings is to liquidate the assets of the undertaking transferred, the transferee automatically takes on the transferor's employees. (See, for the types of proceeding to which this applies, the EAT's decision in *Oakland* v *Wellswood (Yorkshire Ltd)* (2009).) In addition, debts owed by the transferor to its employees will pass to the transferee, except certain debts specified by way of reg. 8. These include items such as arrears of pay, redundancy pay, pay in lieu of notice, and holiday pay. These are paid out of the National Insurance Fund. In addition, in such circumstances there is greater flexibility for the terms and conditions of employment of its employees to be varied. In this event the restrictions noted above on variation of terms and conditions do not apply—reg. 9. (See, generally, *Secretary of State for Trade and Industry* v *Slater* (2007).)

6.6 Employment immediately before the transfer

Only persons employed 'immediately before the transfer' are covered by the Regulations. Initially, this phrase was very restrictively construed by the EAT so that even dismissals carried out hours before a transfer were considered as outside the scope of the Regulations. Gradually, however, the EAT took a different line (see e.g. *Kestongate Ltd* v *Miller* (1986)). A retreat was signalled by the Court of Appeal in *Secretary of State for Employment* v *Spence* (1986) when it held that employees who were dismissed three hours before a transfer were not employed 'immediately before' it. The meaning of that phrase was to be considered as being equivalent to employment at the time of the transfer. A more realistic line was taken later. The leading case is *Litster* v *Forth Dry Dock and Engineering Co. Ltd* (1989). In this case the employees were dismissed just one hour before the transfer. The House of Lords held that they were employed immediately before the transfer. The Regulations were intended to comply with Council Directive (EEC) 77/187, the purpose of which was to protect employees' rights in the event of a transfer of undertaking. To give effect to this purpose, it was necessary to imply into the Regulations words to the effect that the employees must be employed immediately before the transfer or that they would have been so employed if they had not been unfairly dismissed. This implication was necessary, for otherwise it would be easy to evade the Regulations. This wording, since 2006, now appears in reg. 4(3).

The effect of *Litster* (and therefore reg. 4(3)), however, is not as it might initially appear, as Collins has pointed out ((1989) 18 ILJ 144). Although the effect of a dismissal by the transferor will be treated as an automatically unfair dismissal by the transferee in circumstances such as in that case, this is not necessarily to say that continuity is preserved. The dismissals are nevertheless dismissals and effective to terminate the employment relationship. As Collins points out, the House of Lords took the principle of the Regulations merely to mean that pecuniary obligations with respect to dismissed employees are transferred to the transferee and not that the employment relationship persists as if no dismissals had taken place. It is doubtful if this was the intention behind the statement of the ECJ in *P. Bork International A/S* v *Foreningen af Arbejdsledere i Danmark* (1989) that, in these circumstances, workers 'must be considered as still employed by the undertaking at the date of the transfer'. Collins' argument is that the dismissals should be treated as void, not just because to do so preserves continuity, but also because this would avoid forcing the employee into the embarrassing position of bringing an unfair dismissal claim against his new employer in order to receive compensation for the loss of accrued statutory entitlements. (See also *Cornwall County Care Ltd* v *Brightman* (1998); *Re Maxwell Fleet & Facilities Management Ltd* (2000).)

Any purported variation of a contract of employment is void if the sole, or principal, reason for it was the transfer or a reason connected with it that was not an economic, technical or organisational reason entailing changes in the workforce—reg. 4(4).

6.7 Persons employed in an undertaking part-transferred

Clearly, where a whole undertaking is transferred, it will be easy to identify the staff who work for it and, in principle, they will all go across to the transferee. The difficulty arises when only part of an undertaking transfers.

The question of who is transferred when only a part of an undertaking is transferred was considered by the ECJ in the case of *Botzen* v *Rotterdamsche Droogdok Maatschappij BV* (1986). In that case, certain specific departments of a company were sold following a liquidation, and the question arose whether employees employed in general departments (e.g. personnel, porters' services, general maintenance) were also transferred. It was accepted that they carried out certain duties for the benefit of the transferred part of the undertaking, as well as for other departments of the business.

However, the ECJ held that the staff were not transferred merely because they used assets located in the part transferred or carried out work which benefited that part. There had to be more, since they had to be *assigned* to the part transferred. In reaching this conclusion, the ECJ adopted the view of the European Commission which had described the 'decisive criterion' as 'whether or not a transfer takes place of the departments to which they were assigned and which formed the organisational framework within which their employment relationship took effect'.

6.8 Group companies

In *Duncan Webb Offset (Maidstone) Ltd* v *Cooper and Others* (1995) the EAT, in considering the case where a person is employed by X to work on Y's business and Y transfers that business to Z, decided that *prima facie* the Regulations would not apply but that 'tribunals will be astute to ensure that the provisions of the Regulations are not evaded by devices such as service companies or by complicated group structures which conceal the true position'. Tribunals were advised to 'keep in mind the purpose of the Directive and the need to avoid complicated corporate structures from getting in the way of a result which gives effect to that purpose'.

This focuses on evasion and requires the adjudicating body to strip away the veil of incorporation.

An altogether more radical approach was taken by the EAT sitting in Scotland in *Sunley Turriff Holdings Ltd* v *Thomson* (1995). Mr Thomson was employed as company secretary and chief accountant for Lilley Construction Ltd and Lilley Construction (Scotland) Ltd. His contract was with Lilley Construction Ltd. On 18 January 1993, the business of Lilley Construction (Scotland) Ltd was transferred to Sunley Turriff Holdings Ltd. Mr Thomson was not on the list of employees transferred and in effect he claimed that he should have been. He was dismissed on the grounds of redundancy on 1 March 1993 by the receivers of Lilley Construction Ltd and he claimed against Sunley Turriff Holdings Ltd as transferees. It was held that the Regulations applied since the part transferred included Lilley Construction (Scotland) Ltd by which Mr Thomson was employed and Mr Thomson was assigned to the part transferred. The question was whether the claimant was an employee in that undertaking.

The decision in *Michael Peters Ltd* v *Farnfield and Michael Peters Group plc* (1995) is more orthodox. Mr Farnfield was chief executive of Michael Peters Group plc and was responsible for the financial management of all 25 subsidiary companies in the group. The group went into receivership on 27 August and Mr Farnfield was made redundant on that date. Three days later four subsidiary companies were sold to CLK and the subsidiary companies were named as the seller. CLK also acquired part of the assets of the parent company which belonged to the subsidiary companies. Mr Farnfield failed in his claim against the transferee on the ground that he worked for the group as a whole and not exclusively for the subsidiaries sold. He was thus not employed by the transferor.

6.9 Refusing a transfer of employment

In *Katsikas* v *Konstantinidis* (1993) the ECJ decided that Council Directive (EEC) 77/187 did not prevent an employee from refusing the transfer to a transferee of his contract of employment or employment relationship. The Directive does not require member states to provide that the contract of employment should be maintained with the transferor in the event that the employee freely decides not to continue the contract of employment with the transferor. The ECJ said that 'Such an obligation would undermine the fundamental rights of the employee who must be free to choose his employer and cannot be obliged to work for an employer'. Further it left to member states the right to determine the fate of the contract in the event of a transfer. On the basis of this doctrine, the TURERA 1993 amended what is now TUPE, reg. 4(7) and disapplies the automatic transfer principle if the employee 'informs the transferor or transferee that he objects to becoming employed by the transferee' in which case, by reg. 4(8), the transfer operates 'to terminate his contract of employment with the transferor' but he 'shall not be treated, for any purpose, as having been dismissed by the transferor'. To qualify an objection must, however, amount to a refusal and not just an expression of concern, according to the EAT in *Hay* v *George Harrison (Building Contractors) Ltd* (1996).

This provision seems to emphasise the necessity of the employees being informed of the transfer, and in consequence the EAT at first decided in *Photostatic Copiers (Southern) Ltd v Okuda and Japan Office Equipment Ltd* (1995) that it was one of the essential rights of an employee. However, the decision was much criticised on the basis that unscrupulous employers could evade the Regulations by keeping their activities under wraps. The EAT therefore in *Secretary of State for Trade and Industry v Cook* (1997) determined that *Photostatic* was not good law and should no longer be followed. See also *Humphreys v University of Oxford* (2000).

The objection must be made in advance of the transfer since the objection is (by statute) to 'becoming' an employee of the transferee. No reason need be given and no formality is required for the objection to be taken into account. When an objection is made the contract just dissolves; the employee has no right against transferor or transferee. This is becoming very important in the context of garden leave/restrictive covenants, because if there is a transfer in the middle of the notice period, the employee may simply refuse to transfer and the notice dissolves.

6.10 **Pensions**

When a transfer occurs, if employees were members of an occupational pension scheme with a transferor employer, they are entitled to have a scheme provided by the transferee. It need not be an identical scheme, but must satisfy a certain minimum. The transferee must match employee contributions, up to 6 per cent of salary, in a stakeholder pension or equivalent—see Pensions Act 2004, ss 257–258 and the Transfer of Employment (Pension Protection) Regulations 2005 (SI 2005 No. 649). See also Pollard, (2005) 34 ILJ 270.

The TUPE, reg. 10(2) states that aspects of occupational pension schemes which are not concerned with benefits for old age, invalidity or survivors are excluded from being part of a scheme. This is not in breach of EC law (see *Adams v Lancashire CC* (1997); *Frankling v BPS Ltd* (1999); see also Hepple and Mumgaard, (1998) 27 ILJ 309).

6.11 **Restraining a transfer**

The Court of Appeal suggested in *Newns v British Airways plc* (1992) that, in some limited circumstances, a proposed transfer of undertaking might be restrained by an injunction. This interesting possibility depends upon the proposal constituting a breach of the employer's implied duty of good faith. However, the court did not hear detailed argument from counsel on this point in that case and it would go against the general position that TUPE provides for a statutory novation of contract.

6.12 Consultation with recognised unions or elected representatives

6.12.1 The information to be given

Recognised trade unions, elected representatives, and individuals have similar rights to consultation over transfers of undertakings as on redundancies and false representations may attract liabilities in both contract and tort, according to the High Court in *Hagen* v *ICI Chemicals and Polymers Ltd* (2002). The transferor has a duty to inform a union or unions, where members thereof may be affected by the transfer or by 'measures' to be taken in connection with it, of:

(a) the fact that the relevant transfer is to take place;

(b) when, approximately, the transfer is to take place;

(c) the reasons for the transfer;

(d) the legal, economic, and social implications for affected employees;

(e) the measures which he envisages the transferor or the transferee will take or if there will be no such measures, that fact (reg. 13(2)).

The word 'measures' is a curious one, not found in any other area of employment law. In *Institution of Professional Civil Servants* v *Secretary of State for Defence* (1987), Millett J construed the similar language of Dockyard Services Act 1986, s. 1, which mirrored TUPE for the special purpose of the 'privatisation' of the naval dockyards. He considered that 'measures' was a word of wide import, including 'any action, step or arrangement'. 'Envisages' meant 'visualises' or 'foresees'. While manpower projections were not measures, reductions in the level of manpower would be. Where information to be divulged is not factual but is based on appraisal or judgment, such as manpower forecasts, the employer need only divulge the result of his deliberations, the union may not demand information on the calculations or assumptions on which the appraisal or judgment is based.

The relevant information must be given to a 'relevant person...long enough before a relevant transfer to enable the employer of any affected employees to consult all the persons who are the appropriate representatives of any of those affected employees'. The employers need only actually consult if any 'measures' are to be taken, in which case management must consider any representations which the union may make. (See generally on construction of these provisions, *NATTKE* v *Rank Leisure Ltd* (1981). See also *Amicus* v *City Building (Glasgow) LLP* (2009); *Kerry Foods Ltd* v *Creber* (2000); *Alamo Group (Europe) Ltd* v *Tucker* (2003); but *cf. Transport and General Workers Union* v *James McKinnon Jr (Haulage) Ltd* (2001).)

6.12.2 The expanding provision

The original requirement for consultation only with recognised unions was thrown into doubt following the decision by the ECJ in *Commission of European*

Communities v *United Kingdom* (1994). As a result, the Collective Redundancies and Transfer of Undertakings (Protection of Employment) (Amendment) Regulations 1995 (SI 1995 No. 2587) (1995 Amendment Regulations) widened the scope of those to be informed and consulted from representatives of a recognised independent trade union to 'employee representatives elected by' the employees. Until 1 November 1999 whether the employer consulted elected representatives or representatives of a recognised union was entirely a matter for the employer. The Collective Redundancies and Transfer of Undertakings (Protection of Employment) (Amendment) Regulations 1999 (SI 1999 No. 1925) (1999 Amendment Regulations) removed this freedom of choice by requiring the employer to consult union representatives where it recognises an independent trade union in respect of a group of affected employees (reg. 13(2)). It is only where such a recognition arrangement does not exist that the employer is entitled to consult with non-union representatives. If the employees fail to hold an election, the employer will have to give information to each individual employee affected. However, there is no requirement to consult all the affected employees individually (*Howard* v *Millrise Ltd* (2005)).

The 1995 Amendment Regulations established no criteria of independence for the elected representatives. The 1999 Amendment Regulations, however, inserted what is now TUPE, reg. 14, governing the conduct of elections of employee representatives. This imposes a duty on the employer to make such arrangements 'as are reasonably practicable' to ensure that the election is fair. Any employee who may be affected by the proposed dismissals or by measures taken in connection with them is entitled to vote in the election and, if he wants, to stand as a candidate. The election should be conducted, 'so far as is reasonably practicable', in secret and votes must be accurately counted. Representatives' terms of office should be long enough for them to be fully informed and consulted. The TUPE, reg. 14 gives affected employees, employee representatives and the union rights to complain to an ET in circumstances where the employer has failed to perform any of its duties in relation to consultation or elections.

6.12.3 The defence

The only defence for the employer is where he is faced by special circumstances rendering it not reasonably practicable for him to conform. This exception is construed in much the same restrictive manner as under the redundancy consultation provisions. In *Angus Jowett & Co. Ltd* v *NUTGW* (1985) the financial circumstances which gave rise to the appointment of a receiver were neither sudden in onset nor unforeseeable and the tribunal had correctly decided that there was no special circumstance. Regulation 13(4) provides that 'the transferee shall give the transferor such information at such time as will enable the transferor to perform the duty imposed on him . . .'.

Any complaint of default must be made to the ET within three months or such longer period as the tribunal considers reasonable. Subject to the maximum limit of 13 weeks, the tribunal shall award such compensation for breach of the consultation provisions as 'the tribunal considers just and equitable having regard to the seriousness of the failure of the employer to comply with his duty'. The amount is a question of fact with which the EAT is unlikely to interfere (*Angus Jowett*).

6.12.4 **The rights of elected representatives**

There are certain rights which go with the post of elected representative. The elected representative and union representative are accorded the right not to suffer detriment as a consequence of carrying out the functions or activities of an employee representative or a candidate for such elections, and time off for such purposes (ERA 1996, ss 47(1), 61(1)). A dismissal will be automatically unfair if the reason or principal reason is that the employee performed or proposed to perform any functions as an employee representative. The 1999 Amendment Regulations extended these rights to cover any employee dismissed or subjected to a detriment by reason of his participation in an employee representatives' election (ERA 1996, ss 47(1A) and 103(2)).

Further, the employer must provide elected representatives or trade union representatives with access to the affected employees (reg. 13(8)), such as by use of the telephone. In addition, employee representatives should be allowed time off to undergo training in their functions (ERA 1996, s. 61).

SELECTED READING

Freedland, M. (2003), *The Personal Employment Contract*, Oxford: Oxford University Press, 2003, ch. 9

McMullen, J., *Business Transfers and Employee Rights,* London: LexisNexis (looseleaf)

McMullen, J. (1999), 'TUPE: Waiver of Employment Rights and Contract Changes after Wilson', (1999) 28 ILJ 76

McMullen, J. (2006), 'An Analysis of the Transfer of Undertakings (Protection of Employment) Regulations 2006', (2006) 35 ILJ 113

Painter, R. W. and Holmes, A. E. (2010), *Cases and Materials on Employment Law*, 8th edn, Oxford: Oxford University Press, ch. 9, section 5

Wynn-Evans, C. (2006), *Blackstone's Guide to the New Transfer of Undertakings Legislation*, Oxford: Oxford University Press, 2006

Wynn-Evans, C. (2008), 'Service Provision Fragmentation and the Limits of TUPE Protection', (2008) 37 ILJ 371

7

Statutory employment protection on dismissal

SUMMARY

This chapter examines a number of issues that are relevant to the primary statutory employment protection rights of unfair dismissal and redundancy. It considers the multi-stage process by which it needs to be established that a claimant:

(a) is employed;

(b) is not an employee excluded from claiming; and

(c) has a job that has been terminated in a way that in law amounts to dismissal, which can take a variety of forms.

7.1 The scope of statutory protection

In order to be able to bring a claim for both unfair dismissal and redundancy, the first hurdle an applicant must cross is that of eligibility. There are a number of reasons why he or she may be ineligible.

7.1.1 Employment

The first requirement for unfair dismissal and redundancy rights is that the applicant must be an employee. This has been considered in Chapter 2 above, but it should be borne in mind that, for present purposes, the definition of employment is that contained in ERA 1996, s. 230(5). This defines employment (for most purposes under the Act) as employment under a contract of employment. A contract of employment in turn is defined as a contract of service or apprenticeship, whether express or implied, and (if it is express) whether it is oral or in writing (s. 230(2)). An employee is likewise defined as an individual who has entered into or works under (or, where employment has ceased, worked under) a contract of employment (s. 230(1)). It is important to remember that this is a different definition than that used for some other purposes.

7.1.2 Excluded employment

Once it is established that the applicant is an employee of the employer it might be shown that the employee is excluded from the statutory entitlements. Most exclusions, however, go to jurisdiction so that even if neither party raises them, the tribunal itself must enquire (*British Midlands Airways Ltd* v *Lewis* (1978)). It is normally proper for an ET to consider the question as a separate preliminary issue.

Qualifying period

The qualifying period in redundancy payments has throughout the existence of the right been two years' continuous service, but the time for unfair dismissal has varied with the political complexion of the Government of the day. Between March 1975 and October 1979 the relevant period was 26 weeks and it was the Labour Government's intention eventually to reduce it to three months. Between October 1979 and June 1985 an applicant required one year's continuous service up to the effective date of termination in order to claim. An exception was introduced in 1980, in the case of employers who had at no time during the applicant's employment employed more than 20 employees. The provision caused great difficulties of construction. The ERA 1996, s. 108 provided that all employees required two years' continuous employment in order to claim.

These provisions were thrown into some disarray because of the proposition that to require a two-year period indirectly discriminated against women (because a smaller proportion of women could comply with this condition than men) thereby contravening EU sex discrimination law. The point arose in *R* v *Secretary of State for Employment ex parte Seymour-Smith and Perez (No. 2)* (2000).

The qualifying period for unfair dismissal has now been reduced to one year (Unfair Dismissal (Variation of Qualifying Period) Order 1999 (SI 1999 No. 1436)), subject to certain exceptions. For example, if the dismissal is connected with trade union membership or activities, pregnancy or maternity, health and safety, the assertion of a statutory right, a public interest disclosure or the refusal of a retail or betting worker to work on a Sunday, there is no qualifying period required at all (see s. 108(3)). Where the dismissal follows a refusal by the employer to pay an employee who is suspended from work on medical grounds, there is a four-week qualification period.

The calculation of continuous employment has been considered in detail in Chapter 5 above.

Illegality

The general approach of the courts is that an employee cannot claim employment protection rights when his contract is tinged by illegality, for as Bristow J has stated: 'The rights, though creatures of statute…depend on or arise from the contract just as do the common law rights which arise from the contract itself' (*Tomlinson* v *Dick Evans 'U' Drive Ltd* (1978)). Thus, in general, an employee cannot claim unfair dismissal or redundancy payment if his contract is illegal, nor count a week spent on an illegal contract in determining the length of continuous employment. This denial may, however, be out of all proportion to any wrong committed by the employee. (See further Forshaw and Pilgerstorfer, (2005) 34 ILT 158.) All sorts of incidental breaches of the law, whether of statutory provisions or at common law on the ground of public policy, have been held to avoid a contract. In *Napier* v *National Business Agency Ltd* (1951) Evershed MR said:

There is a strong legal obligation placed on all citizens to make true and faithful returns for tax purposes and, if parties make an agreement which is designed to do the contrary, i.e. to mislead and delay, it seems to me impossible for this court to enforce that contract at the suit of one party to it.

Moreover, there appears to be no *de minimis* rule. In *Hannen* v *Ryman* (1979) the tax evaded in four years was just £4, yet the contract was nevertheless declared invalid. Fraud of the Inland Revenue is by far the most common vitiating factor in the employment field, and the doctrine operates most harshly when the evasion of statute is not the fault of the employee at all. The fact that he is excluded from claiming may be somewhat fortuitous. The courts have gone some way to mitigate its effect in various ways.

In *Davidson* v *Pillay* (1979) the EAT stated that the employee must actually participate in the illegality to be fixed with the consequence of it, while in *McConnell* v *Bolik* (1979) the employee's failure to disclose to the Inland Revenue income derived from the sale of two calves did not automatically make the whole contract illegal, since there was nothing to suggest the employee was privy to the arrangement. *Corby* v *Morrison (t/a The Card Shop)* (1980) reflects orthodoxy however: the employer paid the applicant £5 a week which was not subject to tax in addition to her basic wages, but she claimed that she did not know the arrangement was illegal. The EAT nevertheless rejected her contention that she should be able to claim unfair dismissal. May J said: 'In truth it makes no difference whether or not the parties were ignorant that what they were doing was illegal; ignorance of the law is no excuse.' (See too *Salvesen* v *Simons* (1994).) The question was exhaustively discussed by the EAT in *Newland* v *Simons & Willer (Hairdressers) Ltd* (1981). The applicant was paid a weekly cash wage which was falsely recorded at lower amounts in the wage books. She received her tax form showing her annual gross wage completed by the employer, but the EAT held that whether this prevented her enforcing her statutory rights depended on whether she knew of the illegality. May J did, however, warn that: 'The incidence of tax frauds both large and small is so rife that they cannot be brushed aside and the blame for them laid only at the feet of the employers.' However, in *Wilkinson* v *Lugg* (1990) the EAT reaffirmed that an innocent party will not be affected by the illegality. It is not a matter of jurisdiction, so that if illegality is proved the tribunal does not hear the case. On the contrary, it must hear it as a finding of illegality means merely that the contract cannot be enforced by a party who was knowingly party to the illegality. This should mean, as Mogridge has convincingly argued ((1986) 15 ILJ 56), that continuity of employment should be unaffected by illegality, but the EAT has decided to the contrary (see *Hyland* v *J. H. Barker (North West) Ltd* (1985)). As Mogridge pointed out in an earlier article ((1981) 10 ILJ 23), although clearly public policy has a major role to play here, and demands that employees should not be advantaged by illegality, in circumstances where the employee is only marginally involved in the illegality which renders unenforceable not only the contract but also statutory employment protection rights, it is the employer (who often instigates and is responsible for the illegality) who will be the beneficiary. She therefore suggested that statutory rights ought always to be enforceable irrespective of illegality.

Since then there have been signs that the Court of Appeal is willing to adopt a line on public policy which is determined by the relative advantages and disadvantages involved. In *Hewcastle Catering Ltd* v *Ahmed and Elkanah* (1991) the Court of Appeal held that if employees do not gain personal advantage from the illegality, knowledge of it and participation in it will not necessarily deny them a remedy (see Honeyball, (1992) 21 ILJ 143). (See further *Lightfoot* v *D. & J. Sporting Ltd* (1996); Jefferson, (1996) 25 ILJ 234; *Blue Chip Trading Ltd* v *Helbawi* (2009); *Enfield Technical Services Ltd* v *Payne* (2008); and commentary by Pilgerstorfer, (2008) 37 ILJ 279.)

The courts have sometimes allowed severance of illegal terms leaving the remainder of the contract valid and enforceable in respect of employment rights. They have also in some cases permitted the less blameworthy party to the contract to enforce it where he has been the victim of fraud, duress, or oppression by the other party.

Incidental illegality during the course of a contract does not necessarily render it wholly void. An unfair dismissal action may be brought where contractual obligations are capable of being performed lawfully, and were initially intended so to be lawfully performed, but they have in fact been performed by unlawful means. Thus in *Coral Leisure Group Ltd* v *Barnett* (1981) a public relations officer for the appellant's casino operation who claimed that he regularly obtained prostitutes for gamblers who patronised the company's clubs could bring a claim since the intention of the contract was originally lawful; illegality was later and incidental to its performance.

Geographical limitations

The Employment Relations Act 1999, s. 32 abolished the complicated rules on geographical limitations. The exclusions differed between different employment protection rights, and the differences reflected the different history of the rights concerned rather than any clear or apparent differences of policy. Nevertheless it remains the case that territorial restrictions apply, normally requiring employment to be in Great Britain at the time of the dismissal or relevant time, to give employees eligibility to bring claims. This is because legislation, by its nature, is territorially limited in application. (See *Lawson* v *Serco Ltd* (2006); Linden, (2006) 35 ILJ 186; *Crofts* v *Cathay Pacific Airways Ltd* (2005).)

The nature of the employment

Statutory protection of certain employees is modified in several respects.

The definition of Crown servants has already been considered. Employees of central government and Territorial Army Associations in permanent pensionable posts are not covered by the redundancy payment scheme. They have their own rather better special provisions. On the other hand, civil servants are specifically included within the scope of the unfair dismissal provisions (ERA 1996, s. 191) although they and other employees may be excluded by reason of national security (s. 193). Redundancy payments legislation does not apply to any person 'in respect of his employment in any capacity under the Government of an overseas territory' (ERA 1996, s. 160). The doctrine of sovereign immunity applied to a clerk at the Indian High Commission in London since the dismissal was an act done in pursuance of the Republic of India's public function (*Sengupta* v *Republic of India* (1983)).

Domestic servants in a private household where the employer is a close relative are also excluded from the right to claim redundancy payments (s. 161(1)).

Exclusion by agreement

It would render the unfair dismissal provisions virtually meaningless if employers and employees could agree between themselves to exclude their operation, particularly given the greater bargaining power of the employer. Therefore, by ERA 1996, s. 203, any provision in an agreement is void insofar as it purports to exclude or limit the operation of the unfair dismissal provisions or insofar as it precludes any person from pursuing a claim for unfair dismissal. This has a wide scope of application, especially since it may exclude even accepting a contractual variation. Its aim has been described as to 'protect employees from entering perhaps into misguided bargains before their claim is heard by the [employment] tribunal' (*Times Newspapers Ltd* v *Fitt* (1981)). Nevertheless, an employee who enters into such a void agreement which involves a payment to him of a sum greater than the statutory maximum may still bring a claim under the Act, on the grounds that an employee has the right to have his compensation assessed by a tribunal, according to the EAT in *NRG Victory Reinsurance Ltd* v *Alexander* (1992).

In *Tocher* v *General Motors (Scotland) Ltd* (1981) the employers concluded an agreement with the union to deploy employees made redundant on new work removing other employees whose positions were not redundant (a so-called 'bumping' agreement). The applicant lorry driver volunteered for redundancy, but since the employers wished to keep him they put him in the less skilled position of washer operator for which he received £6 per week less. He tried it but resigned after ten days. The tribunal said that his taking the job amounted to an agreed variation of contract, so that on his resignation, since there had been no dismissal, he could not claim a redundancy payment. The EAT allowed an appeal on the ground that, although the agreement was incorporated into the contract of employment, it was rendered void since it purported to exclude or limit the operation of the redundancy payments legislation and deprived the employee of his right to a trial period in the alternative employment.

Notwithstanding the amplitude of s. 203, there are certain strictly defined circumstances in which an agreement, whether collective or individual, might exclude these vital forms of employment protection. We now consider these in turn.

(a) *Dismissal procedure agreements* The Secretary of State may by statutory instrument exclude parties to a dismissal procedure agreement or redundancy payments agreement from the scope of the legislation (ERA 1996, s. 110), and similar provisions apply to handling redundancies and guarantee payments. They are all designed to encourage domestic procedures tailored to the particular needs of different industries. The statutory requirements have proved too stringent for their widespread development. In the case of redundancies, an application must be made by all parties and the agreement must result in submission of disputes to an ET. In the case of unfair dismissal pacts, s. 110(3) requires that every union which is a party to it must be independent, that procedures must be available without discrimination to all employees of the description covered by it, and that the remedies must on the whole be as beneficial as in the statute. There must also be recourse to an independent body or ET in the final stage, and it must be possible to determine with reasonable certainty whether or not a particular employee is covered by the agreement.

The Secretary of State may revoke an order if that is the desire of all the parties to it or it has ceased to fulfil all the statutory conditions.

(b) *ACAS conciliation* The unfair dismissal legislation seeks to promote conciliation. Even though the statute does not normally countenance such an agreement excluding the right to claim, there must be some restricted circumstances in which they may bind the parties. The compromise reached by the statute is that, to be enforceable, agreements must be made under the guidance of an ACAS conciliation officer. This is insurance against an employer using his extra bargaining power to prevail on an employee. Therefore, by ERA 1996, s. 203, any agreement which purports to exclude any person from presenting a complaint to an ET is void unless a conciliation officer has 'taken action' under Employment Tribunals Act 1996, s. 18. This has been in place since the formation of ACAS but was supplemented in 1993 by a more flexible form of compromise agreement in which ACAS do not have to be involved.

The general statutory role of the officer is to endeavour to promote a settlement or where appropriate to seek to promote agreement on a sum in compensation. The conciliator need not do much to have taken action, according to the House of Lords. In *Moore* v *Duport Furniture Products Ltd* (1982) the applicant was suspended on suspicion of stealing from his employers. An ACAS conciliation officer was contacted for advice and eventually the employer and employee agreed on the payment of a lump sum for the latter's resignation in return for the employee withdrawing his claim to the tribunal. The officer took no part in these negotiations, but did record the details of the settlement in the standard ACAS form COT3. Later the employee sought to go back on the arrangement and claimed to have been unfairly dismissed. The House of Lords held that the minimal 'action' taken here by the conciliation officer was sufficient to make the agreement binding. Moreover, there was no duty on the officer to promote a *fair* settlement (as the applicant had argued). It seemed to Cumming-Bruce LJ 'inconceivable or extremely unlikely that Parliament intended to make it impossible for parties who have arrived at a settlement between them before a conciliation officer arrives on the scene to render that settlement valid to exclude a complaint to an industrial tribunal'.

Such agreement need not be in writing, and is enforceable even though the COT3 form is left unsigned (*Gilbert* v *Kembridge Fibres Ltd* (1984)). In *Slack* v *Greenham (Plant Hire) Ltd* (1983), an agreement was not void because the conciliation officer did not advise the employee of the possibility that he could claim future loss of earnings. The officer's duty must depend on the circumstances of each case, and here the applicant was an intelligent man keen to have a settlement without delay. An agreement might, however, be set aside if the officer were to act in bad faith or adopt unfair methods when promoting the settlement. In *Hennessey* v *Craigmyle & Co. Ltd and ACAS* (1986) the Court of Appeal confirmed that the doctrine of duress could apply to settlements of tribunal proceedings, but this will be established only in the most exceptional circumstances. Here the settlement was not invalidated by the fact that at the date of its signing the applicant had not been dismissed or given notice of dismissal.

(c) *Compromise agreements* Since the TURERA 1993, certain other agreements not to take proceedings before ETs have been exempted from the general rule that such agreements are void. By ERA 1996, s. 203(3) certain compromise agreements are effective which comply with the following stringent conditions:

(i) The agreement must be written (s. 203(3)(a)).

(ii) The agreement must relate to the particular proceedings (s. 203(3)(b)).

(iii) The employee must have 'received advice from a relevant independent adviser as to the terms and effect of the proposed agreement and its effect on his ability to pursue his rights before an employment tribunal' (s. 203(3)(c)).

(iv) There must be in force, when the adviser gives the advice, an insurance policy or an indemnity 'covering the risk of a claim by the employee in respect of loss arising in consequence of the advice' (s. 203(3)(d)).

(v) The agreement must identify the adviser (s. 203(3)(e)).

(vi) The agreement must state that the 'conditions regulating compromise agreements under this Act are satisfied' (s. 203(3)(f)).

A 'relevant independent adviser' covers not only qualified lawyers but others certified as competent by trade unions or advice centres, or described as such in an order made by the Secretary of State (s. 203(4)). A single compromise agreement may cover claims under more than one statute (*Lunt* v *Merseyside TEC* (1999)) but it cannot seek to exclude potential claims that have not yet arisen on the off-chance that they might be raised. If a series of claims have been raised by the employee, whether in correspondence or an originating application, all may be covered by a compromise agreement. However, all claims must be identified. A blanket term such as 'all statutory rights' is insufficient—see *Hinton* v *University of East London* (2005).

Police service

A person employed in the police service is excluded from many of the rights in the TULR(C)A 1992 and the ERA 1996 but not discrimination provisions or the right to a written statement of terms, minimum notice, or redundancy payments. 'Police service' here means service as a member of a statutory constabulary or in any other capacity by virtue of which the person has the powers and privileges of a constable. It includes prison officers (*Home Office* v *Robinson and Prison Officers' Association* (1981)).

National security

Where the dismissal occurs for the purposes of securing national security the tribunal is to consider that as automatically fair (ERA 1996, s. 10(1)). In *Council of Civil Service Unions* v *Minister for the Civil Service* (1985) (the GCHQ case, which concerned the removal of employment protection rights and rights to trade union membership because of national security considerations), the House of Lords held that, although ministers acting under prerogative powers might be under a duty to act fairly (or with statutory powers), it was for the Government and not for the courts to decide whether questions of fairness were outweighed by questions of national security. The Government alone has the necessary information to make such decisions, and in any event the judicial process is unsuitable for reaching decisions on national security. However, Lord Diplock did say this:

… if the decision is successfully challenged, on the ground that it has been reached by a process which is unfair, then the Government is under an obligation to produce evidence that the decision was in fact based on grounds of national security.

So long as the reason is shown to be related to national security, whether evidence has to be adduced to prove that or not, the tribunal has no jurisdiction. (It is not necessary that the employer be the government, and private employers may claim exemption under this head according to the EAT in *B* v *BAA* (2005).) As Sandra Fredman has written, the standard of proof in national security cases seems to be markedly lower than before ((1985) 14 ILJ 42 at p. 45).

Dismissal during strike or lock-out

The provisions of the ERA 1996 concerning dismissal during lock-out, strike or other industrial action form a borderline where collective and individual labour law meet. The interconnection is not altogether happy, and the tensions are apparent in the case law. One can see in particular the natural desire of ETs to avoid deciding on the merits of industrial disputes.

If at the time of the dismissal the employer was conducting a lock-out or the employee was taking part in a strike or other industrial action when all so participating are dismissed, and none re-engaged within three months of the dismissal, the tribunal shall not determine whether the dismissal was fair or unfair. In effect, the employer has an immunity. In fact the employer does not have to prove that the industrial dispute was the reason for the dismissal, merely that such termination coincided with the industrial action. The employer may even deliberately provoke the stoppage to remove his workforce with financial impunity.

The general position, in TULR(C)A 1992, s. 238, is subject to an important exception in s. 238(2). If only some of those taking part in official industrial action have been dismissed or have not been offered re-engagement within the three-month period, an unfair dismissal claim may be brought. However, if the action is unofficial being neither endorsed nor authorised by the union in accordance with TULR(C)A 1992, s. 20 (considered in Chapter 15 below), there is no right to complain of unfair dismissal at all (TULR(C)A 1992, s. 237).

In *Hindle Gears Ltd* v *McGinty* (1984) Waite J thought that the general immunity:

is subject … to stringent sanctions, designed to deter employers from abusing the immunity by treating a strike as a pretext for dismissing the unwanted elements in their workforce and retaining the remainder … Motive is irrelevant. Inadvertance makes no difference. The rule is wholly rigid and inflexible. The result (as the authorities show) has been to turn the process of dismissal of a striking workforce into something like a game of hazard in which the winner takes all, in which defeat or victory turns upon the fall of a single card and in which the stakes increase dramatically according to the number involved.

As Browne-Wilkinson J said in *Coates* v *Modern Methods and Materials Ltd* (1982), in s. 238 cases 'it is of great importance to employers that they should so far as possible know the consequences of their acts before they decide to dismiss and who to retain or re-engage'. The costs of getting it wrong from the employer's point of view may indeed be great.

'Strike' is undefined for the purposes of s. 238. Lord Denning's definition in the contractual case of *Tramp Shipping Corporation* v *Greenwich Marine Inc.* (1975) has been applied in this context. The then Master of the Rolls considered that a strike was 'a concerted stoppage of work by men done with a view to improving their wages or conditions or giving vent to a grievance or making a protest about something or other or sympathising with other workmen in such endeavours'. An individual protest did not qualify in *Bowater Containers Ltd* v *Blake* (1981), but the EAT came to the opposite conclusion in *Lewis and Britton* v *E. Mason & Sons* (1994) in which even a mere threat of industrial action by an individual was considered enough to bring the case within s. 238. It would be surprising if this decision were to be followed.

Tribunals and appeal bodies have been reluctant to place a rigid limit on the activities which might constitute other industrial action for the purposes of s. 238. It is a question of fact in each case (*Express & Star Ltd* v *Bunday* (1988)) which, as Brian Napier has written ((1988) 17 ILJ 50 at p. 53) places great faith in those engaged in industrial relations to recognise different forms of industrial action, which at times can be of legal significance. The phrase includes a go-slow, work-to-rule, concerted non-co-operation, and probably a picket of the employer's premises. Most such activity will break the implied contractual duty that an employee shall not disrupt the employer's enterprise (*Secretary of State for Employment* v *ASLEF (No. 2)* (1972)). The phrase is not, however, restricted to such a breach of contract; a concerted withdrawal of co-operation over admittedly voluntary overtime was 'other industrial action' according to the Court of Appeal in *Faust* v *Power Packing Casemakers Ltd* (1983). It was sufficient that the action applied pressure against management, and was designed to extract some benefit from management for the workforce. Controversy has arisen over participation in unauthorised mass meetings. In some businesses, especially television and newspapers, the disruptive union meeting at the peak point of production is a well-worn union tactic.

It appears that an employer may deliberately engineer a dispute and then dismiss without compensation those who participate in it. The test is merely whether the employee was dismissed in the course of the action. Whether the action was the real reason for the sacking is irrelevant to this issue (see *Faust*). This principle has the advantage of keeping the ETs away from the merits of the dispute. Moreover, as Phillips J said in *Thompson* v *Easton Ltd* (1976): 'It is rare for a strike or other industrial action to be wholly the fault of one side or the other. Almost always there is some blame on each side.' (See also *Marsden* v *Fairey Stainless Ltd* (1979).)

Employers who follow this strategy must be careful not to repudiate the contracts of employment of their employees since the workforce might accept such a breach as a constructive dismissal, and then claims would be made on grounds not of the employer's choosing. The question for the ET would then be whether, in breaching the contract, the employer acted reasonably in all the circumstances of the case (the normal ERA 1996, s. 98(4) test of reasonableness for potentially fair dismissals). The fact of going on strike in itself will not, however, be treated as the acceptance by the employee of the employer's repudiation (*Wilkins* v *Cantrell & Cochrane (GB) Ltd* (1978)).

The section has effect only if the dismissed employee was participating in the strike or other industrial action on the date of dismissal. Stephenson LJ in

Coates v *Modern Methods and Materials Ltd* (1982) considered that this vital issue on which the jurisdiction of the tribunal depended was 'just the sort of question which an industrial jury is best fitted to decide' (see to the same effect *Hindle Gears Ltd* v *McGinty* (1984)). This position was criticised with great force by the EAT in *Naylor* v *Orton & Smith Ltd* (1983). There, 33 employees were dismissed for participating in an overtime ban. Two others had voted in favour of such action at a meeting but later signed a form sent out by the employers that they would work normally. The tribunal decided that these two were not to be taken as participating in industrial action, and the EAT president considered that the appeal body could not intervene in the light of the Court of Appeal's pronouncements in *Coates*. It is, however, clear that participation must be personal and direct, and not vicariously through the agency of a shop steward (*Dixon* v *Wilson Walton Engineering Ltd* (1979)).

Whether an employee is taking part in industrial action is not to be determined by whether or not the employer knew that the employee was engaged in such action, according to the EAT in *Manifold Industries Ltd* v *Sims* (1991), reversing its previous line in *McKenzie* v *Crosville Motor Services Ltd* (1989). The later decision would appear to be more in line with the literal wording of TULR(C)A 1992, s. 238, which is not concerned with the reasons for dismissal.

In *Coates* a Mrs Leith went on strike, not because of her support for the cause in dispute, but because she was frightened that she would be abused by her fellow workers if she did not. The tribunal decided that she was nevertheless participating in the strike, so that it had jurisdiction to hear the claims of other workers who had been dismissed while she had been re-engaged after the end of hostilities. Kerr LJ did not think that the employee's reasons or motives for participating in the strike were of any moment. Such an enquiry would not be 'correct or practicable'. It would not be relevant 'to consider whether [the employee's] utterances or actions, or silence or inaction showed support, opposition or indifference in relation to the strike'. Stephenson LJ took the direct view that: 'In the field of industrial action, those who are not openly against it are presumably for it.' Eveleigh LJ, however, dissented on the ground that an employee must act in concert with the strikers to be participating in the strike, and this Mrs Leith did not do.

An employee genuinely on sick leave or holiday during a strike could not normally be said to be participating in it, even though he might have spoken to pickets when attending work to present his sickness certificate (*Hindle Gears Ltd* v *McGinty* (1984)). The position is, however, different if the employee has already taken part in the action before he goes off sick. In *Williams* v *Western Mail and Echo Ltd* (1980) members of the NUJ were given an ultimatum to discontinue industrial sanctions by a certain day or face dismissal. The applicant was away sick at the time but made clear that he would not have submitted to the ultimatum had he been well. Slynn J was not impressed by the argument that he was not to be considered as taking part in industrial action.

A genuine belief by the employer that the employee took part in a strike is not enough to rely on s. 238 in dismissing (*Thompson* v *Woodland Designs Ltd* (1980)). Moreover, the onus is on the employer to prove that the employee took part in the strike, but it is not correct that participation in a strike must be *known* to the employers before it can qualify as conduct taking part in a strike (the *McGinty* case (1984)).

The employee must be taking part in the appropriate action on the date of dismissal for the employer to remain immune from an unfair dismissal claim. The 'date of dismissal' has been construed as the actual time of dismissal. This has important consequences. In *Heath* v *J. F. Longman (Meat Salesmen) Ltd* (1973) a dispute about overtime payments for Saturday working provoked the employer to declare that if the employees did not work on the following Saturday, they would be dismissed. The applicant and two colleagues went out on strike in response to this ultimatum, but after seeing their union representatives, one of them told the employer that the strike of all of them was at an end. Even so, the employer announced that all three were dismissed. The National Industrial Relations Court was of the view that, 'once the men had telephoned and told the employer that they no longer wished to withdraw their labour and wanted to come back to work, they had in our view clearly ceased to be on strike'. The rule that a part equalled the whole day was not appropriate in this context. The essence of the decision was that the return to work had been communicated to the employer.

The employer may not dismiss with impunity those employees who have announced their intention of going on strike but have not yet begun their action (*Midland Plastics* v *Till* (1983)). If, on the other hand, a strike has already begun, and an employee who is off duty states a clear intention to become involved as soon as his shift starts, he is treated as participating from the time at which he makes his intention clear even if his shift has not started at the time of dismissal (*Winnett* v *Semarks Brothers Ltd* (1978)). There are three important questions to be asked. First, by what time does the tribunal decide whether all relevant employees have been dismissed? It appears that the dismissal of all those on strike at the same time as the applicant must have taken place by the time of the conclusion of the tribunal hearing if the employer is to have immunity. If only some have been dismissed by this time, the tribunal must examine whether the employer was fair or unfair in deciding who was to remain and who was to go (*P & O European Ferries (Dover) Ltd* v *Byrne* (1989)). This introduces a certain arbitrary element since the length of time between dismissal and hearing can vary greatly. Moreover, the reason for dismissal of the comparative employees need not be by reason of the strike but may be, for example, because of redundancy.

The second question concerns the position if participants in action have returned to work by the time of the applicant's dismissal. Following the amendments introduced by the Employment Act 1982 (now TULR(C)A 1992, s. 238(3)), any participant in strike action who has returned to work at the time of the applicant's dismissal does not amount to a 'relevant employee'. Thus, the employer need not dismiss all those on strike at any time, but merely all those participating in the disruptive action at the time of the applicant's dismissal. He may thus issue an ultimatum to his employees on strike to return or else. Moreover, only those participating in the action at the establishment 'at or from which' the complainant worked are to be considered.

The final question, whether all the employees need be involved in the same strike, was considered in *McCormick* v *Horsepower Ltd* (1981) where the appellant was one of a number of boilermakers who struck for increased pay. A fitter's mate in a different department (this was before the restriction to establishment was introduced) refused to cross the picket lines of the boilermakers. The appellant claimed that the other employee was a relevant employee for the purposes of what is now TULR(C)A 1992, s. 238 who had not been dismissed. The Court of Appeal disagreed on the ground that there was no agreement between the parties to take industrial action.

As already mentioned, a tribunal must consider whether all participating in a strike or other industrial action have been dismissed and whether some have been re-engaged. If not all have been dismissed or some but not others have been re-engaged the tribunal has jurisdiction to consider the reason for the non-dismissal or re-engagement of some but not others on its merits in each case. An offer of re-engagement is defined as an offer of the same job as that held before dismissal or in a different job which would be reasonably suitable in the case of the employee. This focuses on the nature of the work and the place where it is to be carried on. An offer may so qualify even though it requires that the employee be treated as on the second warning stage of the disciplinary procedure (*Williams* v *National Theatre Board Ltd* (1982)). The question is one of fact and degree for the ET to decide in each case.

Even if the employer were not aware that the employee was previously dismissed for having taken part in industrial action (which is most likely in large organisations with various places of work) such a mistake will not mean there is no re-engagement for the purposes of TULR(C)A 1992, s. 238, according to the EAT in *Bigham and Keogh* v *GKN Kwikform Ltd* (1992), for the employer may have constructive if not actual knowledge of the reason for the dismissal.

Where there is a selective dismissal or re-engagement the employer must reveal the criteria on which he made his choice as to who should go and who should stay. He must show that his selection criteria are fair in all the circumstances of the case so that if the reason for picking and choosing would be invalid if there were no strike, it is likely to be invalid in this situation. The fact that the employee was on strike may be taken into account. The EAT in *Laffin and Callaghan* v *Fashion Industries (Hartlepool) Ltd* (1978) said that 'a valid matter to be considered is the loyalty of those who serve during the strike but…by the same token to give *carte blanche* to the loyalty of those who did work is likely to cause indignation among those who…did not stay loyal to the management'.

Section 238 is subject to an important exception, namely where there is 'protected industrial action'—see p. 158.

7.2 Dismissal

The applicant must also show that there was a dismissal. The definitions are to be found in ERA 1996, s. 95(1) (for unfair dismissal) and s. 136(1) (for redundancy). An employee shall be treated as dismissed only in the following circumstances:

(a) when the contract under which the employee is employed by the employer is terminated by the employer, with or without notice;

(b) when he is employed under a limited-term contract, and that contract terminates by virtue of the limiting event without being renewed under the same contract;

(c) when the employee terminates that contract, with or without notice in circumstances such that he is entitled to terminate it without notice by reason of the employer's conduct.

All three species of dismissal essentially focus on the termination of the contract of employment rather than on the relationship of the employer and employee. One consequence is that an employee can claim to have been dismissed even though taken back by the same employer under a different contract (although it is then unlikely that he could prove unfairness) (*Hogg* v *Dover College* (1990), confirmed in *Alcan Extrusions Ltd* v *Yates* (1996); however, these decisions have been described as contrary to authority, imprecise and impracticable by one writer (see White, (1997) 26 ILJ 252)).

Other forms of termination, which should be contrasted with dismissal, have been considered in Chapter 4 above. It is often difficult to distinguish between, for example, termination by agreement and employer termination.

7.2.1 **Employer termination (ERA 1996, ss 95(1)(a), 136(1)(a))**

The concept of direct dismissal appears obvious in scope at first sight. Some cases, however, are not clear-cut, and courts and tribunals have in particular required that words of dismissal should be unequivocal and set a date for the end of employment. It is essential to distinguish clearly words of dismissal from words which are equivocal or uttered in the heat of the moment. Where words are not obviously words of dismissal but the employee has interpreted them as amounting to a dismissal, tribunals have been counselled to concentrate on the employer's intention and the employee's reaction to it. For example, in *Tanner* v *D. T. Kean Ltd* (1978) the respondent lost his temper on finding that the employee had taken the company's van and he ended his somewhat vitriolic attack by saying: 'You're finished with me'. The EAT decided that these words were spoken in anger, and were not meant to be an effective dismissal. In *Martin* v *Yeoman Aggregates Ltd* (1983) the employee was angrily told to leave when he refused to obtain a spare part for the car of a director. Within five minutes the director had eaten his words and instead suspended the employee without pay so that a more rational decision might be taken about the incident. The employee, however, insisted that he had been dismissed. Kilner Brown J considered that it was a matter of plain common sense vital to industrial relations that an employer and employee should be given the opportunity of recanting from words spoken in the heat of the moment. It was a question of degree for the tribunal in each case to decide whether the change of mind is too late to recover from the unwise and unwonted words. (See too *Kwik-Fit (GB) Ltd* v *Lineham* (1992).) However, in some circumstances, even where the words used are unequivocal and unambiguous, the tribunal is entitled to look at what was meant (*Sovereign House Security Services* v *Savage* (1989)), but it is not altogether clear when this may be justified. It is always advisable to treat even unambiguous termination as requiring written confirmation.

To be effective, a dismissal, although it may be with or without notice, must set a date for termination or at least make it possible to ascertain such a date. Thus a dismissal would be valid which was to take effect on Guy Fawkes Day since that is easily identifiable, whereas a sacking to take effect when Grimsby Town FC win the FA Cup would not be. A vital distinction is thus drawn between an actual dated dismissal and advance warning that a termination may occur (*Hicks* v *Humphrey* (1967)). As Lord Parker CJ stated in *Morton Sundour Fabrics Ltd* v *Shaw* (1967): 'As a matter of law you cannot dismiss an employee by saying "I intend to dispense with your services in the coming months".' This is not to deny that a very long period of notice, even a year in length, may be given, but a final date must always be set and communicated to the individual concerned. In *Doble* v *Firestone Tyre Co. Ltd* (1981) the respondents declared towards the end of 1979 that their Brentford factory would shut on 15 February 1980, and their statement continued with the assurance that: 'Obviously we will be keeping these plans under constant review and any change will be notified to you.' Less comforting was the indication that 'notices of termination will be issued as they become due'. In the atmosphere of insecurity thus engendered, the appellant naturally saw his best course in securing alternative employment as quickly as possible. He took this up on 17 December 1979, and claimed both a redundancy payment and unfair dismissal. The EAT upheld the employer's contention that he had not been dismissed and Waterhouse J echoed Lord Widgery's statement in *Morton* that:

The employee has the perfectly secure right if he thinks fit to wait until his contract is determined, to take his redundancy payment, and then see what he can do in regard to obtaining other employment. If he does, and one can appreciate that there may be compelling reasons, choose to leave his existing employment before the last minute in order to look for a new job before the rush of others competing with him comes, then it is up to him. The effect of the employer's warning is not in any way to derogate from his statutory rights but to give him an alternative which, if he is so minded, he can accept.

(See also *Tunnel Holdings Ltd* v *Woolf* (1976).)

The rule can work with particular harshness when uncertainty descends on a business, yet the employee who leaves has no remedy. An indication that his job is at risk, even that the factory where he works 'will close within a year', is not an anticipatory breach of contract according to the EAT in *Haseltine Lake & Co.* v *Dowler* (1981). (See also *International Computers* v *Kennedy* (1981).) This is because for such a breach it must be inevitable that an actual breach will occur in due course because the other party to the contract has renounced it whether by showing that he intends not to be bound by it or that he has rendered performance impossible by putting it out of his power to perform it. However, a termination with proper notice cannot constitute a repudiation (*Land and Wilson* v *West Yorkshire MCC* (1981)).

The same rules formulated in *Morton* as to dates of dismissal apply to resignations (*Hughes* v *Gwynedd AHA* (1978)), so that a statement that the applicant intended to leave her job to have her baby and would not return would not be sufficient since it would be merely a statement of present intention. On the other hand, an announcement that 'I am resigning' contains no ambiguity according to the Court of Appeal in *Sothern* v *Franks Charlesly & Co.* (1981), and takes effect at once.

There can be a termination by the employer, and thus direct dismissal, when he repudiates the contract of employment. This may be constituted, for example, by his insistence on a change in terms (*Marriott* v *Oxford Co-op Society Ltd (No. 2)* (1970)), or by making it impossible for the employee to continue by closing the factory at which the employee worked (*Maher* v *Fram Gerrard Ltd* (1974)). This is more normally treated as a constructive dismissal, but the fact that it is a termination by the employer within s. 95(1)(a) does have some consequences in respect of effective date of termination and the acceptance of breach.

Termination of one series of tasks where a contract is severable does not amount to a dismissal according to the Court of Appeal in *Land and Wilson* v *West Yorkshire MCC* (1981). Once given, notice of termination may not be retracted without the agreement of the other side (*Harris & Russell Ltd* v *Slingsby* (1973)). The question whether or not there has been a dismissal is one of fact for the ET (*Martin* v *MBS Fastenings (Glynwed) Distribution Ltd* (1983)).

There is also a dismissal when the employer has given notice to the employee, but during that period the employee gives shorter counter-notice—ss 95(2), 136(3). This is to deal with the situation where an employee, who may not have otherwise left his employment, on being dismissed seeks another job which he needs or wants to begin before his notice expires. In such circumstances the reason for the dismissal remains that of the employer had there been no counter-notice.

7.2.2 Limited-term contracts (ERA 1996, ss 95(1)(b), 136(1)(b))

The old presumption of yearly hiring, which was appropriate to a predominantly agricultural community, vanished long ago (e.g. *Richardson* v *Koefod* (1969)), so that most contracts of employment are now of indefinite duration but usually determinable by notice on either side. A significant sector of the workforce is, however, engaged for a fixed term of so many weeks, months, or years. This is especially so among high status professionals employed for specific tasks, like managers or researchers. Unlike the normal type of continuous contracts, those for a fixed term end automatically and the employer need take no steps to terminate them. At common law they are thus discharged by agreement or performance so there is no remedy for wrongful dismissal. However, on enactment of the new statutory jurisdictions it was felt that special rules were essential to assimilate all contracts, so that thousands of workers would not for such rather fortuitous reasons be denied the right to claim a remedy for unfair dismissal or a redundancy payment. Thus the expiry of a limited-term contract of employment without its being renewed is deemed a dismissal.

Can a fixed-term contract (to use the earlier term) be 'unfixed' by earlier notice? In *Wiltshire CC* v *NATPHE* (1980) the Court of Appeal held that it could not. The applicant, a part-time teacher at Swindon College, received a fresh contract of employment at the beginning of every academic year. Each agreement was subject to early termination if interest in the courses she taught did not remain at a satisfactory level. The employer's argument that this amounted to a contract for a particular purpose, and thus not for a fixed term, was rejected since there was a determinable ending point. On the other hand, the court indicated that a seaman engaged for a voyage or a man hired to cut down a certain number of trees would be employed on a contract terminating by performance. A person employed for 'the duration of the present government' would not have a contract for a fixed term. Lawton LJ said: 'A "term" means a period. A "fixed term" means a term with a defined beginning and a defined end.' Lord Denning MR concurred saying: 'If there is a contract by which a man is to do a particular task or carry out a particular purpose then when that task or purpose comes to an end the contract is discharged by performance.' While this cannot be gainsaid on the construction of the Act, the distinction may prove arbitrary in practice. The parties are unlikely to have referred to the issue in deciding whether to give the contract fixed dates. In some cases it may be a mere matter of words. (See too *Dixon* v *BBC* (1978).)

Even assuming a limited-term contract, there is a dismissal under the subsection only where it expires without being renewed under the same contract, and not when it is prematurely terminated or renewed. By s. 235 'renewal' includes extension.

7.2.3 Constructive dismissal (ERA 1996, ss 95(1)(c), 136(1)(c))

The ERA 1996 reflects the common law position that an employee may be entitled to resign in reaction to his employer's behaviour and yet claim to have been dismissed. Otherwise the employer could make life so difficult for the employee that he has to leave, yet escape liability since he has not actually terminated his contract. The most difficult questions raised by the concept concern the nature of conduct which entitles the employee to leave and whether the particular worker has in fact genuinely reacted to that conduct in leaving.

History

The history of the provision is somewhat complicated. It was first introduced by Redundancy Payments Act 1965, s. 3(1)(a) but applied only where the employee was entitled to terminate his contract without notice and did not in fact give such notice. Where the employee gave notice, often because he thought he was under an obligation to do so under his contract, he had to rely on the employer's breach as in itself a termination. Although the Court of Appeal was prepared to countenance the theory of automatic termination in these circumstances in *Marriott* v *Oxford District Co-op Society Ltd (No. 2)* (1970), Lord Denning MR later said that he and his brethren there had 'stretched the law a bit' (*Western Excavating (ECC) Ltd* v *Sharp* (1978)).

A similar judicial development occurred in unfair dismissal, since on its introduction in the Industrial Relations Act 1971 there was no provision for constructive dismissal at all. It was enacted for unfair dismissal in 1974 in what remains its present form. The amendment to the present definition for the purposes of redundancy was effected in 1975.

What conduct entitles the employee to terminate?

For constructive dismissal, the statute requires that the employee be entitled to terminate his contract by reason of his employer's conduct, and two alternative criteria have over time struggled for recognition as the proper construction of 'entitled'. The broad view, propounded *inter alia* in *George Wimpey & Co. Ltd* v *Cooper* (1977), was that the statute required only 'conduct of a kind which in accordance with good industrial relations practice no employee could reasonably be expected to accept'. This test, however, received its quietus in *Western Excavating (ECC) Ltd* v *Sharp* (1978), where the Court of Appeal held that the employer must be in fundamental breach of contract for the employee to be able to claim constructive dismissal. It was a case with particularly strong facts which left the higher courts with little sympathy for the employee. He was originally suspended from work for taking an afternoon off to play cards and in his consequent self-inflicted financial plight he asked the company for his accrued holiday pay or a loan. When the employers refused, he resigned. The tribunal decided in his favour on the preliminary issue of dismissal, but the Court of Appeal found this decision to be perverse. The determination of whether the employee was 'entitled to terminate' was, in their view, a purely contractual matter. Lord Denning MR said:

If the employer is guilty of conduct which is a significant breach going to the root of the contract of employment or which shows that the employer no longer intends to be bound by one or more of the essential terms then the employee is entitled to treat himself as discharged from any further performance. If he does so, then he terminates the contract by reason of the employer's conduct. He is constructively dismissed. The employee is entitled in those circumstances to leave at the instant without giving any notice at all, or alternatively he may give notice and say he is leaving at the end of his notice. But the conduct in either case must be sufficiently serious to entitle him to leave at once.

The employee could not claim to have been constructively dismissed since the appellants had committed no breach of contract. The Court of Appeal gave several reasons for preferring this more stringent contractual approach. First, the statute distinguished between dismissal and unfairness and it was anomalous to have the same test of reasonableness applying to both. The words in subsection (c), 'terminates' and 'entitled', had a legal, and hence contractual, connotation. In any event, the test of unreasonableness was too indefinite by far, and had, according to Lord Denning MR, led to decisions on 'the most whimsical grounds'. Lastly, there was no difficulty in tribunals applying it since anyone of common sense could apply the contractual test.

The reasonableness test appeared to be subtly reintroduced in *Woods* v *WM Car Services (Peterborough) Ltd* (1982), when Watkins LJ commented, in determining whether the employee had been constructively dismissed, that:

Employers must not in my opinion be put in a position where, through the wrongful refusal of their employees to accept change, they are prevented from introducing business methods in furtherance of seeking success from their enterprise.

It appears that this *obiter* remark is confined to the facts of the case since the EAT emphasised in *Wadham Stringer Commercials (London) Ltd* v *Brown* (1983) that neither the circumstances inducing the fundamental breach by the employer nor the circumstances which led the employee to accept the repudiation were relevant to the question of constructive dismissal. However, the contractual test was given further support by the Court of Appeal in *Courtaulds Northern Spinning Ltd* v *Sibson* (1988), when the idea was rejected that an employer's request to an employee to move to another place of work was a constructive dismissal as it was not reasonable. This was not relevant. The court also said that, in order to imply a term into the contract, it was not necessary to examine what the parties would have agreed to before entering into the contract, but to look at what the parties would have agreed to if they were being reasonable. The difference between this and a reasonableness test is in practice of very little effect. Of course it may be necessary for the courts to examine reasonableness in circumstances where it is necessary, for business efficacy, to imply some term into the contract but, as Holland and Chandler have pointed out ((1988) 17 ILJ 253), the courts should not invent terms for the parties. Although the employee's attitude in not agreeing to be moved was difficult to defend on its facts, this should not have detracted from his contractual rights.

Examples of constructive dismissal

There are numerous examples in the case law where a constructive dismissal has been held to have occurred. A deliberate reduction in pay is the repudiation *par excellence*, since: 'The basic rate of pay is a fundamental element in any contract of employment and in our opinion it cannot be said that there is no material breach on the part of an employer who proposes to reduce the basic rate even for good reasons and to a relatively small extent' (*Industrial Rubber Products* v *Gillon* (1977)). This is, however, subject to the *de minimis* rule, so that the sharing out with fellow employees of 1½p per hour bonus for lifting crates of empty bottles, which would at most reduce the applicant's wages by £1.50 per week out of a total of £60, was held not to be fundamental. On the other hand, abolition of a 1 per cent commission was held to be repudiatory, even though the introduction of a new scheme might eventually at least restore that loss. The crucial point was that at the time of resignation this could only be a matter for speculation (*R. F. Hill Ltd* v *Mooney* (1981)). It may be sufficient that the employer fails to increase pay in line with contractual entitlement (*Pepper & Hope* v *Daish* (1980)).

Another example is where an acting manager had his 'most interesting and enjoyable duties' of buying greengroceries removed from him, and this constituted constructive dismissal (*Coleman* v *S. & W. Baldwin* (1977)). The importance of the change is a question of degree and, in assessing the scope of job duties, it is pertinent to examine not only the employee's statement of terms, but also the advertisement by which he was attracted to the post and all surrounding circumstances in order to build up a full picture of what he was employed to do (*Pederson* v *Camden LBC* (1981)). Temporary changes are treated less severely than permanent imposed variations and the EAT has held that:

> If an employer under the stresses of the requirements of his business directs an employee to transfer to other suitable work on a purely temporary basis and at no diminution in wages that may in the ordinary case not constitute a breach of contract. However, it must be clear that 'temporary' means a period which is either defined as being a short fixed period...or which is in its nature of limited duration.

In *Millbrook Furnishing Industries Ltd* v *McIntosh* (1981), where Browne-Wilkinson P enunciated this principle, a transfer of highly skilled sewing machinists in the respondent company's upholstery department to unskilled work in their bedding section was a breach, because it was to last until work picked up in the former section and this could not be at all accurately estimated at the time of application (see also *McNeill* v *Charles Crimin (Electrical Contractors) Ltd* (1984)).

Whether a forced change in the place of work (see *Hawker Siddeley Power Engineering Ltd* v *Rump* (1979); *Courtaulds Northern Spinning Ltd* v *Sibson* (1988)) is a fundamental enough breach of contract 'is a question of degree to be determined according to all the circumstances such as the nature of the work, the circumstances in which it is performed and the circumstances of the place to which the work is to be transferred'. Thus neither the moves in Central London of Times Newspapers from Printing House Square to Grays Inn Road (*Times Newspapers Ltd* v *Bartlett* (1976)), nor of a restaurant from Holborn to Regent Street was a fundamental breach of contract (*Managers (Holborn) Ltd* v *Hohne* (1977)).

Other potentially fundamental breaches include: change in hours of work (*Derby CC* v *Marshall* (1979)); suspension by employer without contractual authority;

failure to provide work where this is an implied term; failure to provide a safe system of work (*Keys* v *Shoefayre Ltd* (1978)); failure to follow a contractual disciplinary procedure (*Post Office* v *Strange* (1981)); punishment out of all proportion to the offence (*BBC* v *Beckett* (1983)).

A constructive dismissal may arise by way of an anticipatory breach. In *Norwest Holst Group Administration Ltd* v *Harrison* (1985), the Court of Appeal decided that an employer who threatened a breach was entitled to withdraw the threat at any time before the innocent party communicated his unequivocal acceptance of the repudiation. The employee was engaged as director and chief engineer, but was told by letter on 14 June 1982 that he would lose his directorship as from 1 July 1982. The employee replied by letter headed 'Without prejudice' that he was not prepared to accept the loss of the directorship. Faced with this, the company withdrew the threat but later on that day the employee sought to accept the repudiation. The Court of Appeal did not think that this could be a constructive dismissal.

A sign that the EAT is willing to stretch the notion of a breach of contract was given in *Greenaway Harrison Ltd* v *Wiles* (1994) when it held that a threat by an employer of a lawful termination itself amounted to a breach of contract. It is difficult to see what term of the contract can have been broken here or, indeed, how this situation can be distinguished from that where the employer gives an employee a warning.

Before a contract of employment can be terminated, there must have been communication by words or by conduct such as to inform the other party to the contract that it is at an end. Thus an employee alleging constructive dismissal must communicate to the employer the fact that he is terminating his employment (*Edwards* v *Surrey Police* (1999)). It is also important, for there to be a breach which amounts to a constructive dismissal, that the employer has not done all in its power to remedy the breach. If it has, then it is not open to the employee to subsequently resign and claim to have been constructively dismissed, according to the EAT in *Bournemouth University Higher Education Corporation* v *Buckland* (2009). In this case, the employer itself had set up an internal enquiry which had completely cleared the employee of any failure, but only later did the employee resign. (See Calibri, (2009) 38 ILJ 403.) However, note that the decision in *Bournemouth* was determined by the finding that the breach had been cured by the employer, and so the issue as to whether any constructive dismissal was fair, and the principles upon which that should be determined, were not necessary to the EAT's decision. There had been no dismissal which needed to be tested for fairness.

The breach must be fundamental

In all these cases the breach in question must be fundamental. This means that the conduct of the employer must be of a serious nature and, in the normal case, occur over a period of time. However, what is not normally a fundamental breach in respect of a new employee may be sufficient to justify resignation where the employee has given long and faithful service. A small straw may break this doughty camel's back. The question is always one of degree, but the following are illustrations of cases where the breach was not fundamental: failure to interview candidates for redundancy in accordance with the appropriate collective bargain (*British Leyland Ltd* v *McQuilken* (1978)); failure to pay the employee on the due date because of cash flow problems, since he was assured of full settlement in the near future

(*Adams* v *Charles Zub Associates Ltd* (1978)); failure by the employers to investigate a complaint against themselves by the employee (*GLC* v *Canning* (1980)); absence of consultation over appointment of a subordinate and not telling an employee of pay increases received by subordinates when his own increment was withheld (*Walker* v *Josiah Wedgwood & Sons Ltd* (1978); *Kenneth McRae & Co. Ltd* v *Dawson* (1984)); and failure to take further measures to limit the risk of criminal attacks at a building society agency (*Dutton & Clark Ltd* v *Daly* (1985)).

There can be no repudiatory breach and therefore no constructive dismissal where there is a dispute about the construction of the contract of employment, according to some decisions. This follows orthodox contractual reasoning, but does not fit well in the employment area. In *Frank Wright & Co. (Holdings)* v *Punch* (1980) the employee resigned when he was not paid cost of living increases. His original contract signed in 1973 had indicated that he was entitled to these rises but his statement of terms issued in 1978 did not. The EAT denied that an expression of intention by one party (here the employer) to carry out the contract only in accordance with its own erroneous interpretation was repudiatory, and thought this was especially so where there was a genuine mistake of law and fact. It placed a strict onus on the employee in this case to prove that the mistake was not genuine, and if followed this would be likely to considerably limit the scope of constructive dismissal. It was, moreover, somewhat unrealistic to expect an employee to bring an action in the county court which alone could clear up any misinterpretations. In *Financial Techniques (Planning Services) Ltd* v *Hughes* (1981) Lawton and Brandon LJJ followed the approach in *Punch*, but Templeman LJ desired to guard himself 'against the implication which might otherwise be read…that if any party to a contract has a plausible but mistaken view of his rights under that contract he may insist on that view and his insistence cannot amount to repudiation'. However, Sir John Donaldson in *Bridgen* v *Lancashire County Council* (1987) took the view that the employer must not intend to be bound by the contract as properly construed. The EAT has more recently given an indication that, at least where the employee is to blame for an employer's misapprehension, that may mean no constructive dismissal has taken place (see *Brown* v *JBD Engineering* (1993)). In other words, an employer's genuine belief may prevent his act from being a repudiatory breach.

Punch does not mean that there is no repudiation where the motive for breach was to preserve the employee's job rather than to terminate the contract; for outside of issues of contractual construction, repudiation is judged on the nature of the breach of contract and its impact on the contractual relationship of the parties and without reference to the subjective intentions of the parties in acting as they did. (See *Ready Case Ltd* v *Jackson* (1981); cf. *BBC* v *Beckett* (1983); *Bliss* v *South East Thames Regional Health Authority* (1985).)

The Court of Appeal in *Woods* v *WM Car Services (Peterborough) Ltd* (1982) decided that there was no rule of law for determining whether a particular set of facts constitutes a repudiatory breach. The EAT should interfere with the decision of the ET only if it is shown that the ET misdirected itself in law so that the decision was such that no reasonable tribunal could reach it (see also *Pederson* v *Camden LBC* (1981); cf. *McNeill* v *Charles Crimin (Electrical Contractors) Ltd* (1984)). There must be evidence that an employee's resignation was really in reaction to, and motivated by, a fundamental breach by the employer, and thus an acceptance, in orthodox theory, of his repudiation. While the worker need not use such technical language, he 'must indicate the reason why he is going and must make it plain that he is accepting a breach on the part of his employers' (*Genower* v *Ealing AHA* (1980)). A long period between breach and resignation will be difficult to explain without good reason, and may amount to waiver of any breach (*Bashir* v *Brillo Manufacturing Co.* (1979)). Lord Denning MR said in *Western Excavating* v *Sharp* (1978) that the employee must make up his mind soon after the conduct of which he complains, for if he continues for any length of time without leaving, he may lose his right to treat himself as discharged. However, this is best seen as a matter of evidence rather than as a rule of law. In other words, even if there is a lengthy gap between the repudiatory breach and the employee's resignation, so long as causation can be proved the right to claim unfair dismissal will not be lost. In *Jones* v *F. Sirl & Son (Furnishers) Ltd* (1997) a series of breaches of contract by the employer began in July 1993, but the employee did not resign until the following November, three weeks after the final breach. Nevertheless, the EAT allowed her claim of constructive dismissal.

In *Reid* v *Camphill Engravers* (1990) the employers committed a breach of statutory obligation about which the employee had done nothing for three years. But this did not disentitle the employee, because it was not within his power to waive a breach of statutory obligation. That is surely not the point. The issue should not have been whether by ignoring the breach the employee was excusing it, but whether his resignation was *caused* by the breach. Delay is very good evidence of the contrary and should perhaps have disentitled him. Had the Scottish EAT so held this would have been quite consistent with pursuing the employer's statutory obligations.

Even if an employee has not treated a breach of an express contractual term as a wrongful repudiation, he is entitled to add such a breach to other actions which taken together may cumulatively amount to a breach of the implied obligation of trust and confidence (*Lewis* v *Motorworld Garages Ltd* (1985)).

The latest time for the employee to accept the employer's repudiatory breach is at the close of his unfair dismissal claim before the ET (*Shook* v *London Borough of Ealing* (1986)). There is however no need for an employee to take the precaution of an express reservation of the right to accept repudiation when the employer has allowed the employee time to make up his mind (*Bliss* v *South East Thames Regional Health Authority* (1985). See further Carty, (1986) 49 MLR 240).

It is not necessary for an employee to give a reason for leaving at the time of leaving, especially in cases where the employer gives outrageous or embarrassing instructions, as the employee may not wish to argue the point there and then. The tribunal should look at each case on its own facts. (See *Weathersfield Ltd* v *Sargent* (1999).)

Who is the employer for these purposes?

It is a necessary element of a constructive dismissal claim that the breach must be the employer's. In many instances the conduct moving the employee to leave will be that of a supervisory employee. In determining whether such conduct is to be treated as the conduct of the employer for these purposes the proper test is not, as might be thought, whether the supervisory employee has the right to dismiss, but whether he or she was acting in the course of employment, according to the EAT in

Hilton International Hotels (UK) Ltd v *Protopapa* (1990). (See too the EAT's decision in *Warnes* v *Trustees of Cheriton Oddfellows Social Club* (1993).)

Constructive dismissal and fairness

It is a commonly held misconception at all levels that a constructive dismissal is necessarily an unfair dismissal. The fact that there has been a breach of contract (however fundamental) by the employer means, however, only that the employee has crossed the first hurdle by establishing dismissal, for the employer may seek to justify the reason for his actions. The proper question was formulated in *Savoia* v *Chiltern Herb Farms Ltd* (1982) as being whether, although in fundamental breach of contract, the employer had in all the circumstances behaved fairly and the facts of that case provide a good example of a positive answer to that question. The employers decided to reorganise their business operation after one of their foremen died. They moved the applicant into the dead man's position because they had certain complaints about his performance in his previous job. He refused what was described by the employers as a 'promotion', claiming that it would expose him to conjunctivitis. The EAT found that the reorganisation was necessary and that the employers had in the circumstances done all that they could to ease the changeover by offering him a higher salary. On the other hand, he had refused to undergo a medical so that they could judge whether his claims of potential sickness were genuine. Thus the constructive dismissal was fair.

7.2.4 Statutory extensions of dismissal

There are three further instances where, although the facts do not neatly sit within the statutory concept of dismissal as just examined, they are nevertheless deemed to constitute dismissal for the purposes of the ERA 1996.

Taking a new job for a trial period

After dismissal from one position with an employer, the employee may take on another with the aim of trying it out. This is particularly so where the termination is by way of the employer's repudiatory conduct. It would penalise the employee who attempted in this way to make a new start if he were not still entitled to claim the statutory remedies if things did not work and he then resigned. At common law, the courts often characterise the employee's acceptance of such a new post after a breach of contract by an employer as qualified and conditional. If he leaves after a reasonable period for assessing the new job, the termination relates back to the employer's original action of repudiation and he can claim his rights. In the EPA 1975, this notion of a 'trial period' was codified into statute and it is now found in ERA 1996, s. 138(3). An employee has four weeks to decide whether he accepts the new terms. This may be extended, although rather restrictively, that extension may be only for the purposes of retraining (s. 138(6)). The period is four calendar weeks, not working weeks (*Benton* v *Sanderson Kayser Ltd* (1989)).

The EAT has held that the legislation supplants the common law, contrary to an early suggestion of the EAT in *Turvey* v *C. W. Cheyney and Son Ltd* (1979)—see *Optical Express Ltd* v *Williams* (2007). This means that a claimant cannot rely on a common law right once the statutory right has expired.

Lay-off and short time

An employee may be left in a state of limbo by his employer, being given little or no work but not actually dismissed. Again statute protects him, but in this respect only allows him to claim he has been dismissed for the purposes of redundancy payments. ERA 1996, ss 147–152 and 154 provide a species of 'implied dismissal' where, for at least four consecutive weeks or at least six weeks spread over not more than 13 weeks, the employee is 'laid off' (no work provided at all for a week—s. 147(1)), or on 'short time' (i.e. where the employee receives less than half a week's pay, not including bonus—s. 147(2)). The employee may then give notice in writing equivalent to the period of notice required by his contract to his employer, indicating his intention to claim a redundancy payment. The employer may react by issuing a counter-notice that he will contest the claim, in which case the matter will be referred to an ET to decide whether 'it was reasonably to be expected that the employee would within four weeks enter on a period of at least thirteen weeks without short time or lay off'.

Implied termination

The ERA 1996, s. 136(5), which provides for 'implied termination', is unique to redundancy, and reads:

(5) Where in accordance with any enactment or rule of law—

(a) an act on the part of an employer, or

(b) an event affecting an employer (including, in the case of an individual, his death),

operates to terminate a contract under which an employee is employed by him, the act or event shall be taken for the purposes [of redundancy] to be a termination of the contract by the employer.

Again this is an example of the statute rather obscurely building on the quicksand of the common law. It comprises all the automatic dismissals including death of a personal employee, dissolution of partnership, appointment of receiver and liquidation of a company, and also a frustrating event affecting the employer such as a fire at his sole place of business, or his imprisonment. This means that even though the employee is not entitled to claim unfair or wrongful dismissal, he may be eligible for a redundancy payment, although only if the frustrating event affects the employer.

7.3 **Date of termination**

Where there has been a dismissal, it is necessary for several statutory purposes to pinpoint the actual date of termination of employment. It is relevant in determining whether the qualifying period of continuous employment has been served, and the relevant age of the employee for the purpose of exclusion from employment protection. It is also relevant in deciding whether the employee has brought the claim in time, and whether the employee is entitled to seek written reasons for his dismissal. Lastly, it is important in establishing the date on which an employee's week's pay should be calculated for the purposes of assessing a basic award or redundancy payment.

This important stage is called the 'effective date of termination' in the unfair dismissal provisions and the 'relevant date' for redundancy payments. In most respects the concepts coincide.

Where the employee is dismissed with notice the effective/relevant date is the date on which the notice expires. If the dismissal is lawfully without notice, that is, summary dismissal for gross misconduct, the effective date of termination is the date (and at the time on that date—see *Octavius Atkinson & Sons Ltd v Morris* (1989)) on which the termination takes effect. This has generally been assumed to be the date when the employer tells the worker he is sacked, but there is scope for argument since this implicitly assumes that the dismissal automatically terminates the contract. If, instead, it is brought to an end only on the other party's acceptance of that breach, it may be that the correct effective date is that of acceptance. In *Robert Cort & Son Ltd v Charman* (1981) the EAT held that, on the authorities, the effective date of termination was that of repudiation. The contract terminated at once for this purpose irrespective of whether, as a matter of contract law, the employer ought to have given notice. A recommendation for this decision was that there should be no doubt or uncertainty as to the proper date; if, however, the employee's approach were accepted, it would depend on the 'legal subtleties of the law of repudiation and the employee would not be able to understand the position'. In *Stapp v The Shaftesbury Society* (1982) the EAT held that the effective date of termination was the actual date of termination of the employment whether the employment was lawfully or wrongfully terminated and this was later supported by the decision of the Court of Appeal in *Batchelor v British Railways Board* (1987). However, it cannot be earlier than the statutory date, even if agreed by both parties, according to the Court of Appeal in *Fitzgerald v University of Kent at Canterbury* (2004).

The EAT dealt with a situation where communication is not instantaneous in *Brown v Southall and Knight* (1980), and held that the effective date of termination when dismissal was by letter was generally the date when the letter was received. Slynn J stated:

In our judgment the employer who sends a letter terminating a man's employment summarily must show that the employee has actually read the letter or at any rate had a reasonable opportunity of reading it. If the addressee of the letter to the employee does not deliberately open it or goes away to avoid reading it he might well be debarred from saying that notice of his dismissal had not been given to him.

In *McMaster v Manchester Airport plc* (1998), the EAT held that where an employee was away from his home, there could be no constructive knowledge of a letter dismissing him. As such, receipt of the letter must mean more than, for example, delivery of a letter to the employee's home. It must mean that the effective date of termination occurs when the employee actually reads the letter, in the absence of a wilful intention not to. The Court of Appeal in *CYF v Barratt* (2009) considered the issue more recently, and decided that, notwithstanding some misunderstandings of the law in the previous line of authority in the EAT, it would not divert from this well-established principle. Although in contract law the dismissal takes effect at the moment of the employer's action to dismiss, this does not mean that the effective date of termination (which is a statutory not common law concept) needs to be determined in the same way. (See too the Court of Appeal's decision in *Kirklees Metropolitan Council v Radecki* (2009).)

In construing a letter of dismissal which contains some ambiguity about the date of termination the tribunal should adopt the construction which a reasonable employee receiving it would understand (see *Chapman* v *Letherby and Christopher Ltd* (1981), *Stapp* v *The Shaftesbury Society* (1982)). The date on which tax form P45 is sent to the employee has no significance at all for these purposes (*London Borough of Newham* v *Ward* (1985)).

Where notice should have been given of a period longer than that which is given or where no notice is given, the proper statutory minimum notice is added to the actual date of the dismissal in order to determine the effective date of termination (ERA 1996, s. 97(2)). This does not, however, apply to summary and constructive dismissal nor the determination of age for the purposes of the scope of statutory protection (*Slater & Secretary for Employment* v *John Swain & Son Ltd* (1981)). The reasoning behind the general statutory extension is that it is unfair that by the employer's own wrongful act in terminating employment in breach of the statutory notice requirement he might reduce the employee's entitlement, whether the amount of basic award or taking into account a later pay rise in calculating the week's pay. Moreover, if the employee's contract provides that a period longer than the statutory minimum notice must be given to the particular employee, only the minimum number of weeks decreed by statute need be added.

This extension provision does not apply to:

(a) the start of the three or six-month period for bringing a complaint to a tribunal;

(b) written reasons for dismissal;

(c) whether the employee was striking at the time of dismissal for the purposes of TULR(C)A 1992, s. 238;

(d) the start of the seven-day period for interim relief;

(e) redundancy consultation;

(f) the requirement that an offer of renewal or re-engagement be made before the ending of the employment.

Where the contract is for a limited term, the effective date is when the limited term expires. If the employee is dismissed by reason of a strike or other industrial action, even when terminated by notice, the effective date is the date on which the notice is given; otherwise the above rules apply, as appropriate.

The courts have generally rejected attempts to extend the effective date of termination to cover periods during which an appeal is being made under an internal disciplinary procedure. In *J. Sainsbury Ltd* v *Savage* (1980) this refusal was notwithstanding that the internal disciplinary procedure provided for 'suspension without pay' pending appeal. Brightman LJ stated that: 'If an employee is dismissed...on terms that he then ceases to have the right to work under the contract of employment and that the employer ceases likewise to be under an obligation to pay the employee, the contract is at an end' (approved by the House of Lords in *West Midlands Co-operative Society Ltd* v *Tipton* (1986)). The same result was reached in *The National Heart and Chest Hospitals Board of Governors* v *Nambiar* (1981), even though there the employee was paid for a ten-month period while his appeal was pending. The principle does not depend on any express term being included in the contract (*Howgate* v *Fane Acoustics Ltd* (1981)), instead resting on the policy reason of the uncertainty of any other course, and the desirability that speed be of the essence in enforcing employment rights.

In special circumstances the parties may agree that a particular date is to be taken as the effective date of termination (*Crank* v *HMSO* (1985)). This can include extension of the date, as well as bringing it forward, according to the EAT in *Mowlem Northern Ltd* v *Watson* (1990).

Where an employee gives counter-notice to take effect before the employer's notice expires, the effective date of termination is that of the counter-notice, according to the EAT in *Thompson* v *GEC Avionics Ltd* (1991). Where, however, the employee requests, under notice, for the date of termination to be brought forward this is possible by withdrawing the original notice and substituting another notice period, according to the EAT in *Palfrey* v *Transco plc* (2004). In reaching this decision, the EAT took the view that an earlier, contrary, decision by the Court of Appeal in *TBA Industrial Products Ltd* v *Morland* (1982) was reached *per incuriam*.

SELECTED READING

Freedland, M. (2003), *The Personal Employment Contract*, Oxford: Oxford University Press, 2003, ch. 8

Linden, T. (2006), 'Employment Protection for Employees Working Abroad', (2006) 35 ILJ 186

8

Unfair dismissal

SUMMARY

This chapter examines the most important statutory remedy employees may have on losing their jobs. It begins by exploring the history of unfair dismissal law. Then the remaining stages to be completed in making a successful claim for the employee, in addition to those considered in the previous chapter, are considered in turn. First, the various reasons for a dismissal that need to be established if a claim is to be made out (or defended as the case may be) are explained. Then the next stage—what has to be established in considering whether or not a dismissal that in law has the potential to be considered unfair is actually unfair—is considered in detail. Then the important issue of remedies is examined. The chapter ends by considering the effects of the legislation in this area and whether it has been successful in its aims.

8.1 Background

The statutory claim for unfair dismissal was introduced by the Heath Administration of the early 1970s in the Industrial Relations Act 1971. It recognises that the common law cannot give adequate protection to employees through the contract of employment, in that the wrongful dismissal claim depends upon a breach of contract by an employer, usually in the form of inadequate notice being given to the employee. Many dismissals can be considered unfair which do not amount to breaches of contract, for the wrongful dismissal claim looks not to intention, motive, or the effect on an employee of a termination of the relationship nor to procedural protections, but merely to the form in which that relationship has been brought to an end.

It is now difficult to imagine a world of labour law without protection against unfair dismissal, but Britain lagged behind most European countries in providing it. Indeed, there had been recognition of the social necessity to introduce such legislation since the International Labour Organisation's (ILO's) Recommendation No. 119, accepted by Britain in 1964. It may seem surprising that this was not achieved until 1971 in that from 1964 until 1970 a Labour Government was in power, but there was still a strong feeling that much could be done through the method of collective bargaining, particularly among the trade unions. The National Joint Advisory Committee of the Ministry of Labour in 1967 also proposed such remedies. It was, however, the Report of the Donovan Commission in 1968 (Cmnd 3623) (London: HMSO, 1968) that moved consensus to a legislative framework of remedies. The legislation thus did not come to be introduced by a Conservative

Government as a product of political perversity. Indeed, as Collins has pointed out ((1982) 11 ILJ 78 at p. 87) the old pattern of national collective bargaining was giving way in the late 1960s to much more fragmented, lower level, bargaining. What he calls 'moral panic' set in over the breakdown of management and union authority. It was particularly this unofficial strike action which led to the proposed legislation, as many stoppages were against dismissals, and it was hoped that statutory unfair dismissal protection would reduce these. But the new protection was not a panacea. (See generally, Collins, (1991) 20 ILJ 227.)

8.2 Outline

The ERA 1996, s. 94 proclaims that, subject to exceptions, 'An employee shall have the right not to be unfairly dismissed by his employer'. The elaboration of this slogan caused Phillips J, after rejecting the idea that it was a common sense concept, to explain: 'It is narrowly and to some extent arbitrarily defined... it is a form of words which could be translated as being equivalent to dismissal "contrary to statute" and to which the label unfair dismissal has been given' (*Devis & Sons Ltd v Atkins* (1977)). Moreover, in some ways the statute does not adopt the most direct approach to the definition of an unfair dismissal. Once eligibility and dismissal have been established (themselves very complicated in concept and which have already been considered above), the determination is twofold. First, the employer must prove the reason or principal reason for the dismissal. Some reasons are automatically unfair (discrimination, union activity and membership, pregnancy), but the most important are only potentially fair reasons. They are: capability or qualifications; conduct; retirement; redundancy; statutory prohibition; and some other substantial reason for dismissal. Secondly, for these potentially fair reasons to be actually fair in any particular case it must be reasonable in all the circumstances for the employer to treat the reason he has given as a reason to dismiss. This process, according to Viscount Dilhorne in the leading case of *W. Devis & Sons Ltd v Atkins* (1977), directs the tribunal to focus on the conduct of the employer and not on whether the employee in fact suffered any injustice. It involves consideration of substance and procedure, the latter being most clearly set out in the ACAS Codes of Practice. (See p. 150 for a schematic depiction of the progress of an unfair dismissal claim.)

The right to bring a claim for unfair dismissal in the tribunal is available even where the employer has agreed to pay a sum equivalent to the maximum compensation under the Act, but without admitting an unfair dismissal, according to the EAT in *Telephone Information Services Ltd v Wilkinson* (1991). This is because the right is not confined to compensation but also to a finding that the dismissal was unfair.

8.3 The reason for dismissal

When it has been established that the applicant is an employee and not excluded from bringing a claim, the onus of proof moves to the employer to establish the reason for dismissal. (See s. 98.) If the employer cannot prove a reason for dismissal,

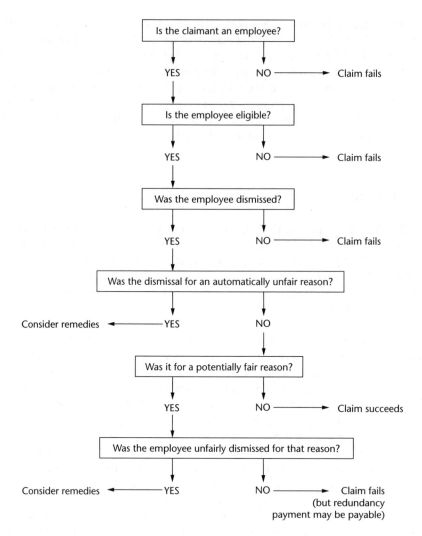

Is the claimant an employee?
- YES
- NO → Claim fails

Is the employee eligible?
- YES
- NO → Claim fails

Was the employee dismissed?
- YES
- NO → Claim fails

Was the dismissal for an automatically unfair reason?
- Consider remedies ← YES
- NO

Was it for a potentially fair reason?
- YES
- NO → Claim succeeds

Was the employee unfairly dismissed for that reason?
- Consider remedies ← YES
- NO → Claim fails (but redundancy payment may be payable)

the dismissal is therefore unfair. Having said that, the courts are sometimes willing to go a long way to assist employers in this regard. For example, in *Ely v YKK Fasteners (UK) Ltd* (1994) the employer was under the impression that the employee had resigned. Nevertheless, the Court of Appeal allowed this misapprehension to operate as a dismissal for 'some other substantial reason'. As the court admitted, this was indeed an illogical conclusion.

The employer's reason for dismissal, of which the ET must determine the fairness, is 'the set of facts known to the employer or beliefs held by him which cause him to dismiss the employee' (*Abernethy v Molt Hay and Anderson* (1974), approved in *Devis & Sons Ltd v Atkins* (1977)). This does not necessarily imply automatic acceptance by the tribunal of the reason put forward by the employer if there are grounds to think that it was not the real cause. Thus, many employers claim that they are dismissing for reasons of redundancy although this is in reality a cloak to be rid of particular employees. The 'reason for dismissal' must be that 'uppermost in the mind of the employer at the time of dismissal'. It may, however, relate to a series of incidents and not only one event (e.g. *Turner* v *Wadham Stringer Commercials (Portsmouth) Ltd* (1974)), and where there is more than one ground the tribunal must establish what was the principal factor motivating the dismissal (*Carlin* v *St Cuthbert's Co-op Association Ltd* (1974)). In *Smith* v *City of Glasgow District Council* (1987) it was held by the House of Lords that if an employer fails to satisfy one of a number of reasons that he has put forward as the reason for the dismissal, the dismissal will be unfair. As Brian Napier has pointed out ((1988) 47 CLJ 21) this makes it difficult for the employer to use a 'blunderbuss' approach by listing a number of reasons for the dismissal in the hope that some will be proved.

8.3.1 The importance of consistency

To be believed the employer must tell a consistent story and may not put forward a different reason at the tribunal from that which he stated in his response nor, on appeal, from that relied upon before the ET (*Nelson* v *BBC* (1977)), nor on an internal appeal from that initially tendered. In *Monie* v *Coral Racing Ltd* (1981) the applicant was dismissed for dishonesty and he exercised his contractual right of internal appeal. This was heard by the managing director who confirmed the dismissal, but since he found no evidence of dishonesty against Mr Monie, he gave as the reason that his failure to exercise the authorised cash control procedures justified dismissal. The court thought that the reason must be that which operated at the time of dismissal. The internal appeal made no difference. If the employer has no reason for dismissal such sacking is unfair.

8.3.2 Alternative grounds

Alternative grounds are tempting but dangerous for the employer. A tribunal is not entitled to find a dismissal fair on a ground not pleaded or argued where the difference in grounds goes to facts and substance of the case and where there would, or might have been, some substantial or significant difference in the way the case was conducted, had another reason been put forward. On the other hand, where the different grounds are different labels for the same facts (such as redundancy or some other substantial reason for dismissal), a tribunal is justified in finding that the true reason for dismissal was one which was not pleaded (*Hannan* v *TNT-IPEC (UK) Ltd* (1986); *Wilson* v *Post Office* (2000)) but where the parties are unrepresented the EAT has said that it is desirable that this is indicated during argument (see *Burkett* v *Pendletons (Sweets) Ltd* (1992)).

In *Hotson* v *Wisbech Conservative Club* (1984) the employers' notice of appearance (response) gave the reason for dismissal as 'inefficiency' but their representative at the tribunal agreed with the chairman's remark that 'in effect what you are claiming is that [the applicant] was dishonest'. The tribunal decided that the employee had been fairly dismissed on the ground of reasonably suspected dishonesty. The EAT would not let the decision stand since the suspicion must be stated at the outset by the employer. While the employer would not necessarily be tied to a 'label' he put on the fact on which he relied, he could not substitute dishonesty for negligence as a substantive reason at so late a stage. It did not give the employee sufficient opportunity to meet the challenge. However, it was suggested by the EAT in *Clarke* v *Trimoco Motor Group Ltd* (1993) that where it is obvious to the employee what the real reason for the dismissal was, that does not render the dismissal unfair. The EAT did recognise that this was on the borderline, but it is suggested it came down on the wrong side of it. The point about *Hotson* is that the employee is disadvantaged in preparing a case if the reason argued at the tribunal is different from that originally given, or stated on the employer's notice of appearance. The force of this reasoning is not diminished if the real reason for the dismissal was known to the employee.

8.3.3 Written reasons for dismissal

Statute facilitates the employee's discovery of the reasons for dismissal by according the right to a written statement of them. This sort of 'anti-reference' was first introduced by the EPA 1975, having no counterpart at common law (*Ridgway* v *Hungerford Market Co.* (1835)).

The employee can request reasons under the ERA 1996 if he is given notice, is dismissed without notice or the employer does not renew his fixed-term contract (but not if he is constructively dismissed, for the obvious reason that the employee resigned in that situation). He must also have completed one year's continuous employment with the employer ending with the last complete week before the effective date of termination (ERA 1996, s. 92(3)) except in the case of a dismissal during maternity leave when no period is required. The period was raised from six months to two years in order to harmonise with the qualifying period at that time for unfair dismissal itself but, as Simon Deakin has pointed out ((1990) 19 ILJ 1 at p. 14), there would appear to be no reason why the two should be the same in that even an employee without unfair dismissal protection should surely be entitled to know the reason for his dismissal and it may assist him in any common law claim.

The employer must, if reasonably possible, reply to an employee's request for reasons within 14 days and give true and adequate particulars (ERA 1996, s. 92(1) and (2) and s. 93(1) and (2)). This document is available as evidence before an ET (ERA 1996, s. 92(5)), and an employer may be effectively estopped from denying the accuracy of the particulars given. The written statement must 'at least contain a simple statement of the essential reasons for the dismissal' (*Horsley Smith and Sherry Ltd* v *Dutton* (1977)), otherwise 'no particular technicalities are involved and no particular form is required. It can be perfectly simple and straightforward' and there need be no statement as to why the employer considered the reason given to be sound (*Harvard Securities plc* v *Younghusband* (1990)). It is only after a request has been refused that a complaint to a tribunal may be made. It therefore follows that if no request is made no complaint may follow, according to the EAT in *Catherine Haigh Harlequin Hair Design* v *Seed* (1990).

A written statement can refer to letters previously written to an employee, according to the Court of Appeal in *Kent County Council* v *Gilham* (1985). The respondent dinner ladies refused to accept terms put forward by the county council to economise on the school meals service. The council sent out an explanatory letter to the dinner ladies giving the reasons for the changes and a week later gave them notice of termination referring back to the earlier letter which was held legitimate. Furthermore, it was adequate compliance with the Act to send the reasons to their representative rather than to the employees personally.

The employee may complain to an ET if there has been an unreasonable refusal by the employer to provide the necessary written statement or the statement given is untrue or inadequate. Any claim must be made during notice of dismissal or within three months after the effective date of termination, although the ET has the usual discretion to extend the time limit if it was not reasonably practicable to comply. If the employer is found to be in default of his obligations, the tribunal must award two weeks' pay to the employee. The provision is generally strictly construed since according to the EAT in *Charles Lang & Sons Ltd* v *Aubrey* (1977), 'it is a penal section. Parliament was intending to impose a penalty on a contumacious employer who decides he is not going to give the employee the required statement.' Thus in *Lowson* v *Percy Main & District Social Club and Institute Ltd* (1979) the employers were not held to have acted unreasonably where the failure was due to a lack of communication with their solicitors and as soon as the solicitors realised that the employee's request had not been complied with, the company gave the reasons. However, a general request to the employer by the police not to communicate with the employee was not a reasonable ground for refusing to provide reasons in *Daynecourt Insurance Brokers Ltd* v *Iles* (1978), but in *Brown* v *Stuart Scott & Co.* (1981) it was held reasonable not to give reasons where the employer had conscientiously formed a belief that there was no dismissal.

If the statement as given is untrue or inadequate the ET may decide what the employer's reasons really were, looking at all the evidence and drawing inferences.

8.3.4 Subsequently discovered reason

The employer cannot dismiss for an insubstantial reason and then hunt round for a reason to justify it. In this there is a vital distinction from wrongful dismissal where this is permissible (*Ridgway* v *Hungerford Market* (1835); *Boston Deep Sea Fishing & Ice Co.* v *Ansell* (1888)). The rule in the statutory jurisdiction was established by the House of Lords in the leading case of *Devis & Sons Ltd* v *Atkins* (1977). The respondent, who managed the appellant's abbatoir, was dismissed on the ground that he refused to implement his employer's purchasing policy. Later they found evidence of much dishonest conduct while he was employed, and sought to advance that as the reason for dismissal, even though they did not know of it at the time. Their Lordships thought that the statutory language that fairness must be determined 'having regard to the reason shown by the employers' could only mean the set of facts known to him at the time of dismissal. However, in *Alboni* v *Ind Coope Retail Ltd* (1998), the Court of Appeal felt that a tribunal was entitled to take into account the period between notification of dismissal and the date of dismissal itself. The *Devis* case could be distinguished because it was not concerned with that period. Michael Rubenstein, however, has argued that the court failed to understand that the statute required it to establish the reasonableness of the dismissal in the sense that it must look to the reason behind the notification, not at the events at and before the time the dismissal takes effect (see [1998] IRLR 107). This would seem to be correct, but in any event there seems to be little justification for distinguishing some very clear *dicta* by the House of Lords in *Devis*. If a subsequently discovered reason cannot be relied upon, it would appear, *a fortiori*, that a reason to consider a dismissal fair that occurs after the notification, and in that sense necessarily subsequently discovered, cannot be relied upon. Justice can be satisfied in these circumstances by reducing the amount of compensation. Indeed, in *Devis* the amount of compensation was reduced by 100 per cent. However, the decision in *Alboni* reflects the Court of Appeal's approach in an earlier case when it held in *Parkinson* v *March Consulting Ltd* (1997) that the reason given for the dismissal had only to be established at the date the dismissal took effect and not when it was given. This would appear to be an even stranger result than in *Alboni*. It is possible to see that hindsight could be thought to operate on the reasonableness of an earlier act even if the new factor were unknown to the employer, but that the reason the dismissal was given can later be altered, when it seems a matter rooted in one particular moment in time, appears illogical.

In *West Midlands Co-operative Society Ltd* v *Tipton* (1986) the House of Lords was confronted with a situation where the employee was denied an appeal after the date that he was dismissed. Applying the principle in *Devis* strictly, it would appear that, as the denial took place after the dismissal, it could not be taken into account in determining its fairness. The House of Lords thought differently however. Equity and the substantial merits of the case, Lord Bridge said, required that it be so considered. A number of reasons support this view. First, *Devis* was concerned with the situation where the employer took into account later-discovered conduct of the employee, which was a different situation altogether. Secondly, in applying, as Deakin has called it (see (1986) 45 CLJ 214 at p. 215) 'a functional approach of the statutory language', the Lords looked to the appeal as part of the process of dismissal, and not subsequent to it. However, as Shrubsall has stated ((1986) 49 MLR 640 at p. 642) this does not fit well with the Lords' approval of the analysis that the dismissal took place not after the denial of the appeal but on the date of termination itself. (Nevertheless, Collins believes that the House of Lords was right on this point—see (1986) 15 ILJ 113 at p. 116.) Neither does it seem logical, as the Lords held, to allow evidence acquired after dismissal which pertains to the actual reason for the dismissal, but not to allow other evidence relating to what might have been a better reason to dismiss.

Although the facts of *Tipton* concerned an appeal which was the employee's contractual entitlement, the principle was extended in *National Coal Board* v *Nash* (1986) to a non-contractual appeal.

8.4 Categories of reason for dismissal

Having established what the reason is for a dismissal, it is important to categorise what type of reason it was. The ERA 1996 makes a twofold decision. The first division is automatically unfair reasons. In other words, once it has been established that the reason was one of these reasons the dismissal is not dependent upon the additional question of whether or not it was also reasonable to dismiss for that reason. However, this is the case with the second category, known as the potentially fair reasons.

We now consider both of these situations in turn.

8.5 **Automatically unfair reasons**

There are various reasons why an employee may be dismissed which are automatically unfair, i.e. do not, having been established, entitle the employer to claim that they were reasonable.

8.5.1 **Dismissal on the grounds of pregnancy or childbirth**

Under the Maternity and Parental Leave Regulations 1999 (SI 1999 No. 3312), an employee is unfairly dismissed if:

The reason or principal reason for the dismissal was connected with:

(a) her pregnancy;

(b) the birth;

(c) an enactment (including delegated legislation) or a recommendation made pursuant to a code of practice issued or approved under health and safety legislation;

(d) the fact that she took, or sought to take or availed herself of ordinary maternity leave (see Chapter 11 below);

(e) the fact that she took, or sought to take, additional maternity leave, parental leave or dependancy leave under ERA 1996, s. 57A (see Chapter 11 below);

(f) the fact that she declined to sign a workforce agreement;

(g) her being a workforce representative or a candidate in an election to become one.

The employee is also taken to be unfairly dismissed if she was dismissed because she was redundant where others in a similar position were not made redundant, for one of the above reasons.

There is no automatic unfair dismissal where the employer has five or fewer employees immediately before the dismissal and it is not reasonably practicable to permit her to return to a suitable and appropriate job after additional maternity leave. Neither, where it is not practicable (other than for redundancy) to permit her to return to a suitable and appropriate job, is there an unfair dismissal if an associated employer offers her a job of that kind and she either accepts or unreasonably refuses the offer.

The need to keep a place open for a pregnant woman to return to would cause problems for an employer if he could not engage a replacement in her position or if he was open to liability in unfair dismissal if he dismissed this replacement. Thus ERA 1996, s. 106 states that he has a substantial reason to justify dismissal if on engaging a replacement he tells the replacement that his or her employment will be terminated on the return to work of the pregnant employee. The tribunal must, however, still consider in this situation whether the employer acted reasonably in all the circumstances in carrying out this dismissal.

8.5.2 Spent offences

The aim of the Rehabilitation of Offenders Act 1974 is that a convicted criminal may put his past behind him and make a fresh start. When the rehabilitation period appropriate to his sentence has elapsed the conviction is 'spent' and should not be taken into account for any purpose including employment. Thus s. 4(3)(b) provides that a spent conviction or the failure to disclose a spent conviction shall be an automatically unfair ground for dismissing someone from any office, profession, occupation or employment, or for prejudicing him in any way. The rehabilitation period depends on the sentence imposed.

The effect is limited by subsequent regulations (Rehabilitation of Offenders Act 1974 (Exceptions) Order 1975 (SI 1975 No. 1023) as amended), which make exemptions from these provisions in the case of certain sensitive professions including medical practitioners, lawyers, accountants, dentists, nurses, police, and social services workers (see *Wood* v *Coverage Care Ltd* (1996)).

8.5.3 Dismissal on transfer of undertaking

The Transfer of Undertakings (Protection of Employment) Regulations 2006 (SI 2006 No. 246) render a dismissal automatically unfair if the transfer or a reason connected with it is the reason or principal reason for dismissal. The only escape for the employer is where the reason or principal reason was 'an economic, technical or organisational reason entailing changes in the workforce of either the transferor or transferee before or after a relevant transfer'. In such a case, the reason is treated as a substantial reason for dismissal. As this covers any substantial reason in ERA 1996, s. 98, it may mean that the dismissal is by reason of redundancy (*Gorictree Ltd* v *Jenkinson* (1984)). This is an exception so wide that it has been called the 'most searing attack' on the principle of industrial justice that a person who loses his job for economic reasons should be entitled to compensation (see Collins, (1985) 14 ILJ 61 at p. 62).

A significant limitation on the scope of this exception to automatic unfairness was revealed by the Court of Appeal's judgment in *Berriman* v *Delabole Slate Ltd* (1984). The employee was constructively dismissed since he would not accept new disadvantageous terms required by the transferee employer who sought to standardise his contract with that of other existing employees. This neither had the object of effecting, nor did it bring about, a change in the workforce as required by the Regulations to fall within the relevant exception. The court thought, however, that a change in the function of the workforce would suffice. This was the position in *Crawford* v *Swinton Insurance Brokers Ltd* (1990) where it was held there was a change in the workforce even though there was no change in personnel. However, the employees were given entirely different jobs. As John McMullen has pointed out, this reasoning has the strange effect that the more disadvantaged an employee is by a change in job function on a transfer, the less well protected he is (see John McMullen, (1992) 21 ILJ 15 at p. 24).

On the face of it, these decisions seem to contradict the general position on reorganisations where there is no takeover. Here the position is that any dismissal of an employee who refuses to accept unilateral variations to his terms and conditions of employment is fair (see e.g. *Hollister* v *NFU* (1979)). But, as Remy Zentar has pointed out ((1986) 15 ILJ 117) the wording of the Regulations clearly demands such an interpretation.

However, the Court of Appeal later took a restrictive view of these provisions. In *Whitehouse* v *Chas A. Blatchford & Sons Ltd* (1999) it held that there were no dismissals connected with a transfer where a number of employees were made redundant by the transferors on the insistence of the transferees prior to transfer. Rather, they were for an economic, technical, or organisational ('eto') reason. This treats the two heads of reasons as separate, whereas it is probably better to see such dismissals as connected with the transfer, but subject to an 'eto' exception.

8.5.4 Trade union membership or activities

Under TULR(C)A 1992, s. 152(1), dismissals are automatically unfair if they are for the reason that the employee:

(a) was, or proposed to become, a member of an independent trade union; or

(b) had taken, or proposed to take, part at any appropriate time in the activities of an independent trade union; or

(c) was not a member of any trade union, or of a particular trade union, or of one of a number of particular trade unions, or had refused or proposed to refuse to become or remain a member.

This is considered in Chapter 13 below, in the wider context of trade union law.

8.5.5 Dismissal for assertion of a statutory right

The ERA 1996, s 104(1) renders the dismissal of employees automatically unfair where they assert that their employer has breached a statutory right. The dismissal is unfair if the reason, or principal reason, was that the employee brought proceedings against his employer to enforce a relevant statutory right, or if they did not do so in fact, nevertheless had the right so to do—see *McLean* v *Rainbow Homeloans Ltd* (2007). No qualifying period of employment is needed in order to claim the right.

In order to exercise the right the employee need not specify the right that he claims has been infringed but need only make it reasonably clear to the employer what the right was that he was alleging had been infringed (s. 104(3)).

The relevant rights are all those which are granted under the ERA 1996 and the TULR(C)A 1992 for which the remedy is a complaint to an ET, in particular:

(a) the rights to written particulars of employment;

(b) guarantee payments;

(c) suspension from work for medical grounds;

(d) protection against dismissal and other detriments in health and safety cases;

(e) time off for public duties and to look for work or to make arrangements for training;

  (f) time off for ante-natal care;

  (g) return to work after pregnancy;

  (h) written statement of reasons for dismissal;

  (i) claim redress for unfair dismissal;

  (j) redundancy payments;

  (k) reclaim unauthorised deductions from wages (including the right to be paid on time—see *Elizabeth Claire Care Management Ltd* v *Francis* (2005));

  (l) require employer to end check-off;

  (m) object to political fund contribution;

  (n) protection against action short of dismissal related to union membership or activities;

  (o) payment for time off for union duties; and

  (p) time off for trade union activities.

It is immaterial for these purposes whether the employee actually has the right or whether it has in fact been infringed or not (s. 104(2)). So long as the employee claims in good faith that the right has been infringed the protection of s. 104 applies (see *Mennell* v *Newell & Wright (Transport Contractors) Ltd* (1997)).

8.5.6 **Protected industrial action**

An employee is deemed to be automatically unfairly dismissed when he is dismissed for taking 'protected industrial action', if he started to take part in that action on or after 24 April 2000 (Employment Relations Act 1999, s. 16 and Sch. 5). The concept of protected industrial action is defined in TULR(C)A 1992, s. 238A. This occurs when the employee takes industrial action which is not actionable in tort under s. 219 (see Chapter 15 below) in three situations. The first is where the date of dismissal is within 12 weeks of the employee taking part in the action. The second is where the date of dismissal is after this 12-week period but where the employee had ceased to take part in it before 12 weeks had elapsed. The third is where the date of dismissal is after the 12-week period, and the employee had taken part in the action for longer than that, but where the employer did not follow a reasonable procedure for resolving the dispute. In determining what is reasonable, no regard is to be had to the merits of the dispute itself and no regard is to be had of days when the employees were locked out. Regard is to be had to such matters as procedures in collective or other agreements, whether the employer or the union had refused to start/re-start negotiations or take part in conciliation or mediation—see s. 238B. The employee's protection is lost if the action ceases to be official, which is to say, where the union repudiates the action.

8.5.7 **Whistleblowing**

Employees who engage in whistleblowing, and who are dismissed for that reason, are considered to be automatically dismissed under the Public Interest Disclosure Act 1998 (see Chapter 12 below).

8.6 **Potentially fair reasons**

In all cases which are not rendered automatically fair or unfair, the tribunal must, after determining the reason for dismissal, consider whether the dismissal was fair or unfair, having regard to the reasons shown by the employer, which shall depend on whether in the circumstances (including the size and administrative resources of the employer's undertaking) the employer acted reasonably or unreasonably in treating it as a sufficient reason for dismissing the employee, and that question should be determined in accordance with equity and the substantial merits of the case (ERA 1996, s. 98(4)). (However, note that this does not apply in the case of retirement dismissals—see below.) ETs should not put any gloss on this phrase. The position was thought to be well established that, in determining fairness, the tribunal was not to decide whether it thought the dismissal fair or unfair, but to determine whether the employer's actions were within the band of reasonable responses, whether it would have acted in the same way. However, this was thrown into some confusion by the decision of the EAT in *Haddon* v *Van den Burgh Foods* (1999) to the opposite effect, and subsequent decisions. Orthodox doctrine has now been restored by the Court of Appeal in *Post Office* v *Foley* (2000); *HSBC Bank plc* v *Madden* (2000); and *Sainsbury's Supermarkets Ltd* v *Hitt* (2003). The 'band of reasonable responses test' applies to all aspects of the dismissal process, according to the Court of Appeal in the latter case.

There is no burden of proof of fairness on the shoulders of the employer but it is instead neutral. An appeal is likely to be upheld if the ET directed itself that the employer must prove fairness (*Howarth Timber (Leeds) Ltd* v *Biscomb* (1986)). Tribunals must have regard to the size of the respondent employer's undertaking (see *Henderson* v *Granville Tours Ltd* (1982)), but the fact that a company is small in scale does not excuse it from carrying out a proper procedure (*MacKeller* v *Bolton* (1979)).

The fairness of a dismissal is essentially a question of fact, and the ET as an industrial jury is best equipped to deal with it, using its industrial experience and knowledge of local conditions. Tribunals have been directed by appeal bodies to approach the matter with common sense and common fairness, eschewing technicalities. The cases which follow are offered merely as examples of the approach of tribunals, and more particularly the EAT and Court of Appeal, in so far as they have offered guidance. They are not binding precedents (*Jowett* v *Earl of Bradford (No. 2)* (1978)). Moreover, the Court of Appeal has recognised that two tribunals may on similar facts reach opposite conclusions, yet this does not necessarily amount to an error of law to be corrected by the appeal bodies (*Kent County Council* v *Gilham (No. 2)* (1985)). As John McMullen has pointed out ((1986) 15 ILJ 49), although this position eschews legalism, if it is at the expense of consistency the result seems unjust. He writes:

The success of [the employees] in Kent was fortuitous. Had they been employed in Exeter or Devon [sic] they would not have been successful despite the fact that their facts were not dissimilar. Such a result seems nonsensical.

He goes on to make the strong argument that the EAT's reluctance to intervene in such issues ignores the special nature of its composition, consisting as it does of a judge and two lay members.

The Court of Appeal set the tone for the current orthodox position in *Bailey* v *BP Oil (Kent Refinery) Ltd* (1980), where Lawton LJ said:

The wording [of ERA 1996, s. 98(4)], which is clear and unambiguous, requires the tribunal, which is the one which hears the evidence, not the one which hears the legal argument, to look at every aspect of the case.... Each case must depend on its own facts. In our judgment, it is unwise for this court or the Employment Appeal Tribunal to set out guidelines and wrong to make rules and establish presumptions for ETs to follow or take into account.

In *The County Council of Hereford and Worcester* v *Neale* (1986) the Court of Appeal re-emphasised the narrowness of the jurisdiction of the role of the EAT in deciding that a judgment of the tribunal was perverse. May LJ said 'Deciding these cases [of unfair dismissal] is the job of [employment] tribunals and when they have not erred in law, neither the EAT nor this Court should disturb their decision unless one can say in effect: "My goodness, that was certainly wrong"'.

Where there has been a misdirection, 'the next question to be asked is not whether the conclusion of the [employment] tribunal is plainly wrong but whether it is plainly and unarguably right notwithstanding that misdirection. It is only if it is plainly and unarguably right notwithstanding the misdirection that the decision can stand.' Otherwise, it must be remitted to the ET according to the Court of Appeal in *Dobie* v *Burns International Security Services (UK) Ltd* (1984) (see further, Schofield, (1985) 14 ILJ 57).

It is difficult to put each case of dismissal into its proper pigeon hole, but the general approach here followed is to discuss the case law on each of the reasons given for dismissal, and then attempt a general overview of the procedures needed for a fair dismissal.

8.6.1 Capability and qualifications

The first potentially fair reason is where the employee is dismissed for a reason relating to capability or qualifications (ERA 1996, s. 98(2)(a)).

The only guidance to be found in the Act in relation to capability as a reason for dismissal is its definition to include 'skill, aptitude, health or any other physical or mental quality' (s. 98(3)(a)). 'Qualifications' means 'any degree, diploma or other academic, technical or professional qualification relevant to the position which the employee held'. The ground put forward by the employer need only relate to capability. It need not prevent the employee performing all work of the kind he was employed to do (*Shook* v *London Borough of Ealing* (1986)).

The employer need only show that the employee was incapable of work. The cause of that incapability is not an issue. So, even if the employer has itself been the cause of the employee's incapability, that does not preclude a finding that the dismissal was fair, according to the Court of Appeal in *Royal Bank of Scotland plc* v *McAdie* (2008).

Incompetence

In so far as incapability through incompetence is concerned, the general rule is that 'the employee's incapacity as it existed at the time of dismissal must be of such a nature and quality as to justify dismissal'. It need not, however, be reflected in any one particular incident but may arise from several indications (*Miller* v *Executors of John Graham* (1978)). Thus, in *Lewis Shops Group Limited* v *Wiggins* (1973) a shop manageress was fairly dismissed when she left her shop dirty and untidy, cash registers failed to operate properly, and stock was not put away.

However, ETs are often not well equipped to measure intangible examples of poor work performance. In *Taylor* v *Alidair Ltd* (1978) Lord Denning said:

Wherever a man is dismissed for incapacity or incompetence it is sufficient that the employer honestly believes on reasonable grounds that the man is incapable or incompetent. It is not necessary for the employer to prove that he is in fact incapable or incompetent.

The case had particularly strong facts since the applicant was an airline pilot, dismissed because he was thought to be at fault for a bad landing which had caused serious damage to the respondents' aircraft. According to the Court of Appeal, the employers had reasonably demanded a high degree of care and fairly dismissed him when he failed to measure up to it on one occasion. He was engaged in a special category of:

activities in which the degree of professional skill which must be required is so high, that the potential consequence of small departures from that high standard is so serious that the failure to perform in accordance with those standards is sufficient to justify dismissal.

The Court of Appeal specifically approved Bristow J's examples of other such employees as, 'the scientist operating the nuclear reactors, the chemist in charge of research into the possible effects of, for example, thalidomide, the driver of the Manchester to London Express, the driver of an articulated lorry full of sulphuric acid'. Few procedural safeguards were then necessary in relation to such employees, but in *ILEA* v *Lloyd* (1981) the Court of Appeal restricted this principle to cases where safety was in question.

Most other cases will have less serious consequences, and there should then be some other evidence besides the *ipse dixit*, or opinion of the employer, of the employee's incapacity. The EAT did say, however, in *Cook* v *Thomas Linnell & Sons Ltd* (1977) that: 'When responsible employers genuinely come to the conclusion that over a reasonable period of time a manager is incompetent, we think that it is some evidence that he is incompetent.' This recognises that although ideally there should be more objective assessments, when one is dealing with such imponderables as quality of management, this may be almost impossible to provide. The tribunal must, however, ensure that the employer's standards are attainable.

One of the most difficult procedural questions in unfair dismissal is how far the stringent guidance found in the ACAS Code on Disciplinary Practice and Procedure, mainly provided for dealing with conduct cases, should apply to dismissal on the grounds of incapacity. This goes to the heart of the policy behind such procedural requirements; if they are enacted because warnings and hearings might lead the employer to change his mind, they are unlikely to be of much value in relation to those employees who have shown themselves manifestly incapable of doing the job in any event. If, on the other hand, the intention is to give the employee a chance to prove or improve himself there is no reason to distinguish between incompetence and misconduct. It is, in fact, often difficult in practice to draw the line. The result is that, according to the NIRC in *James* v *Waltham Holy Cross UDC* (1973):

An employer should be very slow to dismiss upon terms that an employee is incapable of performing the works which he is employed to do without first telling the employee of the respects in which he is failing to do his job adequately, warning him of the possibility or likelihood of dismissal on this ground, and giving him an opportunity to improve his performance.

Without proper appraisal the employer may not be able to prove that he has adequately taken a reasonable view of the employee's incapacity. This is particularly important in cases at opposite ends of the spectrum of experience, that is to say where a long service employee has to adapt to new methods and in the case of a probationer who will need to know what standard he is required to meet. In *Post Office* v *Mughal* (1977) Cumming-Bruce J formulated these tests for tribunals:

> Have the employers shown that they took reasonable steps to maintain appraisal of the probationer throughout the period of probation, giving guidance by advice or warning when such was likely to be useful or fair; and that an appropriate officer made an honest effort to determine whether the probationer came up to the required standard having informed himself of the appraisals made by supervising officers and any other facts recorded about probationers?

A warning is less vital in the case of incapability than for misconduct and is to be treated as only one factor among many in judging fairness. It is most important where the required level of performance is uncertain, and independent judgment thereof difficult. Sir Hugh Griffiths graphically gave the reason in *Winterhalter Gastronom Ltd* v *Webb* (1973) thus:

> There are many situations in which a man's apparent capabilities may be stretched when he knows what is being demanded of him; many do not know that they are capable of jumping a 5-barred gate until the bull is close behind them.

Where the prospects of an employee improving are next to nil, however, a warning and opportunity of improvement can be of no benefit to the senior employee and may constitute an unfair burden on the business (*James* v *Waltham Holy Cross UDC* (1973); *cf. McPhail* v *Gibson* (1976)). Thus in *Lowndes* v *Specialist Heavy Engineering Ltd* (1976) it was considered fair to dismiss after five grievous and costly mistakes by the employee since to have followed proper procedures would have made no difference. This is also the case in situations with very serious consequences, such as a gaming inspector who failed to notice a serious fraud being conducted under his nose (*Turner* v *Pleasurama Casinos Ltd* (1976)). There is no requirement to offer such an employee an alternative position (*Bevan Harris Ltd* v *Gair* (1981)). However, in other circumstances length of service may have the opposite effect in that dismissal may be too serious a sanction for a single act of negligence by a long-serving employee (*Springbank Sand & Gravel Ltd* v *Craig* (1973)).

Health

Cases on dismissal on the grounds of ill-health demonstrate clearly the role of the unfair dismissal provisions in mediating between the economic interest of keeping production moving and maximising profits on the one hand, and humanitarian requirements on the other. The EAT in *Spencer* v *Paragon Wallpapers Ltd* (1977) most generally reconciled this tension by stating that the basic question which has to be determined in every case is whether in all the circumstances the employer can be expected to wait any longer and if so how much longer for an employee to return to work, although not necessarily to his own job (see *Hooper* v *British Railways Board* (1988)). This is not so widely different from the test for frustration on account of sickness discussed earlier (*Tan* v *Berry Brothers and Rudd Ltd* (1974)). In neither case is there a fixed period; the employer has to wait, each situation depending on its own facts.

The most important procedural requirement in health cases is that the employer take an informed view on the basis of proper medical information. The best practice includes consultation with the employee, as stressed in *East Lindsey DC* v *Daubney* (1977). There the employer council's own physician asked a doctor to examine the employee and as a result of his short advice recommended retirement. The procedure was inadequate since the employers had not seen the medical report and had not extended to Daubney the opportunity to obtain and present his own version. The EAT thought that such requirements were far from futile since:

Discussion and consultations will often bring to light facts and circumstances of which the employers were unaware and which will throw new light on the problem, or the employee may wish to seek medical advice which, brought to the notice of the employer's medical advisers, will cause them to change their opinion.

The medical evidence must be more detailed than a mere statement of unfitness if the employer is to take the necessarily 'rational and informed decision'; but at the end of the day dismissal is a personnel and not a medical decision, and in this the employer may have to use his own discretion in choosing between conflicting medical opinions (*BP Tanker Co.* v *Jeffries* (1974)).

The tribunals have significantly lowered the procedural threshold where a series of intermittent absences apparently for illness cause serious hardship to the employer. In *International Sports Co. Ltd* v *Thomson* (1980), the employee had been away for 25 per cent of her last 18 months' employment. She had submitted various medical certificates to cover these absences, specifying dizzy spells, anxiety and nerves, bronchitis, and viral infection. Four warnings were to no avail, and the company claimed that they were excused from having her examined by their doctor, because none of her illnesses could be subsequently and independently verified. The EAT agreed that this was dismissal on the grounds of misconduct rather than ill-health, and Waterhouse J said:

What is required . . . is, firstly, that there should be a fair review by the employer of the attendance record and the reasons for it; and, secondly, appropriate warnings after the employee has been given the opportunity to make representation.

The EAT in *Rolls-Royce* v *Walpole* (1980) took a similar line and found the meager requirements satisfied. The applicant's attendance record was around 50 per cent for the last three years of employment. He received several warnings, and even counselling to discover the reason for his absences, some two years before his actual dismissal, but, on termination, no medical evidence was sought. In a statement of a principle, the EAT declared that:

Frequently there is a range of responses to the conduct or capacity of the employee on the part of the employer, from and including summary dismissal downwards to a mere informal warning, which can be said to have been reasonable.

The employer's reaction could not be said to be outside this spectrum, and the dismissal was fair. Further judicial elucidation is necessary before it is possible to determine when the sickness test with its procedural safeguards ends, and these malingering criteria take over.

A sick note from a doctor may not be conclusive of the genuineness of an employee's illness. In *Hutchinson* v *Enfield Rolling Mills Ltd* (1981) the employee was held fairly dismissed without any procedure being followed when he was seen at a union demonstration in Brighton on a day when certified as off work by reason of sciatica. (See also *Patterson* v *Messrs Bracketts* (1977).) While a medical opinion is normally necessary for fair dismissal in pure sickness cases, it is not quite sufficient. In determining whether the employer was reasonable, an ET can here be expected to have particular regard to 'the size and administrative resources of the employer's undertaking', as directed by ERA 1996, s. 98(4). It is relevant that the employer may have been responsible for the illness when determining the fairness of the dismissal, according to the EAT in *Edwards* v *Governors of Hanson School* (2001), contrary to its previous decision in *London Fire & Civil Defence Authority* v *Betty* (1994).

While a position should be offered even if it is likely that the employee will refuse, e.g. because it carries a lower rate of pay, the authorities fall short of suggesting that there rests a duty on the employer to 'create a special job for an employee however long serving he may be' (*Merseyside & North Wales Electricity Board* v *Taylor* (1975)), nor where to propose it would breach an agreement with a union.

The fact that the employee is dismissed while in receipt of his contractual sick pay does not make the termination automatically unfair. The only relevance of this right to payment is that its duration may be evidence of the period during which the business could do without the employee.

Qualifications

Although 'qualifications' is widely defined in ERA 1996, s. 98(3)(b), it does not extend to the personal characteristic of trustworthiness (*Singh* v *London Country Bus Services Ltd* (1976)) and must be related to 'performing work of the kind which he was employed by the employer to do'. Thus in *Blue Star Ship Management Ltd* v *Williams* (1979) lack of authorisation as a registered seafarer was irrelevant to the employee's position so that this could not be a reason for dismissal. The requirement of a clean driving licence need not be set out in a written contract of employment to be a qualification (*Tayside Regional Council* v *McIntosh* (1982)).

8.6.2 Misconduct

The second type of potentially fair dismissals relate to the conduct of the employee (ERA 1996, s. 98(2)(b)). This can be viewed in various contexts.

Disobedience to reasonable orders

The unfair dismissal jurisdiction maintains the important principle of the contract of employment that the employee must obey the lawful and reasonable orders of the employer. There must, however, be a serious breach of the rules to justify dismissal, and moreover, the employee must not only be warned as to the consequence of a breach of the rule, but also have an opportunity to state his side of the story. More generally, the ACAS Code of Practice for Disciplinary Practice and Procedures in Employment provides that, if they are to be fully effective, rules and procedures need to be accepted as reasonable by those who are to be covered by them and by those who operate them.

The scope of lawful orders must be determined primarily by construing the contract of employment. This may require analysis of the written statement of terms, custom and practice, works rules and collective agreements, particularly with regard to job duties, hours of work, and location. Thus in *Deeley* v *BRE Ltd* (1980) the original engagement gave the right to the respondent company's managing director to transfer the employee to whatever duties he saw fit. Although the advertisement referred to the applicant's post as Sales Engineer Export and he had always been engaged in export sales, a requirement to work on home sales was not in breach of contract. His dismissal for refusal was thus fair.

If an employee is dismissed for refusing or failing to do something which was not within his contractual duties to do, however, the dismissal is likely to be unfair, although any compensation may be reduced because of the employee's contributory fault in failing to react reasonably in the circumstances. In *Redbridge LBC* v *Fishman* (1978) the applicant was appointed to be in charge of the resources centre at a large comprehensive school. At first she did little teaching, but the school's new headmistress informed her that henceforth she would have to take 18 English lessons a week. She refused and was dismissed, in the tribunal's and EAT's view, unfairly, since she had been recruited for special duties which would largely absolve her from general teaching duties. The instruction was not within her contractual duties and she could reasonably refuse it. Phillips J, however, warned against the imposition of a contractual strait-jacket. In particular, the employee's duties may be considerably wider than what he has actually been accustomed to do on a day to day basis. Flexibility may be called for on the part of the employee, particularly in a small business (*Glitz* v *Watford Electric Co. Ltd* (1979); *Coward* v *John Menzies (Holdings) Ltd* (1977); *Simmonds* v *Dowty Seals Ltd* (1978)). This would seem to be reasonable, so long as flexibility is construable as a contractual obligation (possibly through an implied term) but not if it goes beyond the scope of the contract. A contract, after all, is intended to limit, as well as identify, the legal obligations of the parties.

One important way in which the statutory remedy differs from wrongful dismissal is that it focuses on the reasonableness of the employer's order as well as its legality by contract. In *UCATT* v *Brain* (1981) the applicant employee was publications officer of the respondent union when a libel action was brought against him and the union in respect of articles in the union journal. As a part of its settlement, the applicant was required by the union to sign a statement that neither he nor any officers, servants, or agents would repeat the defamatory statement, but he refused on the grounds that he would thereby be making himself liable for the acts of others over whom he had no control. His persistence in this stance led to his dismissal and the Court of Appeal upheld a finding of unfairness on the ground that the order was manifestly unreasonable. This points to the difference from wrongful dismissal where the only question is whether the employer's order was permissible under the contract. Indeed, in *Farrant* v *The Woodroffe School* (1998), the EAT held that, even where an order was unlawful in that it was in breach of contract, this did not render the consequent dismissal necessarily unfair. The logical conclusion, therefore, is that, even if a party acts for self-interested reasons, on occasion the law believes it to be reasonable to act unlawfully. This would seem to be an extraordinary notion.

Determining the scope of fair dismissal for disobeying orders is vital in delimiting the bounds of managerial prerogative. For example, *Boychuk* v *H. J. Symons*

Holdings Ltd (1977) suggests that an employer can dictate his employee's appearance. The applicant, an audit clerk, was held fairly dismissed because of her insistence on wearing badges proclaiming her lesbianism. The EAT considered that: 'a reasonable employer...can be allowed to decide what upon reflection and mature consideration, can be offensive to the customers and the fellow employees'. In another case it was held to be fair to dismiss a woman school cleaner who insisted on bringing her young child to school even though he distracted her attention from her work and had caused accidents (*Lawrence* v *Newham LBC* (1978)).

As in the common law wrongful dismissal, it is not fair to dismiss an employee where he refuses to obey an unlawful order. Thus in *Morrish* v *Henlys (Folkestone) Ltd* (1973) the appellant was sacked for refusing to acquiesce in the alteration of accounts on drawing diesel oil from petrol pumps, and this was held unfair.

Rules

The employer may codify the orders and requirements for his employees into a series of disciplinary rules relating to everything from time sheets and attendance to standards of appearance and rudeness. The employee's written statement of terms must include 'any disciplinary rules that apply'.

In *Pringle* v *Lucas Industrial Equipment Ltd* (1975) the EAT said that 'if employers wish to dismiss automatically for certain misconduct which is short of inherently gross misconduct they must be able to show that management has unequivocally brought to the attention of employees what that conduct is and what its consequences will be'. To cover a series of offences in company rules does not, however, mean that matters falling outside its terms cannot merit dismissal.

It is reasonable for an employer to expect that his workforce is aware of the most obvious prohibitions. This was confirmed with respect to fighting in *C. A. Parsons & Co. Ltd* v *McLoughlin* (1978). Although it was not included in the respondent company's rules as gross misconduct, Kilner Brown J thought that 'it ought not to be necessary for anybody, let alone a shop steward, to have in black and white in the form of a rule that a fight is something that is going to be regarded very gravely by management'. The effects here of an assault near machinery on the factory floor were obviously serious, but the position may be different when the action is not so grave. Thus in *Meyer Dunmore International Ltd* v *Rogers* (1978) summary dismissal for fighting was held unfair and Phillips J declared:

> If employers wish to have a rule that employees engaged in what could properly and sensibly be called 'fighting' are going to be summarily dismissed, as far as we can see there is no reason why they should not have a rule provided—and this is important—that it is plainly adopted, that it is plainly and clearly set out, and that great publicity is given to it so that every employee knows beyond any reasonable doubt whatever that if he gets involved in fighting he will be dismissed.

The distinction between *Parsons* and *Meyer* must be a matter of fact and degree, but several cases have emphasised the need for clear rules in regard to overstaying leave and drinking alcohol during working hours (see *Hoover Ltd* v *Forde* (1980); *Dairy Produce Packers Ltd* v *Beverstock* (1981); *Distillers Co. (Bottling Services) Ltd* v *Gardner* (1982)).

Disciplinary rules are particularly important in emphasising to employees those less serious breaches which the employer is going to visit with the severe sanction of dismissal. In this way the rule acts as a preliminary warning. Instant dismissal has been considered fair following breach of clearly stated rules relating, for example, to clocking on (*Dalton* v *Burton's Gold Medal Biscuits* (1974)), and working for a competitor (*Golden Cross Hire Co. Ltd* v *Lovell* (1979)).

Even where there is a disciplinary rule and it is broken, a tribunal is nevertheless likely to find a consequent dismissal unfair, for example where the rule breached is of no relevance to the employment (*Greenslade* v *Hoveringham Gravels Ltd* (1975)), and where the 'punishment' of dismissal does not fit the 'crime'. Thus in *Ladbroke Racing Ltd* v *Arnott* (1983), where three betting shop employees were summarily dismissed for placing bets on behalf of relatives in breach of a clearly stated rule in the respondent's disciplinary code, the tribunal's determination of unfairness was upheld by the EAT and the Court of Session on the grounds that instant dismissal was an unreasonable response in all the circumstances. The full extent of their misconduct was that one employee had placed just one bet for his brother on one occasion, the second occasionally for two pensioners, and the third was the office manager who had apparently condoned the practice. (See also *Richards* v *Bulpitt & Sons Ltd* (1975).) In *Unkles* v *Milanda Bread Co.* (1973), although rules existed to restrict smoking, dismissal for breach was too severe since the employee's conduct in breaking the rule was inadvertent and not wilful.

Length of service is also relevant when determining on the application of disciplinary rules. In *Johnson Matthey Metals Ltd* v *Harding* (1978) an employee with 15 years' unblemished service was dismissed when found in possession of a fellow worker's wrist watch six months after it had been lost. The EAT held that the amount of previous years' service was 'plainly a matter to be taken into consideration' and held that the dismissal was unfair. Past work did not, however, weigh against the serious and proved misconduct in *AEI Cables Ltd* v *McLay* (1980) where the applicant had made false claims for reimbursement for diesel fuels and had been presenting such fraudulent vouchers for the previous two years.

Where there is no semblance of consistency in application of the rules the likelihood of a finding of unfair dismissal is greater. It may be that breaches of clear disciplinary rules are waived with such regularity that an employee is lulled into a false sense of security. Employers often acquiesce, for example, in breaches of rules prohibiting drinking in the lunch hour. Several decisions have stressed that clear warning is necessary if there is to be a purge on a particular breach. In *Post Office* v *Fennell* (1981) the employee was summarily dismissed after assaulting a fellow employee in the works canteen. His case was that many other workers had been guilty of similar offences but were not punished in this way. The Court of Appeal upheld a decision that the dismissal was thus unfair for that reason. The statutory reference to equity and the substantial merits of the case comprehended the concept that employees who behave in much the same way should receive similar punishments.

In *Hadjioannou* v *Coral Casinos Ltd* (1981) the EAT limited the applicability of this case by stating that an appeal to consistency was relevant only when there was evidence that employees had been led to believe that certain categories of conduct would either be overlooked or at least not dealt with by dismissal and there was evidence in relation to other cases supporting the inference that the employer's purported reason for dismissal was not the real reason if the circumstances in other cases were truly parallel. Here these conditions were not fulfilled so that the EAT upheld a finding by a tribunal that the appellant's dismissal for socialising with customers was in breach of company rules and was fair. It is important for employers to ensure that consistency is achieved for all employees, as it is not enough to show consistency of individual managers where their practices diverge, according to the EAT in *Cain* v *Leeds Western Health Authority* (1990). The employer is entitled to take into consideration aggravating factors such as a poor disciplinary record (*London Borough of Harrow* v *Cunningham* (1996); see also *Paul* v *East Surrey DHA* (1995)).

Offences

Another area where conduct is relevant is plainly where offences have been committed. The tribunals and courts draw a distinction between offences committed at work and those committed outside. Whether the commission of a criminal offence outside his job merits an employee's dismissal depends above all on its relevance to the individual's duty as an employee (see *Securicor Guarding Ltd* v *R* (1994)). The tribunal should take into account the status of the employee, the nature of the offence, the employee's past record, his access to cash, and proximity to members of the public.

The 2009 ACAS Code of Practice on Disciplinary and Grievance Procedures states that:

If an employee is charged with, or convicted of a criminal offence this is not normally in itself reason for disciplinary action. Consideration needs to be given to what effect the charge or conviction has on the employee's suitability to do the job and their relationship with their employer, work colleagues and customers. (p. 35)

The EAT has emphasised that in these cases reasonable employers may reach different decisions, and 'it does not necessarily mean if they decide to dismiss they have acted unfairly because there are plenty of situations in which more than one view is possible' (*Trusthouse Forte Leisure Ltd* v *Aquilar* (1976)).

Tribunals have steered a middle course in relation to dismissal for offences, both at work and outside, between demanding such proof of guilt as would be necessary in a criminal court and allowing dismissal on suspicion. The crucial question (which applies to all misconduct cases) was formulated by Arnold J in *BHS Ltd* v *Burchell* (1978), as whether the employer:

entertained a reasonable suspicion amounting to a belief in the guilt of the employee of that misconduct at that time...First of all, there must be established by the employer the fact of that belief; that the employer did believe it. Secondly, that the employer had in his mind reasonable grounds upon which to sustain that belief. And thirdly, we think that the employer at the stage at which he formed that belief on those grounds, at any rate at the final stage at which he formed that belief, had carried out as much investigation into the matter as was reasonable in all the circumstances of the case.

In approving this test in *Weddel and Co. Ltd* v *Tepper* (1980), Stephenson LJ did, however, emphasise that belief on reasonable grounds entailed that employers must not 'form their belief hastily without making the appropriate enquiries' (*cf.* Griffiths J in *St Anne's Board Mill Co. Ltd* v *Brien* (1973)). Similar principles were applied in the case of suspected serious negligence in *McPhie & McDermott* v *Wimpey Waste Management Ltd* (1981), and generalised in *Distillers Co. (Bottling Services) Ltd* v *Gardner* (1982). More recently, the EAT has stressed that *Burchell* should be understood as a 'guideline not a tramline' (*Boys and Girls Welfare Society* v *McDonald* (1996)). This must be right, as it should be remembered that *Burchell* was decided before the burden of proof on the reasonableness issue was removed from employers, even though there may still be occasions when it is the duty of the employer to provide some evidence (see *Scottish Daily Record and Sunday Mail (1986) Ltd* v *Laird* (1996)). However, this does not amount even to having to produce a *prima facie* case, according to the EAT in *Hackney London Borough Council* v *Usher* (1997). It would seem that this distinction is rather too fine to be properly understood.

The need for a reasonable belief in the guilt of the employee is illustrated by *Ferodo Ltd* v *Barnes* (1976). The applicant was dismissed when it was thought that he had committed an act of vandalism in the company's toilets. The fact that the employers could not prove that the employee had committed the offence was not relevant save as evidence that the employer acted reasonably or otherwise in concluding that the employee had so behaved. The vital question was the state of evidence and information known to the employer at the time of dismissal. Thus a dismissal may be fair even though a criminal court decides that the offence was not in fact committed by the applicant (*Harris (Ipswich) Ltd* v *Harrison* (1978)). One reason is that while the criminal court must be convinced of guilt beyond reasonable doubt, the ET works on the less exacting standard of balance of probabilities (*Lees* v *The Orchard* (1978)). Conversely, in *Earl* v *Slater and Wheeler (Airlyne) Ltd* (1972), it was said that:

If an employer thinks that his accountant may be taking the firm's money but he has no real grounds for so thinking, and dismisses him for that reason, he acts wholly unreasonably notwithstanding that it was later proved that the accountant had been guilty.

In *Scottish Midland Co-operative Society Ltd* v *Cullion* (1991) the Court of Session thought that reasonableness in this context meant merely that the employer held a belief, and that it was one they were entitled to hold. This, of course, if it is not meant to be an empty solecism, merely begs the question in that the authorities tend to suggest that the belief which the employer is entitled to hold is the reasonable belief, albeit by applying a subjective test.

While the law generally rejects blanket dismissals (*Scottish Special Housing Association* v *Cooke* (1979), *Gibson* v *British Transport Docks Board* (1982)), where the net of reasonable suspicion rests on the heads of more than one employee, all may be dismissed. This was established in the difficult leading case of *Monie* v *Coral Racing Ltd* (1980). The appellant worked for the respondent company as an area manager with control and supervision over 19 betting shops, and only he and his assistant knew the combination for the safe in the area headquarters. While Mr Monie was on holiday, his assistant discovered that £1,750 was missing from this safe. There were no indications that either the premises or the safe had been forcibly entered, and the respondent's security officer thus concluded that one or other, or both, must have been involved in the theft. The two were dismissed, and this decision was confirmed by a director. The ordinary application of the *Burchell/Weddel* test demanding reasonable belief in the applicant's guilt would result in a finding that both dismissals were unfair and the EAT so held. On appeal, however, all three Lords Justice confined the principle to those cases in which only one employee is under suspicion. Here, 'looking at the matter as an ordinary businessman', Sir David Cairns thought that the tribunal had correctly inquired 'whether there were solid and sensible grounds on which the employer could reasonably *infer or suspect* dishonesty' (author's italics), and had rightly answered in the affirmative. The fact that the two employees would have the right to be acquitted on a criminal charge of theft on this evidence was immaterial. It is therefore important to concentrate on the reasonableness of the employer's action, rather than on the objective justice for the innocent employee (*Parr* v *Whitbread plc t/a Threshers Wine Merchants* (1990)). It must be stressed that an employer will need to show that the most careful investigation has been undertaken. Moreover, it should not be forgotten in applying its principle that in *Monie* both suspects were in senior positions and handled money in a business in which security and honesty were obviously vital.

The fact that, in such circumstances, not all members of the group under suspicion are dismissed does not mean that those dismissals are unfair, according to the EAT in *Frames Snooker Centre* v *Boyce* (1992). So long as the employer has 'solid and sensible grounds (which do not have to be related to the relevant offence)' for differentiating between members of the group, the dismissals may be fair.

There are no hard and fast rules governing an employer's investigations of criminal offences. The main principle was enunciated by Viscount Dilhorne in *Devis & Sons Ltd* v *Atkins* (1977): 'It cannot be said that the employer acted reasonably...if he only did so in consequence of ignoring matters which he reasonably ought to have known.'

Often there will be agreed procedures for such fact finding processes and if these are followed the dismissal is likely to be fair (see *Bentley Engineering Co. Ltd* v *Mistry* (1978)).

Where a complaint is received about an employee, the employer should enquire whether there has indeed been any misconduct and its gravity and not merely rely on the integrity of the complainant (*Henderson* v *Granville Tours Ltd* (1982)). Dismissal may be unfair because of the employer's delay in instituting proceedings against the employee without good reason for the delay, even though the employee was guilty of conduct meriting dismissal and suffered no prejudice by reason of the delay (*RSPCA* v *Cruden* (1986)).

At this stage of investigation there is no need to involve the employee, but once the facts are fully ascertained they must be put before him at a hearing. The two processes often merge into one, especially when only the employee can give information about the incident; in that case a distinct second stage of hearing is unnecessary. Common sense places some limits on the amount of investigation necessary in some cases.

Some difficulties have arisen when police inquiries and internal procedures are being held simultaneously. Employees have sought to prevent the latter prejudicing them in any criminal charges. *Dicta* (e.g. *Lord Macdonald in Carr* v *Alexander Russell Ltd* (1976)) that employment procedures should be suspended while a prosecution was pending have been later disapproved. There is also no general rule that employees should be suspended on full pay while awaiting the outcome of criminal proceedings, although this commonly happens (*Conway* v *Matthew Wright & Nephew Ltd* (1977)). However, the employee should not be left in a state of uncertainty. Thus in *Portsea Island Mutual Co-op Society Ltd* v *Rees* (1980) the employers were held to have acted unreasonably when at the date of dismissal the incident relied on was six weeks old and the employee had already been reprimanded for it.

It should be noted, in considering cases decided between 2004 and 2009, that during this period statutory procedures existed for the handling of disputes and grievances. These were introduced by the EA 2002 and were contained in the Employment Act 2002 (Dispute Resolution) Regulations 2004 (SI 2004 No. 752). They were repealed by the Employment Act 2008 with effect from 2009 and the common law was resurrected where the regulations previously applied. (See further below.)

8.6.3 **Retirement**

The third type of potentially fair dismissal is retirement, introduced into the list (as s. 98(2)(ba)) by Employment Equality (Age) Discrimination Regulations 2006 (SI 2006 No. 1031), Sch. 8 (see Chapter 10 below). However, the fairness of such dismissals is not to be determined in the ordinary way under s. 98(4), as we have seen, but in accordance with new provisions in the ERA 1996, namely ss 98ZA–98ZG. These state that (in turn):

(a) where the employee is dismissed under the age of 65, or if there is no 'normal retiring age', the dismissal is not to be taken to be for retirement;

(b) where the employee has no normal retiring age but is aged 65 or over, and has been informed that he has the right to request not to retire, the dismissal shall be taken to be for retirement, and no other reason;

(c) where the employee has a normal retiring age but is dismissed before reaching that date, the dismissal shall not be taken to be for retirement;

(d) where the employee has a normal retiring age of 65 or over, has been dismissed on that date, and has been informed that he has the right to request not to retire, the dismissal shall be taken to be for retirement, and for no other reason;

(e) where the employee has a normal retiring age under 65, has been dismissed on that date, and has been informed that he has the right to request not to retire, the dismissal shall be taken to be for retirement, and for no other reason, provided that the lower normal retiring age is objectively justified;

(f) the tribunal is to pay particular regard to whether the employer has notified the employee of the right to request not to be retired, and if so when it did so, and whether it followed, or sought to follow, correct procedures;

(g) if there is a retirement procedure found having applied the above provisions, the dismissal shall be considered fair (i.e. it will be considered automatically fair) unless there has been a failure by the employer to notify the employee of retirement, to consider the employee's request not to be retired, or to consider an appeal against a decision to refuse a request not to be retired.

In other words, in the absence of procedural irregularity, the new provisions will, in many cases, have substantially the same impact on employees over retiring age as they did under the old law when there was a specific age-related exclusion from eligibility to claim.

In considering these provisions, it is clearly important to understand what amounts to the 'normal retiring age'. This is defined in s. 98ZH as the age at which employees in the employer's undertaking who hold, or have held, the same kind of position as the employee are normally required to retire. However, it is a concept that has received a good deal of judicial attention in the past under the old law, and which will still be considered relevant in the future. It is worthwhile examining here, therefore, that position.

The early view regarding the proper construction of 'normal retiring age' was stated in *Ord* v *Maidstone and District Hospital Management Committee* (1974), where Donaldson P thought it meant 'the age at which the employee concerned usually retires'. This was challenged in *Nothman* where Lawton LJ stated:

I construe the word 'retiring'...as having gerundive qualities so as to give the sense of must or should. It follows that the normal retiring age of teachers employed by the local authority is the age at which they would have to retire unless their services were extended by mutual agreement.

This approach brings rather unexpected results, and occasional injustice. The Court of Appeal has emphasised that the vital issue, just as for the definition of 'ordinarily works', is the construction of the contract, not what actually happens in practice. These two can differ widely, especially where the employer has a discretion whether or not to retain an employee above a certain age. This clause is common in the public sector. The terms of employment in the telecommunications branch of the Post Office, for example, laid down a retiring age of 60, but went on to provide that all fit and willing officers would be kept on as long as possible depending on their efficiency, physical fitness, and the best interests of the public service. In *Post Office* v *Wallser* (1981) the evidence showed that a substantial majority of the employees in the same grade as the applicant were retained after 60. Even so, the normal retiring age in the contract was 60 and this was held to be decisive. Only if there is evidence that the policy of retiring at a particular age was generally disregarded could it be said that there was not a normal retiring age. In *Howard* v *Department of National Savings* (1981) another bench of the Court of Appeal accepted that only if the contract did not make the normal retiring age clear should custom and practice be looked at. This opens the somewhat alarming possibility that an employer might insert in a contract a retiring age of 40, subject to the exercise of a discretion to extend it. Even though most employees would be kept on until 60 there would (on the strict interpretation of *Howard*) be no opportunity for an unfair dismissal claim over the age of 40. Ackner and Griffiths LJJ hardly concealed their disapproval of this approach, although feeling bound as to their decision by the House of Lords in *Nothman*. The former admitted that the decision means 'perhaps surprisingly that often the normal retiring age is the minimum retiring age in the sense that it is the earliest date at which there is a contractual liability to retire', while Griffiths LJ thought that in the absence of authority it was not the most obvious construction. (See also *DHSS* v *Randalls* (1981).)

The most important statement of principle is to be found in the House of Lords' decision in *Waite* v *Government Communications Headquarters* (1983). It held that 'normal retiring age' is the age at which employees in a group can reasonably expect to be compelled to retire unless there is some special reason in a particular case for a different age to apply. This is not conclusively fixed by the contract of each member of the group, although there is a presumption to that effect. This presumption may, however, be rebutted by evidence that there is in practice some higher age (but not lower—see *Royal and Sun Alliance Lawrence Group plc* v *Payne* (2005)) at which those employees regularly retire. 'Normal' in this context is not a synonym for usual. The test in *Waite* has proved difficult to apply in practice. As was pointed out at the outset (see John McMullen, (1984) 13 ILJ 57), a personal assurance to an employee that he will be retained at a higher age than that specified in his contract, although it creates an expectation, will not avail that employee if it is not shared by other employees in the same position.

This, indeed, was the situation in *Coy* v *DHSS* (1985) where the EAT held that at most such an undertaking would create an estoppel, which leaves the employee in a very difficult position in that he requires a sword to pursue the claim and not a shield. As Dolding has pointed out (see (1986) 49 MLR 630), this problem became more acute, given the pressure to reduce retirement ages, but now the position is the opposite. The combined appeals of *Hughes* v *DHSS* and *Coy* v *DHSS* also threw up the issue of what was the relevance of past practice in determining employee's expectations. The House of Lords held that it should be irrelevant. It also considered the relevant pool of employees who should be examined in determining who is in the applicant's 'position' and it held that account must be taken of the status of the employee, the nature of the work done and the terms and conditions of the employment. It might seem that the size and composition of the pool should be considered without having regard to a term of the contract of employment that deals only with retirement ages. In other words, in determining whether a pool of employees has a normal retiring age, it would be illogical to *define* that pool by the retiring age of the employees in it. This reasoning appealed to the EAT in *Barber* v *Thames Television plc* (1992) but not to the Court of Appeal, which reversed the EAT's decision. *Barber* itself was not, however, followed in *Bratko* v *Beliot Walmesley Ltd* (1995). The EAT in *Bratko* also decided that the action of the employers in purporting to reduce the normal retiring age below the contractual retirement age was in breach of contract and was not effective for that purpose.

It might be thought that where there is only one employee, because there are no comparators, there can be no *normal* retiring age, nor a pool, but the Court of Appeal disagreed in *Wall* v *British Compressed Air Society* (2004). The policy is to prevent employees from claiming unfair dismissal after their contractual retiring ages and it makes no difference in this regard, the Court said, that an employee is in a unique position. 'Normal' does not connote a norm.

A further problem is this: as employees in the applicant's position will not necessarily be the same age, and will not have started employment at the same time, their expectations as to their retiring ages may be different. An employee in his early thirties may well expect to retire at an earlier age than employees in their late fifties. Rather surprisingly, perhaps, the Court of Appeal in *Brooks* v *British Telecommunications plc* (1992) held that the correct test was to look at the actual expectations of those employees in the applicant's position, and not their expectations had they been his age. This arguably runs counter to the purpose of the provision, which is surely to protect an employee's own reasonable expectations. Part of what is reasonable is to be determined by seeing if others in his position hold the same expectation.

A normal retiring age must be a definite cut-off point and cannot be a band between, for example, 62 and 63. The EAT decided this in *Swaine* v *Health and Safety Executive* (1986). Where employees in fact retired at a variety of ages higher than the contractual retiring age there was no normal retiring age so that the statutory cut-off applied and, as the male appellant was below 65, he could claim. A change in the age at which an employee could expect to be forced to retire could be made orally at an annual staff meeting, even though that policy had previously been contained in written documents. Whether there was a sufficient change was a question of fact which the tribunal had decided in favour of the employer, and the EAT would not interfere.

In *Secretary of State for Scotland* v *Meikle* (1986) the Scottish EAT decided that the tribunal could properly decide that the contractual retiring age of 55 had ceased to be the normal retiring age for prison officers because it was in fact regularly departed from in practice. It was not correct that the presumption that the contractual retiring age was the same as the normal retiring age could only be rebutted when the contractual retiring age had been abandoned altogether. Since there was now a variety of ages for retirement, the tribunal had properly determined that there was no normal retiring age.

The Court of Session had occasion to consider in *Highlands and Islands Development Board* v *MacGillivray* (1986) the scope of those in a similar position to the applicant. In 1975 the appellants reduced the normal retiring age for men to 60, subject to the proviso that they would apply a policy of maximum retention up to 65 for existing male staff. The EAT considered the positions of the 16 administrative officers including the respondent who were covered by this policy. Instead, they should have looked at the positions of all 63 administrative officers in employment at the time of the employee's dismissal. The fact that all those within a group did not have the same contractual retiring age did not mean that they did not remain members of the same group. All 63 had the same status, nature of work and terms and conditions save for the retiring age.

For the position regarding the default retirement age, see Chapter 10 below.

8.6.4 Redundancy

The fourth type of potentially fair dismissal is where the employee is dismissed on the grounds that he was redundant (ERA 1996, s. 98(2)(c)). The definition of redundancy is to be found in s. 139, and will be considered in detail in Chapter 9 below.

Justification

The employer does not have to justify his declaration of redundancy unless it is an obvious sham (*H. Goodwin Ltd* v *Fitzmaurice* (1977)). Thus in *Moon* v *Homeworthy Furniture (Northern) Ltd* (1977) the employees claimed that there was no true redundancy because the factory in which they were working when they were dismissed was still economically viable. Kilner Brown J thought that if the courts were to decide such questions they would be in danger of being utilised as a forum for industrial disputes. Therefore 'there could not...be any investigation into the rights and wrongs of the declared redundancy'. This does not sit well with the Court of Appeal's decision in *James W. Cook & Co. (Wivenhoe) Ltd* v *Tipper* (1990) to the effect that, in assessing compensation for an unfair dismissal, a tribunal may have regard to the genuineness of the closure. It is hard to see why this should not apply to the consideration of whether the dismissal itself was unfair.

Reasonableness

The manner in which the tribunals should approach the question of reasonableness under s. 98(4) in the case of redundancy has never ceased to be highly controversial. In *Atkinson* v *George Lindsay & Co.* (1980) the Court of Session thought that it would 'in most cases be extremely difficult for any tribunal to hold' that a dismissal was unfair under this general test if it survived the hurdle of the agreed selection. These cases have tended to treat the employer as though he were an administrative agency whose decisions in this respect should be challenged only *in extremis.* The same test of perversity has been applied here as to judicial review of administrative action. This is notwithstanding the unambiguously objective terms of the general test of reasonableness. It does, however, reflect the limited options open to an employer at a time of crisis. In *Vickers Ltd* v *Smith* (1977) the EAT thought that the tribunal should have asked 'whether the decision of management was so wrong that no sensible or reasonable management could have arrived at the decision which the employers [reached]'. In *Jackson* v *General Accident, Fire and Life Assurance Co. Ltd* (1976) Lord Macdonald commented, 'while where the ground of dismissal is capability or conduct and there has been some procedural failure...it can readily be seen how the employer could be held to have acted unreasonably...it is not so easy to envisage this where the ground is redundancy' (see *Valor Newhome Ltd* v *Hampson* (1982)).

This trend appeared to be halted in *Williams* v *Compair Maxam* (1982), when the EAT laid down guidelines of good industrial practice in redundancies. The tribunal was directed to consider whether objective selection criteria were chosen and fairly applied, whether the possibility of transfer to other work was investigated, whether employees were warned and consulted and whether the union (if any) was consulted over the most equitable manner of implementing the redundancies.

The EAT in Scotland has scathingly criticised the use of the guidelines in different circumstances. Notwithstanding that the case was approved by the Northern Ireland Court of Appeal in *Robinson* v *Carrickfergus BC* (1983), Lord Macdonald thought that the guidelines were 'becoming overworked and increasingly misapplied' in cases of small non-unionised employers such as in *A. Simpson & Son (Motors)* v *Reid & Findlater* (1983). The facts of the case concerned the dismissal of two out of three employees. In such a context the EAT felt that the guidelines should not be used by tribunals 'like a shopping list'. Further, in *Buchanan* v *Tilcon Ltd* (1983) the Court of Session reverted to the restrictive approach of the *Jackson* case. These latter cases have questioned the appropriateness of the appeal tribunal's role in offering guidelines at all in the light of certain Court of Appeal *dicta*. Browne-Wilkinson J, however, defended this role in *Grundy (Teddington) Ltd* v *Plummer and Salt* (1983) on the ground that it was a useful and proper part of the appeal tribunal's function in a limited number of cases to give guidance on the general approach as to what constitutes reasonable conduct. This was especially necessary since the Code of Practice was falling behind the times. In *Gray* v *Shetland Norse Preserving Co. Ltd* (1985) the Scottish EAT 'welcomed the opportunity of pointing out yet again how very limited the scope of these principles is', and in *Rolls-Royce Motors Ltd* v *Dewhurst* (1985) the

English EAT commented that 'No decision of this court seems to give greater trouble than the decision in *Williams* v *Compair Maxam*'.

The importance of criteria for selection

The employer should have settled criteria for the selection of employees to be dismissed. In *Compair Maxam* the criterion used was those employees 'who in the opinion of the managers concerned would be able to keep the company viable'. This, above all, rendered the dismissals unfair. Browne-Wilkinson J thought that the criteria should be capable of being objectively checked against such matters as attendance record, job efficiency, experience, and/or length of service. (The latter is not discriminatory against younger workers on the grounds of age, according to the Court of Appeal in *Rolls-Royce plc* v *Unite the Union* (2009), when it is a proportionate means of achieving a legitimate aim, which is more likely if there are several other factors which have also been taken into account. See further, Wynn-Evans, (2009) 38 ILJ 113.) In *Cox* v *Wildt Mellor Bromley Ltd* (1978) the EAT held that the employer must 'show how the employee came to be dismissed for redundancy, upon what basis the selection was made and how it was applied in practice'. (See also *Bristol Channel Ship Repairers Ltd* v *O'Keefe* (1977); *Greig* v *Sir Alfred McAlpine & Son (Northern) Ltd* (1979); *Graham* v *ABF Ltd* (1986).) On the other hand, the question for the tribunal should be whether 'the selection [was] one which a reasonable employer could have made, not would we have made that selection' (*BL Cars Ltd* v *Lewis* (1983)), and in *Eaton Ltd* v *King* (1995) the Scottish EAT held that the employer did not have a duty to disclose all the evidence which he used in coming to a decision on selection. However, it is a fine dividing line between that position and relying on the mere assertion of the employer as to the criteria he was relying on. In *British Aerospace Ltd* v *Green* (1995), the Court of Appeal said that:

...in general the employer who sets up a system of selection which can reasonably be described as fair and applies it without any overt sign of conduct which mars its fairness will have done all that the law requires of him....The tribunal is not entitled to embark upon a reassessment exercise...it is sufficient for the employer to show that he set up a good system of selection and that it was fairly administered, and that ordinarily there is no need for the employer to justify all the assessments on which the selection for redundancy was based.

The pool of selection must be reasonably defined so that in *GEC Machines Ltd* v *Gilford* (1982) selection from a section rather than the whole department was held unfair since the work within the department was interchangeable. The idea that the employer has to produce direct evidence to support his selection was, however, challenged in the *Buchanan* case. In the view of Lord Emslie, the employer had only to establish that the selection was fair 'in general terms'.

Consultation

According to the *Compair Maxam* case, the employer must also consult the union as to the best means by which the desired management result of redundancies can be achieved with as little hardship to the employees as possible. This principle receives specific statutory embodiment in TULR(C)A 1992, s. 188 in the case of recognised unions who must be consulted during a specified period before the dismissals begin.

Consultation with the union does not, however, absolve the employer from consulting each individual employee about his future (*Huddersfield Parcels Ltd* v *Sykes*

(1981); *cf. Pink* v *White and White & Co. (Earls Barton) Ltd* (1985)). Consultation is 'one of the fundamentals of fairness' (*Holden* v *Bradville Ltd* (1985); *cf. F. Lafferty Construction Ltd* v *Duthie* (1985)). To fail to consult is not merely a matter of discourtesy to the employee, but rather it deprives the employer of the opportunity to consider whether there may be another slot for the worker to fit into (*Abbotts & Standley* v *Wesson-Glynwed Steels Ltd* (1982)) and how he might ameliorate the blow for the employee (*Graham* v *ABF Ltd* (1986); *Freud* v *Bentalls Ltd* (1982)). In the latter case, Browne-Wilkinson J stressed that 'Consultation is one of the foundation stones of modern industrial relations practice'. In a very important judgment the Court of Session, in *King* v *Eaton Ltd* (1996), ruled that the union should have been consulted at a time when they could have influenced the criteria for selection.

Alternative employment

The principle that the employer should take reasonable steps to seek alternative employment for his employees was first enunciated in *Vokes Ltd* v *Bear* (1974). The respondent company was part of the massive Thomas Tilling group of companies in which there existed several vacancies in the type of senior management positions which the applicant had occupied before his redundancy. The failure to offer such a position rendered the dismissal unfair (*cf. MDH Ltd* v *Sussex* (1986)). In *British United Shoe Machinery Co. Ltd* v *Clarke* (1977), however, the EAT counselled against unreal or 'Elysian standards' being expected of an employer, and in *Barratt Construction Ltd* v *Dalrymple* (1984) the Scottish EAT rather surprisingly decided that the appellant employers did not have to look for alternatives in other parts of the Barratt group for junior jobs. Lord Macdonald thought that the change in the onus of proof in what was then EPCA 1978, s. 57(3) had altered the scope of the *Vokes* principle, and:

> Without laying down any hard and fast rule we are inclined to think that where an employee at senior management level who is being made redundant is prepared to accept a subordinate position he ought, in fairness, to make it clear at an early stage so as to give his employer an opportunity to see if this is a feasible solution.

An employer who can offer alternative employment must make such an offer sufficiently clear so that an employee may make a decision. In some cases, this obligation to consider offering alternative work has meant that another employee has to be dismissed (*Thomas & Betts Manufacturing Co. Ltd* v *Harding* (1980)).

The employer has a duty to provide alternative employment only so long as the employee is in his employment, even if the alternative arises very shortly after the employment has come to an end (*Octavius Atkinson & Sons* v *Morris* (1989)).

8.6.5 **Illegality**

The employer may prove as a reason for dismissal 'that the employee could not continue to work in the position which he held without contravention (either on his part or on that of his employer) of a duty or restriction imposed by or under an enactment' (ERA 1996, s. 98(2)(d)). The statute must in any case be related to the work the applicant was actually employed to do. Dismissal, for example, often follows the disqualification from driving of an employee who must use his car for work.

Even in these cases the resulting dismissal is not necessarily fair. In *Sutcliffe & Eaton Ltd* v *Pinney* (1977), for example, the applicant, a hearing aid dispenser, was sacked when he failed to pass the Hearing Aid Council's examination and was thus removed from the appropriate register of dispensers. It was an offence for him to continue to so act under statute. However, since it was possible for him to obtain an extension of time to take the exam and prosecution was unlikely, his dismissal without the employer inquiring of the likely position was held unfair by the EAT. Reasonableness may also require the employer to offer suitable alternative employment if appropriate. Thus the disqualified driver may be transferred to a stationary task (e.g. *Appleyard* v *F. M. Smith (Hull) Ltd* (1972)).

Dismissal of an employee because he has not obtained a proper work permit often falls under this head, but if the employer is mistaken as to the legality of the permission the dismissal will be fair, for 'some other substantial reason' (*Bouchaala* v *Trusthouse Forte Hotels Ltd* (1980)).

8.6.6 Some other substantial reason

The final category of potentially fair reasons for dismissal is contained in ERA 1996, s. 98(1)(b). This provision has been variously described as a 'dustbin category' or 'employer's charter', intended as a safety net to catch substantial reasons for dismissal which did not fall within other potentially fair gateways to dismissal. It has a 'rubber band' quality which arguably stretches too far. (See Bowers and Clarke, (1981) 10 ILJ 34.) Its language is indeed rather wider than the provisions of ILO Recommendation No. 119 on which most of the unfair dismissal legislation was based.

The general approach of the courts

The test was explained by the Court of Appeal in *Kent County Council* v *Gilham* (1985) as follows:

The hurdle over which an employer has to jump at this stage of an enquiry into an unfair dismissal complaint is designed to deter employers from dismissing employees for some trivial or unworthy reason. If he does so, the dismissal is deemed unfair without the need to look further into its merits. But if on the face of it the reason *could* justify the dismissal, then it passes as a substantial reason, and the enquiry moves on to [what is now ERA 1996, s. 98(4)] and the question of reasonableness.

According to Sir John Donaldson MR, 'different types of reason could justify the dismissal of the office boy from those which could justify the dismissal of the managing director'. (See also *Harper* v *National Coal Board* (1980).) Very few reasons have failed because they are not substantial and there is a tendency in this area to conflate the issue of 'other substantial reason' with the question of whether the employer acted reasonably (see e.g. *Willow Oak Developments Ltd* v *Silverwood* (2006)).

These, and other, developments have important implications for the whole policy of unfair dismissal. For the delicate balance at its heart between employer and employee is subtly tilted in favour of the employer. Central to this imbalance is the fact that rejection of management-instituted reorganisation is often portrayed as an undesirable curb on employer prerogative.

In three respects, more recent decisions have not lived up to what general statements by the NIRC originally and EAT subsequently about 'some other substantial reason'. First, and most importantly, Brightman J in *RS Components Ltd* v *Irwin* (1973), while deciding that the subsection was not to be construed *ejusdem generis* with the other headings, did go on to say that: 'It ought not as a matter of good industrial relations and common fairness to be construed too widely against the employee.' Subsequently, however, a conglomeration of reasons, usually flowing from management-pronounced notions of 'business efficiency', have come through the wide-open door.

Secondly, the NIRC was at pains to keep distinct the employer's reasons for dismissal and the reasonableness thereof. In *Mercia Rubber Mouldings Ltd* v *Lingwood* (1974) Donaldson J commented: 'The reason must be one which can justify dismissal, not one which *does* justify the dismissal.' This has proved rather easier to formulate than apply, as demonstrated by the relative paucity of cases in which 'some other substantial reason' has been found, and yet the dismissal has been subsequently held unfair.

Thirdly, although the EAT declared in *Trusthouse Forte Leisure Ltd* v *Aquilar* (1976) that 'the employer's description of the reason for dismissal is by no means conclusive', this principle has been honoured more in the breach than in its observance. The most extreme expression of non-intervention is to be found in the acceptance by tribunals of the employer's policy on reorganisation. As Arnold J formulated it in *Banerjee* v *City and East London Area Health Authority* (1979):

If an employer comes and says 'we have evolved such and such a policy'...it seems to us that it must inevitably follow that this enunciation by the employer of the policy as a matter of importance...can be seen to be the subject of a substantial other reason.

It may be challenged only on the basis of a complete lack of evidence. This approach rears its head with devastating effect in other areas of unfair dismissal, most notably selection for redundancy, and it undermines the principle that the statutory procedure should ensure that the dismissed employee receives an objective assessment of the basic factual adequacy of accusations made by the employer.

The reasons laid down by statute as being (other) substantial reasons are dismissals of workers: (a) taken on temporarily to replace permanent employees who are medically suspended or pregnant (in both cases the replacement must be warned of the temporary nature of the job on engagement (ERA 1996, s. 106)); and (b) where there are 'economic, technical or organisational reasons entailing a change in the workforce' on a transfer of undertaking (see Chapter 6 above). If an employer wishes to rely on this reason for dismissal, he must expressly raise it before the tribunal, or at the very least relate the full facts establishing it before the tribunal (*Murphy* v *Epsom College* (1983)). We now consider the most important categories of cases under this rubric.

Quasi-redundancies

It is in the area of 'quasi-redundancies'—that is, reorganisations which fail to satisfy the detailed requirements of ERA 1996, ss 135 and 139 for redundancy—that the EAT has found most scope for a dynamic interpretation of s. 98(1)(b). They have allowed the undertaking which reorganises or regroups, and finds that it has surplus staff, to escape both redundancy payments and unfair dismissal. That there should be some flexibility for employers to reorganise cannot be gainsaid, but the threshold for use of this heading has been considerably lowered.

When this notion crystallised is difficult to pinpoint. Phillips J in *Gorman* v *London Computer Training Centre Ltd* (1978), however, dwelt on the 'clear distinction' recognised between redundancy and quasi 'redundancy'. He said:

An employer may say 'I was overmanned, so we had to get rid of someone so A and B had to go, they were redundant'. The wording of [now ERA 1996, s. 139] may show he was wrong, but these grounds may well form a substantial reason.

It is difficult to define the criteria of reorganisation beyond the need for a 'policy', and the need to show the solid advantages of that strategy has steadily diminished. As to the existence of a policy, 'this is not an onus which it is at all difficult to discharge'. Only where there is no evidence at all is the claim open to challenge. In *Banerjee* v *City and East London AHA* (1979) a consultancy had been held jointly by two part-time employees. One left and the authority decided to create a single full-time appointment so that the applicant Dr Banerjee, the other a part-timer, was consequently dismissed. The defendants stated that this was determined in accordance with its 'policy of rationalisation, and the custom and practice of amalgamating part-time posts', but the EAT thought that was not enough and called on the Authority to produce relevant minutes of meetings to prove that due consideration had been given to all relevant matters in formulating the policy. There was no evidence of this at all.

Once there is evidence of a policy, however, the next stage which would appear crucial to the substantiality of the reason has been less strict. In *Ellis* v *Brighton Co-op Society* (1976) there was a reorganisation which had been properly consulted upon and agreed with the trade union and which, if not done, would 'bring the whole business to a standstill'. In *Robinson* v *British Island Airways Ltd* (1978) the EAT required a 'pressing business reason', and in *Hollister* v *NFU* (1979) the Court of Appeal pointed to the necessity for a 'sound good business reason'. After *Banerjee*, however, all that need be shown is that the changes were considered to be 'matters of importance' or to have 'discernible advantages to the organisation'. *Bowater Containers Ltd* v *McCormick* (1980) demands that the reorganisation be 'beneficial'. (See also *Genower* v *Ealing and Hammersmith AHA* (1980).)

It was in *Hollister* v *NFU* (1979) that the Court of Appeal thus formalised the close relation between reorganisation and managerial prerogative. The appellant was one of the respondent union's group secretaries, and received a modest wage and commission on insurance policies sold. The union reorganised its business in a drastic way, so that insurance was no longer dealt with locally, and the appellant's income was substantially cut as a result. On his refusal to sign a new contract, he was dismissed. Not only was this 'some other substantial reason', but the Court of Appeal, differing in this respect from the EAT, decided that there was no requirement for consultation with the employee.

In this area more than elsewhere, the tribunal has to weigh the economic interests of employer and employee. In *Evans* v *Elemeta Holdings Ltd* (1982) the EAT suggested that if it was reasonable for an employee to decline new terms offered by the employer, it would be unreasonable to dismiss him for it. In *Chubb Fire Security Ltd* v *Harper* (1983) the EAT dissented from this view, however, and stressed that the only proper question is the reasonableness of the employer's conduct in dismissing; were the employers reasonable in determining that the advantages to them of implementing the proposed reorganisation of terms outweighed any disadvantage they should have foreseen that the employee might suffer? (See also *Richmond Precision Engineering Ltd* v *Pearce* (1985).) The question as to the fairness or otherwise of the dismissal must be addressed as at the date of the dismissal itself and not as on the date of the offer of the new terms (*St John of God (Care Services) Ltd* v *Brooks* (1992)).

A review of the reorganisation case law shows that the EAT and the Court of Appeal appear to accept as wholly valid employers' claims that to compete efficiently in a free market they must be allowed latitude to trim and make efficient their workforce and work methods, without being hampered by laws protecting their workers. There are, however, indications that tribunals require more evidence on the need for reorganisation.

In *Orr* v *Vaughan* (1981) the EAT stressed that the employers must act on reasonable information reasonably acquired as to their business needs. Here, the employers could not be satisfied on the information available that it was at the particular salon where the respondent was employed that the business was losing money. The employer must provide evidence that there was a need for economy there and it is material for the ET to know whether the company was at the time making profits or losses (*Ladbroke Courage Holidays Ltd* v *Asten* (1981)).

Changes in terms and conditions

Another widespread use of 'other substantial reason' is where an employer insists on a change in the employee's contractual terms and conditions. Thus in *RS Components Ltd* v *Irwin* (1973) the company was losing profits because of the activities of some ex-employees who had set up in competition to them. They thus required their 92 current salesmen to sign a restrictive covenant. Four refused and the NIRC held their consequent dismissal fair. Brightman J posited:

a case where it would be essential for employers embarking, for example, on a new technical process to invite existing employees to agree to some reasonable restriction on their use of the knowledge they acquire of the new technique.

Unfair dismissal provisions have provided no protection against unilateral changes in job content (e.g. *Robinson* v *Flitwick Frames Ltd* (1975)), location (e.g. *Farr* v *Hoveringham Gravels Ltd* (1972)), pay (*Industrial Rubber Products Ltd* v *Gillon* (1977)), and night shift working (*Martin* v *Automobile Proprietary Ltd* (1979)).

These cases emphasise that what would be a constructive dismissal is not necessarily unfair. Yet it is ironic that the unfair dismissal provisions, which were intended to give employees broader rights than at common law, should recognise as a reason for dismissal a compulsory change in contractual terms which would be unlawful at common law and could lead to a claim for wrongful dismissal.

The paradoxical position also arises that if, when faced with a forced contractual variation, the employee stages a personal protest and is dismissed for 'some other substantial reason'. If, on the other hand, he joins official collective action over the change, only if all the strikers are dismissed can that be a gateway to dismissal.

Temporary workers

One of the clearest perceptions of British individual employment law is that it provides a form of 'job security' only to employees who have been with the undertaking for more than a minimal amount of time. This principle might be infringed if employees were too readily held to be 'temporary', and thus not deserving of protection. 'Other substantial reason' has been at times adopted to cover dismissals of temporary workers, but the dangers of an over-extended definition have been recognised. In *Terry* v *East Sussex CC* (1976) the EAT stressed that in every instance the tribunal must ensure that the description was 'a genuine one, where an employee has to his knowledge been employed for a particular job on a temporary basis'. In *Cohen* v *London Borough of Barking* (1976) Slynn J emphasised the scope of review that, while the fact that the contract was not assured of continuance beyond a fixed term was a material factor to be considered, it was not at all conclusive. The temporary employee ought to be given the opportunity of being considered if a full-time position becomes available (*Beard* v *St Joseph's School* (1978)), and tribunals must not omit a 'full consideration of the circumstances surrounding a decision to dismiss at the end of a temporary fixed-term contract'. In the case of *North Yorkshire County Council* v *Fay* (1985) the Court of Appeal dealing with a teacher's contract decided that there was a fair 'other substantial reason' if it is shown that the fixed-term contract was adopted for a genuine purpose and that fact was known to the employee, and that the specific purpose for which the contract was adopted had ceased.

These cases show a welcome recognition of the underlying intentions of the Act, refusing to allow 'some other substantial reason' to deny too easily protection for the temporary employee.

It should be remembered that temporary workers have protection afforded to them outside unfair dismissal law by virtue of the Fixed-Term Employees (Prevention of Less Favourable Treatment) Regulations 2002 (SI 2002 No. 2034)—see Chapter 10 below.

Relationship with other categories of dismissal

The ERA 1996 defines with some particularity conduct, redundancy, and contravention of an enactment, yet tribunals have used the 'other substantial reason' to extend all of these concepts. For example, while conduct connotes active behaviour by the employee, 'some other substantial reason' includes omissions. In *O'Brien* v *Prudential Assurance Co. Ltd* (1979) an employee failed to disclose a long period of mental illness when applying for the job and this was another substantial reason justifying dismissal. The argument that the reason had to be directly referable to the employee's work for the employer failed, as it did in a series of cases in which activities outside and before the job have been included under s. 98(1)(b). These directly raise philosophical issues about how far the managerial prerogative strays into the employee's private life. In *Saunders* v *Scottish National Camps Association* (1980) the Court of Session would not interfere with the determination of fairness once they had found the employers held a common and, it thought, not unreasonable belief that homosexuals were more likely than heterosexuals to interfere with young children. It is hard to imagine that this would be decided the same way today. Where a woman employee had plans to marry a man who worked for a rival travel company this was found to fall within the section notwithstanding that the two clerks had no financial interest in their respective companies (*Skyrail Oceanic* v *Coleman* (1980), overturned by the Court of Appeal on other grounds in 1981). A breakdown in relationships between employees has often been characterised as some other substantial reason, but the EAT in *Turner* v *Vestric Ltd* (1980) counselled that the employer must take reasonable steps to try to improve the relationship and examine all options short of dismissal to obviate the situation.

Outside pressure on the employer to dismiss

There are several decisions in which an outside source of pressure on the employer has been seen as another substantial reason. In *Scott Packaging and Warehousing Co. Ltd* v *Paterson* (1978) the EAT held that it might be justifiable to dismiss an employee in response to an ultimatum from the company's major customer. The US naval authorities refused the applicant's services because of a suspected theft, of which no evidence was presented. This could hardly be a fair dismissal for misconduct, since the employing company had been fully aware of the facts for a full six weeks before dismissal, but it was some other substantial reason. *Moody* v *Telefusion Ltd* (1978) took this further, since the EAT held a dismissal fair because the employee was unable to secure a fidelity bond. In deciding whether the reason was substantial the EAT failed to enquire into the reasonableness of requiring a fidelity bond (see also *Dobie* v *Burns International Security Services (UK) Ltd* (1984)). In *Grootcon (UK) Ltd* v *Keld* (1984) the EAT stressed that the employer must lead convincing evidence as to the outside pressure he was under.

However, the employer cannot argue as a defence or in mitigation of compensation that he was forced to dismiss because of the threat of a strike, whether the pressure was implicit or explicit (ERA 1996, ss 107(2), 123(5)). The former was illustrated in *Colwyn Borough Council* v *Dutton* (1980), where the applicant's trade union branch refused to act as crew of the applicant's dustcart because they considered his driving dangerous, and he was dismissed in consequence. The test propounded in *Ford Motor Co. Ltd* v *Hudson* (1978) was whether:

the pressure exerted on the employers [was] such that it could be foreseen that it would be likely to result in the dismissal of those employees in respect of where the pressure was being brought?

Under TULR(C)A 1992, s. 160 the employer or employee may, however, apply to join the union or other person applying pressure as a third party to proceedings and may obtain a contribution or indemnity for any compensation paid.

8.6.7 Reasonableness and the importance of procedure

In considering whether an employer acted reasonably in dismissing an employee for one of the potentially fair reasons just considered, the procedural aspects of the dismissal are of great importance. As Collins pointed out, however, the emphasis on procedure was not to be found in the wording of what is now the ERA 1996, which merely sets out a broad standard of reasonableness ((1982) 11 ILJ 78 at p. 88). The courts stress procedure as it fits into the main purpose of the legislation as they see it, namely to manage a crisis in industrial relations. To emphasise procedural norms is to give opportunities for second thoughts and conciliation, thereby reducing industrial conflict.

The principles of natural justice also have a part to play in determining procedural fairness (see e.g. Carty, (1989) 52 MLR 449 at p. 451), although it is best to take the Statutory Dismissal and Disciplinary Procedures under the EA 2002 together with the Employment Act 2002 (Dispute Resolution) Regulations 2004 (SI 2004 No. 752) (see below) as a starting point together with the ACAS Code of Practice on Disciplinary and Grievance Procedures 2004. Indeed, in public law a lack of a fair procedure is of lesser importance in determining the fairness of a dismissal (see *R* v *Chief Constable of the Thames Valley Police ex parte Cotton* (1990)). It must also be borne in mind that the Human Rights Act 1998 may have a role to play here, and all pre-HRA decisions should accordingly be treated with some degree of caution—see *Pay* v *Lancashire Probation Service* (2004). (For an interesting discussion on the judicial use of the concept of reasonableness in this area, and a comparison with how it is employed in public law, see Davies, (2009) 38 ILJ 278.)

Procedural defects

From the case of *A. J. Dunning & Sons (Shopfitters) Ltd* v *Jacomb* (1973) the approach developed that a procedural defect would make the dismissal unfair only if the decision might have been different at the end of the day. The trend is to see procedural matters as issues of substance to be weighed in the scales of the overall merits of the case. This became known as the *British Labour Pump* principle after the case of *British Labour Pump Co. Ltd* v *Byrne* (1979). However, this case and the several cases which applied it were overruled in *Polkey* v *Dayton Services Ltd* (1988), when the House of Lords held the proper approach was to consider whether the employer had acted reasonably in deciding that his reason for dismissing the employee was a sufficient reason, and not whether any failure on his part would have made a difference to the decision to dismiss. Lord Mackay said this:

The subject matter for the tribunal's consideration is the employer's action in treating the reason as a sufficient reason for dismissing the employee. It is that action and that action only that the tribunal is required to characterise as reasonable or unreasonable. That leaves no scope for the tribunal considering whether, if the employer had acted differently, he might have dismissed the employee. It is what the employer did that is to be judged, not what he might have done. On the other hand, in judging whether what the employer did was reasonable it is right to consider what a reasonable employer would have had in mind at the time he decided to dismiss as the consequence of not consulting or not warning.

If the employer could reasonably have concluded in the light of the circumstances known to him at the time of dismissal that consultation or warning would be utterly useless he might well act reasonably even if he did not observe the provisions of the code. Failure to observe the requirement of the code relating to consultation or warning will not necessarily render a dismissal unfair. Whether in any particular case it did so is a matter for the industrial tribunal to consider in the light of the circumstances known to the employer at the time he dismissed the employee.

So, in other words, the test reverted more closely to the wording of the statute which required the tribunal to examine whether or not the employer acted reasonably in dismissing the employee, and not to whether or not there had been an injustice done to the employee. *Polkey* was therefore to be preferred as a matter of statutory interpretation, particularly in the light of the fact that the test in *British Labour Pump* was often characterised as involving an examination not of what the employer would reasonably have done had he followed the procedure properly, but whether he *could* have reasonably dismissed, which is altogether different (see Rideout, (1988) 17 ILJ 41). To fall within the exception recognised in *Polkey*, there had to be no conscious decision by the employer to the effect that consultation or some other procedural protection would be utterly useless (*Duffy* v *Yeomans and Partners* (1994)). While the decision in *Polkey* made findings of 'technical' unfair dismissal more likely, as John McMullen pointed out ((1988) 51 MLR 651) following correct procedure is the part of the law of unfair dismissal that differentiates it from the common law.

Warnings

An employee should generally be given a warning about his misconduct or incompetence before being dismissed if that dismissal is to be considered fair—see ACAS Code of Practice. Warning is shorthand for 'efforts to try to make the employee change and an indication to him of the consequence if these efforts are unsuccessful' (*Plasticisers Ltd* v *Amos* (1976)). It is intended to deter and reform the employee, and should be administered to the worker individually, although exceptionally a general warning might be acceptable (*Connely* v *Liverpool Corporation* (1974)). However, a warning given previously, relating to different misconduct, may be taken into account by an employer in considering later misconduct, according to the EAT in *Auguste Noel Ltd* v *Curtis* (1990).

Although the latter stage of the process should be in writing, 'there is no special magic' about it (*McCall* v *Castleton Crafts Ltd* (1979)). Its value is that it invests the process with a more official character. However, the ACAS Code states that, following a meeting, a written note should be given to the employee. To have its proper effect, the warning must be sufficiently specific. If the issue is unsatisfactory work, this should state the performance problem, the improvement required, timescale for improvement, a review date and any support the employee can expect from the employer. If it is because of misconduct a record should be kept, but subsequently discarded. An employer's insistence that 'you undertake these responsibilities and duties forthwith if you are to continue as Deputy Head of the Documentary Credit Department', did not suffice in *UBAF Bank Ltd* v *Davis* (1978). (See also *Littlewoods Organisation Ltd* v *Egenti* (1976).)

In most cases a warning on one ground should not be used as a step in procedure to dismiss on a completely different ground. Although confidential records should be kept at all stages, if the employee improves, the warning should be removed. Usually a 12-month period is reasonable and a specific time will be often inserted in disciplinary rules (*Charles* v *Science Research Council* (1977)). This brings to the forefront the aim to deter and reform. Further, a time limit on the currency of the warning is likely to be strictly construed, so that in *Bevan Ashford* v *Malin* (1995) the 12-month currency of the admonition was not effective when the warning was used by the employers, a firm of solicitors, in a dismissal one day after the year had expired. On the other hand, in *Airbus UK Ltd* v *Webb* (2008) the employer took a previous, expired, warning into account when deciding to dismiss the employee, and this was held by the Court of Appeal not to render the dismissal unfair. It was relevant, in considering the equity, merits and fairness of the employer's actions. It might be thought that this decision means that an employee can never be able to rest in comfort that a previous warning truly has expired.

The general requirement of a warning represents one of the most important improvements in the employee's protection from the law of wrongful dismissal, so that, instead of summary dismissal, the employee is to be given a reasonable opportunity to improve. The ACAS Code indeed urges, as we have seen, that disciplinary procedures should ensure that, except for gross misconduct, no employees should be dismissed for a first breach of discipline. This is particularly important where a rule has lain dormant for a considerable time. Thus the EAT said in *Wilcox* v *Humphreys & Glasgow* (1975):

> If the requirement had been ignored for ages to everyone's knowledge it would not be right without some kind of warning to dismiss the first person to break it after the employers took it into their heads to enforce it.

Many disciplinary procedures have provisions for appeals against a warning and the ACAS Code states that an employee should be told of the possibility of appeal— para. 22. There is, however, no general rule that an employee may not be dismissed while his final warning is under appeal (*Stein* v *Associated Dairies Ltd* (1982)). The tribunal is not to sit in judgment whether the employee should or should not have received such warning. Rather, it is sufficient that the final warning has been issued in good faith and that there was at least *prima facie* ground for following the procedure (see *Tower Hamlets Health Authority* v *Anthony* (1989)). If there was anything to suggest that the warning had been issued for an oblique motive, or that it was manifestly inappropriate, the tribunal could take that into account in reaching its general decision on fairness.

Many works rules attempt to codify what misdemeanours will be treated as gross misconduct by the employer and thus where warnings will not be given. Even when this happens it still remains for the tribunal ultimately to determine whether the conduct was sufficiently serious in the circumstances.

Other circumstances where a warning may be dispensed with can include where the disciplinary rules are so clear as to constitute a warning of dismissal in themselves. This principle is, however, narrowly circumscribed so that in *Meridian Ltd* v *Gomersall* (1977) a notice that 'anyone found clocking cards on behalf of other personnel will render themselves liable to instant dismissal' was held to be insufficiently specific since it did not mean necessarily that the employee would be sacked for one offence.

A warning has been held to be dispensable where the employee knew, or was in a position to know, that he was putting his job in jeopardy by his action or inaction. This may be because of his close relationship with the employer in a small unit (*Brown* v *Hall Advertising Ltd* (1978)—confidential private secretary and managing director). A diametrically opposite view was, however, taken in the strange decision in *McPhail* v *Gibson* (1977). The applicant farm manager had given a grossly inaccurate reference for an employee to a neighbouring farmer. Kilner Brown J thought that a warning was particularly necessary before the dismissal of a person in such a position of trust and that 'instant dismissal even in a case of grave misconduct is very rarely associated with no preliminary step having taken place'. Where there is a specific agreed procedure and a dismissal has proceeded in accordance with it, it is very difficult to persuade an ET that more in the way of warnings is required (*Donald Cook & Sons Ltd* v *Carter* (1977)).

8.7 **Remedies**

The remedies for unfair dismissal are: reinstatement, re-engagement, and compensation. After a finding of unfairness the applicant is required to choose whether or not he wishes to be reinstated, re-engaged, or gain only a monetary award, and the ET must explain to him the consequences of each course (*Pirelli General Cable Works Ltd* v *Murray* (1979)); and if it fails to do so, if there is a possibility of injustice or unfairness the case should be sent back to the tribunal for reconsideration by the EAT, according to the Court of Appeal in *Cowley* v *Manson Timber Ltd* (1995). (For an interesting analysis of the rationale of unfair dismissal compensation, see Hough and Spowart-Taylor, (1996) 25 ILJ 308.)

The first two remedies, for re-employment in some manner, while designed to be the primary remedies, are in fact ordered in very few cases indeed. One assumption is that applicants do not generally want re-employment for the obvious reasons that by the time of the hearing they will have another job, or because they do not desire to return to work for an employer who has already dismissed them and against whom they have successfully pursued a claim for unfair dismissal in an ET. A survey carried out by Evans, Goodman, and Hargreaves (see (1985) 14 ILJ 91) found that while trade union officials tried to ensure that claimants stipulated their desire for re-employment in their applications, this was essentially a tactical move to enhance their bargaining position for compensation.

Hugh Collins has argued that the lack of reinstatement as a viable remedy should not be considered as a serious criticism of the law. He feels that the aims of the legislation are achievable through appropriate levels of compensation. It is important that the remedy is sufficient to deter employers from acting unfairly, and this can be achieved better by compensation than by reinstatement and re-engagement, he argues (see Collins, (1991) 20 ILJ 227). It would appear, however, that the relative deterrence effect is dependent upon variables relating to each employer on which it is difficult to generalise.

8.7.1 **Reinstatement**

Reinstatement is an order that 'the employer shall treat the complainant in all respects as if he had not been dismissed' and must include benefits payable in respect of the period since dismissal and rights and privileges, including seniority and pensions (ERA 1996, s. 114(1) and (2)). It should not be ordered if it is not practicable for the employer to comply with it or it would be unjust to do so because the employee contributed to the dismissal. The general meaning of impracticability was considered by the Court of Appeal in *Coleman* v *Magnet Joinery Ltd* (1974) where, in rejecting the employee's contention that it depended solely on whether a job was available, Stephenson LJ said:

The tribunal ought to consider the consequences of re-engagement in the industrial relations scene in which it will take place. If it is obvious as in the present case that re-engagement would only promote further serious industrial relations strife, it will not be practicable to make the recommendation.

The matter is one pre-eminently for the tribunal's independent discretion, and appeals are only reluctantly entertained. The employer does not need to show that it is impossible to comply with the orders. Practicability must be seen in the light of the circumstances of the business, according to the Court of Appeal in *Port of London Authority* v *Payne* (1994) (see Bennett, (1994) 23 ILJ 164). The EAT would not order reinstatement where, for example, it would poison the atmosphere in a factory either generally or among particular workers (*Coleman* v *Toleman's Delivery Service Ltd* (1973)), or where a genuine redundancy or reorganisation has arisen in the position since dismissal (*Trusler* v *Lummus Co. Ltd* (1972)). Neither will it be awarded if it would lead to strike action (*Langston* v *AUEW* (1974)). However, the test is one of practicability, not reasonableness. Even if it would be unreasonable to comply with the order, so long as it is practicable to do so it should be considered, according to the EAT in *Wood Group Heavy Industrial Turbines Ltd* v *Crossan* (1998).

The most important general restriction was introduced in *Enessy Co. SA* v *Minoprio* (1978), where Lord McDonald said, *obiter*:

> In our view it was not realistic to make an order of this nature in a case where the parties involved were in close personal relationships with each other such as they were in the present situation. It is one thing to make an order for reinstatement where the employee concerned works in a factory or other substantial organisation. It is another to do so in the case of a small employer with a few staff.

The fact that the employer has engaged a permanent replacement for the dismissed employee before the tribunal hears the case is irrelevant and does not make it impracticable to reinstate unless the employer shows that it was not practicable for him to arrange for the dismissed employee's work to be done without engaging a permanent replacement for him, and he engaged the replacement after the lapse of a reasonable period without having heard from the dismissed employee that he wished to be reinstated or re-engaged, and that when the employer engaged the replacement it was no longer reasonable for him to arrange for the dismissed employee's work to be done except by a permanent replacement (ERA 1996, s. 116(5) and (6)).

8.7.2 Re-engagement

Re-engagement resembles reinstatement in its effect except that the employee does not necessarily return to the same post. The job must be comparable and suitable and, so far as is reasonably practicable, as favourable as the previous position (ERA 1996, s. 115). It may, however, be with an associated or successor employer and the tribunal decides what terms should apply and the date by which compliance must be made.

The tribunal has no power to commit to prison for contempt of court, nor fine the employer if he ignores an order to reinstate or to re-engage, but the sacked worker may apply for an 'additional award'—a special form of exemplary or punitive damages—amounting to between 26 weeks' and 52 weeks' gross pay as extra compensation (s. 117) minus any award made for a procedural failure (s. 117(2A)). An order to re-employ is not satisfied if the applicant is re-employed on less favourable terms (*Artisan Press* v *Strawley and Parker* (1986)). (See David Lewis, (1986) 15 ILJ 203.)

Any order for re-engagement must put the applicant as far as possible in the position he would have been in had he not been dismissed. An ET may not order that an employee be re-engaged upon terms significantly more favourable than those he would enjoy if reinstated (*Rank Xerox (UK) Ltd* v *Stryczek* (1995)). There is an entitlement to pay between dismissal and re-engagement (*City and Hackney Health Authority* v *Crisp* (1990)).

8.7.3 Compensation: basic award

Since the EPA 1975 unfair dismissal compensation has consisted of two components, the basic and compensatory awards (ERA 1996, s. 118) and both may be reduced owing to failure to mitigate the loss or contributory fault. The unfairly dismissed employee claims as basic award so many weeks' pay for each year of continuous employment with his own or any associated or predecessor employer before the effective date of termination, irrespective of whether the unfair dismissal has caused any loss to him. This head was first introduced by EPA 1975 and is intended at the same time to convey disapproval of the employer's action and also to compensate for the loss of job security. It performs a similar function to a redundancy payment and it is appropriate that they should be calculated in almost the same way (ERA 1996, s. 119).

It has been described as reflecting the loss of the employee's 'paid-up insurance policy' against the loss of a job, but the House of Lords in *Devis & Sons Ltd* v *Atkins* (1977) saw it in a different negative light. Their remarks were wholly *obiter*, since the case was decided on the earlier law, but Lord Diplock said that: 'The compensation provisions are therefore converted into a veritable rogues' charter, for the tribunal would be bound to award to a fraudulent employee because he had successfully concealed his fraud a basic compensation which might well amount to a substantial sum.'

The amount of basic award depends on the age of the employee in this way:

(a) each year which consists wholly of weeks in which the employee was over 41, one and a half weeks' pay; and

(b) each year which consists wholly of weeks not within (a) but in which the employee was not below 22, one week's pay;

(c) any year wholly consisting of weeks under 22, half a week's pay (s. 119(2)).

No account is to be taken of any time beyond 20 years (s. 119(3)) or of any week's pay over a sum fixed by Order from time to time (presently £380). The maximum is therefore £11,400. The amount is based on the national minimum wage if the actual figure paid is lower, according to the EAT in *Paggetti* v *Cobb* (2002).

There is no minimum basic award, except in trade union membership cases (TULR(C)A 1992, s. 156(1), when it is £4,700). It may be reduced if the employee had unreasonably refused an offer of reinstatement (ERA 1996, s. 122(1)), or because of any conduct before the dismissal (s. 122(2)). The latter is designed to mitigate the effect of the *Devis* v *Atkins* sort of case where the dismissal is unfair because the employer did not know at the time of the facts for which he could reasonably dismiss. Unlike contributory fault in assessing the compensatory award, it does not matter under this subsection whether there was a causal link between the applicant's conduct and the dismissal.

There is a two weeks' maximum of basic award where the reason for dismissal was redundancy and the employee unreasonably refuses to accept a renewal of the contract or suitable alternative employment or where the employee during a trial period unreasonably terminates the contract (ERA 1996, s. 121). Because the basic award performs the same function and is assessed in a similar way, any redundancy pay is fully deducted from it (ERA 1996, s. 122(4)). However, the EAT in *Chelsea Football & Athletic Club Co. Ltd* v *Heath* (1981) held that the basic award was not automatically to be reduced by any money paid by the employer *ex gratia* although it was presumed referable expressly or impliedly to the basic and compensatory award.

8.7.4 The compensatory award

The compensatory award provides what is just and equitable as compensation having regard to the loss suffered as a result of the dismissal (ERA 1996, s. 123(1)). This is subject to a maximum which is varied each year–£65,300 from February 2010. However, there is no maximum where whistleblowers or health and safety representatives are dismissed—see s. 124. The maximum should be applied only as a last step in the calculating process, and therefore after any deductions have been made, according to the EAT in *Walter Braund (London) Ltd* v *Murray* (1991). It would, indeed, be difficult to see how s. 124 could be read in any other way. The test for assessing the award within the maximum has remained consistent since the introduction of unfair dismissal in 1971. In *Devis & Sons Ltd* v *Atkins* (1977), Viscount Dilhorne thought that it had two elements:

[Section 123(1)] does not...provide that regard should be had only to the loss resulting from the dismissal being unfair. Regard must be had to that but the award must be just and equitable in all the circumstances, and it cannot be just and equitable that a sum should be awarded in compensation when in fact the employee has suffered no injustice in being dismissed.

This means that if the employee has suffered no loss because, for example, he has immediately gained a better paid job and he would nevertheless have been dismissed if all the necessary procedural protections had been provided to him, he can claim nothing under this head, although he may still be entitled to the basic award (see *Chaplin* v *H. J. Rawlinson Ltd* (1991)). However, obtaining a new job does not mean the employer's liability is necessarily at an end. If the employee were to be dismissed from his new job after a short period, without compensation, his subsequent loss could be taken into account, according to the Court of Appeal in *Dench* v *Flynn and Partners* (1998). It also meant that there was nothing to preclude tribunals from making awards for injury to feelings and similar heads irrespective of any financial loss, according to Lord Hoffmann in *Johnson* v *Unysis Ltd* (2001), but this was ruled to be *obiter* by the House of Lords in *Dunnachie* v *Kingston-upon-Hull City Council* (2004)—see Barnard, [2006] CLJ 27. The rule in *Norton Tool Co. Ltd* v *Tewson* (1972) that only economic loss was recoverable was still good law. (See Bowers and Lewis, (2005) 34 ILJ 83; Brodie, (2004) 33 ILJ 349.)

In *British United Shoe Machinery Co. Ltd* v *Clarke* (1978), where a redundancy dismissal was held unfair because there was no consultation, the EAT would not give the employee compensation because he would have been made redundant at a later stage anyway. Phillips J commented:

In some cases it will happen that the industrial tribunal reaches the conclusion that had everything been done which ought to have been done it would not have made the slightest difference...where the industrial tribunal finds that the dismissal was unfair it will be necessary for them to proceed to assess compensation and for that purpose to make some estimate of what would have been the likely outcome had that been done which ought to have been done. This is often a difficult question, but one which the industrial tribunal in their capacity as industrial jury are well suited to answer, and in respect of which they will not go wrong if they remember that what they are trying to do is to assess the loss suffered by the claimant and not punish the employer for his failure in industrial relations.

On the other hand, the degree of unfairness is not a relevant consideration in the assessment of what award is just and equitable. The tribunal is not entitled at this stage to take into consideration that the employers had no wish to treat the employee in anything other than a fair manner (*Morris* v *Acco Co. Ltd* (1985); *cf. Townson* v *The Northgate Group Ltd* (1981)). The tribunal often has to calculate the chance of the employee retaining his job if he had been granted all proper procedural protections (e.g. *O'Dea* v *ISC Chemicals Ltd* (1995)).

Tribunals have also been counselled not to act 'in a general benevolent manner according to the conception of what they think will be fair in the circumstances' (*Lifeguard Assurance Ltd* v *Zadrozny* (1977)). The burden of proving loss is firmly on the complainant, although: 'It is not therefore to be expected that the precise and detailed proof of every item of loss will be presented' (*Norton Tool Co. Ltd* v *Tewson* (1972) per Donaldson J). The *Norton* case also required tribunals to set out their findings in appropriate subheadings, and these remain generally the same today despite much subsequent elaboration. The EAT has frequently called upon tribunals to take a broad brush approach to compensation questions, and will interfere with a decision on this matter only if it is perverse (e.g. *Manpower Ltd* v *Hearne* (1983)). Moreover, in *Courtaulds Northern Spinning Ltd* v *Moosa* (1984), Browne-Wilkinson J accepted that 'the assessment of compensation in [employment] tribunals cannot be as scrupulously accurate as, say, in an action for personal injuries in the High Court'. In any event, there are some who believe that such an approach is contrary to the 'just and equitable' approach required by the statute (see e.g. Collins, (1991) 20 ILJ 201).

Many of the criteria derive from the principles adopted in awarding special damages for personal injuries.

Immediate loss of earnings

This heading replaces loss of net earnings from the date of dismissal to the hearing, and receipt of jobseekers' allowance is ignored for this calculation because the Government can recoup such benefits from the employer of a successful applicant. It was at one time thought that no deduction was to be made for anything which was or could have been earned during the notice period (*Everwear Candlewick Ltd* v *Isaac* (1974); *Norton Tool Co. Ltd* v *Tewson* (1972)), so that where proper notice was not given, payment in lieu thereof was the irreducible minimum to be awarded as compensation. This was, however, doubted in *Tradewinds Airways Ltd* v *Fletcher* (1981), where the EAT confirmed that compensation is to be awarded for actual financial loss, and if, as in the instant case, the employee proceeds to take another position within the notice period, earnings therefrom must be fully deducted. This would seem particularly justified in the case of constructive dismissal perhaps, where the employee has terminated the contract (see the Court of Appeal's decision in *Peters Ltd v Bell* (2009)), although it has to remembered that the employee has resigned as a consequences of the employer's repudiatory breach in these circumstances. But this may not be so in every case. (See e.g. *Babcock FATA Ltd v Addison* (1987); cf. *Horizon Holidays Ltd v Grassi* (1987), where pay in lieu and an *ex gratia* payment were deducted from the award. See too *Hardy v Polk (Leeds) Ltd* (2004) and *Langley v Burlo* (2006).) Likewise, any incapacity benefit paid is to be deducted, and in full—see *Morgans v Alpha Plus Security Ltd* (2005); cf. *Voith Turbo Ltd v Stowe* (2005).

Future loss of earnings

The amount of this element depends on how long the dismissed worker is likely to be unemployed, and whether he will have to take a job at a lower rate than in his previous employment. The proper comparison is between net (and not gross), pay in the two positions. According to the judgment in *Tradewinds Airways Ltd v Fletcher* (1981) tribunals must:

compare his salary prospects for the future in each job and see as best they could how long it would have been before he reached with [the second employer] the equivalent salary to that which he would have reached if he had remained with his old employers. Then the amount of shortfall during the period before he reached parity would be the amount of his future loss.

Normally the tribunal adopts a multiplier and multiplicand, as in tort cases, so that the proper sum to be awarded is the difference between earnings in the new job and the old multiplied by a reasonable estimate of how long any shortfall will last. In *Cartiers Superfoods Ltd v Laws* (1978), since the shortest period the applicant would work was two to three years and the longest ten, the tribunal was held correct in applying a multiplier of three. (See also *Adda International Ltd v Curcio* (1976).) There may be a discount for accelerated receipt of earnings which may as a lump sum be invested and bear interest, and to take account of a whole range of possible future contingencies, although the EAT criticised over-complicated analysis. If the employee has not found other employment before the tribunal hearing, the tribunal may consider certain circumstances. If the employee is in poor health or has defective eyesight (*Fougère v Phoenix Motor Ltd* (1976); also *Penprase v Mander Bros Ltd* (1973)) or was injured in a fight which led to his dismissal (*Brittains Arborfield Ltd v Van Uden* (1977)), it may prove more difficult for him to find other work, so that a higher award is appropriate, and again this resembles a common law principle—of taking the victim as one finds him. The tribunal may award compensation for a time beyond the normal retiring age if it finds that the employee would probably have stayed in a job beyond that time (*Barrel Plating Co. Ltd v Danks* (1976)).

If the employee might have been fairly dismissed in the near future, the period of future loss will be thereby reduced to last only until the date of fair dismissal. In *Evans v George Galloway & Co. Ltd* (1974), for instance, the applicant was dismissed because of poor productivity. The tribunal thought that the five weeks he had been given to improve his performance was insufficient, but that he was hardly likely to turn the corner given a longer period. They thought six months was a reasonable period to test his capabilities and that he could have been fairly dismissed at the end of it, so they limited future loss of earnings to this period. (See also *Winterhalter*

Gastronom Ltd v *Webb* (1973).) In some cases this may mean that no compensation at all is awarded although the practice has proved very controversial, not least because it renders a finding of unfairness virtually useless. Even so, in *Devis & Sons* v *Atkins* (1977), the House of Lords rejected the applicant's argument that the statutory provision that the tribunal 'shall' award compensation precluded a nil award. They did this on the ground that in the circumstances of the subsequently discovered fraud it was neither just nor equitable to award compensation.

It is important to ask when the compensation 'clock' should stop ticking in a case where the employee gets another job and promptly loses it. In *Fentiman* v *Fluid Engineering Products Ltd* (1991) the EAT decided that compensation should only be granted up to the time the employee secures alternative employment if the employee has moved to a higher paid job. In other cases, the relevant period is up to the date of the hearing, with deductions made for earnings from the new employment (*Ging* v *Ellward (Lancs) Ltd* (1978)). A tribunal was wrong to limit compensation to be paid to school dinner ladies on the basis that without the reduction in numbers the school meals service would have closed in 12 months' time through lack of funds (*Gilham* v *Kent County Council (No. 3)* (1986)).

Loss of fringe benefits

By ERA 1996, s. 123(2) recoverable loss includes any 'expenses reasonably incurred by the complainant in consequence of the dismissal, and...loss of any benefit which he might reasonably be expected to have had but for the dismissal'. This has covered, in various cases, a company car (*Mohar* v *Granitstone Galloway Ltd* (1974)), commission, free housing, food, special travel allowance, and benefits under a share participation scheme (*Bradshaw* v *Rugby Portland Cement Co. Ltd* (1972)).

It is not proper to take into account loss of allowances paid free of tax in the former employment since they go to reimburse the employee for expenses necessarily incurred in the course of his job and there is no profit element thereon (*Tradewinds Airways Ltd* v *Fletcher* (1981)). Similarly nothing can be awarded where a company car was to be used only for business purposes. On the other hand, where the employee has lost tied free accommodation, the loss will be the rent which he has to pay on new accommodation (*Scottish Co-operative Wholesale Society Ltd* v *Lloyd* (1973)).

Expenses in looking for work

The sacked employee may have to move to get appropriate work and will inevitably have other expenses, such as travel and buying trade journals to search the appointments vacant columns (*CWS* v *Squirrell* (1974)). This is part of his necessary mitigation of loss and he may claim for it. Legal expenses in fighting a claim are not, however, recoverable under this head, although they may, in certain restricted circumstances, be included in a costs order. The tribunal may also in a proper case award expenses incurred in a reasonable attempt to set up a new business (*Gardiner-Hill* v *Roland Berger Technics Ltd* (1982)).

Pension rights

Loss of pension entitlement can in some cases be a very large sum, and its calculation often proves difficult, particularly as it is, in effect, a deferred entitlement. A deduction must be made if there is such a high turnover of the employer's staff that it is in the highest degree unlikely that the employee would have stayed until retirement age even if not dismissed at the time he was dismissed (*Manpower Ltd* v *Hearne* (1983)).

There is no reason why pension rights should be treated any differently from other parts of the remuneration of the employee in considering compensation, according to the Court of Appeal in *Aegon UK Corp Services Ltd* v *Roberts* (2009).

Receipt of an early pension on dismissal should not be taken into account so as to reduce a compensation payment, according to the EAT in *Knapton* v *ECC Card Clothing Ltd* (2006). It is a form of deferred pay.

There are basically two forms of pension loss which may be suffered; the loss of pension position earned thus far, and loss of future pension opportunity (*Copson* v *Eversure Accessories Ltd* (1974)). Usually it is most appropriate to base the sum lost on the amount of the employee's and employer's contributions made to a future pension (*Willment Brothers Ltd* v *Oliver* (1979)), and this is reached by applying the conventional multiplier and multiplicand method. Where, however, the employee is approaching retirement, tribunals may instead determine how much it would cost to purchase an annuity to produce the pension which he has lost and award this amount subject to a discount for accelerated payment (*Smith, Kline and French Laboratories Ltd* v *Coates* (1977)). In *Powrmatic* v *Bull* (1977) it was also necessary to take into consideration that the 32-year-old employee was unlikely to remain in the same job for the next 33 years and that he might go on to another job with much better pension prospects, the scheme might be altered or he might die prematurely. A multiplier of 15 was adopted instead of the actual number of years to take account of these contingencies. A withdrawal factor as high as 70 per cent may be justified in recognition of the high probability that an employee's poor performance would sooner or later result in his dismissal (*TBA Industrial Products Ltd* v *Locke* (1984)).

Loss of employment protection

It will take a sacked employee a further year in a new job to obtain statutory employment protection. A fairly nominal sum, usually about £350, is awarded because of loss in respect of unfair dismissal while the basic award is intended to serve this purpose for loss of redundancy payment. The tribunal may also take into account the fact that an employee's dismissal may deprive him of his entitlement under the employer's redundancy scheme through lack of service (*Lee* v *IPC Business Press Ltd* (1984)). The EAT has declared that an amount to reflect loss of notice entitlement in a new job is especially necessary in a time of high unemployment (*Daley* v *A. E. Dorsett* (1981)).

8.7.5 Additional award

Where an employer fails to comply with a reinstatement or re-employment order, an additional award may be made of between 26 and 52 weeks' pay, i.e. to a maximum of £19,760. The employer may avoid an additional award under ERA 1996, s. 117(3) if he satisfies the tribunal that it was not practicable to comply with an order for reinstatement or re-engagement. The criteria are different from the determination in respect of the order for reinstatement itself. Then practicability is merely one consideration among others; here the onus is on the employer to prove impracticability, and if he cannot the additional award will be made (*Freemans plc* v *Flynn* (1984)). As David Lewis pointed out ((1985) 14 ILJ 115), to avoid this employers will frequently dismiss another employee in order to accommodate the complainant; a practice known as 'bumping'. Then, of course, the issue arises as to whether compliance with a tribunal order renders the dismissal of the displaced employee fair on the basis that it was reasonable so to do. The actual amount awarded in a particular case is in the discretion of the ET, but it is clear that it is not based on loss to the employee (see *Electronic Data Processing Ltd* v *Wright* (1986)).

8.7.6 Deductions

Contributory fault

A deduction for contributory fault allows a tribunal a wide discretion to reduce compensation in a case where they find the applicant employee at fault in a way which has contributed to his dismissal. By ERA 1996, s. 123(6), if 'the dismissal was to any extent caused or contributed to by any action of the complainant' compensation may be reduced by such amount as is just and equitable. The tribunals possess a slightly differently worded power to deduct for contributory fault from a basic award (ERA 1996, s. 122(2)). Viscount Dilhorne called it an industrial form of contributory negligence in *Devis & Sons Ltd* v *Atkins* (1977).

Sir Hugh Griffiths said in *Maris* v *Rotherham Corporation* (1974) that the concept 'brings into consideration all the circumstances surrounding the dismissal, requiring the tribunal to take a broad common sense view of the situation, and to decide what, if any, part the applicant's own conduct played in contributing to his dismissal and then in the light of that finding, decide what, if any, reduction should be made in the assessment of this loss'. The onus lies on the employer to prove that the employee contributed to his dismissal by conduct which is 'culpable or blameworthy' and unreasonable in the circumstances. His action need not, however, amount to a breach of contract or tort (*Nelson* v *BBC (No. 2)* (1979); *Gibson* v *British Transport Docks Board* (1982)). In the *Nelson* case Brandon LJ thought that it 'includes conduct which is...perverse or foolish or, if I may use the colloquialism, bloodyminded. It may also include action which, though not meriting any of those more pejorative epithets, is nevertheless unreasonable in the circumstances'.

It is only the employee's action that must be considered in determining whether to reduce an award, according to the Court of Appeal in *Parker Foundry Ltd* v *Slack* (1992). The employee's misdeeds need not relate to the reason given by the employer for the dismissal (see *Robert Whiting Designs Ltd* v *Lamb* (1978)) but according to the EAT in *Hutchinson* v *Enfield Rolling Mills Ltd* (1981) there must be 'a causal link between the actions of the employee and the dismissal'. In that case, the employee was dismissed for attending a union demonstration in Brighton, notwithstanding that he had presented a sick note for the day to his employers in which he gave sciatica as the reason for absence. The EAT considered that the tribunal was wrong to take any of the following as contributory fault: that he had been a 'troublemaker' throughout his employment; that he intended to picket his union leaders in Brighton; and that his political views were affecting his work. None of these was causative of the dismissal, but his attendance in Brighton was and in itself justified a reduction for contributory fault. It also follows that acts of the employee following dismissal are not relevant in determining deductions (see *Soros* v *Davison* (1994)). It is not appropriate to make such a deduction for mere participation in industrial action according to the House of Lords in *Crosville Wales Ltd* v *Tracey (No. 2)* (1997). There is the important *caveat* that where complainants have been shown to be responsible for some additional conduct of their own over and above mere participation in the industrial action, the fact that such conduct occurred during and as part of the industrial action does not preclude the ET from examining it separately and considering whether it contributed to the dismissal.

It was held by the EAT in *Holroyd* v *Gravure Cylinders Ltd* (1984) that it would be only in exceptional circumstances that a reduction would be made in cases of constructive dismissal since the finding involves a fundamental breach by the employer. However, in *Polentarutti* v *Autokraft Ltd* (1991) it went the other way on the basis that the EPCA 1978 did not make such a stipulation. So, in this case, the tribunal was right to reduce an award by two-thirds where the employer had constructively dismissed the employee by withholding overtime payments due to the employee's shoddy workmanship. (See too *Garner* v *Grange Furnishing Ltd* (1977).)

Once a causal link has been established, the amount of deduction is at large for the tribunal. It takes a percentage from such compensation as the employee would otherwise be entitled to. In extreme cases the award may be reduced to nil, but this should only occur where the unfairness is highly technical, perhaps a minor breach of procedure, and the employee's own conduct was highly provocative. There has been a major difference of opinion as to the acceptability of large deductions. Although the English EAT reduced compensation by 100 per cent in *Maris* v *Rotherham Corporation* (1974), it commented in *Trend* v *Chiltern Hunt Ltd* (1977) that reductions should rarely exceed 80 per cent. Lord McDonald, on the other hand, in the Scottish EAT in *Courtney* v *Babcock & Wilcox (Operations) Ltd* (1977) could see nothing wrong in principle or practice with a 100 per cent reduction, adding that the English EAT's approach savoured of a tariff. This line was indeed approved by the House of Lords in *Devis & Sons Ltd* v *Atkins* (1977). The question of what is just and equitable is directed to the proportion of the reduction and not whether there should be any reduction at all, which is simply a question of causation (*Warrilow* v *Robert Walker Ltd* (1984)).

There has been some conflict of authority as to whether a tribunal errs in law in making a reduction for contributory fault from only the compensatory award while leaving intact the basic award. The Northern Ireland Court of Appeal in *McFall & Co. Ltd* v *Curran* (1981) thought that this showed unacceptable inconsistency, but the EAT in *Les Ambassadeurs Club* v *Bainda* (1982) saw no objection. This would seem to be the better view, as the basic award is not subject to the just and equitable test. In most cases the same percentage should be deducted from both awards (*RSPCA* v *Cruden* (1986)).

The EAT will generally not intervene in a tribunal's finding of contributory fault, still less in the amount of deduction. In *Hollier* v *Plysu Ltd* (1983), the Court of Appeal advised tribunals to take a broad common sense view. It was a matter of 'impression, opinion and discretion'. (See also *Warrilow* v *Robert Walker Ltd* (1984); *Yate Foundry Ltd* v *Walters* (1984); *F. C. Shepherd & Co. Ltd* v *Jerrom* (1985).)

The EAT has said, however, in *Slaughter* v *C. Brewer & Sons Ltd* (1990), that ill-health will rarely justify a deduction under the contributory fault ground in ERA 1996, s. 123(6), although it may justify a reduction under the general just and equitable ground in ERA 1996, s. 123(1) where it is clear that the employee is incapable of doing the job.

The relationship between the reductions that may be made under ERA 1996, s. 123(6) and (1) was also considered by the Court of Appeal in *Tele-Trading Ltd* v *Jenkins* (1990). It held that where the contributory conduct of the employee was known to the employer at the time of the dismissal, a reduction should be made, if at all, under s. 123(6). However, in other circumstances it should be made under s. 123(1). A tribunal would therefore not err in circumstances where the employee's conduct was known to the employee at the time of the dismissal if it did not consider reducing the award under s. 123(1).

A deduction for contributory fault under s. 123(6) should be made before any deduction under s. 123(1), according to the Court of Appeal in *Rao* v *Civil Aviation Authority* (1994), as a deduction under s. 123(6) may affect what is just and equitable in any further deduction.

Mitigation

Reduction in compensation will be made if the employee failed to take reasonable steps to get another job or otherwise keep down his loss, as at common law (ERA 1996, s. 123(4)). The onus of proof of failure of mitigation rests on the employer (*Sturdy Finance Ltd* v *Bardsley* (1979)), and the duty arises only after dismissal, so that a refusal to accept other employment before that date is irrelevant (*Savoia* v *Chiltern Herb Farms Ltd* (1981), *McAndrew* v *Prestwick Circuits Ltd* (1988)).

The employee cannot, however, sit back and mount up his losses in the confident expectation that they will be met by the respondent. The proper test for tribunals to apply was set out by the Court of Appeal in *Bessenden Properties* v *Corness* (1974) as whether, 'if the complainant had had no hope of recovering compensation from anybody else and if he had consulted merely his own interests and had acted reasonably in all the circumstances, would he have accepted the job in mitigation of the loss which he had suffered'. (See also *Archbold Freightage Ltd* v *Wilson* (1974).) This is a question of fact in each case, and reference may be made to the authorities on the similar question for wrongful dismissal (see Chapter 4 above).

Broadly, although the employee need not take the first job that comes along (*Gallear* v *Watson* (1979)), it may be reasonable after a period of unemployment to accept a post at a lower rate of pay than before (*Daley* v *A. E. Dorsett* (1981)). To make one application in eight weeks has been held to be unreasonable (*O'Reilly* v *Welwyn and Hatfield District Council* (1975); *Sweetlove* v *Redbridge & Waltham Forest AHA* (1979)). The proper approach involves assessing how long the employee would be out of work if he had properly mitigated, rather than reducing the global sum by a percentage as in contributory fault (*Smith Kline & French Laboratories Ltd* v *Coates* (1977)). A similar process is to be applied to loss of pension rights.

Tribunals realistically recognise that a former employee who starts a new business after dismissal will probably earn little in the initial period but this does not mean that he is not reasonably mitigating his loss. In *Gardiner-Hill* v *Roland Berger Technics Ltd* (1982) the applicant was dismissed from his position as managing director of the respondent consultancy service when he was 55 years old and decided then to set up on his own account. In the six and a half months between dismissal and tribunal hearing he had earned only £1,500. The employers argued that this did not reflect a reasonable attempt to mitigate his loss and the tribunal decided that since he was spending some 90 per cent of his time on the new business and not looking for alternative employment his compensation should be reduced by 80 per cent. The EAT thought that the applicant's strategy was a reasonable one and that in any event it was wrong to make a percentage reduction in relation to mitigation. Rather the tribunal should have decided on a date when if the ex-employee had used reasonable efforts he would have gained other employment at a similar level. (See also *Lee* v *IPC Business Press Ltd* (1984).) A failure to follow the internal appeals procedure laid down at the place of work is not a failure to mitigate (*William Muir (Bond 9) Ltd* v *Lamb* (1985)). An employee is well advised to keep a list of all jobs he has applied for and the answers he has received in order to demonstrate to a tribunal that he has tried as hard as he can to find alternative work.

Ex gratia payments

Employers must give close attention to how they structure *ex gratia* payments if they envisage the possibility of an unfair dismissal claim. The EAT in *Chelsea Football Club & Athletic Co. Ltd* v *Heath* (1981) held that if an employer admits that he has unfairly dismissed an employee and pays him an amount specifically referable to the basic award the employer may properly contend that he has made a basic award and need not pay again. Whether a general payment covers the basic award is 'a question of construction in each case'. Here the letter was really an offer without prejudice to legal rights. In *Boorman* v *Allmakes Ltd* (1995), an employee was paid an *ex gratia* sum expressed to include statutory redundancy payment, but it was held that it did not fall to be deducted from the basic award when he was ultimately found to have been unfairly dismissed on a ground other than redundancy.

Discrimination legislation

The ERA 1996, s. 126 states that where compensation falls to be awarded under unfair dismissal and discrimination statutes, an ET must wholly offset the compensation under one head against the others. However, that does not mean that an employer is not liable for discrimination when there is liability for a later unfair dismissal, the compensation for which is capped, according to the EAT in *HM Prison Service* v *Beart (No. 2)* (2005). A tortfeasor should not benefit from committing a second wrong.

Redundancy payments

Where a redundancy payment has been made in excess of the employee's statutory entitlement, and the employee is unfairly dismissed (for example because the proper consultation procedure has not been followed), the excess is deducted in full after any percentage reduction has been made. It is not subject to the percentage deduction because the employer is entitled to a pound for pound recompense, according to the Court of Appeal in *Digital Equipment Co. Ltd* v *Clements (No. 2)* (1998). The court felt that this was in line with the clear language of what is now ERA 1996, s. 123, but it also seems to have the advantage that this reading prevents the employee from being compensated in part twice over. On the other hand, it is unclear if this could be sustained where the employee had every reason to expect an award in the event of any redundancy in excess of the statutory entitlement. In such circumstances there may be no generosity on the part of the employer involved at all.

Pensions

If an employee takes an early pension following a dismissal, that pension is not deductible from a compensatory award, being a form of deferred pay, according to the EAT in *Knapton v ECC Card Clothing Ltd* (2006).

Tax rebates

A tax rebate need not be deducted (*MBS Ltd v Calo* (1983); *cf. Lucas v Lawrence Scott & Electromotors Ltd* (1983)).

Procedure

Even where there has been a reduction of compensation due to the employee's contributory fault, the tribunal may make a further reduction where there has been an unfair dismissal finding due to the failure to follow a proper procedure. In such circumstances, according to the Court of Appeal in *Rao v Civil Aviation Authority* (1992), a further deduction may be made where the tribunal is of the opinion that, had the proper procedure been followed, the dismissal would have been fair.

8.7.7 The effect of the legislation

The legislation has generally been a success and now forms the major source of employment protection for most employees. Although the remedies of reinstatement to the employee's old job, or re-engagement by the same employer in a different job, have not been widely used, this is by no means to be considered as indicative of the failure of the legislation, but merely a reflection of industrial realities (see P. Lewis, (1981) 19 BJIR 316). What is, perhaps, more significant is the fact that many more claims fail than succeed. What this may show is that, among other things, applicants do not understand the nature of the claim, its procedure and limitations, or are often incapable of presenting a claim at a tribunal adequately without the representation which most still do not have (see Smallcombe, *Lay Representation At Industrial Tribunals*, unpublished Ph.D. thesis (University of Exeter, 1988); Genn and Genn, *The Effectiveness of Representation at Tribunals* (London: Lord Chancellor's Department, 1989); and Latreille, Latreille, and Knight, (2005) 34 ILJ 308). In addition, many claims are settled before they come to a hearing. But some blame must lie beyond the parties themselves, particularly in the tribunal procedure itself which is too adversarial, and with the law which is at times very complex.

Empirical research studies have certainly tended to indicate that the legislation had significant impact on employers' practices. Most notably perhaps, written disciplinary procedures grew rapidly in number, particularly in larger firms (see Evans, Goodman and Hargreaves, (1985) 14 ILJ 91 at p. 96). But some perceived impacts have perhaps been overstated. For example, the oft-repeated argument that the legislation had a dampening effect on recruitment would not seem to be well-founded (see Daniel and Stilgoe, *The Impact of Employment Protection Laws* (London: Policy Studies Institute, 1978)). But it does seem to be true generally of deregulation in employment protection (particularly for atypical workers such as those on temporary contracts) that significant economic effects follow, particularly in income distribution (see Deakin and Wilkinson, *The Economics of Employment Rights*, 2nd edn (London: Institute of Employment Rights, 1991)).

If the success of the legislation is to be gauged not by the empirical data of numbers of claims and their success rate, but by the extent to which employees now enjoy greater employment protection than hitherto, that can be a matter of some debate. Certainly this is the case if one were to view the role of unfair dismissal law as providing such protection, because that is not, as we have seen, historically accurate. The greater concern at the inception of the legislation was with reducing the potentiality of industrial conflict. As time went on a debate ensued as to the extent the courts were interpreting the legislation in favour of employees by being concerned with providing checks on the unfettered exercise of the managerial prerogative. There were those, such as Patrick Elias (see (1981) 10 ILJ 201) who thought the law successful in those terms obliging employers 'to adopt a pluralist rather than a unitary perspective'. On the other hand, there were those, such as Hugh Collins (see (1982) 11 ILJ 78 at p. 170) who disagreed with that, arguing that the legislation promoted a more or less unbridled discretion for the employer to exercise discretionary powers. And then there were those, such as Humphrey Forrest (see (1980) 43 MLR 361), who took the view that there had been no great sea change in managerial prerogative, but that the interests of employees were considered as more important than hitherto in securing managerial and financial objectives. He saw any further development in employee protection coming not from the law, but from managerial practice.

Since then things have moved on, with the gradual further erosion of protection in small piecemeal ways, such as the extension of periods of continuity of employment requirements, and the failure of the compensation remedy to keep pace with the actual financial and other loss suffered by unfairly dismissed employees, particularly in times of high unemployment. In recent years, therefore, alternative ways of securing employment protection have been examined.

Traditionally the method of securing such protection came through the processes of collective bargaining, but it was the products of the failure of that which principally led to the introduction of unfair dismissal legislation, as we have already seen. There are now few who would advocate a return to that method as the principal viable alternative. However, some have suggested a fresh look at the contract of employment as a source of protection in addition to the possibilities thrown up by public law, which we have already briefly examined.

Most interesting, perhaps, is Keith Ewing's suggestion of the incorporation of particular terms into the contract (see (1989) 18 ILJ 217). He suggests a term providing that employees shall be dismissed only for specified reasons and in a specified manner. Such a clause had judicial endorsement, by the House of Lords, in *McClelland* v *Northern Ireland General Health Services Board* (1957). He also advocates a clause providing that employees have a right not to be unfairly dismissed—an idea borrowed from Australian labour law. The contractual remedies may not at first glance appear as attractive as the statutory protection, but when one considers that contract law has no eligibility requirements, no compensation ceilings, and that injunctive relief may be available (at least to restrain a dismissal), the idea appears more attractive. Indeed, it it possible to trace already the willingness of the courts to award the non-pecuniary remedies (e.g. injunctions and declarations) for employment contracts, which is an essential prerequisite if such an approach is to succeed (see Carty, (1989) 52 MLR 449 at p. 456). (See also Fraser Davidson, (1984) 35 NILQ 121 at p. 124.) The difficulty, of course, remains that the only way by which such terms are likely to be incorporated into the contract of employment is by the old route of collective bargaining.

SELECTED READING

Bowers, J. and Clarke, A. (1981), 'Unfair Dismissal and Managerial Prerogative: a study of Some Other Substantial Reason', (1981) 10 ILJ 34

Collins, H. (1993), *Justice in Dismissal*, Oxford: Clarendon Press 1993

Davies, A. C. L. (2009), 'Judicial Self-Restraint in Labour Law', (2009) 38 ILJ 278

Davies, A. C. L., *Fairness at Work* (1998) Cm. 3968

Painter, R. W. and Holmes, A. E. (2010), *Cases and Materials on Employment Law*, 8th edn, Oxford: Oxford University Press, ch. 8

Sanders, S. (2009), 'Part One of the Employment Act 2008: "Better" Dispute Resolution?', (2009) 38 ILJ 30

9

Statutory redundancy payments and consultation procedures

SUMMARY

This chapter examines the circumstances in which it may be possible for an employee to bring a claim against the employer for a statutory redundancy payment. Having established that the employee is an employee eligible to bring a claim and who has been dismissed (considered in Chapter 7 above) it is necessary to explore what amounts to redundancy under statute. So, having outlined the justification of the statutory scheme, the definition of redundancy is considered and later the circumstances in which the employee might lose a right to claim a redundancy payment. Matters consequent on finding a redundancy are also examined, namely offers of new employment and the effects of a refusal. Finally, the method of calculating redundancy payments is considered, together with an examination of what the legal position is when the employer is insolvent and perhaps where there is a rescue in prospect. In so doing, the position of trade unions and employee representatives is also examined.

9.1 Introduction

The redundancy payments scheme was introduced under the Redundancy Payments Act 1965 as the first of the substantial statutory individual employment rights. The current law has been consolidated in the ERA 1996. The original structure remains intact and provides a lump sum payment designed to tide an employee over the period of uncertainty and hardship after dismissal or redundancy. The amount of payment increases, as does the basic award for unfair dismissal with which it shares many similarities, with the number of years' continuous service of the employee. His entitlement is in the bank, as it were, only maturing at dismissal, but payment is denied if the employee unreasonably refuses a suitable alternative offer of employment from his employer, his successor, or an associated employer. A measure of the importance of the scheme is that many people receive such payments each year. The *ACAS Annual Report & Accounts 2008/9*, (London: The Stationery Office, 2009) stated that ACAS had referred to it from ETs 3,938 cases, a sharp rise on the previous year of 2,891. The figure had been slowly declining for several years, but the credit crunch was inevitably the cause of the sharp increase in that year. This is despite the fact that the maximum statutory entitlement to a redundancy payment is very low, presently capped at £11,400 for a very long-serving older employee.

9.1.1 **The nature of the scheme**

Various justifications of the scheme have been proffered, but few explain all its many and curious features. Some have described it as establishing a 'proprietary interest in the job'. Thus, the President of Industrial Tribunals in *Wynes* v *Southrepps Hall Broiler Farm Ltd* (1968) said:

Just as a property owner has a right in his property and when he is deprived, he is entitled to compensation, so a long-term employee is considered to have a right of property in his job, he has a right to security and his rights gain in value with the years.

It seeks to assist training and resettlement and thus stimulate mobility of labour, the lack of which has been diagnosed as one of the major problems of Britain's economy. However, as Elias, Napier, and Wallington pointed out (*Labour Law: Cases and Materials* (London: Butterworths, 1981), p. 646) this is difficult to sustain as a primary function, since the way in which payments are assessed means that 'the most money goes to the older, longer-serving workers who are the least likely, as a group, to be prepared to leave their homes and families in search of new work'.

Other commentators have seen the payment less idealistically as a 'bribe' to employees to go quietly. In particular, Fryer ((1973) 2 ILJ 1) argued that the legislation is a positive inducement to insecurity of work by encouraging abandonment by workers of protective attitudes to job security, which were often manifested in so-called 'restrictive practices'. It certainly stimulated the negotiation with unions of redundancy agreements, which were formerly anathema to them. Yet Fryer argued that the scheme was of little use as a cover to employees losing their jobs, since only less than one third of redundant employees actually qualified for statutory payments.

Grunfeld described the scheme more pragmatically. He wrote:

The original Act's purpose was to mitigate the resistance of individual employees (and their unions) to the extensive changes which have accompanied and will continue to accompany the response of British industry, commerce and finance to the searching demands of world trade and competition . . . the new legislation tempered the wind of industrial and commercial change to the redundant employee by providing an additional pecuniary cushion against the ancient hardship of loss of employment. The principal end of the Act was the national economic one of facilitating higher standards of efficiency and effectiveness in industry and commerce; the means used are of a social character, an extension on a selective basis of the social security system dealing with unemployment.

(*Law of Redundancy*, 3rd edn (London: Sweet & Maxwell, 1989), p. 2.)

The scheme was a product of the 1960s—a decade of hope, relatively full employment and the 'white heat of the technological revolution' as the Prime Minister, Harold Wilson, put it. The numbers of redundancies then rose with ever-changing technological developments. In particular, any optimism about redundancy overcoming malutilisation of labour appeared to be dashed.

Many apparent contradictions in the case law can often be traced back to the particular viewpoint taken on this by the tribunal in question. Many believe that the scheme achieves none of its manifold objects with any degree of success.

Another analysis sees the rationale of redundancy in a mixture of the ideal of job security and the allocation of economic loss where it is most sustainable and justified. An example of this is Collins's statement that:

We can no more permit casual dissolution of the employment relationship than we can countenance impulsive divorce or capricious eviction. A progressive society moves not from contract to status, but from contract to trust; that is, to the recognition of a duty to take into account the interests of another. Correlative to the duty of the employer to respect the interests of the employee lies the right to job security. This right is analogous to an equitable interest, defended by specific relief in the form of reinstatement against unreasonable dismissal, but merely entitling an employee to compensation when the dismissal results from economic exigencies.

Who should pay this compensation? It should be paid by those persons standing to benefit from the business reorganisation, for otherwise they will be unjustly enriched. In the first place this includes the employers as agents of the owners of capital, who expect to receive greater profits or reduce losses. Often, however, a business reorganisation accrues to the benefit of the whole community as well, since more efficient production leads to cheaper goods and services for the domestic consumer and competitive advantages in international markets. One man's redundancy is another man's price cut. Thus some proportion of the compensation should be paid out of general taxation.

(Collins, (1985) 14 ILJ 61.)

The case law also demonstrates tension in another rather subtle way, for those seeking to prove redundancy as a reason for dismissal have over time changed sides. In the beginning, it was in the interests of employers to disprove redundancy since that was the only reason for dismissal which would cost them money, but with the Industrial Relations Act 1971 and its introduction of unfair dismissal, management began to put it forward as a potentially fair reason for dismissal. The battle lines were redrawn; the decisions drew different distinctions and the patchwork became more complicated.

9.2 Definition of redundancy

Redundancy is much more strictly defined in the ERA 1996 than the concept as it is referred to in ordinary speech. It is not uncommon to hear that a person has been 'made redundant' when in fact there has really been a dismissal for some other reason. The Act uses the same definition for the purposes of determining entitlement to redundancy payments and establishing a potentially fair reason for dismissal. The definition formerly applied to consultation with unions but this was amended by the TURERA 1993.

Under ERA 1996, s. 139(1) an employee is dismissed for redundancy where the dismissal is attributable wholly or mainly to:

(a) the fact that his employer has ceased, or intends to cease, to carry on the business for the purposes of which the employee was employed by him, or has ceased, or intends to cease, to carry on that business in the place where the employee was so employed; or

(b) the fact that the requirements of that business for employees to carry out work of a particular kind, or for employees to carry out work of a particular kind in the place where he was so employed, have ceased or diminished or are expected to cease or diminish.

9.2.1 Eligibility

An employee does not have any right to a redundancy payment unless he has been continuously employed for a period of not less than two years ending with the relevant date—ERA 1996, s. 155. The age limit previously in place has been abolished by Employment Equality (Age) Regulations 2006 (SI 2006 No. 1031), Sch. 8, para. 30.

9.2.2 Dismissal and proof

A dismissal is a condition precedent to a redundancy payment just as it is the basis for a claim of unfair dismissal. Its definition has already been considered and the slight differences in respect of redundancy payments noted. However, it should be emphasised here that the frequently used term 'voluntary redundancies' is apt to be misleading, since for a claim to succeed the initiative must come from the employer; an employee who resigns is not entitled to a redundancy payment.

After dismissal has been proved, for the purposes of redundancy payment alone and not unfair dismissal, redundancy is presumed to be the reason unless the contrary is proved by the employer (ERA 1996, s. 163(2)).

9.2.3 Total cessation of the employer's business

There are three discrete parts to the definition of redundancy. The first limb applies when a worker's employer completely closes the business in which the applicant is employed. Business, by statute, includes any trade or profession or activity carried on by a body of persons, and it is not necessary to prove that the employer owns the business in question in order to succeed in claiming a payment on its closure. Thus, in *Thomas* v *Jones* (1978), the applicant was hired and fired by a sub-postmistress, although the Post Office actually owned the business in which she worked. The EAT held that the former was correctly named as respondent.

Early decisions refused to countenance a redundancy payment where an employee was in effect himself responsible for the redundancy caused (*Marsland* v *Francis Dunn Ltd* (1967)). However, this was rejected as authority for any general principle of self-induced redundancy in *Sanders* v *Ernest A. Neale Ltd* (1974), where dismissal followed a strike.

9.2.4 Cessation of business at place of employment

If the employee works at a particular factory, office or shop of the employer company or firm which closes, his dismissal then will be for redundancy notwithstanding that the employer continues to carry on business elsewhere. This puts into focus the *place* of employment and, according to the NIRC: 'These words do not mean "where he in fact worked". They mean "where under his contract of employment he could be required to work".' In the case where this principle was established, *UK Atomic Energy Authority* v *Claydon* (1974), the employee's conditions reserved to the employing Authority 'the right to require any member of their staff to work at any of their establishments in Great Britain or in posts overseas'. The applicant, a draughtsman, was originally employed at Orford Ness, and was dismissed when the work on which he was engaged moved to Aldermaston and he refused to go with it. The court upheld the employer's contention that requirements for workers had not ceased 'in the place where he was employed', since he was under an obligation to work at any place in Great Britain where the employers so chose.

A mobility clause will only rarely be implied. In *O'Brien* v *Associated Fire Alarms Ltd* (1968), the employing company installed fire and burglar alarms throughout the UK, but the applicant electrician worked for its north western area, which covered a very large area (at least 200 miles long) and was controlled from the Liverpool Office. He lived in Liverpool and generally worked within commutable distance of home. When requirements in that area diminished, the management sought to compel him to work 120 miles away in Barrow-in-Furness claiming that it was implied in his contract that he would work anywhere in the north west. They thus claimed that there was no diminution in the place he was required to work. The Court of Appeal would imply a term that the employee should work only within daily travelling distance of his home and no more. His dismissal by reason of the employer's repudiation was thus due to a diminution of work in the relevant place where he was employed. Further, in *Bass Leisure Ltd* v *Thomas* (1994) the EAT held that the place of work was to be determined by reference to where the employee actually worked and any contractual term evidencing this. Any contractual mobility clause was irrelevant.

Where there is a clear term requiring mobility on the part of an employee and an employee's refusal to move results in his dismissal the statutory reason will be disobedience to orders, i.e. misconduct, and not because his employer has ceased to carry on business at a place where he is employed, so that he cannot claim redundancy (*Rowbotham* v *Arthur Lee & Sons Ltd* (1974)). (See further on mobility clauses, pp. 50–51.)

9.2.5 Diminution in requirements of the business

The third limb of redundancy comprises a reduction in requirements for employees because of, say, a fall off in demand or rationalisation of the business, or because fewer men and women as opposed to machines or new techniques are necessary. This has proved most difficult to construe.

Diminution in employer's requirements

Only if the requirements for employees doing the particular work the employee was contracted to perform have ceased or diminished is the employee redundant under this heading. The NIRC declared it to mean 'work which is distinguished from other work of the same general kind by requiring special aptitudes, special skills or knowledge' (*Amos* v *Max-Arc Ltd* (1973) and *O'Neill* v *Merseyside Plumbing Co. Ltd* (1973)). This involves fine lines sometimes having to be drawn to characterise the particular kind of work involved, and the EAT and Court of Appeal have frequently stated that it is a matter of fact and degree for the ET (e.g. *Murphy* v *Epsom College* (1984)).

In *Vaux and Associated Breweries Ltd* v *Ward* (1968), for example, the employers decided to relaunch one of their hotels and to give it a new image by employing young 'bunny girls' in place of older barmaids. The vital question in deciding whether one of the dismissed middle-aged barmaids was entitled to a redundancy payment concerned whether 'the work that the barmaid in the altered premises was going to do was work of a different kind to what the barmaid in the unaltered premises had been doing'. The Divisional Court found that the work was not so different, even though the type of person required to fill the position was not entitled to a redundancy payment. On the other hand, in *Archibald* v *Rossleigh Commercials Ltd* (1975), the tribunal held that the work of an emergency night mechanic who worked unsupervised could be distinguished from that of an ordinary mechanic. The test clearly focuses on the characteristics of the job and whether these have gone, rather than the aptitudes of the employee filling it (*Pillinger* v *Manchester AHA* (1979)).

It is important to note that it is the requirement for employees doing particular work that must diminish for the statutory test to apply, rather than that the work itself is diminishing. Indeed, the work may actually be increasing but the employer may economically employ other methods (e.g. mechanisation) to do that work (*McCrea* v *Cullen & Davison Ltd* (1988)).

The scope and extent of the business in which a redundant employee is employed is a question of fact for the tribunal to determine. Partners who operate more than one enterprise may be regarded for redundancy purposes as operating a single business. The relevant factors include the similarity of the work done at each establishment, the skilled nature of the work, and the degree of interchangeability between members of staff (*Babar Indian Restaurant* v *Rawat* (1985)).

The test

The EAT in *Haden Ltd* v *Cowen* (1982) derived from *Nelson* v *BBC* (1977) the principle that the tribunal should focus not on the work that the employee actually did before dismissal, but rather on the work which he could be expected to do under his contract of employment. The case of *Safeway Stores plc* v *Burrell* (1997) further developed the law when the EAT held that both this contract test and the test based purely on the actual function of the employee were flawed. In this case, the applicant was employed as a petrol station manager but, following reorganisation of the business, his job disappeared and he was instead asked to apply for the job of petrol filling station controller at a lower salary. The applicant refused this offer and presented a complaint of unfair dismissal, claiming that the new position was exactly the same in substance to his old job so that he was not redundant. The essential question was whether a redundancy had occurred. The EAT held that neither the contract test nor the function test touched on whether there was a diminution in the employer's requirements for employees (not the applicant) to carry out work of a particular kind, or any expectation of such a diminution in the future, which is a requirement of ERA 1996, s. 139(1). The shift in emphasis meant that, in a situation such as *Safeway Stores*, one should ascertain how many employees carrying out a particular kind of work are needed by an organisation, rather than what work generally is required to be done or what the employee's contract stipulates. The instant case was thus remitted to a differently constituted ET to determine this question.

Safeway Stores was followed by *Church* v *West Lancashire NHS Trust* (1998). In this case the EAT held that, in determining whether an employee was employed to do the particular kind of work in respect of which the needs of the business have ceased or diminished, the proper test was neither contractual nor functional but a sensible blend of the two. The employee's contractual obligations may therefore be relevant in determining whether a redundancy has taken place.

There was definitive approval of *Safeway Stores* in the House of Lords' decision of *Murray & Anor* v *Foyle Meats Limited* (1999). Lord Irvine, the Lord Chancellor, agreed with the analysis in *Safeway Stores* and, cutting a swathe through the previous authorities, stated that the two questions to ask were:

(a) Were the requirements of the employer's business for employees to carry out work of a particular kind diminished irrespective of the employee's own functions or the terms of his contract?

(b) Was the dismissal wholly or mainly attributable to that state of affairs?

It may be that an employee who is dismissed could have been redeployed, or was carrying out work unaffected by the diminution of the employer's need for work of a particular kind, but the establishment of a causal link under the second part of Lord Irvine's test is an issue of fact not one of law. (See also *Shawkat* v *Nottingham City Hospital NHS Trust* (1999); *BBC* v *Farnworth* (1998).)

Redundancy and reorganisations

The courts have excluded from the scope of redundancy a mere reorganisation of work. Thus, where duties are different or hours have been changed, but the overall needs for the persons doing the collection of those duties, (i.e. the job), are not less, the courts have not awarded a redundancy payment. The essential question is whether the process 'results in the employee's work being encompassed in other posts and whether the employer's business is such that it no longer has a requirement for a separate and additional employee to carry out the work' (*Sutton* v *Revlon Overseas Corporation Ltd* (1973)). Further, in *Frame It* v *Brown* (1993) the EAT held that even though work could be carried out with fewer employees there was no redundancy where an employee's duties were redistributed to three other employees. The work had not ceased or diminished but had merely been reallocated.

The employee's skill and qualifications and hours of work are generally irrelevant to this question. Night shift as opposed to day shift work may, however, be work of a particular kind (*Macfisheries Ltd* v *Findlay* (1985)). The distinction between the job description and the job itself is often difficult to draw. The most that perhaps can be done is to accept Phillips J's statement in that case that: 'In truth all these cases of redundancy claims ultimately raise questions of fact and the decided cases are only of value in enunciating the principles.'

In *Chapman* v *Goonvean and Rostowrack China Clay Co. Ltd* (1973), for example, seven workers used to travel to work each day on a bus provided by the employers. As this became uneconomic it was decided to cut off the service. The employees claimed to be constructively dismissed by reason of redundancy and argued that if they had not been dismissed the employers would be running the business at a loss which would eventually have led to redundancy. Lord Denning, however, said that, 'the requirements of the business—for the work of these seven men—continued just the same as before. After they stopped work the firm had to take on another seven men to replace them…it would be necessary to import the words on the existing terms and conditions to justify the employees' arguments'. Redundancy did not cover a change of terms. The Master of the Rolls was pleased to reach this result since it accorded with his view of public policy:

It is very desirable in the interests of efficiency that employers should be able to propose changes in the terms of a man's employment for such reasons as these so as to get rid of restrictive practices; or to induce higher output by piece work; or to cease to provide free transport at an excessive cost…the employers can properly say to the men…'you have lost your job because you live so far away that it is not worth our while paying the costs of bringing you here…'

(See also *Lesney Products & Co. Ltd* v *Nolan* (1977).)

The distinction between different terms and different jobs is further illustrated by the decision in *Johnson* v *Nottinghamshire Combined Police Authority* (1974). The two applicant women employees had worked as clerks in one of the respondent's police stations for some years, coming in between 9.30 a.m. and 5.30 p.m. or 6 p.m. from Monday to Friday. In 1974 the Authority sought to introduce a shift system of 8 a.m. to 3 p.m. and 1 a.m. to 8 a.m., which both women refused, and they were dismissed. The Court of Appeal decided that the sacking was not by reason of redundancy, since the clerical work for which they were employed had neither ceased nor diminished, even though there was no need for women doing those hours. The NIRC declared: 'Work of a particular kind refers to the task to be performed not to the other elements which go to make up the kind of job which it is.' Moreover, 'an employer is entitled to reorganise his business so as to improve its efficiency'. Since it was 'the same job done to a different time schedule', the dismissal was not attributable to redundancy.

Replacing employees

If an employee is directly replaced there can be no redundancy. Thus, in *Wren* v *Wiltshire County Council* (1969), no payment could be claimed where an unqualified teacher was replaced by one with qualifications; the employers still required the same kind of work. It is, however, only the requirement of the business for *employees* that need cease or diminish; if they are replaced by self-employed workers, there would probably be a redundancy (*Ladbroke Courage Holidays Ltd* v *Asten* (1981)).

Knowledge of the employee

It also does not matter for this purpose that the employee knows from the beginning of his job that his work is going to diminish, as shown by *Nottinghamshire CC* v *Lee* (1979), where the employee was offered a post as a temporary lecturer for one year, at the end of which period the post was extended for another 12 months. He knew that there would be no further extension since the college's requirements had already ceased. Slynn J found that this was not included in the statutory definition since the employer's requirements had not diminished during his second period of employment and that it would be unfair in the circumstances if a redundancy payment were required. The Court of Appeal overruled this interpretation, applying the exact words of the Act. The appellant's contract was not renewed because the employer's requirements for employees had diminished. The Act did not mean that the requirement must cease or diminish during the period of employment. The case also serves to re-emphasise that fairness has nothing to do with entitlement to redundancy payment.

Diminution

The diminution in requirements must arise in the job being done, so that, as in *North East Coast Shiprepairers Ltd* v *Secretary of State for Employment* (1978), there is no redundancy where an apprentice is not taken on at the end of his apprenticeship as a journeyman because there is not enough work for him to do. There is a redundancy, however, where the employer takes on additional workers in the hope of increased production which never in fact materialises.

Place of work

The place in which the work is done is to be determined by a consideration of factual circumstances which obtained until the dismissal, and there is no warrant for determining that this place always extends to every place where the employee may by reason of his contract be required to work. If, however, the work of the employee has involved a change of location such as where the nature of the work required the employee to go from place to place, the contract may be helpful to determine the extent of the place where he worked (*High Table Ltd* v *Horst* (1997)).

Associated employers

By ERA 1996, s. 139(1) and (2), if the employee is dismissed because of an overall reduction in requirements within a group of associated employers, he can claim a redundancy payment even if there is no redundancy on his particular employer's part. Further, it is enough that redundancy is the main reason where there is more than one cause for dismissal, or that requirements are expected to cease or diminish in the future, so that a claim may be brought before the closure actually takes place.

Redundancy as the cause of dismissal

The redundancy situation must be a cause of the dismissal. In *Baxter* v *Limb Group of Companies* (1994) a majority of the Court of Appeal held that there was no dismissal on grounds of redundancy where dock workers had been dismissed as a result of industrial action and, rather than being replaced, their work had been put out to other companies in the group. While there was a redundancy situation, this was caused by the dismissal on grounds of industrial action and could not be said to have caused the dismissal.

9.3 **Offer of new employment**

9.3.1 **The statutory provisions**

If the employee accepts the renewal of his contract on the same terms as before, he is not entitled to a redundancy payment, and the same applies if he is re-engaged in a suitable alternative position (ERA 1996, ss 138 and 141). In either case the offer is also valid if it comes from an associated employer, from the transferee on transfer of the business, or involves a move to Crown service. Any renewal or re-engagement must, in order to qualify, take effect either immediately on the end of the previous employment or not more than four weeks thereafter and then his service will be treated as unbroken and continuous. Where the old job ends on a Friday, Saturday or Sunday, it suffices if the new employment begins on the following Monday or within four weeks of that Monday (ERA 1996, s. 146(2)).

Section 138 applies only for the purposes of redundancy pay. It does not apply to unfair dismissal (*Hempell* v *W. H. Smith & Sons Ltd* (1986)). The section is merely designed to provide a defence for an employer faced with a claim for a redundancy payment in circumstances where the employee even before dismissal has obtained another job with the same or an associated employer.

9.3.2 **Trial period**

If the proffered new contract differs as to capacity or place of employment, the offer must be made before the redundancy takes effect, and the employee is entitled to a trial period of up to four weeks to test the new terms (ERA 1996, ss 141 and 146). This does not apply where the differences are *de minimis* (*Rose* v *Henry Trickett & Sons Ltd (No. 2)* (1971)), but it does not matter that the new conditions are better than the old (*Baker* v *Gill* (1971)). The aim is that during the four weeks the employee can decide whether to take the new position or leave. If he finds it disagreeable and resigns, he can claim a redundancy payment, being treated as dismissed, and the statutory reason for dismissal is the reason for the original dismissal, that is, before the trial period began. Further, the four-week trial period may be extended for such longer period as is agreed between the employer and employee or his representative in writing, providing that the agreement is reached before the employee starts the work, the extra time is for training only and the parties specify the date of the end of the longer period and the terms and conditions to apply after it. Moreover, the employer can end the trial period if he can show a reason connected with or arising out of the change in terms, such as reorganisation or redundancy or the employee's incompetence in the position (ERA 1996, s. 138(2)(b)). If the employer takes this step the original dismissal stands and the employee may claim a redundancy payment unless the employer makes a more successful offer of suitable alternative employment at that stage.

The four-week period is in terms of calendar weeks regardless of the actual period of working during those weeks (*Benton* v *Sanderson Kayser Ltd* (1989)). If the employee leaves after the four-week period of grace he is treated as having resigned in the normal way and cannot claim a redundancy payment or unfair dismissal. The strictness of the rule is shown by *Meek* v *J. Allen Rubber Co. Ltd and Secretary of State for Employment* (1980). The employee used to drive a lorry for the first respondent on a shuttle between Lydney and Whitecroft and when the latter depot was closed down, he was offered the alternative of a London to Lydney route. Part of the deal was that he might try it out for at least six months and at the end of this period he decided that it was not for him. Notwithstanding the six months offer, it was held that he could not claim a redundancy payment when he then resigned, since he was taken to have accepted the offer of alternative employment after the four statutory weeks had gone. It was open to the relevant Government department, which was not party to the arrangement, to refuse a redundancy rebate.

The EAT also rejected a submission that his acceptance of the new route was conditional on his satisfaction.

9.3.3 Acceptance or refusal of job offer

If the employee accepts the job offered there is no problem as there is no redundancy. The fact that it may be wildly unsuitable and he is thereafter forever unhappy about the decision is irrelevant. He retains his continuous service, provided that, if there are changes in conditions, the offer was made before the former redundant employment terminated.

If, on the other hand, the employee refuses the new offer the situation is complicated. Where the new terms do not differ from the old (ERA 1996, s. 141(3)(a)) the tribunal must decide whether his refusal was reasonable and it is for the employer to prove that it was not. If the proffered terms do differ, the employer must prove that the offer was one of suitable alternative employment and that the employee was unreasonable in refusing it, if he is to avoid liability to make a redundancy payment (s. 141(3)(b)). The offer of new terms must be sufficiently certain, unconditional and duly communicated (*Havenhand* v *Thomas Black Ltd* (1968)), although it may be addressed to a group of workers (*McCreadie* v *Thomson & MacIntyre (Patternmakers) Ltd* (1971)), rather than solely to the individual. The offer need not be in writing but must contain specific information about 'the capacity and place and other terms and conditions of employment' (*Roberts* v *Essoldo Circuit (Control) Ltd* (1967)). The Act does not apply where an offer is made by a third party, unless he is a transferee or associated employer of the employer (*Farquharson* v *Ross* (1966)). It is not intended to prevent the award of a redundancy payment simply because the redundant worker gains another job. The employer must have a reasonable expectation of fulfilling the offer made (*Kane* v *Raine & Co. Ltd* (1974)); it is not good enough to pluck a post out of the air in a desperate effort to avoid a redundancy payment.

The question is one of fact in every case, and Bridge J suggested in *Collier* v *Smith's Dock Ltd* (1969) that appeal bodies should not interfere with the decisions of ETs, apart from cases where a job is so obviously unsuitable that the tribunal must have misdirected itself or where the tribunal has failed to take account of relevant circumstances. In *Carron Company* v *Robertson* (1967) the court gave this general survey:

Now suitability is an imprecise term, but I accept that in deciding as to the suitability of employment in relation to an employee, one must consider not only the nature of the work, hours and pay, the employee's strength, training, experience and ability but such matters as status in the premises of the employer.

Neill LJ in *Spencer* v *Gloucestershire County Council* (1985) considered that it was confusing to 'draw too rigid a distinction between' suitability and reasonableness because 'some factors may be common to both aspects of the case'.

This was brought out neatly in *Cambridge and District Co-operative Society Ltd* v *Ruse* (1993) when the EAT held that, even though the tribunal felt that the alternative job offered was suitable, where the employee considered it was not (due to his perceived drop in status), that did not mean that his refusal to accept the offer was unreasonable. Reasonableness did not relate merely to personal factors of the employee which were extraneous to the job.

The most important factors to be considered have emerged in these cases. In *Kennedy* v *Werneth Ring Mills Ltd* (1977) the EAT held that the most important criterion of pay concerns what is actually earned in the new position, and not the basic wage alone. In *Taylor* v *Kent County Council* (1969), the headmaster of a boys' secondary school was, on its closure, offered a post in a pool of mobile staff, meaning that he would have to teach in any school where he was required. Although he would still be remunerated on his old scale as a headmaster, the Divisional Court held that this was not suitable because of the serious loss of status, and the judges drew a comparison with a company director being expected to work as a navy.

It is for the employer still to go on to show, even if he has established that the alternative offer was suitable, that the employee's rejection of it was unreasonable (*Jones* v *Aston Cabinet Co. Ltd* (1973)). Tribunals take into account, in assessing the reasonableness of the employee, the existence of other local employment (*John Laing & Son Ltd* v *Best* (1968)), but have held that an offer is not in itself unreasonable because it is in an industry, for example, coal, which is contracting so that the new job in it is unlikely to be permanent (*James and Jones* v *National Coal Board* (1969)). This was notwithstanding that the tribunal thought that the applicants had made a wise decision to leave the declining industry and appeared rather sympathetic to the worker who, having just undergone one trauma, does not wish to uproot himself again. It may be inevitable, however, at a time of recession when so many industries are in sharp decline. For similar reasons, the refusal of an offer which 'on any view was to last 12 to 18 months' though not necessarily for ever (*Morganite Crucible Co. Ltd* v *Street* (1972)), was held unreasonable. It is a matter of degree, so that in *Thomas Wragg & Sons Ltd* v *Wood* (1976), on the other hand, uncertainty about the future, combined with the fact that the employee was 56, had accepted a job elsewhere, and that the offer came very late, provided valid grounds for refusal. The Court of Appeal in *Spencer* v *Gloucestershire County Council* (1985) disagreed with a judgment of the EAT to the effect that it was not legitimate for school cleaners to refuse reduced hours of work on the ground that they did not consider that they could do a satisfactory job in the time and with the numbers available. The Court of Appeal considered that there was no rule of law that questions of standards were irrelevant to the decision; it was rather in each case a question of fact and the EAT should not have interfered with their decision that the employees were not unreasonable in refusing the offered positions.

Where the TUPE apply, the transferee must continue the employee's contract exactly as before (see Chapter 5 above).

9.4 Disqualification from redundancy payment

An employee may for various reasons lose his entitlement to redundancy payment in full or in part even though he satisfies other requirements so far considered.

9.4.1 Misconduct

The first situation is where the employer is entitled to terminate the employment by reason of the employee's misconduct (ERA 1996, s. 140(1)). For this to apply,

214 Statutory redundancy payments and consultation procedures

the contract must be terminated either without notice, or with shorter notice than was contractually necessary. Where the misconduct occurs before notice of redundancy the employer must either sack the employee instantly or give a written statement that he is entitled to dismiss at once. This is a strange provision, since if the employer dismisses the employee for cause, whether for incapability or misconduct, that is not a dismissal for redundancy. The reason the provision was inserted may have been because the Redundancy Payments Act 1965, in which it is first found in exactly the same form, predated the wider unfair dismissal jurisdiction. Its continuance now is more problematic and it has given rise to difficulties of interpretation. *Sanders* v *Ernest A. Neale Ltd* (1974) suggests that the subsection is intended to apply where the employee is dismissed in fact for redundancy when he could have been sacked for cause.

9.4.2 Strike action

If the employee takes part in a strike within the period of notice of termination which the employer must give, and the employer then terminates the contract for that reason, s. 140 does not apply and he remains entitled to a redundancy payment (s. 140(2)). If the employer dismisses for any other reason during this time, an ET may award the whole or part of the redundancy payment to which the employee would have been otherwise entitled if this appears just and equitable (s. 140(3) and (4)). By ERA 1996, s. 143(2), where a redundant employee goes on strike the employer may require him 'by notice of extension' to make up the time lost in the strike if he is still to be entitled to redundancy payment. It must warn that the employer will dispute the employee's right to redundancy payment if he does not comply (s. 143(2)(c)).

9.4.3 Counter-notice

If the employee is under notice of redundancy and wishes to leave before the notice runs out, for example to start another job, he may himself give notice. If the employer objects to him leaving early, he can request the employee to withdraw the notice and warn him that he will contest his redundancy payment. The ET must then decide whether to award all or part of the redundancy payment, reviewing all the circumstances (ERA 1996, s. 142). The provision appears to have been little used.

9.5 Calculation of redundancy payment

Redundancy pay, like the basic award in unfair dismissal, is based on the week's pay in accordance with ERA 1996, ss 220–229. Calculation depends first on whether or not the employee has normal working hours and, secondly, whether he is paid by time, piece or is on shift or rota work. First the mode of calculation will be explained, and then the vocabulary.

9.5.1 **The method of calculation**

The appropriate redundancy payment is reached by multiplying the week's pay by a multiplier depending on age, being 1½ for every year during the whole of which the employee was 41 or over, 1 for every year during the whole of which the employee was between 22 and 40, and ½ for every year between 18 and 21. The maximum payable is thus 30 weeks and this would be appropriate where an employee has been working for 20 years' continuous employment over 41. The amount of remuneration to be awarded for redundancy payment, as for unfair dismissal basic award, is subject to a maximum limit, and the Secretary of State must alter this sum annually in line with the retail price index. The present maximum stands at £380 per week as from 1 October 2009 and this clearly reduces the compensation which would otherwise have been awarded to a large section of the workforce. The maximum payment is thus now £11,400.

Payment of an earlier redundancy payment breaks continuity (ERA 1996, s. 214(2)(a)). Where, however, there is a gap of up to four weeks or renewal of employment following a redundancy, and the offer of an alternative job or renewal of the old one, this counts towards continuity. Just as with ordinary weekly pay, the employer must give the redundant worker a written statement setting out how his amount of redundancy payment has been calculated (ERA 1996, s. 165(1)). This is not required where the computation has been carried out by an ET. An employer in default (unusually for employment law provisions) is liable to a fine, and if no statement is given the employee may in writing demand it by a specified date giving at least one week to reply (ERA 1996, s. 165(2)–(4)).

9.5.2 **Normal working hours**

The ERA 1996, s. 234(3) defines normal working hours as being those where the contract fixes the number, or the minimum number, of hours in a week, whether or not those hours can be reduced in certain circumstances. The number must be included in the written statement of terms. The working of overtime involves manifold complications. It is unusual to find hours of overtime expressly fixed by a contract of employment, and the more common situation was examined by the Court of Appeal in *Tarmac Roadstone Holdings Ltd* v *Peacock* (1973). The employee's standard hours were 40, but his contract also stated that 'workers shall work overtime in accordance with the demands of the industry', and in fact they regularly worked 57 hours. The court considered that the decisive issue was whether the contract not only obliged the employee to work overtime, which it did, but also the employer to provide it, which was not so here. A unilateral obligation on the employer is, in fact, much more frequent. The 'normal working hours' were held to be 40 and the applicant's redundancy pay consequently amounted to less than the amount he normally took home in his pay packet each week.

Moreover, the EAT is reluctant to infer a variation of contract by reason of practice (*Friend* v *PMA Holdings Ltd* (1976); *cf. ITT Components (Europe) Ltd* v *Kolah* (1977)) although this is not unknown. In *Dean* v *Eastbourne Fishermen's and Boatmen's Protection Society Ltd* (1977), for example, the applicant worked fixed bar sessions and at other times as and when his employer needed him. The regular periods demanded amounted to less than the 21 hours which was then necessary to gain employment protection. The EAT held that in the absence of any express term as to number of hours the ET should have inferred a term from what happened in practice; and that since the evidence was that during the two years necessary to qualify for the redundancy payment he was claiming he had worked for more than the statutory minimum on 86 occasions, he was entitled to claim.

9.5.3 Remuneration

Having worked out the normal hours, it is then necessary to determine the contractual rate of pay for them. For these purposes the week is deemed to end on Saturday, unless pay is calculated on a weekly basis, in which case the week ends on the day on which the employee is regularly paid.

The relevant remuneration is by statute 'money paid under the contract of employment by the employer' *(Lyford v Turquand* (1966)), with the qualification that if the employee is paid less than the sum to which he is entitled, it is the latter which is the relevant figure *(Cooner v P. S. Doal & Sons* (1988)). The concept refers to the gross amount of weekly pay *(Secretary of State for Employment v John Woodrow & Sons (Builders) Ltd* (1983)). The week's pay certainly does not include the value of, for example, a company car or free accommodation but does cover bonuses, allowances and commission, if they are provided for by an express or implied term in the contract of employment (e.g. *Lawrence v Cooklin Kitchen Fitments Ltd* (1966)). This was justified in *Weevsmay Ltd v Kings* (1977), on the ground that tribunals must interpret the word in a commonsense way.

The ERA 1996, s. 228(1)–(3) provides that if bonuses are annual payments, or in any other way do not coincide with the periods of normal pay, a proportionate amount is to be included *(J. & S. Bickley Ltd v Washer* (1977)). A Christmas bonus payable *ex gratia* is clearly excluded *(Skillen v Eastwoods Froy Ltd* (1967)) but an incentive bonus is to be included *(British Coal Corporation v Cheesbrough* (1988)), while the treatment of tips depends on their precise nature. Where a restaurant levied a compulsory service charge, and shared this out each week between its waiters, their right was contractually enforceable and included in the relevant remuneration *(Tsoukka v Potomac Restaurants Ltd* (1968)), but tips paid direct to the employee, on the other hand, are not reckoned *(S. & U. Stores Ltd v Lee* (1969)) since they are not money paid by the employer. (See also *Cofone v Spaghetti House Ltd* (1980).) A tribunal assessing the week's pay must look to the realities of any payment made, and this is particularly apposite in view of the massive range of payment systems in use.

For similar reasons state benefits are not included *(Wibberley v Staveley Iron & Chemical Co. Ltd* (1966)), while holiday pay is outside the definition since it is referable to weeks of absence and not normal working time *(Secretary of State for Employment v Haynes* (1980)). Items described as expenses are taken into account only where they represent a profit over actual outlay *(S. & U. Stores Ltd v Wilkes* (1974)), but nothing is awarded where the relevant arrangement is illegal as a fraud on the Inland Revenue *(Nerva v R. L. & G. Ltd* (1997)).

9.5.4 **Calculation date**

The relevant pay and hours for redundancy payment purposes are those governing at the 'calculation date' as specified in ERA 1996, ss 225 and 226. This is generally the last date of working under the employee's contract of employment, but some modification is made to prevent employers escaping liability to pay higher amounts (because of a pay rise) by giving shorter notice than that to which the employee is entitled by contract. The calculation date is then the date on which notice would have expired had the employer given the minimum notice as required by ERA 1996, s. 86. The proper method is to find the statutory period and work back from the relevant date of termination. Thus, if the employee has worked for 10 years and is dismissed in week 20, the calculation relates to week 10, whether or not the necessary 10 weeks' notice has in fact been given. If the employee has worked two years the calculation date is week 18.

Doubts surround the treatment of a pay agreement backdated to the calculation date; an example would be when the agreement is announced in week 25 but starts in week 15 and the employee is dismissed in week 20. Since the vital words are 'is payable' it is thought that it should be included in the remuneration to be so calculated. This view has been upheld (*obiter*) in *Leyland Vehicles Ltd* v *Reston* (1980), where there was evidence that wages were annually increased on a particular date, and it may be confined to these special facts. In fact the particular applicant was not entitled since he was not employed on the starting date. If the backdated agreement is announced after the calculation for redundancy payment falls to be made, a new claim may be submitted (*Cowan* v *Pullman Spring Filled Co. Ltd* (1967)).

9.5.5 **Week's pay of particular workers**

We now apply these general provisions in the concrete situation of particular workers, that is, time workers, piece workers, and shift workers.

A time worker has normal working hours and his 'remuneration for employment in normal working hours, whether by the hour or week or other period, does not vary with the amount of work done in the period' (ERA 1996, s. 221(2)). His week's pay is that 'payable' under the contract of employment in force on the calculation date.

A piece worker is an employee who has normal working hours, but his pay varies with the amount of work done; this may take the form of payment for every piece of work he does, an incentive bonus, or a commission related to output. One arrives at his 'week's pay' by multiplying the normal hours worked by the average hourly rate of remuneration in the 12 weeks before the last complete week before the calculation date (s. 221(2)). It does not matter whether these previous weeks were full working weeks or not (*Sylvester* v *Standard Upholstery Co. Ltd* (1967)), although any week in which no pay at all was received in the relevant 12-week period is ignored and an earlier week used. Overtime premium rates are to be excluded even when the hours are counted.

Shift and rota workers are those whose hours 'differ from week to week or over a longer period so that the remuneration payable for . . . any week varies according to the incidence of the said days or times' (s. 222(1)). Here one multiplies the average weekly hours by the average hourly rate of remuneration. Both calculations are again made by taking an average of the 12 weeks preceding the calculation date if that date is the last day of a week, or otherwise ending with the last complete week before the calculation date. The average hourly rate of remuneration is the average pay for the hours actually worked in the 12 weeks preceding the calculation date, if that should be the last day of the week, or in other circumstances the last complete week before the calculation date. Again, the remuneration to be considered is only that paid in respect of hours 'when the employee was actually working', so excluding rest days (see *British Coal Corporation* v *Cheesbrough* (1990)).

Some employees have no normal working hours at all. University academics, sales staff on commission, and those employed in a managerial, administrative, or professional capacity are examples. These employees are normally not employed on a strict 9 a.m. to 5 p.m. basis. Here again, an average of a 12-week period is taken. There are, however, some cases in which the employee has not been employed in the same job for 12 weeks, yet is still able to claim employment protection rights, because continuity is preserved from a previous employment. If this is so, the weeks of that previous job are taken into account but if this would not be appropriate or is impossible, the ET is directed to reach a computation it considers just in all the circumstances.

9.6 Claiming a redundancy payment

Unless there is a dispute about whether the employee is dismissed for redundancy, the employer usually offers the correct redundancy payment to his employee without any formal claim being necessary. In the event of a dispute the employee should submit a written claim, making it clear to the employer what he is seeking. If this does not succeed, the next step is to refer the matter to an ET within six months of the relevant date of dismissal by submitting an originating application (ERA 1996, s. 164). If the employee fails to take any of these steps within six months he may have an extension of up to six months, but only if the ET thinks it to be 'just and equitable...having regard to the reason shown by the employee' for the delay (s. 164(2)). A complaint of unfair dismissal presented within six months may entitle the applicant to a redundancy payment if the tribunal decides that the reason for dismissal was redundancy even where there is no claim as such for a redundancy payment (*Duffin* v *Secretary of State for Employment* (1983); see also *Secretary of State for Employment* v *Banks* (1983)). If the employee has died in the meantime the right to redundancy payment devolves with his estate, and a special representative may be appointed solely for the purposes of tribunal proceedings.

9.7 Insolvency and corporate reconstruction

9.7.1 Adoption of contracts by administrator

Where there is an attempt to rescue the employer company by means of an appointment of either a receiver or an administrative receiver, it is possible to enforce a claim against the receiver. In *Powdrill* v *Watson* (1995), the receivers had sent to employees letters stating that they were not to be taken to have adopted the employees' contracts of employment. Lord Browne-Wilkinson, however, decided that under Insolvency Act 1986, s. 19(5) a contract of employment was adopted if the employee continued in employment for more than 14 days after the appointment of the administrator or receiver, and that it is not possible to avoid this result or alter its consequences unilaterally by informing employees that their contracts are not being adopted, or adopting them only on terms. However the consequence of adoption is to give priority only to liabilities incurred by the administrator or receiver during his tenure of office. The decision also affected receivers since under Insolvency Act 1986, s. 44(1)(b) receivers are also personally liable.

In respect of both receivers and administrative receivers the effect of this was very soon ameliorated by the Insolvency Act 1994 which limited their liability in relation to contracts of employment adopted after 15 March 1994 to 'qualifying liabilities', namely obligations to pay wages or salary or contributions to an occupational pension scheme, and not, for example, unfair dismissal. As Davies observes ((1994) 23 ILJ 141), while seeking to encourage rescues, the 1994 Act reflects a policy which prioritises the interest of the chargeholder and, because the interest of receiver or administrative procedure is in maximising the funds for the chargeholder rather than simply maximising receipts, this approach may not encourage the efficient use of resources.

9.7.2 Preferential creditor status

A worker whose employer becomes insolvent risks losing all his employment protection rights in the financial wreck of the company, partnership, or individual. He does, however, have preferential creditor status in the assets of the insolvent employer, so that he ranks to be paid out of company funds, along with PAYE tax and VAT, that is before anything goes into the pool for ordinary trade creditors. This may mean that the employees are paid in full or pro rata. Employee's preferential debts under Insolvency Act 1986, s. 175 and Sch. 6 are the employee's remuneration (by way of wages or salary) for a period of up to four months subject to the maximum set by the Secretary of State from time to time, and any holiday pay. Remuneration specifically includes any guarantee payment (under ERA 1996, s. 28(1)–(3)); remuneration on suspension on medical grounds (ERA 1996, s. 64(1) and (2)); payment for time off for trade union duties and ante-natal care (TULR(C)A 1992, s. 169(3); ERA 1996, s. 56(1)); and any protective award for failure to consult over redundancies (TULR(C)A 1992, s. 189). Any other sums due and owing may be claimed as an unsecured debt and proof of debt forms may be gained from the trustee or liquidator, but the process may take a very long time.

9.7.3 Direct payment by Department for Business, Innovation and Skills

The ERA 1996 offers three further ways of ensuring that the employee's position is to some extent protected where an individual has been declared bankrupt or has made a composition or arrangement with his creditors; an individual's estate is being administered in accordance with an order under Insolvency Act 1986, s. 421; or a company is wound up by a shareholders' resolution (ERA 1996, s. 183). The provisions do not go so far as to cover an individual firm or company which is only unable to meet its debts as they fall due (*Pollard* v *Teako (Swiss) Ltd* (1967)). Further, the fact that one of two partners in the firm by which a person was employed had been adjudged bankrupt was not sufficient to establish that the employer was insolvent within the meaning of the Act; in such a case both partners would have to be adjudged as bankrupts (*Secretary of State for Trade and Industry* v *Forde* (1997)).

Speedy and safe recourse may be made to the Government's National Insurance Fund (ERA 1996, s. 182) in the case of the following debts (ERA 1996, s. 184):

(a) up to eight weeks' wages, including guarantee pay, medical suspension pay, union duties pay, ante-natal care pay, statutory sick pay, and protective award;

(b) minimum pay during notice under ERA 1996, s. 86 or damages for failure to give such notice, but not including the appropriate holiday pay during notice according to the EAT in *Secretary of State for Employment* v *Haynes* (1980) (see also *Secretary of State for Employment* v *Jobling* (1980));

(c) up to six weeks' accumulated holiday pay during the last 12 months preceding the relevant date;

(d) a basic award made by an ET for unfair dismissal;

(e) reimbursement of premiums or fees paid for apprenticeship or articles of clerkship.

Item (d) may be reclaimed in full, but the other payments are subject to a maximum of £330 per week for, it would appear, each type (ERA 1996, s. 186(1)). This is subject to a reduction if the employee earns from another source or receives state benefits during the period of his notice. Further, in the unusual case where the employer has a cross-claim against the employee, for example in respect of a loan, this may be set off (*Secretary of State for Employment* v *Wilson and BCCI* (1996)). Days covered by payments made under the insolvency provisions do not count in establishing eligibility to social security benefit. The Department for Business, Innovation and Skills (BIS) may apply the limit before making deductions in respect of income tax and National Insurance contributions (*Morris* v *Secretary of State for Employment* (1985); *Titchener* v *Secretary of State for Trade and Industry* (2002)).

The claims arise on the 'relevant date' which is defined as the latest of the following dates: when the employer becomes insolvent; when the employment came to an end; and where the debt is a basic award for unfair dismissal or a protective award for failure to consult the union over redundancies, the date when the award was made.

Gaining these payments involves a mass of form filling. A written application must be first made to BIS certifying that one of the appropriate debts was owing on the 'relevant date'. The payments are not actually made until a trustee or liquidator is appointed, since he must then submit to the Department a statement of what is due to each employee as soon as reasonably practicable. If there is no such statement within six months of the submission of the written request, the Department has a discretion to pay without it but if the Department refuses to pay what the employee claims he is entitled to, he can refer the matter to an ET within three months of the alleged default.

The right to unpaid employers' pension contributions from the Department extends to arrears accrued within 12 months prior to insolvency, arrears certified by an actuary to be necessary to pay employees' benefits on dissolution of the scheme and 10 per cent of the last 12 months' payroll for the employees covered by the scheme. The maximum is the lowest of these figures. Again, the Department defers until a trustee or liquidator is appointed before paying, and recourse is to an ET in the event of dispute.

An employee can claim a redundancy payment direct from the National Insurance Fund where he is entitled to such a payment in the usual way, and he has taken all reasonable steps to obtain payment besides resorting to legal proceedings, or the employer is insolvent as defined in ERA 1996, s. 166(5), (6), and (7). The worker then receives his normal redundancy payment less any payment already made towards it by the employer. The employee's rights and remedies are taken over by (subrogated to) the Secretary of State (s. 167(3)(a)), who may take proceedings against the employer while disputes over these payments may be referred to an ET (s. 170).

9.8 Consultation

The redundancy consultation legislation has an English mother and a European father. The Council Directive (EEC) 75/129 was the chief European impetus, while the British genesis is found in the Donovan Commission Report. It remains an unusual hybrid of collective and individual enforcement. Consultation over redundancy was from the outset embodied in the Code of Industrial Relations Practice but only in an advisory capacity.

From the same European source derives a parallel obligation to inform representatives of recognised unions about takeovers and mergers, enacted in TUPE (see Chapter 5 above).

The EPA 1975, Part IV for the first time extended collective bargaining to cover consultation over redundancies. It is now re-enacted as TULR(C)A 1992, s. 188 and imposes the duty on employers who recognise a trade union to consult with its 'authorised representatives' when even only one employee of the class for which the union is recognised is to be made redundant, and whether or not the worker(s) in question is a member of the union. The sanction on the employer for default is a protective award, and this will be ordered unless there are special circumstances explaining his omission. The provision was substantially amended by the TURERA 1993 to reflect the judgment of the ECJ that UK law was incompatible with EU law (*Commission of the European Communities* v *United Kingdom* (1994)). The Collective Redundancies and Transfer of Undertakings (Protection of Employment) Amendment Regulations 1995 (SI 1995 No. 2587) (1995 Amendment Regulations) extend the definition of those to be consulted to 'employee representatives elected by them'. They must be employees at the time when they were elected, so it is not possible to draft in someone from outside the employing company.

The UK Government moved a step closer towards fulfilling its obligations under Council Directive (EEC) 75/129, replaced and revoked by Council Directive (EC) 98/59, by issuing the Collective Redundancies and Transfer of Undertakings (Protection of Employment) (Amendment) Regulations 1999 (SI 1999 No. 1925) (1999 Amendment Regulations). The 1999 Amendment Regulations strengthen the position of union-authorised representatives and include new arrangements designed to under-pin the independence of representatives elected by the employees. (See Hall and Edwards, (1999) 28 ILJ 299.)

Different groups of workers may have different representatives to be consulted, whether elected or union representatives. By the 1995 amendments, if there were both elected representatives and a recognised trade union for employees of a particular description, the employer could choose which representatives he consulted. The 1999 Amendment Regulations remove this freedom of choice by requiring the employer to consult union representatives where it recognises an independent trade union in respect of a group of affected employees (new TULR(C)A 1992, s. 188(1B)). It is only where such a recognition arrangement does not exist that the employer will be entitled to consult with non-union representatives.

The representatives need not be elected specifically for the purposes of consultation about redundancies to qualify as such elected representatives, but if they may have been elected for other purposes it must be appropriate for the employer to consult them over redundancies. Thus, it would be appropriate for the employer to consult members of a works council, but probably not those elected as canteen representatives. The employer also has a duty to allow appropriate representatives, whether from the recognised union or as elected by employees, 'access to the employees whom it is proposed to dismiss as redundant' and they must be given 'such accommodation and other facilities as may be appropriate'. The elected representatives and candidates for such posts have a right not to be subjected to detrimental treatment or to dismissal on the grounds of their functions or activities and to reasonable time off with pay, for the purposes of their activities.

The 1995 Amendment Regulations required that the employer invite employees to select representatives, and nothing more. If the employees failed to take the employer up on his invitation, he would not face legal liability for a failure to consult, so long as the invitation was issued in good time (*R* v *Secretary of State for Trade and Industry ex parte Unison* (1996)). However, the 1999 Amendment Regulations inserted s. 188(7B) into the TULR(C)A 1992, which provides that, in the absence of an election, the employer must consult instead with all the affected employees individually.

The 1999 Amendment Regulations also inserted s. 188A into the TULR(C)A 1992, governing the conduct of elections of employee representatives. This imposes a duty on the employer to make such arrangements 'as are reasonably practicable' to ensure that the election is fair. Any employee who may be affected by the proposed dismissals or by measures taken in connection with them is entitled to vote in the election and, if he wants, to stand as a candidate. The election should be conducted, so far as is reasonably practicable, in secret and votes must be accurately counted. Representatives' terms of office should be long enough for them to be fully informed and consulted in accordance with s. 188.

The right to be consulted is one thing. The subject-matter of the consultations is another. In *UK Coal Mining Ltd* v *NUM (Northumberland Area)* (2008) the EAT held that the duty goes beyond the need to consult about the consequences of redundancies, but goes to the reasons for making those redundancies. This is a significant distinction for trade unions in this regard.

9.8.1 Definition of redundancy

In the period between the introduction of the legislation and passage of the TURERA 1993, the same definition of redundancy served for the purposes of consultation over redundancy as applied to statutory redundancy payments. Under the impulse of the relevant European Directive, however, the definition was altered in relation to consultation to 'dismissal for a reason not related to the individual concerned or a number of reasons all of which are not so related' (TULR(C)A 1992, s. 195) which is clearly much wider than statutory redundancy—see *GMB* v *Man Truck & Bus UK* (2000). Indeed in *Commission of the European Communities* v *United Kingdom* (1994) the UK Government conceded that prior to the amendment the UK definition of redundancy had failed to give full effect to Council Directive (EEC) 75/129.

9.8.2 Recognition

Under the first statutory scheme the obligation to consult also arose only once a trade union had been recognised. However, in *Commission of the European Communities* v *United Kingdom* (1994) the ECJ held that this constituted a breach of Council Directive (EEC) 75/129 in that the Directive required the UK to provide a mechanism for the designation of workers' representatives in an organisation where the employer refuses to recognise such representatives. Reliance cannot be placed directly upon the Directive even as against an emanation of the State. In *Griffin* v *South West Water Services Ltd* (1995) it was held that, although the defendant was an emanation of the state, the Directive was not sufficiently precise as to be directly enforceable, since it gave member states a wide discretion as to the designation of the 'workers representatives' to be consulted. It remains necessary to identify whether there is sufficient recognition by management of a trade union to trigger the consultation requirements. Whether there is recognition in any particular case is a mixed question of fact and law. The only general definition of this concept, important though it is throughout modern labour law, is to be found in TULR(C)A 1992, s. 178(3). It survived the repeal of the statutory recognition provisions in the EPA 1975, but is self-reflexive, and of no great assistance, citing 'recognition of the union by an employer to any extent for the purpose of collective bargaining'. Collective bargaining is defined in TULR(C)A 1992, s. 178(1) as negotiations relating to or connected with the subject matter of a collective agreement, as there detailed.

The matter is straightforward in the paradigmatic case of recognition by a written agreement, or where a declaration of recognition is made by the CAC under the statutory procedure. At the other end of the scale, however, a right to be consulted about terms and conditions is not enough. Much more problematic is the situation arising in the leading case, the Court of Appeal decision in *National Union of Gold, Silver and Allied Trades* v *Albury Brothers Ltd* (1978), where the union sought to prove recognition on the ground that the company was a member of the British Jewellers' Association, which had negotiated a series of agreements on terms and conditions with it. The Court of Appeal emphasised the high burden of proof resting on the union since 'recognition was such an important matter involving serious consequences on both sides'. In the absence of an actual agreement, only clear and distinct conduct signifying implied accord would suffice and Eveleigh LJ thought 'a point must be reached where one can use the expression "it goes without saying"'. That position was not reached on the facts.

What more is required is illustrated in *National Union of Tailors and Garment Workers* v *Charles Ingram & Co. Ltd* (1977), where not only was the employer a member of a bargaining trade association, but the manager of the factory in question had 'over a substantial period of time' discussed terms and conditions of employment, and grievances raised by the shop steward, with the local union official. It was powerful evidence also that the employer had stated on a government form that the union was recognised. In *Joshua Wilson & Bros Ltd* v *USDAW* (1978) the union qualified as recognised because management followed Joint Industrial Council wage agreements, allowed the shop steward to put up a notice announcing a particular increase and consulted with the shop steward over changes in employees' duties. The company had also talked with an area organiser of the union.

There is no place for automatic recognition to be thrust on an employer by a third party employers' association or Government Minister. In *Cleveland County Council* v *Springett* (1985) the Association of Polytechnic Teachers claimed that they were recognised at Teesside Polytechnic because, although they had been refused recognition despite requests over many years, enquiries by union representatives concerning conditions at work were answered and the union was encouraged to send representatives to meetings of the Polytechnic Health and Safety Committee. Further, in 1981 the Secretary of State for Education decided that it should be represented on the Burnham Pay Committee. The EAT thought that the action of the Secretary of State was in no way decisive as the tribunal had thought that it was, and that the other matters did not add up to recognition for the purposes of the statute.

Unions have attempted to cut through the generally restrictive interpretation of recognition by arguing that use of the words 'recognition to any extent' signified acts preliminary to the completed act of recognition. In *Transport and General Workers' Union* v *Dyer* (1977) this contention was supported by the fact that negotiations about procedure and machinery for collective bargaining (talks about talks) were comprised in the Act's definition of collective bargaining. However, the argument was rejected here as it was in *NUGSAT* v *Albury Bros Ltd* (1978), where the EAT held that the words referred to an employer recognising a union, say, for the purpose of discussing wages but not holidays or pension rights.

The cases make clear that discussion about matters of mutual interest on a 'one-off basis' is not enough. Thus in *NUGSAT* v *Albury Bros Ltd* there were a few letters and one meeting, while in *TGWU* v *Dyer* (1977) very limited and unwilling contact over the reinstatement of a union member did not found an inference of recognition. As Lord McDonald put it, there must be *consensus ad idem* on recognition, and this must be without any misapprehension, the employer realising the significance of the step he is taking (*TGWU* v *Courtenham Products Ltd* (1977)).

9.8.3 Consultation 'in good time'

By TULR(C)A 1992, s. 188 as originally enacted, the overriding duty on an employer when he proposed to dismiss employees as redundant, was to begin consultation with the recognised union 'at the earliest opportunity'. By virtue of the 1995

Amendment Regulations, s. 188(1A) now states that the consultation when the employer proposes to dismiss 'shall begin in good time', a less exacting test. There must be consultation, even if the employer believes that it would make no practical difference to the outcome (*Sovereign Distribution Services Ltd* v *TGWU* (1989); *Middlesbrough Borough Council* v *TGWU* (2002)) and even if the employees are not actually members of the recognised trade union (*Governing Body of the Northern Ireland Hotel and Catering College* v *NATFHE* (1995)).

The obligation begins when the employer proposes to dismiss. 'Proposal' here means more than that there is at the time a remote possibility of dismissal (*National Union of Public Employees* v *General Cleaning Contractors Ltd* (1976)), and requires, as the EAT put it in *Association of Patternmakers and Allied Craftsmen* v *Kirvin Ltd* (1978), 'a state of mind directed to a planned or proposed course of events'. The employer must thus have formed some view of how many employees are to be dismissed, when this is to take place and how it is to be arranged. But, according to the EAT in *Hough* v *Leyland DAF Ltd* (1991) there is no need to consult until a specific proposal to dismiss employees as redundant has been reached. This is a later stage than the mere diagnosis of a problem, for which a possible solution may be the declaring of redundancies—see too *Scotch Premier Meat Ltd* v *Burns* (2000).

The requirement to consult only from the point when the employer 'proposes' to dismiss falls foul of the Directive which refers to the time when the employer is 'contemplating' collective redundancies, which could be a good deal earlier, according to the EAT in *MSF* v *Refuge Assurance plc* (2002). It also decided that the Regulations could not be read in accordance with the Directive, and therefore the UK is in breach of the Directive. As Rubenstein points out ([2002] IRLR 310) this would appear to mean that there are different rules for the public and private sector here as Directives have direct effect against emanations of the State. That s. 188 is in breach of EU law and has now been highlighted by the ECJ in *Junk* v *Kühnel* (2005). Consultation must take place before notices of dismissal have been issued. However, it would not appear to be necessary for the whole 90-day period to have elapsed before notices of dismissal are issued.

In *E. Green & Son (Castings) Ltd* v *ASTMS & AUEW* (1984) the employers claimed that they had consulted on the day that redundancy notices were issued, and that this constituted the start of statutory consultations. The EAT reiterated their decision in *National Union of Teachers* v *Avon County Council* (1978) that this could not constitute consultation in any meaningful sense of the word. It was also insufficient to inform the unions that the criteria for selection would 'be determined in consultation with union representatives'. The employers had to inform the unions of their proposed method before consultation began, and this had to be done before notices of dismissal were dispatched, for union representatives had to be enabled to properly consider the proposals put to them. In *Transport and General Workers' Union* v *Ledbury Preserves (1928) Ltd* (1985) dismissal notices were sent out half an hour after a meeting with union representatives at which redundancy proposals were put to them for the first time. The EAT had little difficulty in deciding that this exercise was a sham.

Minimum periods of time for consultation are laid down by TULR(C)A 1992, s. 188(2): where 100 or more employees are to be made redundant at one establishment within a period of 90 days or less, at least 90 days must be left for consultations, before the first of the dismissals takes effect. Thirty days must be allowed for this process where between 20 and 99 employees are to be dismissed within 30 days. The Secretary of State for Work and Pensions has power to vary further this provision (TULR(C)A 1992, s. 197(1)) as long as he does not reduce it to less than 30 days.

Where a proposal to make redundancies is shelved but later resurrected, so long as this is not a fresh proposal, there is no need to re-consult, according to the EAT in *Vauxhall Motors Ltd* v *TGWU* (2006). Clearly, though, there is going to be a period after which the tribunal should not consider such consultations as extant and evergreen.

9.8.4 Meaning of 'establishment'

The minimum amount of time for consultation depends on the number of persons employed at the 'establishment' in question. This term derives from Council Directive (EEC) 75/129 and is by no means a term of art in British labour law. *Barratt Developments (Bradford) Ltd* v *UCATT* (1978) yields few clues. The employers were a building company which operated on 14 sites in Lancashire, and made 24 employees at eight of these places redundant at the same time. In deciding the appropriate number in an establishment, the tribunal was advised to consider the matter as an 'industrial jury', using their common sense on the particular facts of the case. Since here the sites were all administered from one base at Bradford, the EAT upheld the tribunal's decision that there was only one establishment.

In *E. Green & Son (Castings) Ltd* v *ASTMS & AUEW* (1984) the three appellant companies were all subsidiaries of the same holding company, operated from the same site and shared the same accounting and personnel services. The tribunal sought to decide the number of employees to be made redundant at one establishment by aggregating the numbers employed by the three companies on the one site. Nolan J considered that this approach was misconceived. The first question is the identity of the employer, and only within the one company can numbers at a particular establishment be aggregated.

'Establishment' must be understood as a matter of EU law as designating the unit to which the worker made redundant was assigned to carry out his duties (*Rockfon A/S* v *Specialarbejderdrbundet i Danmark* (1996)). For a more detailed description, see the ECJ's decision in *Athinaiki Chartoppoiia AE* v *Panagiotidis* (2007).

9.8.5 Informed consultation

There was no statutory definition of 'consultation' beyond the vague instruction that the employer must consider any representation made by trade unions' representatives and reply to them (TULR(C)A 1992, s. 188(6)) until amendments made by TURERA 1993, s. 34(2). There is still no exhaustive definition but consultation must include consultation about 'ways of (a) avoiding the dismissals; (b) reducing the numbers of employees to be dismissed; and (c) mitigating the consequences of the dismissals'. Further, the employer must undertake the consultation 'with a view to reaching agreement with the trade union representatives', foreshadowing a finding of the ECJ that the absence of such a requirement constituted a breach of Council Directive (EC) 98/59. A breach of this provision is difficult to substantiate, for it is not clear how far actual bargaining must take place. However, talks must proceed on an informed basis, so that the employer is required at the beginning (TULR(C)A 1992, s. 188(4)), inserted in 1993 to disclose in writing to union representatives the reason for the loss of jobs, the number, although not the names, of those to be dismissed, the total number of workers employed and the proposed method of selection.

The details should also include how much notice the employer intends to give, and whether he will be making any enhanced severance payments. The employer's attempt to comply with the Act in *Electrical and Engineering Association* v *Ashwell-Scott* (1976) was not enough, since their letter only gave general notification of impending redundancies, and went on 'if there is any further information you should require please communicate...'. However in *MSF* v *GEC Ferranti (Defence Systems) (No. 2)* (1994) the EAT held that a failure to provide information under s. 188(6) will not necessarily be considered as a serious default. Whether information has been provided which is adequate to permit meaningful consultation depends on the particular facts of each case.

Some tribunals have sought guidance on the meaning of consultation. In the administrative law case, *Rollo* v *Minister of Town and Country Planning* (1947), it was decided that it means the communication of a genuine invitation, extended with a receptive mind, to give advice.

9.8.6 The defence of 'special circumstances'

An employer may plead 'special circumstances' as a partial exemption from the requirement to consult with a recognised union, although he must still 'take all such steps towards compliance...as are reasonably practicable' (TULR(C)A 1992, s. 189(6)). The employer may not, however, rely upon 'a failure on the part of that person controlling the employer (directly or indirectly)...to provide information to the employer' (TULR(C)A 1992, s. 188(7) inserted in 1993). The defence reflects the problems which affect particular trades and industries, especially construction. In *Amalgamated Society of Boilermakers* v *George Wimpey M. E. & Co. Ltd* (1977), the employers contended that it was not reasonably practicable for them to comply since the building site at Grangemouth, where the redundancies were declared, was subject to resignations, unexpected delays, uncertain weather, and design changes. These were precisely the arguments unsuccessfully used in Parliament to justify an amendment excluding the building trade altogether from the scope of the provisions, and the EAT decided that such matters could provide an acceptable excuse, but did not in this case, since the employers had not done their best to comply in the circumstances. Yet in denial of the principle that for the breach of a right there exists a remedy, no protective award was granted to the employees. On the other hand, in what may seem a harsh decision, where a builder was wrongly informed by the relevant Government department that he could make a man redundant without first consulting the union, this misleading advice was held not to be a 'special circumstance' (*Union of Construction Allied Trades and Technicians* v *H. Rooke and Son (Cambridge) Ltd* (1978)).

The most common set of special circumstances to have come before tribunals concerns the last breaths of a dying business. The employers in *Clarks of Hove Ltd* v *Bakers' Union* (1978) had carried on business for many years as manufacturers and retailers of confectionery. By the early autumn of 1976 they were in grave financial difficulties, but in October it was apparent that their last hopes had failed. Yet it was only two hours before the night shift came to work on the final day at 7 p.m. that a notice was posted on their numerous factory and bakery premises announcing that the workforce were then dismissed. The Court of Appeal confirmed the opinion of the tribunal that 'special' circumstances must be out of the ordinary or uncommon and in this context commercial and financial events such as the destruction of the plant, a general trading boycott or a sudden withdrawal of supplies from the main supplier. Insolvency alone was not 'special' but it might be so if it were proved that the employer had continued trading in the face of adverse economic pointers in the genuine but nonetheless reasonable expectation that redundancies would be avoided. Here, on the other hand, the company's management knew of the closure plans long before the date of dismissal and they ought to have seen that there was little chance that they could ward it off, and thus should have consulted the unions earlier.

In *Association of Patternmakers and Allied Craftsmen* v *Kirvin Ltd* (1978) Lord Macdonald drew a valuable distinction between a foreseeable insolvency as in the *Clarks* case, which could not be a special circumstance, and carrying on in the reasonable hope that the company would be sold as a going concern, which would obviate the need for redundancies and which might be within the scope of the excuse. The EAT thought the *Kirvin* case was in the latter category. Here, there were potential purchasers in the field, and Government subsidies in the background, and it was accepted that consultation would be fatal to delicate negotiations surrounding a 'rescue operation'. It might be thought that this was exactly the sort of circumstances for which the procedures section was envisaged, but Lord Macdonald did warn that an employer will not prove special circumstances 'if he shut his eyes to the obvious'. *Hamish Armour* v *ASTMS* (1979) applied the same principle and was taken as a precedent in rather less stringent circumstances in *Union of Shop, Distributive and Allied Workers* v *Leancut Bacon Ltd* (1981). The respondent company's directors had for some time been negotiating for the purchase of its shares by a third party. On the breakdown of these talks, the receiver declared redundancies without the necessary consultations taking place. This was held to be a special circumstance, even though, unlike in *Hamish Armour*, where the future depended on the discretion of a Government department, all factors were within the employer's knowledge.

9.8.7 Protective award

The remedy for failure to comply with the duty to consult on any of the procedural requirements of the section lies in the 'protective award' (TULR(C)A 1992, s. 189(3)). This is an unusual hybrid in that it may only be sought in an ET by a recognised union or an elected employee representative, but is in favour of, and can ultimately be enforced by, the individual employee dismissed as redundant. It is an entitlement 'to be paid remuneration by the employer for the protected period' (TULR(C)A 1992, s. 190(1)), conditional upon, in the main, the employee's being available for work should management wish to use his services. The only guidance provided for ETs is that the award must be 'just and equitable in all the circumstances having regard to the seriousness of the employer's default' (TULR(C)A 1992, s. 189(4)). The maximum in all cases is 90 days' pay, by virtue of the 1999 Amendment Regulations. In deciding on the amount, the tribunal should take into account the seriousness of the employer's breach and any mitigating circumstances, according to the EAT in *Amicus* v *GBS Tooling Ltd* (2005). It is intended to be a sanction against an employee rather than compensation for the employee, according to the Court of Appeal in *Susie Radin* v *GMB* (2004).

An application must be presented 'before the proposed dismissal takes effect or before the end of the period of three months beginning with a date on which the dismissal takes effect' or within a further period which the tribunal finds it just and equitable to grant, by way of extension. The question of whether an individual employee who may not be a trade union member can force the recognised union to make a claim on his behalf remains unanswered.

The primary judicial guidance on the size of the award is to be found in *Talke Fashions Ltd* v *Amalgamated Society of Textile Workers and Kindred Trades* (1977) where the EAT emphasised that it was discretionary and in no way penal. Tribunals should weigh the loss suffered by the employees and the seriousness of the employer's conduct in relation to them. Kilner Brown J referred to the experience of the penal provisions of the Industrial Relations Act 1971, saying: 'We regard the imposition of penalties for bad behaviour as a retrograde step.' Moreover, he said the seriousness of the default ought to be considered in its relationship to the employees and not in its relationship to the trade union representative who has not been consulted. In *Barratt Developments (Bradford) Ltd* v *UCATT* (1978) the EAT thought the appropriate award was the 'amount of money, either by way of wages or in lieu of notice, that the employee would have got if the proper consultation procedures required by the Act had been applied'. This was adopted by Slynn P in *Spillers-French (Holdings) Ltd* v *USDAW* (1979) where the employers argued that they were not liable to make an award to redundant employees at 13 of the bakeries which they had closed, because they had immediately secured jobs with the transferee company. The EAT remitted the case to the tribunal for it to examine the number of days consultation lost and the seriousness of their default. On the latter issue, it pointed to a difference of substance between disclosing certain matters orally which should have been put in writing and failure to give reasons for the redundancy at all, and went on:

> If the employer has done everything that he can possibly do to ensure that his employees are found other employment...a tribunal may well take the view that either there should be no award or if there is an award it should be minimal.

It is still open to an ET to make no protective award where it finds the employer in breach of his duties. Thus in *Association of Scientific, Technical and Managerial Staffs* v *Hawker Siddeley Aviation Ltd* (1977) the parties had already agreed on payment by the employer of wages in lieu of notice so that, even though the first employee left only nine days after the beginning of consultation, the tribunal awarded no compensation. Also, where the breach was only the lack of written information where the union had been told orally of the substance, this was treated as a technical default only, since the workers were in fact kept fully informed albeit orally; and the EAT made no protective award (*Amalgamated Society of Boilermakers* v *George Wimpey M. E. & Co. Ltd* (1977)). Moreover, the employee loses entitlement to a protective award if, during the period which would otherwise be covered by such an award, he is not ready and willing to work, goes on strike, is fairly dismissed for a reason other than redundancy, unreasonably terminates his contract, is offered suitable new employment, or his old contract is renewed to take effect before or during the protected period. It is not possible to set off in respect of an insolvent employer in relation to failure to consult over redundancies sums not paid for failure to give statutory minimum notice (*Secretary of State for Employment* v *Mann* (1996)).

The employee cannot claim jobseeker's allowance for the period covered by a protective award. The normal situation in practice is that benefit is paid in the first instance because of uncertainty whether an award will be made but when made it is subject to recoupment as ordered by the ET. The award must not be paid to the relevant employees until social security received has been returned to the Department for Work and Pensions. They are not treated as wages or salary (*Krasner* v *McMath* (2005) but are treated as golden handshakes for tax purposes and are thus usually exempt.

Since the only remedy provided by statute is the protective award, there is no right to injunctive relief to enforce the right to consultation. Indeed in *Griffin* (1995) the court emphasised that even if Council Directive (EEC) 75/129 had been directly effective, injunctive relief would not have been granted because, *inter alia*, the UK had been given a choice of remedies and was entitled to choose damages.

9.8.8 The union's authorised representatives

It is difficult in some cases to decide who are the appropriate representatives of the union who should be consulted, in the absence of a legally created plant-level body such as exists on the Continent. TULR(C)A 1992, s 196 identifies an official or other person authorised to carry on collective bargaining with the employer in question by that trade union. In *General and Municipal Workers' Union* v *Wailes Dove Bitumastic Ltd* (1977) a tribunal rejected the union's complaint that the employer had not discharged his statutory duty because he had consulted the shop steward with whom he bargained over plant matters, rather than the full-time organiser of the union, since the latter had never carried on collective bargaining with the company.

The autonomy of collective bargains on redundancy consultations is preserved so that where there exists a procedure which is on the whole at least as favourable to employees as that contained in the Act, the Secretary of State may order by statutory instrument that the statute is not to apply. The agreement must be no less favourable to the employer than the statutory provisions (TULR(C)A 1992, s. 198(2)).

SELECTED READING

Freedland, M. (2003), *The Personal Employment Contract*, Oxford: Oxford University Press, 2003, ch. 8

McMullen, J. (ed.) (2010), *Redundancy: The Law and Practice,* 3rd edn, London: Sweet & Maxwell

Painter, R. W. and Holmes, A. E. (2010), *Cases and Materials on Employment Law*, 8th edn, Oxford: Oxford University Press, ch. 9

Wynn-Evans, C. (2009), 'Age Discrimination and Redundancy', (2009) 38 ILJ 113

10

Discrimination

SUMMARY

This chapter concerns the ever-growing legal protection for workers who are discriminated against at work for a variety of reasons. After considering the theoretical foundations of legislating against discrimination, and the history of such legislation, the various forms of discrimination (such as direct and indirect versions) are examined. The scope of the legislation is then considered, to determine who may be covered. The sex, married status, and race grounds of discrimination covered by statute are examined along with the various exceptions, defences, enforcement mechanisms, and remedies available. This leads to a consideration of the law on disability discrimination at work and other forms, namely discrimination against part-timers, fixed-term workers, religion, belief, sexual orientation, pregnant workers and those on maternity leave and the recent law on age discrimination.

IMPORTANT NOTE

At the time of writing in early 2010 the Equality Bill is making steady progress through Parliament. The Bill on becoming law will amount to a thorough overhaul of statutory discrimination legislation. It will attempt to provide a single home for all discrimination legislation, within a more logical and consistent framework. In order to do so, the language of much of the existing law will change, although will remain largely recognisable to those familiar with the present law. But the Bill also goes further in that it contains significant changes to the present law, with expanded rights and duties, as well as new areas of coverage.

Although the Bill is presently at an advanced stage in its progress through Parliament, amendments are still being introduced and proposed clauses and amendments are being dropped. It remains controversial in several areas, not least at the time of writing in the field of religion and the idea of a default retirement age (DRA). Although it seems likely that the Bill will reach the Statute Book, there does remain the real possibility that it may be lost due to the Prime Minister calling a General Election earlier than he is required to do. In that event it is not likely that, even should a Labour Government be returned to power, the Bill would then become law in its form as at the election, or indeed by the time of the publication of this edition in late 2010.

The discussion of the law of discrimination in this chapter, and on equal pay in the next, has therefore proceeded on the basis that the present law is in force at the time of publication. The possibility was considered of giving an account of the Bill in its present state, but the conclusion has been reached that this would be of little use to the readers of this book should either the Bill become law (in a probably further-amended condition) but particularly if it does not. Should, however, the Bill become an Act, as seems highly likely, by the time this edition appears, or shortly afterwards, the reader is referred to the Online Resource Centre at **www.oxfordtextbooks.co.uk/orc/honeyball11e/,** *where there will be fully-revised and up-to-date coverage. In any event, of course, most of the discussion of the existing case law will remain relevant to the interpretation of the new law.*

online
resource
centre

10.1 **Introduction**

It is of the essence of all discrimination that a person, or group of people, is treated differently from others in a similar position (or from how they would themselves have otherwise been treated) for a reason which should not be considered to be a relevant consideration. When a detriment results in such circumstances we usually view discriminatory treatment as wrong (*cf.* T. Macklem, *Beyond Comparison: Sex and Discrimination* (Cambridge: Cambridge University Press, 2003); Réaume, (2005) 25 OJLS 547).

However, it is not always considered right to legislate against discrimination, for the reason that a number of conflicting principles are at work in this context. For example, there is the principle inherent in liberal democracies that the law should keep away from such areas as a general rule, requiring positive reasons to intervene in order to retain the maximum possible individual freedom. These reasons are frequently a matter of dispute. It may be that we consider the law should intervene only in circumstances where the harm resulting from discrimination is so great that it justifies such interference. On the other hand, we may feel that anti-discrimination legislation is justified on the basis of distributive justice. There are many other principles at work, and those just mentioned are all readily identifiable with the liberal point of view. For these reasons alone, any legislation in this area is likely to be of great complexity, but historical accident (such as that behind the late inclusion of indirect discrimination in the legislation) and a failure fully to work out the theoretical basis of discrimination has compounded this. Thus it is possible to trace different philosophies within the legislation, attempting to work together, but in fact constituting very unhappy bedfellows (see Gardner, (1989) 9 OJLS 1; Brest, (1976) 90 Harv LR 1).

One consequence of these competing philosophies is that the law has been used in this area only where social concern has been significant, primarily with regard to race and sex. However, in recent years, there have been increasingly powerful lobbies to secure legislation with regard to age discrimination and the disabled (see Doyle, (1993) 22 ILJ 89). The latter proved successful in 1995, and the former in 2006. The Amsterdam Treaty of 1997 incorporated a new art. 13 into the Treaty of Rome. The Council of Ministers was empowered to take action to combat discrimination based on sex, racial or ethnic origin, religion or belief, disability, age, or sexual orientation. The British Government, however, announced that it would not be introducing legislation on age discrimination, preferring instead to proceed by way of a Code of Practice. (See further, Bell, (2000) 29 ILJ 79; Waddington, (1999) 28 ILJ 133.) However, a Directive (Council Directive (EC) 2000/78) was adopted in November 2000 that obliged member states to enact legislation in all these areas by the end of 2006. The UK has now complied with all of these.

The history of discrimination legislation is a short one and early moves towards anti-discrimination provisions were not altogether laudable by modern standards. Thus, the TUC's initiative in 1888 to secure equal pay seems to have been motivated more by a desire to prevent women from under-cutting men than by any great desire to right a moral wrong. The only piece of relevant legislation in the early part of the last century was the Sex Disqualification (Removal) Act 1919 which removed any disqualification by way of sex or marriage for those who wished to exercise a public function, hold a civil or judicial office or post, enter any civil profession or vocation or be admitted to any incorporated society. However, it had very little impact. Gradually the UK collected international obligations to introduce anti-discrimination legislation, most notably under the ILO Convention No. 111, the UN International Convention on Social and Cultural Rights, and the European Convention for the Protection of Human Rights and Fundamental Freedoms (European Convention on Human Rights), and major legislation subsequently resulted.

In one sense the issue is of much greater importance than before in that a larger number of women are now working, and a greater proportion of the workforce is now made up by women, many of whom are the principal, or even sole, earners in the household. Approximately twice as many men as women work full-time and almost four times as many women than men work part-time.

Various problems abound for the legislator in this field. One is that it is not altogether clear what it is that the law should seek to secure. If it is equality, that is not a clear notion. (See e.g. Barmes and Ashtiany, (2003) 32 ILJ 274; Honeyball, 'The Principle of Non-discrimination as a Fundamental Value', in *Fundamental Values* (Oxford: Hart Publishing, 2000), at p. 47.) Some writers even challenge the moral value of equality and the principle of non-discrimination—see e.g. Cavanagh, *Against Equality of Opportunity* (Oxford: Clarendon Press, 2002); Holmes, (2005) 68 MLR 175. It does not necessarily mean identical treatment, but if not an evaluation exercise has to be undertaken. That is a difficult task. Furthermore, there are occasions when it may be right to treat people differently and even more favourably. This is less obvious with regard to race but rather more obvious with sex. It is not clear, for example, that it is wrong to treat women more favourably with regard to pregnancy and childbirth. Some go further and argue for positive discrimination, so that in areas where one group has traditionally been disadvantaged compensating discrimination is seen as legitimate—see e.g. Barmes (2009) 68 CLJ 623. The ECJ seems to be attracted to this view (see *Marschall* v *Land Nordrhein-Westfalen* (1998); *cf. Kalanke* v *Freie Hansestadt Bremen* (1996): see Schiek, (1996) 25 ILJ 239; Szyszczak, (1996) 59 MLR 876; Fredman, (1997) 113 LQR 575) and art. 157 of the Treaty on the Functioning of the European Union (art. 157 TFEU) (ex art. 141 of the Treaty of Rome (ex art. 141 EC)) also allows member states to adopt positive discrimination measures. There are also the difficulties that there have been traditional differences with regard to the work that different groups do. Dress codes are often different for men and women without being discriminatory (see Flynn, (1995) 24 ILJ 255; Cunningham, (1995) 24 ILJ 177; *Smith* v *Safeway plc* (1996)) although they may now raise issues of human rights (see Chapter 16 below).

Women have traditionally had lower status jobs and part-time work, for example, and there are still important reasons why women's average pay is significantly lower than men's. Sometimes that is out of choice because of a societal, biological, and personal leaning towards women as the partner to take the major role in raising children in their early years. But how much should this difference be treated as reflecting inequality, and how much is it discriminatory? If it is discriminatory, is it possible to legislate against it? Who may sue and who should be sued? What state of affairs would mean that the discrimination had been removed? Should past inequalities be balanced by future inequalities on the other side, by a process of positive discrimination, for example? (See e.g. Barmes, (2003) 32 ILJ 200.)

Such issues are highly complex, and it is not altogether obvious that the law really has a major part to play in practice in remedying discrimination. There is a widespread perception that success is difficult to achieve and that the price of success is too high. On the whole this perception is well-founded (see on sex claims Leonard, *Judging Inequality* (London: Cobden Trust, 1987), and on race claims Lustgarten, (1986) 49 MLR 68. See too generally, Honeyball, *Sex, Employment and the Law* (Oxford: Blackwell, 1991), ch. 1). This in part may be because it has never been clear whether the aim of the legislation has been primarily to grant individuals remedies or to make sea changes in social perceptions of race and sex.

10.2 **History**

Modern anti-discrimination law began with the Race Relations Act 1965. This was modelled on the American Civil Rights Act 1964, and was stimulated by a series of reports on the low status of blacks in Britain and the first racial violence. It was, however, mainly concerned with public order and incitement to racial hatred, and outlawed discrimination only in places of public resort. It was extended to employment three years later, and the new Act also introduced the definition of direct discrimination which still exists today. The Race Relations Board, however, was still the sole enforcement mechanism, and it was only in 1976 that an individual right of access to tribunals was introduced. The Race Relations Act 1976 (RRA 1976), which is still in force although amended in some respects, also established the CRE, not only to advise and assist individual complainants but also to concentrate on a collective, strategic role.

Sex discrimination law began with the Equal Pay Act 1970 which came into force in 1975 with the Sex Discrimination Act 1975 (SDA 1975). Those two Acts form a homogenous code, the 1970 Act being concerned with discrimination in the contract of employment, and the SDA 1975 with other forms of discrimination in employment. The SDA 1975 set up the Equal Opportunities Commission (EOC) with similar powers to those of the CRE (see Townshend-Smith, *Sex Discrimination in Employment: Law, Practice and Policy* (London: Sweet & Maxwell, 1989), p. 213; Sacks, (1986) 49 MLR 560). The EOC issued a press release in January 1998 calling for an overhaul of the legislation, particularly the introduction of one clear, comprehensive statute. (See further for a powerful argument on this, Hepple *et al.*, *Improving Equality Law: The Options* (London: Justice and the Runnymede Trust, 1997); and Wintemute, (1997) 26 ILJ 259.) As yet, only small progress has been made towards this, although the Equality Act 2006, setting up a single Commission to cover all areas of discrimination (as well as human rights), is a step in the right direction in this regard.

The legislation was considered by the ECJ to be inadequate with regard to the implementation of EC Directives. It was necessary in 1986 to pass another Sex Discrimination Act to comply with the EEC Equal Treatment Directive (Council Directive (EEC) 76/207) outlawing sex discrimination in, *inter alia*, collective agreements and by small employers (see *Commission of the European Communities* v *United Kingdom* (1984), and Fredman, (1984) 13 ILJ 119. See too *Johnston* v *Chief Constable of the RUC* (1986); Shrubsall, (1987) 16 ILJ 118; Paisley (1987) 38 NILQ 352.) Two further important pieces of legislation were passed in 1989. The Employment Act

1989 removed further restriction on women working in certain occupations, particularly in factory and mines legislation dating from the 19th century (see for a useful analysis of the Act, Deakin, (1990) 19 ILJ 1). In addition, the Social Security Act 1989 requires equal treatment between the sexes with regard to occupational pension schemes.

The most recent item of primary legislation prior to the 2006 Act was the Disability Discrimination Act 1995 (DDA 1995), closely modelled on the sex and race discrimination statutes, which seeks to outlaw discrimination against disabled people in the workplace and elsewhere. However, despite its similarity to earlier legislation, we shall consider the DDA 1995 separately towards the end of this chapter because some of the concepts used are quite different, especially the notion of reasonable adjustments and the wider use of the defence of justification.

In 2000, however, the Government introduced some secondary legislation to deal with discrimination against part-time workers, in the form of the Part-time Workers (Prevention of Less Favourable Treatment) Regulations 2000 (SI 2000 No. 1551). These were introduced in response to Council Directive (EC) 98/23 on Part-time Workers, and will be considered towards the end of this chapter. Since then there has been further delegated legislation to protect fixed-term workers from discrimination, as well as other measures relating to discrimination on the grounds of sexual orientation, religion or belief—see Fixed-Term Employees (Prevention of Less Favourable Treatment) Regulations 2002 (SI 2002 No. 2034), Employment Equality (Sexual Orientation) Regulations 2003 (SI 2003 No. 1661), Employment Equality (Religion or Belief) Regulations 2003 (SI 2003 No. 1660), and Employment Equality (Age) Regulations 2006 (SI 2006 No. 1031) respectively.

It thus continues to be the case that anti-discrimination legislation is introduced piecemeal. Some countries in the Commonwealth, and some outside it (such as South Africa) have introduced general discrimination laws. Whilst there are occasional calls for this to be done in the UK—see e.g. Hepple, *Equality: A New Framework* (Oxford: Hart Publishing, 2000 (the Hepple Report)), and review by Harrington, (2001) 64 MLR 757—the latest trends have been away from making the approach in the legislation similar. There are even growing differing approaches between the two earlier pieces of legislation so that, for example, there are different definitions of indirect discrimination, according to context.

It is not surprising that in 2005 the Government announced a comprehensive review of discrimination law in the form of an Equalities Review and a Discrimination Law Review. Both of these reviews recommended the introduction of a Single Equality Act covering all of the present heads of discrimination in law. (See McCrudden, (2007) 36 ILJ 255.) Together with the completion of the requirements of the EU Equal Treatment Framework Directive, Council Directive (EC) 2000/78 with the introduction of the Regulations on age discrimination, and the Equality Act 2006, which places a general duty on public authorities to have due regard to the need to eliminate sex discrimination, it can be seen that major advances in discrimination measures are presently being made. The trend towards simplification was further signposted at EU level in 2006 by the publication of the Equal Treatment Recast Directive, Council Directive (EC) 2006/54, which consolidates the existing Directives on equal pay, equal treatment, and burden of proof in discrimination cases.

In this chapter we shall consider the legislation other than as it affects sex discrimination in the contract of employment which is within the purview of the

Equal Pay Act 1970. This will be considered in Chapter 11 below, along with maternity rights. We shall begin with the scheme, jointly shared by the sex and race legislation, and then consider other forms of prohibited discrimination.

10.3 Forms of discrimination

There are two main forms of prohibited sex and race discrimination—direct and indirect. Common to both is the factor of comparison, and the legislation decrees that like must be compared with like so that the 'relevant circumstances are the same or not materially different' between comparators (SDA 1975, s. 5(3); RRA 1976, s. 3(4)).

10.3.1 Direct discrimination

Direct discrimination is the most blatant form of racism or sexism and occurs when one person treats another less favourably on the grounds of their sex, on the grounds of marital status or on racial grounds than he treats or would treat another (SDA 1975, ss 1(1)(a) and 3(1)(a); RRA 1976, s. 1(1)(a)). The SDA 1975 also covers transsexuals intending to undergo, or those undergoing, gender reassignment, by virtue of the Sex Discrimination (Gender Reassignment) Regulations 1999 (SI 1999 No. 1102) inserting s. 2A.

Hypothetical comparison

The comparison may be with a hypothetical person, since the provisions cover not only actual treatment but also a comparison with how another person would be treated. It is not necessary to adduce evidence as to the hypothetical situation, and a tribunal therefore does not err if it decides against an employer without taking his evidence to the contrary, according to the EAT in *Leeds Private Hospital* v *Parkin* (1992). It is, however, necessary where an applicant unsuccessfully seeks to make a comparison with a real comparator for the tribunal to consider the hypothetical comparison, according to the Court of Appeal in *Balamoody* v *UK Central Council for Midwifery and Health Visiting* (2002). It is, however, vital to prove that the treatment was caused by the sex or marital status of the complainant and not on other grounds, but in the case of race discrimination, this need only be on the grounds of race in general (see *Weathersfield Ltd* v *Sargent* (1999)). For the sake of convenience here we shall assume that the applicant is a woman or black person, but of course the legislation applies to both sexes and all races.

It is an extremely difficult process in making a hypothetical comparison to attribute the comparator with the necessary and sufficient characteristics to make the comparison meaningful. Clearly, to compare A with B in order to determine if A has been treated less favourably than B entails ensuring that any difference in treatment between them has been caused by a reason recognised by statute as discriminatory (a protected reason) and not by some other (in that context) irrelevant factor. We shall examine this when we consider the issue of motive next. However, it is particularly important when it comes to drawing a hypothetical comparator, for the irrelevant factors are not given then as a matter of fact, but if they creep into the comparison are likely to be there because the tribunal has failed to apply the right tests. Although in one sense it might be easier for a tribunal to make a hypothetical rather than an actual comparison, as it is not distracted by given irrelevant factors, on the other hand it has to construct a model comparator who has all the relevant attributes, and none of the irrelevant. What this exercise might show, however, is that the comparison need not, in principle, be between two different people, as the identity of the applicant and the comparator are rarely relevant. It might be a better approach to compare the treatment of the applicant with how she may herself have been treated had she not had the characteristics that are relevant to placing her (if she is) within the protected category. All other distinguishing features between her and any actual or hypothetical comparator are irrelevant. However, the legislation does not generally proceed on that basis.

Motive

In the controversial sex discrimination case, *Peake* v *Automotive Products Ltd* (1978), the Court of Appeal appeared to require a hostile motive on the part of the employer. The male appellant complained that he was discriminated against because he had to stay at work until 4.30 p.m., although female staff could leave at 4.25 p.m. Lord Denning MR, however, accepted the employer's contention that the reason for the difference was the safety of workers as they left the factory, and that there was thus no illegal discrimination. He continued more generally that: 'It would be very wrong if this statute were thought to obliterate the differences between men and women and to do away with the chivalry and courtesy which we expect mankind to give to womankind.'

Shaw LJ also thought that motivation was centrally relevant, saying that discrimination 'involves an element of something which is inherently adverse or hostile to the interests of the persons of the sex which is said to be discriminated against'. This threatened to limit greatly the scope of the Act and was subjected to severe academic criticism. It is now regarded as a heresy. Lord Denning, however, soon joined in the narrowing of the *ratio* of the decision in *Ministry of Defence* v *Jeremiah* (1980). The applicants were again men, this time employed at the appellant's ordnance factory. They had volunteered for overtime, which meant that they had to work in very dirty conditions in the 'colour bursting shell shop', making shells which exploded in red or orange for artillery practice. Women did not have to do this, partly because it was thought that such conditions would affect their hair. The Court of Appeal upheld the men's claim of discrimination; Lord Denning MR accepted that *Peake* could be considered correctly decided only on the basis that there the difference in treatment (five minutes less work per day) was *de minimis*. In fact, if taken over a year-long period, the concession to the women in effect gave them the equivalent of an extra two days' holiday.

After this decision it is irrelevant whether the motive for less favourable treatment is good, bad, or indifferent, the only question being causation (see also *R* v *Commission for Racial Equality ex parte Westminster City Council* (1985); *Din* v *Carrington Viyella Ltd* (1982); *cf. Barclays Bank plc* v *James* (1990) where the EAT seemed to suggest that the correct approach is to examine the reason for the less favourable treatment being on the grounds of sex. However, the parties in that case took the highly unusual step of issuing a joint statement to the effect that they accepted that there were two errors of law in the EAT's decision, one of which was this particular point). In *Greig* v *Community Industry* (1979) the director of the respondent company failed to employ the appellant because he genuinely believed, as a result of previous experience, that it was unwise for her to be the only girl in their painting and decorating group. Nevertheless, he was found to have unlawfully discriminated. The House of Lords has (but by the barest majority) sanctioned this view in *James* v *Eastleigh Borough Council* (1990). In that case the defendant council charged for admission to a swimming pool according to the state pension age, which was held directly discriminatory against men aged between 60 and 64. Why the council applied that policy was irrelevant. The sole question was whether the men would have been treated differently *but for* their sex. This decision must be right, as tribunals would otherwise be faced with the difficult task of assessing the motives and intentions of the parties. In any event, the purpose of the legislation is not primarily punitive but designed to achieve equality in treatment between the sexes, and to that end a subjective approach seems inappropriate. The 'but for' test applied in *James* was one enunciated by Lord Goff in the House of Lords in *R* v *Birmingham City Council ex parte EOC* (1989). He had been criticised for failing to distinguish adequately in that case between various ideas such as motive and intention (see Gelowitz, (1989) 18 ILJ 247; see too Ellis, (1989) 52 MLR 710) but in *James* he made it clear he thought it important that tribunals should not have to grapple with elusive concepts of that nature. However, he did also say that, although motive was irrelevant, it was necessary to have an element of intention. But this went so far only as an intention to treat the other less favourably. As Geoffrey Mead pointed out, it was essential here that the concept of intention was adequately spelled out, as SDA 1975, s. 66(3) stated that damages for indirect discrimination were, at the time, payable only if there was an intention to discriminate (Mead, (1990) 19 ILJ 250). Since March 1996 the position has been that tribunals are given the power, where they think it would be just and equitable to do so, to award compensation even if there were no intention to discriminate (see Sex Discrimination and Equal Pay (Miscellaneous Amendments) Regulations 1996 (SI 1996 No. 438)).

The House of Lords' decisions in these cases should have made proving discrimination somewhat easier than hitherto, but the approach in some cases has not been so enlightened. For example, in *Dhatt* v *McDonalds Hamburgers Ltd* (1991) the Court of Appeal held that it was not discriminatory for an employer to require evidence of the right to work in the UK of overseas applicants, when this was not necessary for those from the EC (see Ross, (1991) 20 ILJ 208). This is despite the fact that RRA 1976, s. 3(1) expressly includes nationality within its definition of 'racial grounds'. The reason was one of expediency—that employers should be entitled to require such evidence. This may be true, but the point is that they are entitled to know that of EU nationals too. It is just that in that case such evidence is assumed. Applying the 'but for' test it is difficult to see how the Court of Appeal could have come to its conclusion except on the basis of the employer's motive. But it should not be thought that the 'but for' test makes discriminatory mere differences in treatment between the sexes. On the contrary, it requires that sex be the *reason* for that difference in treatment, even if it is not the *motive* for it, a point reiterated by the EAT in *Amnesty International* v *Ahmed* (2009). So, where in *Bullock* v *Alice Ottley School* (1992) differences in retirement ages between one group consisting of men and another consisting almost entirely of women were caused by difficulties in recruiting and retaining the group to which most of the men belonged, these differences were justified, according to the Court of Appeal. Although disparate impact between the sexes was the effect of applying different retirement ages, that was not the reason for it. This makes sense. Otherwise the employer would have to have the same retirement ages for all his workers, doing a number of different jobs, if the sexes were not evenly distributed among them.

Assumptions

The words of the statutes also cover cases where the reason for discrimination is a generalised assumption that people of a particular sex, marital status, or race possess or lack certain characteristics. In *Coleman* v *Skyrail Oceanic* (1981) a booking clerk in the respondent's travel agency was dismissed when she married a man employed by a rival tour operator, even though she promised not to divulge confidential information, and there was no evidence that she had done so during her engagement. The EAT found the dismissal unfair because of its abruptness but overturned the decision of the tribunal that her treatment constituted unlawful discrimination, on the grounds both of sex and marital status since Mrs Coleman might have given away information, and was not the breadwinner of the family. Slynn J also thought the treatment not discriminatory since other employees with close relationships, such as brothers and sisters or engaged couples, might have been treated in the same way (see also *Moberly* v *Commonwealth Hall (University of London)* (1977)). The decision was, however, overturned by the Court of Appeal (with Shaw LJ dissenting), on the ground that the assumption that the man was the breadwinner without further investigation of the personal situation was, in itself, discriminatory. The husband in fact was earning only a modest wage, and there was no evidence that his employers were reluctant to dismiss him. The court also noted that in 56.2 per cent of households married women contributed to their income.

It was also unlawful for the respondents in *Horsey* v *Dyfed CC* (1982) to refuse to second the applicant to a training course in the London area where her husband was employed because they assumed that she would remain in London when her course was completed and not return to work for the respondents in Wales. It was an inescapable inference that the respondents would have treated a married man differently from the way in which they treated the applicant. The EAT did not, however, say that an employer could never act on the basis that a wife would give up her job to join her husband. What the employer could not do was to *assume* that this was so. He must look at the particular circumstances of each case. (See further on each of these points, *Reed and Bull Information Systems Ltd* v *Stedman* (1999).)

10.3.2 **Indirect discrimination**

The concept of indirect discrimination, which was first introduced in the SDA 1975 and then included in the RRA 1976, recognises that inequality does not result only from intentional overt acts, the model (although not identical with it) of direct discrimination. Some of the most insidious institutional discrimination operates at a more subtle level, by indirect means which, although applying to both sexes or all races, in effect discriminate against one. This is often the legacy of past discrimination. The US Supreme Court found the concept implicit in the very fabric of the prohibition against discrimination in the Civil Rights Act 1964. The essence of its leading judgment in *Griggs* v *Duke Power Co.* (1971) is that 'Practices, procedures, tests…neutral on their face…cannot be maintained if they operate to freeze the status quo of past discrimination'. Thus a height requirement in a company rule book may indirectly discriminate against women, although those who inserted the provision did not at all advert to its effect on them, and short men would be treated similarly. (For a comparative discussion of the approaches to UK and US discrimination see McGinley, (1986) 49 MLR 413.)

The British statutes provide that indirect discrimination occurs in either of two ways. First, under SDA 1975, s. 1(1)(b) (which does not apply in the employment field) where a person applies a requirement or condition which he applies or would apply equally to a man but:

(i) is such that the proportion of women who can comply with it is considerably smaller than the proportion of men who can comply with it, and

(ii) which he cannot show to be justifiable irrespective of the sex of the person to whom it is applied, and

(iii) which is to her detriment because she cannot comply with it,

then indirect discrimination is made out. Likewise, under RRA 1976, s. 1(1)(b), a person indirectly discriminates against another if he applies to that other a requirement or condition which he applies or would apply equally to persons not of the same racial group as that other but:

(i) is such that the proportion of persons of the same racial group as that other who can comply with it is considerably smaller than the proportion of persons not of that racial group who can comply with it, and

(ii) which he cannot show to be justifiable irrespective of the colour, race, nationality or ethnic or national origins of the person to whom it is applied, and

(iii) which is to the detriment of that other because he cannot comply with it.

For many years the definition of indirect discrimination was limited to these formulations. They proved to be rather narrower than was probably intended. For example, if part-timers were discriminated against compared with full-timers it was hard to see always that they had the protection of the legislation. One could not say, without doing violence to the meaning of the words, that there was a 'requirement or condition' to be full-time that a larger proportion of women compared to men could not satisfy. It was merely a fact that those employees were part-time and not the consequence of a requirement or condition at all. Many other types of potential claimants found themselves outside the Act too. For this reason, the definitions were expanded by two pieces of delegated legislation.

The SDA 1975 was modified by the Sex Discrimination (Indirect Discrimination and Burden of Proof) Regulations 2001 (SI 2001 No. 2660) inserting a new s. 1(2) (b) and then again by the Employment Equality (Sex Discrimination) Regulations 2005 (SI 2005 No. 2467). This now states that, in employment cases, a person indirectly discriminates against another where:

(b) he applies to her a provision, criterion or practice which he applies or would apply equally to a man, but—

(i) which puts or would put women at a particular disadvantage when compared with men, and

(ii) which puts her at that disadvantage, and

(iii) which he cannot show to be a proportionate means of achieving a legitimate aim.

An equivalent amendment has been made to SDA 1975, s. 3 to cover indirect discrimination on the grounds of a person's married status (see below). The previous misnomer of 'marital' status—a misnomer because the section does not apply to discrimination against people on the grounds that they are single—has thus now been recognised as such.

It was unfortunate that the widened definition was not extended likewise to race cases, but this was corrected in 2003 with the Race Relations Act (Amendment) Regulations 2003 (SI 2003 No. 1626). This inserted a new s. (1A) which is in equivalent terms to the new provision in the SDA 1975.

The position now is therefore somewhat confusing. The 'old' definition of indirect discrimination no longer applies in the employment field. The 'new' definition (as amended) does and, containing as it does entirely different terminology, will continue to need new case law in order to give further light as to its meaning in that it places greater emphasis on the disparate impact of the employer's act than, under the old definition, on the difference in treatment of the victim. We do know that the Burden of Proof Directive, Council Directive (EC) 97/80, would seem to require that cases falling within the old test should be included in the wider test—see *British Airways plc* v *Starmer* (2005). However, the old test still applies in other areas of discrimination law. Given these two latter points, the old (as far as employment cases are concerned) law will continue to be of relevance in developing these new tests.

To complicate matters even further, although the new definition in employment matters covers all discrimination on grounds of race, sex, age, sexual orientation, and religion or belief, it covers race only in areas other than nationality or colour, so that race or national or ethnic origins continue to come under the old test.

With these considerations in mind, let us examine how the courts have approached the concept of discrimination.

Provision, criterion, or practice

This aspect of what will here be called the 'new' test is somewhat wider than the wording in what will here be called the 'old' test, but which is still relevant in other circumstances, as we have seen. The concepts of 'provision, criterion or practice' were originally a 'requirement or condition'. This proved to be too narrow in policy terms, in that some examples of indirect discrimination which clearly should have been covered by the Act simply fell through the definitional net. For example, if an employer discriminated against part-time workers in some way, that would very often be indirectly discriminatory against women because a greater proportion of women than men undertake part-time working. However, in such circumstances it would be stretching language beyond breaking-point to say that the employer applied a requirement or condition that those workers be part-time. It was merely that part-time workers were disproportionately affected by some factor that had the effect of treating women as a whole in that position less favourably than men. The notion of a 'provision, criterion or practice' would be more likely to bring part-time workers within the ambit of protection. It would be easy to think of many other examples.

It follows that some of the case law under the old test is inapplicable under the new, but only to the extent that some areas of indirect discrimination were not caught under that test. So, for example, it was thought that to be a requirement or condition indicated a 'must'. So, employers could easily escape the effects of the Act by stating, for example, that a certain factor was desirable, advantageous, or welcomed. These ideas do not connote something that 'must' be complied with. Some tribunals and courts refused to follow this line, but it was by no means uniform. (Contrast e.g. *Falkirk Council* v *Whyte* (1997); *Bhudi* v *IMI Refiners Ltd* (1994).) In *Home Office* v *Holmes* (1984) a request that the employee return to work full-time was held to be a requirement or condition, as was an employer's decision in *Clarke and Powell* v *Eley (IMI) Kynoch Ltd* (1983) that part-time workers should be dismissed first under a redundancy selection agreement. Other stipulations considered as requirements or conditions included the situation where work was to be allocated by reference to the seniority of employees (*Steel* v *UPOW* (1977)), and where school pupils were subjected to uniform regulations requiring the applicant to cut his hair and remove his turban (*Mandla* v *Dowell Lee* (1983)).

Particular disadvantage

In *Mandla* v *Dowell Lee* (1983) the House of Lords understood the element in the old test to establish indirect discrimination that a smaller proportion of one sex 'can comply' with the requirement or condition meant 'can consistently [comply] with the customs and cultural conditions of the racial group' rather than the restricted meaning of 'can physically' comply. In *Price* v *Civil Service Commission* (1978) the EAT thought that the phrase was to be interpreted broadly. 'It should not be said that a person "can" do something merely because it is theoretically possible for him to do so; it is necessary to see whether he can do so in practice. (*Cf. Jones* v *University of Manchester* (1993).) The new test clearly goes a good deal further than this in that the claimant need merely show that they are at a 'particular disadvantage' along with others in the protected group. It may not be that the group, and the claimant, find the provision, criterion or practice very difficult to negative, so long as they are at a particular disadvantage because of it.

The relevant time for making the comparison is at the date on which the provision, criterion, or practice has applied to the claimant. So, where gypsies were barred from a pub on the ground that no 'travellers' were admitted, it was irrelevant that at some prior date the applicants could have ceased to be travellers in order to comply (*Commission for Racial Equality* v *Dutton* (1989)).

The choice of the relevant pool for comparison is clearly crucial to the exercise of finding indirect discrimination. The EAT decided in *Kidd* v *DRG (UK) Ltd* (1985) that this was a question of fact for the tribunal. (See further *O'Donovan* v *Szyszczak*, (1985) 14 ILJ 252.) This was surprising, as it meant that different tribunals may come to different conclusions on the same statistical data. This could produce some absurd results, as in *Greater Manchester Police Authority* v *Lea* (1990) where the EAT felt that it was not possible to interfere in the tribunal's finding that 95.3 per cent was considerably smaller than 99.4 per cent. In the United States the relevant figure is 80 per cent—in other words, that no more than 80 per cent of those in the disadvantaged group were able to comply. The difficulty with any set figure, however, is that it is less meaningful when small numbers exist in the relevant pool. (See e.g. the decision of the Court of Appeal in *London Underground Ltd* v *Edwards (No. 2)* (1988) when it held that 95.2 per cent was a significantly smaller proportion than 100 per cent, representing 20 out of 21 women who could comply with the requirement compared with all of the 2,023 men who could do so.) The notion of 'particular disadvantage' should do away with this difficulty in large measure, because it concentrates on the extent of the disadvantage to the individual and to each individuals in the relevant group to which the claimant belongs, rather than to the proportion of those in the relevant groups who can and cannot comply.

In *Rutherford* v *Secretary of State for Trade and Industry (No. 2)* (2006) Baroness Hale said that 'we should not be bringing into the comparison people who have no interest in the advantage in question'. In *Somerset County Council* v *Pike* (2009) the Court of Appeal reaffirmed that this was the correct way to proceed in identifying the pool. However, it is by no means clear that the House of Lords in *Rutherford* did in fact apply this approach, and it has been a source of some confusion since then as to what the correct approach should be. However, as a matter of simple logic it would seem irrelevant to make comparisons with the treatment of those who have no interest in it.

Proportionate means of achieving a legitimate aim

It is open to the employer to construct a defence on the basis that the disparate treatment applied to the different groups amounts to proportionate means of achieving a legitimate aim. Some provisions, criteria and practices exist on quite reasonable grounds, and it is considered unfair to prohibit them simply because they may have an adverse impact on certain groups. The employer may thus impose criteria which have an adverse impact if they satisfy both the test of proportionality and legitimacy. So, proportionality plays a role in the new definition of indirect discrimination but a different one to that it played in the old test. It now goes to providing a defence rather than establishing whether the provision, criterion, or practice is discriminatory in the first place. The old test was based on 'justification'. The House of Lords held in *Orphanos* v *Queen Mary College* (1985) that justifiable meant 'capable of being justified', necessitating a balance to be struck between the discriminatory effect of the requirement and the needs of the party who applied it. (See Leigh, (1986) 49 MLR 235.) This meant that the employer needed to show that there was a real necessity for the requirement, be it economic or administrative efficiency or some other reason, according to the Court of Appeal in *Hampson* v *Department of Education and Science* (1991), later reversed by the House of Lords, but not on this point. (See Bourn, (1989) 18 ILJ 170; Napier, (1989) 48 CLJ 187).

In *Redcar & Cleveland Borough Council* v *Bainbridge*; *Surtees* v *Middlesbrough Borough Council* (2008), the Court of Appeal held that if the historical reason for the inequality evidenced there arose because of direct sex discrimination, any gradual nature of the phase out of the discrimination would be unlawful, but if it were indirect discrimination it could be objectively justified if proportionate to achieving a legitimate aim. But this would depend upon how much the employer knew of the discriminatory treatment before the phase out began and how much it did about it.

It should be noted, as *Redcar* illustrates, that there is a defence of proportionate means achieving a legitimate aim only in indirect discrimination cases. There is not, at present, such a defence for direct discrimination although it has been argued that there should be a defence of justification in those cases in sex discrimination law—see Bowers and Moran, (2002) 31 ILJ 307; *cf.* Gill and Monaghan, (2003) 32 ILJ 115, and the reply by Bowers, Moran, and Honeyball, (2003) 32 ILJ 185.

10.3.3 **Discrimination by association**

The general discrimination prohibition has been somewhat extended to include sacking an employee for serving a black customer (*Zarczynska* v *Levy* (1979)). This appears to be a sort of transferred discrimination or discrimination by association—dismissal not because of the employee's colour but rather that of the customer. Further, in *Showboat Entertainment Centre Ltd* v *Owens* (1984) the applicant, a white man, claimed that he was dismissed as manager of an amusement centre because he refused to carry out the employer's instruction to exclude young blacks. The EAT decided that the subsection covered all cases in which an employee was treated less favourably on racial grounds even though the race in question was that of another person. One ground for this decision was that it would place the applicant in an impossible position if he had to choose between being party to illegality and losing his job.

It should be noted that the RRA 1976 explicitly allows discrimination by association because the applicant has to be discriminated against on the grounds of race. This is not so under the SDA 1975, which requires the applicant to be discriminated against on the grounds of *her* sex (see too *Redfearn* v *Serco Ltd* (2006).) (See Cariolou, (2006) 35 ILJ 415.)

It is, though, also the case with the Regulations on religion and belief—see *Saini* v *All Saints Haque Centre* (2009, considered below). More potentially far-reaching in practice is the application of the principle of associative discrimination to cases of disability discrimination. This is shown by the facts of the leading case in this area. In *Coleman* v *Attridge Law* (2008) the issue was whether an employee who found it necessary to care for her disabled son, and thought that she was directly discriminated against and harassed because of that by her employer, could bring a claim under the Disability Discrimination Act 2005 even though she was not herself disabled. The ECJ held that she could. (See the earlier Honeyball, [2007] WebJCLI, issue 4; Pilgerstorfer, (2008) 37 ILJ 384.) It was held by the EAT later that, in order to comply with this decision of the ECJ, it was necessary to go further than merely interpret the Disability Discrimination Act 2005 to reach this end, but to insert an extra provision into the Act to the effect that: 'A person also directly discriminates against a person if he treats him less favourably than he treats or would treat another person by reason of the disability of another person.' (See *EBR Attridge Law* v *Coleman* (2010).)

10.3.4 **Sexual orientation**

The Court of Appeal held, in *R* v *Ministry of Defence ex parte Smith* (1996), that discrimination on grounds of sexual orientation was not sex discrimination. This was the view of the ECJ too in *Grant* v *South West Trains* (1998) and ultimately the House of Lords in *MacDonald* v *Advocate General for Scotland* (2003). (See Manknell, (2003) 32 ILJ 247.) However, the passing of the Employment Equality (Sexual Orientation) Regulations 2003 (SI 2003 No. 1661) means that discrimination on this ground is, in any event, unlawful as a separate head of discrimination. The scheme of the Regulations is that under the SDA 1975. The tests of direct and indirect discrimination, victimisation, harassment, the scope of protection in the employment field, and the genuine occupational defence are in the same terms in these Regulations as in the SDA 1975 for claims in the employment field (see p. 273 below).

10.4 The scope of prohibited discrimination

The scope of unlawful discrimination is very widely drawn and encompasses every stage of employment. Thus an employee may complain if discriminated against in any of the several following ways.

10.4.1 Pre-employment discrimination

By virtue of RRA 1976, s. 4, and SDA 1975, s. 6, an applicant can claim if put off applying for a job by reason of, for example, the way an interview is set up, the questions asked there, or being left off a short list *(Saunders* v *Richmond-upon-Thames LBC* (1977)). It is no defence that the employer has so made arrangements in order to keep an overall balance between the sexes or races. In *Brennan* v *J.H. Dewhurst Ltd* (1983) a tribunal found that the conduct of the local manager of a butcher's shop at an interview suggested that he did not want a woman for the job on offer, but that there was no discrimination since no one had ultimately been appointed to the job. The EAT thought differently since the subsection covered the discriminatory operation of arrangements for selection as well as discriminatory selection.

Discriminatory advertisements may not be included under the rubric 'arrangements for recruitment', according to the EAT in *Cardiff Women's Aid* v *Hartup* (1994), but the CEHR also has general powers to seek an injunction to restrain 'victimless' advertisements. (There is very little else that can be done to prevent discriminatory treatment in domestic law where there is no identifiable victim, unlike the position in other European countries—see *Centrum voor gelijkheid van kansen en voor racismebestrijding* v *Firma Feryn NV* (2008).) Proof is facilitated in the SDA 1975 by special rules on the use of words with a sexual connotation: thus the description 'sales girl or waitress' is taken to indicate an intention to discriminate unless it is made clear that the position is open to both sexes. Otherwise the correct test is the likely response of the ordinary reader (s. 38). In *CRE* v *Associated Newspapers Group Ltd* (1978) (under the similarly worded Race Relations Act 1968, s. 6(1)), an advertisement for nurses in South African hospitals included the words 'all white patients', but the Court of Appeal held that that would not reasonably be taken to mean that only white applicants would be considered. Moreover, the publisher of any such advertisement escapes liability if he proves that he acted reasonably in reliance on a statement by the person effecting the publication that it would not be unlawful.

It may be possible for a potential employee to claim also where there is a refusal or deliberate omission to offer employment (SDA 1975, s. 6(1); RRA 1976, s. 4).

10.4.2 Post-employment discrimination

Past employees may claim for post-employment discrimination by virtue of RRA 1976, s. 27A; SDA 1975, s. 20A; DDA 1995, s. 16A—see *Rhys-Harper* v *Relaxion Group plc* (2003); but *cf. Coutinho Rank nemo (DMS) Ltd* (2009). Previous authority had stated the opposite—see *Nagarajan* v *Agnew* (1994); *Adeyake* v *Post Office* (1997). The Regulations covering religion, belief, and sexual orientation have equivalent provisions.

10.4.3 Terms and conditions of employment

If there is discrimination with respect to the terms and conditions of employment the position with regard to race is straightforward, but difficulties arise in respect of sex discrimination because of the mismatch between the two statutes in the field. The Equal Pay Act 1970 is relevant when a job has been offered and accepted, but if the prospective employee is deterred from accepting the job at all because of the terms offered, the SDA 1975 is the proper statute (SDA 1975, s. 6(6)). However, it may be possible that claims can be brought under the SDA 1975 with regard to inequalities in contractual terms due to discriminatory collective bargains, according to Lester and Rose (see (1991) 20 ILJ 163).

10.4.4 Benefits

Where there is discrimination against women or ethnic minorities concerning access to transfers, promotion or training, this is unlawful by virtue of SDA 1975, s. 6(2)(b), and RRA 1976, s. 4(2)(b). This applies also to other fringe benefits.

10.4.5 Disparate treatment

Sometimes what may appear to be objectively fair treatment may nevertheless be unlawful if a person in another racial group, or of the opposite sex, is treated differently. So where two employees have stolen from the employer and one culprit is white and one black, but only the black is dismissed, the latter may have a claim under the RRA 1976 (s. 4(2)(c)). A similar position pertains under the SDA 1975 (s. 6(2)(b)). These provisions give protection to employees who are discriminated against by being dismissed. (Whether this covers constructive dismissal is unclear following two conflicting EAT decisions within the space of a few months but in seeming ignorance of each other—see *Commissioner of Police of the Metropolis* v *Harley* (2001); *Derby Specialist Fabrication Ltd* v *Burton* (2001); and the commentary by Rowland, (2001) 30 ILJ 381.) Normally it would be easier to claim unfair dismissal but an employee might not be qualified to do so because he has not served for a sufficient period of continuous employment or is over the normal retiring age. Further, compensation under the SDA 1975 recommendations may be made to prevent such acts occurring in the future.

10.4.6 Any other detriment

It is also unlawful discrimination to subject the applicant to any other detriment (SDA 1975, s. 6(2)(b), and RRA 1976, s. 4(2)(b)). Although 'detriment' is a word of wide import and this is a residual subsection, some action is too insignificant to fall within its scope. Thus, in *Peake* v *Automotive Products Ltd* (1978), as already mentioned, the Court of Appeal decided that the rule allowing women to leave five minutes early was not serious enough and this *ratio* survives *Jeremiah* (1979). In *Schmidt* v *Austicks Bookshops Ltd* (1978) Phillips J held that a prohibition on female employees wearing trousers did not constitute a detriment since it must 'have something serious or important about it'. This may be a mere matter of opinion, and in *Ministry of Defence* v *Jeremiah* (1979), where the requirement that men undertake particularly dirty work was sufficient, Brandon LJ paraphrased the word to mean 'putting under a disadvantage'. It was irrelevant that the employers paid an extra 4p an hour to compensate for the dirty work, since they could not thus buy a right to discriminate. In order for there to be a detriment, the acts complained of do not have to amount to a constructive dismissal. However, it is not necessary for the claimant to be aware that he was suffering a detriment, but enough that he was in fact disadvantaged, according to the Court of Appeal in *Garry* v *London Borough of Ealing* (2001). The House of Lords held, in *Shamoon* v *Chief Constable of the Royal Ulster Constabulary* (2003) that an act which a reasonable employee might feel places them at a disadvantage would amount to a detriment. It is not necessary that it has either physical or economic consequences.

Examples of cases where a detriment has been found are where there was a transfer to a less interesting job (*Kirby* v *Manpower Services Commission* (1980)), failure to investigate an allegation of discrimination (*Eke* v *Commissioners of Customs and Excise* (1981)), a requirement of full-time working (*Home Office* v *Holmes* (1984)) and, a restriction on females standing at the bar of a Fleet Street wine bar (*Gill and Coote* v *El Vinos Co. Ltd* (1983)). On the other hand there was no detriment within the Act when a manager said in the hearing of the black applicant 'get this typing done by the wog' (*De Souza* v *Automobile Association* (1986)). This was because it was difficult to find a disadvantage to the employee in his employment conditions. As Lord Wedderburn remarked, such attitudes 'display a disturbing absence of social experience and imagination' (Wedderburn, *The Worker and the Law*, 3rd edn (Harmondsworth: Penguin, 1986), p. 522. See too Hough, (1986) 15 ILJ 123; and *cf.* Carty, (1986) 49 MLR 653 at p. 655 who points out that *De Souza* reflects the landmark American decision on harassment). It is thought that the approach in *De Souza* would not be followed today. In *BL Cars* v *Brown* (1983) the EAT upheld a tribunal's determination on a preliminary point that a requirement imposed by BL that all black workers should be checked as they came through the works security gate could constitute a 'detriment'. Whether it did in a specific case, however, depended on all the facts relating to the issue of the instructions and the particular circumstances of the employee.

10.5 Grounds of discrimination

We all differentiate between things or between people every day. To be discriminating in some senses is considered a virtue, and it remains perfectly lawful to reject an applicant for a job because for example, he cannot spell, is a member of the Labour Party, supports Colchester United Football Club, or has green hair. Discrimination is prohibited only when the reason is one of the forbidden grounds under the legislation. However, it should be noted here that the courts seem to be willing to entertain remedies for forms of discrimination other than those proscribed by the legislation, such as where an employer has an equal opportunities policy which can be taken to be incorporated into the employee's contract of employment. (See *Secretary of State for Scotland* v *Taylor* (1997), a case concerned with age discrimination.) In such cases, the remedies will, of course, be in contract.

10.5.1 **Sex**

The SDA 1975 applies when a woman is discriminated against because of her sex, either directly or indirectly, as we have seen. The Act, of course, applies also to discrimination against men (SDA 1975, s. 2) although only one in 20 sex discrimination claims in ETs are brought by men. Unlike the race relations legislation, however, the sex in question must be that of the applicant, and not sex in general. An employer does not discriminate unlawfully under the SDA 1975, for example, when he orders the employee to discriminate against one sex, for in that instance the employee's own sex is irrelevant. However, there would be discrimination under the race relations legislation in the parallel context there (see *Showboat Entertainment Centre Ltd* v *Owens* (1984) and possibly in other areas of discrimination—see Honeyball, [2007] WebJCLI, issue 4).

10.5.2 **Gender reassignment**

The EAT held in *Chessington World of Adventures Ltd* v *Reed* (1997) that discrimination on grounds of sex included discrimination on the grounds of transsexuality, and that this did not require a comparative approach as the grounds were sex-based. The comparative approach should be let go only when the discrimination was gender-specific, as with pregnancy (see *Webb* v *EMO Air Cargo (UK) Ltd (No. 2)* (1995)). It is hard to see how transsexualism could be placed within that category. As we have seen, the SDA 1975 now includes specific protection against less favourable treatment on the ground of gender reassignment by virtue of the Sex Discrimination (Gender Reassignment) Regulations 1999 (SI 1999 No. 1102)—SDA 1975, s. 2A. However, the Court of Appeal held in *Croft* v *Royal Mail Group plc* (2003) that, although all transsexuals are entitled not to be discriminated against on the grounds of their gender reassignment, regardless of what stage that had reached, that did not mean that all transsexuals were automatically entitled to be treated for all purposes as if they were of their chosen sex. So here the employer was entitled to refuse a male-to-female pre-operative transsexual use of the female toilet facilities. When the employer would not have been entitled to refuse, however, is unclear. (See further, the decision of the ECJ in *Richards* v *Secretary of State for Work and Pensions* (2006).)

10.5.3 **Married status**

The SDA 1975 applies to discrimination against married persons, although only in respect of employment (s. 3(1)). It also applies to civil partners. It remains lawful, however, to discriminate against single people in any way. In *Bick* v *Royal West of England Residential School for the Deaf* (1976), the applicant could not claim when she was sacked because she intended to marry the next day, for at the appropriate time she was not married. Hence, the purpose behind the provision seems to be to protect married persons against discrimination, a seemingly unnecessarily restrictive interpretation.

Not only does this detract from the general symmetry of the discrimination statutes, but it may not wholly fulfil Britain's obligations under Council Directive (EEC) 75/117 that 'there shall be no discrimination whatsoever on grounds of sex, either directly or indirectly in particular by reference to marital or family status'.

Note that to discriminate against a person according to their married status may also amount to discrimination on the grounds of sex if a person of the opposite sex is or would be treated differently—SDA 1975, s. 3.

10.5.4 **Pregnancy and maternity leave**

For many years there was broad agreement that discrimination against women because they were pregnant should attract legal protection. What was not agreed was the form of discrimination that should be or the method by which it could be achieved. (See further the eighth edition of this book at pp. 245–248.) The ECJ took the view that such discrimination was direct sex discrimination *per se* as only women could get pregnant. Therefore a comparative analysis as to how men would be treated was not required—see e.g. *Dekker* v *Stichting Vormingscentrum voor Jonge Volwassenen-Plus* (1991). Others took the view that pregnancy discrimination was sex discrimination, but indirect rather than direct as the requirement not to be pregnant was one which disproportionately affected women—see e.g. Wintemute, (1998) 27 ILJ 23. A third view was that it was not sex discrimination at all, but that protection should be afforded by way of a stand-alone head of claim and that it should not require a comparative approach between individuals—see e.g. Honeyball, (2000) 29 ILJ 43.

The latter view has now prevailed. A new s. 3A is inserted into the SDA 1975 by virtue of the Employment Equality (Sex Discrimination) Regulations 2005 (SI 2005 No. 2467). The new section states that a person discriminates against a woman if, during a 'protected period', on the grounds of her pregnancy, that person treats her less favourably than he would treat her had she not become pregnant. The protected period begins when she becomes pregnant (on the meaning of this, see the ECJ's decision in *Mayr* v *Bäckerei und Konditorei Gerhard Flöckner OHG* (2008)) and ends when her ordinary (or additional, if appropriate) maternity leave ends, or earlier if she has already returned to work. If she is not entitled to ordinary maternity leave (for example, because of a miscarriage) the protected period ends at the end of the two weeks beginning with the end of the pregnancy. Illness because of pregnancy is to be treated as for pregnancy, and discrimination arising because the woman is exercising, or seeking to exercise, statutory rights to maternity leave is also covered in the same way.

The issue remains as to how discrimination against women because of pregnancy, but which falls outside the protected period, is to be treated. This may occur, for example, because a woman *has* been pregnant, has announced that she *intends* to get pregnant or indeed, perhaps, that she has *not* become pregnant. In such circumstances it may be thought that she would have to show that there was direct or indirect sex discrimination. If that is so, then some of the old case law on pregnancy discrimination may still apply. However, it is not clear how far it would, if at all, given that the context in which such cases arise is normally that the claimant has become pregnant.

10.5.5 **Racial grounds**

The RRA 1976 includes within the definition of racial grounds differentiation on the grounds of 'colour, race, nationality or ethnic or national origins' (s. 3(1)). Although the meaning of this phrase has been little elaborated by the courts, certain points have been clarified. Religions as such are not covered under these grounds, but now come under the Employment Equality (Religion or Belief) Regulations 2003, considered at para. 10.12 below. However, discrimination on ethnic origins may include disparate treatment of Jews (*Seide* v *Gillette Industries Ltd* (1980)). That Sikhs are included was finally determined by the House of Lords in *Mandla* v *Dowell Lee* (1983). The adjective 'ethnic' did not (as the Court of Appeal had thought) require the group to be distinguished by some fixed or inherited racial characteristic. The concept was appreciably wider than the strictly racial or biological divide. The group need only regard itself and be regarded as a separate and distinct community by virtue of characteristics commonly associated with a common racial origin. Such a group could include converts to a religion. However, Rastafarians are not a separate group for these purposes, according to the Court of Appeal in *Dawkins* v *Department of the Environment* (1993).

The distinction between nationality and national origins causes some confusion. Nationality includes discrimination against Scots or Irish and, indeed, the English—see *BBC Scotland* v *Souster* (2001). Although one's nationality and national origins are likely to be the same, a person may have a different nationality to his national origins, if, for example, he was born in the West Indies but has now gained British citizenship. Nationality was added to the definition in 1976 because of the narrow interpretation of 'national origins' (which alone had been in the Race Relations Act 1968) in *Ealing LBC* v *Race Relations Board* (1972). There the plaintiff was a British citizen but of Polish origin. The defendant council admitted discriminating against him on the grounds of his origins in establishing its housing waiting list, but the House of Lords held that this was not illegal since it was not included in the definition of nationality.

10.5.6 **Segregation**

It is unlawful to maintain separate facilities for members of different races, even though they are equal in quality (RRA 1976, s. 1(2)). There is thus no room for any form of apartheid in English law. The decision in *Pel Ltd* v *Modgill* (1980) shows that the section does not impose positive obligations on the employer to pursue actively integration between racial groups. The employers were thus not at fault in failing to insist that Asians go into the mainly white paint shop of their factory in order to remove *de facto* separation. There is no comparable provision as to the keeping apart of members of different sexes.

10.5.7 **Victimisation**

Unlawful victimisation arises where a person is treated less favourably because he brings proceedings, gives evidence or information, alleges a contravention or otherwise acts under the Equal Pay, Sex Discrimination or Race Relations Acts or intends to do any of these things (SDA 1975, s. 4(1); RRA 1976, s. 2(1)). In so determining, the motive of the alleged discriminator is not relevant, according to the House of Lords in *Nagarajan* v *London Regional Transport* (1999), overturning the Court of Appeal. This is consistent with other areas of discrimination law.

It is not enough that the complainant is treated disadvantageously because of bringing proceedings, but he must also show that someone who had not done any of the above acts would have been treated differently (see the Court of Appeal's decision in *Cornelius* v *University College of Swansea* (1987)). That clearly is a difficult test to satisfy, but is a matter of causation. Thus, where a person was expelled from an association for making secret tape recordings for use in discrimination proceedings, as others would have been treated in the same way in the situation where there was no discrimination claim, the complainant could not succeed (*Aziz* v *Trinity Street Taxis Ltd* (1988)). It is also not enough that the complainant shows he would have been treated differently 'but for' bringing proceedings, according to the House of Lords in *Chief Constable of West Yorkshire Police* v *Khan* (2001)—see Connolly, (2002) 31 ILJ 161. It must be shown that it was the reason for the victimisation. However, contrary to the impression given in *Khan*, it is important to concentrate on the effect of the employer's action on the employee, not on the reasonableness and honesty of the employer, according to the House of Lords in *St Helens MBC* v *Derbyshire* (2007). (See Connolly, (2007) 36 ILJ 364.)

The House of Lords held in *Waters* v *Commissioner of Police of the Metropolis* (2000), overturning the courts below, that an employer failing to prevent acts of employees against a fellow-employee as a result of bringing allegations may itself amount to an act of victimisation under the Act. (See Barrett, (2001) 30 ILJ 110.)

A claim may even lie for events after the termination of employment, according to the EAT in *Coote* v *Granada Hospitality Ltd (No. 2)* (1999), giving effect to the ECJ's earlier decision in the same case. Therefore, as in this case, it is open to the employee to claim that she was victimised by her employer failing to provide her with a reference because of earlier proceedings brought against it.

For a very thought-provoking examination of the present law on victimisation, and some suggestions for change, see Connolly, (2009) 38 ILJ 149.

10.5.8 Sexual harassment

It has long been recognised that sexual harassment is a form of sex discrimination. (See *Porcelli* v *Strathclyde Regional Council* (1985) and generally, Hazel Houghton-James, *Sexual Harassment* (London: Cavendish Publishing Ltd, 1995).) However, there have been many drawbacks in this not being a free-standing claim, not least in that it was difficult to see how a person who harassed female as well as male employees equally could come within the tests of sex discrimination. Therefore, in 2005, by virtue of the Employment Equality (Sex Discrimination) Regulations 2005 (SI 2005 No. 2467), a new s. 4A was introduced into the SDA 1975. This states that a person subjects a woman to harassment if, on the grounds of her sex, he engages in unwanted conduct that has the purpose or effect of violating her dignity or of creating an intimidating, hostile, degrading, humiliating, or offensive environment for her. (It should be noted, however, that the causative element, suggested by 'on the grounds of' does not seem to go so far as art. 2(2) of the Equal Treatment Directive, Council Directive (EEC) 76/207, requires—see *R (EOC)* v

Secretary of State for Trade and Industry (2007). This is also the case if he engages in any form of unwanted verbal, nonverbal or physical conduct of a sexual nature that has the same effect. So the Act now covers both harassment on the grounds of sex, and conduct of a sexual nature. He is also taken to harass her if he treats her less favourably because she has rejected or submitted to any such form of conduct but not, it seems, if she chooses to ignore it. This is curious because it does not necessarily signify that she is not detrimentally affected by such conduct. If the conduct cannot reasonably be considered as having the effect described it will, however, not amount to harassment. These provisions cover the situation where the victim is a man and are also extended to the situation where the reason for harassment is the claimant's gender reassignment. Section 6 (2A) makes it clear that this provision applies to the employment field.

The SDA 1975, s. 41(1) states that an act done by an employee in the course of employment shall be treated as done by his employer as well as by him, whether or not it was done with the employer's knowledge or approval. This is particularly important in sexual harassment claims where employers frequently do little or nothing to prevent acts of harassment by their employees (see e.g. *Enterprise Glass Co. Ltd* v *Miles* (1990)). Some employers tried to sidestep this provision by arguing that harassment cannot be seen as being perpetrated 'in the course of employment'. However, this loophole was closed by the Court of Appeal in *Jones* v *Tower Boot Co. Ltd* (1997) by saying that those words should have their everyday meaning, which is presumably to say that if the harassment is carried out at work, during work time, by employees the employer will be liable (see Mullender, (1998) MLR 85, *Waters* v *Commissioner of Police of the Metropolis* (2000)). In any event, it was held by the EAT in *Chief Constable of the Lincolnshire Police* v *Stubbs* (1999) that an act can be considered to be in the course of employment even if it took place in a social context after work hours. Such an event is an 'extension' of employment. It is hard to see how anything may be seen to be in the course of employment if it does not occur at a time for which the employee is entitled to payment. (*Cf.* the then test for vicarious liability at common law, applied in *ST* v *North Yorkshire CC* (1999).)

The SDA 1975 required amendment following the decision of the High Court in *Equal Opportunities Commission* v *Secretatry of State for Trade and Industry* (2007). It was held that the Act, in failing to extend the employer's duty to protect employees from harassment by third parties, was in breach of the Equal Treatment Directive, Council Directive (EEC) 76/207. The Government therefore introduced the Sex Discrimination Act 1975 (Amendment) Regulations 2008 (SI 2008 No. 656) amending SDA 1975, s. 4A to protect workers against unwanted conduct that is related to her sex or that of another person which has unwanted effects, including the violation of the worker's dignity.

See further, Clarke (2006) *Legal Studies* 347; Clarke, (2006) 35 ILJ 161.

10.6 Applicants and respondents

10.6.1 Applicants

The anti-discrimination statutes are slightly wider in scope than most employment protection legislation in terms of both potential applicants and respondents. Both the SDA 1975 and RRA 1976 protect not only employees but also a person who has a contract to 'personally execute any work or labour' even though as an independent contractor. This includes a painter or a plumber; a trainee solicitor (*Oliver* v *J. P. Malnick & Co.* (1983)); and a self-employed salesman of fancy goods on a pitch in a department store remunerated on a commission basis (*Quinnen* v *Hovells* (1984): see Leighton, (1985) 14 ILJ 54, who describes the case as 'somewhat curious'). Also included now are members of the armed forces (see Sex Discrimination (Complaints to Employment Tribunals) (Armed Forces) Regulations 1997 (SI 1997 No. 2162)). It also includes office-holders, since 2005—s. 10A and unpaid Government interns on short-term work placements—see *Treasury Solicitor's Department* v *Chenge* (2007). It excludes: a postmaster, since he is responsible merely for seeing that the work of the Post Office is carried on and does not have to perform any of the duties himself (*Tanna* v *Post Office* (1981)); an independent wholesale newspaper distributor who enjoyed an agency for the Mirror Group (*Mirror Group Newspapers Ltd* v *Gunning* (1986); see Leighton, above); a doctor who was not under a contractual arrangement but rather was linked by the statutory scheme with the Family Practitioner Committee or Medical Practitioners Committee (*Wadi* v *Cornwall & Isles of Scilly Family Practitioner Committee* (1985)); and partners in a firm where the firm is the contracting party rather than any particular individual (*Loughran and Kelly* v *Northern Ireland Housing Executive* (1998)).

Contract workers supplied by an agency which employs them (e.g. temporary secretaries, cleaners, building workers) are also expressly included (SDA 1975, s. 9; RRA 1976, s. 7). This is necessary because normally it is the client company for whom the 'temp' works (although he is employed by the agency) who has the scope for discrimination. It is not necessary that the work be done under the managerial control of the principal, and so covers the contractor's own employees, according to the Court of Appeal in *Harrods Ltd* v *Remick* (1998). It is not, however, sufficient under this head that work is done by one person for the benefit of another unless there is an undertaking to supply the work. It thus does not include a taxi owners' collective which patrons phone to ask for a taxi (*Rice* v *Fon-a-Car* (1980)).

Discrimination claims may not be pursued by an applicant's estate after his or her death, according to the EAT in *Lewisham & Guys Mental Health Trust* v *Andrews (dec'd)* (1999). This is a matter of construction of the discrimination statutes, but it does create an anomaly with regard to other remedies.

As we have already seen, following decisions by the House of Lords to the same effect, the discrimination legislation has been amended to allow past employees to claim with respect to post-employment discrimination—see the Sex Discrimination Act 1975 (Amendment) Regulations 2003 (SI 2003 No. 1657) (2003 Amendment Regulations) inserting new SDA 1975, s. 20A; Race Relations Act 1976 (Amendment) Regulations 2003 (SI 2003 No. 1626) inserting new RRA 1976, s. 27A; Disability Discrimination Act 1995 (Amendment) Regulations 2003 (SI 2003 No. 1673) inserting DDA 1995, s. 16A.

10.6.2 Respondents

The prohibitions extend beyond employers to:

(a) Partnerships of six or more partners in the treatment of fellow partners. For reasons not at all clear, exception for small partnerships applies only in the case of race discrimination (RRA 1976, s. 10).

(b) Trade unions, employers associations, professional and trade associations (SDA 1975, s. 12; RRA 1976, s. 11) which refuse membership, make it more difficult for such an applicant to join, offer inferior terms of membership, offer less favourable terms on being received into membership, or subject the member to any detriment.

(c) Qualification bodies for trades or professions (SDA 1975, s. 13; RRA 1976, s. 12) e.g. Law Society, licensing justices, and even the British Judo Association in its capacity of awarding national referee's certificates (*British Judo Association* v *Petty* (1981)), but not the Labour Party in its capacity as selector of candidates (*Ahsan* v *Watt* (2008)). Such bodies must not refuse a licence or make it more difficult to obtain one or grant it on inferior terms or withdraw the licence on discriminatory grounds. Appeals by complainants must be made in this case to the normal appeal body, e.g. the Privy Council in the case of the British Medical Association, and not to tribunals or courts.

(d) Employment agencies (SDA 1975, s. 15; RRA 1976, s. 14); (see *Commission for Racial Equality* v *Imperial Society of Teachers of Dancing* (1983)). However, the person to whom the employee is supplied may also be liable under the Act even though not in an employment relationship with the applicant (see *BP Chemicals Ltd* v *Gillick* (1995)).

(e) The Crown (SDA 1975, s. 85; RRA 1976, s. 75): 'Service for the purpose of a Minister of the Crown or Government Department, other than a person holding statutory office', but this does not extend to the selection of Justices of the Peace (*Knight* v *Attorney-General* (1979)), or rent officers (*Department of Environment* v *Fox* (1979)).

(f) Any provider of training for employment in connection with access to training or related facilities, in terminating training or subjecting a person to detriment in the course of training (Employment Act 1989, s. 7, substituting SDA 1975, s. 14).

One who aids discrimination or pressures another to discriminate may be restrained under the two Acts (SDA 1975, s. 42; RRA 1976, s. 33) and this includes the situation where the party is doing more than something so insignificant as to be negligible, according to the House of Lords in *Anyanwu* v *South Bank Students' Union and South Bank University* (2001). More than a general attitude of helpfulness and co-operation is required, however—see *Hallam* v *Cheltenham Borough Council* (2001). The RRA 1976, s. 31 renders it unlawful to 'induce, or attempt to induce, a person to do any act which contravenes Part II' of the statute. An employer is liable if an employee or agent of his has discriminated unless he can prove he did all that was reasonably practicable to prevent it (SDA 1975, s. 41; RRA 1976, s. 32). The employee who committed the act is also liable under these provisions, even though he himself is the perpetrator. It is not that he is aiding his own act, but he is aiding and abetting his employer's vicarious liability, according to the EAT in *AM* v *WC and SPV* (1999). Although it is welcome that guilty parties should not escape liability, this decision does seem to do violence to the logic of these provisions and this seems to be shown by the fact that the employee is liable even if the employer has no vicarious liability—see *Yeboah* v *Crofton* (2002).

Following the ECJ ruling in a case brought by the European Commission against the UK, Sex Discrimination Act 1986, s. 6 renders void discriminatory provision in collective agreements, internal rules of undertakings, and rules governing independent occupations and professions. Section 6(4A) allows ETs to make a declaration that a discriminatory term or rule in a collective agreement is void, if the employee is either presently, or may in the future be, affected by it—see the decision of the EAT in *Unison* v *Brennan* (2008).

10.6.3 Territorial limitations

The legislation applies to all employment unless it is wholly outside Great Britain (SDA 1975, s. 10; RRA 1976, s. 8; Equal Opportunities (Employment Legislation) (Territorial Limits) Regulations 1999 (SI 1999 No. 3163)). It is where the employee actually works that is important (see *Carver* v *Saudi Arabian Airlines* (1999)).

10.7 Exceptions

There are several exceptions to both the RRA 1976 and the SDA 1975, so that if an employer falls within one he may treat a member of one race or sex less favourably than another whether in the arrangements he makes for filling a job, refusing a job, or denying an employee opportunities for promotion, or transfer to, or training for, the job.

10.7.1 Genuine occupational qualification

The most important exception is where being of one sex or race is a genuine occupational qualification as defined by the Act; then an employee may justifiably be refused a position on grounds of race (RRA 1976, s. 5) or sex (SDA 1975, s. 7). This does not, however, allow discrimination in the terms and conditions provided he or she is, in fact, offered employment. The appropriate provisions of the Equal Pay Act 1970 and the RRA 1976 still apply here with full force. Moreover, the qualifications concentrate on the individual rather than the particular job. For, even where sex or race is a genuine occupational qualification, the employer must consider whether it would be reasonable for him to use existing employees of the appropriate sex or race to carry out the relevant duties, and thus take on either a woman or member of a minority group.

We will deal here with the exceptions under the two Acts separately, although the provisions overlap to a certain extent and have the same underlying policy.

Sex and genuine occupational qualification

The SDA 1975, s. 7 provides that an employer may discriminate on the grounds of sex, although not marital status, if, but only if, he can prove he did so because of one of the following circumstances:

(a) The essential nature of the job calls for a man because of his physiology, for example, to work as a model, although greater strength and stamina alone are not enough as qualifications. As David Pannick pointed out, physiology being the study of natural objects, another term is perhaps more appropriate, although his suggestion of 'physiognomy' would also not seem to be accurate. (Pannick, *Sex Discrimination Law* (Oxford: Clarendon Press, 1985), p. 237.) Perhaps 'physical appearance' is better.

(b) A man is required for authenticity in entertainment: a casting director need not interview women for the part of Iago.

(c) Decency or privacy requires the job to be done by a man because, for example, there are men 'in a state of undress' at the workplace, e.g. a lavatory cleaner. This also applies if customers or other employees might reasonably object to physical contact with a person of the opposite sex as an employee. This exempts, for example, masseurs, but would probably not extend to doctors or chiropodists. Discrimination is unlawful where there are enough employees of the other sex to perform these duties (s. 7(4)). Thus, in *Wylie* v *Dee & Co. (Menswear) Ltd* (1978), a refusal to employ a female in a menswear shop was not permitted under this rubric since it was not often necessary to measure an inside leg, and then one of the seven male assistants could be summoned to do so. However, there would appear to be a serious gap in the law here. If a business is being set up, and at the time of refusal of employment there were not in fact members of the opposite sex in employment, the applicant will not succeed. The words of the statute are clear, and the EAT felt it could not intervene to give a purposive interpretation in *Lasertop Ltd* v *Webster* 1997).

(d) The job is likely to involve the holder of the job doing his work or living in a private home and needs to be held by a man because objection might reasonably be taken to allowing a woman the degree of physical or social contact with a person living in the home, or the knowledge of intimate details of such a person's private affairs (added by Sex Discrimination Act 1986, s. 1(2)).

(e) The nature of the establishment makes it impracticable for the holder of the job to live elsewhere than in premises provided by the employer and the only such premises available are inhabited by men and it is not reasonable to expect the employer to build other premises for women (see *Timex Corporation* v *Thompson* (1981)). In *Sisley* v *Britannia Security Systems Ltd* (1983) the respondents ran a security console station where the operators were employed in shifts. The employers foresaw problems arising if both sexes worked together in the confined spaces and so hired only women. The case was held not to fall within the 'live in' exception since this involved actual residence either temporary or permanent, and not merely serving in the premises for a limited period.

(f) The job is at a single-sex establishment where people require special care, supervision, or attention, e.g. a prison.

(g) The employee provides personal services towards the welfare or education of others and they can be provided 'most effectively' by a man, e.g. a probation officer or member of a social work team.

(h) The job involves work abroad which can be done only by a man. This means that a recruiting agency for, say, the Middle East can take into account the recipient country's views about the role of women.

(i) The job is one of two which are to be held by a married couple, e.g. a pub manager.

For an interesting, if slightly dated, analysis of SDA 1975, s. 7, including an account of the problems of drafting encountered in its progress through Parliament, see Pannick, (1984) OJLS 198.

Race and genuine occupational qualification

An employer is allowed to differentiate on the grounds of race in fewer situations than in the sex discrimination area. Similar exceptions to categories (b) and (g) above, apply, however, so that it would be lawful to choose an Indian social worker to work in an Indian area or to refuse a white for the part of Othello (RRA 1976, s. 5). In addition, an employer can discriminate where a member of a particular race is required for reasons of authenticity in art or photography or a bar or restaurant has a particular ambience. This preserves the prerogative of a Chinese or Indian restaurateur in his choice of 'ethnic' waiters. (See *Tottenham Green Under Fives Centre* v *Marshall* (1989), and the discussion by Jeremy Lewis, (1991) 20 ILJ 67.) The defence is not, however, available to an employer if he already has employees of the appropriate race and they are capable of carrying out the duties of the job necessary to be performed by that race, it would be reasonable to employ them, and there were enough to meet the employer's requirements.

10.7.2 Other general exceptions under both the RRA 1976 and SDA 1975

There are also general exceptions under both statutes. Acts done to safeguard national security are exempt (SDA 1975, s. 52; RRA 1976, s. 42 but under the RRA 1976 needs to be justified which is not the case under the SDA (Race Relations (Amendment) Act 2000, s. 7(1)).

Charitable instruments are also excepted (RRA 1976, s. 34; SDA 1975, s. 43): in *Hugh-Jones* v *St John's College* (1979) the EAT held that the respondent all-male college need not offer positions to women due to the charitable status of the college statutes which barred them from membership.

10.7.3 Other exceptions to the SDA 1975

The SDA 1975 has further restrictions in that it does not apply to clergy, if the doctrines of religion in point provide, or the strongly-held religious convictions of a significant number of its followers are such that they should be all of one sex or particular marital status (s. 19); police in respect of height, uniform, equipment, pregnancy, and pensions (s. 17); and prison officers in respect of height (s. 18); and 'special treatment afforded to women in connection with pregnancy or childbirth', in line with the similar exemption in the Equal Pay Act 1970.

Neither does it apply in respect of provisions in relation to an occupational pension scheme (s. 6(4)). The ECJ's decision in *Barber* v *Guardian Royal Exchange Assurance Group* (1990) is an important decision in this regard, for it decides that occupational pension schemes count as 'pay' for the purposes of direct effect (that is to say, applicable to individuals' claims under domestic legislation). The result is that any inequalities with regard to occupational pension schemes that were permitted by virtue of s. 6 are not permitted. In other words, s. 6 in these respects is overriden by the decison in *Barber.* The court said that, for the purposes of art. 157 TFEU (ex art. 141 EC), pay comprised any consideration, whether cash or in kind, whether immediate or future, provided that the worker received it, albeit indirectly, under the contract of employment. (See further, Honeyball and Shaw, (1991) 16 ELR 47; Shrubsall, (1990) 19 ILJ 244; Deakin, (1990) 49 CLJ 408; Fitzpatrick, (1991) 54 MLR 271.)

10.7.4 **Exceptions in respect only of race discrimination**

The RRA 1976 does not apply to immigration rules, or civil service regulations which restrict Crown employment on grounds of birth, nationality, descent, or residence. A person is not eligible for the civil service unless he or she is a British subject, a Commonwealth citizen or a citizen of the Irish Republic, and additional restrictions apply to the Cabinet Office, Ministry of Defence, and the Diplomatic Service.

The Act also fails to protect a person who applies abroad for employment on any ship (s. 9(1)), unless the employment is concerned with the exploration of the seabed or subsoil of the continental shelf. Selection for national and local teams for any game or sport is lawful on the basis of nationality, birthplace, or length of residence.

The exception for acts done under statutory authority (s. 41(1)) is for those done under any enactment or Order in Council and there is no limitation on the date when that Order was enacted.

10.8 **Enforcement mechanisms**

The Race Relations Act 1965 channelled all complaints of racial discrimination through the Race Relations Board, and it was the unsatisfactory working of this system, particularly the delay and complaints that the Board was not taking up proper grievances, which stimulated the granting of an individual right of action in tribunals under both the Sex Discrimination Act and the Race Relations Act. Difficulties of proof are, however, formidable and the number of claims under both Acts has not been as great as might have been expected. Besides the individual actions the CEHR retains a strategic but infrequently utilised enforcement role through formal investigations. The various methods and procedures of enforcement will now be examined.

10.8.1 **Individual complaint**

An individual's application must be presented within three months of the act complained of to an ET, unless the tribunal considers it just and equitable to extend the limit (SDA 1975, s. 76; RRA 1976, s. 68). It should only do so in exceptional circumstances according to the Court of Appeal in *Robertson* v *Bexley Community Centre* (2003). This power to extend is rather different from the analogous provision in respect of unfair dismissal. In *Hutchison* v *Westward TV Ltd* (1977) the judge emphasised the width of discretion and 'deprecated [the] very simple wide words becoming encrusted by barnacles of authority'. The EAT would only interfere if the decision of the ET was wrong in law or perverse. In a discriminatory dismissal case, the 'act complained of' (from which point time starts to run) arises when the applicant found himself out of a job rather than the date on which he was given notice (*Lupetti* v *Wrens Old House Ltd* (1984)). The period does not begin to run until the employer is in a position to offer employment, according to the EAT in *Swithland Motors plc* v *Clarke* (1994). Where a discriminatory rule or practice is maintained by an employer, however, that constitutes a continuing act according to the House of Lords' decision in *Barclays Bank plc* v *Kapur* (1991). In that case it was held that a refusal to count an employee's previous period of service was a continuing act, and time did not run from the refusal as a deliberate omission. However, according to the Court of Appeal in *Sougrin* v *Haringey Health Authority* (1992) the House of Lords was referring merely to the situation where there was a *policy* of discrimination, which there was not on the facts of the instant case where regrading had occurred which was a one-off case. It is difficult to see how this can be so. At every moment that an applicant is on a lower grade than she might be but for discrimination, there appears to be continuing discrimination. There is no repeated act of discrimination, but that is not necessary where one act of discrimination has a continuing effect. As Rubenstein has pointed out (see [1992] IRLR 391) the Equal Pay Act 1970 does not have time limits for current employees presumably because such discrimination should properly be regarded as continuing. The discrimination ceases on the termination of employment, and therefore it is only in that circumstance that the application of a time limit becomes applicable. The EAT took a more liberal view in *Littlewoods Organisation plc* v *Traynor* (1993) when it held that, where an employer had promised remedial action, and the employee had waited for this for over three months, he was not time-barred as that was a continuing act of discrimination. It would seem difficult to reconcile this decision with the legislative wording in that the failure to remedy was surely a different discrimination to the act complained of which the remedial action would have prevented from recurring. However, as Rubenstein has argued (see [1993] IRLR 147), it is also the common-sense approach to be welcomed.

Where the act complained of is one in a series of repeated similar acts of discrimination, even though it may not be seen as an act of continuing discrimination, nevertheless the time flows from the last occurrence of that act, according to the Court of Appeal in *Rovenska* v *General Medical Council* (1997).

It will sometimes occur that the employee will be fully aware of the discriminatory act but unaware that it is discriminatory until a later date, for example, when a person of the opposite sex or another colour is appointed to the job previously refused the applicant. In such circumstances the EAT has held in *Clarke* v *Hampshire Electro-Plating Co. Ltd* (1992) that the time should run from the later date. Moreover, if the employee is aware that there is a cause of action at the earlier date, the period should be extended if a failure to make a complaint to a tribunal was as a result of the employee's belief that he could not prove discrimination until further evidence came to light, such as an appointment being made. Where there has been delay because of the employee's attempt to exhaust internal remedies first, that too should be considered a just and equitable reason for extending the time limit, according to the EAT in *Aniagwu* v *London Borough of Hackney and Owens* (1999) but the Court of Appeal has decided that this is not necessarily so, in *Apelogun-Gabriels* v *London Borough of Lambeth* (2002). It is only one factor to be taken into account. (See too *Robinson* v *Post Office* (2000) and *Virdi* v *Commissioner of Police of the Metropolis* (2007).)

It may be that a claimant may wish to bring a claim out of time because of a later interpretation of EU law. For example, in *Biggs* v *Somerset CC* (1996), the employee wanted to make a claim for unfair dismissal after the time limit for that claim subsequent to decisions of the ECJ that discrimination against part-timers may be discriminatory contrary to art. 157 TFEU (ex art. 141 EC). The Court of Appeal did not think that this came within the 'not reasonably prac-ticable' exception to that exclusion, in the interests of legal certainty, and the employee could have brought art. 157 (ex art. 141 EC) proceedings at the earlier date. It would appear that this test would be universal, covering all out-of-time complaints, but the EAT in *British Coal Corporation* v *Keeble* (1997) held that this did not apply to an out-of-time claim under the SDA 1975 because there the test is somewhat wider, allowing such claims if it is just and equitable so to do. Although to be welcomed in principle, this decision does leave the law in a somewhat confused and illogical state.

The individual applicant may be financially assisted by the CEHR when it thinks he has a test case raising a matter of principle or it is 'unreasonable . . . to expect the applicant to deal with the case unaided or if there is any other special con-sideration' (RRA 1976, s. 66; SDA 1975, s. 75). However, there is no appeal if the Commission refuses its aid, which may take the form of seeking a compromise, settlement, preliminary advice, or any other assistance it considers appropriate.

An ACAS conciliation officer is involved in attempting to settle all employment discrimination complaints before a full ET hearing, and the rules under which he operates apply in the same way as to unfair dismissal and redundancy claims.

10.8.2 **Problems of proof**

In many ways the applicant is like a fettered runner in discrimination cases. Those most prone to suffer acts of racial discrimination are likely to have language diffi-culties, and to find the English legal system a hostile maze. Application and success rates compare most unfavourably with the analogous jurisdiction in unfair dis-missal cases and American experience of not dissimilar provisions (see Lustgarten, (1977) 6 ILJ 212).

Those charging discrimination may be met by a smokescreen defence and all sorts of alternative and spurious reasons put forward for the less favourable treat-ment meted out. The burden of proof in sex discrimination cases was altered by the Sex Discrimination (Indirect Discrimination and Burden of Proof) Regulations 2001 (SI 2001 No. 2660) and the Race Relations Act 1976 (Amendment) Regulations 2003 (SI 2003 No. 1626). Where the claimant proves facts from which the tribunal could infer that unlawful discrimination has occurred, the burden moves to the employer to prove that he did not commit that act. If it cannot do so, the tribunal must (not may) find in favour of the claimant, according to the Court of Appeal in *Igen Ltd* v *Wong* (2005). (See Cunningham, (2006) 35 ILJ 279; *Madarassy* v *Nomura International plc* (2007); *Barton* v *Investec Henderson Crosthwaite Securities Ltd* (2005); cf. *Madden* v *Preferred Technical Group CHA Ltd* (2005).) The original judicial view was that the evidential burden of proof was on the employer. (See Geoffrey Mead, (1992) 21 ILJ 217.)

The complainant may submit a special questionnaire to the respondent employer and, if the latter fails to reply or gives an evasive or equivocal response, the tribunal may draw inferences as to the existence of discrimination.

Statistical evidence is clearly most important in indirect discrimination claims, but it may be relevant also in direct discrimination cases. In *West Midlands Passenger Transport Executive* v *Jaquant Singh* (1988), the Court of Appeal held that, in direct discrimination cases, statistical material was relevant in that it might establish a discernible pattern of treatment by the employers towards the applicant's racial group, from which discrimination might be inferred. (See further Gardner, (1989) 105 LQR 183.) While an employer cannot be required to conduct a survey to pass over the necessary information, adverse inferences may be drawn in the event of a failure to give satisfactory answers to enquiries (*Carrington* v *Helix Lighting Ltd* (1990)).

It may be vital for the applicant to see documents drawn up by the respondent even though they are of a confidential character, for only then can it be shown whether the complainant had as good reports and references as the successful applicant with whom he or she was competing. In the leading case of *Science Research Council* v *Nassé* (1979), the House of Lords heard together Mrs Nassé's complaint of sex discrimination against the SRC and Mr Vyas' application against British Leyland on the grounds of race. Both applicants sought details of employment records of all other persons interviewed for jobs they had sought. These were to include service records, personal history forms, personal assessment records, and details of commendations together with their application forms for the post advertised. This produced a clash of two important principles: facilitating proof of discrimination and preserving the confidentiality of staff reports. Although all members of the House of Lords agreed that there was no principle of law that documents are protected from discovery by reason of confidentiality alone, their relevance, although a necessary condition, is not by itself sufficient. The test was whether discovery 'is necessary for disposing fairly of the proceedings'. Lord Wilberforce went on to say:

> The process is to consider fairly the strength and value of the interest in preserving confidentiality and the damage which may be caused by breaking it, then to consider whether the objective to dispose fairly of the case can be achieved without doing so and only in the last resort to order discovery.

In especially sensitive cases, tribunals and courts cover up parts of the relevant documents, insert anonymous references, or proceed *in camera*.

In the first important decision post-*Nassé*, *Perera* v *Civil Service Commission* (1983) the EAT gave its principle ample scope. In order to prove that he had been turned down several times for jobs with the Civil Service because of his race, the applicant sought discovery of all documents relating to those applications. Notwithstanding that the assembly of the necessary information would be difficult and expensive since there were 1,600 applicants, Slynn J called for sufficient material to be disclosed so that the applicant could pursue his relevant inquiry whether other candidates had as high qualifications as he possessed. In particular, the application forms of 78 candidates interviewed in 1977 should be revealed, together with details of nationality and fathers' nationalities and their final reports and assessment. Any identifying material was to be blacked out.

In *Selvarajan* v *ILEA* (1980) the applicant sought to refer, in support of his claim of discriminatory promotion, to a series of abortive applications between 1961 and

1976 for jobs with the respondents, since he alleged continuing discrimination. The EAT held that these could be logically probative and disagreed with the industrial tribunal's cut off point of 1973. Since the request was limited to the application forms of the appointed candidates, minutes of appointment, and Selvarajan's own file, no unfairness or oppression would result to the respondents.

10.8.3 Remedies

Where an ET upholds a complaint under either of the discrimination statutes, it may grant any of three types of remedies.

Declarations and recommendations

First, it may make a declaration of the rights of the parties. (On all the remedies see SDA 1975, s. 65(1); RRA 1976, s. 56(1).) Secondly, the tribunal may make a recommendation (but not order) that the respondent should, within a specified period, take such action as the tribunal deems practicable in order to obviate or reduce the adverse effect of the act complained of. If, without reasonable justification, the respondent fails to comply with this recommendation, the tribunal may increase any compensation awarded. The recommendation is, however, restricted to remedying the specific act of discrimination and cannot be more wide-ranging. Moreover, it cannot be used to 'top up' compensation as the tribunal appeared to suggest in *Irvine* v *Prestcold Ltd* (1981), when it recommended an increase in wages to the applicant who had been discriminated against by not being promoted. The Court of Appeal thought that: 'The words "action within a specified period" are inapt to cover a recommendation as to payment of a particular remuneration during a period which might extend over several years.' The ET cannot, moreover, recommend positive action so that in *Ministry of Defence* v *Jeremiah* (1980) its suggestion that the employers provide showers for women was overturned. Again in *Bayoomi* v *British Railways Board* (1981), the tribunal refused to make a general recommendation affecting the employer's recruitment policies on the ground that it could only obviate or reduce the adverse effect on the applicant; instead, it decreed the entry of a reference on the applicant's personal file explaining that his dismissal was due to discrimination. Likewise, the tribunal cannot make a recommendation that the complainant be promoted to the next suitable vacancy, according to the EAT in *British Gas plc* v *Sharma* (1991), because this would amount to positive discrimination. However, as Rubenstein has pointed out ([1991] IRLR 99), this is not the case as the position would not be reversed for a person because of their race or sex, but because that person has been the victim of a discrimination, involving a wrong that should be righted.

Compensation

Compensation may be ordered. This is no longer subject to a maximum. Since the ECJ's ruling in *Southampton & South West Hampshire AHA* v *Marshall (No. 2)* (1993), any compensation awarded must be adequate, enabling the loss and damage actually sustained to be made good, which included a requirement that interest be awarded (see further McColgan, (1994) 23 ILJ 226; Arnull, (1995) 24 ILJ 215). This applies to both sex and race discrimination claims (Race Relations (Remedies) Act 1994, s. 1(1)). The measure of compensation is the same as that adopted by the ordinary courts (SDA 1975, s. 65(1)(b); RRA 1976, s. 56(1)(b)) and should be restitu-tionary (*Alexander* v *Home Office* (1988)), except that it may expressly include injury to feelings (SDA 1975, s. 66(4); RRA 1976, s. 57(4)). In *Skyrail Oceanic Ltd* v *Coleman* (1980) the EAT and Court of Appeal thought that no more should be awarded for injury to feelings than is given in defamation cases, and rejected the tribunal's award of £1,000. Their Lordships thought that there could be no damage to the applicant's reputation on the facts and that £100 was thus suitable. However, in *Noone* v *North West Thames Regional Health Authority* (1988), the Court of Appeal awarded £3,000 for injury to feelings, but in reducing an award originally for £5,000; and in *Sharifi* v *Strathclyde Regional Council* (1992) the EAT felt that £500 was at or near the minimum. However, in *Doshoki* v *Draeger Ltd* (2002) the EAT thought, in a race discrimination case, that £750 was at the very bottom or very close to it, and substituted an award of £4,000. In *Orlando* v *Didcot Power Station Sports and Social Club* (1996), the EAT held that £750 is not so low as to be perverse and that the removal of the maximum of compensation did not affect the princi-ples to be applied. The median at the time of writing is about £5,000 depending on the claim—it is lower for sex discrimination claims than race cases—although the EAT in 2002 reduced an award for injury to feelings from £50,000 to the max-imum. In *Vento* v *Chief Constable of West Yorkshire Police (No. 2)* (2003) the Court of Appeal stated that an award of more than £25,000 should be made only in the most exceptional cases, and under £500 never at all. The point between less ser-ious cases and serious cases it put at £5,000, with the most serious cases attracting a minimum of £15,000. The EAT, in pursuance of the principles behind the Court of Appeal's decision in *Vento*, has now said that these figures should be increased by a fifth to reflect present-day values—see *Da'Bell* v *NSPCC* (2010). It will be rare for a discrimination case by its very nature not to involve injury to feelings to some extent. (For an example of a case where £25,000 was considered appropriate, see *Miles* v *Gilbank* (2006).)

Where the damage extends beyond emotional distress to psychiatric illness the Court of Appeal has decided in *Sheriff* v *Klyne Tugs (Lowestoft) Ltd* (1999) that dam-ages for personal injury may be awarded by ETs. There is no necessity for a separate tort claim in the ordinary courts.

It might also be possible for an employee to be awarded compensation for the stigma that is attached should an employer dismiss them and subsequently be pur-sued for discrimination. In *Chagger* v *Abbey National plc* (2010) the Court of Appeal held that an employee who had been turned down in 111 applications following their claim against their former employer could succeed. This was so, even though there had been no claims against the employers receiving those applications. It might be thought that this is not really an example of stigma damages at all in that the employee has not been tainted by their previous action but become someone of whom potential future employers have become wary due to their discrimination action record. As such, this might better be seen as an instance of victimisation. Nevertheless, the actions of the dismissing employer have had a detrimental effect on the employee in that, without the dismissal, the employee would not have found it necessary to bring the action in the first place.

No compensation could formerly be awarded for indirect discrimination unless the employer intended the discrimination to occur. To found the necessary inten-tion it had to be shown that the employer intended discriminatory consequences to follow from his acts, knowing that those consequences would follow and wanting them to follow, according to the EAT in *J. H. Walker Ltd* v *Hussain* (1996). However, tribunals may award compensation even though there is no intention to discriminate where it would not be just and equitable to grant other remedies alone (see Sex Discrimination and Equal Pay (Miscellaneous Amendments) Regulations 1996 (SI 1996 No. 438)).

It is not possible to award exemplary damages in discrimination cases, according to the EAT in *Deane* v *London Borough of Ealing* (1993). (See Rowland, (1994) 23 ILJ 64.) However, as Tom Linden has pointed out ((1991) 20 ILJ 139), in many instances the power to award aggravated damages for injured feelings will be an adequate alternative, and this will be in addition to any sum payable for injury to feelings, according to the Court of Appeal in *Scott* v *Commissioners of Inland Revenue* (2004).

The Court of Appeal has held in *Ministry of Defence* v *Wheeler* (1998) that the calculation of compensation should be made in the following order. First, after the gross amount has been assessed (the sum the employee would have earned), any deduction for sums in fact earned elsewhere should be made, this figure then being reduced by any percentage reduction reflecting the assessment of the chances that the employee might have left the employment in any event. If this were to be gone through in a different order, radically different final totals would be reached.

Void contractual terms

By SDA 1975, s. 77 and RRA 1976, s. 72, a term of a contract is void where:

(a) its inclusion renders the making of the contract unlawful by virtue of the Act;

(b) it is included in furtherance of an act rendered unlawful by the Act; or

(c) it provides for the doing of any act which would be rendered unlawful by the Act.

This applies if the term is directly or indirectly discriminatory against men, women, or married persons by reason of sex or marital status. This provision has existed in the same form since the Acts were passed but was rarely used.

10.9 Disability discrimination

There were more than a dozen attempts to introduce legislation addressing discrimination against the disabled, but it was not until the DDA 1995 was passed that the necessary Governmental backing was secured. Since then, claims under the Act have increased at a steady rate. The Act is a reasonably comprehensive measure in the sense that it is a fairly recognisable sibling of the legislation outlawing sex and race discrimination. While many of the concepts and approaches of the DDA 1995 are similar to those of the earlier legislation, there are nevertheless important differences which reflect the special difficulties thrown up by disability. There are also important differences which occur because of the Government's reluctance to provide the full panoply of protection given in the sex and race provisions. (See generally Davies and Davies, (2000) 29 ILJ 347.) Nevertheless, the scope of legislation protection has been extended recently with the Disability Discrimination

Act 2005, which widens the coverage of conditions protected by the DDA 1995 as well as creating important new duties on public bodies to promote equality of opportunity for the disabled (s. 49(A)). In addition, the human rights aspect of disability is beginning to be explored—see Lawson, (2005) 56 NILQ 462 on the role of European Convention on Human Rights, art. 3.

10.9.1 **The meaning of 'disability'**

The DDA 1995 extends protection against discrimination to those who have a 'disability' (or, by virtue of s. 2, who have had a disability), which is defined in s. 1 as a physical or mental impairment which has a substantial and long-term adverse effect on that person's ability to carry out normal day-to-day activities (see *Law Hospital NHS Trust* v *Rush* (2001); *Paterson* v *Commissioner of Police of the Metropolis* (2007)), or would do but for the fact of medical treatment *(Kapadia* v *London Borough of Lambeth* (2000)). That the adverse effect needs to be 'likely' but for the treatment means no more than that there would be a 'significant' risk of it occurring, not necessarily more probable than not, according to the House of Lords in *SCA Packaging Ltd* v *Boyle* (2009). What is a normal day-to-day activity, and what is substantial, are matters for the tribunal and not medical advice, according to the EAT in *Vicary* v *British Telecommunications plc* (1999). Further explanation of this definition is contained in Sch. 1 to the Act, which enables the definition to be changed as necessary by the Government through delegated legislation.

In fact the provision was most significantly extended in the Disability Discrimination Act 2005, which now includes within the definition of a disabled person those with cancer, multiple sclerosis, and HIV (Sch. 1, para. 6A). Nor is it any longer a requirement that those with a mental illness only come within the definition if they suffer from a 'clinically well-recognised' condition. (Indeed, the idea of 'impairment' in the Act in any context is not restricted to a clinical condition. Rather, it is functional, according to the EAT in *Ministry of Defence* v *Hay* (2008).) However, those with short-term depressive illnesses may still be excluded from the definition by virtue of the continued necessity to show that it is 'long term'. The requirement that the condition be 'substantial' appears on the face of it to be somewhat more stringent than the Government intended. During the Committee stage of the Bill's progress through Parliament the Government made it clear that the provision was intended to exclude only minor or trivial conditions. However, it should be noted that it is the effect which the wording requires to be substantial and long term, and not necessarily the condition itself, although clearly the two will go hand-in-hand most frequently. An effect will be long term by virtue of Sch. 1 if it has lasted, or is likely to last 12 months, or would have been likely to but for the fact that death is likely to intervene, to be assessed at the time of the alleged discriminatory act *(McDougall* v *Richmond Adult Community College* (2008)). The very different situation where a person is diagnosed as having a disabling condition that will not have a significant impact on that person's life for the time being is one that is difficult. Because such a person may nevertheless suffer from discrimination as a result of the diagnosis, Sch. 1 includes him or her within the definition so long as some effect has materialised. It is difficult to see why this should be necessary.

The meaning of 'disability' is also governed by the Disability Discrimination (Meaning of Disability) Regulations 1996 (SI 1996 No. 1455). These state that certain mental impairments are not to be considered as disabilities. These are:

(a) addiction to alcohol, nicotine or any other substance unless it is addiction which was originally the result of administration of medically prescribed drugs or other medical treatment;

(b) a tendency to set fires;

(c) a tendency to steal;

(d) a tendency to physical or sexual abuse of other persons;

(e) exhibitionism;

(f) voyeurism;

(g) seasonal allergic rhinitis (e.g. hay fever).

If, however, these are manifestations of a disability, it was thought these could be taken into account—see *Murray* v *Newham Citizens Advice Bureau Ltd* (2003). See further Wells, (2003) 32 ILJ 253 who argues that the definition adopted in the UK is unduly restrictive, and too medically-based, leading to many people suffering from disability discrimination falling outside the protection of the law. However, the High Court held in *Governing Body of X Endowed Primary School* v *Special Educational Needs and Disability Tribunal* (2009) that there was no reason to make this distinction between a disability and a consequence of it, which in any event would be difficult to distinguish clearly in practice.

10.9.2 Scope of the Act

The scope of the Act is, as one would expect, very similar to that of the race and sex discrimination legislation. That is to say, by way of s. 4, it covers discrimination against the disabled in respect of recruitment (see too, s. 16B on the liability of employers and publishers for discriminatory advertisements), terms of employment, promotion, transfers, training and other similar benefits, as well as termination of employment or similar detriment. Reference should be made to the case law under the equivalent sections of the other discrimination legislation which is very likely to be considered of relevance here. However, an area of special concern as far as the disabled are concerned is that of medical examinations before employment. Pressure was put on the Government during the passage of the Bill through Parliament to include provisions specifically related to this subject, but it may be that most instances of concern are covered by s. 4(1)(a), which makes it unlawful to discriminate against a disabled person in the arrangements an employer makes for the purpose of determining to whom employment should be offered.

10.9.3 Meaning of 'discrimination'

The meaning of 'discrimination' is covered by s. 3A of the Act (inserted by the Disability Discrimination Act 1995 (Amendment) Regulations 2003 (SI 2003 No. 1673). Again, this is similar to that in the race and sex discrimination legislation, but is different in several important respects. The concept of direct discrimination is present in almost identical terms (see s. 3A(5)). There is also disability-related discrimination, which is similar to indirect discrimination in other legislation, except that it does not require disparate treatment—see s. 3A(1). It is subject to a justification defence. However, even then it will not be justified unless the able-bodied comparator's abilities are materially different from the disabled person's. This is because, unlike sex and race, disability will frequently have an impact on a person's ability to do a job successfully. According to the Code of Practice, the relevant circumstances must relate to the individual circumstances and must not be trivial or minor (para. 4.6). This is a very undemanding test. If the employer is unaware that the applicant is disabled, this is irrelevant in determining whether there has been discrimination on the grounds of disability, according to the EAT in *H J. Heinz Co. Ltd* v *Kenrick* (2000) and several other authorities. An objective test should be applied—that is to say, the tribunal should consider whether the discrimination was related to the disability, not whether the employer knew of it. This is a matter that should be left to considering whether that discrimination was justified. However, in a later case to go before the EAT on this point, *Callagan* v *Glasgow City Council* (2001), it felt that this went too far. The text should be akin to the 'range of reasonable responses test' in unfair dismissal law, according to the Court of Appeal in *Jones* v *Post Office* (2001). (See too *Williams* v *J. Walter Thompson Group Ltd* (2005), and Davies, (2003) 32 ILJ 164 who argues that this interpretation of the test is complex and inappropriate, leading to poor success rates.)

In considering if there has been discrimination, it must be established that the employee has been treated less favourably than others are treated, or would be treated, for a reason related to that person's lack of disability. The House of Lords held in *London Borough of Lewisham* v *Malcolm* (2008) that the proper comparator here was someone who was in the same position to that of the claimant, but for the latter's disability. (See too the EATs decisions in *Stockton on Tees Borough Council* v *Aylott* (2009); *Child Support Agency* v *Truman* (2009).) This is a much more restrictive test than had been laid down before by the Court of Appeal in *Clark* v *TGD Ltd t/a Novacold* (1999). For example, under the test in *Clark*, if a disabled employee were absent from work due to disability, a comparison had to be made with other employees who were not absent. After *London Borough of Lewisham* the comparison has to be made with other absent employees who are not disabled. This will normally be a much easier test for an employer to satisfy, although of course it depends on the facts in each case. (See further, Horton, (2008) 37 ILJ 376.)

10.9.4 Reasonable adjustments

Section 4A places a duty on an employer to make reasonable adjustments where a provision, criterion, or practice is applied by or on behalf of an employer, or any physical feature of premises occupied by the employer, places the disabled person concerned at a substantial disadvantage in comparison with persons who are not disabled. The employee should inform the employer as to what reasonable adjustments in his or her view might be required, unless the employer reasonably should know without being so told (see *Ridout* v *TC Group* (1998) perhaps after undertaking a risk assessment, according to the EAT in *Mid-Staffordshire General Hospitals NHS Trust* v *Cambridge* (2003)). The employer should be made aware of the broad nature of the adjustment proposed, without necessarily giving the claimant the task of giving details—see the EAT's decisions in *Project Management*

Institute v *Latif* (2007); *HM Prison Service* v *Johnson* (2007). However, it is important to remember that the duty is on the employer (see *Cosgrove* v *Caesar Howie*
(2001)). In determining what it is reasonable for the employer to do, s. 18 B(1)
states that regard shall be had, *inter alia*, to the extent to which taking a particular step would prevent the discriminatory effect, the extent to which it is
practicable for the employer to take the step, the financial and other costs of so
doing, the employer's financial resources and the financial and other assistance
available to him in doing so—see *O'Hanlon* v *HMRC* (2006). Most adjustments are
likely to cost little or nothing, however, and the Government's advice was that
in those few cases where an adjustment would involve cost, this is unlikely to go
above a few hundred pounds. An example might be to allow an employee who has
become disabled to apply for posts reserved, under company policy, to employees
made redundant (see *Kent CC* v *Mingo* (2000); *Kenny* v *Hampshire Constabulary*
(1999)). However, where a disabled employee becomes totally incapable of doing
the job they are employed to do, it may be a reasonable adjustment to transfer
the employee to another job, according to the House of Lords in *Archibald* v *Fife
Council* (2004)—see Hughes, (2004) 33 ILJ 358.

It must be reasonable, in all the circumstances of the case, for the employer to
have to undertake these adjustments in order to prevent the provision, criterion,
practice, or feature from having effect. This is an objective test but ultimately one
for the ET, according to the Court of Appeal in *Smith* v *Churchill Stairlifts plc* (2006).
Naturally, the employer must be aware that the employee has the disability in
question in order for the adjustment to be considered reasonable but there is no
requirement on the employer to consult the employee on what adjustment should
be made according to the EAT in *Tarbuck* v *Sainsbury's Supermarkets Ltd* (2006).

Section 3B, introduced by the 2003 Amendment Regulations, protects disabled
employees from harassment because of their disablement. It defines 'harassment'
as unwanted conduct having the purpose or effect of violating the applicant's
dignity, or creating an intimidating, hostile, degrading, humiliating, or offensive
environment for that person. A mixed subjective and objective test is applied in
order to determine this.

10.9.5 Exception

One of the most controversial aspects of the Act in its original form was that it
did not apply to employers with fewer than 15 employees, by virtue of s. 7. While
over four-fifths of employees were already covered by the Act in that they worked
for businesses where the employer has more than 15 employees, in fact most
employers (over 95 per cent) escaped the effect of the Act because they employ
fewer than 15 employees. Furthermore, associated employers (such as wholly-
owned subsidiaries) were not to be taken into account, according to the EAT in
Hardie v *CD Northern Ltd* (2000). Although this was in line with the Conservative
Government's policy to reduce burdens on business, and particularly small
businesses, it was difficult to see the justification for it in what is basically a
moral-based piece of legislation. Furthermore, there was not the same exemption in other anti-discrimination legislation. The 2003 Amendment Regulations
thus repealed s. 7, and no small employer exemption has therefore existed since
October 2004.

10.9.6 **Enforcement**

Enforcement of the Act is similar to that in other anti-discrimination legislation. Complaint should be made to an ET within three months from the date of
the act complained of, under s. 17A. The tribunal may, if it finds the case well-
founded, make a declaration, an order for compensation, or a recommendation
to the respondent. Compensation, which is calculated in the same way as for
damages for breach of statutory duty, may include compensation for injury to
feelings.

10.10 **Discrimination against part-time workers**

As we have seen, in 2000 the Government introduced the Part-time Workers
(Prevention of Less Favourable Treatment) Regulations 2000 (SI 2000 No. 1551) in
response to the EC's Part-time Workers Directive, Council Directive (EC) 98/23.
This gives protection on similar (but not identical) lines against other forms of
discrimination considered above.

This additional stand-alone right protects those workers who cannot avail
themselves of an indirect sex discrimination claim. In many instances, therefore,
this gives protection in particular to male part-timers. This concept has graphically been referred to as 'diagonal' discrimination—see Davies, (2005) 25 *Legal
Studies* 181.

Regulation 5 gives a part-time worker the right not to be treated by his employer
less favourably than he treats a comparable full-time worker regarding the terms of
his contract or by being subjected to any other detriment by any act, or deliberate
failure to act, of his employer. This is the case only if the less favourable treatment
is on the ground that the worker is part-time, and only where it is not objectively
justifiable. The latest authority (*Sharma* v *Manchester City Council* (2008)) suggests
that it is not necessary that the discriminatory treatment is caused solely by the
employee working part-time. However, this decision of the EAT would appear to
be *per incuriam* in that the opposite was stated to be the case by the ECJ in *Wippel* v
Pek and Cloppenburgh GmbH (2005), as well as by the Court of Session in Scotland
in *McMenemy* v *Capita Business Services Ltd* (2007), both of which cases the EAT in
Scharma made no mention of. Less favourable treatment is determined by applying a *pro rata* test, so that if, for example, the employee works 20 hours a week, and
full-timers work 40, then any treatment of the full-timer more than twice as beneficial will give rise to a claim. Likewise, if a full-time employee would not be given
time off in lieu of a bank holiday falling on a day of the week not normally worked,
there is no discrimination against part-time workers in this regard, according to
the Court of Session in *McMenemy* v *Captia Business Services Ltd* (2007).

A number of points are noteworthy here. One is that the Regulations refer to
workers (being anyone who undertakes to perform services personally for another)
rather than employees, as they originally did in draft form. References to an
'employer' however, are to be taken as referring to anyone who employs employees
and workers, and is not to be restricted to the narrower category (reg. 1).

A second point is that, unlike other discrimination legislation, there is a require-ment here for the comparator to be real and not hypothetical. This is an unfor-tunate feature, and takes out many possible claimants from the protection of the Regulations. (See *Carl* v *University of Sheffield* (2009).)

Thirdly, the terminology is in many respects identical to that used in other dis-crimination legislation, and it is legitimate in construing the Regulations to refer to case law in those other areas. Thus, workers can only be compared if they are doing the same or broadly similar work. If significant differences exist between full and part-time workers, a claim will not lie according to the House of Lords in *Matthews* v *Kent & Medway Towns Fire Authority* (2006). However, in making the comparison, the focus should be on the similarities, not the differences, between the work that the full-timers and part-timers do.

A part-time worker is defined in reg. 2 as someone who 'is paid wholly or in part by reference to the time he works and, having regard to the custom and practice of the employer in relation to workers employed by the worker's employer under the same type of contract, is not identifiable as a full-time worker'. A full-time worker is defined as someone who 'is paid wholly or in part by reference to the time he works and, having regard to the custom and practice of the employer...is identifiable as a full-time worker'. It is likely that the Department for Business, Innovation and Skills will remove the references to 'same type of contract' in the near future to allow part-time workers on fixed-term contracts to compare themselves with full-time workers on permanent contracts and, of course, *vice versa.*

As with unfair dismissal, if a worker feels he has suffered unfavourable treat-ment, he is entitled to a written statement as to the reasons for the treatment, under reg. 6. This must be given within 21 days of his request. Regulation 7 gives protection against further detrimental treatment by his employer arising out of the worker pursuing his rights under the Regulations.

Any complaint must be made to the ET within three months of the less favour-able treatment, but the tribunal can extend this if it considers it just and equitable to do so (reg. 8). The usual remedies apply, which is to say a declaration and com-pensation as is just and reasonable, but without an element for injury to feelings. The tribunal is also empowered to recommend remedial action.

10.11 **Discrimination against fixed-term workers**

Under EA 2002, s. 45 the Secretary of State was empowered to make regulations for the purpose of ensuring that fixed-term employees are not treated less favour-ably than employees in permanent employment. These, the Fixed-Term Employees (Prevention of Less Favourable Treatment) Regulations 2002 (SI 2002 No. 2034) came into effect in October 2002. (See, for analysis of the Regulations, McColgan, (2003) 32 ILJ 194.)

The scheme is much the same as for other discrimination legislation in gen-eral and part-time workers in particular. The Regulations seek to protect employ-ees (being those employees not on permanent contract—see reg. 1(2)) against less favourable treatment, as compared with a permanent employee, on the grounds of their fixed-term contract status, unless the employer can provide objective justification for that treatment. The Regulations cover less favourable treatment as regards the terms of the contract and the employee's subjection to any other detriment by the employer (reg. 3). It was thought that the former did not cover terms relating to pay as art. 153 TFEU (ex art. 137 EC), whilst conferring powers on the EU to legislate on matters concerned with working conditions, did not specifically extend to pay. However, the ECJ has ruled that it does, in *Del Cerro Alonso* v *Osakidetza-Servicio Vasco de Salud* (2007). The consequence is that employees on fixed-term contracts may bring equal pay claims using permanent employees as their comparators. There are similar rights to a written statement of reasons for the less favourable treatment (reg. 5), and a right to claim unfair dismissal in the event of being dismissed for such a reason (reg. 6). There is also protection against other detriment that does not amount to dismissal.

However, there are some important differences between protection for fixed-term employees and discrimination protection in some other areas. A major one is that the Regulations only relate to 'employees' (but not apprentices nor agency workers) rather than to the wider category of 'workers'. This will take many people out of the scope of the Regulations who could have benefited from them, and there are over a million fixed-term workers. It may thus be that the Regulations, if they remain unamended, will be considered to fail to implement the EC Fixed-Term Contracts Directive, Council Directive (EC) 99/70, which refers to 'workers'.

A contract for a fixed term is nevertheless such even if it contains provision for earlier determination by notice, according to the EAT in *Allen* v *National Australia Group Europe Ltd* (2004).

There is also a provision to deal with the problem of adverse treatment of employees on successive fixed-term contracts. Under reg. 8 where a fixed-term contract has been renewed once, any reference in any further renewal to fixed-term status will be of no effect, and the contract will be considered to be one of indefinite duration, so long as the employment has been for four years or more and no objective justification for fixed-term status was present. (See the decision of the ECJ in *Adeneler* v *Ellinikos Organismos Galaktos* (2006).) This was an issue which was particularly troubling the Government. The result of this will be, however, that the employee will be subject to the minimum period of notice relevant to him under ERA 1996, ss 86–91. Some employees, particularly in the public sector, may in fact be in an inferior position in consequence. Further, the Court of Appeal has held that the mere fact of not renewing a fixed-term contract does not constitute grounds for a claim, as that would undermine the legality of fixed-term contracts as such—see *Department for Work and Pensions* v *Webley* (2005).

There are further variations from discrimination law in some other fields. First, although there is the usual comparison required, unlike the SDA 1975 the comparator must be a real permanent employee, and not hypothetical—reg. 2. Likewise, unlike under the Equal Pay Act 1970, the comparison can be made overall and not necessarily term-by-term—reg. 4. So, a more favourable term may be balanced against a less favourable term to get parity of overall treatment or even global advantage to the fixed-term employee. In such cases no claim will be made out.

There is a defence of objective justification under reg. 4. This will occur 'if the terms of the fixed-term employee's contract of employment, taken as a whole, are at least as favourable as the terms of the comparable permanent employee's contract of employment'.

10.12 **Discrimination on the grounds of religion or belief**

The Employment Equality (Religion or Belief) Regulations 2003 (SI 2003 No. 1660), in force from December 2003, give protection against discrimination on the grounds of religion, religious belief, or philosophical belief—reg. 2. (See for analysis of the Regulations, Vickers, (2003) 32 ILJ 188. See too Howes and Wank, (2005) 21 IJCLLIR 571; McColgan, (2009) 38 ILJ 1.) Originally the reference to philosophical belief was restricted to similar philosophical beliefs, but that was altered by Equality Act 2006, s. 77. Now any philosophical belief is covered. This was done in order to include philosophical beliefs about religion that did not involve religious beliefs, such as atheism and humanism. However, the effect would seem to be to cover a wide variety of beliefs which have nothing to do with religion, such as political beliefs, so long as they are rooted in a political philosophy, such as Marxism, communism and free-market capitalism, according to the EAT in *Grainger plc* v *Nicholson* (2010). It is difficult to think that this can have been an intended consequence, although an obvious one. The difficulty for the courts in the future is clearly going to be how to restrict the concept of 'philosophical belief' to an idea that does not produce an overly-wide ambit of claims, and to provide protection against misuse of the idea. In *Grainger* the belief, which was held to come within the definition, concerned climate change and the environment. In addition, even with regard to religious belief, it is not necessary for the belief to be widely-held, and indeed it may be entirely a personal one, according to the EAT in *Eweida* v *British Airways plc* (2009).

The definition of discrimination is similar to that for the race and sex discrimination with the definition of indirect discrimination being the new form adopted there. So, under reg. 3, A discriminates against B if:

(a) on the grounds of the religion or belief of B or of any other person except A (whether or not it is also A's religion or belief) A treats B less favourably than he treats or would treat other persons; or

(b) A applies a provision, criterion or practice which he applies or would apply equally to persons not of the same religion or belief as B, but:

(i) which puts or would put persons of the same religion or belief as B at a particular disadvantage when compared with other persons,

(ii) which puts B at that disadvantage, and

(iii) which he cannot show to be a proportionate means of achieving a legitimate aim.

If B has brought proceedings, and is discriminated against on that basis, then there is a claim in victimisation, as under the sex and race legislation—reg. 4. There is also a claim for harassment under reg. 5 if A, on the grounds of religion or belief, engages in unwanted conduct which has the effect or purpose of violating B's dignity or creating an intimidating, hostile, degrading, humiliating, or offensive environment for B, and it is reasonable to regard it as such.

The Regulations apply in similar circumstances to the operation of the SDA 1975 and the RRA 1976. So it covers, for example, discrimination relating to offers of employment, terms of employment, transfer, training and other benefits, and dismissal—see reg. 6. Likewise, under reg. 7, there is a defence of 'genuine occupational requirement' (GOR) similar to that of 'genuine occupational qualification' in the earlier legislation. Where being of a particular religion or belief is a genuine *and determining* requirement for the job, even if the employer does not have an ethos based on religion or belief, he will have a defence—reg. 7(2). Where he does have such an ethos, however, there is no necessity for a determining requirement, so long as it is genuine—reg. 7(3). The latter category would seem to cover, for example, churches and denominational schools.

There are two exceptions to the Regulations. The first is to safeguard national security (reg. 24), and the second is where positive action is undertaken in order to redress previous religious imbalance (reg. 25).

10.13 Discrimination on the grounds of sexual orientation

The Employment Equality (Sexual Orientation) Regulations 2003 (SI 2003 No. 1661) give protection against discrimination on the grounds of sexual orientation on the same model as the above Regulations on religion and belief, and so we will not rehearse the detail here except to consider the definition of 'sexual orientation' for the purposes of the Regulations. (See generally, Oliver, (2004) 33 ILJ 1.) Regulation 2 states that 'sexual orientation' means sexual orientation towards:

(a) persons of the same sex;

(b) persons of the opposite sex; or

(c) persons of the same sex and of the opposite sex.

The definition thus covers heterosexuals, homosexuals, and bisexuals, but seemingly not those without any sexual orientation. However, it goes wider than that in that it is not necessarily the applicant's orientation that need be the ground of discrimination. In this way, the Regulations resemble the RRA 1976 rather than the SDA 1975. Indeed, homophobic abuse of a person known by the discriminator not in fact to be gay may still come within the Regulations, according to the Court of Appeal in *English* v *Thomas Sanderson* (2009)—see Eastwood, (2009) 38 ILJ 222; Connolly, (2009) 68 CLJ 265.

Neither was it intended to cover discrimination on the grounds of taste or preferences other than orientation, such as a liking for sado-masochism. However, the Administrative Court took the view in *R (Amicus—MSF section)* v *Secretary of State for Trade and Industry* (2004) that sexual orientation also included its manifestation in the form of sexual behaviour.

For the general approach to be adopted by the courts in considering the Regulations, see *R (Amicus—MSF section)* v *Secretary of State for Trade & Industry* (2007).

10.14 Discrimination on grounds of age

The final stage of the UK Government's implementation of the requirements of the EU Equal Treatment Framework Directive was the Employment Equality (Age Discrimination) Regulations 2006 (SI 2006 No. 1031). The model, with some exceptions, is very closely that of the Regulations on sexual orientation and religion and belief already considered and will not be rehearsed here. However, there are some important differences. For example, under the Regulations on age:

(a) A discriminates against B if he treats B less favourably than he treats or would treat other persons because B has not carried out an instruction to discriminate, or because B complains to A about the instruction—reg. 5;

(b) it is possible to have a defence of justification for direct discrimination (where the employer is able to show that there is a proportionate means of achieving a legitimate aim by such discrimination, a defence allowed elsewhere only for indirect discrimination)—see reg. 3(1). This is because age will be a relevant factor justifying discrimination in many more instances than in other heads of discrimination; (See the decision of the Court of Appeal in *Royce plc* v *Unite the Union* (2009)—selection criteria for redundancy including length of service not discriminatory. However, it is important to bear in mind the balance between the legitimate business interests of the employer and the disparate impact on the employee—see the decisions of the EAT in *Loxley* v *BAE Systems Land Systems (Munitions and Ordnance) Ltd* (2008); *MacCulloch* v *Imperial Chemical Industries plc* (2008); and the commentary by Wynn-Evans, (2009) 38 ILJ 113.)

(c) it is not unlawful to discriminate in order to comply with other statutory requirements—reg. 27;

(d) when drawing a comparison between the claimant and a comparator, the latter need merely belong to the same 'group', and need not be of exactly the same age, for obvious reasons—reg. 3. However, the term is not defined except to identify it as referring to a particular age or 'range' of ages—reg. 3(3)(a).

The Regulations contain an important, specific example of age discrimination which is not unlawful, namely where applicants for a job under a contract of employment are already over the normal retiring age or, where there is none, over 65, or who will be in six months time—reg. 7(5). Regulation 30 has the effect that to dismiss employees in this category is not unlawful on grounds of age, and this has proved to be very controversial. (See further Chapter 7 above.) Many people who reach the DRA wish to continue working, for a variety of reasons, including of course financial, personal, and social. The feeling of discontent with that continued existence of the DRA, even though it would seem to be manifestly inconsistent with the spirit of the age discrimination legislative principle, resulted in the famous Heyday case (*R (on the application of Age UK)* v *Secretary of State for Business, Innovation and Skills* (2009)) when the High Court held that the DRA was still lawful, even though Blake J was of the opinion that the DRA of 65 could no longer be justified. Employer confidence was a social policy factor that was important to take into account, and the Regulations had not been unlawful when they were introduced in 2006. It is clear he had in mind the likely change in the law that will occur following the Government's own review which was due to be completed in 2011 but which was brought forward to 2010. (See further Connolly, (2009) 38 ILJ 233.)

The Regulations apply to employees, but not to the wider categories of workers, such as partners—see the EAT's decision in *Seldon* v *Clarkson Wright & Jakes* (2009).

SELECTED READING

Connolly, M. (2009), 'Rethinking Discrimination', (2009) 38 ILJ 149

Doyle, B. (2005), *Disability Discrimination: Law and Practice,* 5th edn, Bristol: Jordan Publishing Ltd

Fredman, S. and Spencer, S. (2004), *Age as an Equality Issue*, Oxford: Oxford University Press

Manfredi, S. and Vickers, L. (2009), 'Retirement and Age Discrimination: Managing Retirement in Higher Education', (2009) 38 ILJ 343

Monaghan, K. (2005), *Blackstone's Guide to the Disability Discrimination Legislation*, Oxford: Oxford University Press

Oliver, H. (2004), 'Sexual Orientation Discrimination: Perceptions, Definitions and Genuine Occupational Requirements', (2004) 33 ILJ 1

Painter, R. W. and Holmes, A. E. (2010), *Cases and Materials on Employment Law*, 8th edn, Oxford: Oxford University Press, chs 5 and 6

Rubenstein, M. (2004), *Discrimination: The New Law: A Guide to the New Regulations on Race, Religion or Belief, Sexual Orientation and Disability,* London: LexisNexis

Vickers, L. (2008), *Religious Freedom, Religious Discrimination and the Workplace*, Oxford: Hart Publishing

11

Equal pay and family rights

SUMMARY

This chapter examines first the earliest statutory sex discrimination protection for workers, namely the Equal Pay Act 1970, which gives protection for all discrimination on grounds of sex in contracts of employment, not just in pay. The history behind the legislation is examined and also its practical effect. Then the scheme of the Act is explained, and the various ways in which a claimant can found a claim are explored. After looking at the avenues open to an employer to mount a defence to such a claim, matters concerned with making a claim are considered. Finally on equal pay, protection afforded by EU law is explored.

Following this, various legislative rights supporting the family with regard to employment are considered, namely those relating to maternity and parenting, including adoption.

IMPORTANT NOTE

Should the reader be approaching this chapter before reading the previous chapter on discrimination law, attention is drawn to the Important Note which appears following the chapter summary, on p. 231. The reader is referred to the Online Resource Centre at **www.oxfordtextbooks.co.uk/ orc/honeyball11e/.**

11.1 Equal pay

11.1.1 Introduction

The aim of the Equal Pay Act 1970, as stated in its preamble, is to 'prevent discrimination as regards terms and conditions of employment between men and women'. It is mainly intended to eliminate the clearly lower pay which has been given to women for centuries, and is the first legal embodiment of the equal pay principle which became TUC policy in 1888, was the subject of a Royal Commission in 1944–46, and has been ILO policy for decades. In the 1970s this became more pressing; nearly 40 per cent of the labour force was female and more than half the women between the ages of 16 and 59 were in work. The Equal Pay Act 1970 also represents Britain's enactment of the directly enforceable obligation originally contained in art. 119 of the Treaty of Rome, equal pay for equal work. (This article was later renumbered to be art. 141 (art. 141 EC) until December 2009 when on the Treaty of Lisbon coming into effect, it became art. 157 of the Treaty on the Functioning of the European Union (art. 157 TFEU).) The courts have on several occasions referred cases to the ECJ for interpretation of the principle in the European legislation, although the effect on construction of the Act is rarely settled.

The Equal Pay Act 1970 was brought into force on 29 December 1975 (giving employers a five-year transitional period), but was immediately amended by the SDA 1975. Together these two statutes are intended to form one code (see e.g. *Shields* v *E. Coomes (Holdings) Ltd* (1978); *Jenkins* v *Kingsgate (Clothing Productions) Ltd (No. 2)* (1981)). The borderline between the two Acts is, however, a potent cause of confusion and some injustice, and in many respects it would have been more efficient to have but one enactment (see *Oliver* v *J. P. Malnick & Co. (No. 2)* (1984)). The EOC has occasionally called for this, and the CEHR may also do so.

Some matters relating to discrimination during employment, such as promotion, transfer and non-contractual benefits, as we have seen, come within the SDA 1975 while the Equal Pay Act 1970 relates solely to what is gained by way of contract (and, as such, is a claim in contract rather than a statutory tort—see *City of Newcastle upon Tyne* v *Allan* (2005)), although this extends beyond pay mentioned in its title to such elements as bonuses, concessionary coal and mortgage repayment allowances (see *NCB* v *Sherwin* (1978); *Sun Alliance and London Insurance Ltd* v *Dudman* (1978)). (See too Chapter 10 above for a discussion of protection given to part-time workers in regard to, *inter alia*, discrimination related to their contracts.) The terms of the earlier statute are somewhat narrower than the SDA 1975 since the Equal Pay Act 1970 does not prohibit discrimination against married persons or, on the face of it, indirect discrimination. Although primarily introduced to promote equality for women, both Acts are open to applicants of either sex. For the sake of convenience, the applicant will be here assumed to be female.

The Equal Pay Act 1970 was amended in 1984. The amendments were introduced after the ECJ ruled that the 1970 Act did not satisfy the requirement that 'the principle of equal pay for men and women…means for the same work and for work to which equal value is attributed, the elimination of all discrimination on grounds of sex with regard to all aspects and conditions of remuneration' (*Commission of the European Communities* v *United Kingdom* (1984); see Shaw, (1984) 47 MLR 348; Napier, [1984] CLJ 40).

The scope of the Equal Pay Act 1970 extends not only to employees but also to all who are 'employed under a contract of apprenticeship or a contract personally to execute any work or labour' (s. 1(6)(a)), and specifically covers Crown service (s. 1(8)). The ECJ made it clear in *Allonby* v *Accrington & Rossendale College* (2004) that rights under art. 157 TFEU (ex art. 141 EC) are to cover 'workers', but the definition in s. 1(6)(a) is probably wide enough to satisfy that. By virtue of s. 1(6A) the Act now covers office-holders since 2005. (See on *Allonby*, Fredman, (2004) 33 ILJ 281.) There is no qualifying period. The Act and Regulations are complex and are now surrounded by much difficult case law, but the CEHR has published a Code of Practice on Equal Pay to guide interested parties in this area.

Although the Equal Pay Act 1970 applies only to discrimination based on sex, it is possible to bring proceedings for equal pay based on race under the RRA 1976 (see e.g. *Wakeman* v *Quick Corporation* (1999)).

11.1.2 **Effect of the Act**

Although there has been some improvement since the 1970s as a result of the legislation, the relative position of men's and women's pay appears to be only marginally better now than then. The latest statistics show that the median weekly pay for female employees working full time was £426 and for male employees working full time, £531. The rate of increase in women's pay is faster than that of men at 3.5 per cent per annum compared with 1.8 per cent for men (2009 Annual Survey of Hours and Earnings, National Statistics). Some commentators have taken the view that these disparities are in part due to direct discrimination. It may be, however, that the figures are not quite as bad as they initially appear, because the removal of discrimination would leave women's earnings substantially lower than men's. This is for a number of reasons, although it should be remembered that while some of these reasons do not betray discrimination on an employer's part, they may reflect discrimination rooted in societal attitudes. For example, it is still much more likely that the mother rather than the father will be considered as the natural parent to look after the child in the pre-school years.

The work that men and women do differs markedly. Twice as many men as women are self-employed. Of these, more men work full-time and women part-time. This is a discrepancy which is likely to grow as more and more people become self-employed. There are still some occupations that are predominantly single-sexed. Most obviously the construction industry and the 'caring professions' are populated by single-sex workforces. This is clearly important when one considers that the caring professions are accounting for close to one-third of all female employment.

If disparities in pay occur for these reasons, it may be thought that a possible cause is the sex of those doing the work. Likewise with the fact that women tend to work lower in the hierarchy then men. However, this may partly be due to the fact that women have career breaks due to child-bearing, and often return to part-time work which tends to be lower paid and lower graded.

The proportion of women in part-time work is clearly an important factor in lower pay rates compared with men. About half of all married women in work are on part-time work, and perhaps surprisingly, a quarter of all non-married women. Only about 4 per cent of men with dependent children, and 9 per cent without, work part-time according to the Labour Force Survey of the Office for National Statistics. Not only does part-time work result in less pay, at lower rates (which is indirectly discriminatory) but clearly can result in slower occupational advancement.

11.1.3 The equality clause

By Equal Pay Act 1970, s. 1(1), an 'equality clause' is implied into the contract of every woman who is employed on 'like work'; 'work rated as equivalent' or 'work of equal value' with a man, at the same establishment, or at an establishment where similar terms and conditions are applied. This means that if any aspect of the woman's conditions is or becomes less favourable to the woman than a term of a similar kind in the man's contract, the term is modified so as to be as favourable; if there is no corresponding term, the contract is deemed to include one (s. 1(2)). Thus, if men have a right to four weeks' holiday and women to three, and the women are found to be engaged on like work, their entitlement must be increased to four. If women have no right to holidays at all, a term to that effect must be inserted. However, it is necessary to be able to compare oneself with a man in order to found a claim.

Where this is not possible, as with pregnant women who are not comparable either to men or women at work once they have begun maternity leave, equal pay cannot be claimed. The ECJ has held time and again that the comparison that used to be made with sick employees is unsustainable. This means that a claim that maternity pay is less under an employee's contract than disability pay given to employees who are sick cannot succeed, according to the Northern Ireland Court of Appeal in *Todd* v *Eastern Health and Social Services Board* (1997). This seems a strange result, and one which has been heavily criticised (see Rubenstein, [1997] IRLR 377), but is in fact logical given the legislation and art. 11(3) of the Pregnant Workers Directive, Council Directive (EC) 92/85, which requires only that maternity pay be no lower than *statutory* sick pay (see *Gillespie* v *Northern Health and Social Services Board (No. 2)* (1997) decided with *Todd*). It is also consistent with the Court of Appeal's decision in *Clark* v *Secretary of State for Employment* (1997) that an employee absent from work on maternity leave was not 'incapable of work because of sickness' for the purposes of construing what has now become ERA 1996, s. 88(1).

The applicant for equal pay may choose with whom she is to be compared (*Ainsworth* v *Glass Tubes and Components Ltd* (1977)), but the search for a precise comparator has proved very difficult in those areas where women are generally underpaid, and for which the statute was most needed. In particular, employment in many offices, textile, catering and retail businesses is the preserve of women, so that no man is employed on like work. This problem had led to the desire of women to compare their wages with a man who was no longer employed at the time of a tribunal application, and this important issue was resolved eventually by the ECJ in *Macarthys Ltd* v *Smith* (1980). The woman applicant was a stockroom manageress who sought to compare her wages with her predecessor in the post. The Court of Appeal restrictively interpreted the English statute: its use of the present tense in their view precluded the applicant's desired comparison. The European Court, however, decided that the applicant could compare herself with the predecessor under art. 157 TFEU (ex art. 141 EC). It stated that the concept of equal pay '…is not exclusively concerned with the nature of the service in question and may not be restricted by requirements of contemporaneity' and the EAT extended this by allowing comparison with a successor, in *Diocese of Hallam Trustee* v *Connaughton* (1996). Nevertheless, the decision in *Hallam* was held by a later EAT to be *per incuriam* and wrongly decided in *Walton Centre for Neurology and Neurosurgery NHS Trust* v *Bewley* (2008) in that it had misinterpreted a passage in the judgment by the ECJ in *Macarthys* to be its own, rather than from the Commission's submissions which it had specifically rejected.

One particular difficulty to which the failure to allow hypothetical comparisons gives rise is that the Act is restricted to giving redress only in cases where there should be similarity of treatment, not where there is unfairness because there is not dissimilar treatment. A woman who has greater experience than her male comparator in the same position may, in all justice, be entitled to more than he is paid. But all she is entitled to in law is not to be treated less favourably than he, not in the sense that she is entitled to be paid what he will receive when he has the same level of experience, but in the sense that she is entitled only to receive what he is now being paid. (See the Court of Appeal's decision in *Evesham* v *North Hertfordshire Health Authority* (2000).) This highlights one of the major deficiencies of the Act, in that in establishing equality it seeks to treat people of equal worth equally, rather than to treat those of unequal worth unequally in a fair and proportionate manner. (See further, Honeyball, 'The Principle of Non-Discrimination as a Fundamental Value', in Economides *et al.* (eds), *Fundamental Values* (Oxford: Hart Publishing, 2000), ch. 4.)

The comparator must be in the same employment as the applicant. Under s. 1(6) this means at the same establishment or where common terms and conditions (i.e. terms and conditions substantially comparable on a broad basis: *British Coal Corporation* v *Smith* (1996)) are observed either generally or for employees of relevant classes, and not just between the employee and her comparator, for that would require something that is the very basis of the applicant's claim—that a common term or terms are missing (see *Leverton* v *Clwyd County Council* (1989). See too *Robertson* v *DEFRA* (2005); Steele, (2005) 34 ILJ 338). The House of Lords thought in *Leverton* that it might be sensible and rational, for geographical or historical (rather than sex-related) reasons, for an employer to operate separate different employment requirements at different establishments, but of course, this is not necessarily so. (See further Mead, (1989) 18 ILJ 119.) The Court of Session in *South Ayrshire Council* v *Morton* (2002) decided that it is not necessary for the comparator to have the same employer as the applicant in circumstances such as in that case where both fell under the same national collective agreement. (See too *South Tyneside MBC* v *Anderson* (2007); *Galloway Council* v *North* (2009).)

The Act requires that a comparison be made between respective terms of the applicant's and comparator's contracts of employment. The issue arose in *Hayward* v *Cammell Laird Shipbuilders Ltd (No. 2)* (1988) whether this was the case when there was, taking the contract in the round, no disadvantage to the applicant, or indeed even an overall greater benefit. The House of Lords held that the Act must be construed literally, and that a term-by-term comparison must be made, even if this resulted in leapfrogging claims. This approach has its merits but, as Evelyn Ellis has pointed out, may create difficulties where the same subject-matter is treated in wholly different ways in the applicant's and comparator's contracts. This is particularly the case in equal value claims where *ex hypothesi* there need be no congruity whatsoever between the jobs or contracts compared, she argues (see Ellis, (1988) 51 MLR 781). It also enables some claimants to pick and choose between different aspects of their remuneration package to enable them to have an overall advantage compared to any of their comparators.

It is important to bear in mind throughout that an equal pay claim is concerned solely with sex-based discrimination in relation to terms of the contract of employment. So, even if discrimination concerned aspects of pay, other than in contractual terms, the claim cannot be brought as an equal pay claim but as a sex discrimination claim. So, where an employee is denied a settlement to an equal pay claim, and this amounts to discrimination, this is a sex discrimination, not equal pay, claim. (See the decision of the EAT in *Hartlepool Borough Council* v *Llewellyn* (2009).)

11.1.4 **Like work**

'Like work' is defined in s. 1(4) as where '[the applicant's] work and [the comparators'] is of the same or broadly similar nature, and the difference (if any) between the things she does and the things they do are not of practical importance in relation to the terms and conditions of employment'. This definition is generally a matter of degree (e.g. *Durrant v N. Yorkshire AHA* (1979)), and it was suggested in early cases, such as *Capper Pass Ltd v Lawton* (1977), that the words should be interpreted broadly in order to make the Act workable. Employment tribunals were advised not to undertake too minute an examination, or be constrained to find work to be dissimilar because of insubstantial differences. Thus, there was like work between a female cook who made ten to 20 lunches for directors in their dining room, and two assistant male chefs who provided rather more meals in the works canteen. The crucial point was that the basic processes were the same. Thus, it is important to look at what is done, rather than when it is done. However, the time during which the work is done may mean that there is added responsibility and this factor may mean that the employee and the comparator are not employed on like work. In *Thomas v National Coal Board* (1987) this was held to be so when the comparison was made between day and night shifts. The Court of Appeal gave general guidance in *Shields v E. Coomes (Holdings) Ltd* (1978), where the applicant was employed as a counterhand in the respondent's betting shop. She was paid 62p per hour, while the men received £1.06, but the employers alleged that there was a difference in duties which justified the large variation in pay, for by contract the men were expected to help in case of trouble. This was not enough. The ET should first ask whether the work was the same or broadly similar, then, using its industrial experience, examine the nature and extent of any differences, and especial emphasis should be placed on the frequency or otherwise with which differences occurred in practice. In fact, there was no evidence here that a man ever had to deal with a disturbance or incidents of violence, and every indication that the women had their own ways of dealing with difficult customers. Indeed, Lord Denning said: 'He may have been a small nervous man who would not say "boo to a goose". She may have been as fierce and formidable as a battle axe.'

In *British Leyland UK Ltd v Powell* (1978) the EAT formulated the proper test as 'whether the two employments would have been placed into the same category on an evaluation exercise', and Phillips J took a similar approach in the complex case of *Electrolux Ltd v Hutchinson* (1977). Men and women worked on the same track in the manufacture of refrigerators and freezers, but while all the men were paid on grade 10 rates, 599 out of the 600 women received rather lower wages in class 01. The company argued that the men had additional contractual obligations in that they had to transfer to totally different tasks on demand, and work overtime as and when required. The EAT focused on how frequently the men in fact did other work, how often they were required to work on Sunday and what kind of work they did in these unsocial hours. They came to the conclusion that in reality the work was like work. In *Eaton Ltd v Nuttall* (1977), however, a male production scheduler handling 1,200 items worth between £5 and £1,000 each and a woman scheduler handling 2,400 items below £2.50 were not engaged on broadly similar work—for an error on the part of the man would be of much greater consequence. Handling substantial sums of money may prevent work being like, as may involvement on heavier work.

11.1.5 **Work rated as equivalent**

A second way by which an equality clause can be inserted under s. 1(2) is where there has been a job evaluation study rating the applicant's and her comparator's work as equivalent. Section 1(5) states:

A woman is to be regarded as employed on work rated as equivalent with that of any men if, but only if, her job and their job have been given an equal value, in terms of the demand made on a worker under various headings (for instance effort, skill, decision), on a study undertaken with a view to evaluating in those terms the jobs to be done by all or any of the employees in an undertaking or group of undertakings...

A job evaluation scheme is thus an alternative route to equal pay and attempts to be as scientific and objective as possible. Its criteria are commonly agreed between management and unions and are of particular application to white collar staff. Yet its limitations must be appreciated, since it classifies jobs not the people who fill them. It must be followed by a subjective merit assessment of the individual's qualities. A job evaluation study merely provides a building block to indicate the underlying structure of wages on which individual variations may then be built.

The chief types of job evaluation schemes generally in use are:

(a) Job ranking where each job is considered as a whole and is then given a ranking in relation to all other jobs.

(b) Paired comparisons, where points are awarded on a comparison between pairs of jobs and then a rank order produced.

(c) Job classification, whereby all other jobs are compared with benchmark grades.

(d) Points assessment, the most common system, which breaks down each job into a number of factors—for example, skills, responsibility, physical and mental requirements and working conditions.

(e) Factor comparison, which differs from points assessment only in that it uses a limited number of factors based on key jobs with fair wages (see discussion in *Eaton Ltd* v *Nuttall* (1977) and ACAS job evaluation information (2008).)

The main legal questions concern the meaning of, and the challenges to, job evaluation study, and the necessity of putting schemes into effect when completed.

According to *Eaton Ltd* v *Nuttall* (1977) the subsection requires 'a study thorough in analysis and capable of impartial application'. Further, 'it should be possible by applying the study to arrive at the position of a particular employee at a particular point in a particular salary grade without taking other matters into account'. It must not require management to take a subjective view as to the grading of an employee. The scheme must therefore be analytical, and comparisons must be made under the various headings set out in s. 1(5). Relative weightings or 'whole-job' comparisons are thus inadequate for this purpose, according to the Court of Appeal in *Bromley* v *H. & J. Quick Ltd* (1988) (see further Mead, (1988) 17 ILJ 244).

The study can only be challenged if there is 'a fundamental error in it...or a plain error on the face of the record'. A broad attack was attempted in *England* v *Bromley LBC* (1978) where the widely used 'London Scheme' was adopted to grade the respondent council's employees, but it was adjusted for 'special factors'. The male applicant clerks received the same number of points in the main scheme as their female comparators, but were awarded less for 'special factors'. Phillips J closed the door to challenge saying: 'What the claimant cannot do is to base his claim on the footing that if the evaluation study had been carried out differently...he would be entitled to the relief claimed. He must take the study as it is.' (See also *Arnold* v *Beecham Group Ltd* (1982).) The single exception is where the factors used in making the evaluation are in themselves discriminatory.

In *O'Brien* v *Sim-Chem Ltd* (1980) the court had to determine whether, once a study had been carried out, it must be implemented. This depended on the meaning and effect of the appropriate enforcement provision which modifies the contract of employment where 'any term.... determined by the rating of the work' becomes less favourable. The appellants, all women employees of the respondent company, had been informed of a new grading and appropriate salary range as a result of a job evaluation study carried out by awarding points for each element of their job. All that remained was to complete a merit assessment of each individual after which their exact pay would be decided. Before this could be done, however, the Government announced a 'voluntary incomes policy' which discouraged such increases, and the appellants were never actually paid in accordance with the new structure. The question for the court was thus whether any 'term' had indeed been 'determined by the rating of the work', as required by s. 1(5) for the implementation of the job evaluation scheme. Cumming-Bruce LJ in the Court of Appeal thought that the word 'determined' must be given its 'normal causative meaning', and since here there was no contractual condition actually brought about or effected by the study, it was not compulsory. The House of Lords, however, overturned this decision. Examining the structure of the Act, Lord Russell of Killowen said:

> Once a job evaluation study has been undertaken and has resulted in a conclusion that the job of the woman has been evaluated under s. 1(5) as of equal value with the job of the man, then the comparison of the respective terms of their contracts of employment is made feasible and a decision can be made...

This is much more in line with the EC principle of 'equal pay for work of equal value' than the approach taken by the Court of Appeal, which would also make a job evaluation study defeasible on the whim of management. According to *Arnold* v *Beecham Group Ltd* (1982), however, a job evaluation study is not completed unless and until the parties who agreed to carry out the study have accepted its validity.

Section 1(5) applies where the work of the claimant and that of her comparator has been rated as 'equivalent'. However, it would clearly be contrary to the purposes of the provision if she were not able to bring a claim because her job had been rated as being of greater value than that of her comparator. Nevertheless, it has taken litigation to make this the accepted position—see the decisions of the ECJ in *Murphy* v *Bord Telecom Eirann* (1988), and the Court of Appeal in *Redcar and Cleveland Borough Council* v *Bainbridge* (2007).

In similar vein, if the difference in the comparison in the job evaluation study between the jobs of the applicant and comparator is marginal, it is open to the tribunal nevertheless to find that they are equivalent, according to the Court of Appeal in *Hovell* v *Ashford and St Peter's Hospitals NHS Trust* (2009). On the other hand equal means just that—not nearly equal. It is thus a matter of degree.

11.1.6 **Equal value claims**

As already mentioned, since the Equal Pay (Amendment) Regulations 1983 (SI 1983 No. 1794) amended the Equal Pay Act 1970, an applicant may request a job evaluation study to be carried out by an independent expert appointed from a panel nominated by ACAS if hers is not like work or work rated as equivalent. The tribunal is not required to refer the case to an expert and may determine the issue itself—see Equal Pay Act 1970 (Amendment) Regulations 2004 (SI 2004 No. 2352).

The complaint must, however, be stopped where there has already been a job evaluation study which has accorded different values to the work of the applicant and comparator and there are no reasonable grounds for determining that the study discriminated on the grounds of sex. This may happen at any time up to the final hearing (*Dibro Ltd* v *Hore* (1990)). If there has been a job evaluation study involving workers in another undertaking or group of undertakings, that study cannot prevent an equal value claim from proceeding, even if the work and the pay structures are the same, according to the Northern Ireland Court of Appeal in *McAuley* v *Eastern Health and Social Services Board* (1991).

The burden of proof that there has been discrimination lies on the employee, and the test is whether there is good reason to suppose that any comparative value set by the system on any demand or characteristic ought to have been given a more favourable value if those determining the values had not consciously or unconsciously been influenced by consideration of the sex of those on whom the demands would chiefly be made. There would be sufficient reason if a traditionally female attribute were undervalued (*Neil* v *Ford Motor Co. Ltd* (1984)).

It is for the applicant to choose with whom she wishes to be compared. If there has been no job evaluation scheme in relation to them both, and they are not engaged on like work, an equal value claim may be pursued even if there are other male employees of whom that is not true, according to the House of Lords in *Pickstone* v *Freemans plc* (1988). The importance of this has been thought to be that it prevents employers from employing a token male on the same work as potential women claimants in order to avoid the effect of the Act. However, as Peter Schofield remarked, one wonders how likely a scenario that is. He saw the significance of the decision in the fact that it opened up the potential for leapfrogging claims (see Schofield, (1988) 17 ILJ 241).

Provided that the study is not discriminatory, there is no limit on the time within which that study may provide a defence. It would, however, be surprising if the study was based on a set of job duties which had been superseded.

If the case does not fall at this first hurdle, the tribunal must invite the parties to 'apply for an adjournment for the purpose of seeking to reach a settlement of the claim' but not in order to allow the employer to carry out the job evaluation (*Avon County Council* v *Foxall* (1989)). If the conciliation procedures fail, and the tribunal has reasonable grounds for determining that the work is of equal value and decides to refer the case to an expert (see *Sheffield Metropolitan District Council* v *Siberry* (1989)), the tribunal must require an expert's report in writing, stating particulars of the precise question on which he is required to report and the persons with reference to whom the question arises. However, the finding of the report is not conclusive or binding on the tribunal. (See *Tennants Textile Colours Ltd* v *Todd* (1989).)

The applicant is still able to choose her comparator and there is no provision to change this if the expert finds a more appropriate man.

The expert has an inquisitorial function, but must take account of all representations made to him and, before drawing up his report, must produce and send to the parties a written summary of information supplied and representations made and invite further representation on this basis. A brief account of such representations must be included in his report together with the reasons for his conclusion. The expert may not concern himself with the material factor defence (see below) unless it is specified in the reference. He labours under a general duty to 'act at all times fairly', and should produce the report in 42 days after which time the tribunal (whose proceedings are adjourned in the meantime) may ask for an explanation of delay and information as to progress. His task is facilitated by tribunal rules that the tribunal may require any person whom it believes may have relevant information to furnish it and to produce any documents which are in his possession, custody, or power. The tribunal will send such material to the expert. He has no power, however, to require a person to give oral evidence before him, nor to gain access to the workplace. The latter may prove a significant handicap.

Copies of the report must be sent to all parties, and before accepting it in evidence, the tribunal must hear representations and decide whether the expert has complied with the procedural requirements, the conclusion contained in the report is one which, taking due account of the information supplied and representations made to the expert, could not reasonably have been reached, or whether for some other material reason the report is unsatisfactory. The report must not be excluded merely because of 'disagreement with a conclusion that the applicant's work is or is not of equal value or the reasoning leading to that conclusion'. If the report is excluded for one or more of these three valid reasons, the tribunal should appoint another expert. In deciding this preliminary issue of admissibility, the tribunal may 'permit any person to give evidence upon, to call witnesses and to question any witnesses upon any matter relevant thereto'. The expert is a compellable witness in such a hearing.

If and when the report is accepted in evidence, the tribunal holds a hearing at which the expert may be cross-examined on his conclusions. The Rules allow any party on giving reasonable notice to 'call one witness to give expert evidence on the question on which the tribunal has required the [official] expert to prepare a report', but no other person 'may give evidence upon or question any witness upon any matter of fact upon which a conclusion in the report of the [official] expert is based' save in respect of the genuine material factor defence. The expert's report is not conclusive but it is rare for a tribunal to reject its conclusions.

11.1.7 Genuine material difference

The employer has a defence if he can prove that a difference in contractual treatment was genuinely due to a material difference (other than sex) between her case and his (s. 1(3)). This demonstrates that the Act is aimed at differences in terms due to sex alone, for it would be a strange result if there was no possibility of different wages to recognise that a man (although employed on a similar job) in fact deserved more than the woman because of personal qualities or qualifications.

It is quite possible for something to amount to a genuine material difference even if that same factor did not amount to a difference making the jobs of the applicant and her comparator unequal, according to the EAT in *Christie* v *John E. Haith Ltd* (2003). Michael Rubenstein sees force in the contrary view. He writes (at [2003] IRLR 637): 'It is illogical that a difference...should not be sufficiently important to make two jobs of unequal value and yet the same difference should be treated as sufficient to negate the equal pay claim of applicants employed on work of equal value'.

What has to be shown?

The courts ask two basic questions (but *cf.* Kilpatrick, (1994) 23 ILJ 311). First, has the employer shown that any variation was genuinely due to (i.e. caused by) a material difference between the two? Secondly, has he shown that the material difference is genuinely due to a reason other than sex? Apart from the burden on the employee to show in indirect discrimination cases that there has been disproportionate adverse impact (see *Nelson* v *Carillion Services Ltd* (2003)) the burden of proof is on the employer throughout—see *Byrne and others* v *Financial Times Ltd* (1991); *Financial Times Ltd* v *Byrne and others (No. 2)* (1992). At first it was thought that a heavier burden than usually demanded in civil cases here rested on the employer, but this heresy was scotched in *National Vulcan Engineering Insurance Group Ltd* v *Wade* (1978). It is not, however, enough that the employers did not intend to discriminate (*Jenkins* v *Kingsgate Clothing Ltd (No. 2)* (1981); *McPherson* v *Rathgael Centre for Children and Young People* (1991)), but a genuine mistake may suffice according to the EAT in *Tyldesley* v *TML Plastics Ltd* (1996). Nor is it adequate merely to show that the reason for the disparate treatment was not due to sex. It must also be shown that the difference was caused by a *material* factor, and that the material factor goes only so far as necessary to explain the disparate treatment—see for example the EAT's decision in *Cumbria County Council* v *Dow (No. 1)* (2008).

However, that does not necessarily mean that the factor is one that has to be justified, so long as it is not the difference of sex, the House of Lords held in *Strathclyde Regional Council* v *Wallace* (1998). That the variation between the woman's and the man's contract is material is an issue of causality not justification. In other words, materiality is an issue of the reason for the difference in treatment, not the excuse for it. The purpose of the legislation is to eliminate discrimination on the grounds of sex, not to eradicate all discrimination. To require an employer to show that the non sex-based reason for the disparate treatment was justified would be to interpret the Act in just this way. It is therefore enough to show that the reason for the variation was not grounded in sex. This would seem to be right, although Lord Browne-Wilkinson's further comment, that if the reasons for disparate treatment were based on sex nevertheless a defence of justification would be available, even for direct discrimination, seems to go too far, and was made *obiter*. However, the other four members of the House deciding the case agreed with him. The wording of s. 1(3) would not seem to justify this, as it extends the defence only to those situations where the material difference is not the difference of sex, but there are arguments that the section must be so seen in order to be consistent with the SDA 1975 and art. 157 TFEU (ex art. 141 EC).

A similar situation to that in the *Strathclyde* case arose in *Glasgow City Council* v *Marshall* (2000). In this case the House of Lords held that the reasoning in the earlier case applied not only where the employer showed that the reason for the discriminatory treatment was not sex-based but even where it was not shown what the reason for the discriminatory treatment was, other than an historical one. So long as the tribunal is satisfied that there is no *sex* discrimination, the claim fails. The legislation is not there to tackle discriminatory treatment but to outlaw sex discrimination. (See too the Court of Appeal's decision in *Armstrong* v *Newcastle upon Tyne NHS Hospital Trust* (2006).) However, the EAT has taken the view that this may be contrary to art. 157 TFEU (ex art. 141 EC)—see *Sharp* v *Caledonia Group Services Ltd* (2006). But see, too, the support of the EAT for the approach in *Armstrong* in *Middlesborough BC* v *Surtees* (2007). One difficulty with the suggestion that objective justification is only in issue if the employer cannot show that sex was not a factor (i.e. the lack of objective justification for a non-sex-based factor is not the law's concern) is that this seems to be inapplicable to indirect discrimination as, by definition, it is not discrimination based on sex—see Rubenstein, [2007] IRLR 838. (On the inclusion of indirect discrimination in the Equal Pay Act 1970, see below.)

Beyond the personal equation

The Court of Appeal placed a vital, but temporary, restriction on the concept of genuine material difference in *Clay Cross (Quarry Services) Ltd* v *Fletcher* (1979). The applicant, Mrs Fletcher, was a clerk earning £35 per week, but since the comparator male had received £43 per week in his existing job, Clay Cross paid him more in order to attract his services. They claimed the previous pay constituted a genuine material difference, but the court held that only 'the personal equation' might justify such discrimination, since the subsection went on to say that the distinction was 'between her case and his'. Here extrinsic market forces were in effect determining the rate for the job, and Lord Denning remarked that, 'an employer cannot avoid his obligations under the Act by saying: "I paid him more because he asked for more", or "I paid her less because she was willing to come for less".' To do so would render the statute virtually impotent. He went on: 'These are the very reasons why there was unequal pay before the statute.'

However, the House of Lords took a wider view in *Rainey* v *Greater Glasgow Health Board Eastern District* (1987). When a prosthetic fitting service was set up within the Scottish NHS, it was agreed that the prosthetists would be paid on the Medical Physics and Technicians pay scale, but in order to attract a sufficient number of experienced prosthetists from the private sector, they were offered the same pay as they had been receiving. Further, a different structure of increase was adopted. A woman complained that a man who had joined from the private sector was paid £2,790 more than she was for the same work. The Court of Session, with one dissentient, thought that the circumstances of the higher pay were sufficiently 'personal' to fall within s. 1(3), and were similar to the 'red circle' cases (see below). The House of Lords held that it was possible to go beyond the 'personal equation' and to look at all the relevant circumstances of the case. The materiality of the difference was present if it was significant and relevant, and to be a difference between the two cases it need not be one which is necessarily to be found by looking at their personal circumstances alone. Consideration of a person's case must necessarily involve consideration of all the circumstances of that case.

Although *Clay Cross* has long not been good law, as Hazel McLean showed ([1987] CLJ 224) Lord Denning had a point. The social subordination of women may lead to their being offered and accepting lower wages than men for the same work. If market forces are to be included in the concept of genuine materiality, that seems to undermine the purpose of the 1970 Act. However, as she also points out, the House of Lords, following the ECJ's decision in *Bilka-Kaufhaus GmbH* v *Weber von Hartz* (1987), required that the employer show objectively justified grounds for the difference in treatment. There must be a real need on the part of the business for the difference (a point underlined by the ECJ in a parallel decision concerning fixed-term workers—*Del Cerro Alonso* v *Osakidetza-Servicio Vasco de Salud* (2007)) and it is not enough to show that the reason for the difference was not discriminatory. This was later underlined by the ECJ in *Enderby* v *Frenchay Health Authority* (1994) (see Fredman, (1994) 23 ILJ 37; Cunningham, (2009) 38 ILJ 209). Nevertheless, that there must be a need for the difference does not mean that it need be the only possibility, according to the Court of Appeal in *Barry* v *Midland Bank* (1998). The House of Lords also makes it clear in *Rainey* that such reasons could include administrative efficiency in a concern not engaged in commerce or business. But perhaps the most significant aspect of the case is that, as Richard Townshend-Smith stated, the House of Lords' decision means that indirect discrimination, although not as such catered for in the Equal Pay Act 1970, is now equally applicable to equal pay claims (see Townshend-Smith, (1987) 16 ILJ 114). However, the House of Lords has made it clear that the Equal Pay Act 1970 is not to be interpreted as including the distinction between direct and indirect discrimination (see *Ratcliffe* v *North Yorkshire County Council* (1995); but cf. the House of Lords' later decision in *Strathclyde Regional Council* v *Wallace* (1998), when it was stated that this 'must not be carried too far'). In so doing, it narrowed significantly the scope of the s. 1(3) defence. Lord Slynn said that the fact that the employers paid women employees less than their male comparators because they were women constituted direct discrimination and *ex hypothesi* could not be shown to be justified on grounds 'irrespective of sex'. This is particularly important here because a male employee doing the same work would also have been paid the lower rate, but the employees as a whole were women and that meant that they were as a group paid less than if they had been men. Even in this situation, the House of Lords held, there was necessarily direct discrimination. (See further McColgan, (1995) 24 ILJ 368.)

Examples of differences

There are several distinct 'differences' which the courts have considered on many occasions. Greater length of service is clearly a material difference (*Capper Pass Ltd* v *Lawton* (1977)) but working at different times of the day is not (*Dugdale* v *Kraft Foods Ltd* (1977)). In *NAAFI* v *Varley* (1976) a distinction in hourly pay between workers based in London and the rather cheaper Nottingham area was held to be a genuine material difference. However, the fact that a union has agreed to a collective bargain that results in discriminatory impact when compared with the effect of the treatment of other employees is not sufficient to amount to a defence, according to the EAT in *British Airways plc* v *Grundy (No. 2)* (2008). Most controversy has surrounded treatment of part-time workers, protected earnings called 'red circles', and grading systems.

Part-time work

The treatment of part-timers was in the nature of a test for the Act because of the predominance of women in the part-time labour market, and some of the early cases did much to retard their progress towards equal pay. In *Handley v H. Mono Ltd* (1979), for example, a female machinist, who worked a basic 26-hour week, claimed an equal hourly rate with a man who worked 40 hours. It was conceded that they were engaged on like work, but the fact that the woman worked substantially fewer hours, was entitled to overtime rates earlier, and that all '26-hour workers' were paid at the same rate, together established a genuine material difference. Slynn J also referred to the different value of their contribution to the productivity of the company. In the case of part-time employees, machinery in the respondent's clothing factory laid idle. It was thus a less efficient method of business. In *Jenkins v Kingsgate (Clothing Productions) Ltd* (1981), however, the EAT took a more radical view holding that the employer has to show that the difference in pay between full-time male workers and part-time women is reasonably necessary in order to obtain some result which the employer desires for economic or other reasons. A bare statement to this effect by the employer was not enough, and the case was remitted to the tribunal to determine whether the difference in pay was indeed necessary in order to enable the employers to reduce absenteeism and to obtain maximum utilisation of their plant as claimed.

The House of Lords considered the position of part-timers in *Barry v Midland Bank plc* (1999). The case involved a security of employment agreement whereby redundant employees were paid a sum, based on their final salaries, to support them in the immediate period after redundancy, rather than as remuneration for past service. It was claimed this indirectly discriminated against part-time workers in that it did not take into account previous full-time service. The House of Lords disagreed. The purpose of the payment was relevant. Only earnings at the point of dismissal were relevant to this and, with all employees treated the same in this regard, there was no disparate treatment. In any event, the scheme was objectively justified. The decision has been criticised (see Rubenstein, [1999] IRLR 507) on the basis that the purpose of the treatment was considered relevant in considering whether there was less favourable treatment rather than being reserved to the issue of justification. It is difficult to see the force of this criticism. Examining what the subjective reasons for a scheme are, and whether those reasons can be objectively justified, are two quite different questions. (See further, Thomas, (2000) 29 ILJ 68.)

Red-circling

Earnings are 'red-circled' when jobs are regraded, or a long-serving employee is moved, and his pay protected at the previous rate in order to avoid breach of his contract, or perhaps industrial unrest. New employees performing the same function will, however, receive the normal lower rate for the grade. Very often the long-serving or sick employee is a man, and the grade in which he is placed is solely or mainly female. A good example of the phenomenon is *Snoxell and Davies v Vauxhall Motors Ltd* (1977). As part of a major company pay restructuring in 1970, designed partly to facilitate equal pay, the position of quality controller was downgraded but the males then in post had their wages protected in their inferior jobs. The claimant women who had been employed for many years as inspectors of machine parts sought equal pay with these men who were now doing a similar job. The EAT stated that the red circle was not a decisive defence: the correct approach entailed eliciting and analysing all the circumstances of the case, including the situation prior to the formation of the protected class. An employer could never establish a genuine material difference if past discrimination blatantly contributed to the now protected differential, as indeed it had in the *Snoxell* case. Phillips J, moreover, thought it desirable 'whenever possible for "red circles" to be phased out and eliminated'. Other relevant factors included 'whether [the red circle] group…is a closed group; whether the red circling has been the subject of negotiations with the representatives of the work people, and the views of the women taken into account; or whether the women are able equally with the men to transfer between the grades'. It is legitimate for a higher rate to continue to be paid where a man is transferred for reasons of illness or age. In *Methven and Mussolik* v *Cow Industrial Polymers Ltd* (1980) Dunn LJ emphasised that the issue was one of fact for tribunals who should not be mesmerised by the label 'red circle' (see also *Outlook Supplies Ltd* v *Penny* (1978), and *Avon & Somerset Police Authority* v *Emery* (1981)). However, once the reason for the difference in treatment has been removed, there is no continued justification for it. As such the courts will no longer treat the difference as material and genuine. In *Benveniste* v *University of Southampton* (1989) a woman university lecturer was appointed in times of financial constraint which later eased. Although the original reason that her pay was lower than her male comparator was not discriminatory, the university could not show that there was a difference which was material at the time of her claim. (See also *Barclays Bank plc* v *Kapur* (1991); and the commentary on both cases by Hazel McLean, (1991) 20 ILJ 61; *Fearnon* v *Smurfit Corrugated Cases (Lurgan) Ltd* (2009).) (See further on sex discrimination in collective agreements, Lester and Rose, (1991) 20 ILJ 163; Gay, (1989) 18 ILJ 63; Dickens *et al.*, *Tackling Sex Discrimination through Collective Bargaining* (London: HMSO, 1988).)

A particular difficulty arises where a re-grading or re-structuring pay exercise is undertaken, perhaps to avoid inherent sex discrimination, or for some other reason. This troubled the Court of Appeal in the practically highly-significant case of *Redcar & Cleveland Borough Council* v *Bainbridge; Surtees* v *Middlesbrough Borough Council* (2008). This involved wide-scale local government re-grading, whereupon several employees were required to take drops in pay. However, the effect was cushioned by being effected over a period of time. As such, any previous inequalities because of sex-based reasons were perpetuated whilst gradually being phased out. The Court of Appeal held that if the historical reason for the inequality was by way of direct sex discrimination, the gradual nature of the phase out was unlawful, but if it were indirect discrimination it could be objectively justified if proportionate to achieving a legitimate aim. But this would depend upon how much the employer knew of the discriminatory treatment before the phase out began and how much it did about it.

Grading systems

The courts have also experienced some difficulty in dealing with grading systems in a series of cases starting with *Waddington* v *Leicester Council for Voluntary Service* (1977). The applicant there was a female community worker who had responsibility for a male play leader. She was, however, paid some £400 less than he because she was on a different local authority pay scale. Phillips J stated: 'Where men and women are employed on like work, and the variation is in the rate of remuneration and the remuneration is fixed in accordance with a nationally or widely negotiated wage scale...there will usually be a strong case for saying that the case falls within s. 1(3).' While the scales are not conclusive, 'when one is dealing with nationally negotiated scales, in general use by local authorities, it seems unlikely that a problem caused by grading is very likely to give rise to a remedy under the Equal Pay Act'.

This case was approved by the Court of Appeal in *National Vulcan Engineering Insurance Group Ltd* v *Wade* (1978). The EAT had found fatal in the appellant's grading scheme the fact that 'the assignment of a particular individual, and therefore his remuneration, depended upon the personal assessment of the individual, which was of necessity a subjective judgement'. Lord Denning, however, overruling this decision took a much less interventionist stance; employers will have a defence under s. 1(3) provided only that any scheme is 'genuinely operated'. It was a matter of policy, since 'a grading scheme according to skill, ability and experience is an integral part of good business management...If it were to go forth that these grading systems are inoperative and operate against the Equal Pay Act, it would, I think, be disastrous for the ordinary running of efficient business'.

The defence in s. 1(3) in respect of like work and work rated as equivalent cases operates where there is a material difference between the man's case and the woman's but in equal value claims it is not necessary that there be a material difference between her case and his. However, after the House of Lords' decision in *Rainey*, there is no longer any significant practical difference between the two cases (see further Honeyball, *Sex, Employment and the Law* (Oxford: Blackwell, 1991), pp. 48–49).

11.1.8 Claiming equal pay

A claim for equal pay may be referred by a court or the Secretary of State to an ET at any time before the expiration of six months after leaving the relevant employment (which is to say, the *job* in question—see *National Power plc* v *Young* (2001); *Cumbria County Council* v *Dow (No. 2)* (2008)), and then arrears of remuneration may be awarded (s. 2(1)). However, there is confusion as to whether or not there is a time limit for former employees making claims. One division of the EAT held in *British Railways Board* v *Paul* (1988) that the wording in s. 2(4) imposing a time limit did not apply to employees' claims because it makes reference to a claim which is *referred* to an ET. Employees do not make references to an ET—only the Secretary of State does that. Another division of the EAT in *Etherson* v *Strathclyde Regional Council* (1992) decided that this assumed a precision in the statutory language which was unwarranted, and came to the opposite conclusion. While sympathy may be felt with the view that common sense should dictate a time limit, in accordance with other similar statutory claims, it might also be thought that an applicant should not be barred from bringing what may be a worthy claim by an argument that states that the language was not intended to be precise when he may have relied on its precision. There have been numerous other cases, however, when the six-month time limit has been assumed, including the decision of the House of Lords in *Preston* v *Wolverhampton Healthcare NHS Trust* (1998). The question was referred to the ECJ as to whether s. 2(4) breached art. 157 TFEU (ex art. 141 EC) as being excessively difficult or impossible in practice to comply with and it held that it did in 2000.

Since the 'equality clause' acts as an implied term of the contract of employment, an action may also be brought in the county court. Like most discrimination actions, while the proceedings are individual in nature, they are usually in the nature of test cases, the pay of hundreds of other similarly placed employees commonly depending on the outcome. This is reflected in the power accorded to the Secretary of State for Work and Pensions to bring a complaint if it appears to him that it is not reasonable to expect individual employees concerned to do so. There are, however, no reported instances of his so doing. Moreover, the CEHR may also provide general advice and assistance to applicants.

Until 1999, it was not possible to bring a claim under the Act for arrears of pay arising from the lack of an equality clause for periods beyond two years of the date when proceedings were instituted, by virtue of s. 2(5). However, the ECJ held, in *Levez* v *T. H. Jennings (Harlow Pools) Ltd* (1999), that s. 2(5) was unenforceable being contrary to EU law, and this has now been reiterated by the House of Lords in *Preston* v *Wolverhampton Healthcare NHS Trust (No. 2)* (2001) following the earlier ruling in the same case by the ECJ.

The Government responded to these cases by introducing the Equal Pay Act (Amendment) Regulations 2003 (SI 2003 No. 1656) which, for standard new cases, extends the period up to six years. However, whether the employer has concealed information from the applicant without which he or she could not reasonably have been expected to have brought the claim, then the case is considered non-standard, and no back limit on arrears applies. A clear difficulty that arises from backdating claims, however, is that it is not just the date of the claim that is relevant for determining what constitutes equality as there may have been material changes in the relevant comparison in that period. Nevertheless, a day-by-day comparison is required, even though that might be an onerous task—see the EAT's decision in *Potter* v *North Cumbria Acute Hospitals NHS Trust* (2009).

The EA 2002, s. 42 placed upon the Secretary of State an obligation to draw up regulations containing questionnaires enabling the employee to obtain information from the employer, and enabling the employee to respond to the complainant's questions. These are contained in the Equal Pay (Questions and Replies) Order 2003 (SI 2003 No. 722). They are admissible in evidence in proceedings. If the employer omits to reply, or is evasive or equivocal, the tribunal is entitled to make any inference it considers just and equitable. The Regulations make the gathering of evidence before an equal pay claim much easier to obtain and should expedite proceedings before tribunals.

11.2 EU law

Although the European Union is basically an economic unit, the social as well as political dimensions of its future nature have recently markedly come to the fore, most notably in the Maastricht Treaty of 1992 and the Amsterdam Treaty of 1997. But the social aspects of the European Union have always been present. Various Articles of the Treaty of Rome 1957 are concerned with such issues. Bob Simpson has remarked that perhaps the most important aspect of the EC's social policy has been the pursuit of equal treatment for men and women in matters relating to employment, and it would seem difficult to disagree with that view. But, as he points out, this has not always been conceived of as a social rather than as an economic issue, as art. 157 TFEU (ex art. 141 EC) enshrining the equal pay principle was primarily motivated by economic causes, notably the need to reduce competitive advantage brought about by lower labour costs. (See Simpson, (1984) 52 MLR 445.) Indeed, as Christopher Docksey has argued, the ECJ has perhaps been too willing to limit the principle of equality where member states have stressed the negative economic or financial consequences of a decision in a particular case (see Docksey, (1991) 20 ILJ 258 at p. 274, and Docksey, (1992) 21 ILJ 715). However, art. 157 TFEU (ex art. 136 EC) and the Preamble do make it clear that social objectives were also in mind.

EU law may be relevant to an equal pay claim in two ways. First, it may be relevant in the interpretation of domestic legislation through the concept of 'indirect effect' (see further, Shaw, (1990) 19 ILJ 228), and secondly it may be possible to bring a claim relying on EU law directly. (In this event, the fact that a claim based on domestic law only has already been heard does not prevent a new hearing based on EU law alone, according to the EAT in *Methilhill Bowling Club* v *Hunter* (1995).) For these reasons, EU law should always be kept in mind when considering the domestic legislation, but for ease of exposition it will be considered separately here.

11.2.1 The Treaty of Rome

The most fundamental source of EU anti-discrimination law is art. 157 TFEU (ex art. 141 EC) of the Functioning on the European Union. In its amended form following the ratification of the Amsterdam Treaty it states that:

Each Member State shall ensure that the principle of equal pay for male and female workers for equal work or work of equal value is applied.

The most important amendment lies in the addition of work of equal value, although, as we have seen, this has been protected since the Equal Pay Directive in 1975 (Council Directive (EEC) 75/117), and it has long been clear that it derived from art. 157 TFEU (ex art. 141 EC) itself rather than being an extension brought about by the Directive (see, e.g. *Worringham* v *Lloyds Bank Ltd* (1981)).

Comparison with domestic legislation

The provision is thus somewhat narrower than domestic legislation which demands equality with regard to every term of the contract of employment. However, in other respects it is wider in that it permits comparison with a man previously employed (*Macarthys Ltd* v *Smith* (1980)). It is also wider in that some exclusions from domestic employment protection legislation which adversely affected women, such as the minimum hours requirement for part-time work, contravene the article unless justified by objective factors unrelated to sex according to the ECJ in *Rinner-Kühn* v *FWW Spezial-Gebäudereinigung GmbH* (1989). (See Szyszczak, (1990) 19 ILJ 114. See too, the ECJ decisions in *Vroege* v *NCIV Instituut voor Volkshuisvesting BV and Stichting Pensioenfonds NCIV* (1995); *Fisscher* v *Voorhuis Hengelo BV and Stichting Bedrijspensioenfonds voor de Detailhandel* (1995).)

Direct effect

In *Defrenne* v *SABENA* (1976) the ECJ made it clear for the first time that art. 157 TFEU (ex art. 141 EC) is directly effective in national courts, but only where there is 'direct and overt discrimination which may be identified solely with the aid of criteria based in equal work and equal pay'. In *Jenkins* v *Kingsgate (Clothing Productions) Ltd* (1981) the ECJ held that paying an hourly rate to part-time workers was not covered by art. 157 TFEU (ex art. 141 EC). It was not discriminatory *per se* provided that the hourly rate was applied to each category without discrimination based on sex. Any further prohibition was a matter for national legislatures. However, if the difference in pay were merely an indirect way of reducing the level of the part-timers on the ground that they were exclusively or predominantly women the position would be different. If the pay policy could not be explained by factors other than discrimination based on sex, then that would nevertheless be enough to show discrimination. (See too, *Krüger* v *Kreiskrakenhaus Ebersberg* (2000).)

Pay

What amounts to pay is clearly of importance. The article defines it as:

the ordinary basic or minimum wage or salary or any other consideration, whether in cash or in kind, which the worker receives, directly or indirectly, in respect of his employment from his employer.

Continued payment of wages during illness is pay for this purpose because it derives from the employment relationship (*Rinner-Kühn* v *FWW Spezial Gebäudereinigung GmbH* (1989)). However, it is not necessary that the contract of employment be still subsisting for the definition to apply. For example, in *Garland* v *British Rail Engineering Ltd* (1982), it was held to cover concessionary travel arrangements for retired staff. The benefits were nevertheless paid in respect of employment even though there was no contractual obligation to supply them. So *ex gratia* payments were held by the ECJ in *Barber* v *Guardian Royal Exchange Assurance Group Ltd* (1990) to come within art. 157 TFEU (ex art. 141 EC) (see Honeyball and Shaw, (1991) 16 ELR 47). It may also cover pension schemes supplemental to the state pension schemes (*Bilka-Kaufhaus GmbH* v *Weber von Hartz* (1987)—see Shrubsall, (1987) 16 ILJ 52). However, in *Newstead* v *Department of Transport and HM Treasury* (1988) the European Court held that where a civil servant had to pay part of his gross salary into a compulsory pension scheme, unlike his female counterparts, this did not fall within art. 157 TFEU (ex art. 141 EC), being concerned with a deduction of contributions from pay, and not a difference in pay itself (see Grief, (1988) 17 ILJ 119; Szyszczak, (1988) 51 MLR 355). In *Barber* the central issue was whether entitlement to an occupational pension could be linked to the state retirement ages which were different for men and women. On the one hand to entitle both men and women to pension benefits at the same number of years before the state retirement ages does not appear discriminatory. However, the ECJ held it was. The entitlements must be the same for men and women of the same age. This may have a strange effect, particularly with regard to bridging pensions paid to early retirers before they are entitled to the state pension, where the qualifying ages for each sex are different (see e.g. *Birds Eye Walls Ltd* v *Roberts* (1994)). In *Coloroll Pension Trustees Ltd* v *Russell* (1995) the ECJ held that art. 157 TFEU (ex art. 141 EC) may be used against trustees of occupational pension schemes as well as employers—an important extension. Article 157 TFEU (ex art. 141 EC) also extends to survivors of employees who receive pensions, as the payment is one derived from the employment relationship, according to the ECJ in *Ten Oever* v *Stichting Bedrijspensioenfonds voor het Glazenwassen-en Schoonmaakbedrijf* (1993) (see further Fitzpatrick, (1994) 23 ILJ 155). (See generally on occupational pension schemes in EC sex discrimination law, Tether, (1995) 24 ILJ 194.)

The EAT in *Secretary of State for Employment* v *Levy* (1989) held that statutory redundancy payments were not pay for the purpose of what is now art. 157 TFEU (ex art. 141 EC) but the ECJ in *Barber* stated that they were. Merely because such payments do not derive from the contract of employment itself does not mean that they constitute a social security benefit and not pay. (See also, *Cannon* v *Barnsley MDC* (1992).) This reasoning is in line with the ECJ's earlier decision in *Defrenne* v *Belgium* (1971) that the article applied to discrimination arising directly from legislative provisions. The Court of Appeal logically extended this concept of 'pay' to unfair dismissal compensation in *R* v *Secretary of State for Employment ex parte Equal Opportunities Commission* (1993).

In *Defrenne* v *Belgium* (1971) the ECJ held that social security schemes or benefits which are directly governed by legislation and which are compulsory without any element of agreement (in particular retirement pensions) could not amount to pay. Where the scheme is financed by the employer, or by the employer and his employees, this does constitute pay for the purposes of art. 157 TFEU (ex art. 141 EC) in that such schemes form part of the consideration offered by the employer, according to the ECJ in *Barber*. However, in *Bestuur van het Algemeen Burgerlijk Pensioenfonds* v *Beune* (1994) the ECJ took the view that payments under schemes which are occupational, but nevertheless set up under statute, are pay within art. 157 TFEU (ex art. 141 EC).

Time limits

Where a claim is brought directly under art. 157 TFEU (ex art. 141 EC), one *prima facie* difficulty seems to be that no time limit is specified. However, the EAT has held in *Rankin* v *British Coal Corporation* (1993), following the ECJ's decision in *Emmott* v *Minister for Social Welfare* (1991), that it is in the interests of legal certainty that there be a limit, and that this should not be greater than the period applying to claims generally under domestic legislation. For claims in an ET this would suggest somewhere between three and six months as those are the relevant periods under sex discrimination legislation. An earlier suggestion by the EAT in *Cannon* v *Barnsley Metropolitan Borough Council* (1992), that it is the relevant limit made under what is now ERA 1996, in the case of discriminatory treatment for redundancy selection, that is, three months, would not seem to be the most logical approach. (See further Barnard, (1993) 22 ILJ 50.)

The remedial action

In two important decisions of the ECJ, *Smith* v *Avdel Systems Ltd* (1994) and *Van den Akker* v *Stichting Shell Pensioenfonds* (1994), the court has made it clear that, to eliminate the discrimination, it is necessary to bring the level of the disadvantaged to that of the advantaged, which, in the case of retirement ages or pension entitlement ages, will involve the lowering of the higher age. However, where they are identical, it seems that they may both be revised without involving a discrimination. Although both of these ideas seem reasonable in isolation, taken together there seems to be a logical contradiction in approach here. One writer has called this 'a curiously self-defeating conclusion to the *Barber* litigation' (Deakin, (1995) 54 CLJ 35).

Supplementary

The amended art. 157 TFEU (ex art. 141 EC) contains two more important provisions. The first is that the Council of Ministers is required to adopt measures to ensure the application of the principle of equal opportunities and equal treatment of men and women regarding employment and occupation, including equal pay for equal work or work of equal value. With regard to this, it is noteworthy that the UK was prepared to allow qualified majority voting. The second is that member states are empowered to adopt measures involving positive discrimination to make it easier to pursue vocational activities or to compensate for disadvantages in professional careers. The Declaration attached to this states that, in the first instance, it should be women who are the beneficiaries of art. 157 TFEU (ex art. 141 EC). (See further, Barnard, (1997) 26 ILJ 275.)

11.2.2 **Equal Pay Directive**

The Equal Pay Directive (Council Directive (EEC) 75/117) states that:

> The principle of equal pay for men and women outlined in Article 141 . . . means, for the same work or for work to which equal value has been attributed, the elimination of all discrimination on grounds of sex with regard to all aspects and conditions of remuneration.

Directives in European law are 'binding as to the result to be achieved' but cede to the national authorities 'the choice of form and methods'. They are capable of direct enforcement in national courts (*Van Duyn* v *Home Office* (1975)), at least where they are 'clear, precise and admit of no exceptions and of [their] nature need no intervention by national authorities'. The Court of Appeal in *O'Brien* v *Sim-Chem* (1980) thought that the Equal Pay Directive was not directly effective. The ECJ decided that Directives are only directly enforceable by individuals against Government institutions or emanations thereof. This might include an area health authority, as in *Marshall* v *Southampton and South West Hampshire Health Authority* (1986). (See Grief, (1986) 15 ILJ 187; Atkins, (1986) 49 MLR 508.) British Gas, prior to privatisation, was also included, according to the ECJ and the House of Lords in *Foster* v *British Gas plc* (1990), as it provided a public service under the control of the State. However, the Court of Appeal held in *Doughty* v *Rolls-Royce plc* (1992) that Rolls-Royce was not included as control was only one of a number of factors; not only did it not provide a public service, but also it did not claim special powers. It is important to note that it is not the body itself that need be under the control of the state, but the public service which it provides (see *Griffin* v *South West Water Services Ltd* (1995); Eady, (1994) 23 ILJ 350, although this decision must now be doubted in the light of the ECJ's decision in *Bestuur* (see above)). (However, see too the Court of Appeal's decision in *NUT* v *Governing Body of St Mary's Church of England (Aided) Junior School* (1997), that the governing body of a voluntary aided school is an emanation of the State, providing as it does a public service while not being under State control (see Eady, (1997) 26 ILJ 249).)

There is the further question of forum. In *Amies* v *ILEA* (1977) the EAT held that since it was set up by statute it had power to hear only issues of discrimination arising from the SDA 1975 and not from the EEC Treaty or Directives: the proper forum for the assertion of such a right would be the High Court. In *Macarthys* v *Smith* (1980) the Court of Appeal seems to have assumed that European rights can be enforced in tribunals although the point was not extensively argued (see also *Albion Shipping Agency* v *Arnold* (1982)).

Handels-Og Kontorfunktionaerernes Forbund i Danmark v *Dansk Arbejdsgiverforening (acting for Danfoss)* (1989) had a radical effect on the structure of many incremental pay schemes. The court stated that a number of criteria used by employers to justify incremental pay differentials would have to be justified. Where differentials were due to the flexibility of employees, if this were used to reward quality of work, and would systematically disadvantage women, this can only be because of unjustified discrimination, for women's work is not of lower quality to that of men. If differentials are due to adaptability with regard to when and where the work is done, employers must also justify this as being important for the performance of the employee's duties. Likewise if increments are based on vocational training. However, the ECJ said if increments are due to seniority, this does not require special justification in that generally experience enables workers to work better. This was surprising in that, in many manual jobs, this is not necessarily so at all. However, in *Nimz* v *Freie und Hansestadt Hamburg* (1991) the ECJ said that payments based on seniority did require to be justified but the ECJ reverted to the *Danfoss* position in *Cadman* v *HSE* (2006). (But see the decision of the Court of Appeal in *Wilson* v *Health and Safety Executive* (2010) to the effect that it does not mean that employers can act in a purely arbitrary way in this regard.)

In *Angestelltenbetriebsrat der Wiener Gebietskrankenkasse* v *Wiener Gebietskrankenkasse* (1999) the ECJ considered the similar situation where workers have different qualifications and different pay, but are nevertheless doing the same tasks. It held that in such circumstances these workers are not doing the same work for the purposes of art. 157 TFEU (ex art. 141 EC) and the Equal Pay Directive. It is therefore justified to pay those who have higher qualifications more than those who do not, even though women constitute a higher proportion of the latter category. This was a surprising decision. Although it would seem arguable that there is justification for different pay levels due to differing qualifications, it seems contrary to common sense to argue that those performing exactly the same tasks are nevertheless not employed on the same work.

11.3 **Family rights**

Many women have neither the desire nor the financial circumstances to enable them to interrupt their employment for significant periods in order to raise children. However, all employed women who are pregnant need to have time off work in order to give birth, to be paid during this period, and a large proportion of these will wish to return to work shortly after the pregnancy is over. In recent years it has also come to be recognised that fathers need rights with regard to childbirth. There are occasions, particularly during the early school years, when parents need time off work in order to care for their children, but this is something that also applies with regard to other members of the family in need of care. English law has, somewhat slowly and with a great deal of prompting by the European Union, come to recognise the importance of providing legal rights in these respects, and we now turn to look at each of these rights.

11.3.1 **Maternity leave**

The law on maternity leave entitlements originally was very complex, particularly when considered in the context of other entitlements a woman has in relation to childbirth. However, the law was later greatly simplified, if not made simple, by the introduction of the Maternity and Parental Leave etc. Regulations 1999 (SI 1999 No. 3312) as amended by Amendment Regulations in 2002 (SI 2002 No. 2789). These were made under the authority of ERA 1996, ss 71–75, as amended by Employment Relations Act 1999, s. 7 and EA 2002, s. 17. (See further McColgan, (2000) 29 ILJ 125; Mair, (2000) 63 MLR 877.)

The Regulations introduced a number of concepts. The first is that of Ordinary Maternity Leave (OML)—see reg. 4. A woman may take OML, regardless of length of service or hours of work. The entitlement is to 26 weeks' leave—see reg. 7. However, in order to be entitled to take the leave, the woman normally must notify her employer, at least by the end of the 15th week before the expected week of childbirth (EWC) of her pregnancy and the date on which she intends the OML to begin. This date cannot be more than 11 weeks before the EWC. The employer may request a certificate from a registered medical practitioner or midwife stating the date of the EWC. The period can be shorter if sufficient notice is given. Notice is not required if the OML begins within four weeks before the EWC (including where it begins on the date of the birth itself), although the woman must tell her employer as soon as is reasonably practicable that she is absent from work wholly or partly due to the pregnancy. The OML begins with the date of notification, or absence if earlier, in such circumstances—see reg. 6. Notification in all cases must be in writing if the employer so requests. Failure to notify will be a disciplinary offence, but is not directly related to the right to return to work after the birth.

The second concept introduced by the Regulations is that of Additional Maternity Leave (AML)—see reg. 4. An employee who qualifes for OML will be entitled to AML which begins after the expiry of OML and continues for 26 weeks—see reg. 7. Since the Work and Families Act 2006, it is no longer necessary to have 26 weeks' continuous employment.

Sometimes a birth is late. If the employee has exhausted her 26 weeks of OML by this period (and clearly this will be in only rare circumstances) she will be entitled to Compulsory Maternity Leave (CML)—see reg. 8. In such circumstances the OML is extended until the birth, and then an additional two weeks' CML are added.

Where an employee takes AML, reg. 17 states that, during the period of leave, the parties are entitled respectively to the implied obligations of trust and confidence and good faith, and are bound by any terms relating to notice, redundancy compensation, disciplinary and grievance procedures, disclosure of confidential information, the acceptance of gifts or other benefits and the employee's participation in any other business. Where she takes only OML the employee is entitled to the benefit of all the terms of the contract, bar remuneration (i.e. salary and wages—reg. 9)—see ERA 1996, s. 71(4), (5). However, following the decision of the High Court in *Equal Opportunities Commission* v *Secretatry of State for Trade and Industry* (2007), the SDA 1975 will need to be amended. It was held there that the AML, even though going further than the Pregnant Workers Directive Council Directive (EC) 92/85, required, nevertheless constituted maternity leave for the purposes of the Directive and should afford full contractual rights to the employee for the length of its duration. This followed the reasoning of the ECJ in *Land Brandenburg* v *Sass* (2005).

Where the employee has taken, or has sought to take, or availed herself of OML, or has sought to take AML, parental leave or dependant's leave under ERA 1996, s. 57A, she is entitled not to be subjected to any detriment or failure to act—see reg. 19. This is also the case if she suffers this because she is pregnant, has given birth, is the subject of a maternity suspension for legal reasons (e.g. health and safety reasons), has declined to sign a workforce agreement, or because she is a workforce representative or is a candidate in an election to become one.

It was held in *Visa International Service Association* v *Paul* (2004) that the employer's failure to inform an employee then on maternity leave of a vacancy she would have applied for had she been aware of it, amounted to a breach of the implied term of trust and confidence. It is difficult to see why this should not also apply to employees on other types of leave.

11.3.2 The right to return to work after maternity leave

An employee whose pregnancy is over may wish to return to work. If she has taken OML only then there is no need to notify her employer of her intention to return. Where OML or AML is taken, the employee is entitled to return to the job she had before her absence. However, if this is not reasonably practicable after AML, she is entitled to another job which is suitable for her and appropriate in the circumstances—see reg. 18 and ERA 1996, s. 71; *Blundell* v *Governing Body of St Andrew's Catholic Primary School* (2007).

After OML the employee is entitled to return with her seniority, pension and other rights as they would have been had she not been absent and on terms and conditions no less favourable—see reg. 18A. Where the employee is made redundant during OML or AML she is entitled to be offered any available suitable alternative employment before the termination of her existing contract of employment. This may be with her existing employer or successor, or an associated employer. The employment must be suitable to her and appropriate to her circumstances and not substantially less favourable than her previous contract—see reg. 10.

Where the employee wishes to return before the end of the OML or AML, as the case may be, she must give at least eight weeks' notice—see reg. 11. If she does not do this, the employer is entitled to postpone her return to the end of her leave period and, if she does return having been notified that she is not to return to work, refuse to pay her.

11.3.3 Suspension on maternity grounds

The TURERA 1993, s. 25 and Sch. 3 introduced new rights with regard to suspension from work on maternity grounds where the employee is prohibited from continuing working (ERA 1996, ss 66–68).

If an employee is suspended from work by her employer because she is pregnant, has recently given birth or is breastfeeding a child, she has a number of rights where the suspension is in consequence of any requirement imposed by or under any relevant provision of any enactment or of any instrument made under any enactment or any recommendation in any relevant provision of a code of practice issued or approved under Health and Safety at Work, etc. Act 1974, s. 16 (ERA 1996, s. 66(1)).

The first right which a woman has where she cannot continue working as a result of any requirement or recommendation is that she should be offered any suitable alternative work which is available before she is suspended (s. 67(1)). If the woman is not offered work, then she may complain to an ET which may make an award of such compensation as it considers just and equitable having regard to the employer's infringement and any loss attributable to that breach (s. 70). Any complaint must be lodged within three months of the first day of the suspension unless it is not reasonably practicable to present a complaint within three months (s. 70(5)).

If the employee is actually suspended pursuant to s. 70(5) then she is entitled to be paid remuneration by her employer while she is suspended (s. 68(1)). The suspension lasts as long as the employee continues to be employed but is not provided with work or—excepting alternative work under s. 67—does not do the work she did before suspension.

Complaints of breaches of s. 68(1) must be brought within three months of any day on which remuneration is not paid, unless the ET considers that it was not reasonably practicable to complain within this period (s. 70(2)). If the tribunal finds that the complaint is well-founded then it must order the employer to pay the amounts of remuneration which it finds due to the woman (s. 70(3)).

11.3.4 Ante-natal care

The right to time off for ante-natal care was introduced by Employment Act 1980, s. 13 (inserted as ERA 1996, ss 55–57), following concern at the extent of peri-natal mortality and handicap expressed, in particular, by reports of the House of Commons Select Committee on Social Services. It found the UK figure to be one of the highest in the Western world. The right is available to all women employees irrespective of length of service or hours of work. In order to claim it, the employee may, however, be required to produce a doctor's or midwife's certificate of pregnancy, and appointment card. If she does, she should be paid at the appropriate hourly rate for the time taken off, and if this is unreasonably refused, she may complain to an ET within three months. It may be reasonable to refuse such time off if an employee can reasonably make arrangements for an appointment outside normal working hours (*Gregory* v *Tudsbury Ltd* (1982)).

11.3.5 Time off for dependants

The Employment Relations Act 1999 introduced a right into the ERA 1996 that gives entitlement to time off work in order to care for dependants. Although this would normally be for a family member, this is not necessarily the case. The ERA 1996, s. 57A(3) defines a dependant as a spouse or civil partner, child, parent, or person living in the same household as the employee, except employees, tenants, lodgers and boarders, and any people who reasonably rely on the employee for assistance in the event of illness, injury, or assault—see s. 57A(4).

The right (by virtue of s. 57A(1)) is to a reasonable amount of time off work in order to take action which is necessary:

(a) to provide assistance when a dependant falls ill, gives birth or is injured or assaulted;

(b) to make arrangements for the provision of care for a dependant who is ill or injured;

(c) in consequence of the death of a dependant, but not if it amounts to compassionate leave—*Forster* v *Cartwright Black* (2004);

(d) because of the unexpected disruption or termination of arrangements for the care of a dependant (see *Royal Bank of Scotland plc* v *Harrison* (2009)); or

(e) to deal with an incident which involves a child of the employee and which occurs unexpectedly in a period during which an educational establishment which the child attends is responsible for him.

The employee must inform the employer of the absence as soon as practicable and, if relevant, how long he expects it to be—see s. 57A(2). The right is to time off only—the Act does not state that the employee is entitled to be paid during this period.

The remedy is intended to cover arrangements to deal with an immediate crisis, not to provide longer-term care for the dependent, according to the EAT in *Qua* v *John Ford Morrison Solicitors* (2003).

Remedy lies by way of complaint to an ET within three months, which is extendable by the tribunal where it is not practicable to present within that time. A declaration is to be made if the right has been infringed, and there is an additional power to award compensation.

11.3.6 Statutory maternity pay

The Social Security Contributions and Benefits Act 1992 (as amended by EA 2002, ss 17–21) and, *inter alia*, the Statutory Maternity Pay (General) Regulations 1986 (SI 1986 No. 1960) entitle some employees to statutory maternity pay. The scheme applies only to those who have been earning at least the lower limit for making National Insurance contributions. If, by the 15th week before the expected week of confinement, the employee has been working for that employer for a minimum of 26 weeks, she will be entitled to statutory maternity pay for 39 weeks. The Government intended to extend this to 52 weeks under powers derived from the Work and Families Act 2006, but it has now postponed this indefinitely. The rate is fixed by regulation, but for employees who have been working for at least two years for the employer at the qualifying week, for the first six weeks of that 39 the rate will be nine-tenths of their week's pay and for the remaining weeks is £123.06, or 90 per cent of average weekly earnings if that comes to less than £123.06 per week.

The employee must notify the employer at least 28 days before she intends to cease work. The employer may recoup the sums paid from the state by making deductions from National Insurance contributions.

Rights to maternity pay are not lost for any day (up to a maximum of ten) the employee works during the statutory leave period. These are known as KIT (keeping-in-touch) days, and allow the employee not to miss out on training, for example. (See Caracciolo di Torella, (2007) 36 ILJ 315.)

Any employee who does not qualify is entitled to receive a maternity allowance, payable under the scheme in operation prior to the introduction in 1987 of the scheme (as amended in 2007) in the Social Security Act 1986.

11.3.7 Parental leave

The Maternity and Parental Leave etc. Regulations 1999, regs 13–16 as amended by the Maternity and Parental Leave (Amendment) Regulations 2001 (SI 2001 No. 4010) were made pursuant to the Parental Leave Directive (Council Directive (EC) 96/34). An employee who has been continuously employed for at least a year by his present employer and who has, or expects to have, parental responsibility (within the meaning of Children Act 1989, s. 3), or is the parent named on the birth certificate or is the adoptive parent, is entitled to parental leave in order to care for the child. In the last case, and where the child is entitled to disability living allowance, the child must be under 18, and in the former cases, under five years old. Leave is for 18 weeks for each parent in respect of any child. (This is rather curious, because it would appear that consecutive leave may be taken in respect of children born in multiple births—hence, parents working for the same employer having triplets are entitled to 18 months when one of them is off work at any given time.) Where the employee's working week varies from time to time, the period of entitlement is calculated by dividing the total periods required to be worked over a year by 52. Entitlement runs for five years from birth; or in the case of an adopted child, from the date of placement with the parents. The leave must be taken in weeks, and may not be broken down into days, according to the Court of Appeal in *Rodway* v *South Central Trains Ltd* (2005).

During the period of leave, the employee is entitled to the same benefits and is subject to the same obligations as the employee who takes AML, discussed above.

The employee has the right to return to the same job as he or she held before or, if that is not practicable after leave of more than four weeks, to a similar job which has the same or better status, terms and conditions. Where parental leave is taken for four weeks or less after AML, the entitlement is to return to the employee's old job unless it would not have been reasonably practicable for her to return after AML as well as at the end of parental leave. In this event, she is entitled to return to another suitable and appropriate job.

11.3.8 Flexible working

A further area of innovation to the end of making the balance between working and family life as easy as possible, close to the Labour Government's legislative heart, is the enhancement of flexible working rights granted by EA 2002, s. 47. (See Anderson, (2003) 32 ILJ 37.) This introduces a new s. 80F into the ERA 1996 supplemented by the Flexible Working (Eligibility, Complaints and Remedies) Regulations 2002 (SI 2002 No. 3236) and the Flexible Working (Procedural Requirements) Regulations 2002 (SI 2002 No. 3207). Under these provisions, 'qualifying' employees may apply, in writing to their employer for changes in their terms and conditions relating to hours, times, and place of work. The employer must hold a meeting with the employee within 28 days and inform him or her of the decision within a further 14 days.

The employee, to be qualified for the right, must be the mother, father, adopter, guardian or foster parent of the child, or married to, or be the partner of, such a person. The child must be under the age of six, or 18 if disabled, and the qualified employee must expect to have responsibility for the child's upbringing. Carers of persons requiring care over the age of 18 are also eligible if they are married to, the civil partner of, the relative of, or living at the same address as, the employee. Continuous employment of 26 weeks is required to be eligible—see Flexible Working (Eligibility, Complaints and Remedies) (Amendment) Regulations 2006 (SI 2006 No. 3314).

The employer is able to refuse an employee's application on numerous grounds. These are:

   (i) the burden of additional costs,

   (ii) detrimental effect on ability to meet customer demand,

   (iii) inability to reorganise work among existing staff,

   (iv) inability to recruit additional staff,

   (v) detrimental impact on quality,

   (vi) detrimental impact on performance,

   (vii) insufficiency of work during the periods the employee proposes to work, planned structural changes, and

   (viii) such other grounds as the Secretary of State may specify by regulations.

This is clearly a very wide list, and will be rather easy hurdles for employers to set up. The hapless employer who falls foul of these provisions, however, may only be required to reconsider the employee's application, following a declaration by the ET (ERA, 1996, s. 80(1)) but may have to pay compensation as the tribunal considers just and equitable, to a maximum of eight weeks' pay.

The employee has an additional right under ERA 1996, s. 47E not to be subjected to any detriment, other than dismissal, arising from exercising these rights, or certain acts preparatory to that, as specified. Where the employee is dismissed in these circumstances, that will be considered to be an automatically unfair dismissal—ERA 1996, s. 104C. This will be the case even if the employee is engaged in official or unofficial industrial action. There is evidence that large employers have adopted practices that give employees rights that go further than the legislation here demands—see Croucher and Kelliher, (2005) 21 IJCLLIR 503.

11.3.9 Paternity and adoption leave and pay

The EA 2002, s. 1 introduced the concept of paternity leave into domestic law. It did so by inserting a new s. 80A into the ERA 1996, followed by the Paternity and Adoption Leave Regulations 2002 (SI 2002 No. 2788).

The regulations apply to fathers of children born on or after 6 April 2003. Entitlement is dependent on the father having no less than 26 weeks of continuous employment 15 weeks before the expected date of the child's birth. The father must have, or expect to have, responsibility for the upbringing of the child, and must either be the natural father or married to, or the partner of, the child's mother.

The entitlement also exists where the child has died, and there will be no multiple entitlement in the event of multiple births. The father is entitled to up to two weeks' leave on statutory paternity pay (to be supplemented by 26 weeks' unpaid leave where the child's mother returns to work before the end of her maternity leave entitlement, by virtue of the Work and Families Act 2006, known as additional paternity leave, but at the time of writing this has been postponed indefinitely) to be taken at one time within the first 56 days of the child's life so long as written notice has been given at least 15 weeks before the child's expected date of birth, or if that is not reasonably practicable, as soon as is reasonably practical. While the father is on paternity leave, he is entitled to the benefit of terms and conditions of his employment as if he had not been on leave (most importantly, pay), may not suffer any detriment because he has taken it (see *Atkins* v *Coyle Personnel plc* (2008)) and will be entitled to return to work after his leave has expired.

Similar provisions apply to fathers adopting children, and in addition it is possible for either adoptive parent to take paid adoption leave of 26 weeks in the first instance, with a possible additional period of 26 weeks unpaid.

In addition to leave there are also entitlements for new fathers (both natural and adoptive), to Statutory Paternity Pay and this is in addition to contractual remuneration. (See the Statutory Paternity Pay and Statutory Adoption Pay (General) Regulations 2002 (SI 2002 No. 2822).)

SELECTED READING

Hepple, B. and Szyszczak, E. (eds) (1992), *Discrimination: the Limits of the Law,* London: Mansell, 1992

Honeyball, S. (2000), 'The Principle of Non-Discrimination as a Fundamental Value', in K. Economides, *et al* (eds), *Fundamental Values*, Oxford: Hart Publishing 2000

James, G. (2006), 'The Work and Families Act 2006: Legistation to Improve Choice and Flexibility?', (2006) 35 ILJ 272

Kilpatrick, (1994), 'Deciding When Jobs of Equal Value Can be Paid Unequally', 1994 23 ILJ 311

Lester, A. (1994), 'Discrimination: What Can Lawyers Learn from History?', [1994] *Public Law* 224

Painter, R. W. and Holmes, A. E. (2010), *Cases and Materials on Employment Law*, 8th edn, Oxford: Oxford University Press, ch. 4

12

Statutory rights regulating
the employment relationship

SUMMARY

In this chapter we consider the following rights which an employee may have against his employer which are derived from, or influenced by statute:

(a) the itemised pay statement;

(b) deductions from pay;

(c) time off work;

(d) patents;

(e) lay-off and short-time working;

(f) the minimum wage;

(g) restrictions on working time;

(h) rights under the Public Interest Disclosure Act 1998;

(i) grievance procedures;

(j) protection from harassment.

12.1 Itemised pay statement

The ERA 1996, s. 8 gives every employee the right to a written pay statement at or before every payment of wages or salary. It must distinguish the gross amount of wages or salary, the net amount payable, where different parts of the net amount are paid in different ways, the amount and method of each part payment, and any variable or fixed deductions therefrom. In the case of fixed deductions (for example, union contributions, or payments in respect of fines or maintenance), a new statement need not be given at each time of payment. Instead a single communication may cover a maximum of 12 months, but should always be specific. The label 'miscellaneous deductions' was found to be inadequate (*Milsom v Leicestershire County Council* (1978)). It should include the amount of the deduction, the intervals at which it is to be made and its purpose (s. 9). Not all income comes within the scope for this purpose of wages. For example, it has been held that waiters' tips are not wages as the employee cannot know the precise sum involved, so that the taking of sums by the employers in accordance with an internal company agreement is not a deduction which has to be notified (*Cofone v Spaghetti House Ltd* (1980)).

If the statement is not produced or there is a dispute over the terms it contains, an ET may declare the particulars which should have been included (*Coales v John Wood and Co.* (1986)) and order the employer to make up the unnotified deductions which have been taken up to a period of 13 weeks immediately preceding the application. The courts have recognised this to be a penal provision and thus one to be construed restrictively. In *Scott* v *Creager* (1979) the tribunal took into account that the respondent was a dentist with a busy professional practice, short of time to fulfil his statutory duty, that the requirement was then new and that he had to pay the solicitors for the costs of defending the claim.

12.2 Deductions from pay

Employees have had some statutory protection against the employer making deductions from wages for a very long time. Under the Truck Act 1831 a worker had to agree in writing to deductions made in respect of such matters as food, rent, and fuel. The Truck Act 1896 permitted deductions only if certain stringent conditions were met. However, the courts were adept in sanctioning ways to circumvent the Act. For example, in *Sagar* v *Ridehalgh & Son* (1931) deductions which were made for poor work were held not to be deductions at all, but merely a method by which the amount of wages due could be calculated. It became clear that the various Truck Acts were in need of repair, and in 1986 the Wages Act was passed (now ERA 1996, ss 13–27).

The provisions of the ERA 1996 apply to all workers, including employees, apprentices, and independent contractors who undertake to perform services personally, other than professionals or business people working for clients or customers. Remedies are only by way of complaint to an ET under s. 23. The tribunal may make an order as it thinks appropriate under s. 24 that the employer pay such sum as the tribunal thinks appropriate to compensate the worker. There is thus no need to make a separate county court claim to recover such sums.

Deductions from wages may only be made in the circumstances laid down in ERA 1996, s. 13(1). These include the many deductions made under the sanction of statute, such as for National Insurance contributions, tax, attachment of earnings orders and so on. These may be deducted by the employer irrespective of the authorisation of the employee. But in other circumstances such express authorisation is required. This may arise in one of two ways.

First, deductions may be made where the employee has agreed in writing to their being made. This type of authorisation must occur prior to the actual deduction being made from the employee's wages, and prior to the occasion which gives rise to the deduction (s. 13(6); see *Discount Tobacco and Confectionery Ltd* v *Williamson* (1993)). It must be clear from the authorisation that wages are the source from which the deduction is to be made. A general authorisation to recover a loan is thus, for example, not sufficient for these purposes, according to the EAT in *Potter* v *Hunt Contracts Ltd* (1992).

Secondly, deductions may be allowed if the contract of employment itself so authorises the deduction provided that this is done in advance of the deduction being made. In many instances, however, the authorisation to make a deduction may arise from a variation to the employee's contract of employment by way of a collective agreement. Where this is the case, even if the collective agreement is oral only, that is sufficient authorisation, according to the EAT in *York City & District*

Travel Ltd v *Smith* (1990). Nevertheless, there must be some written notification of this fact to the employee. In *Davies* v *Hotpoint Limited* (1994), however, there was no authorisation for a deduction pursuant to a collective agreement because on its true construction any such variation required union consent.

It is not enough for the employer to show only that the deduction has been authorised in the manner in which the Act allows. It must also be shown that the deductions were justified in fact, according to the EAT in *Fairfield Ltd* v *Skinner* (1993). This rather wide purposive reading of the Act is sound in principle. The employer in that case argued that it was entitled to make a deduction for alleged damage to a van and for telephone calls and mileage in excess of an agreed figure without substantiating the allegations. The EAT held that, even though these were categories which were authorised under the contract, deductions were lawful only if they were justified in fact in the particular case and here they were not.

12.2.1 **Retail workers**

An upper limit of ten per cent of gross weekly wages on a given pay day is imposed in the case of retail workers. Deductions from wages are frequently made for cash shortages and stock deficiencies, and special further provision is made so that such deductions must be made within 12 months following the employer's discovery of the shortage or deficiency, or (if earlier) the date on which such discovery ought to have been made (ERA 1996, s. 18(2) and (3)).

12.2.2 **Payments**

Section 15 contains provisions to cover the situation where, instead of deductions being made by the employer, a payment is made to the employer by the employee. These mirror those which apply to deductions, requiring prior written authorisation by the employee. However, s. 16 states that s. 15 does not apply in the following situations:

(a) overpayment of wages or expenses (see *Home Office* v *Ayres* (1992));

(b) disciplinary proceedings held by virtue of any statutory provison (but this does not apply to private employers: *Chiltern House Ltd* v *Chambers* (1990));

(c) statutory requirements (for example, regarding underpayment of tax);

(d) check-offs (deductions for trade union subscriptions) and similar arrangements;

(e) industrial action (because the legality of industrial action is thought to be best left to the courts);

(f) court orders.

12.2.3 **What are wages?**

A number of cases have concerned the vexing question of what amounts to wages for this purpose. One particular problem is whether a payment in lieu of notice can amount to wages within the statutory definition, and therefore whether failure to make such payment entitles the employee to make a claim under the ERA 1996. The definition includes 'any sums payable to the worker by his employer in connection with his employment'. In *Delaney* v *Staples* (1992) the House of Lords held that it referred to payments for work done or to be done under a contract of employment. It therefore followed that, where the employer had unlawfully terminated the contract, payments in lieu of notice were not wages but were, depending on the terms of the contract, damages for breach of contract. This was despite the fact that such payments were properly construed as being made in connection with employment, contrary to the view of the Court of Appeal whose overall decision the House of Lords nevertheless upheld. (This aspect of the decision has already been considered in Chapter 4 above.)

It should be noted that ERA 1996, s. 27(1) refers to any sums *payable in connection with* employment. It would therefore appear that 'wages' may include payments which are not contractual. The issue arose in *Kent Management Services Ltd* v *Butterfield* (1992) when the EAT decided that commission, described as discretionary and *ex gratia*, was nonetheless wages if it was within the reasonable contemplation of both parties that it would be payable. Rubenstein has argued (see [1992] IRLR 389) that s. 13(3) of the Act (then s. 8(3) of the Wages Act 1986) suggests the opposite conclusion, in that it states that a deficiency shall be treated as a deduction from wages only where it is 'properly' payable. This, he says, indicates a payment under a legal duty. But this is not at all clear. A legally 'proper' payment is surely one that can be lawfully made, which is wider than one made under a duty. Furthermore, if the intention had been in s. 13(3) to equate proper and contractually obligatory payments, then that terminology could surely have been used.

Discretionary payments, once declared, are wages, even though they are non-contractual according to the EAT in *Farrell Matthews & Weir* v *Hansen* (2005). It is not necessary to count as wages that the deduction should already have been paid.

It is important when stating that a payment, such as a bonus, is discretionary to indicate clearly what is meant by that. Various aspects of the payment might be discretionary, but others not. For example, it may be in the discretion of the employer whether to pay it or not, or it might simply be that the amount, the method of its calculation or the time of its payment, are the discretionary elements. (See *Small* v *Boots Co. plc* (2009).)

A further point raised in *Delaney* v *Staples* in the Court of Appeal (but not subject to appeal in the House of Lords) was whether a total failure by the employer to pay anything at all could amount to a deduction. Certainly the term could connote something less than non-payment. A deduction could be distinguished from non-payment on the basis of the reason why the deduction is made. For example, if no payment is made because the employer does not believe it to be due, that could be considered non-payment. On the other hand, if the employer retains the money because he thinks it in some way represents a sum owed to him, that could be considered a deduction. However, the Court of Appeal in *Delaney* held that a non-payment was a deduction and therefore denied the distinction. This must be the right decision in practice, by-passing a number of difficulties (see Honeyball, (1991) 20 ILJ 143). The EAT also decided in *McCree* v *London Borough of Tower Hamlets* (1992) that an employer cannot achieve a reduction in pay by absorbing a sum into pay increases so that there appears to be no deduction as such.

As part of its decision on this point, the ET may have to answer complex questions about the way in which wages are assessed and apportioned. In *Thames Water Utilities* v *Reynolds* (1996), for example, when the employee was made redundant he was owed eight days' holiday pay. He had been employed on an annual salary, and the employers paid him 8/365ths of that salary for the holiday. The employee brought a deduction claim before the tribunal, arguing that the apportionment should have been made on the basis of the number of *working* days in a year (not calendar days), which would have meant that he should have been paid 8/260ths of his salary. The tribunal, applying Apportionment Act 1870, s. 2, upheld his claim, but the EAT allowed the employers' appeal. The correct interpretation of the section (which states that, unless the contrary is intended, money due is to be 'considered as accruing from day to day') is that it applies to calendar days, not working days.

Only sums that are identifiable amounting to a quantified loss are able to be claimed in ETs under the ERA 1996, according to the Court of Appeal in *Coors Brewers Ltd* v *Adcock* (2007). Other sums will have to be recovered by way of a claim in the county court, which is a potentially much more expensive, and slower, method. It remains to be seen how this will work in practice, as the line between sums that are identifiable and those that are not is not a clear one. It is more a matter of degree.

12.2.4 **Payment when contract only part completed**

Considerable problems surround the right at common law to payment of an employee who completes only part of his contract. Confusion primarily derives from the 18th-century case of *Cutter* v *Powell* (1795). A second mate on a voyage from Jamaica to Liverpool was to be paid 30 guineas, provided he completed the voyage, but he died three weeks before the end of the two-month journey. The Court of King's Bench held that his widow was not entitled to any payment on a *quantum meruit* action or otherwise in respect of the part he had completed. Although the decision might have been different had there not been an express term for completion included on a promissory note, the statement of law was generalised in later cases. Thus in *Boston Deep Sea Fishing and Ice Co.* v *Ansell* (1888) it was held that, at common law, an employee was not entitled to pro rata payment in respect of any uncompleted period of service. This means that, if X is employed and paid Monday to Friday, and leaves on the Wednesday, at common law he can recover no wages for days worked. An exception has, however, developed where the employer has received substantial performance even though not all the services bargained for are completed (*Hoenig* v *Isaacs* (1952); *Bolton* v *Mahadeva* (1972)).

Further, the injustice of the general rule is mitigated somewhat by Apportionment Act 1870, s. 2, which provides that 'all annuities (which includes salaries and pensions)... and other periodical payments in the nature of income... shall... be considered as accruing from day to day, and should be apportioned in respect of time accordingly'. Thus, generally, a proportion of the contractual amount can now be gained.

It should be noted that the position is different when the part-performance by the employee is a form of industrial action. This is considered in Chapter 15 below.

12.2.5 **Sick pay**

There is no presumption in law that sick pay is payable. At common law the position depends primarily upon the terms of the contract. In the absence of any conclusive evidence the tribunal should not assume that sick pay is to be paid, according to the Court of Appeal in *Eagland* v *British Telecommunications plc* (1992) overturning the earlier suggestion by the same court in *Mears* v *Safecar Security Ltd* (1982) to the contrary effect. In the majority of instances, however, employees will be entitled to sick pay under their contract of employment.

The common law position is, however, of less consequence since the introduction of statutory sick pay. The Social Security and Housing Benefits Act 1982 effectively rendered the employer an agent of the Department of Social Security to administer the sickness pay rights of his employees. The Act was later amended and largely consolidated in the Social Security Contributions and Benefits Act 1992, and has been amended by the Statutory Sick Pay Act 1994.

In outline, the scheme provides that the employer must pay sick pay for the first 28 weeks of illness and only after that is the employee entitled to incapacity benefit. The employer may recover the amount of statutory sick pay that exceeds 13 per cent of gross National Insurance contributions payable by both employer and all his employees in any tax month. These are recoverable from NI and PAYE payments. The employee may not claim statutory sick pay for the first three days of any period of sickness, and the following employees are excluded altogether from claiming it: pensioners, employees for less than three months, those who earn too little to pay National Insurance contributions and a person not employed by reason of a stop-page of work due to a trade dispute at his workplace unless the employee had no direct interest in its outcome.

To claim, the employee must be suffering from some disease or physical or mental disablement rendering him incapable of performing any work which he can reasonably be expected to do under his contract. Two periods of incapacity are treated as one if they are separated by not more than eight weeks. Where an employee's contract is terminated in order to evade the employer's liability for sick pay, the entitlement continues as long as the sickness. Although most workers labour from Monday to Friday, there are many variations to this theme, and the employer and employee should agree what are qualifying days for sick pay. In the absence of agreement, the Regulations lay down the agreed normal working days as qualifying days.

The amount payable is a daily rate but depends on normal weekly earnings. The general rule takes the last normal pay day before the entitlement to statutory sick pay arises and then averages the weekly earnings over the period of at least eight weeks before that date. The rates are reviewed annually. The payment is taxable and the claimant must pay National Insurance contributions on it. Payments by the employer for statutory sick pay serve to reduce any contractual entitlement to sick pay by an equivalent amount.

To claim statutory sick pay, the employee or his agent has to inform the employer that he is unfit for work. The employer can fix a time limit for notification, but must give reasonable publicity to it. In the absence of a published time limit, the employee has seven days to give notice, with a discretionary extension for good cause up to 90 days. Although the employer cannot require that the sick employee notifies him in person of his illness, the employer may lay down the mode of notification. He cannot, however, require medical evidence or notification on a special form. In due course, the employer may seek other relevant information, such as medical evidence, from the employee. The employee may conversely ask for a statement of his entitlement to statutory sick pay. Most issues of contributions are ruled on by the Department for Work and Pensions in the first instance with a question of law referred to the High Court by way of case stated. In other cases, entitlement is decided by an adjudication officer with appeal to the Social Security and Child Support Appeals Tribunal and then to a Commissioner.

Once an employee's entitlement to sick pay is exhausted, it is not possible to claim holiday pay, according to the Court of Appeal in *Commissioners of Inland Revenue* v *Ainsworth* (2005) as this presupposes the employee is on leave from work. When on sick leave there is no work to take leave from.

12.2.6 Medical suspension pay

As part of its policy of preserving income during difficult periods for employees, the EPA 1975 (now ERA 1996, ss 64 and 65) gave the right to payment to an employee who is suspended by his employer on medical grounds, subject to some exceptions.

The reason for suspension may be statutory requirements or any Code of Practice issued under Health and Safety at Work etc. Act 1974, s. 16. These demand suspension in the event of certain dangers arising from, for example, the handling of tin, enamel, chemicals, etc. The employee must then be paid while suspended for a period up to 26 weeks (ERA 1996, s. 64(1)) 'only if, and so long as, he continues to be employed by his employer, but is not provided with work, or does not perform the work he normally performed before the suspension' (s. 64(5)).

12.3 Time off work

Statute provides certain rights for employees to take time off. Two of these rights, of trade unions officials to carry out their duties and of trade union members to participate in trade union activities, are more appropriately considered as examples of the legal encouragement to collective bargaining. Another permits time off for ante-natal care, and is dealt with under maternity provision. Time off to care for dependants has already been considered above.

Others are more widely available. The ERA 1996, ss 52–54 accord an employee who has served over two years, and who is dismissed for redundancy, reasonable time off at the normal hourly rate to look for other work or make arrangements for training. What is 'reasonable' depends on the prospects of getting other work, but it is not essential for the employee to give details of his proposed interviews as a precondition of being released (*Dutton* v *Hawker Siddeley Aviation Ltd* (1978)). The employer is liable for up to 40 per cent of a week's pay.

The ERA 1996, s. 50 permits reasonable time off to an employee who is a member of, for example, a local authority, statutory tribunal, a relevant health body, or a school governor. This provision is designed to encourage a broader cross-section of society to serve on such bodies. The criteria for determining the reasonable amount of time off include consideration of how much time off is required for the performance of the relevant office, how much the employee has already been permitted, the circumstances of the employer's business, and the effect of the employee's absence. There is no obligation on the employer to pay for such time off since most of these public bodies provide loss of earnings allowances. It is not enough, on the other hand, for the employer merely to alter the times of work so that, for example, lecturer's times of lectures do not clash with council meetings—the employee must actually have time off (*Ratcliffe* v *Dorset CC* (1978)).

Another is the right introduced by EA 2002, s. 43 as a new TULR(C)A 1992, s. 168A, allowing trade union members who are learning representatives to take time off for various purposes. These are:

(i) analysing learning or training needs,

(ii) providing information and advice about learning or training matters,

(iii) arranging learning or training, and

(iv) promoting the value of learning or training,

and consulting the employer about them, as well as preparing for them. Written notice must be given to the employer. The employee is also entitled to time off to train for these purposes. The amount of time off is such as is reasonable in the circumstances having regard to any Code of Practice produced by ACAS or the Secretary of State.

12.4 **Patents**

The common law duty of fidelity used to provide the legal basis of the ownership of inventions made by the employee in his employer's time. The courts emphasised that the employer had first call on the employee's time and any designs made during working hours thus belonged to the employer (*British Reinforced Concrete Co. Ltd* v *Lind* (1917), *British Syphon Co. Ltd* v *Homewood* (1956)). Often collective agreements and individual bargaining modified its scope and now the Patents Act 1977 and the Copyright, Designs and Patents Act 1988 cover the field and greatly improve the position of the employee.

The Patents Act 1977, s. 39 provides that an invention made by an employee shall between him and his employer be taken to belong to the employer only if:

(a) the invention was made in the course of the normal duties of the employee and the circumstances were such that an invention might reasonably be expected to result from the carrying out of his duties; and

(b) the employee has a special obligation to further the interests of the employer's undertaking because of his duties and particular responsibility arising therefrom; or

(c) although the invention was not made in the normal course of duties it was made in the course of duty specifically assigned to the employee such that an invention would be expected to result.

In all other cases the patent vests in the employee.

In *Reiss Engineering Co. Ltd* v *Harrison* (1985) Falconer J decided that an employee's normal duties under the Act are those which he is actually employed to carry out. The plaintiff, a manager of a valve department, was not employed to design or invent. He had no special obligation within the statute to further the interests of the employer's undertaking. The extent of the latter depended on the status of the employee and his attendant responsibilities and duties. The plaintiff's invention accordingly belonged to him.

Even where it is lawfully patented by the employer, a worker may apply to a court or the Comptroller of Patents on the grounds that the patent is of 'outstanding benefit' to the employer and for that reason the employee deserves compensation for his effort (s. 40). He is then entitled, by s. 41(1), to a 'fair share (having regard to all the circumstances) of the benefit which the employer has derived, or may reasonably be expected to derive, from the patent'. It has been argued by K. R. Wotherspoon that this test too greatly favours the employer and that 'substantial benefit' merely should be shown (see (1993) 22 ILJ 119).

Under the Patents Act 1977, compensation may be awarded more generally where the employee has assigned to the employer for inadequate return any of the employee's rights in the invention belonging to himself (s. 40). Again, the appropriate compensation is such as will secure for the employee a 'fair share' of the benefit the employer has derived or may reasonably be expected to derive from the patent. The one exception to the above rules is where there is a relevant collective agreement in force concerning the issue, and there is no requirement that this arrangement be more favourable to the employee than statute. On the other hand, an employee may not validly contract out of the rights conferred by the Act.

12.5 Lay-off and short-time working

It is a common industrial phenomenon that employees are placed on short time with reduced or no pay, due to lack of orders, recession, or natural breaks in production. This practice is particularly widespread in the older industries like shipbuilding and construction where the legacy of casual working is still most apparent. The practice raises important legal problems in respect of the employer's contractual right to lay off workers, and employees' maintenance of income during such periods.

12.5.1 Lay-off at common law

At common law, an employer is in breach of contract if he lays off an employee without pay, unless there is an express term permitting lay-off (*Warburton* v *Taff Vale Railway Co.* (1902); *Hanley* v *Pease & Partners Ltd* (1915)). A lay-off with pay is lawful since the employer is under no duty to provide work, but he must continue to pay employees even in the absence of their actually working. As A. L. Smith MR put it in *Turner* v *Sawdon & Co.* (1901): 'It is within the province of the [employer] to say that he will go on paying wages, but that he is under no obligation to provide work.' In *Browning* v *Crumlin Valley Collieries Ltd* (1926), a mineowner was held not to be in breach of contract in laying off his colliery workers when repair work had to be done to return the mine to a safe condition.

The courts have, however, gone some way to imply a duty on the employer to provide work in three broad categories:

(a) where the consideration for the employee's work is 'a salary plus the opportunity of becoming better known', as in the case of an actor (*Herbert Clayton and Jack Waller Ltd* v *Oliver* (1930));

(b) where the employee is engaged on skilled work, such as a chief engineer, and his skills may only be maintained with a reasonable amount of work (*Breach* v *Epsylon Industries Ltd* (1976); *Bosworth* v *Angus Jowett and Co. Ltd* (1977), sales director; and *William Hill Organisation* v *Tucker* (1998));

(c) where remuneration is partly by way of commission, so that the depriving of work reduces the amount earned, e.g. a commercial traveller (*Turner* v *Goldsmith* (1891)), or journalist (*Bauman* v *Hulton Press Ltd* (1952)). In *Devonald* v *Rosser & Sons* (1906) the employee's wages fluctuated with the number of items she completed, and when the employer refused to let her work during the period of notice to which she was entitled, she succeeded in an action for breach of contract. Although decided before *Browning*, this exception is more attune with modern ideas on lay-off than is the general principle. Thus in *Jones* v *H. Sherman Ltd* (1969) the court held that the employer had no right at common law to lay off a bookmaker manager when there was no racing.

An obligation not to put workers on short time has also been held to arise in other cases by way of trade custom (*Bird* v *British Celanese Ltd* (1945)); collective agreements (*O'Reilly* v *Hotpoint Ltd* (1970)); or statute (*Wallwork* v *Fielding* (1922); cf. *Waine* v *R. Oliver (Plant Hire) Ltd* (1978)). An express contractual right to lay off is likely to be restricted to lay-off for a reasonable time (*A. Dakri & Co. Ltd* v *Tiffen* (1981)).

There have also been various generalised *dicta* about an implied 'right to work' in cases concerning entry to trade unions and professional bodies. It was in this context that Lord Denning in *Langston* v *AUEW* (1974) tentatively suggested that in the case of skilled workers there is an obligation to provide a reasonable amount of work. He said:

We have repeatedly said in this court that a man has a right to work which the courts will protect...I would not wish to express any decided view but simply state the argument...In these days an employer when employing a skilled man is bound to provide him with work. By which I mean that the man should be given the opportunity of doing his work when it is available and he is ready and willing to do so...

When the case was remitted to the National Industrial Relations Court, Donaldson P declined to implement this tentative but radical essay of the law, and instead decided the case in favour of the plaintiff on the narrower ground that Mr Langston must be given an opportunity to work since he was paid by the piece. Hepple has convincingly shown that there are insuperable problems involved in implying a general right to work—see (1981) 10 ILJ 65.

12.5.2 Guarantee pay required by statute

The uncertainty of these rights at common law, and the difficulty of enforcing them in the county court and High Court, stimulated the development in collective agreements of a guaranteed week securing payment during short time. Such provision is particularly widespread in the engineering industry, although it is often subject to suspension, and, of course, it generally does not exist in areas of weak trade unionism. The EPA 1975 thus stepped in to imply a restricted right to guarantee payments in every contract of employment, and in doing this the Government had the secondary aim of transferring some of the liability for loss due to intermittent work from the State to employers.

Conditions of entitlement

Now contained in ERA 1996, ss 28–35, the guarantee payment is in a sense a temporary daily redundancy payment. In the normal case an employee is entitled to it if he has at least one month's continuous employment, ending with the last complete week before the workless day. The claim must be made in respect of a 'workless day', i.e. a period of 24 hours from midnight to midnight (s. 28(4)), when the employee would normally have worked, so that like unemployment benefit it does not apply to a normal idle day or holiday. The reason for the lack of work must be either the diminution of the employer's need for the kind of work the employee does, or any other occurrence which affects the normal working of the business. This rather vague phrase has been little elucidated by litigation, but appears to embrace at least a fall in orders, lack of raw materials, power failure, bad weather, and the bankruptcy of a major customer. It does not, according to the tribunal in *North* v *Pavleigh Ltd* (1978), extend to the lay-off without pay because of the employer's desire to comply with Jewish holidays.

Exclusions

The right to payment is forfeited if:

(a) The workless day is due to a trade dispute affecting any employee of the employer or an associated employer (s. 29(3)). This exception is now wider than the exclusions for unemployment and income support.

(b) The employer has offered suitable alternative employment and the employee has unreasonably refused it (s. 29(4)). It is irrelevant that the employee is not contractually obliged to perform the tasks, and a job may be suitable for a short time but not permanently (see *Purdy* v *Willowbrook International Ltd* (1977)).

(c) The employee does not comply with reasonable requirements imposed by the employer (s. 29(5)).

(d) The employee has been engaged for a period of less than one month (s. 29(1)).

A gap in the legislative framework appears to be revealed in relation to casual workers by the difficult decision in *Mailway (Southern) Ltd* v *Willsher* (1978). The applicant was registered as a part-time packer with the respondent company and worked in accordance with their needs while she was having a baby. Although she otherwise fulfilled all the requirements for guaranteed pay during lay-off, she was not able to claim because she was not required to work in accordance with her contract of employment as necessary under what is now s. 28. Rather, according to Kilner Brown J, she was invited to work, being told that work was available if she presented herself.

Where a contract is varied in connection with short-time working, under s. 31(6) the number of days' payment is still to be controlled by the original contract notwithstanding supervening idle days (see *Trevethan* v *Stirling Metals Ltd* (1977); *cf.* a permanent alteration in *Daley* v *Strathclyde Regional Council* (1977)).

Amount of payment

The employee is entitled, where none of the above exclusions applies, in any period of three months, to as many days guaranteed payments as days usually worked in a week, subject to a maximum of five (s. 31(3)). Thus if the employee normally has Friday, Saturday, and Sunday off work, there would be an entitlement to up to four days in any quarter, but if a six-day week were normally worked, his entitlement would still be five.

The appropriate amount of payment is calculated by multiplying the employee's normal working hours by the 'guaranteed hourly rate'. For those who work regular hours each week, one divides the basic rate of pay, plus bonus commission and contractual overtime, by the hours worked (s. 30(2)). If, on the other hand, he is on shift work, or works different hours each week, a 12-week average is taken (s. 30(3)(a)). The figures thus produced are subject to a daily maximum payment, reviewed annually (ss. 31(1) and 208(1)(a)) and standing at present at £21.50. From this must always be deducted any contractual entitlement, whether by guarantee week agreement or otherwise, but only a payment which derives from the employer and not, say, a trade union or sickness benefit (s. 32(2)) (see *Cartwright* v *G. Clancey Ltd* (1983)). The statutory payment is also subject to income tax.

If an employer does not comply with his obligations under these provisions, the employee may present a complaint to an ET within three months of the default, and the tribunal may then order the employer to pay the amount due (s. 34). If, in the meantime, the employee has claimed benefit, the Department has power to recoup the sum so paid out. Since it may be a considerable time before the guarantee payment complaint is adjudicated, the worker can claim benefit and then pay back the State from the money eventually received as guarantee pay.

12.5.3 Rights on lay-off or short time

Normally a dismissal is a prerequisite for claiming a redundancy payment. An employee sacked with the expectation that he will be re-employed if and when work picks up is still dismissed and there is no problem about claiming a redundancy payment. Further, where a lay-off is in breach of contract, the employee is entitled to react to the employer's breach by resigning and claiming constructive dismissal (e.g. *Puttick* v *John Wright & Sons (Blackwall) Ltd* (1972); *Jewell* v *Neptune Concrete Ltd* (1975)). Where the employer is in breach of contract in that he has laid off the employee for more than a reasonable period, the employee may claim a redundancy payment even though he has not complied with the elaborate statutory procedure (*A. Dakri & Co. Ltd* v *Tiffen* (1981)).

Even without a statutory dismissal a time must come when the employee can say 'enough is enough' and claim a redundancy payment. Otherwise the employer might effectively exclude his liability by waiting for employees to resign due to long periods of intermittent work rather than sacking them. The legislative extension provides the only circumstance where an employee can simply resign, not reacting to his employer's contractual breach, and still claim his statutory right to a redundancy payment.

By ERA 1996, s. 147 an employee may mount the first hurdle towards a redundancy payment when there has been a stipulated period of short time and/or lay-off. The statute provides that an employee is laid off if in any week he is entitled to no pay and on short time when he earns less than half his normal week's pay. The provisions relate solely to an employee who is paid only for work which he does and depend on pay rather than hours worked. Thus if an employee is entitled to three quarters of his normal weekly remuneration even though he works only on one day in the week (perhaps by reason of a collective agreement), he is not treated as on short time. This applies only to contractual remuneration and not to what he might receive by way of guarantee payment, jobseekers' allowance, or income support. Continuity of employment is also preserved during times of short time and lay-off since they will be periods of 'temporary absences from work' although absence caused wholly or mainly by a strike or lock-out is disregarded.

The employee can commence this long route to a redundancy payment after: (i) four or more consecutive weeks of short time or lay-off; or (ii) six or more such weeks in any period of 13 weeks. The weeks may consist partly of lay-off, partly of short time, and he must then give notice to his employer within four weeks of the end of these respective periods that he intends to claim a redundancy payment (s. 148). An employee's claim will be rejected if he has been laid off for less, even one day less, than four weeks at the time he presents his claim (*Allinson* v *Drew Simmons Engineering Ltd* (1985)). The notice acts as conditional resignation, but actually to gain payment he must give one week's notice of actual termination of his contract of employment or such longer period as is expressly required in the contract of employment. The employee is able to see whether his claim to payment will be disputed before taking the drastic step of resigning, for the employer may serve, within seven days of the employee's communication, a counter-notice that he will contest liability to payment. Full-time work may soon resume again and as part of the statutory compromise the employer may resist payment if it is reasonably to be expected that the employee will, within four weeks, enter into 13 consecutive weeks without either short time or lay-off (s. 152(1)) (see *Neepsend Steel & Tool Corporation Ltd* v *T. Vaughan* (1972)). He may expect new orders to come in, or that the business will be taken over. However, if the employee for the next four weeks is laid off or on short time at all, he is conclusively presumed to be entitled to a redundancy payment. Few tribunals will convene to decide the issue before this period has elapsed, so that the matter may be reviewed *ex post facto*.

Example
Othello was employed by Shakespeare Enterprises for five days a week at eight hours per day. His contract stated that he was to be paid only for hours worked and that the employer had the right to lay him off. Due to lack of orders for his employer, his record of service over a 15-week period was (and this is by no means atypical in some trades):

Week	Time worked (days)
1	3
2	5
3	2
4	5
5	3

6	2
7	nil
8	5
9	1
10	4
11	5
12	5
13	$\frac{1}{2}$
14	2
15	1

His rights are as follows:

   (a) *Guarantee payment* He may claim for two workless days in week 1 and three in week 3, and then not until week 14, when he is entitled to three days in that week and two in week 15.

   (b) *Jobseekers' allowance* Othello may claim this allowance on the fourth day of week 6. He cannot claim in weeks 1 and 3 because he receives guarantee payments, nor in weeks 2 and 4 since he is then working for the normal full extent, five days per week. In week 5 he is unemployed for two days and he can carry those forward for the next eight weeks to link in with a further two days in order to fulfil the three waiting days. In fact, he is unemployed for three days in week 6 and can claim the second of those.

   (c) *Redundancy payment* Othello may claim a redundancy payment in week 14 since he has been on short time or lay-off for six out of the preceding 12 weeks; there is no consecutive four-week period. Since he is on short time for the next four weeks the employer cannot argue with his entitlement unless for one of those weeks the short time was as the result of a strike.

12.6 The minimum wage

The first move towards widening the scope of low pay provisions came under the special impulse of wartime. Order 1305, the Conditions of Employment and National Arbitration Order 1940, required employers to observe any terms and conditions which had been reached by collective agreement for the particular trade in the district, and operated by way of an implied term in the individual contract of employment. Any dispute was referred to the National Arbitration Tribunal. This package served as a *quid pro quo* for a virtual ban on strikes during the war and its immediate aftermath and came to an end in 1951.

A laissez-faire approach then continued unabated until 1959 when Terms and Conditions of Employment Act, s. 8 reinstated a right to complain (to the Industrial Court) where an 'employer was not observing the terms and conditions of employment which had been established generally or in any district by an agreement between employers and employees'. The EPA 1975, Sch. 11 took this further since it also allowed recourse where, in the absence of agreed terms, an employer was paying wages less favourable than the general level observed for comparable workers in the same trade or industry. The Thatcher Government completely repealed Sch. 11 by Employment Act 1980, s. 19 and also the similar provision in the Road Haulage Wages Act 1938, and put nothing in their place. Wages councils were abolished by TURERA 1993, s. 35.

The National Minimum Wage Act 1998 is a much more general provision as it covers the whole gamut of workers as defined, for example, in the deductions from wages provisions, and the Secretary of State may also make regulations under which other classes of persons are added. (See generally Simpson, (2004) 33 ILJ 22; Davidov, (2009) 72 MLR 581.) Special provision is made for home workers and agency workers, while agricultural workers will receive at least the national minimum wage as part of the agricultural minimum rate. A pupil barrister does not qualify as a worker for these purposes (*Edmonds* v *Lawson* (2000)). The coverage is workers over compulsory school age and who ordinarily work in the UK. Former workers may claim against their former employer for a period of up to six years back-dated, as may existing employees, following the serving of an enforcement notice by an enforcement officer—see National Minimum Wage Act 1998, s. 19 as amended by Employment Act 2008, s. 9.

The minimum wage is a single hourly rate of currently £5.73 to be calculated over a pay reference period. There is one overall rate so that it is not possible to treat differently different areas, different sectors, undertakings of different sizes, persons of different ages or different occupations. There are, however, exceptions for au pairs and family members who work in a family business. There is also a rate of £4.77 for those who have attained the age of 18 but not yet 22. For those who are 16 or 17 the rate is £3.53.

There are complex rules for assessing the actual level of remuneration which is actually paid by the employer. The total of remuneration is the money payments determined in accordance with reg. 30 of the National Minimum Wage Regulations 1999 (SI 1999 No. 584). Benefits in kind are not included except for accommodation—see *Leisure Employment Services Ltd* v *Commissioner for HMRC* (2007). Four different types of work are identified for consideration, each with different methods of calculation. They are:

(a) time work, which is paid for according to set or varying hours or periods of time;

(b) salaried hours work, where the worker is entitled to no payment in addition to annual salary other than a performance bonus; salaried work is an entitlement to be paid for an ascertainable basic number of hours in a year and where the employee is paid by equal weekly or monthly instalments regardless of how many hours he or she works in that period;

(c) output work, which is paid wholly by reference to the number of pieces made or processed by the worker or some other measure of output such as sales made or transactions completed;

(d) unmeasured work, which is work which does not fall within any of the other categories.

(See regs 3–7.)

There are then complex calculations which have to be made to find what work is actually 'paid for' work. For time work and salaried hours work this covers time spent actually working (see *Walton* v *Independent Living Organisation Ltd* (2003)) or on call (when the worker is available at or near his place of work for the purpose of doing time work and is required to be available for such work). Time spent by the worker travelling will normally be included. The primary difference between the treatment of hours under time work and salaried hours is that for salaried hours work there are special provisions for training. For output work travelling time is treated as time working unless it is time spent in travelling between the worker's effective home and the premises from which he works.

The Low Pay Commission must be consulted on various matters before the Secretary of State makes regulations, that is the overall rate, the pay reference period, the method of calculating the hourly rate, whether special provision should be made for those under 26, and whether any categories should be added to the definition of 'worker'. The Commission in performing these tasks must have regard to 'the economy of the United Kingdom as a whole and competitiveness'. The Secretary of State may in due course add to these criteria.

Employers must keep and preserve records of the wages paid to their staff. The enforcement process may be commenced by any worker who has reasonable grounds to believe that he is not paid the national minimum wage, requiring the employer by notice to produce the records which the worker may then inspect and copy. In default of compliance, the worker may complain to the ET which may order the errant employer to pay to the worker 80 times the hourly rate of the minimum wage.

Workers who are paid less than the minimum wage have a contractual right to be paid the difference, and may bring that claim in either the county court or the ET. There is a presumption that the worker is remunerated at a rate less than the minimum wage unless the contrary is established by the employer. The employee may be able to cover arrears of pay he is owed—see National Minimum Wage Act 1998, s. 17.

Workers also have protection from detriment on the grounds that they or any person on their behalf have taken action to secure rights under the minimum wage legislation. Any dismissal for that reason will be automatically unfair.

The enforcement mechanism is supported by the provision for officers who have the power to require production of minimum wage records and require an explanation of them. Unusually for the enforcement of employment rights, they have the power to enter premises in order to carry out their duties. When such an officer believes that an employer has been paying workers at less than the minimum wage, he can serve an enforcement notice under s. 19 on the employer requiring that employer to pay in future a rate at least equal to that wage and to pay arrears due. (However, this does not apply in respect of past-workers—see *Inland Revenue Wales & Midlands* v *Bebb Travel plc* (2002).) The employer has a right of appeal against such notice to the ET. Should the employer fail to comply with an enforcement notice, however, the officer may bring proceedings on behalf of one or more of the workers affected to the ET or county court in order to recover the outstanding sums. Alternatively, he may serve a penalty notice requiring the employer to pay a penalty for the period specified in the notice. The penalty will be twice the hourly national minimum rate for each employee on the date of failure to comply. Again appeal is to the ET.

There are also criminal offences under s. 31 punishable on summary conviction by a fine not exceeding level 5 of the standard scale of fines for such matters as refusal or wilful neglect to pay the minimum rate, knowingly keeping false records, or refusing to answer a question, furnish information or produce documents when required to do so by an officer.

12.7 Restrictions on working time

The Working Time Regulations 1998 (SI 1998 No.1833) implement the Working Time Directive (Council Directive (EC) 93/104) and certain provisions of the Young Workers Directive (Council Directive (EC) 94/33). The Regulations came into force in 1998, and impose a statutory maximum on the number of average weekly working hours. There is doubt whether the Working Time Directive was directly effective (in whole or in part) before the Regulations came into effect. The Court of Appeal in *Gibson* v *East Riding of Yorkshire Council* (1999) decided that the provisions on annual leave were not sufficiently precise to be directly effective but other parts of the Directive may be.

Only a worker has rights under the Working Time Regulations 1998. 'Worker' is widely defined in reg. 2 to include any person who has entered into or works under any kind of contract, whether express or implied, oral or written, whereby 'the individual undertakes to do or perform personally any work or services for another party to the contract whose status is not by virtue of the contract that of a client or customer of any profession or business undertaking carried on by the individual'. A distinction is made between a 'young worker', who is between the ages of 15 and 18 and over compulsory school age, and a 'worker', who is over 18, as the two are treated slightly differently by the Regulations.

Certain workers, such as junior doctors and those working in the air, rail, road, and marine industries, were originally excluded from the Regulations but many of these workers are now covered by the Regulations following the coming into force, in August 2003, of the Working Time (Amendment) Regulations 2003 (SI 2003 No. 1684).

For several purposes under the Regulations it is necessary to calculate what precisely working time is. 'Working time' is defined as 'any period during which [a worker] is working, at his employer's disposal and carrying out his activity or duties'. The Department of Trade and Industry Consultation Document which accompanied the Regulations when they appeared suggested that workers 'on call' will not be working for the purposes of the Regulations and that a lunch break will generally not be included unless it is a working lunch. However, the ECJ has held in *Landeshauptstadt Kiel* v *Jaeger* (2003) that, for the purposes of the Working Time Directive, workers on call are on 'working time'. Travelling may be included, depending on the circumstances in which the travelling took place.

12.7.1 The 48 hours restriction

The primary restriction is contained in reg. 4(1), which states that '...a worker's working time, including overtime, in any reference period which is applicable in his case shall not exceed an average of 48 hours for each seven days'. A 'reference period' is defined as a period of 17 weeks in the course of the worker's employment, and reg. 4(6) lays down a specific formula for determining the worker's average working time for each seven days during the reference period.

The first important case to be decided concerning reg. 4 was *Barber & others* v *RJB Mining (UK) Ltd* (1999)—see Edwards, (2000) 29 ILJ 280. Pit deputies employed by the respondent were required to work in excess of the statutory maximum in the 17 weeks following the coming into force of the Regulations. The pit deputies argued that reg. 4(1) created a free-standing right that could be the subject of civil proceedings in the High Court, and that they should not be required to work again until such time as their average working hours fell within the limit specified in reg. 4(1). The High Court accepted this argument, further stating that Parliament clearly intended that reg. 4(1) should be incorporated into all contracts of employment (subject to the exceptions already mentioned). However, the High Court did not accept the pit deputies' other arguments, namely that the court had jurisdiction to decide whether the respondent had taken reasonable steps to ensure compliance with the 48-hour limit under reg. 4(2), or that it could grant injunctions to prevent the respondent from subjecting the pit deputies to detriment and to restrain the respondents from requiring the pit deputies to work. This was the exclusive preserve of ETs and the procedures specifically detailed in the Regulations.

The Regulations allow for collective agreements to be made between the workforce and the employer, provided that the agreement is in writing and its effect does not exceed five years (Sch. 1 to the Regulations). The employer must provide all workers to whom such an agreement is intended to apply with copies and any guidance which the workers might reasonably require in order to understand it fully.

12.7.2 Opt-out clause

There is an important opt-out clause in the Regulations. Regulation 5 provides that the statutory maximum will not apply to a worker who has agreed with his employer in writing that it should not apply in his case. The worker is entitled to terminate the agreement but, subject to the agreement, the employer is entitled to ask for a maximum three-month notice period before termination. Without such an agreement, the employer is entitled to a minimum of seven days' notice. However, the opt-out has had the effect of rendering the Regulations largely ineffective in reducing the long-hours culture in the UK—see Barnard, Deakin, and Hobbs, (2003) 32 ILJ 223. Nevertheless, an attempt in the Council of Ministers to remove the UK's right to include this opt-out failed in June 2005.

12.7.3 Night workers

Night work means a period the duration of which is not less than seven hours and includes a period between midnight and 5 a.m., and when the worker is on call but not actually doing any work (see *British Nursing Association* v *Inland Revenue* (2001)). This period may be determined by a relevant agreement, or if not so interpreted is the period between 11 p.m. and 6 a.m. A night worker is someone who 'as a normal course works at least three hours of his daily working time during night time' or 'who is likely during night time to work at least such proportion of his annual working time as may be specified' in a collective or workforce agreement (see consideration in *R* v *Attorney-General for Northern Ireland ex parte Burns* (1999)).

A night worker's normal hours of work in any reference period must not exceed an average of eight hours for each 24 hours, and the employer must take all reasonable steps to ensure that this limit is complied with (reg. 6(1), (2)). Workers must also have the opportunity to undergo free health assessments before being assigned to night work, and at further appropriate intervals (reg. 7).

12.7.4 Annual leave

Workers are entitled to 5.6 weeks' paid leave per year—see Working Time (Amendment) Regulations 2007 (SI 2007 No. 2079). Pay for these purposes is defined in the same way as the week's pay for the purpose of redundancy payments. The right cannot be excluded or modified by a relevant agreement and is not lost when the worker is on sick leave and contractual sick pay entitlement has ceased, according to the EAT in *Kigass Aero Components Ltd* v *Brown* (2002). The ECJ came to the same conclusion in *Stringer* v *HMRC* (2009) and later (in *Pereda* v *Madrid Movilidad SA* (2009)) decided that the employer could not require the employee to take that leave whilst off sick, which would defeat the purpose of the Working Time Directive. That leaves open the question, however, as to whether the employee may opt to do so, and thus place themselves under pressure from the employer. However, there is only entitlement to public holidays within these extended periods—i.e. the employer is not required to give these additional holidays when there is already an equivalent contractual entitlement to public holidays off. The extension to 4.8 and then 5.6 weeks in 2009 was intended to cover public holiday entitlement. The leave year begins for these purposes on a date stated in a relevant agreement or, in default of such agreement: (i) if the worker's employment commenced before 1 October 1998 on 1 October 1998, and each subsequent anniversary of that date; or (ii) if the worker commenced after 1 October 1998, on the date of the commencement of the employment (reg. 13(3)). The employee originally needed to accrue 13 weeks' continuous employment to be entitled, but this was removed by the Working Time (Amendment) Regulations 2001 (SI 2001 No. 3256). If the worker's employment is terminated during the course of the leave year and he has not yet taken the proportionate leave, the employer must make him a payment in lieu of the leave not taken (reg. 14(2)) but there is no duty on the employee to account for taken leave greater than the contractual entitlement, in absence of agreement to the contrary, according to the EAT in *Hill* v *Chapell* (2003). There are also provisions by which the employer can require the worker to take leave on particular days (reg. 15(2); see *Sumsion* v *BBC (Scotland)* (2007).

The employee's entitlement to a claim for annual leave once his entitlement to sick pay has been exhausted may also be brought under ERA, s. 23. This is because it also amounts to an unlawful deduction from wages, according to the House of Lords when *Stringer* was referred back by the ECJ—see *HMRC* v *Stringer* (2009).

Sometimes employers include within pay a sum to cover holiday pay. These are lawful, so long as the amount that represents holiday pay is specified in actual or percentage terms, and where it is allocated to and paid during, immediately before, or immediately after, the holiday leave—*Marshalls Clay Products Ltd* v *Caulfield* (2003); *Smith* v *A. J. Morrisroes & Sons* (2005). The employer cannot unilaterally decide that the remuneration he is paying is to be taken as including an element for holiday pay—*Blackburn* v *Gridquest* (2003).

Rolled-up holiday pay, by which employers pay additional payments to employees during working weeks rather than pay during holidays actually taken, is unlawful (as contrary to the Working Time Directive) according to the ECJ in *Robinson-Steele* v *R. D. Retail Services Ltd* (2006). This is because it may discourage employees from taking their holiday entitlement.

One issue which remains unclear is the periods to which the term 'annual leave' is meant to apply. Most employees working a standard working week would appreciate that a week's leave would cover both the days on which they would ordinarily be at work, but also those days when they would not, such as weekends. It is not always so clear for workers who have more abnormal contracts. If work is done on a basis of two weeks on, followed by two weeks off, throughout the year, would the employer be entitled to require the employee to take annual leave during those weeks when he is not working? That would seem to contradict common sense in theory—it would seem to allow other employers require their employees to take annual leave at weekends—but was the conclusion reached by the EAT in *Craig* v *Transocean International Resources Ltd* (2009). The alternative would be to entitle employees who work half the weeks of the year to additional statutory entitlement weeks. That seems equally illogical.

12.7.5 **Rest breaks**

By reg. 12 an adult worker is entitled to a rest break where the daily working time is more than six hours (reg. 12(1)). The EAT made it clear in *The Corps of Commissionaires Management Ltd* v *Hughes* (2009) that this does not mean a rest break for each six hours of working. It said also that, as the Regulations were silent on the matter, it was a matter of agreement between the parties as to whether this period was paid or not. Although the employer is not required to ensure that employees take their rest breaks, they must do nothing to dissuade them from doing so. So, the employer should, for example, actively schedule rest periods—see the decision of the ECJ in *Commission of the European Communities* v *United Kingdom* (2006). The rest break must be for an uninterrupted period of not less than 20 minutes and the worker is entitled to spend that time away from the work station. Details of the rest break may be set out in a collective or workforce agreement. Where the pattern of work puts the health and safety of a worker at risk, in particular because the work is monotonous or the work rate is pre-determined, the employer must ensure that the employee is given adequate rest breaks (reg. 8). Under reg. 21(c) the employer has a defence if 'the worker's activities involve the need for continuity of service or production'. However, the employer cannot escape liability purely by not employing enough workers to cover breaks, according to the Court of Appeal in *Gailagher* v *Alpha Catering Services Ltd* (2005).

12.7.6 **Enforcement**

The enforcement of the Regulations is the domain of the Health and Safety Executive and, in some limited circumstances, local authorities (reg. 28(2)). An employer failing to comply with the 'relevant requirements' of the Regulations will commit an offence and may face fines of up to a statutory maximum on summary conviction or unlimited fines on conviction on indictment. A worker is entitled to complain to an ET if Regulations relating to rest and holiday pay are breached by the employer or the worker has suffered detriment due to asserting his rights under the Regulations (reg. 31, which inserts a new s. 45A into the ERA 1996).

Records must be kept which are adequate to show whether time limits for maximum weekly working time, night working and assignment to night work are complied with (reg. 9), and they should be retained for two years from the time when they were made.

12.7.7 Exclusions

The primary duties do not apply to those engaged in air, road, rail, sea, inland waterway or lake transport, sea fishing or other work at sea. Doctors in training are excluded, as are some activities of the armed forces, police and civil protection services which 'inevitably conflict with the provisions of [the] Regulations' (reg. 18). Further, the limits on maximum weekly working time, night work, daily rest, weekly rest or rest breaks do not apply to those workers who are engaged in 'unmeasured working time'. Regulation 20 defines this rubric as 'where, on account of the specific characteristics of the activity in which [the worker] is engaged, the duration of his working time is not measured or predetermined...by the worker himself'. Examples are given of managing executives, other persons with autonomous decision-taking power, family workers, and church workers. The provisions on night workers, daily and weekly rest breaks are excluded in several cases, including where a worker's activities are such that his place of work and place of residence are distant from each other or the worker is engaged in security and surveillance activities.

12.8 The Public Interest Disclosure Act 1998

The Public Interest Disclosure Act 1998 (which inserts Part IVA into the ERA 1996) was implemented to protect individuals who make disclosures of information in the public interest. It is irrelevant that such information is protected by a duty of confidentiality in a contract of employment (ERA 1996, s. 43J), and the worker is able, under ERA 1996, ss 47B and 48 to take his employer to the ET if he suffers any detriment as a result of his protected disclosure or is dismissed on this ground (see Bowers, Lewis, and Mitchell, *Whistleblowing; the New Law* (London: Sweet & Maxwell, 1999); Lewis, (2001) 30 ILJ 169; Lewis (ed.), *Whistleblowing at Work* (London: Athlone Press, 2001); and Lewis, (2005) 34 ILJ 239. In the latter piece the author argues that greater benefits would accrue to workers if the legislative scheme were more like the anti-discrimination legislation). The term 'worker' is very widely defined and includes third party contractors and trainees (ERA 1996, s. 43K).

Protected disclosures include disclosures concerning crime, breach of a legal obligation (including, rather surprisingly, breaches of the contract of employment—see *Parkins* v *Sodexho Ltd* (2002)), miscarriage of justice, danger to health or safety or to

326 Statutory rights regulating the employment relationship

the environment, and attempts to conceal any of the above (ERA 1996, s. 43B(1)). A disclosure which itself amounts to a criminal offence (e.g. under the Official Secrets Act) does not qualify. However, it is only disclosures themselves that are protected, with activities leading to disclosures, such as hacking into a computer to obtain information, according to the Court of Appeal in *Bolton School* v *Evans* (2007). (See Lewis, (2007) 35 ILJ 324.) Likewise, an allegation that does not amount to the mere disclosing of information will not be protected by the Act, according to the EAT in *Cavendish Munro Professional Risks Management Ltd* v *Geduld* (2010). Employees must therefore take extreme care in this type of case, which is common. The solution, however, would seem to be to separate any allegation from the disclosure of factual data as opposed to (even well-justifed) opinion, in which event it would seem that there could be protection.

It is not necessary that the wrongdoing or failure the whistleblower discloses be that of the employer or a co-worker. It might be that of a third party, as in *Hibbins* v *Hesters Way Neighbourhood Project* (2009) where an employee made a disclosure about a person whom she had interviewed during the course of her work.

There are different regimes for regulation dependent on the person to whom disclosure is made. The worker is entitled to disclose a relevant failure to his employer (or ex-employer—see *Woodward* v *Abbey National plc* (2006)) if he has a reasonable belief that malpractice has occurred and acts in good faith (ERA 1996, s. 43C) without a predominant, antagonistic, ulterior motive for making the claim—see *Street* v *Derbyshire Unemployed Workers' Centre* (2004). The same applies if the disclosure relates to the conduct of a person other than the employer and that person has legal responsibility for the matter about which the disclosure is made. A qualifying disclosure is made to a legal adviser if the disclosure is in the course of obtaining legal advice (ERA 1996, s. 43D). The worker is further entitled to disclose relevant information to a person prescribed by an Order made by the Secretary of State specifically for this purpose (such as the Financial Services Authority and Serious Fraud Office for matters within their respective remits), provided that he reasonably believes 'that the information disclosed, and any allegation contained in it, are substantially true' (ERA 1996, s. 43F). He must also reasonably believe that the relevant failure falls within any description of matters in respect of which that person is so prescribed.

There are also more tightly regulated and complex circumstances in which workers may gain statutory protection for a disclosure made to others, including the media. Section 43G provides that where the worker makes the disclosure to any other person in good faith, believes that the information is substantially true, is not making the disclosure for purposes of personal gain and meets one of the following conditions, the disclosure will be protected provided that it is reasonable for the worker to make the disclosure in all the circumstances of the case. The conditions are as follows:

(a) that at the time he makes the disclosure, the worker reasonably believes that he will be subjected to detriment by his employer (perhaps vicariously for the acts of another employee—see *Cumbria County Council* v *Carlisle-Morgan* (2007)); (see Lewis, (2007) 36 ILJ 224) if he discloses the relevant failure either to his employer or to a prescribed person; or

(b) that, in a case where there is no prescribed person, the worker reasonably believes that it is likely that evidence relating to the relevant failure will be destroyed if he discloses information to his employer; or

(c) that the worker has already made the disclosure to his employer or to a pre-scribed person (ERA 1996, s. 43G(2)).

Criteria which are specifically laid down to determine the reasonableness of the disclosure include the identity of the person to whom the disclosure is made, the seriousness of the disclosure and whether the failure detailed in the disclosure is likely to occur in the future (ERA 1996, s. 43G(3)). The employee need only have a reasonable belief in the truth of the facts he is disclosing. It is not necessary for them in fact to be true (*Darnton* v *University of Surrey* (2003)) or that the employee is in fact in breach of a legal obligation (*Babula* v *Waltham Forest College* (2007)).

There is further provision where the worker discloses information concerning an exceptionally serious failure. The requirements are less stringent, and do not require him to believe that he would be victimised or to have already raised his concerns with his employer or a prescribed person (ERA 1996, s. 43H). If the reason or principal reason why an employee is dismissed is that he has made a protected disclosure, the dismissal is automatically unfair and the employee may claim com-pensation without any maximum limit (ERA 1996, s. 103A). Interim relief is avail-able (ERA 1996, s. 128(1)). Further, the employee must not be subjected to any detriment for this reason (ERA 1996, s. 47B).

12.9 Protection from harassment

The Protection from Harassment Act 1997 gives some protection to, amongst others, employees who are bullied at work. (See generally Quill, (2005) 21 ICJLLIR 645.) Under this Act, unless an act is lawfully and reasonably done to prevent a crime, an act of harassment may constitute an offence under ss 1 and 2. Regardless of the perpetrator's own belief, if a reasonable person in that position would have considered it to amount to harassment, it will do so. Having said that, the Court of Appeal said in *Sunderland City Council* v *Conn* (2008) that whether something amounts to harassment depends upon the context in which it occurs. This would not appear to be a correct reading of the legislation.

Harassment includes alarming another or causing that person distress, and it may consist of speech alone (s. 7). The penalty is a maximum term of imprison-ment of six months or a fine not exceeding level 5 on the standard scale, or pos-sibly both. It is also possible to bring civil proceedings under s. 3 for an actual or apprehended act of harassment, and damages may be awarded. In addition an injunction may be made by the county court or High Court and the victim may apply, under oath, for a warrant for the arrest of the perpetrator. In this event the latter is liable to be sentenced for a maximum of five years and/or fined if convicted on indictment or, on summary conviction, imprisoned for a period of up to six months or fined. Repeated actions causing another to fear violence may be liable to the same penalties under s. 4. In addition the court has the power under s. 5 to make a restraining order. Again, the same penalties apply as above on the breach of such an order.

It was some time before the courts considered the possibilities for the application of this Act in the employment context, designed as it was primarily for the purposes of dealing with stalkers. However, it also clearly has relevance for employees who are bullied at work, but frequently the bully concerned is not the employer but a fellow employee. In *Majrowski* v *Guy's and St Thomas's NHS Trust* (2006) the House of Lords held that it was nevertheless possible for the Act to come to the victim's aid in such circumstances. There was nothing in the Act to prevent the employer from being vicariously liable for the acts of the bully, so long as there was a sufficient connection to the employment. (See further Stevens, (2007) 123 LQR 30.) This was an important finding in that the options open to bullied employees in such circumstances before were very limited, relying as they would have to on other, inappropriate, areas of law, such as constructive dismissal. (See Barrett, (2006) 35 ILJ 431; *Banks* v *Ablex Ltd* (2005).)

SELECTED READING

Barnard, C., Deakin, S., and Hobbs, R. (2003), 'Opting Out of the 48-Hour Week: Employer Necessity or Individual Choice? An Empirical Study of the Operation of Article 18(1)(b) of the Working Time Directive in the UK', (2003) 32 ILJ 223

Deakin, S. (1992), 'Logical Deductions? Wages Law before and after Delaney v Staples', (1992) 55 MLR 848

Lewis, D. (1995), 'Whistleblowers and Job Security', (1995) 58 MLR 208

Lewis, D. (1998), 'The Public Interest Disclosure Act', (1998) 27 ILJ 325

Lewis, D. (2005), 'Protecting Rights for Whistleblowers: Would an Anti-Discrimination Model Be More Effective?', (2005) 34 ILJ 239

Simpson, B. (2004), 'The National Minimum Wage Five Years On: Reflections on Some General Issues', (2004) 33 ILJ 22

13

Trade unions

SUMMARY

This chapter moves away from individual employment rights to collective labour law. The main focus of that is the trade union. The chapter begins by looking at what a trade union in law is. The legal status of trade unions is then examined, and the importance of being an 'independent' trade union is explored. Then follows an examination of the legal aspects of certain matters regarding the internal affairs of trade unions, namely its accounts, political funds, amalgamations, and the rule book. The law concerning union elections to its principal executive committee are then dealt with. Finally, the rights to union membership and union activities are considered, and then the law on the union's right to discipline its members.

13.1 Definition of trade union

The term 'trade union' is in constant and popular use, and it is usually clear whether a body is or is not a union. However, a statutory definition is necessary in order to determine what are the organisations which are eligible for the various rights and duties accorded such bodies. Thus TULR(C)A 1992, s. 1 primarily characterises as a union, 'an organisation (whether temporary or permanent) which consists wholly or mainly of workers of one or more descriptions and is an organisation and whose principal purposes include the regulation of relations between workers of that description or those descriptions and employers or employers' associations'. The statute thus stresses collective bargaining as the indicator of an organisation being a trade union as opposed to other major functions. Constitutional formality distinguishes an organisation from a mere collection of individuals. Moreover, it is the principal purposes of the organisation which must be within the scope of the section, so that in *Midland Cold Storage Ltd* v *Turner* (1972), although a shop stewards' committee drawn from the members of various unions in London docks was an organisation of workers, it was not a trade union since its main objects did not include regulating industrial relations between employers and employees. Rather the court found, 'its most apparent activity seems to be recommending the taking or abandonment of industrial action'. It did not take part in negotiation of terms on the resumption of work, but instead ceded that role to the official unions' structure. A group engaged in political activities which may indirectly influence industrial relations is not thereby a trade union.

The definition of 'workers' in TULR(C)A 1992, s. 296 is particularly important in that it includes, in addition to employees (including government employees) all those who agree to perform personally any service for another, except where the relationship is that of professional and client. Specified health practitioners such as doctors are included by express provision (s. 279). This serves, however, to exclude from the definition of trade unions organisations of solicitors (*Carter* v *Law Society* (1973)) because they are professionals; and authors (*Writers' Guild of Great Britain* v *BBC* (1974)) and students since they are under no obligation to provide services.

The statutory definition of a trade union also expressly includes federations or confederations of unions, such as the International Transport Workers Federation (*NWL Ltd* v *Woods* (1979); *Universe Tankships Inc. of Monrovia* v *ITWF* (1980)), and probably the TUC itself. A branch or division of a trade union may itself constitute a trade union where it meets the statutory criteria, even though members of that branch are also members of the main trade union.

Membership of trade unions is now most pronounced in the public sector. The main problem for the unions has been the sharp decline in union density from 39 per cent of the workforce in 1989 to 27.4 per cent of the workforce in 2008 according to National Statistics—see www.stats.bis.gov.uk. The reverse is probably as a result of the statutory recognition procedures introduced in the Employment Relations Act 1999, the decline of the closed shop, the changing composition of the work force (in particular the decline in manufacturing and the growth of the part-time service sector), and limited bargaining opportunities and derecognition, in particular at new sites.

13.2 Employers' associations

There are many employers' associations in various sectors of the economy, performing functions as diverse as pay bargaining, tribunal representation, and supervising disputes procedures. An employers' association is entitled to certain statutory privileges like unions, and is primarily defined as: 'an organisation (whether temporary or permanent) which consists wholly or mainly of employers or individual owners of undertakings...and whose principal purposes include the regulation of relations between employers...and workers or trade unions' (TULR(C)A 1992, s. 122(1)). This is the mirror image of the definition of trade unions and extends to constituent and affiliated organisations or their representatives.

The National Federation of Self Employed and Small Businesses was an 'organisation of employers' notwithstanding that not *all* of its members were employers, because its members were *predominantly* employers (*National Federation of Self Employed and Small Businesses Ltd* v *Philpott* (1997)).

An employers' association, unlike a trade union, may be an incorporated or an unincorporated association, but if it is the latter, it has the same quasi-corporate benefits as does a trade union.

13.3 Special Register organisations

The Special Register is a leftover from Industrial Relations Act 1971, s. 34, where it provided a home for bodies active in industrial relations, and even collective bargaining, but among whose principal objects could not be said to fall regulation of relations between employers and employees. They include the British Medical Association and the Royal College of Nursing, and are usually incorporated. The list is now closed, although the advantage of such registration remains that such bodies obtain the same immunity from restraint of trade as do trade unions, but only in so far as their activities are concerned with the regulation of labour-management relations.

13.4 **The legal status of trade unions and employers' associations**

A trade union is an unincorporated association at common law, which means *prima facie* that it is not a separate entity from its members, so its property must rest in the hands of trustees. It is in this respect more like a Members' club than a company, although several cases have suggested that it has a quasi-corporate status and it may be sued as such by reason of TULR(C)A 1992, s. 10(1). The most notorious decision, which galvanised the modern trade union movement, was in *Taff Vale Railway Company* v *Amalgamated Society of Railway Servants* (1901), which concluded from the fact that they were registered under the Trade Union Act 1871 that unions could be sued in tort, although only Lord Brampton went as far as ascribing to them full corporate status.

The issue next arose in the rather different context of deciding whether an employee could sue for breach of rules by union officers. In *Bonsor* v *Musicians' Union* (1956) Lord Morton said that a union was 'a body distinct from the individuals who from time to time compose it'; Lord Parker thought it 'an entity, a body, a "near corporation"'. As part of its aim to make unions pay for the consequences of their industrial action, the Industrial Relations Act 1971 went further and imposed corporate status on all unions. This was, however, reversed by the Trade Union and Labour Relations Act 1974 (TULRA 1974), and indeed unions are now forbidden to register under company law (TULR(C)A 1992, s. 10(3)) and other provisions, and may not be treated as if they had even quasi-corporate status (TULR(C)A 1992, s. 10(2)). The only exception is for the Special Register bodies.

Although the legal form is different from corporate entities, the reality underneath is not, since TULR(C)A 1992, ss 10 and 12 confers on unions many of the characteristics of legal corporate status, as indeed did the pre-1971 Acts. These provisions have the effect that:

(a) a union is capable of making contracts in its own name;

(b) proceedings may be brought against a union for a criminal offence;

(c) all union property must be vested in trustees who hold it in trust for the trade union—if they were ordinary unincorporated associations it would be in trust for the members or otherwise void as a purpose trust and perpetual;

(d) a union is capable of suing or being sued in its own name;

(e) a union is liable for enforcement of judgments as though it were a body corporate.

There are, however, some residual consequences of unincorporated status. Thus a trade union does not have the necessary legal personality to suffer injury to its reputation and thus cannot sue for libel (*Electrical, Electronic, Telecommunication and Plumbing Union* v *Times Newspapers Ltd* (1980)).

13.5 **Restraint of trade**

The common law view was that trade unionism itself was an unreasonable restraint of trade since unions sought to restrict freedom of contact between employer and employee, most particularly in the taking of strike action and the closed shop (*Hornby* v *Close* (1867)). The consequence was that the contract of union membership was void and unenforceable. This potentially severe brake on union development was alleviated initially by the Trade Union Act 1871, and TULR(C)A 1992, s. 11(2) now provides that no trade union purposes or rules should be unlawful or unenforceable on this ground alone. The provision specifically legalising union rules was added in 1974 because of the potential restriction of the word 'purposes' in the definition in *Edwards* v *SOGAT* (1970), where Sachs LJ said that if a rule was 'capricious or oppressive' it might not be made pursuant to the proper purposes of the union. The same immunities also apply for similar reasons to employers' associations (TULR(C)A 1992, s. 128).

13.6 **Listing**

Before 1971, the Registrar of Friendly Societies had the responsibility of maintaining a register of trade unions and most unions complied with this harmless formality without demur. The Industrial Relations Act 1971, however, introduced the office of Registrar of Trade Unions and made registration the pathway to any organisational benefits to be gained under the Act. Since it also involved manifold interventions in the internal affairs of the union and control of the rule book by the courts (the so-called 'guiding principles'), only a very few (mainly white collar) unions in fact registered. The TUC, indeed, led a strenuous campaign against registration, around which constituent organisations rallied as the centrepiece of resistance to the Act they detested. Those unions which registered were expelled from the TUC.

The TULRA 1974 reverted to the substance of the pre-1971 law but changed the personnel. Now by TULR(C)A 1992, ss 2(1) and 123(1) the Certification Officer (CO) of ACAS is charged with the duty of keeping a voluntary list of trade unions and employers' associations. The CO grants a listing if he is satisfied the organisation comes within the appropriate definition. He retains a copy of the rules, a list of officers, and its address and the union pays the prescribed fee. Further, to be registered a union's name must not be too similar to an existing union's appellation nor likely to deceive the public (TULR(C)A 1992, s. 3(4)).

The CO may remove a union from the list, which is open to public view, if it ceases to fall within the definition or to exist altogether (TULR(C)A 1992,

s. 4(1), (2)). An appeal against either refusal to register or against removal from the register lies to the EAT on a point of fact or law (TULR(C)A 1992, s. 9(1), (3)).

There are only minor differences between listed and non-listed unions, in that listing provides a precondition for a certificate of independence which itself confers many additional benefits, entitlement to tax relief on income and chargeable gains applied for provident benefits (Income and Corporation Taxes Act 1988, s. 467), and *prima facie* evidence that the organisation is a trade union, should the matter arise in any legal proceedings (TULR(C)A 1992, s. 2(4)–(6)).

13.7 Independence of trade unions

13.7.1 Purpose

An employer who fears that a union is about to gain strength among his employees has several cards up his sleeve to resist it. For example, he may pay more than the union rates in order to convince his workers that there is no need for outside intervention or he might stimulate and nurture a staff association (a quasi-union active solely within his firm). The latter is often controlled by middle management who do not wish to blot their copy book with senior executives. Such a 'house union' often represents its members only feebly, being rather more of a sophisticated tool of personnel management. This is a frequently adopted tactic in the United States and has been attempted in the UK too. There is no law banning the existence of such weak associations. However, the consequence of their dependence is that they cannot claim the advantages of important statutory rights.

This idea that such groups of workers do not merit the privileges accorded to unions derives from the ILO Convention No. 98 of 1951, and was embodied in Industrial Relations Act 1971, s. 153(1) as part of the little-used registration provisions. Now, under the TULR(C)A 1992 the characterisation rests with the CO, with a right of appeal by the union to the EAT on both law and fact. It is vital for conferring the rights to take part in trade union activities, to gain information for collective bargaining, to secure consultation over redundancies, to insist on time off for trade union duties and activities and to appoint health and safety representatives.

13.7.2 Definition of independence

By ERA 1996, s. 235(1) (repeated in TULR(C)A 1992, s. 5) a union is independent if it is not under the domination or control of an employer and not liable to interference by an employer (arising out of provision of financial or material support or by any other means tending towards such control). The second limitation is the more difficult to apply since it demands a subjective approach and a good deal of speculation about the union's likely future performance. In *Squibb UK Staff Association* v *Certification Officer* (1979) the Court of Appeal determined that the proper question was whether the union was 'exposed to, vulnerable to, or at the risk of, interference'. Shaw LJ continued:

If the facts present a possibility of interference tending towards control, and it is a possibility which cannot be dismissed as trivial or fanciful or illusory, then it can properly be asserted that the union is at risk of, and therefore liable to, such interference. The risk need be no more than one which is recognisable and capable in the ordinary course of human affairs of becoming an actuality.

In *Government Communications Staff Federation* v *Certification Officer* (1993) a five-member EAT held that the staff federation, set up at the Government Communications Headquarters at Cheltenham (GCHQ) after trade union membership and employment protection rights famously had been removed, was properly denied a certificate of independence because this state of affairs was likely to continue and the federation was therefore 'liable to interference'.

There is no statutory requirement that a union be effective in its activities and many trade unions have criticised the CO for his liberality in granting certificates.

13.7.3 Criteria of independence

Although each case must ultimately depend on its own facts, the process of determining independence calls for a subtle assessment, and the main criteria are most helpfully set out in the CO's Report for 1976. This was approved by the EAT in *Blue Circle Staff Association* v *Certification Officer* (1977), and provides the basis for treatment of the subject here.

(a) *History*: where the union was set up at the behest of management, the more recent the connection with the employer's coat tails the less likely it is that the union is genuinely independent. Thus in the *Blue Circle* case it was important to the EAT's decision refusing independence that the Association had been formed only six months earlier with complete employer control; the change of rules since then was treated as a mere facade. The CO did, however, state that 'it was not unusual for a staff association to start as a creature of management and grow into something independent'.

(b) *Membership base*: a single-company union is more vulnerable to employer interference than one which draws its membership from many sources.

(c) *Finance*: a low bank balance may make a union dependent, while a direct employer subsidy would probably be decisive against independence.

(d) *Employer-provided facilities*: a major influence in the refusal of a certificate in the *Squibb* case (a decision ultimately approved by the Court of Appeal) was the fact that the employer accorded, *inter alia*, time off with pay for its officials, free use of office accommodation, free stationery and internal mailing facilities. This suggested dependence on the employer, yet the irony is that when a union has established its independence the employer is actively encouraged to make provision of this sort. Generally, the CO should enquire into the effects of the removal of employer-provided facilities from a small organisation.

(e) *Collective bargaining record*: although the CO has taken the view that a robust attitude in negotiation is regarded as an item on the credit side, in *Blue Circle* the EAT 'deplored any suggestion that a record of bad relations is an index of freedom from domination or control'.

(f) *Organisation and structure:* one of the major elements arguing against independence in *Blue Circle* was the limited role which ordinary members might play in the union. Only employees of three years or more were eligible for election as area committee representatives, the employer could insist on the withdrawal of credentials of a union representative on the Joint Central Council the chairman of which was always nominated by the employer. The EAT said:

> The main requirement is that the union should be organised in a way which enables the members to play a full part in the decision-making process and excludes any form of employer involvement or influence in the union's internal affairs.

(See also *A. Monk and Co. Staff Association* v *CO* (1980).)

13.7.4 Procedure for determining independence

In deciding on independence the Certification Officer (CO) may make such enquiries as he thinks fit and should take into account any relevant information submitted to him by any person including, it appears, the comments of rival unions. At least a month must elapse between application and his decision, to allow proper soundings. While the burden lies on the union to prove its independence (*Association of HSD (Hatfield) Employees* v *CO* (1978)) the CO often helpfully recommends changes which will increase the union's prospects of being considered independent at a later date. However, as the EAT said in *Blue Circle SA*:

> There must be a heavy onus on such a body to show that it has shaken off the material control which brought it into existence, and fostered its growth and which finally joined in drafting the very rules by which the control appears to be relaxed.

Although they can make representations to the CO, rival unions do not have a right of appeal to the EAT against his decisions, however much the characterisation may affect them indirectly (*General and Municipal Workers' Union* v *CO* (1977)). The CO also makes periodic checks that a union is maintaining its independence since he may withdraw certificates if the characterisation of the union changes. If doing so, he must notify the union concerned and receive any appropriate representations. An appeal from the CO to the EAT takes the form of a full re-hearing and 'the parties are not limited to the material presented to or considered by the CO in the course of his enquiries. The tribunal considers the facts as they are at the date of the hearing before it' (*Blue Circle Staff Association* v *CO* (1977)). The CO's position is then very delicate. He is not to be cross-examined on appeal as to the reasons for reaching his decision—rather the Treasury Solicitor should represent his interest as *amicus curiae*.

In order to preserve the single channel of adjudication in the CO, if the question of independence arises in any legal proceedings (whether in the ET, EAT, CAC, or ACAS), those proceedings must be stayed until the CO has decided whether or not to issue a certificate of independence (TULR(C)A 1992, s. 8(4), (5)). The certificate is conclusive evidence that the union is independent (s. 8(1)–(3)).

13.8 Union accounts

The TULR(C)A 1992 lays down detailed rules for the organisation of unions' and employers' associations' financial affairs. These have close similarities to the obligations imposed on limited companies with the same end in view, that of protecting the organisations' membership. The rules were tightened by the TURERA 1993 which legislated by inserting new provisions into TULR(C)A 1992.

Primarily the union must make annual returns to the CO (TULR(C)A 1992, s. 32), including a profit and loss account, a balance sheet, an auditor's report, and any other documents or particulars he may require. All must be approved by auditors who should be, as with companies, independent and professionally qualified. Their overriding obligation is to present figures which are a 'true and fair view of the state of affairs of the union and explain its transactions' (s. 28(2)). The union must include in the return a statement of the number of names on the register of names of members at the end of the period to which the return relates (s. 32).

Strict rules apply to union superannuation schemes, in particular to ensure that they are run on actuarily sound bases and are dealt with in separate funds. Thus every union must have its plan examined by an actuary at least every five years, and the CO must receive a copy of his report relating to matters set out in s. 32(3).

The duty of trustees of a union pension fund is to act in the best interests of their beneficiaries whatever their political beliefs. A power of investment has to be exercised so that the funds yield the best return by way of income and capital appreciation judged in relation to the risks being considered. This must pay no regard to the trustees' personal views of the companies to be invested in or their moral reservations about the most suitable investments (*Cowan* v *Scargill* (1984)).

The Government in 1988 was concerned that trade union members had only a right to inspect post-audit accounts, whereas it felt there was a legitimate interest in the current state of the union's financial affairs. The Employment Act 1988 therefore placed upon unions the duty to allow their accounts to be inspected for at least a six-year period following their creation (see now TULR(C)A 1992, ss 29–31, 45–45D). The right to inspect is given only to a member of the union who may be accompanied by a qualified accountant. The member, and any accountant who may accompany him, must be allowed to see the records within a 28-day period running from the date the request was made for an inspection. In default, the court may make such an order as is necessary for compliance, which will usually be a declaration, but may be an injunction.

A union must also include in the annual return details of the salary paid to and other benefits provided to or in respect of:

(a) each member of the executive (and this includes any person who under the rules or practice of the union may attend and speak at some or all of the meetings, whether that person in fact does so or not, other than persons who attend to provide the executive with factual or professional advice: TULR(C) A 1992, s. 32(7));

(b) the president; and

(c) the general secretary (s. 32(3)).

The union must also provide a statement of the number of names on the union's register as at the end of the period covered by the return and the number of names not accompanied by the member's address (s. 32(3)(d)).

Trade unions were also subjected by the 1993 Act to new safeguards in respect of their financial probity. By TULR(C)A 1992, s. 37A the CO may if he thinks there is good reason to do so give directions to a trade union or a branch or section thereof, requiring it to produce such relevant accounting documents as may be specified by him. The CO may also appoint inspectors to investigate the financial affairs of a trade union (s. 37B(1)) if it appears that the financial affairs have been conducted for a fraudulent or unlawful purpose, the trade union has failed to comply with any statutory duty in relation to its financial affairs, or a rule of the union itself has not been complied with. Inspectors have power to call any official or agent of the trade union before them. Such a person has no privileges against self-incrimination. The report of an inspector must be published and can be used in subsequent proceedings.

The TURERA 1993 tightened up greatly on the abuse by trade union officials in relation to the financial affairs of the trade union. By TULR(C)A 1992, s. 45B, the union must secure that a person does not at any time hold a position in the union of executive committee member, president, or general secretary if that person has been convicted of an offence under s. 45, within periods of five or ten years beforehand. The time period depends on the nature of the offence. If the trade union fails to comply with the requirements to remove a disqualified officer, any member of the union may apply to the CO or to the court for a declaration (s. 45C).

13.9 **Political fund**

13.9.1 **Background**

The nascent Labour Movement saw as one of the foremost ways of solidifying its power the election for the first time of working class MPs and representatives on orthodox official bodies. The only way workers could afford this was by union subsidy. In *Amalgamated Society of Railway Servants* v *Osborne* (1910), however, the House of Lords decided that the use of union funds for political purposes was illegal, since unions were empowered to pursue only those objects permitted in the Trade Union Act 1871 and this was not one of them. This put a significant brake on the development of the Labour Party, but three years later their allies in the Liberal Government secured the passage of the Trade Union Act 1913, which permitted unions to pursue any object sanctioned by their constitution, although it placed restrictions on the funds which could be used for political purposes. Substantial amendments were introduced by the Trade Union Act 1984. The Conservative Government threatened to reintroduce the contracting-in system, but this was shelved in favour of a requirement that unions must ballot their members every ten years as to whether they wished to maintain a political fund. The law is now consolidated in TULR(C)A 1992.

13.9.2 **Political purposes and the political fund**

The most fundamental rule relating to the political fund (TULR(C)A 1992, s. 71(1)) is that payment for political purposes 'applied directly or in conjunction with another trade union, association or body, or otherwise indirectly' can be made only from a separate political fund. Political objects are then defined by TULR(C) A 1992, s. 72(1). The definition covers contributions to the funds and expenses of a political party, provision of any service or property for a political party, expenditure in connection with the registration of electors, the candidature of any person or the selection of any candidate, the maintenance of any holder of a political office (including an MP, MEP, local councillor, or party office-holder), and hold-ing a party political conference or meeting (including sending observers or other non-participants). Every form of political advertising is covered, following con-troversy over the advertising campaign by National Association of Government Officers (NALGO) during the 1983 General Election. The definition extends to 'the production, publication or distribution of any literature, document, film, sound recording or advertisement the main purpose of which is to persuade people to vote' for or against a political party or candidate (TULR(C)A 1992, s. 72(1) (f)). This would probably include a special election edition of a union's journal (*cf. McCarthy* v *APEX* (1980)).

The CO took a narrow view of the meaning of 'political' in *Coleman* v *Post Office Engineering Union* (1981). A member of the respondent union sought to restrain his union branch from affiliating to the Canterbury and District Trades Council Campaign against the Cuts with money out of its general rather than political fund. The CO, however, thought this was not a political activity since the adjective required expenditure on literature or meetings held by a politi-cal party which has or seeks members in Parliament, or directly and expressly in support of such party. It was not enough here that the Committee distrib-uted literature and held meetings at which views on matters of public concern were expressed, and those opinions were of one particular persuasion. The fac-tors weighing against political status included the heterogeneous nature of the Campaign's constituents, and its active support from unions not affiliated to the Labour Party. The overall approach may be contrasted with *Richards* v *NUM* (1981) where the CO held that money spent on a march and Parliamentary lobby against Government cuts should have come from the union's political fund. Contributions to the funding of the Labour Party Headquarters also had to be borne out of the political fund since this was a political rather than a commer-cial investment (*Association of Scientific, Technical and Managerial Staffs* v *Parkin* (1984), and *Richards* v *NUM* (1981)).

13.9.3 Establishing the fund

The TULR(C)A 1992 contains strict safeguards for those who oppose the idea of a union political fund. A resolution to establish a fund recognised by TULR(C)A 1992 must be passed strictly in accordance with the union's own procedure for rule changes, or by a majority of members or of delegates at a meeting called for the purpose. A ballot of members must then be held under rules approved by the Certification Officer (CO) and under the scrutiny of an independent scrutineer (s. 49). The CO must determine that the requirements set out in ss 75–78 have been satisfied, relating to appointment of the scrutineer, entitlement to vote, voting, and the scrutineer's report (s. 74(1)).

The CO must also sanction the political fund rules themselves and his strin-gent requirements, in particular, protect those who contract out of contribution. Section 82(1) provides that a member may be exempted from the obligation to contribute if he gives due notice, and he must be told of this right to be exempted. Furthermore, the contribution to the political fund shall not be a condition of admission to the union. If the political levy is not kept separate from the general union subscription, each member has a right to know how much of his contribution goes to that purpose (*McCarthy* v *APEX* (1979); *Reeves* v *TGWU* (1980)).

Under s. 73(3) the union must ballot its members at least every ten years on whether they wish to retain the union's political fund. If it fails so to do, or the resolution is defeated in the ballot, the fund lapses. The union must not confine the voting constituency to those who presently contribute to the fund. Only over-seas members may be excluded. All members must furthermore be free to vote without interference or constraint by the union or any of its members, officials or employees. The voting must be by the marking of a paper, state the scrutineer's name and be numbered. There must be no constraints on voting and the voter must not have to bear any cost. The paper must be sent to the home address or another nominated address and must be postal and secret (s. 77).

The rules apply to the conduct of political fund ballots, requirements similar to those for union executive elections. An independent person is required to store, distribute, and count the votes. The scrutineer must inspect the register of names and addresses of union members or examine the copy of the register whenever appropriate, and in particular when a request has been made by a union member who suspects that the register is not or was not accurate during the 'appropriate period', or by a member who suspects that the register is not or was not accurate and up to date. The union is under an obligation to ensure that nothing in the independent person's appointment would make it reason-able for anyone to call into question that person's independence in relation to the union. The union must respond to all reasonable requests by that inde-pendent person which he or she makes in carrying out his or her function and ensure that there is no interference with that performance that would make it reasonable for anyone to call into question the independence of the person. The scrutineer's report is to include a statement of the name of the person, or persons, appointed as the independent person and, if no one was so appointed, then that fact.

If the political fund lapses because of a contrary vote or no vote being held, the union must at once discontinue the political levy on its members, and any sum collected after that date must be refunded to the member concerned. No property may be added to the fund other than that which accrues to the fund in the course of administering its assets, and the union may, whatever its rules or trust provides, transfer the whole or part of the fund to another union fund.

The forum for complaints about the holding of ballots is the High Court and anyone who was a member at the relevant time may seek a declaration that the law has not been complied with. The court can order that the collection of contribu-tions to the political fund should be discontinued (s. 90).

13.9.4 Protection of the non-contributor

Most importantly, a member who does not contribute to the political fund must not suffer any disadvantage compared to other members save that the rules may exclude him from the control or management of the political fund itself (s. 82(1)). The extent of this exception fell to be considered in *Birch* v *NUR* (1950), where the respondent union's rules provided that a non-contributor should be ineligible to occupy any office or representative position involving any such control or management of the political fund. When the union's national executive declared invalid on this ground the election of a branch chairman who was a non-contributor, Danckwerts J found this unlawful discrimination, since 'an exempted member might find himself excluded from practically all activities of his branch'. On the one hand, some detriments are too trifling to amount to discrimination. This includes a refund of the political funds contributions in arrears (*Reeves* v *TGWU* (1980)), and a requirement that the employee had to forward his union money himself rather than having the subscription automatically deducted by computer, as it would have been had he contracted in (*Cleminson* v *POEU* (1980); *cf. Richards* v *NUM* (1981)). On the other hand, in *McCarthy* v *APEX* (1979), the CO thought that it was illegal that the employee was expected to pay 5/13ths of a penny per week to the fund which was only returned at the end of the quarter.

In the event of a successful complaint under these provisions the CO may order the repayment of any political levy improperly demanded and that the member in question be treated as exempt from the levy. The CO may make 'such order as he thinks just under the circumstances', which can then be enforced as though it were an order of the county court (s. 82(4)). An appeal may be made on a question of law to the EAT. In *Reeves*, however, the EAT said it had no jurisdiction to decide that fund rules were in breach of the statute as *ultra vires*, which is a matter for declaration by the civil courts, especially the Divisional Court of the Queen's Bench.

13.9.5 **Political fund and 'check off'**

Sections 86 and 87 deal with those union members whose subscriptions are collected by their employers under the 'check off' system. The employer must not deduct any part of the political levy from the pay of a member who gives the appropriate certificate in writing that he is exempt from the political levy or that he has sent to the union a notice of objection to paying the levy. Further, the employer must not discriminate between exempt and non-exempt members of the union by operating a check off for the latter while denying the facilities to the former. If the employer fails to live up to these duties, the relevant employee may apply to the county court for a declaration and an order requiring the employer to take such steps within a specified time to prevent a repetition of such default.

13.9.6 **Remedies**

In the event of a failure to comply with the political fund ballot rules, an application may be made to the CO or the High Court for a declaration. If granted, the declaration must specify the grounds on which the union has failed to comply. If the declaration is granted by the High Court, that court may make an enforcement order requiring steps to remedy the failure. Application may be made by persons who are members of the union at the time of the application and, if there has been a ballot, at that time also (s. 79(2)).

13.10 **Trade union amalgamations**

13.10.1 **The background**

As we saw in Chapter 1, the early British unions were primarily organised among skilled craft workers before the general unions began to operate at the turn of the century. This distinction still remains, and a third type of union, the white collar sector, has emerged to add to the multiplicity of unions and the illogicality of their structure. This presents a different picture from that on the continent of Europe, where unions are generally organised on industrial lines, with one union per industry and one industry per union. The closest to that degree of exclusive jurisdiction over every occupational group was the National Union of Mineworkers (NUM), but even that has competition from the National Association of Colliery Overmen, Deputies and Shotfirers (NACODS) and the breakaway Union of Democratic Mineworkers. On the other hand, a large company may have to negotiate with 20 or more unions.

Many argue that much better industrial relations would result from the elimination of multi-unionism and a movement towards industrial unions. In recent years this has spurred the development of single-union deals which have been especially favoured by electricians' and engineers' unions. John Hughes, in the 1960s, saw as 'the central structural problem of British unionism the multiplicity of unions and overlapping unions in particular sectors or occupations' (*Trade Union Growth and Government*, Research Paper, Donovan Report, Part I). Hugh Clegg later identified four problems to which this patchwork gives rise: demarcation disputes as to allocation of work between unions; inter-union rivalry exacerbating pay disputes; complexity in collective bargaining; and the allocation of work on bases determined by union structure rather than on functional lines (Clegg, *The System of Industrial Relations in Great Britain* (Oxford: Blackwell, 1979)). Criticism of its effect provided one of the main themes of the Donovan Commission's Report and the Labour Government's White Paper, *In Place of Strife*, which followed it. In fact, the number of unions has been gradually reduced. This process has been facilitated by the Trade Union (Amalgamation) Act 1917 and the Trade Union (Amalgamations etc.) Act 1964 (now consolidated in TULR(C)A 1992), but the statutes have done little to influence the structure to be arrived at.

There have been two major periods of amalgamation. The first was after the easing of the process by the 1917 Act, and saw the formation of the enormous Transport and General Workers Union (TGWU) in 1921 and the General and Municipal Workers Union in 1924. In recent years the second wave has seen giant unions fast absorbing some of their smaller brethren. Such unions as the Union of Construction, Allied Trades, and Technicians (UCATT), and the Managerial, Scientific and Finance Union (MSF) were created in this way. The TGWU solidified its presence in the motor industry by taking over the Vehicle Builders, and the Electricians have merged with the Plumbers and Engineers. The Amalgamated Union of Engineering Workers (AUEW, then renamed AEU), the second largest conglomerate, was created in a most stormy marriage of convenience, with several disputes reaching the courts. It was divided into four parts: technical and super-visory, foundry workers, and constructional and engineering sections, but the technical and supervisory section split away. There was then a further merger, with the EETPU, to form the Amalgamated Engineering and Electrical Union (the AEEU). The trend towards merger has accelerated as smaller unions find it harder to survive. This process has, however, done little to create industrial unions, partly because the unions best able to invite mergers have been those with a trade group structure, that is, separate conferences and staffs for different interest groups, so that the concerns of little fish transferors are not submerged in the larger pond of the transferee. These have tended to be the general unions. Unite is an example.

13.10.2 **The Trade Union and Labour Relations (Consolidation) Act 1992**

There are two ways to achieve a merger under the 1992 Act, which also applies to employers' associations (s. 133). The first is by amalgamation which must be sup-ported by a separate ballot of both transferor and transferee union. The second is by a transfer of engagements which requires approval only by a vote of the trans-feror's membership. The ballot in either case must conform strictly to guidelines laid down in statutory regulations. Moreover, any alteration in the union rules to smooth the progress of the merger must be passed in accordance with the exist-ing provisions in the union rules to change them, so that if the union rule book requires an 80 per cent majority before the negotiations for merger can take place then an 80 per cent majority must be gained. Ballots on union mergers are to be fully postal and subject to independent scrutiny. There are requirements providing for the appointment of scrutineers and independent persons. Further, the notice sent out to members about the merger should not contain any comment about the merits of it.

Where there is a transfer of engagements of a union, the rules of the transferee may be altered by the executive committee by memorandum in writing, so far as necessary to give effect to the proposed transfer (s. 102). The Act ensures the full and informed participation of union members in that each amalgamating organi-sation must hold a ballot (s. 100) and all its members must be sent a copy of a notice approved by the CO at least a clear week before voting (s. 99) fairly setting out the issues at stake. Each member is entitled to vote (s. 100(1)).

13.10.3 **Hearing objections**

Objections may be made to the CO by any member of the organisations concerned that the ballot was improperly conducted, or that a vote to reject amalgamation has been construed as in fact favouring it. The CO must ensure that the rules of the new union are in line with the instrument of transfer, and may not register it until he has considered such complaint (s. 101), allowing six weeks to elapse so that any challenge may be formulated. This requirement is, however, directory only and does not avoid an amalgamation if it is not followed (*Rothwell* v *APEX* (1976).

There is an appeal from the CO's determination on point of law to the EAT (s. 104) but, if all goes smoothly, the property of the old union(s) is automatically vested in the new organisation as from the date of registration (s. 105(1)).

By s. 107(1) a union may change its name even if there is no provision to this effect in its rule book.

There is no specific statutory provision on dissolving a union but it might be regarded as an unregistered company and wound up under companies legislation, or killed off by the High Court's inherent jurisdiction to dissolve an unincorporated association.

Where some members of a union secede from it, and perhaps form another union, the court will not order that a proportion of the union's funds be paid over to them, for to do so would amount to an unjustified intervention in the affairs of the union, according to the High Court in *Burnley Nelson Rossendale and District Textile Workers' Union* v *Amalgamated Textile Workers' Union* (1987).

13.11 The union rule book

13.11.1 The rule book and the judges

The basis for legal control within unions is the rule book, on the terms of which the contract of membership is made. The process of incorporation is analogous to the way in which the law implies into the contract of employment any relevant collective bargain. The similarity goes further in that neither contract is an entirely equal agreement, and the courts have often intervened to protect the individual. One question in the trade union case is whether in doing so the courts have ignored the need of a properly functioning union for solidarity in collective actions. Lawyers trained in a laissez-faire individualism often find this aim difficult to understand. Indeed, Sir Otto Kahn-Freund commented, 'the trade unions are entitled to claim, especially in this country, that their norms and institutions express a subculture and that the courts have in the past shown their inability to understand it' ((1970) 33 MLR 241). For the courts' general reluctance to intervene in the affairs of voluntary associations, in particular not enjoining 'mere irregularity in the form of [their] conduct' (*Edwards* v *Halliwell* (1950)), has not always extended to trade unions because of the powers they are thought to possess. Lord Denning saw the rules of the unions not as agreements whose terms the law allows the members to determine, but instead rather more like by-laws, that is:

...a legislative code laid down by some members of the union to be imposed on all members of the union. In those circumstances the rules are to be construed not only against the makers of them, but, further, if it should find that if any of those rules is contrary to natural justice...the courts would hold them to be invalid.

(See also *Bonsor* v *Musicians' Union* (1956).) These can be controlled if unreasonable, as in administrative law, and he went on to suggest that unions wield powers as great as, if not greater than, those exercised by the courts of law: 'They can deprive a man of his livelihood. They can bar him from the trade in which he has spent his life and which is the only trade he knows.' The height of judicial intervention was reached in the rules of the NUM during the prolonged miners' strike of 1984–85 but the abolition of all legal support for the closed shop since then has meant that the underlying rationale for this approach has, of course, largely disappeared. (For an illuminating analysis of the court's approach to the rule book during that strike, see Ewing, (1985) 14 ILJ 160.)

The right of action is somewhat restricted by the fitful application to trade unions of the rule in *Foss* v *Harbottle* (1843), well known in company law. This provides that the proper plaintiff in a wrong done to a corporate organisation is the company itself and not individual members. Even if it should be applied to unincorporated associations like unions, its scope is restricted in the trade union area because most union litigation is to restrain *ultra vires* action or infringement of the personal rights of members, both of which are exclusions from the general rule (*Edwards* v *Halliwell* (1950); *Wise* v *USDAW* (1996)).

13.11.2 **Contents of the rule book**

An initial problem in construing union rule books is that they, again like the contract of employment, are often little more than the sum of accretions of custom and practice. Kahn-Freund described them as 'no more than the tip of the iceberg' (Davies and Freedland, *Labour and the Law*, 3rd edn (London: Sweet & Maxwell, 1983), p. 214). Many are ill-drafted if not chaotic and the Donovan Commission suggested that much improvement was necessary. They rarely have the precision beloved by lawyers and Lord Wilberforce judicially acknowledged this in *Heatons Transport (St Helens) Ltd* v *TGWU* (1973):

Trade unions' rule books are not drafted by parliamentary draftsmen. Courts of law must resist the temptation to construe them as if they were; for that is not how they would be understood by the members who are the parties to the agreement of which the terms, or some of them, are set out in the rule book, or how they would be and in fact were understood by the experienced members of the court.

(*Cf. Goring* v *British Actors' Equity Association* (1987).) Custom and practice could thus supplement the written rules 'particularly as respects the discretion conferred by the members upon committees or officials of the union as to the way in which they may act on the union's behalf'. It would also take into consideration in this respect statements made by union officials, committee minutes, agreements with employees, and union shop stewards' handbooks. Lord Denning himself recognised in *Marley Tile Co. Ltd* v *Shaw* (1980) that 'the rules of a trade union are not to be construed like a statute. They grow by addition and amendment.'

13.11.3 **Legal control over the rule book**

Between 1974 and 1984 unions had virtually complete freedom over what went into their rule books save as regards the political fund and the right to resign. The history has been chequered. While the Trade Union Act 1871 laid down various innocuous requirements, potentially intrusive statutory intervention came with the Industrial Relations Act 1971. This required the rules of each registered union to state the body by which instructions could be given to members to take industrial action, the conduct rendering a member liable to discipline and the procedure for such action. This had little practical effect, since the vast majority of unions chose not to register and it was repealed by TULRA 1974, which also prevented the avoiding of rules as being in restraint of trade. The one rule now specifically guaranteed by statute is an 'implied term conferring a right on the member, on giving reasonable notice and complying with any reasonable conditions, to terminate his membership of the union' (s. 69).

More generally, the discrimination statutes have some effect on rule books, rendering it unlawful to discriminate on the grounds of race or sex in membership applications, access to benefits, or by subjecting members to any other detriment (e.g. RRA 1976, s. 11; SDA 1975, s. 12; DDA, s. 13). A union must also not discriminate against EC nationals or disabled persons.

Some union rules may be held to be illegal at common law. Thus, in *Drake* v *Morgan* (1978), the House of Lords thought that a general union policy to pay the fines of members who were convicted of unlawful picketing would be unlawful, although on the facts they did not declare void a National Union of Journalists (NUJ) resolution to indemnify members since it had been passed after one particular event, and did not encourage an assumption that future breaches of the law would be treated in the same way. (It is now, however, unlawful under statute to make such payments by virtue of TULR(C)A 1992, s. 15.) In *Porter* v *NUJ* (1980) the House of Lords held that a union can validly provide for its members to take strike or other industrial action in breach of their contracts of employment. Further, in *Thomas* v *National Union of Mineworkers (South Wales Area)* (1985), one of the cases arising out of the 1984–85 miners' strike, Scott J decided that while it would be *ultra vires* the rules of the union for its officials to embark upon and finance a form of picketing that would be bound to involve criminal acts, it was not *ultra vires* if the picketing was merely capable of involving criminal acts. In the instant case a resolution that 'any subsequent fines would be paid by the union' was declared void. The union did, however, have power to relieve members who were arrested for picket line offences in individual cases, if it thought that this was in the interests of the union and its membership as a whole. In such a case, the court would intervene only if the decision of the union was so perverse that no reasonable person could suppose that it was indeed in the interests of the union.

13.11.4 Implied terms in the contract of membership

Like other contracts, the common law implies into union contracts of membership constituted by the rule book terms to which any bystander, if asked whether they formed part of it, would say, 'of course'. Thus the courts have required reasonable notice to be given to members of important meetings (*MacLelland* v *NUJ* (1975)), and that a right to demand a referendum of the union's membership in respect of a General Meeting resolution should be exercised in reasonable time (*British Actors' Equity Association* v *Goring* (1978)). A power to discipline members will not usually be implied in the absence of an express term. However, an exception was made in the case of *McVitae* v *Unison* (1996). McVitae infringed the rules of her own union and disciplinary proceedings were pending when the union merged with another. Her conduct was also against the rules of the amalgamated union; however, these made no provision for disciplinary proceedings to be carried over from the time before the merger. Harrison J nevertheless held that the amalgamated union had an implied right to discipline McVitae for conduct which was both an offence according to the rules of the amalgamating union and an offence according to the rules of the amalgamated union. On the other hand, the courts have refused to imply that members be entitled to vote by proxy (*Goring*), or that a member should abide by all reasonable directions of the union (*Radford* v *NATSOPA* (1972)).

Many unions provide legal advice and representation for members. *Bourne* v *Colodense Ltd* (1985) raised the novel point of the union's responsibilities to the other party in the event that a union-supported claimant were unsuccessful. National Society of Operative Printers, Graphical and Media Personnel (NATSOPA) supported a test case for damages for personal injuries against the defendants who employed one of the union's members. The defendants were successful and secured a costs order of over £50,000. Since the individual plaintiff could not afford such a sum, the defendants sought the appointment of a receiver by way of equitable execution to take proceedings in the plaintiff's name against his union for an indemnity by way of costs. The Court of Appeal considered that this was a proper application. Although no one on behalf of the union had expressly told the plaintiff that the union would give him an indemnity against any costs he might be ordered to pay, the court should have regard to the surrounding circumstances including general practice over many years in such claims. This showed an understanding, amounting to a contract, that the union would discharge any liability for costs which the plaintiff might incur, although it is perhaps difficult to see what constituted the consideration for such an agreement (see Kidner, (1985) 14 ILJ 124).

The union does not owe a duty of care to its members individually if this amounts to a conflict with the collective interests of the union, according to the Court of Appeal in *Iwanuszezak* v *General, Municipal, Boilermakers and Allied Trade Union* (1988). So, in that case, the complaint of a disabled worker who had to give up work when a new shift system was introduced by his employers was struck out. He had argued that the union did not do enough to prevent the shift change.

13.12 **The government of trade unions and the rules**

The union rule book, like the articles of association of a company, provides for the institutions which govern the union, and there are often several bodies which have conflicting and coordinate jurisdiction. The courts must sometimes restrain a union organ which acts beyond its legal capacity (*ultra vires*). Annual conferences and national executives are frequently at variance over certain issues, and in a series of cases the courts have been concerned to ensure that the correct union body takes the relevant decision. *Hodgson* v *NALGO* (1972) is a good example of conflicting jurisdictions. NALGO's annual conference resolved against Britain's entry to the EEC, but the union's National Executive Council (NEC) did a *volte-face* and instructed its delegates to the forthcoming TUC to vote for entry. Goulding J granted an injunction to dissatisfied members to prevent such a vote since this was a matter which the rule book placed in the hands of an annual conference.

The courts have also ensured that industrial action is called in accordance with the union's procedures. In *Porter* v *National Union of Journalists* (1980) the NUJ was in protracted dispute with provincial newspapers and called a strike of its 8,500 members, and 200 at the Press Association. Some journalists who refused to strike were expelled from membership. The plaintiff succeeded in having this declared void on the ground that, while the National Executive had the exclusive right to call a strike, it was under an obligation to ballot its members if there was to be 'a withdrawal from employment affecting a majority of the members of the union'. Although there were only 8,500 provincial journalists out of 30,000 members, the House of Lords held that the strike affected other members, both those whose earnings would be reduced by the strike, and those who would have to break their contracts of employment in the secondary blacking of local papers. Although it was not clear how many members would be affected, since it was quite likely to be at least half the members, an interlocutory injunction against expulsion was granted on the grounds of the balance of convenience.

This jurisdiction was much used during the 1984–85 miners' strike. In *Clarke* v *Chadburn* (1984) Megarry V-C issued a final declaration supported by an interim injunction that a resolution of the NUM conference changing the disciplinary rules without an appropriate prior meeting of the Nottinghamshire Area Council as provided for in the rules was void for illegality. He commented that 'as long as [the NUM] disregards its own rules and the democratic process for which the rules provide, it must not be surprised if it finds that any changes of rules by these means are struck with invalidity'.

In *Taylor* v *National Union of Mineworkers (Derbyshire Area)* (1985) the plaintiffs obtained a declaration that the miners' strike called by the NUM was in breach of the Derbyshire union's rules and went on to seek damages against the union's secretary and treasurer for breach of contract and/or breach of trust for misapplying the union's funds. The rule in *Foss* v *Harbottle* (1843) (that the proper plaintiff where there are procedural irregularities should be the union itself and not a member) did not apply since the transaction was *ultra vires* the union and could not be ratified by it (a generally recognised exception to the rule), although there is a strong argument that, being unincorporated associations, trade unions should not be subject to the *ultra vires* doctrine (see Wedderburn, (1985) 14 ILJ 127). Any member of the union had an interest in preserving the funds of the union and was entitled to insist that the union's funds be used exclusively in furthering the objects within its constitution. The defendant union officers had sanctioned payments of over £1.7 million to unofficial strikers and were liable to reimburse the union. Vinelott J refused to give summary judgment, however, since a majority of the members, if they thought it right in the interests of the union to do so, could resolve that no action should be taken to redress the wrong thus done to the union. He took note that 85 per cent of the members of the union were indeed then on strike and that the payments had not been made in conscious breach of the rules or for the personal private benefit of the defendants.

Hopkins v *National Union of Seamen* (1985) was another case on *ultra vires* to arise out of the year-long miners' strike. The Executive Council of the National Union of Seamen (NUS) approved payments of £15,000 to the NUM and also introduced a by-law into the union's rules to raise a levy on members. Scott J decided that there was no power in the NEC to raise such a levy and it was thus *ultra vires* the union. He rejected the plaintiff's broader contention that it was beyond the union's powers to support a strike which had been declared unofficial. Rather, it was within the powers of the union if the NEC formed the view that the alleviation of hardship and distress among the families of striking miners was something that would further the interests of its own members in enhancing the possibilities that more collieries would stay open and that there would be more coal for transport around the coast, and the enhancement of employment prospects for NUS members. Since, however, the money of the NUM was subject to a sequestration order at the time there could here be no benefit to the NUS.

13.13 Union elections and ballots

Two types of ballots, concerning amalgamations and the political fund, have for some time been under statutory control, and have already been described. The attitude of the law to other instances has changed over time. The Donovan Report in the late 1960s rejected compulsory strike ballots which many had advocated, on the ground that experience in North America showed that they almost always favoured strikes and they gave negotiators less room for manoeuvre. Even so the Industrial Relations Act 1971 sought to use them as a means of mobilising moderate trade unionists. The NIRC could direct that no steps be taken in calling specified industrial action until a ballot of the workers affected had been held, where there were reasons for doubting whether the workers concerned wanted to strike or the effect of the strike would be very serious. The only ballot in fact ordered by the NIRC, during the railways strike of 1972, produced a massive majority in favour of continued industrial action. This procedure was repealed by the TULRA 1974. The Conservative Government elected in 1979 sought again to encourage trade union ballots and provided subsidies from public funds by Employment Act 1980, s. 1. This was repealed as from April 1996. The Trade Union Act 1984 went much further and required ballots to be held, before industrial action, for the principal executive committee, and on retaining the political fund. These provisions are now consolidated in TULR(C)A 1992 and the Labour Government has left them largely intact.

13.13.1 Elections of principal executive committees

By TULR(C)A 1992, s. 46, every voting member of the principal executive committee of a trade union must be elected every five years. This refers to the main executive body, whatever its name might be (s. 119). The Act overrides anything currently provided in the rule book of the union, and a union in default may face an enforcement order in the High Court. The Act also overcomes any provision to the contrary in a contract of employment of an executive committee member about his tenure of that office. There is, however, a special exemption for older, long-serving members and federated unions.

The 1984 Act originally covered only a voting member of the committee, being a member who has the right to attend meetings of the executive and vote on any matter. This opened the net wide enough to cover the president or general secretary of the union who may have a casting vote only. The Employment Act 1988 extended the requirement to non-voting members who may attend and speak at some or all of the meetings otherwise than for the purpose of providing the committee with factual information or with technical or professional advice (now s. 46(3)). If that were not enough to catch presidents and general secretaries, they are specifically mentioned as included. However, if presidents on appointment have been validly elected to another position on the PEC, it is not necessary to hold another election until the original five-year period has expired—s. 46(4A).

The requirements in the Act, however, do not apply where there is an amalgamation of unions, where there has already been an election within a previous five-year period, and there are also provisions relating to officials who are close to retirement age.

The TULR(C)A 1992 defines the franchise of voters in such ballots with the broad aim of ensuring that all union members may vote save for 'overseas Members' that is, those 'outside Great Britain throughout the period during which the votes may be cast' (s. 60(2)). Within this general principle the union may formulate various constituencies for its executive as it chooses. The executive may thus consist of representatives of particular areas, industries or trade groups, but such representatives may not be indirectly elected by the regional trade group or industry conference as often happened in the past.

Ground rules are prescribed for such elections. The voter must mark the voting paper in secret and vote without interference from or constraint by 'the union or any of its members, officials or employees'. Neither should the member so far as reasonably practicable be put to any direct cost to himself. The member must be sent by the union a list of candidates and be given a 'convenient opportunity of voting by post'. The result of the election must in all cases be 'determined solely by counting the number of votes cast directly for each candidate' (s. 51(6)). The result need not be by the first-past-the-post method—a single transferable vote system is permitted.

It is essential to the election process that the union maintain a register of the proper names and addresses of its members, and keep it up to date. This is required by s. 24. Certain classes of membership may be excluded from the right to vote by union rules. These are the unemployed, those in arrears with their subscriptions, apprentices, trainees, students, or new members of the union. If these categories are excluded by the rules from voting, however, all such persons must be left out; it is not lawful to pick and choose, for example between those unemployed members who can and those who cannot vote. The votes must be fairly and accurately counted, but the court may disregard any inaccuracy in counting if it is accidental and insufficient to affect the result of the election.

The union member has a right not to be unreasonably excluded as a candidate for election, and must not be required to join a political party in order to stand. A rule excluding particular groups of members (e.g. Communists or British National Party members) is not, however, outlawed.

The union has the obligation to appoint a qualified independent scrutineer before the ballot is held, and to ensure that he carries out his functions free from interference. Independence from the union might be thought to be undermined if the union is required to supervise the scrutineer in his functions, but both duties are unqualified (s. 49). Solicitors and accountants qualified to be auditors may be appointed scrutineers, as may the Electoral Reform Society, the Industrial Society and Unity Security Balloting Services Ltd, by virtue of delegated legislation made by the Secretary of State under s. 49 (Trade Union Ballots and Elections (Independent Scrutineer Qualifications) Order 1988 (SI 1988 No. 2117)). The scrutineer must perform certain duties outlined in s. 49 (such as supervising the production and distribution of all ballot papers) and he must make a report giving details of the election, including the voting figures. Under s. 51(2)(a) the voting paper must now state the name of the scrutineer, which must also be separately notified to the members prior to the scrutineer beginning to carry out his functions (s. 49(5)).

The list of duties to be performed by scrutineers, in s. 49 was amended in 1993 to require that they either inspect the register of names and addresses of the members of the union or examine a copy of the register, whenever it appears appropriate to do so (s. 49(3)(aa)). This should be done, in particular, when there is a request to inspect the register or the copy from a union member or candidate within the 'appropriate period' who suspects, on well-founded grounds, that the register is not, or at the 'relevant date' was not, accurate and up to date (s. 49(3A)). The appropriate period, defined in s. 49(3B), begins with the first day on which a person may become a candidate in the election or, if later, the day on which the scrutineer is appointed, and ends with the day before the day on which the scrutineer makes the report to the union.

The union also has the duty to provide every candidate at an election with the opportunity of preparing an election address in his own words and of submitting it to the union to be distributed to the persons who are accorded entitlement to vote in the election (s. 48). Only the candidate remains liable for its contents, such as defamatory statements. There is no limitation in the Act on the content of the address, and the union does not have the right to reject an address on the basis that it does not have anything to do with the election, unless it were able to argue that such material did not amount to an election address at all. The union also has the duty, so far as is reasonably practicable, to distribute the address with the voting paper by post at each member's postal address.

By s. 51A, a union must ensure that the voting papers in an executive election are stored and distributed, and the votes counted, by one or more 'independent persons'. This may be the scrutineer or any other person or body whose competence and independence cannot reasonably be called into question.

Although the union rule book forms the contract between the member and the union, it appears that the statutory remedy disentitles the member from pursuing any claim in contract for irregularities, because those are within the purview of the independent scrutineer (*Veness and Chalkey* v *NUPE* (1991)). It has been held that a union has no implied power to set aside the result of an election ballot after the result has been declared *(Douglas* v *GPMU* (1995)).

13.13.2 Enforcement

To have the capacity to complain, whether in the court or before the CO, where an election has been improperly held, the complainant must have been a member on the date of the election and when he makes his application to the court. When the complaint is that an election has not been held, the vital date is when the application is made. In any event, the action must be taken within a year from the default. The declaration should specify the provisions with which the union has failed to comply, and the court may make an enforcement order unless it considers it inappropriate to do so. Such an order will require the union to hold an election, to 'take such other steps to remedy the declared failure as may be so specified within a certain time', or to abstain from certain acts in the future. The order may be enforced by contempt proceedings. Since TULR(C)A 1992 excludes any other form of enforcement, there can be no application for an injunction (s. 56).

The procedure before the CO is less formal. He has express power to regulate his own procedure, but should 'ensure that an application so far as is reasonably practicable…is determined within six months' (ss 25(6), 55(6)). If the CO requests information from any person and it is not forthcoming, he may determine the application without it. The making of an application to the CO does not 'prevent the applicant or any other person, from making a subsequent application to the High Court…in respect of the same matter'. If he does so, the court shall 'have due regard to any declaration, reasons or observations' of the CO (ss 26(2), 56(2)).

The CO's responsibilities were enlarged by provisions contained in the Employment Relations Act 1999. The TULR(C)A 1992, Chapter VIIA gives the CO jurisdiction to hear complaints by members that their trade union (or any branch or section of the union) is in breach, or threatens to be in breach, of its own rules in respect of any of the following matters:

(a) the appointment or election of a person to, or the removal of a person from, any office;
(b) disciplinary proceedings by the union (including expulsion);
(c) the balloting of members on any issue other than industrial action;
(d) the constitution or proceedings of any executive committee or of any decision-making meeting;
(e) such other matters as may be specified in an order made by the Secretary of State (s. 108A(2)).

Any order made under (e) above must be made by a statutory instrument, approved by positive resolution of both Houses of Parliament (s. 108A(13)).

This procedure provides a trade union member with an alternative to full-blown court proceedings. By applying to the CO under s. 108A, the member will bar himself from taking his claim to court (and vice versa) (s. 108A(14) and (15)).

A trade union member has six months in which to apply to the CO under s. 108A, starting with the day of the breach or threatened breach in question. The only exception will be where the member has invoked an internal union grievance procedure, in which case the six months will begin to run when that procedure concludes or one year after the procedure was invoked (s. 108A(6) and (7)). Trade union members are encouraged to exhaust internal remedies first, since a failure to do so may cause the CO to reject an application (s. 108B(1)).

The CO will endeavour to determine an application within six months of its being made. In that time, it shall make such enquiries as it thinks fit and give both sides a chance to be heard (s. 108B(2)). Where the member succeeds in establishing his case, the CO may issue a declaration to the effect that the union is in breach, or threatens to breach, its own rules and, if so, will usually also make an enforcement order requiring the union to take appropriate steps to remedy or abstain from the breach in question (s. 108B(3)). Both a declaration and an enforcement order made by the CO under these provisions will have the same force as if they had been issued by a court (s. 108B(6) and (8)). An appeal on a question of law from the decision of the CO will lie to the EAT (s. 108C).

13.14 **Membership rights**

Trade unions are voluntary associations, and the regulation of workers' rights is essentially based upon the contract that exists between the members and the union, where traditionally abstentionist, laissez-faire ideas have prevailed. It may thus be thought that there are very few rights in law regarding membership. In fact that is not the case. Trade unions are a peculiar form of voluntary association in that they have power and influence far beyond their own internal activities. Until recently they also had the effective power to deny employment, for where a closed shop obtained refusal of union membership was tantamount to a refusal of a job. Now that legal support for the closed shop has disappeared that is no longer the case, but the other considerations remain relevant.

Rights pertaining to membership of trade unions take a variety of forms. There is the right to join a union, the right to remain a member, and the right to leave a union. These rights may be relevant as against an employer or against the union itself. Because of the closed shop, most case law is concerned with providing remedies against the union for refusal of membership or for expulsion. As against the employer the provision is mainly statutory, in the form of protection against dismissal or other action for union membership, non-membership, or union activities, which is considered below. We shall therefore here concentrate on the rights against the union, both at common law and under statute.

13.14.1 **The common law and the 'right to work'**

In controlling admission the difficulty for the common law is that the prospective union member cannot claim that any contract has been broken by reason of refusal of his application. His grudge is rather that there is no contract of membership and he wants one. He complains of deprival of an expectation for which, in the absence of a previous relationship or tort, there is normally no legal remedy. In an Irish case on this point (*Tierney* v *Amalgamated Society of Woodworkers* (1959)) the judge commented appositely:

He is certainly not deprived of any right of property nor is he deprived of any other right, be it work or otherwise, which he had before. He is, at most, only deprived of acquiring a right.

The Court of Appeal, and in particular Lord Denning MR, however, in several cases suggested that the so-called 'right to work' provides a basis for judicial control of the admission process and that natural justice applies to such dashing of legitimate expectations. The genesis of this principle can be traced to the case of *Nagle* v *Feilden* (1966). The plaintiff claimed that she had been refused a trainer's licence by the Jockey Club solely because she was a woman, notwithstanding her experience in the sport and the fact that her head lad was accorded such permission. The power of the defendant resided in the rule that no horse could be entered for a race on the flat unless the Club had licensed its trainer. The Court of Appeal would not accept that the plaintiff's claim was grounded in contract as she had contended, but called in aid the unruly horse of public policy. The Master of the Rolls' *dicta*, relying *inter alia* on the 17th-century decision in the case of *Tailors & Co. of Ipswich* (1614), ranged wider than the facts before him when he said:

When an association, who have the governance of a trade, take it upon themselves to license persons to take part in it, then it is at least arguable that they are not at liberty to withdraw a man's licence—and thus put him out of business—without hearing him. Nor can they refuse a man a licence—and thus prevent him from carrying on his business—in their uncontrolled discretion. If they reject him arbitrarily or capriciously, there is ground for thinking that the courts can intervene.

The limitations of this case should be noted. The facts did not concern a trade union, although *dicta* did dwell on this area. It appears to run contrary to the House of Lords' decision in *Weinberger* v *Inglis* (1919) which held it lawful for the Stock Exchange to refuse membership to a broker on the grounds of his German origins, and also fails to deal with the question of appropriate remedies.

Lord Denning repeated his remarks in *Edwards* v *SOGAT* (1971), a trade union expulsion case, and addressed himself specifically to a closed shop. He said:

I do not think that the trade union or any other trade union can give itself by its rules an unfettered discretion to expel a man or withdraw his membership. The reason lies in a man's right to work...The courts of this country will not allow so great a power to be exercised arbitrarily or capriciously or with unfair discrimination, neither in the making of rules nor in the enforcement of them...A man's right to work at his trade or profession is just as important to him as, perhaps more important than, his rights to property.

Such a decision would be capricious if based on personal animosity, spite or pure prejudice, but might be legitimate if it seeks to cut down the number of entrants to a trade or industry for valid reasons. This was strictly *obiter* since the only issue before the court was the amount of damages for an admittedly unlawful expulsion. It did, however, serve to clarify somewhat the character of the action. Lord Denning thought the union could not rely on its immunity from restraint of trade claims since the union's action was *ultra vires* in destroying the right of the individual to earn his living. Sachs LJ drew a distinction that 'a rule that enabled such capricious and despotic action [cannot be said to be] proper to the "purposes" of this or indeed of any trade union'. This argument is now unavailable by reason of the widening of the restraint of trade immunity in TULR(C)A 1992, s. 11 to include rules specifically.

Perhaps the idea of a right to work in legal terms is too radical and vague to become an important source of protection at common law. Certainly, there are doubts as to what is meant by the term. It would have to meet the objection raised by Megarry V-C in *McInnes* v *Onslow Fane* (1978) (not a trade union case) that 'the right to work can hardly mean that a man has a "right" to work at whatever employment he chooses, however unsuitable he is for it'. Hepple ((1981) 10 ILJ 65) has directed trenchant criticism at the whole concept, arguing that such a right could be meaningless, encouraging a 'false consciousness' among workers. The provisions we now examine mean that it is less likely to be pressed into service although the statute expressly does not exclude the development of the common law.

13.14.2 **Statute**

The Industrial Relations Act 1971, s. 65 made it illegal to exclude 'by arbitrary or unreasonable discrimination an appropriately qualified worker' of the description that a trade union branch was wholly or mainly composed of. This was not confined in its operation to the closed shop, and was repealed by the Trade Union and Labour Relations (Amendment) Act 1976.

The Thatcher Government was not satisfied with self-regulation of the process by the unions themselves which filled the void after 1976. The Employment Act 1980, s. 4 thus reverted broadly to the position under the Industrial Relations Act 1971, although applying only where the relevant employer operates a union membership agreement, or closed shop (see now TULR(C)A 1992, ss 174–177). The Act accords the employee a right not to be unreasonably refused, or excluded from, membership of a trade union. As it is now virtually impossible to operate a closed shop, this right is of little practical importance.

The TUC traditionally sought to police issues of inter-union disputes, over rights to organise in particular workplaces or descriptions of workers, primarily to prevent poaching from one union by another and the multiplication of small breakaway unions. Both pose threats to orderly industrial relations and union solidarity. To this end it operated a series of principles known as the Bridlington rules after the seaside town in which they were first adopted in 1939. They were, in fact, extended in the less salubrious surroundings of Croydon Town Hall in 1969, mainly to avoid legislation on inter-union unofficial disputes by the Labour Government's controversial White Paper, *In Place of Strife*. Minor amendments were made in 1979. Jurisdiction over their observance rests with the TUC Disputes Committee, consisting of three senior union officials, and constituted under TUC rules 12 and 13. The ultimate sanction involved expulsion from the TUC. The TURERA 1993 has made these provisions unenforceable. (See further Simpson, (1993) 22 ILJ 181.)

The exclusion or expulsion of an individual from a trade union is permitted only when that member does not satisfy an enforceable membership requirement; does not qualify for membership because the union operates only in a particular part of Great Britain; and, in the case of a trade union whose purpose is confined to a particular employer or group of employers, the member is not employed by that employer or the exclusion or expulsion is entirely attributable to that person's conduct. This excludes the possibility of exclusion or expulsion in reliance on agreement between trade unions for regulation of their relationships with each other which were enshrined in the Bridlington principles. A requirement is enforceable for these purposes only if it restricts membership solely by reference to one or more of the following criteria (by TULR(C)A 1992, s. 174(3)): employment in a specified trade, industry or profession; occupational description (including grade level or category of appointment) and possession of specified trade, industrial or professional qualifications or work experience. Suspension from the benefits of union membership (*NACODS* v *Gluchowski* (1996)) is not covered.

Section 137 also makes it unlawful to refuse a person employment (being employment under a contract of service or apprenticeship) because he is or is not a member of a union, or because he is unwilling to accept a requirement to take steps towards membership or non-membership as the case may be, or to be penalised financially in the event of non-membership. Refusal to employ includes omitting to process an application, bringing about a withdrawal of an application, offering a job on such terms as no reasonable employer who wished to fill the post would offer it, or withdrawing the offer (s. 137(4)). If an advertisement is published which indicates, or might reasonably be understood as indicating, that the job is open only to union members, or non-members, there is a conclusive presumption that the refusal is unlawful (s. 137(3)). The remedy is by way of a complaint to an ET (s. 137(2)). The tribunal makes a declaration if it finds that the complaint is well-founded and an order for such compensation as it considers just and equitable, subject to the same maximum as applies in unfair dismissal. It may also make a recommendation that certain action be taken, or not taken. The complaint may be brought against employers, but also against employment agencies who discriminate likewise (s. 138). An exception is made in the case of appointment or election to an office in a union, in which case union membership may be a legitimate requirement (s. 137(7)). It should be noted that there are no rights to protect refusal of employment on the grounds of trade union activities, which is essential if the law is to give the same level of protection in this area to members as to non-members. As Richard Townshend-Smith remarked, in many instances it may be less significant to an individual and his prospective employer that the employee has been a member than what he has done with that membership ((1991) 20 ILJ 102 at p. 107).

We shall shortly consider how the law protects members in their trade union activities, but first, other sources of statutory protection for the right not to join a union must be considered.

Under s. 146(1) an employee has the right not to have action short of dismissal taken against him for the purpose of compelling membership of any, or a particular, trade union, or one of a number of unions. This includes the making of any payment or deductions whether under the contract of employment or not. The failure to pay a wage increase to non-union employees only would come under this section according to the Court of Appeal in *Ridgway and Fairbrother* v *NCB* (1987). The employee also has the right not to have inducements offered to him by his employer to join, or not join, a union—s. 145A.

Under s. 152 a dismissal is to be regarded as automatically unfair, and is an inadmissible reason in selecting for redundancy if the reason was that the employee was, or proposed to become, a member of an independent trade union, or had refused, or proposed to refuse, to become or remain a member of a non-independent trade union. An employee so dismissed can claim even though he does not have the length of service normally required to apply or because he is over the normal retiring age. Moreover, interim relief (under s. 161) in the form of reinstatement or suspension on full pay until final determination of the complaint is available.

Lastly, trade union immunities for certain torts committed while taking part in industrial action, accorded by s. 219, will be removed if the action is taken because of the belief that the employer is employing, has employed, or might employ non-union labour, or is failing to discriminate against such people (s. 222). It is not necessary that the belief be held by the tortfeasor, nor that the action be in support of a closed shop, although these may not be the intended effects of s. 222.

13.15 Protection of trade union activities

Section 152 states that a dismissal is to be regarded as automatically unfair for the purposes of an unfair dismissal claim, and is an inadmissible reason in selecting an employee for redundancy, if the reason was that the employee had taken, or proposed to take, part at any appropriate time in the activities of an independent trade union. Action short of dismissal is covered by s. 146(1) and may lead to a declaration and an order for compensation being made.

13.15.1 **Activities**

The interpretation of the phrase 'activities of an independent trade union at any appropriate time' is of the utmost importance to ss 146 and 152 rights. However, in some cases its construction, which derives little assistance from further statutory definition, has failed to accord full scope to the underlying policy of the provisions. The aim is to protect trade unionists, and ultimately to provide a freer atmosphere to develop the strong unions necessary to creative collective bargaining. This is the golden thread running through the legislation and could be seen most strongly in the recognition procedures and duties of ACAS. The underlying tension this creates in the case law was well expressed by Phillips J in *Lyon & Scherk v St James Press Ltd* (1976) (a dismissal case):

The special protection afforded to trade union activities must not be allowed to operate as a cloak or an excuse for conduct which may ordinarily justify dismissal; equally the right to take part in the affairs of a trade union must not be obstructed by too easily finding acts done for that purpose to be a justification for dismissal.

In *Dixon and Shaw v West Ella Developments Ltd* (1978), the same judge said:

[Section 152] was intended, and must have been intended, to discourage employers from penalising participation in activities of a fairly varied kind ... and should be reasonably, and not too restrictively, interpreted.

He gave little guidance to expound this statement and few hints can be gleaned from the ACAS Code of Practice on Time Off for Trade Union Duties and Activities (1991). This defines 'activities' rather restrictively in paras 21 and 22 as including attendance at meetings, and voting in ballots and elections. (See generally, McColgan, (1991) 20 ILJ 281.) However cases have established that the following activities are protected: collecting union subscriptions; discussing union affairs (*Zucker v Astrid Jewels Ltd* (1978)); seeking advice from union representatives on industrial issues (*Stokes and Roberts v Wheeler-Green Ltd* (1979)); posting union notices (*Post Office v UPW & Crouch* (1974)); speaking at a recruitment forum (*Bass Taverns Ltd v Burgess* (1995)); and seeking recognition for a union (*Taylor v Butler Machine Tool Ltd* (1976)). Included is criticism of the union itself (*British Airways Engine Overhaul Ltd v Francis* (1981)), and union recruiting activities even where, as in *Lyon & Scherk v St James Press Ltd* (1976), the employees went about their attempt to start a union chapel with utmost secrecy, and thus caused considerable ill feeling in the small respondent firm. The EAT did say, however, that unreasonable and malicious acts done in support of trade union activities might be a valid ground for dismissal.

A controversial issue concerns the holding of union meetings in company time, with consequent loss of production. On one view, this is tantamount to a strike, yet an employer should give reasonable time to his employees to attend union meetings necessary for the proper functioning of collective bargaining. In *Marley Tile Co. Ltd v Shaw* (1980) Goff LJ was 'inclined to doubt' whether this was a protected activity where the caller of the assembly in question was an unaccredited shop steward. Eveleigh LJ, however, thought that nothing should be done to fetter the judgment of members of tribunals. All the judges agreed that the question should 'not be dressed up as a point of law'. However, it is difficult for ETs to decide this issue, since the Court of Appeal gave no guidance as to criteria, even though in the instant case it criticised the 'industrial jury' for their 'broad brush approach'. The ACAS Code advises that meetings are protected where to hold the meeting is 'reasonable because of the urgency of the matter or where to do so would not adversely affect production or services'.

'Activities of an independent trade union'

An assault has been made on the generality of 'activities of an independent trade union' from various directions. The first, a distinction between the activities of a union and a trade unionist owes its provenance to *Gardner* v *Peaks Retail Ltd* (1975). The applicant there was dismissed for having made various complaints to management about the unsatisfactory state of the staff room. She was not protected since 'individual complaints may be of a trouble-making kind . . . if supported by a union this provides some guarantee that they have substance'. Kilner Brown J made the point forcefully in *Chant* v *Aquaboats Ltd* (1978):

The mere fact that one or two employees making representations happen to be trade unionists and the mere fact that the spokesman happens to be a trade unionist does not make such representations a trade union activity.

In this case a round-robin petition protesting against unsafe machinery was held not to be a trade union activity.

What authorisation must proceed from the union for the activities, and in what form, is left unclear. It is not enough, however, that the applicants are trade union officers and considered a course of conduct to be in the interests of their members (*Stokes and Roberts* v *Wheeler-Green Ltd* (1979)). A difficult case arises where there may be a union policy, contained in a conference resolution, to resist a particular management decision on the ground that such is inimical to employers' obligations regarding health and safety. If the union member wrongly takes that as a sanction for resisting management, is his action included? In *Drew* v *St Edmundsbury BC* (1980) a parks gardener was dismissed because of his refusal to clear snow during an official go-slow and his long-standing one-man campaign against the council's health and safety record. The EAT rejected his contention that he had been sacked for an inadmissible reason, first, because the tribunal had no jurisdiction where he was dismissed during industrial action even though this constituted a continuation of his own campaign. The second ground was that he had no official standing in the union. It is submitted that a more suitable interpretation is that the protection should cover activities of the sort carried out by a trade union, even if in the particular circumstances the precise *modus operandus* has not been referred to, nor received express approval from, the official union hierarchy. This would at once recognise the independent power of shop stewards, and deal more satisfactorily with the type of situation that arose in *Chant*.

The second potential restriction on trade union activity relates to the position where the union activity is contrary to a particular union rule. This was accepted as a principle in *Marley Tile Co. Ltd* v *Shaw* (1980) although, on the facts, the court held that the action did not infringe rule 13 of the AUEW. Moreover, the point was made by Goff LJ that rule books of this sort were not to be construed like statutes.

The Court of Appeal in *Therm-A-Stor Ltd* v *Atkins* (1983) narrowly construed the provision so that it did not apply to employees dismissed because the employer objected to the recognition of their union. Rather the section was concerned only with the individual employee's activities in the trade union. This should be contrasted with that in *Farnsworth* v *McCoid* (1999), where the employer objected not to the union but to the conduct of a particular individual while he was acting as shop steward. In these circumstances, the Court of Appeal concluded that action was taken against him as an individual, not against the trade union as a whole.

Strike action does not amount to trade union activities for this purpose. This is made explicit in the statute only in the case of s. 170(2): the right to time off for trade union activities specifically exempts industrial action. Even so, this phrase may prove difficult to construe. One possibility is that it includes anything done in breach of contract, but does a refusal to work voluntary overtime, which may not involve breach of contract, come within it? Is it confined to collective union action, or does it comprise individual protests? Would a demonstration to protest at government policy be included? An argument was raised in *Winnett* v *Seamarks Bros* (1978), a case on what is now s. 170(2), that the strike is a well-recognised activity of an independent trade union, but this was summarily rejected. Two rationales have been put forward for this result. In *Brennan* v *W. Ellward (Lancs) Ltd* (1976) it was held that the activity was not at 'an appropriate time: The [legislation] cannot extend to...suddenly downing tools and leaving the premises, in order to consult their union officials elsewhere'. However, in *Drew* v *St Edmundsbury District Council* (1980) the EAT based its *obiter* conclusion on the fact there is a different provision in the legislation for strike dismissals.

The appropriate time for trade union activities is defined as not only occasions 'outside the employee's working hours' but also time 'within working hours at which, in accordance with arrangements agreed with, or consent given by, his employer, it is permissible for him to take part in [those] activities' (ss 146(2), 152(2)). In *Post Office* v *UPW* (1973) Lord Reid declared that 'it does not include periods when in accordance with his contract the worker is on his employer's premises, but not actually working'. He went on to cut down the scope of his judgment by saying that 'the incursion of these rights on the employer's rights...must be reasonable' and the employer must not be caused substantial inconvenience. He continued: 'It is a very different matter to use facilities which are normally available to the employer's workers or to ask him to submit to some trifling inconvenience'.

Arrangement and consent

The question of interpreting 'arrangement' and 'consent' in the definition was central to the *ratio* in *Marley Tile Co. Ltd* v *Shaw* (1980). The EAT had held that a meeting of maintenance men to protest about the shop steward's lack of credentials during working hours was 'at an appropriate time', because the legislation had to be construed in the light of 'actual industrial practice'. The Court of Appeal, however, disapproving of this 'broad brush approach', viewed the issue more narrowly. While consent might be implied, it could not arise by way of extension from other factories, custom and practice at the plant in question, nor the employer's silence. The EAT and ET were overruled because they 'considered too much the reasonableness of the behaviour and the reactions of the employees'. Yet it is submitted that this view ignores the fundamental importance of informal works rules, of which there was here adequate evidence. It takes the sort of strict contractual rights position which the House of Lords found unsatisfactory in the *Post Office* case and leaves unclear what are the circumstances from which consent might be inferred outside the obvious cases.

The Court of Appeal decided in *Fitzpatrick* v *British Railways Board* (1991) that previous trade union activities can be relevant under s. 152, contrary to the heavily criticised decision of the EAT in *City of Birmingham District Council* v *Beyer* (1977). However, such previous activity must be relevant to the present employment, from which the employee claims he was unfairly dismissed, in that it must relate to how the employer views the likely conduct of the employee in his present employment. (See Wynn-Evans, (1992) 21 ILJ 67.)

13.15.2 Action short of dismissal

The protection of trade unionists and their activities extends to action short of dismissal, since otherwise the employer could make life miserable for the trade unionist without going as far as sacking him. Section 146(1) thus prohibits action against a trade unionist because he is a trade unionist by preventing him or deterring him from being or seeking to become a member or penalising him for doing so, or for participating in its activities, whether by means of the 'velvet glove of bribery...or the mailed fist of coercion' (B. Bercusson, *Current Law Statutes Annotated* (London: Sweet & Maxwell/Stevens, 1978), vol. 2). Dismissal in this context bears the same meaning as in relation to dismissals by reason of trade union activities so that the section is intended to prevent discrimination during the course of employment (*Johnstone* v *BBC Enterprises Ltd* (1994)).

It is provided that 'action' includes refusal to confer a benefit on a worker, but doubt has surrounded the question of whether it also comprises a threat. In *Brassington* v *Cauldon Wholesale Ltd* (1977) the EAT in *obiter dicta* (since the only question was the assessment of damages) doubted whether a threat to close down a factory, sack the workforce and open under a different name if the workers joined a union, sufficed.

In *Carlson* v *Post Office* (1981) the EAT held that a failure to give a member of a small union a car parking permit at his place of work because its allocation was determined between the employers and the Council of Post Office Unions, of which his union was not a member, could amount to action penalising him. Slynn J thus overturned the tribunal's holding that this was *de minimis,* and said that the provision was not restricted to 'the imposition of what may be called a positive punishment on to a financial penalty'. However the prevention or deterrence of union activity must be an objective which the employer desires or seeks to achieve. It is not sufficient that the employer's action merely has this effect. In *Department of Transport* v *Gallacher* (1994) the Court of Appeal held that there was no breach of s. 146 where a full-time union official was refused a promotion because he had insufficient managerial experience and he could acquire the relevant experience only by taking a post which would involve reducing his trade union activity. There is, however, no requirement that the employee prove malice or a deliberate decision to get rid of a union activist (*Dundon* v *GPT* (1995)).

Frequently employers offered personal contracts as a way of discouraging union membership. The leading cases, which were heard together, are *Palmer* v *Associated British Ports* and *Wilson* v *Associated Newspapers Ltd* (1995). Both employers offered financial inducements to those employees who were prepared to sign new contracts in the context of derecognition of trade unions. Under s. 145A (inserted by Employment Relations Act 2004, s. 29) employees now have the right not to be offered such inducements designed to deter membership, non-membership or union activities. Section 145B extends this to the situation where an employer offers inducements to employees to take their terms and conditions outside a collective bargain. The tribunal will make a declaration and an award of £2,500 in such cases—s. 145E.

13.15.3 **Proof**

Discrimination on any grounds is, as we have already seen, most difficult to prove. Unless the employer blatantly says, 'no trade unionists here', the evidence is likely to take the form of inferences, nods and winks. This helps to explain the low success rate of applicants for all these types of discriminatory treatment, and why there is a case for placing the burden of proof on the employer since he knows the grounds for dismissal or action short of dismissal. Lord Denning MR was attracted to this view, when, dissenting in *Smith* v *Hayle Town Council* (1978), he said that the weight of the burden at least must depend 'on the opportunities and knowledge with respect to the facts to be proved which may be possessed by the parties respectively'. The other two Lords Justice took the orthodox approach, confirming *Goodwin Ltd* v *Fitzmaurice* (1977), that the burden fell squarely on the applicant. The latter case also stands as authority for the rule that a tribunal must first decide whether the dismissal was for trade union activities before examining whether it was redundancy or some other ground. (See also *Maund* v *Penwith DC* (1982).)

In the light of the difficulties of proof much will depend on the inferences which the tribunal is persuaded to draw from the primary facts, just as in sex and race discrimination cases. In particular, where there is a departure from good industrial relations practice, such as in relation to redundancy, the tribunal must consider what, if any, weight is to be given to this. It is not necessarily an answer for the employer merely to rely upon the absence of any legal duty to act otherwise (see *Driver* v *Cleveland Structural Engineering Co. Ltd* (1994)).

Another problem concerns collective decisions. In *Smith*, the employee was dismissed by a one vote majority of the respondent council. Although he proved that at least one councillor was motivated by his dislike of trade unionists, this did not prove that it was the principal reason for the decision to dismiss.

13.15.4 **Time off**

Employees may be entitled to time off work, either paid or unpaid, in various circumstances. It should be noted that the right is to undertake these activities during working hours, and not to take time off work in lieu of the time spent in such pursuits. So, where an employee was due to start work at 3 p.m. and finish at 11 p.m., and his training course for which he was entitled to have time off began at 9 a.m. and finished at 4 p.m., he was entitled to the time from 3 p.m. to 4 p.m. only, plus such other time spent travelling, for example, to enable him to attend the course. He could not take further time off in the evening in lieu of the time spent on the course outside working hours, according to the EAT in *Hairsine* v *Kingston upon Hull City Council* (1992).

Particular complications arise with regard to rights to time off for part-time workers. If the same amount of time off is accorded to full-timers and part-timers that would seem to discriminate against full-timers. If the amount of time off is to the limit of their respective working hours, this appears to discriminate against part-timers where they, for example, attend the same training courses as full-timers lasting, of course, for the same period of time. As compensation is not generally paid to those attending courses for longer than their working hours, this would seem to discriminate against part-timers where a course is longer than the part-timers' working hours, but not so long as the full-timers' working hours. In this situation there is discrimination against the part-timers and, because that group consists proportionately of more women than men, there would be sex discrimination against women contrary to art. 157 of the Treaty on the Functioning of the European Union (ex art. 141 of the Treaty of Rome) according to the ECJ in *Arbeiterwohlfahrt der Stadt Berlin* v *Bötel* (1992). See also *Davies* v *Neath Port Talbot BC* (1999).

Paid time off for trade union duties

The TULR(C)A 1992, ss 168 and 169 recognise that it is not conducive to the public policy of an improvement of industrial relations that shop stewards and other union officials should have to devote their spare time without pay to their duties. Where his union is recognised, such an official is thus entitled to time off with pay to carry out *duties* concerned with negotiations with the employer that are related to matters in s. 244(1) (which is the subsection detailing the matters which a dispute must be about in order to attract the tortious immunities), in relation to which the union is recognised by the employer and other duties concerned with functions in relation to these matters which the employer has agreed may be performed by the union. This can include time off for meetings prior to negotiations as well as for the negotiations themselves, according to the EAT in *London Ambulance Service* v *Charlton* (1992). If the employer refuses the time off, the official can complain to the ET which may make a declaration and award compensation. 'Official' is defined as any officer of the union or branch and any other person elected under the union rules to represent the members (s. 119), thus clearly including a shop steward.

The time taken off must be reasonable in the circumstances when it is taken. The ACAS Code of Practice on Time Off directs attention in determining reasonableness to, *inter alia*, the exigencies of production, services and shifts in process industries, the size of the enterprise and the size of the workforce. An employer may also properly consider the occasions on which an applicant had previously enjoyed time off in assessing the reasonableness of a further request. In *Wignall* v *British Gas Corporation* (1984) the applicant had already been granted 12 weeks' leave for union business when he sought a further ten days for the preparation of a union district monthly magazine. The EAT upheld the tribunal's decision that it was reasonable for the employers to refuse the further time.

In *Thomas Scott & Sons (Bakers) Ltd* v *Allen* (1983) the Court of Appeal emphasised that the question of the reasonableness of the time off sought was a matter of fact for the tribunal, and the Court of Appeal would accordingly not interfere with the tribunal's view that it was unreasonable to seek leave for all 11 shop stewards at the same time. Moreover, May LJ appeared to suggest that the tribunal had to decide not only whether it was reasonable for them to attend the meeting, but also whether it was reasonable that they should be paid for so doing. This analysis is difficult to square with the wording of the section.

A trade union official cannot, however, claim to have been refused time off if the employer did not know of the request for that time off to be taken (*Ryford Ltd* v *Drinkwater* (1996)).

Unpaid time off for trade union activities

By TULR(C)A 1992, s. 170, a trade union member is to be allowed reasonable time off during working hours without pay to take part in the activities of an independent trade union recognised by the employer for the purposes of collective bargaining. These activities need have nothing to do with industrial relations, providing they are reasonable. As the ACAS Code of Practice states:

To operate effectively and democratically, trade unions need the active participation of members.

Time off for industrial relations training

Reasonable time off must also be given to a trade union official for training which is relevant to industrial relations duties and which is approved by the TUC or the applicant's own union (on relevance see *Ministry of Defence* v *Crook and Irving* (1982)). However, approval by the union alone is not sufficient and this was the important message demonstrated by *Menzies* v *Smith & McLaurin Ltd* (1980). The EAT decided that an employee had been properly refused time off to attend a union course on redundancy because its syllabus was not relevant to industrial relations duties, being far too general in scope. It covered issues like North Sea Oil, import controls and responses to the EEC and the employee had failed to establish that anything he learned on the course would be of direct value to him in negotiations with the company. He was allowed time off as a union activity but he had no right to be paid for it.

Time off for health and safety representatives

A duly appointed health and safety representative has a right to reasonable time off with pay to perform his function and to train therefore (Safety Representatives and Safety Committee Regulations 1977 (SI 1977 No. 500), reg. 4). Where the employer provides an adequate internal course it is not necessarily reasonable to seek time off also to attend a TUC-sponsored school (*White* v *Pressed Steel Fisher Ltd* (1980)).

The Code of Practice issued by the Health and Safety Commission states that safety representatives should be given basic training as soon as possible after appointment and such further training thereafter as may be appropriate.

13.15.5 **Remedies**

If the applicant has mounted the foregoing hurdles, the remedies potentially available to him are several, depending on the precise way in which his rights to participate in union activities have been infringed.

Action short of dismissal

A declaration may be granted and compensation which is 'just and equitable in all the circumstances having regard to the infringement complained of' (TULR(C)A 1992, s. 149). *Brassington* v *Cauldon Wholesale Ltd* (1977) determined that compensation for the employee, not a fine on the employer, however tactfully wrapped up, is the basis of the award. The applicants could thus recover their expenses in going to the tribunal, and also non-pecuniary losses such as 'the stress engendered by such a situation' and compensation if a 'deep and sincere wish to join a union...had been frustrated' with all the benefits of help and advice which that might entail. (See too *Skiggs* v *South West Trains Ltd* (2005).) The normal provision for reasonable mitigation of loss applies, and the remedy can be sought by complaint within three months to a tribunal (see *Adlam* v *Salisbury and Wells Theological College* (1985)). Unusually there is no maximum on the compensation which may be awarded. The employer or employee may reclaim such compensation by joining in proceedings any union or person pressing him to take such action (s. 150).

Time off

Breach of this provision similarly entitles the complainant to a declaration and just and equitable compensation.

Dismissal

The usual remedies of compensation, reinstatement, and re-engagement are available on a dismissal for trade union membership or activities. The TULR(C)A 1992, s. 158 used to contain the same provisions for enhanced payments as applied to closed shop dismissals, but now the only difference from normal awards for unfair dismissal is a minimum basic award of £4,700. The applicant may also claim interim relief, a special emergency procedure which reflects the serious industrial relations consequences that often ensue in these situations. It does not, however, apply to selection for redundancy for an inadmissible reason.

An application must be made to the ET within seven days of the effective date of termination, supported by a written certificate signed by an official of the employee's union who is specifically so authorised. This should contain the reasons why the claim falls within the scope of interim relief (*Stone* v *Charrington & Co.* (1977)), although tribunals have eschewed technicalities in its interpretation. Thus it was accepted that a union regional organiser was an authorised official notwithstanding he had been formally appointed (*cf. Farmeary* v *Veterinary Drug Co. Ltd* (1976)). Moreover, the tribunal may read together an application lodged within the time limit which does not comply with s. 161(2) and a letter presented after the period has expired which does so comply (*Barley* v *Amey Roadstone Corporation Ltd* (1977)). Where, however, the authority of the official to give such a certificate is challenged by the employers before the tribunal, the onus lies on him to prove that he has actual or implied authority to sign the certificate, and if he had not, the certificate is defective and the claim must fail (*Sulemany* v *Habib Bank Ltd* (1983)).

The tribunal must hear an interim relief application within seven days of the effective date of termination (s. 161), and to expedite matters its chairman may sit alone. The crucial issue in deciding whether to grant interim relief is whether it is 'likely' that the tribunal will, at the end of the day, make a finding of unfair dismissal on account of an inadmissible reason. If so, it should at this stage order a reinstatement or re-engagement pending final determination (s. 163(2)). 'Likely' has been interpreted as demanding more than a reasonable chance of success; the prospects must be 'pretty good' (*Taplin* v *C. Shippam Ltd* (1978)). On the other hand, Slynn J did not 'think it right in a case of this kind to ask whether the applicant has proved his case on a balance of probabilities'.

13.15.6 Protection of health and safety activities

The ERA 1996, s. 44(1) gives an employee 'the right not to be subjected to any detriment by any act, or deliberate failure to act, by his employer' on the grounds that:

(a) having been designated by the employer to carry out activities in connection with preventing or reducing risks to the health and safety of employees at work, he carried out or proposed to carry out any such activities;

(b) if a representative of employees on matters of health and safety at work, he performed or proposed to perform any functions as such;

(ba) the employee took part (or proposed to take part) in consultations with the employer pursuant to the Health and Safety (Consultation with Employees) Regulations 1996 or in the election of representatives of employee safety within the meaning of those regulations (whether as a candidate or otherwise);

(c) being an employee at a place where—

(i) there was no such representative or safety committee, or

(ii) there was such a representative or safety committee but it was not reasonably practicable for the employee to raise the matter by those means,

he brought to his employer's attention, by reasonable means, circumstances connected with his work which he reasonably believed were harmful or potentially harmful to health or safety;

(d) in circumstances of danger which the employee reasonably believed to be serious and imminent and which he could not reasonably have been expected to avert, he left (or proposed to leave) or (while the danger persisted) refused to return to his place of work or any dangerous part of his place of work; or

(e) in circumstances of danger which the employee reasonably believed to be serious and imminent, he took (or proposed to take) appropriate steps to protect himself or other persons from the danger.

The right is given to a worker to complain to an ET, and the onus is on the employer to show the ground on which any act or failure to act was done (s. 48(2)).

Any such complaint must be presented before the end of three months beginning with the date of the act or failure to act to which the complaint relates, or where the act or failure is part of a series of similar acts or failures, the last of them (s. 48(3)(a)). There is the normal power to extend time also found in applications, for example, for unfair dismissal, where it was not reasonably practicable for the complaint to be presented within the three-month period, in which case it must be presented within such further period as the ET considers reasonable (s. 48(3)(b)). A deliberate failure to act is treated as done when it was decided upon (s. 48(4)(b)), that is, when he does an act inconsistent with doing the failed act or if he does no such inconsistent act when the period expires within which it might reasonably have been expected to do the failed act if it was to be done.

An ET has power to award compensation and this award of compensation is made on a similar basis to compensation for unfair dismissal, that is, what the tribunal considers 'just and equitable in all the circumstances having regard to the infringement complained of and to any loss which is attributable to the act or failure which infringed his right' (s. 49(2)). That loss includes any expenses incurred and the loss of any benefit which the applicant 'might reasonably be expected to have had but for that failure' (s. 49(3)). The principles of mitigation and contributory fault apply just as they do in analogous unfair dismissal proceedings (s. 49(4) and (5)).

This is a species of automatically unfair dismissal like the remedies for dismissal on trade union grounds. A selection for redundancy on these grounds is also automatically unfair (s. 105(3)). This is achieved in respect of dismissal by s. 100 but there is an exception in that the dismissal is not to be regarded as unfair if the employer shows that it was or would have been so negligent for the employee to take the steps which he took or proposed to take that a reasonable employer might have dismissed him for taking or proposing to take them (s. 100(3)). There is no qualifying period required in order to make a claim (s. 108).

13.15.7 **Pension fund trustees**

Since 1996, pension fund trustees have also enjoyed protection from any detriment short of dismissal by any act or deliberate failure to act by the employer done on the ground that they are trustees of a relevant occupational pension scheme (s. 46(1)). A dismissal on such ground is also automatically unfair (s. 102).

Pension fund trustees have rights to time off to perform their duties and to undergo training similar to those of trade union officials. In determining the reasonableness of the time off sought, however, the ET must consider 'the circumstances of the employer's business and the effect of the employee's absence on the running of that business' (s. 58(2)(b)).

13.16 **Discipline of union members**

13.16.1 **Construing union disciplinary rules**

All unions have some provision for disciplining members. This is no different from most voluntary organisations but is especially necessary to maintain union solidarity, and to ensure that the union can 'deliver' on industrial agreements which it has entered into. Any such disciplinary action must be carried out in accordance with the union's own rule book, and these are read restrictively with a view to protecting the member. Breaches are usually restrained by way of an injunction or a declaration that an offending action is void, and damages are occasionally awarded. Most cases which reach the courts naturally arise in connection with expulsion from the union rather than any lesser sanctions.

The judges, as part of the policy to protect the member, are reluctant to allow a domestic union tribunal to be final arbiters of legal questions of construction of its constitution, and also intervene if there is no evidence to support a finding of fact found by any disciplinary committee (*Lee* v *Showmen's Guild* (1952); also *Partington* v *NALGO* (1981)). Thus in *MacLelland* v *NUJ* (1975), where the appellant was disciplined for failing to 'attend' a union meeting as required by its rule book, the court avoided this result on the ground that 'attend' meant only that the member should sign on, and not that he remain glued to his chair for the whole undoubtedly riveting assembly.

In *Kelly* v *NATSOPA* (1915) the court held that taking a part-time job could not constitute 'conduct prejudicial to the union's interests', even though the union's own tribunal had decided that it was. Similarly, general rules providing discipline for conduct injurious to the union do not extend, for example, to a refusal to do overtime which was persisted in after the member had been censured once.

13.16.2 Natural justice

Trade union bodies must comply with the rules of natural justice when acting in a disciplinary capacity (but not when simply acting as an employer (*Meacham* v *AEU* (1994)). This is because 'although the jurisdiction of a domestic tribunal is founded on contract, express or implied, nevertheless the parties are not free to make any contract they like' (*Breen* v *AEU* (1971)). It is thus impossible to exclude, even by an express and unambiguous rule, the right of a member to be heard in his defence before disciplinary action is taken against him. Lord Denning MR made this general statement about a disciplinary union tribunal in *Breen*:

Even though its functions are not judicial or quasi-judicial but only administrative, still it must act fairly. Should it not do so the courts can review its decisions just as they can review the decisions of a statutory body. The courts cannot grant the prerogative writs such as *certiorari* and *mandamus* against domestic bodies, but they can grant declarations and injunctions which are the modern machinery for enforcing administrative law.

This applies not only to the deprival of rights of members, but also when their legitimate expectations are dashed (*Schmidt* v *Home Secretary* (1969); *McInnes* v *Onslow Fane* (1978)).

The content of natural justice 'depend[s] on the circumstances of the case, the nature of the enquiry, the rules under which the tribunal is acting, the subject matter that is being dealt with and so forth' (*Russell* v *Duke of Norfolk* (1949)). In union affairs it has focused on the following elements which cannot be excluded by union rules (*Radford* v *NATSOPA* (1972)).

Notice

A member must be given notice of any charge which he has to meet and potential penalties therefore. In *Annamunthodo* v *Oilfield Workers' Trade Union* (1961) the plaintiff's expulsion from the defendant union was declared void because he had no knowledge of the precise charge on which it was based. Such notice must also be specific except where the case is simple and already well known to all (*Stevenson* v *URTU* (1977)), and even then the member should have sufficient time to prepare his defence.

Opportunity to be heard

The member must be given the chance to reply to any allegations against him even though the case may superficially appear unanswerable. The hearing should thus be held at a time reasonably convenient to him, although if the member decides not to take the opportunity offered that is his misfortune (*Annamunthodo's* case). The hearing is normally to be conducted orally (see e.g. *University of Ceylon* v *Fernando* (1960); *R* v *Hull Prison Board of Visitors ex parte St Germain (No. 2)* (1979)) and allows the member to call evidence on his own behalf and cross-examine witnesses for the other side.

The rule against bias

The normally very strict rules against bias in judicial or quasi-judicial proceedings are modified in the case of domestic tribunals, since often the roles of prosecutor and judge are expressly and necessarily combined under the rule book. The rather less stringent principle which applies in this situation was summarised by Viscount Simon in *White* v *Kuzych* (1951):

> What those who considered the charge against the respondent and decided that he was guilty ought to bring to their task was a will to reach an honest conclusion after hearing what was urged on the other side and a resolve not to make their minds up beforehand on his personal guilt, however firmly held their conviction as to union policy and however strongly they had joined in previous adverse criticism of the respondent's conduct.

Here the plaintiff was expelled from the union because of his vehement opposition to its closed shop policy, but the fact that those hearing the complaint against him had already spoken out in favour of the principle did not disqualify them. They were not expected to have 'the icy impartiality of Rhadamanthus'. The member must instead 'put up with the fact that, as members of the union, and as officers, the members of the tribunal itself are rightly and properly concerned to uphold the union and its officers'.

On the other hand, blatant instances of prejudgment should be avoided. In particular, justice must be seen to be done. In *Roebuck* v *NUM (Yorkshire Area)* (1977) the bystander would not have thought it was. The plaintiff was disciplined for allegedly misleading the respondent union's solicitors in a case involving its area president, Arthur Scargill. Yet it was the latter who presided over both the initial disciplinary process and the confirming Area Council after he had already condemned the parties. This action was held to break the general injunction to act fairly and it made no difference that the union rules generally required the president to chair the meeting since he could vacate it in special circumstances and should have done so here. In *Taylor* v *National Union of Seamen* (1967), where the union's general secretary dismissed an official and then presided at his appeal, his decision was quashed.

Legal representation

The cases on whether natural justice requires the individual to have the right to legal representation before union and other voluntary association organs are somewhat difficult to reconcile. There is, for example, authority for the proposition that an accused may have a qualified right to representation where an adverse decision may ruin him (*Pett* v *Greyhound Racing Association Ltd (No. 1)* (1969)) but, even that qualified right may be taken away by the rules of the union or association (*Enderby Town FC v Football Association* (1971)).

13.16.3 Ousting the jurisdiction of the court

The relationship of a union with its members largely reflects its contractual basis. This means that the courts are, on the whole, reluctant to interfere in the contract more than is necessary. However, if the rule book were to contain a rule that the member could not take grievances to the courts, or that he should exhaust internal remedies first, then a potential conflict arises between the doctrine of freedom of contract and the court's disapproval of attempts to oust their own jurisdiction. Lord Denning put this very clearly in *Lee v Showman's Guild* (1952) when he said:

> If the parties should seek by agreement to take the law out of the hands of the courts and put it into the hands of a private tribunal without any recourse at all to the courts in case of error of law then the agreement is to that extent contrary to public policy and void.

The courts have taken the same view in a number of cases subsequently (e.g. in *Leigh v NUR* (1970); *Lawlor v UPW* (1965)). However, in *Lee* there was an attempt at complete ouster. Where there is merely an attempt at postponement until internal remedies have been exhausted, the courts have tended to allow this if not unduly prejudicial to a member's interests (see e.g. *White v Kuzych* (1951)).

With regard to trade unions, the position is now covered by TULR(C)A 1992, s. 63. Under this provision, if the relevant rule is void (that is, is a complete ouster) the court will not take into account that rule. Where there is a postponement, then the court may give effect to the rule for up to six months after an application has been made to the union to have the matter settled in accordance with its rules. After that date, if court proceedings are commenced, then the court will take no cognisance of the rule.

13.16.4 Internal disciplinary hearings

The courts insist that meetings to dispense discipline must be properly called, so that an expulsion has been held void because two members of the branch committee who decided to expel the plaintiff did not receive the papers relating to his case (*Leary v NUVB* (1971)), and a similar result was reached where a meeting was called with only a few minutes' notice (*MacLelland v NUJ* (1975)).

The courts will not normally, however, review the facts as found by the internal tribunal (*Weinberger v Inglis* (1919)), as long as it acts honestly, in good faith and in accordance with its own rules (*Maclean v Workers Union* (1929)), although there is no presumption to this effect. The exception is where the tribunal reaches a decision at which no reasonable tribunal could arrive. *Radford v NATSOPA* (1972) provides a good example. The employers and unions in the printing industry agreed to a scheme under which those made redundant could choose between alternative employment in the industry, in which case they would lose their right to a redundancy payment, and departure from printing whereby they would receive a larger award. The plaintiff sought to stay in the industry and claim his payment. He was thus charged with 'taking action against the union' and expelled. The union claimed that this was a matter for them to decide and not for the courts. Plowman

J, however, dismissing the interests of union solidarity, held that there was no evidence to support the charge and declared the expulsion void. (See also *Esterman* v *NALGO* (1974).)

13.16.5 **Unjustifiable discipline**

Before the Employment Act 1988, if union members were unjustifiably disciplined by their union, particularly for not taking part in industrial action, there was little possibility of legal redress. Compare the view of Ewan McKendrick ((1988) 17 ILJ 141 at p. 149) who states that members who refused to strike enjoyed 'extensive protection' prior to the Act (but *cf.* McKendrick, (1986) 6 *Legal Studies* 35)). Lord Denning MR in *Nagle* v *Feilden* (1966) attempted to introduce the novel concept in English law of a right to work, in order to enable a woman to be admitted to the Jockey Club, so that she could work as a trainer. However, despite one or two cases (such as *Edwards* v *SOGAT* (1970)), which are sometimes taken to support the idea, it has not developed. The rule book may give a remedy, but if it does not, there is little the member can do. One further possibility is to rely on the rules of natural justice which apply even if the union has adhered strictly to its rules. (See e.g. *Lee* v *Showman's Guild of Great Britain* (1952).) If the union were to expel the member unreasonably, TULR(C)A 1992, s. 174, gives the member a remedy. Due to the decision of the European Court of Human Rights in *ASLEF* v *UK* (2007) the government was compelled to amend s. 174 to make it clear that membership of a political party could justify expulsion from a union on the grounds that trade unions have the right of freedom of association under European Convention on Human Rights art. 11. This it did by way of Employment Act 2008, s. 19, which has been subject to some powerful criticism—see e.g. Ewing, (2009) 38 ILJ 50. This right does not cover action short of expulsion. (See the discussion above.)

The right in TULR(C)A 1992, s. 64, is more extensive in that it protects against unjustifiable discipline by the union for certain types of specified conduct. If the member fails to support or participate in industrial action, or seeks to assist or encourage others to break their contracts, or makes assertions that the union, its official representatives or trustees are infringing the union's rules or the law, or because the CO has been approached about this, or because the member proposes to do any of these things (against the union's determination or otherwise) then he may have a remedy if disciplined in consequence. (As to the meaning of 'industrial action' in this context, see *Knowles* v *Fire Brigades Union* (1997).) The TURERA 1993 extended the scope of unjustifiable discipline by proscribing the following discipline, that is, for failing to agree to the making of a deduction of subscriptions arrangement; resigning from one union to join another; working with individuals who are not members of that union or another union; working for an employer who employs or has employed individuals who are not members of that union or another union; or requiring the union to do an act which the union is, pursuant to the TULR(C)A 1992 required to do on the requisition of a member.

A recommendation of discipline is not sufficient for this purpose, in that it does not amount to a 'determination' as the Act requires, according to the EAT in *TGWU* v *Webber* (1990) (see Kidner, (1991) 20 ILJ 284). Discipline which subjects the member to one of the listed detriments will be relevant discipline for this purpose, but the section lists a number of types specifically, being expulsion, firing (directly or indirectly), deprivation of access to benefits, services or facilities of the union, or where another union is encouraged or advised not to accept him into membership. If the member succeeds in proving such unjustified disciplining he may get a declaration and compensation (up to the unfair dismissal maximum) and the union must put the member in the same position he was in before the unjustifiable discipline, according to the EAT in *NALGO* v *Courteney-Dunn* (1992). So, as in this case, it was for the union to ensure that a check off arrangement was restored.

SELECTED READING

Bogg, A. (2009), *The Democratic Aspects of Trade Union Recognition*, Oxford: Hart Publishing, 2009

Elias, P. and Ewing, K. (1987), *Trade Union Democracy, Members' Rights and the Law*, London: Mansell, 1987

Ewing, K. (2005), 'The Function of Trade Unions', (2005) 34 ILJ 1

Morris, G. and Archer, T. (2000), *Collective Labour Law*, Oxford: Hart Publishing, 2000

Painter, R. W. and Holmes, A. E. (2010), *Cases and Materials on Employment Law*, 8th edn, Oxford: Oxford University Press, ch. 10

14

....

Collective bargaining

SUMMARY

In this chapter the law on agreements between employers and trade unions is examined. After describing the process of collective bargaining, the legal status of such agreements is explained. The importance, both to the union and its members, of trade union recognition by employers is considered in this context. The rights of trade unions to information and consultation are examined, followed by a consideration of European Works Councils. Finally, some observations on the role of ACAS and the CAC in this area are made.

14.1 Introduction

Britain has one of the most developed systems of collective bargaining in the world, reflecting the long history of the institution, especially among manual workers. (See Sciarra, 29 Comp. Lab. L. & Pol'y J (2007)) At its peak in the 1970s it covered a high percentage of workers and its sophistication is one of the central reasons why British workers traditionally pressed less for the statutory provision of basic rights in the workplace than their Continental brethren. Many trade unionists still prefer to put a grievance 'through procedure' rather than go to an ET.

This is partly due to the traditional scepticism that trade unions have had towards the law, deriving largely from many conservative decisions of the judiciary in the 19th century. However, as the industrial power of trade unions has weakened, most unions have come to a realisation that the law does have an important role to play in industrial relations, and the extent to which the absence of law is distinctive of British industrial relations came to be the subject of much academic debate. Writers like Kahn-Freund had argued that Britain was distinctive in this way (see Wedderburn, Lewis, and Clark (eds), *Labour Law and Industrial Relations* (Oxford: Clarendon Press, 1983), ch. 1), whereas others (such as Simitis) have argued that the trend towards law (or 'juridification') is a feature of all democratic industrial societies, including Britain (see Clarke, (1985) 14 ILJ 69). Not all are convinced that if this latter view were true it would be a good thing, or at least that the law is up to the tasks which modern industrial relations throw up (see e.g. Wood, (1988) 17 ILJ 1; see generally Wilson, (1984) 13 ILJ 1). The Labour Government has introduced a legal right to recognition in certain limited circumstances which may improve the standing of trade unions and extend collective bargaining, but it is still the case that most workers are not covered by collective bargains. The Government's emphasis remains on enhancing individual rights—see Pollert, (2005) 34 ILJ 217.

14.1.1 **Substance and procedure**

It is necessary to make various distinctions between forms of bargaining for a full understanding of the complex picture. The first relates to the difference between substantive and procedural collective agreements. Kahn-Freund (Davies and Freedland, *Labour and the Law*, 3rd edn (London: Sweet & Maxwell, 1983), p. 124) described the latter as 'an agreement on the relation between the collective bargaining partners as such on the institutions and methods designed to be used for the prevention or settlement of disputes and thus for the making of substantive norms'. On the other hand, the substantive rules actually set wages, bonus rates, hours, and all other conditions of employment. There are differences in emphasis between procedural and substantive aspects in particular agreements, but Clegg broadly distinguished between the statute and common law models of bargaining (*The Changing System of Industrial Relations in Great Britain* (Oxford: Basil Blackwell, 1979), p. 117). In the former, the substantive clauses are paramount, covering in detail all matters subject to joint regulation to the end of the specific fixed term. There are only exiguous procedural sections to deal with disputes about the interpretation of ambiguous clauses.

The drawback of this approach, which seeks to put everything in black and white, is its rigidity. It is not well adapted to rapid changes in circumstances or multi-level bargaining, where many terms are determined at the plant level. For this type of bargaining, the alternative common law model is most usually adopted so that, under the broad umbrella of a general agreement, most effective terms arise out of detailed disputes procedures which resolve differences between the parties on a day-to-day basis. These procedures are often very complicated and the parties commonly agree to resort to industrial action only when they have failed to produce a satisfactory settlement through these channels. Bargaining arrangements in the manufacturing and particularly engineering industries adopt this model and it provides a very dynamic system. The Donovan Commission Report (Royal Commission on Trade Unions and Employers' Associations, 1968, Cmnd 3623) noted (para. 471):

Collective bargaining is not in this country a series of easily distinguishable transactions comparable to the making of a number of contracts by two commercial firms. It is in fact a continuous process in which differences concerning the interpretation of an agreement merge imperceptibly into differences concerning claims to change its effect.

This remains true today.

14.1.2 **Different levels of bargaining**

There may be many levels of collective bargaining. Agreements may be struck at a national level between either one union or a confederation of unions on the workers' side, and a single employer or an employers' association representing management.

The Donovan Report stated (p. 36):

The formal system assumes that collective bargaining is a matter of reaching written agreements. The informal system consists largely in tacit agreements and understandings.

There is often a multiplicity of overlapping and conflicting agreements, overlaid in turn with accretions of custom and practices and plant level bargaining which deals with basic issues, for example, piece-work.

Most national bargains deal only with minimum terms and conditions and are the tip of a very large iceberg. This is the ambit of domestic bargaining, which usually consists of the shop steward reaching understandings with middle management: a written agreement to last for a fixed period is the exception. The modem influence of domestic bargaining is undoubted but the Donovan Commission Report heavily criticised its structure, or rather lack of it, talking of 'the challenge from below'. It pointed to:

the central defect in British industrial relations... [as]... the disorder in factory and workshop relations and pay structures promoted by the conflict between the formal and informal systems.

In particular, there was an 'absence of ready, clear and effective disputes procedures' and this swelled the outbreak of unofficial strikes, which often occurred when workers and management differed on what was agreed between them. The Report noted 'the tendency of extreme decentralisation and self-government to degenerate to indecision and anarchy', and sought:

a change in the nature of British collective bargaining and a more orderly method for workers and their representatives to exercise their influence in the factory.

The way forward was not to make 'the present inadequate procedure agreements legally enforceable', because such a move 'would be irrelevant and would divert attention from and hinder action to remedy the real causes' (para. 268). Instead it proposed a statutory standing body to assist voluntary reform, and that task was soon given, in 1969, to the Commission on Industrial Relations, whose work has now been superseded by ACAS. Its proposal that companies employing over 5,000 employees should register their agreements was not, however, implemented.

The recent trends in bargaining are primarily the continued movement from national to local bargaining and from basic pay to incentive-based arrangements such as share options and performance-related pay.

14.1.3 Shop stewards

Domestic bargaining is the main preserve of shop stewards, who are elected by their fellow workers and are often more in touch with the 'shop-floor' than is the full-time union hierarchy. In bigger unionised plants there may be a shop steward superstructure, headed by a convenor who might spend most or all of his time on union business. Most stewards, however, carry out their duties in their spare time.

The origin of the position can be traced back to the 'father of chapels' in work place union branches, mainly at first in the printing industry. The practice spread to the manufacturing and engineering industries after the First World War, and has now taken root in virtually every manual occupation and increasingly in the white collar sector, although they are there often known by different names, for example, staff representative.

There are some who regard the steward as a militant 'mole', leading unwilling workers into strike action at the slightest provocation. The Donovan Report considered, however, that he was 'more a lubricant than an irritant'.

14.2 **Enforcement of collective bargains**

The central legal question raised by collective bargaining is whether agreements can be enforced in the courts. Most controversy has surrounded the issue whether the employer can sue the union for taking strike action before the procedure for settling disputes laid down in the collective bargain has been pursued. There is no problem with privity here: the vital question is instead whether collective bargains are intended to have legal effect.

Collective agreements in Britain are not normally drafted with the precision to which a lawyer is accustomed, rarely covering all eventualities, and this is particularly so at local level. It was primarily for these reasons that, in the leading case at common law, *Ford Motor Co. Ltd* v *AEU* (1969), Geoffrey Lane J found that the Ford Motor Company's collective agreement was not intended to create legal relations, and therefore not open to construction and enforcement by the courts. He also referred to 'the general climate of opinion on both sides of industry' and 'the vague aspirational wording' of the agreement before him (see Hepple, (1970) 39 CLJ 122), and went on: 'Agreements such as these, composed largely of optimistic aspirations, presenting grave practical problems of enforcement and reached against a background of opinion adverse to enforceability are, in my judgment, not contracts in the legal sense.' He said, on the general issue of intention:

> If one applies the subjective test and asks what the intentions of the various parties were, the answer is that so far as they had any express intentions they were certainly not to make the agreement enforceable at law. If one applies an objective test and asks what intention must be imputed from all the circumstances of the case the result is the same.

This is not to deny that a different conclusion might be reached in the case of a differently worded collective bargain. Moreover, from time to time there have been attempts to make collective bargains enforceable by statute. The Royal Commission on Labour recommended such a move in 1894 and several Bills were introduced to this effect in the inter-war years. Although the Donovan Commission, on balance, rejected such calls, Industrial Relations Act 1971, s. 34 reversed the generally understood common law position by making a presumption that such bargains were intended to be enforceable. It became an unfair industrial practice to procure breach of a collective bargain unless the intention to render it legally enforceable was excluded by the parties. In fact most collective bargains during the period did include a clause stating 'This is not a legally enforceable agreement' (TINALEA). Therefore the reversion to the common law in TULRA 1974, s. 18 had little practical effect. The TULR(C)A 1992, s. 179, replacing it, states that bargains are unenforceable in the courts 'unless the agreement is (a) in writing and (b) contains a provision which (however expressed) states that the parties intend that the agreement shall be a legally enforceable contract.' Very few agreements, in fact, contain such a statement. In 1981 a Green Paper of the Thatcher Government concluded that without significant changes in bargaining practices, the law would be evaded. Although the idea was revived in the Green Paper *Industrial Relations in the 1990s*, it was again dropped.

Some agreements may, however, fall outside the statutory definition of collective agreements (TULR(C)A 1992, s. 178), in which case the common law as revealed in the *Ford* case still applies. The result is that in general, unlike the position in many other countries, the employer cannot sue the union which is party to a collective agreement for failing to honour obligations they have undertaken collectively, in particular that employees will take disputes through procedure before striking— the so-called 'peace obligation'.

A further limited exception is created by the recognition provisions introduced by the Employment Relations Act 1999. Where the CAC has already made a dec- laration of recognition, there is a further procedure under which either side may subsequently apply to it to impose a 'method of collective bargaining' (in effect a bargaining procedure), where the parties have failed to arrive at such a method voluntarily. The method imposed by the CAC has the force of a binding contract between the union and the employer, and is enforceable by an application to the civil courts for specific performance. Similar provisions apply where the CAC imposes a method of collective bargaining on parties who have entered into a semi-voluntary form of recognition known in the Act as an 'agreement for recog- nition'; where the parties agree to vary a method of collective bargaining imposed by the CAC; and where, following a change in the bargaining unit, the parties' established method of collective bargaining transfers across to the new bargain- ing unit.

14.3 Recognition

The treatment of trade union recognition is in many ways a case study of the approach of the law to collective bargaining at various stages of development. Until 1971 recognition of unions by management so that bargaining could take place was, like most industrial relations issues, one which the parties thought the law should leave well alone. Recognition spread mainly by custom and practice, although, increasingly, comprehensive management-union agreements were drawn up. These were valuable in that they specified in detail who the employer would negotiate with, where, and over what issues, and also such subsidiary questions as trade union facilities on the employer's premises, and the automatic deduction of union subscriptions from the employee's pay packet (the 'check-off').

The only relevant legal provisions concerned recognition in the public sector where Parliament inserted in several statutes a duty on employers to consult with 'organisations appearing to be appropriate with a view to establishing negotiating and consultation machinery' (e.g. Coal Industry Nationalisation Act 1946, s. 46(1)). There was also a wide-ranging duty on the Secretary of State for Education to con- sult those associations 'which appear to him to represent teachers' (Remuneration of Teachers Act 1965, s. 1), which led to the formation of the important Burnham Committee to determine teachers' pay, but this was abolished in 1987.

The Industrial Relations Act 1971, consistent with its policy of bringing the law into the centre of industrial relations, introduced an element of compulsion into this process; if there was a majority in favour of recognition in a particular work place, the employer was bound to accord the rights, and the National Industrial Relations Court had jurisdiction to enforce recognition. The complex procedure provided was little used in practice, however, since it was a necessary condition that the union was registered and, as we have already seen, few unions did register.

The measure was abolished by TULRA 1974 but re-enacted in an even more complicated form in the EPA 1975, the initial decision on recognition now being taken by ACAS. Recognition also became, and remains, the threshold for various statutory rights including information relevant to collective bargaining, consultation over redundancies (although now it shares those with elected representatives) and time off for trade union activities. The rather unhelpful statutory definition of the concept was 'recognition of the union by an employer, or two or more associated employers, to any extent for the purpose of collective bargaining' (EPA 1975, s. 126(1) now TULR(C)A 1992, s. 178). Collective bargaining was then defined as negotiations related to or connected with the same matters as may be the subject of a trade dispute (for which, see TULR(C)A 1992, s. 244(1)).

Charges of bias were levelled against ACAS from all sides, and this bedevilled its constructive mediatory role in other areas. For ACAS to work properly it had to be like Caesar's wife, above suspicion. Thus few dissented when the then Chairman of ACAS, Jim Mortimer, wrote in 1979 to the incoming Conservative Government that its general 'essentially voluntary role does not sit with the statutory duties in [the recognition provisions in the legislation]'; and, when the procedure was abolished by the Employment Act 1980, it was little lamented.

Recognition reverted from 1980 onwards to being a matter for voluntary agreement between unions and employers. However, this changed in June 2000 with the coming into force of the recognition provisions of the Employment Relations Act 1999. These are mainly contained in Sch. 1 to the Act, which are inserted in TULR(C)A 1992 as Sch. A1. (See generally Simpson, (2000) 29 ILJ 193.)

14.3.1 Statutory recognition

Part I of the Schedule sets out a procedure under which an independent trade union has the right to apply to the CAC for a declaration awarding it recognition for collective bargaining purposes in respect of a particular 'bargaining unit' (i.e. group of workers). If the CAC does issue such a declaration, the award of statutory recognition should, if all goes well, last for a minimum of three years, and can normally only be ended through one of the derecognition procedures described below. (See generally Wright, (2005) 34 ILJ 345; Dukes, (2008) 37 ILJ 236.)

'Collective bargaining' in Sch. A1 has a much narrower meaning than elsewhere in the TULR(C)A 1992. For the purposes of statutory recognition, it refers only to negotiations about 'pay, hours and holidays' (the core topics) and nothing else, although the union and the employer will be free to add to this list by mutual agreement (para. 3). If they do so, it will not be regulated by statute.

With the exception of provisions on the derecognition of non-independent unions, the Schedule is not intended to affect voluntary recognition arrangements, either those entered into before its coming into force, or after. Part II of the

Schedule is, as we shall see, involved with a hybrid form of recognition which is, perhaps, better described as 'semi-voluntary'.

The statutory recognition procedure, under Part I of the Schedule, begins when a union sends a request to an employer to recognise it as entitled to conduct collective bargaining on behalf of a particular 'bargaining unit' (i.e. group of workers)—para. 4. This request will be valid only if the union possesses a certificate from the Certification Officer that it is independent and the employer employs at least 21 workers (paras 6 and 7). The procedure allows the parties to agree recognition voluntarily at this stage, but, failing this, the union will normally then be entitled to apply to the CAC (paras 10–12).

The CAC will accept the union's application for further consideration only if it complies with the various admissibility criteria set out in paras 33–42. One of the most important of these is the requirement that ten per cent of the workers in the bargaining unit must already belong to the union (or unions) making the application and that a majority of workers in the bargaining unit 'would be likely' to vote in favour of recognition of the union in a ballot (para. 36). In order to discourage competing applications by rival unions, the CAC will normally reject applications covering any part of the same bargaining unit (paras 38 and 51). However, it will accept a single, joint application made by two or more unions where they can show that they will co-operate with each other and will accept 'single-table bargaining' if this is what the employer wants (para. 37).

Once the CAC has accepted an application as admissible, its next move will depend on whether or not the parties have already agreed the appropriate unit for collective bargaining purposes. Where they have done so, the CAC will go on to consider the issue of recognition straightaway (see below). Otherwise, it must first help the parties to try once more to agree the bargaining unit. If a voluntary solution still proves elusive, the CAC will have to select the bargaining unit itself and impose this on the parties. In doing so, it will have to take various factors into account, but the overriding consideration must be the compatibility of the unit with effective management (paras 18 and 19).

A union's entitlement to recognition will depend on the amount of support it has within the bargaining unit in question, usually measured by means of a secret ballot of all the workers in the unit. However, a ballot may be unnecessary where a majority of the bargaining unit are already union members. If this is the case, the CAC will issue a declaration ordering the employer to recognise the union without further ado, unless it decides that a ballot should be held anyway, because the CAC believes it has credible evidence that a significant number of union members do not support the union conducting collective bargaining on their behalf, or because there are doubts that the membership want the union to bargain on their behalf or 'in the interests of good industrial relations' (para. 22).

Where union membership within a bargaining unit as defined is short of a majority of the workforce in that unit, the CAC will hold a secret ballot to determine the level of support for recognition within the bargaining unit (para. 23). The CAC does not conduct the ballot itself, but instead delegates this task to a 'qualified independent person', whom it must appoint. The ballot may take place either by post or in the workplace or workplaces concerned, and, in certain circumstances, the CAC will be able to specify a mixture of methods (para. 25). In order to ensure the fairness of the balloting process, the Schedule imposes a number of duties on the employer, including a general duty to co-operate within the union and the independent person and an obligation to allow the union 'reasonable' access to the workforce during the run-up to the ballot itself (para. 26). Where an employer fails to fulfil any of its duties under para. 26, the CAC has the power initially to issue an order requiring it to do so, and, where the employer persists in its default, may issue a declaration granting the union recognition without the need for a ballot (para. 27). The costs of the ballot are to be shared equally between the employer and the union, and where two or more unions are involved the 'union half' will be apportioned equally between them unless they indicate a contrary intention to the person conducting the ballot (para. 28). The CAC has the power to order a re-run of the ballot where not all workers have been given sufficient opportunity to vote—see *R (on the application of Ultraframe (UK) Ltd) v CAC* (2005).

Once all the votes have been counted, the qualified independent person will notify the CAC of the result of the ballot. The CAC will issue a declaration awarding the union recognition only if a majority vote in favour of this, and the number so voting constitute at least 40 per cent of the total number of workers in the bargaining unit. Any other result will cause the CAC to issue a declaration that the union is not entitled to statutory recognition (para. 29).

A declaration of recognition by the CAC will not, however, be the end of the whole process. The union and employer will then have to move on to negotiations about the contents of what the Schedule calls the 'method of collective bargaining' (para. 30). In effect, this will be the bargaining procedure that the parties will undertake to observe during the lifetime of the statutory recognition arrangement (i.e. covering such matters as when collective bargaining negotiations are to take place, who is to attend, what provisions are to be made in the event of a failure to agree, etc.). The CAC can be asked to impose a method of collective bargaining where the parties are unable to agree—see Trade Union Recognition (Method of Collective Bargaining) Order 2000 (SI 2000 No. 1300) for this purpose (para. 31). Even when the parties have had a method of collective bargaining imposed on them in this way, the Schedule allows them to vary this by mutual agreement in writing (para. 31(5)).

The method imposed by the CAC will have the force of a binding contract between the union and the employer, unless the parties agree otherwise in writing (para. 31(5)). However, the only means of enforcing a legally binding method of collective bargaining will be by an application to the civil courts for specific performance (para. 31(6)), although the parties may apply to the CAC for 'assistance' in certain circumstances (para. 32).

Part III of the Schedule contains important provisions covering the situation where a change occurs that may affect the continued viability of statutory recognition. The change in question can be any of the following:

(a) a change in the organisation or structure of the business carried on by the employer;

(b) a change in the activities pursued by the employer in the course of business carried on by him;

(c) a substantial change in the number of workers employed in the original bargaining unit.

Where either side believes that, because of one of these changes, the original bargaining unit is no longer appropriate, it may apply to the CAC, which will (if the parties are unable to reach their own agreement) determine if this is in fact the case and, if so, select a new bargaining unit (or units) as appropriate to the changed circumstances (paras 66–73). Under a similar procedure, the union has the right to make an application to the CAC where the employer informs it that he believes the original bargaining unit to have ceased to exist on account of one of the changes listed above and wishes to bring statutory recognition to an end (paras 74–81). Where the CAC imposes one or more new bargaining units under either of these procedures, it must be satisfied that this does not disrupt any other collective bargaining arrangements (either statutory or voluntary) and that the difference between the original and new bargaining units is not such as to require a fresh test of support for recognition (paras 82–86). Where the CAC is not satisfied of the latter, it will hold a ballot of workers in the new unit, organised along much the same lines as before (paras 88–89). However, a ballot will not be necessary where a majority of workers in a new unit already belong to the union, unless (on the same grounds as in para. 22 above) the CAC decides to hold a ballot anyway (para. 87). The CAC will issue a new declaration awarding the union statutory recognition in respect of the new bargaining unit if the new unit has a majority of union members, or the union wins majority support for recognition in a ballot.

14.3.2 Voluntary recognition

Part II of the Schedule gives the union the option, once it has invoked the statutory recognition procedure under Part I, to bring it to an early halt on the ground that the employer has agreed to recognise it voluntarily. This 'semi-voluntary' form of recognition is referred to in the Schedule as an 'agreement for recognition'. From the union's perspective the main advantages of recognition under Part II over entirely voluntary recognition are:

(a) that the employer may not bring the former to an end before three years are up (whereas the union may terminate the agreement for recognition at any time); and

(b) recognition under an agreement for recognition allows either side to apply to the CAC to impose a method of collective bargaining in the same way as for statutory recognition (see above).

That said, doubts have been expressed, both inside Parliament and without, about whether any union would want to enter into an agreement for recognition—if the employer's good faith is seriously questioned, is it not better for the union to persevere with its application for statutory recognition under Part I?

14.3.3 Derecognition

Parts IV–VII contain various procedures allowing either the employer or workers in the bargaining unit to apply to the CAC to bring statutory recognition to an end after a period of three years. These provisions do not, however, apply to 'voluntary' recognition under Part II.

Generally speaking, these procedures take a form very similar to that for statutory recognition under Part I, including the ultimate test of a secret ballot of all the workers in the bargaining unit concerned. Under Part IV, the employer may apply for derecognition on the ground that he now employs fewer than the threshold figure of 21 workers (paras 99–103), or that there is no longer majority support for recognition within the bargaining unit (paras 104–111). One or more workers in the bargaining unit can also apply to end the statutory bargaining arrangements on the ground that there is no longer majority support for recognition within the bargaining unit (paras 112–116). Part V provides the employer with a slightly different procedure in cases where the CAC originally awarded the union 'automatic' statutory recognition (i.e. on the basis that a majority of workers already belonged to the union, without the need for a ballot). Under this procedure, the CAC will first examine whether the union has in fact lost majority membership within the bargaining unit and, if so, will hold a ballot to test whether it nevertheless enjoys majority support (paras 122–133).

Part VI of the Schedule is almost unique, in that it allows the CAC to interfere with purely voluntary recognition arrangements, which, as we already have seen, are normally out-of-bounds to it. Paragraph 137 allows one or more workers to apply to the CAC to end an employer's voluntary recognition of a non-independent trade union in respect of the bargaining unit to which they themselves belong. The procedure after this largely follows that for derecognition under Part IV, including the ultimate test of a secret ballot of all the workers in the bargaining unit (paras 134–148). Part VII is relatively brief. Put simply, it covers the situation where a previously independent trade union loses its certificate of independence (a virtually unheard-of occurrence). The effect of such a loss will be to convert any statutory recognition arrangement that the union has into a voluntary recognition arrangement. In principle, this would leave the union open to attack by a disgruntled workforce by means of an application for derecognition under Part VI.

The balloting provisions for Parts IV–VI of the Schedule are mainly contained in paras 117–121. They are, for the most part, a mirror image of those for statutory recognition, described above.

14.3.4 Detriment/dismissal in relation to recognition or derecognition

Part VIII contains provisions to protect 'workers' suffering a detriment on grounds related to recognition or derecognition under the Schedule: para. 156(1) states that a worker must not be subjected to a detriment by any act or any deliberate failure to act by his or her employer which takes place on any of the following grounds:

(a) the worker acted with a view to obtaining or preventing the employer recognising a union under the Schedule;

(b) the worker indicated that he or she supported or did not support the employer recognising a union under the Schedule;

(c) the worker acted with a view to securing or preventing the ending of bargaining arrangements under the Schedule;

(d) the worker indicated that he or she supported or did not support the ending of bargaining arrangements under the Schedule;

(e) the worker influenced or sought to influence the way in which votes were to be cast by other workers in a ballot arranged under the Schedule;

(f) the worker influenced or sought to influence other workers to vote or to abstain from voting in such a ballot;

(g) the worker voted in such a ballot; or

(h) the worker proposed to do, failed to do, or proposed to decline to do, any of the above.

The employer will not be liable for inflicting a detriment in cases where the worker's act or omission (as described above) is deemed to have been unreasonable (para. 156(3)).

Where a worker alleges that he or she has suffered a detriment in breach of para. 156, the only remedy available is to make a complaint to an ET. This should be done within three months of the act or failure complained of, unless the tribunal is satisfied that it was not reasonably practicable for the worker to do so, in which case it will accept the complaint so long as the worker manages to present it within whatever further period the tribunal regards as reasonable (para. 157). The burden of proof lies on the employer to show the ground on which it has acted or failed to act (para. 158). If the tribunal finds the worker's complaint well-founded it must make a declaration to this effect and may order the employer to pay compensation. The amount awarded should be whatever 'the tribunal considers to be just and equitable in all the circumstances having regard to the infringement complained of and to any loss sustained by the complainant which is attributable to the act or failure which infringed his [or her] right', including but not limited to:

(a) any expenses reasonably incurred by the complainant in consequence of the act or failure to act complained of; and

(b) loss of any benefit which the complainant might reasonably be expected to have had but for that act or failure (para. 159).

The tribunal may reduce an award of compensation where the complainant has failed to mitigate his loss or where action by the complainant caused or contributed to the employer's detrimental act or failure to act. There is a limit on compensation in cases where the detriment complained of is the termination of a contract other than a contract of employment. In this situation, a successful complainant will be entitled to a sum no higher than the total of the basic and compensatory awards he or she would have received if the claim had been one for unfair dismissal under ERA 1996, Part X (para. 160).

Paragraph 161 prohibits dismissal of an employee on grounds relating to recognition or derecognition under the Schedule. Such dismissal is automatically unfair.

14.4 The closed shop

14.4.1 The institution

The justifiability of the closed shop and compulsory union membership raised fundamental issues about trade unionism. It was criticised by some as an attack on fundamental freedoms and supported by others as an essential accompaniment of strong collective bargaining. It has claimed the critical attention of the European Court of Human Rights and, as a result of the climate of hostility, the Employment Acts 1980, 1982, 1988, and 1990 abolished all legal support for it as we have already seen (see now TULR(C)A 1992). The closed shop illustrates in the strongest form the tension between the interest of the union in collective solidarity as a counterweight to management, and the individual need for freedom of association, which is an essential element of a free society.

14.4.2 Flexibility of operation

Before the law first turned its attention to the institution of the closed shop, most were informal and flexible arrangements which had grown up over time, often supported only by custom and practice in the work place or industry concerned. It was, rather ironically, the Industrial Relations Act 1971 which induced a measure of formality into the practice. With the introduction of unfair dismissal provisions, it was provided that an employer who dismissed a non-unionist in accordance with a valid closed shop agreement (and few were valid) had dismissed fairly. The concept of the 'union membership agreement' was later pressed into service to define the institution but the Employment Act 1988 removed the legal underpinning for closed shops so that dismissals for failure to belong to a closed shop are now automatically unfair. The closed shop itself remains lawful but it has become very difficult in law to maintain (TULR(C)A 1992, ss 137, 138, 152, 174–177, and 222).

14.4.3 The debate on the closed shop

Many employers and trade unions alike favoured the closed shop simply because it eliminated multi-unionism, which is said to be the bane of British industrial relations and leads to damaging inter-union strikes and notorious 'who does what' disputes. This perhaps explained its growth, with at least the acquiescence of management, in periods when the legislative background was not at all auspicious. There was no greater threat to its continuance than during the currency of the Industrial Relations Act 1971, yet B. Weekes and his colleagues found (*Industrial Relations and the Limits of the Law* (Oxford: Blackwell, 1975), p. 42):

Every manager whom we interviewed, who had a direct responsibility for collective bargaining, whether in the private or in the public sector worked to preserve the *status quo* where there were closed shops. No company at any level issued direct instructions to the contrary.

However, the closed shop was by no means a prescription for industrial peace, as the Donovan Commission pointed out; and indeed, many of the most damaging and bitter disputes in the 1970s and early 1980s occurred in corporations with 100 per cent trade unionism, such as British Leyland, British Railways, and the National Coal Board.

One argument is that some groups of workers are so scattered that they are impossible to organise without compulsory unionism, and consequently collective bargaining could not be carried on in those areas without the institution of the closed shop. This argument led to the exemption, in the Industrial Relations Act 1971, for certain workers, such as seamen and actors, to be in 'approved closed shops' but even these did not survive the reforms of the Thatcher Government's legislation.

All employees take the gains of collective bargaining negotiated for their particular workgroup by a union, whether or not they are members of it. It is, accordingly, strenuously argued by some trade unionists that workers should not take such benefits without having the counterpart burden of contributing to the funds of the union which provides the negotiators and the extensive back-up they require. This was recognised in the Industrial Relations Act 1971, and in several individual closed shop agreements, in a clause that workers who refuse to join a union should give the equivalent money to charity.

Another aspect of this argument was expressed in the TUC's publication, *Trade Union Organisation and the Closed Shop*, that the closed shop: 'defends hard-won terms and conditions and security of employment from being undermined by persons willing to work for worse terms and conditions'. Moreover, to ensure delivery by the union on the collective bargains, they must sometimes discipline their members and this would be immeasurably strengthened by the closed shop.

These arguments must be set against the opposite claim of the opponents of the closed shop—that it abused human rights, and that individual liberty must come before any potential industrial relations gains. They contend that consistent with a right to belong to a trade union, a symbol of a free society and now protected in law, goes a right to dissociate. It is indeed for this reason that the closed shop, or some forms of it, are banned in several Continental nations, including Italy, Belgium, and Switzerland. The Donovan Report, however, drew a distinction:

The two are not truly comparable. The former condition [right not to belong] is designed to frustrate the development of collective bargaining which it is public policy to promote, whereas no such objection applies to the latter.

The European Court of Human Rights has held that the closed shop, at least as operated before the reforms of the Employment Act 1980, breached European Convention on Human Rights, art. 11, which provides that:

Everyone has the right to freedom of peaceful assembly and to freedom of association with others, including the right to form and join trade unions for the protection of his interests.

The Court was passing judgment on the cases of *Young, James and Webster* v *United Kingdom* (1981), three staunch non-unionists who were dismissed by British Rail in 1976 as a result of the signing of a closed shop agreement between their nationalised employers and the three rail unions. Trade unionism became thereby a compulsory term of their contracts and one they could not stomach. The court did not find it necessary to deal separately with the applicant's other contentions that the closed shop was in breach of arts 9 and 10, which guarantee freedom of thought and conscience, and freedom of expression, respectively. (See for a full discussion of the case Forde, (1982) 11 ILJ 1; and see *Sibson* v *United Kingdom* (1994).)

14.5 Right of trade unions to information

A vital factor in facilitating collective bargaining is the provision of information so that discussion may proceed on an informed basis. The Industrial Relations

Act 1971 made provision for the disclosure of information but the appropriate section was not brought into force. It was only with the EPA 1975 that the disclosure of information so long advocated in trade union circles became a reality, and then arguably in a most attenuated form. One major defect of the legislation (now TULR(C)A 1992) is that, based as it is on a threshold of recognition, an employer can resist the disclosure of information on a particular subject by refusing to bargain on that issue (*General and Municipal Workers' Union et al. & BL Cars Ltd*, CAC Award No. 80/65). Difficulties in reconciling rights to confidentiality on the one hand, and rights to know on the other, are also responsible for the vagueness of the provisions as enacted.

The employer must disclose to any recognised union information without which the trade union representative would be to a material extent impeded in carrying on with him collective bargaining and which it would be in accordance with good industrial relations practice that he should disclose to them for the purposes of collective bargaining (TULR(C)A 1992, s. 181(1)). Collective bargaining is defined by TULR(C)A 1992, s. 178(2) as concerned with:

(a) terms and conditions of employment or the physical conditions in which any workers are required to work;

(b) engagement or non-engagement or termination or suspension of employment or the duties of employment of one or more workers;

(c) allocation of work or the duties of employment of one or more workers;

(d) matters of discipline;

(e) the membership or non-membership of a trade union on the part of a worker;

(f) facilities for officials of trade unions;

(g) machinery for negotiation or consultation and other procedures relating to any of the above matters, including the recognition by employers or employers' associations of the right of a trade union to represent workers in any such negotiation or consultation or in the carrying out of such procedures.

However, there is difficulty in applying the test. Information which is commonly disclosed in one part of industry may be considered highly sensitive in another.

Moreover, it may be difficult for a union to say it is impeded in collective bargaining through lack of information when it has *ex hypothesi* managed without it for many years past. The general test was stated in CAC Award No. 78/353, para. 20: 'Is the information sought in this case relevant and important in general terms?' Later, in its Annual Report for 1979, the CAC said: 'As a general point, the relevance of information under any of the categories...increases when jobs are at risk.'

The ACAS Code of Practice on Disclosure of Information (para. 10) directs negotiators to:

take account of the subject matter of the negotiations and the issues raised during them; the level at which negotiations take place (department, plant, division, or company level); the size of the company; and the type of business the company is engaged in.

Joint understandings are especially encouraged. The Code (para. 11) sets out the following list of subjects but they are not the only evidence of good practice; they serve neither as a checklist nor are they intended to be exhaustive:

(a) pay and benefits: principles and structure of payment systems etc.;

(b) conditions of service: policies on recruitment, redeployment, redundancy, training, equal opportunities and promotion; appraisal systems; health, welfare and safety matters;

(c) manpower: numbers employed analysed according to grade, department, location, age and sex; labour turnover; absenteeism; overtime and part-time; manning standards; planned changes in work methods, material, equipment or organisation; available manpower plans; investment plans;

(d) performance: productivity and efficiency data etc.;

(e) financial: costs structures; gross and net profit; sources of earnings; assets; liabilities; allocation of profits; details of Government financial assistance; transfer prices; loans to parent and subsidiary companies and interest charged.

This does not extend to commercial information about market share of products, cash flow and Government assistance, and in a survey it was shown that few applications for information about profits, non-labour costs and redundancy plans have met with success (Gospel and Willman, (1981) 10 ILJ 10).

The details sought must be relevant for the description of workers in which the union is recognised, and the application must be made in writing by a representative of the union, defined as: 'an official or other person authorised by the trade union to carry on such collective bargaining' (TULR(C)A 1992, s. 181(1)), thus including a shop steward. It is not, however, sufficient to disclose material to representatives only on condition of its not being available to full-time officers of the union or denying access to individual members (*IPC Ltd and the National Union of Journalists*, CAC Award Nos 80/4, 78/711, 80/73). The union may require the information to be given in writing but not that any particular documents be produced.

There is a list of exceptions from the right to information which must normally be proved by the employer (TULR(C)A 1992, s. 182). They relate to cases where:

(a) Disclosure of information would be against the interests of national security.

(b) Disclosure would contravene a prohibition imposed by or under any enactment. This served, for example, to exclude a survey of earnings in an industry since the copyright was in the surveying company (*Joint Credit Card Co. & NUBE*, CAC Award No. 78/2/2).

(c) Information has been communicated to the employer in confidence or where he has obtained it in consequence of the confidence reposed in him by another person. In *Civil Service Union v CAC* (1980) the cost of transferring cleaning operations to outside contractors had been conveyed on a form marked 'in confidence', and this suggested that the person communicating it was relying on its remaining secret.

(d) Information relates to an individual, unless that person has consented to its disclosure. This arises particularly where grading schemes are in issue. While the CAC in *Rolls-Royce Ltd & ASTMS*, CAC Award No. 80/30 said that such information should be given even where it might enable an individual to be identified, in No. 79/121 an application for information about a directors' pension scheme was refused since it related only to individuals.

(e) Disclosure would cause substantial injury to the employers' undertaking. The Code of Practice suggests as examples where the employer might lose customers to competitors, where suppliers will refuse to supply necessary materials, and where the ability to raise funds to finance the company would be seriously impeded. It does not, however, allow the argument that the use of the information in negotiations would merely harm the company.

(f) The information has been obtained for the purpose of bringing or defending any legal proceedings.

To gain a remedy for failure to provide information is a curious, complicated, and lengthy process. Like the right itself, it is a hybrid between collective and individual enforcement (TULR(C)A 1992, s. 183) and consists of various stages. The union applicant first makes a complaint to the CAC. The CAC may refer the matter to ACAS for settlement by conciliation, failing which the CAC conducts a hearing at which anyone whom it considers to have a proper interest in the matter may be heard and the CAC must give reasons for its findings. If the Committee upholds the complaint it may make a declaration of the information which ought to be disclosed and a final date by which this must be done. If the employer still fails to comply the union may make a further complaint, and also seek changes in those parts of the individual contract in respect of which the union is recognised (s. 184).

The Act states merely that the Committee may award the terms claimed or others as it considers appropriate. There is no appeal from this finding (except by way of judicial review where the CAC has breached administrative law—see *Fullerton Computer Industries Ltd* v *Central Arbitration Committee* (2001)) and it does not apply to the Crown.

The policy appears to be that if the union does not have information to achieve meaningful collective bargaining, the CAC will arbitrate the bargaining for it.

14.5.1 Health and safety

Provided that a safety representative gives the employer reasonable notice, he may inspect and take copies of any document which the employer is required to keep by virtue of statutory health and safety provisions. There is also the more general duty on the employer to make available to him information which is within his knowledge and which is necessary for the safety representative to fulfil his functions. The Health and Safety Executive's Code of Practice exemplifies plans and performance of the undertaking, and any changes affecting the health and safety at work of the employees, technical data about hazards and necessary precautions, and accident records. Such information may also be revealed by an inspector. There is no small firm exception, and an alternative route is to consult all employees directly.

14.6 **Information and consultation in large undertakings**

The Information and Consultation of Employees Regulations 2004 (SI 2004 No. 3426) were passed to give effect to Council Directive (EC) 2002/14. (See generally Hall, (2005) 34 ILJ 103; Dukes, (2007) 36 ILJ 330.) They give rights to employees working for large undertakings to be given information about the business that they work for and in some circumstances to be consulted about how it is run. They apply to undertakings that have 50 or more employees, as from April 2008. The number of employees is determined by taking an average over a 12-month period, or less if the undertaking has not been in existence that long—reg. 4. Part-time workers can be counted as half-time if they have worked as such over the whole month in the calculation. Employees are entitled to be informed as to how many employees are in the undertaking in order to determine if it comes under the Regulations—reg. 5. Any disagreement about this may be taken to the CAC for a declaration—reg. 13.

An undertaking is defined as 'a public or private undertaking carrying out an economic activity, whether or not operating for gain'—reg. 1. The idea is to catch legal entities, but not parts of such entities. The approach is similar to that in the Acquired Rights Directive, Council Directive (EEC) 77/187. The Regulations apply to those undertakings which have their registered or head office or, in the absence of such an office, their principal place of business, in Great Britain.

Employers may start a process to negotiate an Information and Consultation Agreement (which I shall refer to as an ICA)—reg. 11. Otherwise employees may request it themselves—reg. 7. At least ten per cent must make the request, subject to a minimum of 15 and a maximum of 2,500. It must be in writing, identify the employees making it and be sent to the employer, or to the CAC if they wish to remain anonymous. If the undertaking is of sufficient size the employer will be required to negotiate an ICA with employee representatives. However, if there is one already in place the employer, on giving one month's notice, is entitled to ballot the workforce to determine whether they endorse the request—reg. 8. If a majority of those voting endorse the request it must be complied with, so long as that represents at least 40 per cent of the workforce. Any such pre-existing agreement must be in writing, cover all the employees of the undertaking, set out the information to be given and have been approved by the employees. Disputes about the existence of any purported pre-existing agreement may be determined by the CAC—reg. 10. If upheld, a new agreement would then have to be reached.

If an agreement is reached, no further requests by employees may be made. If no agreement is reached, which needs only to be approved by union representatives if they represent the majority of employees (see *Stewart* v *Moray Council* (2006)), standard provisions to inform and consult apply as a form of default—regs 18–20. If a process is begun to reach agreement this must be completed within three months. The employer must arrange for employees to elect or appoint their representatives. The employer must inform the workforce as to the identity of the representatives and then invite them to enter into negotiations to reach an ICA. The parties are required to negotiate in a spirit of co-operation taking into account the interests of the undertaking and the employees—reg. 21. Negotiations must be complete after a further six months after the expiry of the three-month period, although this is extendable by agreement. ACAS may assist in this process.

There are very few requirements in the Regulations as to what an ICA should contain. This is left largely to the parties. The agreement must specify the circumstances in which employees will be informed and consulted, but does not specify what these circumstances should be. The ICA must, however, be in writing, dated, signed and cover all the employees in the undertaking.

If an employer has failed to abide by an ICA, application may be made to the EAT in which event the employer is liable to a penalty of up to £75,000. This is payable to the Secretary of State. The first time this has been imposed was in 2007, against Macmillan Publishers. Where there has been a finding by the CAC in circumstances where a dispute has been referred to it (under reg. 24) an appeal may be made on a point of law to the EAT.

14.7 **European Works Councils**

In December 1997, the Government finally signed up to the European Works Council Directive (Council Directive (EC) 94/45), previously subject to the UK's 'opt-out' from the EU Social Chapter. This requires organisations employing at least 1,000 staff across the European Economic Area (the 30 EU states, plus Norway, Iceland, and Liechtenstein), and at least 150 in two or more states, to establish a mechanism at European level for informing and consulting staff about transnational issues. The UK was obliged to implement the Directive's provisions into national law by 15 December 1999. It was enacted into domestic law by the Transnational Information and Consultation of Employees Regulations 1999 (SI 1999 No. 3323), which came into force on 15 January 2000.

14.7.1 **Scope**

The Regulations apply to all multinationals of the requisite size, by virtue of inclusion of UK staff, whose central management is located in the UK—estimated to be around 100 companies. They do not apply to organisations which establish a European consultative body voluntarily, in accordance with art. 13 of the Directive; nor to multinationals which have already come under an obligation to establish a European Works Council by virtue of their staff in other EEA states where the Directive has been implemented for some time.

14.7.2 **Establishing the European Works Council**

If no voluntary European Works Council agreement exists, either 100 employees, their representatives or management may trigger a process leading to negotiations to set up a European Works Council or equivalent body. These should take place between central management and employee representatives in a Special Negotiating Body (SNB). The regulations propose that the SNB should consist of one representative from each EEA state where the company operates plus, where appropriate: one extra seat for a state where between 20 per cent and 40 per cent of the workforce within the EEA is employed; two extra for 40–60 per cent; and three extra for over

60 per cent. UK members of the SNB are to be elected by a general ballot of the UK workforce, although where more than one SNB seat is allocated to the UK, management has the option of dividing the workforce into equal constituencies.

If management refuses to enter talks about setting up a European Works Council within six months of a request by the employees or their representatives, or fails to negotiate a European Works Council within three years thereof, a statutory European Works Council will be set up in accordance with the Annex to the Directive, which is attached to the regulations.

14.7.3 Employee representatives

Employee representatives (including representatives of an independent trade union recognised for collective bargaining purposes) who are in place prior to the formation of a Special Negotiating Body (SNB) or European Works Council have the right to request information concerning staff numbers to ascertain whether a company is covered by European Works Council legislation; to submit a written request to management for the creation of a European Works Council, or equivalent procedure; and to elect or appoint from their own ranks members of the European Works Council who represent the whole workforce.

Members of the SNB and European Works Council will receive rights to paid time off to perform their duties, and protections against detriment and unfair dismissal under ERA 1996. Management may withhold information from the SNB or the European Works Council if disclosure could be harmful to the company. SNB and European Works Council members are also forbidden to disclose information provided to them in confidence.

14.7.4 Disputes and enforcement

Disputes arising in the UK about matters prior to the establishment of a European Works Council are referred to the CAC. Disputes about the operation of a European Works Council, or the failure to set one up within the three-year period, are handled by the EAT, except for challenges to the withholding of information, which are referred to the CAC.

14.8 The Advisory, Conciliation and Arbitration Service

It is in the interests of everyone, above all the general public, that industrial disputes are resolved peacefully and quickly. From earliest times Government services have therefore been made available to assist independently warring industrial parties. The role used to be filled mainly by the Ministry of Labour but its functions were transferred in 1969 to the quasi-autonomous Commission for Industrial Relations (CIR), the brainchild of the Donovan Commission. ACAS took over all the CIR's functions in 1974, originally on a non-statutory basis, although its constitution was soon laid down by EPA 1975 and it was given the duty of promoting the improvement of industrial relations, and in particular of encouraging the extension of collective bargaining and the development, and where necessary, the reform of collective bargaining machinery. ACAS's duty has been simplified, however, to just 'the improvement of industrial relations' since the amendment to TULR(C)A 1992, s. 209 came into effect in 1999.

ACAS's main strength in this respect lies in its manifest independence both of the two sides of industry and of the Government. TULR(C)A 1992 clearly provides that it is not to be 'subject to directions of any kind from any Minister of the Crown as to the manner in which it is to exercise any of its functions under any enactment' (s. 247(3)). The Service is instead governed by a Council which is responsible for policy matters and consists of nine members serving part-time, although its chairman is full-time and holds office for five years. All are appointed by the Secretary of State for Trade and Industry—three after consultation with employers and three on the recommendation of the unions, while the rest sit as independents. The Council was thus intended, like ACAS itself, to reflect whatever consensus exists in British industrial relations, and to be the constructive side of dispute management.

The most important role of ACAS is its peace-keeping and fire-fighting function—trying to prevent industrial action at the earliest stages. It must strike a fine balance between intervening too readily in disputes and yet being available if the parties positively desire its assistance. It thus has power where a trade dispute (as defined) exists 'by way of conciliation or by other means to offer assistance to the parties to the dispute with a view to bringing about a settlement'.

14.8.1 Conciliation

There is a long history to the independent conciliatory approach now provided by ACAS. The Conciliation Act 1896 gave power to the Board of Trade to inquire into the causes of any dispute and 'take such steps as to the Board may seem expedient'. These were extended, after the experience of wartime and the Whitley Report, by the Industrial Courts Act 1919 and this function duly passed to ACAS in 1975. Conciliation involves not so much making suggestions to the two parties, but rather providing a forum for discussion and procedural guidance to bring them together. Thus the Service does not involve itself in a dispute unless both sides agree, and not until internal procedures under the collective bargain have been exhausted (TULR(C)A 1992, s. 210(3)). The hope is that it can then flexibly react to particular problems involved.

In the past the Government itself intervened in particularly contentious disputes, in the person of the Secretary of State for Employment or the Prime Minister; the semi-ritual of marathon sessions at No. 10 Downing Street in the 1970s, punctuated by beer and sandwiches, led to the settlement of many disputes, but was not a practice which was continued by the Conservative Government nor the subsequent Labour administrations.

ACAS conciliation officers are also involved in conciliation on an individual level, since every complaint to an ET is examined by them to see whether a settlement is feasible.

14.8.2 Mediation

Mediation is a more intrusive and active process than conciliation, for the mediator, who may or may not come from the ACAS staff, makes recommendations of his own for a way out of an industrial dispute, and the parties then consider his suggestions.

14.8.3 Advice

ACAS may offer advice to employers, employers' associations, workers and trade unions on matters concerned with and affecting, or likely to affect, industrial relations (TULR(C)A 1992, s. 213). Included are a telephone advice service and a comprehensive industrial relations handbook. The TURERA 1993 gave it the power to charge for its services.

14.8.4 Inquiry

The offer of a far-ranging independent inquiry has sometimes defused an apparently intractable industrial dispute by providing a calmer atmosphere in which to review all the underlying issues involved (TULR(C)A 1992, s. 214). The generally held convention is that the parties called off their strike or lock-out pending the results of the inquiry although this has been observed less fully of late, with unions anxious not to lose the momentum built up behind their strikes. Section 215 accords power to the Secretary of State for Trade and Industry to refer any matter connected with a trade dispute to a court of inquiry conducted either by one person or a board. Such 'courts' have been set up to consider some of the most damaging industrial disputes; thus Lord Wilberforce's court investigated the miners' strike of 1972 and Lord Scarman attempted to untangle the events in the Grunwick affair a few years later. There have been no inquiries of this nature, however, in recent years. The hearing before the court is invariably formal in procedure and it has power to compel witnesses, whose evidence may be heard on oath. It may otherwise generally regulate its own procedure, but it must lay a report before Parliament.

14.8.5 Arbitration

Arbitration is an important step to take for the parties in dispute since it in effect delegates the autonomy of both sides to a third party over whom they can have no control. Even so, some industries have long had a settled system of arbitration as a safety valve to prevent strikes, and this is especially so in the public sector.

The general independent arbitration role was initiated in the Conciliation Act 1896, although traces may be found as far back as the Combination Act 1800 and the Masters and Workers Arbitration Act 1824. Now a trade dispute may be referred to arbitration by ACAS with the consent of all parties and provided that internal bargaining procedures have already been adopted, unless there is a 'special reason' for by-passing such procedures. Further, ACAS must have considered the likelihood of the dispute being settled by conciliation (TULR(C)A 1992, s. 212(2)). The Service may itself appoint an arbitrator or a board of arbitrators but none of them should be on the ACAS staff, so that the independence of the institution is not compromised s. 212(1)). Alternatively, the case may be referred to the CAC. The latter's chairman appoints a panel consisting of one member from each of the three lists of employers' representatives, employees' representatives, and independent persons. ACAS looks on arbitration as a matter of last resort, urging the parties not to abdicate responsibilities but to reach agreement between themselves. Little use has been made of these facilities.

14.9 **Central Arbitration Committee**

The CAC replaced the Industrial Arbitration Board in 1975 but it traces its descent to the Industrial Court set up in 1919 and continues to act as an independent focus for arbitration, along with various statutory jurisdictions (TULR(C)A 1992, ss 259–265).

Between 1975 and 1980 the CAC had jurisdiction in respect of claims for the extension of collectively bargained and general level terms and conditions. Both these provisions were abolished by the Employment Act 1980, leaving the CAC with only the responsibilities of reviewing collective agreements and pay structures which contain terms 'applying specifically to men only or women only' under the Equal Pay Act 1970 and adjudicating on complaints of failure to disclose information to a recognised trade union for the purposes of collective bargaining—ss 183, 184). The CAC lost its jurisdiction over fair wages claims in 1983. It may still, however, provide voluntary arbitration facilities.

Like ETs, the CAC consists of a chairman sitting with 'wingmen' who are representatives of employers and employees; they seek to reach unanimous decisions, but where this is impossible the chairman acts as an umpire, his decision binding even if outvoted by the wingmen. As befits a body well versed in industrial relations, its procedure is flexible, and the Arbitration Acts do not apply. It has no power to summon witnesses nor to punish for contempt and usually first considers written representations which are then amplified at a formal hearing, normally held in public. While there is no appeal, its decisions are subject to judicial review by the Divisional Court of the Queen's Bench Division where there is an error of law or procedure. The judges have generally not intervened in the CAC as they have to correct ACAS. Lord Widgery CJ inferred from the lack of any appeal that 'Parliament intended these matters to be dealt with without too much assistance from the lawyers' (*R v CAC ex parte TI Tube Division Services Ltd* (1978)).

Like most administrative bodies, it is not obliged to give reasons for its decisions (except when upholding a complaint of failure to disclose information for collective bargaining purposes—ss 183(4), 184(2)), but it has now broken from the former practice and sets out the 'general considerations' behind its awards. They are, however, to be read by the parties as a guide, not as a precise legal judgment.

The CAC plays the central role in the statutory recognition system contained in TULR(C)A 1992, Sch. A1. The various procedures set out in the Schedule are far more prescriptive than anything the CAC has had to deal with up till now, although the established pattern of three-member panels continues (s. 263A).

The Employment Relations Act 1999 also introduced changes to the way in which individuals are appointed to the CAC. It is not necessary for the Secretary of State to select members from a list of nominees prepared by ACAS, although those he does select must be experienced in industrial relations and have a background representing either workers or employers. The Secretary of State must also consult ACAS before making an appointment, and may consult other interested bodies, such as the CBI and TUC (s. 260).

14.10 **Codes of Practice**

Codes of Practice are a fertile source of 'quasi-law' in the industrial relations area. A distinction must be drawn in procedure and effect between codes promulgated by ACAS and the Department of Trade and Industry. The TULR(C)A 1992, s. 199 requires that ACAS provide guidance by codes of practice on disclosure of information and time off for trade union activities both of which were only vaguely defined in the statute. In the exercise of its discretion it has also published a Code on Disciplinary Practice and Procedures. All these are intended as authoritative statements of proper practice.

The TULR(C)A 1992, ss 203–206 give co-ordinate power to the Department for Business, Innovation and Skills also to issue Codes of Practice. The procedure here requires the Secretary of State to consult ACAS, issue a draft, consider representations, if necessary amend the draft, and then lay it before Parliament for approval. Perhaps significantly, the statutory aim of the Codes is stated by TULR(C)A 1992, s. 203(1), to be the improvement of industrial relations and there is no parallel duty as for ACAS to promote the extension of collective bargaining.

The TULR(C)A 1992, s. 207 states that a failure on the part of any person to observe any provision of a Code of Practice shall not of itself render him liable to any proceedings but any such code is admissible in evidence, with the same persuasive but not decisive authority as the Highway Code has in road traffic cases. An important difference between ACAS and Secretary of State's Codes is that the latter may be referred to in the courts as well as ETs and the CAC. This may be particularly important with regard to picketing, which often strays into the criminal area (see use of the Code in *Thomas* v *NUM (South Wales Area)* (1985)). Moreover, a Code issued by the Secretary of State may expressly supersede one put out by ACAS.

If an employer fails to comply with a Code of Practice, any award the tribunal makes to the employee may be increased by up to a quarter. Likewise, if the employee should not comply, any such award may be reduced by the tribunal by up to a quarter. The tribunal will make such increases or reductions if reasonable, just and equitable to do so. (See s. 207A.) The jurisdictions to which s. 207A applies are laid out in TULR(C)A 1992, Sch. 2A.

The CEHR and Health and Safety Executive also have similar powers under their respective enabling Acts.

14.11 **The right of public sector employees to be consulted about changes in terms of employment**

The House of Lords' decision in *R* v *Secretary of State for Foreign and Commonwealth Affairs ex parte Council of Civil Service Unions* (1985) raised fundamental questions about the right of Crown employees to be consulted about changes in their terms. The case concerned a challenge by the unions represented at GCHQ to the

Government's decision without consulting them to remove the right of employees to join unions of their choice. Instead they were allowed only to join an approved staff association. The House of Lords decided that since the Crown might at any time change the conditions of service of civil servants, they and their unions had no right to prior consultation when there were changes. They would, however, have a legitimate expectation to be so consulted because of the practice to this effect ever since the establishment of GCHQ. The courts would protect this right in a proper case by an application for judicial review. Here, however, the interests of national security overrode the normal right in this regard. It was made clear that these rights did not relate to employees in the private sector. Lord Fraser said that 'if no question of national security arose, the decision-making process in this case would have been unfair' but 'the judicial process is unsuitable for reaching decisions on national security'.

SELECTED READING

Hall, M. (2005), 'Assessing the Information and Consultation of Employees Regulations', (2005) 34 ILJ 103

Morris, G. and Archer, T. (2000), *Collective Labour Law*, Oxford: Hart Publishing, 2000

Wedderburn, L. (2000), 'Collective Bargaining or Legal Enactment? The 1999 Act and Union Recognition', (2000) 29 ILJ 1

15

....

Industrial action

SUMMARY

This chapter considers the law relating to the breakdown in collective relations between the employer and the workforce. After the practical context is explained the legal analysis of industrial action is explored. The fundamental position in contract, its unimportance of itself but also its role in relation to particular torts are explained. However, the possibility for trade unions then to claim immunities for relevant torts is explored. The particular issues raised by, for example, secondary action, and the requirement of supporting ballots and the position of consumers are examined. Finally, the legal consequences and remedies of taking part in industrial action are considered, followed by an examination of the law that relates particularly to picketing in industrial disputes.

15.1 Right to take industrial action

15.1.1 Background

It is virtually impossible in modern Britain to take industrial action which is lawful. In some circumstances and for certain legal purposes immunities will be accorded to strikers and trade unions; but in particular contractual liability will almost always remain, giving the right to employers to sue their employees for damages caused by industrial action. For reasons we will examine later, it might be true to say that it is only possible to take lawful industrial action if it constitutes a ban on voluntary overtime, but even that is doubtful. So, in general, industrial action, taken for whatever reason, is unlawful in Britain.

The consequences of this are naturally serious. To take part in industrial action may mean the worker can be dismissed, or lose pay and lack qualification for jobseekers' allowance or other benefits. This is so even if the employer is totally to blame for the breakdown in relations that leads to the action. In addition, the illegality may be something on which to pin other forms of liability (as in the case of the indirect torts which are most important in practice), and forms the rationale on which the legal requirements for strike ballots and the rights of dissentients who wish to work, in particular, are based. For those who argue for the right to strike, the last two decades of the last century were bad ones. Take, for example, Roger Welch who argued for a number of legal rights he believed trade unions and their members should have, including the rights to organise industrial action, to participate in it in solidarity with other workers, free from the threat of dismissal, and to engage in non-violent picketing at any workplace. He contended that his proposals would require a total repeal of the legislation passed by the Conservative Government, and may seem radical to some, but 'represent no more than the legal position that many trade unionists and lawyers thought existed for the best part of this century, that is since the Trade Disputes Act 1906' (Welch, *The Right to Strike: A trade union view* (Liverpool: Institute of Employment Rights, 1991), p. 41). But there has been no possibility of this occurring under the recent Labour administrations.

15.2 Industrial action and the individual contract

The effect of strikes and other industrial action on the individual contract of employment is, paradoxically, rarely of direct importance. Employers normally do not wish to disturb post-strike calm by resorting to the courts to sue individual workers, but it is still vital indirectly, for it provides the basis of the illegality which is central to the economic torts of intimidation, inducing breach of contract and conspiracy. In this way management may seek redress from strike leaders and unions unless they are acting in contemplation or furtherance of a trade dispute as defined. The most valuable remedy, other than damages after a strike, is an injunction to prevent a strike taking place.

15.2.1 Notice to terminate

There is now a statutory minimum of one week for an employee's notice (ERA 1996, s. 86(2)) but longer periods are usually required by the individual contract. If such notice is given in a strike by each employee, the effect would seem to be the employee has resigned, although this rarely happens in practice since the object of industrial action is not to sever relations with the employer but to impose different terms on which that relationship is to be continued. As Donovan LJ said in *Rookes* v *Barnard* (1963), in the Court of Appeal:

It would, however, be affectation not to recognise that in the majority of strikes no such notice to terminate the contract is either given or expected. The strikers do not want to give up their jobs; they simply want to be paid more for it or to secure some other advantage in connection with it. The employer does not want to lose his labour force; he simply wants to resist the claim. Not till the strike has lasted some time, and no settlement is in sight, does one usually read that the employers have given notice that unless the men return to work their contracts will be terminated and they will be dismissed.

Lord Denning MR recognised that (*J. T. Stratford & Son* v *Lindley* (1965)):

The strike notice is nothing more nor less than a notice that the men will not come to work. In short, that they will break their contract...

There might be difficulties in a union giving notice to terminate on behalf of its members, not only because it is not acting as their agent but also because different employees may have to give different periods of notice. Davies LJ, dissatisfied with the ramifications of the notice idea, saw strike notices as notices to terminate the present contractual conditions coupled with an offer to work on new terms (*Morgan* v *Fry* (1968)). Thus the striker does not intend to put an end to the employment altogether. Only if the employee is subject to a non-strike agreement between his employer and union, would he then be acting in breach of contract. It would thus not be a rule of law that notice to strike is notice of breach. However, in *Miles* v *Wakefield Metropolitan District Council* (1987), the House of Lords suggested that all forms of industrial action are repudiatory of the contract of employment as there is generally an intention to harm the employer's business. This would seem to point to the motive with which the notice is given as being relevant to its legality. That was a major development in the law, for the law of contract traditionally merely required the form to be complied with (the correct notice to be given) for lawfulness to be preserved. The motive with which a lawful act is done should arguably be irrelevant in determining its legality in contract in accordance with the principle enunciated by the House of Lords in *Allen* v *Flood* (1898) (see below). (See further, Ferran, [1987] 46 CLJ 412; Morris, (1987) 16 ILJ 185.)

15.2.2 **Suspension of contract**

Another contention that has at times attracted the courts is that a strike suspends the contract of employment. This focuses on the fact that there is clearly no right to pay during a strike. Thus, in *Morgan* v *Fry* (1968), Lord Denning MR held that there was an implied term that each side to a contract agreed to its suspension by strike action after the giving of notice which could determine the contract. He said: 'If a strike takes place the contract of employment is not terminated. It is suspended during the strike and revives again when the strike is over.' The Donovan Commission in the late 1960s rejected the general adoption of this idea on the ground of 'considerable technical difficulty', including problems over its application to unofficial, unconstitutional strikes and other forms of industrial action like a go-slow and work-to-rule. It is also unclear what would happen if a strike were never settled, or if the employer sought to dismiss all the strikers.

15.2.3 **Repudiatory breach**

The courts thus generally view a strike with or without proper contractual notice (and it usually takes place without such notice) as a repudiation of their contracts by the strikers. The EAT in *Simmons* v *Hoover Ltd* (1977), said: 'It seems to us to be plain that it was a [repudiation] for here there was a settled, confirmed and continued intention on the part of the employee not to do any of the work which under his contract he had been engaged to do; which was the whole purpose of his contract.' Phillips J thought that *Morgan* v *Fry* was not 'intended to revolutionise the law on this subject' and held to the view that a strike is a repudiatory breach, citing *Bowes & Partners* v *Press* (1894), for it is a failure by the employee to perform the most fundamental duty under his contract—to work.

The employer has a choice whether or not to accept the repudiation by the strikers; if he does accept it, he reacts by dismissing them and this counts as a termination of contract by the employer. Those cases which suggested that a strike, and indeed any other repudiatory breach, automatically brings the contract to an end as a form of 'constructive resignation' later came to be regarded as unsound (*London Transport Executive* v *Clarke* (1981)). The law on dismissal during the course of industrial action is considered in Chapter 8 above.

15.2.4 **Damages**

The employer may also sue strikers for damages, but a major difficulty arises in their calculation. The courts have rejected an aliquot share of overhead expenses during lost days as the appropriate measure (*Ebbw Vale Steel, Iron and Coal Co. v Tew* (1935)). In *National Coal Board v Galley* (1958) the Court of Appeal ignored the breaches of contract by other employees, and awarded the employers of the defendant, a colliery deputy engaged on safety work, only the cost of hiring a substitute—the princely sum of £3 18s 2d—and not a proportional amount of the whole loss as they had claimed. If the factory were running at a loss only nominal damages could be secured, and sometimes strikes may even enhance a company's chance of profitability by reducing wage costs at a time of slack demand. In reality very few employers take the risk of further exacerbating industrial relations by suing for damages after the end of a dispute. As the CBI said in evidence to the Donovan Commission (para. 413 of the Report): 'The main interest of the employer is in the resumption of work and the preservation of good will.' Most employers will also seek to make deductions from the pay of strikers (*Wiluszynski v Tower Hamlets LBC* (1989)). A deliberate refusal in advance of performance to work under the contract as normal completely defeats the employee's contractual claim to wages or salary, and this continues for as long as the refusal to perform goes on. The employer may resist any claim to part-payment on the basis that he makes it clear that he refuses to waive his right to receive full performance.

15.2.5 **Other forms of industrial action**

There are various other forms of industrial action and the effect on the contract of employment depends on which form is in point.

The work-to-rule and go-slow were particularly common on the railways. Employees meticulously follow work rules. Forms may be completed in great detail, and usually-ignored safety provisions activated. All this slows down the rate of work progress and we have already seen that the Court of Appeal have held that this withdrawal of co-operation can amount to a breach of contract (*Secretary of State for Employment v ASLEF (No. 2)* (1972)).

Overtime bans have occurred most frequently in the newspapers and electricity supply industries but constitute a breach of contract only if overtime is compulsory, which is rarely the case. This tactic is often combined with a ban on shift working. It is not a breach of the implied term of co-operation to operate a ban on voluntary overtime, even if this is done with a motive to be disruptive to the employer's business. Employees need have no good reason for refusing to undertake tasks which they are not contractually required to do—see the decision of the Privy Council in *Burgess v Stevedoring Services Ltd* (2002).

Employees may work normally but refuse to perform the particular duty about which they are protesting. Thus, bus drivers on one-man buses may refuse to collect fares, and teachers may refrain from dinner duties (*Gorse v Durham County Council* (1971)), or refuse to cover for absent colleagues (*Sim v Rotherham Metropolitan Borough Council* (1986). See Morris, (1987) 16 ILJ 185; Napier, [1987] 46 CLJ 44).

Sit-ins, which normally take place after the termination of the contract of employment, constitute the tort of trespass and can be restrained by injunction. In general, an employee is not entitled to remain on his employer's property without the employer's consent (*City and Hackney Health Authority* v *NUPE* (1985)).

15.3 The legality of industrial action: the questions to be asked

The court must ask itself three questions to test the legality of most industrial action. The stages were first adumbrated as such by Brightman LJ in *Merkur Island Shipping Corporation* v *Laughton* (1983) and approved by Lord Diplock and repeated in *Dimbleby & Sons Ltd* v *NUJ* (1984). The questions are, first, whether the employers have a cause of action at common law, and secondly, whether the defendants are acting in contemplation or furtherance of a trade dispute against the claimant. If so, TULR(C)A 1992, s. 219 accords immunity in tort for acts which induce a person to break a contract of employment; threaten that a contract of employment will be broken; interfere with the trade, business or employment of a person; or constitute an agreement by two or more persons to procure the doing of any such act. The final question is to consider whether the immunity is removed by further provisions in TULR(C)A 1992. If the answer to the second is in the affirmative, and the action is not taken against the primary employer in the dispute, to be immune it must fall within the narrow area of protected secondary action left lawful by s. 224; that is secondary picketing. Further, in order to retain the immunity from certain torts, there must be an affirmative ballot among those likely to be called out in the action. Action to enforce 'union labour only' clauses is also in itself unlawful.

The liability of trade unions for the acts of its officials in tort will then be discussed. Lastly we turn our attention to the remedies available to an employer and a consumer to restrain unlawful industrial action, and contempt of court. We will first consider the main economic torts used in strike claims, and then turn to the immunities.

15.4 Inducing breach of contract

15.4.1 The importance of the tort

This centrally important tort is committed where a person directly or indirectly induces a party to a contract to break it without legal justification. It will be almost always committed in a strike which breaches not only the contracts of employment of the strikers, but also commercial contracts entered into by the employer struck against.

In the first authority on inducement, *Lumley* v *Gye* (1853), the defendant theatre owner persuaded an opera singer to sing for him at Her Majesty's Theatre, thus inducing breach of her exclusive engagement for three months to the plaintiff at the rival Queen's Theatre. The court held that there was a cause of action and thus generalised the existing action for enticement of a servant. (For an interesting account of this case see Waddams, (2001) 117 LQR 431.) Since then it has been applied to all manner of agreements. Lord Watson later stated the principle in *Allen* v *Flood* (1898) that:

He who wilfully induces another to do an unlawful act which, but for his persuasion, would or might never have been committed, is rightly held to be responsible for the wrong which he procured.

15.4.2 **Different modes of committing the tort**

Most commonly in strikes, the tort is committed when a shop steward or union official directly persuades an employee to breach his contract of employment. This, and other similar forms, may be called direct inducement.

However, another common fact-situation is the case of a boycott or 'blacking' where union organisers take action against suppliers or distributors of the employer with whom it is in dispute and so induce breach of the employer's commercial contracts. This is an essential feature of solidarity action. *Torquay Hotel Co. Ltd* v *Cousins* (1969) is a good example of this form, which may be called indirect inducement as the union does not operate directly on the party in breach. The owner of the plaintiff hotel company had criticised the defendant union's action in an inter-union dispute already affecting other hotels in the area. The defendants thus contacted the drivers for Esso Ltd, which supplied the plaintiff hotel with fuel, and stated that they would prevent all oil supplies reaching the hotel. The non-delivery of oil was a result of the employees' inducement and a majority of the Court of Appeal held there was a breach of the commercial contract. The breach was induced indirectly, however, and for indirect action to be illegal, unlawful means must be used. There were unlawful means, in the information conveyed to Esso Ltd that if they did not cut off oil supplies, the union would be calling on its members in that company to break their contracts of employment.

The situation can be described diagrammatically where employers are represented by R and employees by E. Vertical lines represent employment contracts and horizontal lines represent commercial contracts.

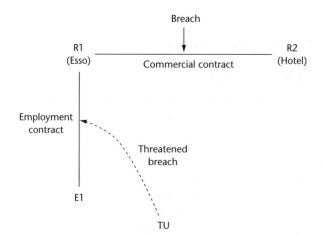

The indirect tort described is an example of the situation where the inducement consists in persuading someone to break a contract. However, there may be inducement where the party is put into breach for reasons outside his control, which may be called the procurement of a breach of contract. (See further Simester and Chan, (2004) 63 CLJ 132.) Blacking the goods of a particular employer is the example *par excellence* of procurement, and often two contracts will thereby be broken: that of the employee who procures it, and the employer's agreement with the outside party. *J. T. Stratford and Son v Lindley* (1965) provides a good illustration of this *modus operandus*. The plaintiff, Stratford, was the chairman of Companies A and B. A owned Thames motor barges while B hired them out to firms, C, which employed their own crews. Forty-five of A's employees were members of the TGWU, while three belonged to the much smaller Waterman's Union (WU). Both organisations sought negotiating rights with Stratford for A & Co. When the TGWU made a breakthrough in negotiations, the WU sought to use whatever industrial muscle they had to compel the same end. They had no power to attack Company A directly since they had very few members there, and instead they put pressure on B by calling on their members in C not to return them to the moorings when the contracts ended. The breaches of these agreements were thus achieved indirectly but were no less successful in achieving their end. The High Court granted an injunction, since the union had induced the hirers' employees to act in breach of their contracts of employment in order to procure a breach of contract between their employers and Company B on whom the union was seeking to exert pressure. Procuring breach of contract most commonly constitutes secondary action, the restriction on which is considered later.

The *Stratford* case can be described diagrammatically as shown below.

In *Thomson & Co. v Deakin* (1952) Jenkins LJ essayed a statement of general principle that for this variant of the tort to be committed it must be shown:

first, that the person charged with actionable interference knew of the existence of the contract and intended to procure its breach; secondly that the person so charged did definitely

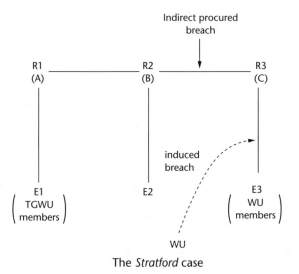

The *Stratford* case

and unequivocally persuade, induce or procure the employees to breach their contracts of employment with the intent mentioned; thirdly, that the employees so persuaded, induced or procured did in fact break their contracts of employment, and fourthly, that the breach or the contract forming the alleged subject of interference ensued as a necessary consequence of the breach of the employees concerned of their contracts of employment.

This *dictum* was approved by the House of Lords in *Merkur Island Shipping Corporation* v *Laughton* (1983).

15.4.3 Knowledge of contract

Economic torts all require intention by the defendant, which means that he must foresee the possibility of a breach of contract and desire that result. The older cases demanded that the defendant have actual knowledge of the contract breached and some cognisance of its terms (*Thomson* v *Deakin* (1952); also *Long* v *Smithson* (1918); *Smithies* v *National Association of Operative Plasterers* (1909)), but the threshold has been reduced over time. Ignorance will not always excuse liability for inducement. Thus in *Cunard SS Co. Ltd* v *Stacey* (1955) strike organisers were taken to know that, on their calling a strike, union members would thereby break their articles as seamen. The Master of the Rolls took the objective view in his wide statement of principle:

Even if [the defendants] did not know of the actual terms of the contract, but had the means of knowledge which they deliberately disregarded—that would be enough.

Jenkins LJ thought that the defendant is liable if he intends to have the contract ended by breach if it cannot be ended lawfully; again, motive enters the field. He could not 'turn a blind eye to it', and Parker LJ agreed. Here they found that the defendants did intend a breach for, even though the defendants said they assumed that the contracts could be terminated lawfully, they were in the end indifferent whether they did so or not. (See also *British Industrial Plastics Ltd* v *Ferguson* (1938); *Emerald Construction Co. Ltd* v *Lowthian* (1966); *Merkur* (1983).) In *Greig* v *Insole* (1978) Slade J said:

It will suffice for the plaintiff to prove that the defendant knew of the *existence* of the contract, provided that he can prove also that the defendant intended to procure the breach of it...ignorance of the precise terms may in particular circumstances enable him to satisfy the court that he did not have such intent; ignorance of this nature, however, does not alone suffice to show absence of intent to procure a breach.

One case where the union was held to have insufficient knowledge was *Timeplan Education Group Ltd* v *National Union of Teachers* (1997). The National Union of Teachers (NUT) was in dispute with T Ltd, a teachers' supply agency. After the union persuaded a New Zealand teachers' magazine to stop carrying T Ltd's advertisements, the company sued the NUT for unlawful interference with its continuing advertising contract with the magazine. The Court of Appeal rejected the claim. Although the union was aware of the contract and the law did not require knowledge of precise terms, there was no evidence that the NUT knew there was a continuing contract. The union reasonably assumed that T Ltd would have paid for advertisements placed in the past; but there was no suggestion that it ever occurred to the union that there was a subsisting contract extending to future advertising. The court rejected T Ltd's submission that the union was under a duty to make enquiries about whether there was such a contract.

15.4.4 **Inducement**

Although inducement must be carefully distinguished from the giving of friendly advice the line of distinction is difficult to draw. It is not enough that a union official tells employees that the boss is going to cut overtime payments from next week, and they immediately strike in protest. The Court of Appeal thus held that there was no actionable inducement in *Thomson* v *Deakin* (1952) because the defendants simply stated the facts as they knew them. In *Torquay Hotel Co. Ltd* v *Cousins* (1969) Winn LJ, however, thought that mere advice could be an inducement, going on to say:

A man who writes to his mother-in-law telling her that the central heating in his house has broken down may thereby induce her to cancel an intended visit.

In *J. T. Stratford & Son* v *Lindley* (1965) Lord Pearce abstracted from the case law the proposition that:

The fact that an inducement to break a contract is couched as an irresistible embargo rather than in terms of seduction does not make it any the less an inducement.

It would be enough if the union members were threatened with loss of their union membership if they did not take part in particular action.

In *Camellia Tanker SA* v *ITF* (1976) it was held that the defendants, in informing their members of negotiations with the plaintiff, did not induce them to break their contract in support, since there was no 'pressure, persuasion or procuration'. The breach of the commercial contract was not the necessary result of the union's action, only being reasonably likely, and this was not sufficient.

15.4.5 **Breach of contract**

A breach of contract is a fundamental requirement for the commission of this tort. Thus in *Allen* v *Flood* (1898) the defendant boilermakers' action in informing management that they would knock off work if the plaintiff shipwrights were not dismissed was not unlawful since they were free to leave at any time without breaking their contracts. The fact that the motive for their leaving was to injure the plaintiffs was irrelevant. The tort also has no application where the term of the contract breached is itself void for illegality, nor is there 'a tort of wrongfully inducing a person not to enter into a contract'. (See Megarry J in *Midland Cold Storage Ltd* v *Steer* (1972); *Solihull Metropolitan Borough* v *NUT* (1985); *Hadmor Productions Ltd* v *Hamilton* (1983).) Breach of an equitable duty suffices, however, so that in *Prudential Assurance Co.* v *Lorenz* (1971) trade union members who refused to submit insurance premiums they had collected to their head office were enjoined from this course of action since it was inducing breach of their equitable duty to account, which they owed as agents to their principal, the claimant.

15.4.6 **Causation**

Thomson v *Deakin* (1952) shows the need for a chain of causation between inducement and breach of contract. The claimant printers had a policy of refusing to employ trade unionists and they required workers to sign a written undertaking that they would not join a union. This was challenged by NATSOPA (then the print union) who called out on strike their 75 secret members at the company (Bowaters) and asked other unions to disrupt the company's activities as a sign of solidarity. TGWU members at Bowaters responded that they would not deliver paper to Thomson and another union refused to load it. In fact, the threats never materialised into a breach of contract by the employees, although there was a breach of the contract to supply between Bowaters and Thomson. This was held not to be due to any inducement of the employees but to Bowater's decision not to supply, for it could not be proved conclusively that this had been caused by messages from the union. Lord Evershed said: 'The links in the chain which connect the defendants with the plaintiffs are...very insubstantial.' In any event, the employees were not in breach of their contracts so that the necessary unlawful means were not present. Jenkins LJ said:

A person who advocates the objects without advocating the means is [not] to be taken to have advocated recourse to unlawful means.

The fact that the contracted party may be perfectly willing to break the contract does not mean that the inducement is not effective.

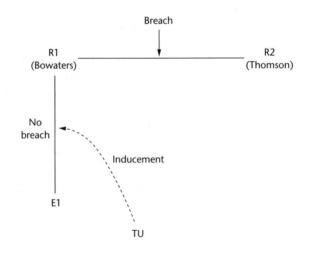

15.4.7 Unlawful means

Unlawful means are necessary in the indirect variants of the tort. Unlawful means may be committed by way of tort, breach of contract or any other form of civil liability. This is a vital restriction because of the enormous potential width of this tort if it were not observed. Otherwise, for example, a wholesaler's action in persuading a retailer to cancel his supply contract with a competitor because of its lower prices might be illegal if it amounted to a breach of contract, yet this is generally considered fair in a free market economy.

Lord Denning suggested that there was a tort even if lawful means were adopted in *Daily Mirror Newspapers* v *Gardner* (1968), but he retracted this view a year later in *Torquay Hotel Co. Ltd* v *Cousins* (1969) with the salient comment that the 'distinction [between lawful and unlawful means] must be maintained, else we should take away the right to strike altogether'. He went on to explain:

Nearly every trade union official who calls a strike...knows that it may prevent the employers from performing their contracts. He may be taken even to intend it. Yet no one has supposed hitherto that it was unlawful; and we should not render it unlawful today. A trade union official is only in the wrong when he procures a contracting party directly to break his contract or when he does it indirectly by unlawful means.

Unlawful means in the indirect inducement of breach of commercial contracts may be found in the direct inducement of breach of employment contracts, as *Emerald Construction Co. Ltd* v *Lowthian* (1966) shows. The main contractors for a CEGB power station had entered into a lump labour contract with the plaintiffs, but this was not to the liking of the union's officers, who were opposed to such arrangements in principle. The union called its bricklayer members out on strike, and as a result the work fell behind, which put the plaintiffs in breach of their contract with the main contractors. The Court of Appeal held that there was a *prima facie* case that the union's action was intended to procure a breach of contract; the unlawful means used were the inducement of the employees' breaches. Moreover, there was no statutory protection at the time, since the breach indirectly induced was not of a contract of employment.

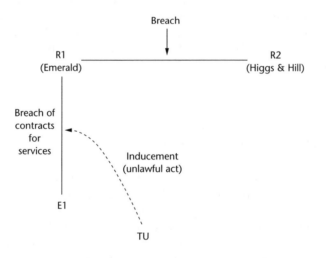

Moreover, the Court of Appeal has indicated that inducing breach of statutory duty may constitute unlawful means (*Meade* v *Haringey LBC* (1979)), notwithstanding that some such breaches are only technical and almost incidental to the strike action. In *Associated Newspapers Ltd* v *Wade* (1979) the defendant and the Executive of the National Graphical Association ordered the blacking of all advertisements of advertisers who continued to use the Nottingham Evening Post with which the union was engaged in a bitter industrial dispute. This incidentally made it difficult for many public bodies to fulfil their statutory duties to make public announcements, and provided the unlawful means for indirect inducement. Further, Lord Denning MR thought the action would anyway have been unlawful as an infringement of European Convention on Human Rights, art. 10, which secures freedom of expression. Inducing such a breach of statutory duty lies outside the trade dispute immunity which refers only to inducing breach of *contract*. The availability of this tort depends crucially on the true construction of the appropriate statute (*Lonrho* v *Shell Petroleum Ltd (No. 2)* (1982), and *Associated British Ports plc* v *TGWU* (1989)).

15.4.8 Justification

Justification is more narrowly circumscribed as a defence to inducement than to the other economic torts. Indeed, it has succeeded only in *Brimelow* v *Casson* (1924), and there in very special circumstances. Chorus girls employed by the defendant, a notorious impresario at the time, were paid so little that they had to resort to immorality to make ends meet. A strike in protest at these conditions was held justified in the circumstances, even though it induced breach of the employer's contract to perform his 'King Wu Tut Tut' review for the good burghers of Dudley.

The wider argument that the defence is always available where there is no ill-will towards the employer was scotched in *South Wales Miners' Federation* v *Glamorgan Coal Co. Ltd* (1905). Moreover, in *Greig* v *Insole* (1978), where the International Cricket Council were found to have induced breach of cricketers' contracts with the Kerry Packer World Cricket Series, Slade J held that the Council's contention that they had acted from 'disinterested and impersonal motives' did not amount to justification. (See for a powerful argument in favour of widening the justification defence, Howarth, (2005) 68 MLR 195. See too, generally, on the theoretical foundation of the torts, Lee, (2009) 29 OJLS 511; Deakin and Randall, (2009) 72 MLR 519.)

15.5 Interference with contract

Lord Denning MR on several occasions stated that a wide tort exists of interference with contract by unlawful means, of which inducement of breach and intimidation are but two examples. This opened a much wider liability—there need be no breach of contract and the claimant need not be a party to the contract broken, but need only have an interest capable of protection. It may also extend to the prevention of an expectation that a contract would be made (*Brekkes Ltd* v *Cattel* (1972)). The central significance of such a development is that it lay outside the trade dispute immunity in that it was not one of the specified torts granted immunity in what is now TULR(C)A 1992, s. 219. In *Merkur Island Shipping Corporation* v *Laughton* (1983) Lord Diplock regarded the tort of 'interfering with the trade or business of another person by doing unlawful acts' as a 'genus of torts' of which procuring breach of contract is a 'species'. (See further Carty, (1988) 104 LQR 250; Carty, (2008) 124 LQR 641.)

The history of the tort is a complex one and its definition is still imprecise. The House of Lords in *Allen* v *Flood* (1898) said that an individual was not liable *per se* for intentionally inflicting economic loss on another, if the means used were otherwise lawful. The presence of malice or bad motive did not constitute the border post between lawfulness and unlawfulness. Thus the defendant union official could with impunity threaten to call on the boilermakers who worked for the plaintiff to strike unless shipwrights also so employed were dismissed. Neither action was in breach of contract and so was quite legal even though the reason was to punish the shipwrights. This was always difficult to reconcile with *Quinn* v *Leathem* (1901), also a decision of the House of Lords, where it was held that a conspiracy to cause harm to another without lawful justification would constitute a tort. There were some straws in the wind before Lord Denning's series of pronouncements. For example, in *J. T. Stratford & Son* v *Lindley* (1965), Lord Reid doubted whether breach of contract was essential to constitute a tort, although Lord Donovan thought this argument 'novel and surprising'.

The issue arose directly in *Torquay Hotel Co. Ltd* v *Cousins* (1969), the facts of which have already been given. There was a clause in the agreement between the fuel suppliers and the hotel that the former, Esso, would not be liable in contract for failure to supply should that be due to industrial dispute. Such clauses are known as *force majeure* clauses, and the issue arises as to whether they excuse a party in breach from that breach, or merely limit the ambit of obligation so that non-performance will not amount to a breach. Russell LJ narrowly interpreted this as 'an exception from liability for non-performance' (so that there was a breach of contract) and considered it as an ordinary inducement of breach of contract. Winn LJ suggested that if the contract allowed performance in mode A or mode B it would be tortious to prevent performance in mode A even if it could still be performed in mode B, that is to say, even if no breach of contract resulted. (See also *Greig* v *Insole* (1978).) However, Lord Denning, disagreeing, said:

...if one person deliberately interferes with the trade or business of another, and does so by unlawful means, that is, by an act which he is not at liberty to commit, then he is acting unlawfully.

He thought this was the properly understood basis of *J. T. Stratford & Son* v *Lindley* (1965) and *Rookes* v *Barnard* (1963) (where the threat to call a strike was itself held to be actionable, and constituted intimidation), and defined the requirements of the tort of interference in some detail:

First, there must be interference in the execution of a contract. The interference is not confined to the procurement of a *breach* of contract. It extends to a case where a third person prevents or *hinders* one party from performing his contract, even though it be not a breach. Second, the interference must be deliberate. The person must know of the contract, or, at any rate, turn a blind eye to it and intend to interfere with it...Third, the interference must be *direct*. Indirect interference will not do.

(See further on the necessity for intention the discussion in the House of Lords' decision in *OGB Ltd* v *Allen* (2007); Simpson, (2007) 36 ILJ 468. However, this was not an industrial action case.)

Indirect interference can be restrained only if unlawful means are adopted. Interference appears to include any hindrance upon the freedom of either party to perform the contract. In *Torquay Hotel* the majority held that they were breaches of contract but Lord Denning MR returned to a similar theme in *BBC* v *Hearn* (1977) and *Beaverbrook Newspapers Ltd* v *Keys* (1978) where he said that coercive interference with another's freedom of action was unlawful. In *Associated Newspapers Group* v *Wade* (1979) he widened the principle still further by suggesting that some matters (here interference with freedom of the press) could be so contrary to public policy that they could themselves amount to unlawful means. Thus the National Graphical Association's blacking of advertisements in a local newspaper with which it was in dispute was held to be unlawful means, partly because it prevented some public authorities and local councils from complying with their statutory duties to publish formal notice of proposed actions. It did not matter that neither party could enforce the unlawfulness by independent cause of action.

The existence of the tort was affirmed by the House of Lords in *Hadmor Productions Ltd v Hamilton* (1983) where the plaintiff alleged that Association of Cinematograph Television and Allied Technicians (ACTT) officials threatened to persuade union members to refuse to transmit television programmes produced by the plaintiff. They claimed that this was interference with the plaintiff's business by unlawful means. Thames TV had acquired a licence to transmit the programmes but was not contractually bound to do so. The House of Lords accepted the plaintiff's proposition that it could complain since the company's commercial expectation that the programmes would be broadcast was 'shattered' by the 'blacking'.

The tort was rationalised in *Merkur Island Shipping Corporation v Laughton* (1983). The facts followed the familiar pattern in shipping cases. The International Transport Workers Federation (ITF) organised blacking of the plaintiff's Liberian registered ship after a crew member complained of low wages. When the ship sought to leave the port of Liverpool, tugmen and lock-keepers refused to assist its free passage. The House of Lords agreed with Parker J that the tort of 'interfering by unlawful means' consisted of 'procuring the tugmen and the lockmen to break their contracts of employment by refusing to carry out operations on the part of the tugmen and the port authorities that were necessary to enable the ship to leave the dock'. The contractual duty under the charter was to 'prosecute voyages with the utmost dispatch'. The plaintiff could not rely on procurement of breach of contract since there was a *force majeure* clause. This provided an exclusion from liability, *inter alia*, 'in the event of loss of time due to boycott of the vessel in any port or place by shore labour or others'. Lord Diplock distinguished for these purposes between the primary obligations of the parties to perform under the contract, and their secondary obligations, to pay damages for breach, and said:

All prevention of due performance of a primary obligation under a contract was intended to be included [in the definition of interference] even though no secondary obligation to make monetary compensation thereupon came into existence, because the second obligation was excluded by some *force majeure* clause.

As to knowledge of the contract breached, Lord Diplock thought that there 'can hardly be anyone better informed than the ITF as to the terms of the sort of contracts under which ships are employed'. (See also *Dimbleby & Sons Ltd v NUJ* (1984), *Thomas v NUM (South Wales Area)* (1985), and *Messenger Newspaper Group Ltd v NGA* (1984).)

The distribution of leaflets outside supermarkets urging members of the public to boycott the employer's mushrooms (*Middlebrook Mushrooms Ltd v TGWU* (1993)) did not, however, amount to this tort. The employer was not able to prove a causal connection between the defendant's action and a contract breaker. Since the leaflet was directed at the public and not the management of the supermarkets, any pressure or inducement to act in breach of contract would come from the public and only indirectly from the defendants, so that the action was not tortious at all. To be tortious the persuasion had to be directed at one of the parties to the commercial contract in issue.

15.6 **Intimidation**

15.6.1 **The tort**

In 1793 the master of a slave trading ship (A) in the Cameroons fired at a canoe which was about to do business with another vessel (B), and the natives in panic ceased to trade with B as a result of the volley. On an action by vessel B the Court of Common Pleas held that the defendant, the master of ship A, was liable in damages for intimidation since the plaintiff had lost financially as the result of a threat of violence (*Tarleton* v *McGawley* (1793)). This may seem far removed from the modern industrial dispute, but in *Rookes* v *Barnard* (1964) the House of Lords developed this tort to include threat of a breach of contract or other unlawful act as well as threats of violence. This was highly controversial and the result was reached notwithstanding that Pearson LJ in the Court of Appeal had described the tort as 'obscure, unfamiliar and peculiar'. The case arose when the Association of Engineering and Shipbuilding Draughtsmen threatened to withdraw their labour if a non-unionist was not removed by the British and Overseas Airways Corporation (BOAC) within three days, in order to preserve their informal closed shop. Inducement of breach of contract was not here available as a cause of action since the employee was lawfully dismissed with notice, but the House of Lords held that this anyway constituted the tort of intimidation and awarded exemplary damages to the employee concerned. The unlawful threat was contained in threatening to act in breach of contract, since it had been conceded by counsel for the union that a no-strike clause of a collective agreement had been incorporated into the contracts of individual workers. More generally, Lord Devlin commented that:

I find nothing to differentiate a threat of breach of contract from a threat of physical violence or any other illegal threat. All that matters to the plaintiff is that, metaphorically speaking, a club has been used. It does not matter to the plaintiff what the club is made of—whether it is a physical club or an economic club or tortious club or an otherwise illegal club.

The objection that allowing breach of contract to be a threat enabled a person not a party to a contract to sue on it was summarily rejected by the House of Lords. The principle seems to be that the claimant can sue the defendant for intimidation if he could succeed in a claim for breach of contract had the defendant carried out the threat. Liability in *Rookes* was for an unlawful threat against BOAC, a third party which indirectly but unintentionally caused the plaintiff loss. The decision gave rise to much controversy, both academic (e.g. Hamson, [1964] CLJ 159; Hoffmann, (1965) 81 LQR 116), and political. It was not clear why the defendant, a full-time union official should be held liable when he was not an employee of BOAC and could thus not have threatened a breach of contract. Neither was it clear what the unlawful act was. Furthermore if the union members had actually gone on strike, they would have not been liable in tort in that they were granted statutory immunity, so that the decision portended a greater liability for threats than for carrying out the action itself. (Threats are now covered by the immunity granted by TULR(C)A 1992, s. 219.)

There must be proof of loss to constitute the tort. There must be a threat and damage resulting therefrom—if a union organiser says to the employer that if he does not concede higher wages he will paralyse the company's operations, and the employer does not give an increase and the union leader finds his fierce words not backed up by his Members' actions, the employer has no cause of action in intimidation. *Hodges* v *Webb* (1920) defined a threat as 'an intimation by one to another that unless the latter does or does not do something, the former will do something which the latter will not like'. The difficulty is to distinguish between a threat and a warning or mere advice.

The party who submits to a threat may claim the loss flowing therefrom (*DC Builders* v *Rees* (1966)). This is known as two party intimidation. It is probably necessary that the defendant must then have the claimant directly in mind when making the threat. However, the threat must be 'of sufficient consequence to induce the other to submit' (Lord Denning in *Morgan* v *Fry* (1968)).

15.7 Conspiracy

It was only a few years after the abolition of the criminality of trade unions for conspiracies (Conspiracy and Protection of Property Act 1875, s. 3) that the courts developed a tort of conspiracy with precisely similar components. Since injunctions were granted freely its effects were also similar. It was described by Willes J in *Mulcahy* v *R* (1868) as consisting 'in the agreement of two or more to do an unlawful act, or to do a lawful act by unlawful means'. A conspiracy to commit a crime or a tort is clearly included in this class, but it is less certain whether it includes agreement to commit a breach of contract.

It is, however, the second part of the definition—'unlawful means' conspiracy—which is the most difficult and invidious, because it makes unlawful when done by two or more what would have been quite lawful when performed by an individual, e.g. *Kamara* v *DPP* (1974). A conspiracy to injure is an agreement to cause deliberate loss to another without cause or excuse with the intention of injuring the claimant (e.g. *Huntley* v *Thornton* (1957)). The unlawful means of pursuing the strike must, however, be integral to the aims of the conspirators and not peripheral. For example, that the strike organiser broke the speed limit as he raced to a mass meeting would not constitute the unlawful act.

In *Quinn* v *Leathem* (1901) officials of the union asked the respondent to dismiss a non-unionist, and on his refusal to do so told him that an important customer would be warned to cease dealing with him under threat of strike if he persisted in denying their request. The matter went before a jury which found that the union's motive was to injure the respondent and not to promote the interests of the union. On appeal, the majority of the House of Lords decided that this was actionable as a tortious conspiracy notwithstanding that the defendants had not committed any otherwise unlawful act in inducing the butcher no longer to trade with the plaintiff; there had been no crime, tort, or breach of contract. This decision was also reached notwithstanding that *Allen* v *Flood* (1898) showed that an action done with the desire to injure was not in itself necessarily tortious. (There was an attempted reconciliation in *Thomas* v *NUM (South Wales Area)* (1985).) In *Mogul Steamship Co. Ltd* v *McGregor, Gow and Co. Ltd* (1892), the House of Lords delineated the three-fold requirements of the tort as combination by at least two persons; intentionally causing loss; with the predominant purpose not to further a legitimate interest. The claimant must always prove an agreement between the parties, not merely coincidental action on their part. In *Lonrho plc v Fayed* (1991), the House of Lords held that in every conspiracy it was necessary to demonstrate that the defendants acted with intent to injure the claimant but intent is different from purpose. If the defendants intentionally use unlawful means in order to harm the claimant, that constitutes the tort of conspiracy, whatever their motive or purpose in so acting; but if the defendants intentionally inflicted harm on the claimant by means lawful in themselves, they nevertheless committed the tort of conspiracy if they acted with the predominant motive or purpose of inflicting harm on the claimant.

This would also be so if the defendants inflicted harm on the claimant by means which are lawful in themselves but where the defendants had acted with the predominant motive or purpose of inflicting harm on the claimant.

15.7.1 Justification

Traders often combine in an attempt to create a monopoly and this has received the blessing of the common law in, for example, the *Mogul Steamship* case, where it was said that 'otherwise most commercial men would be at risk of legal liability in their legitimate trading practices and competition would be dead'. The most important justification case involving trade unions is *Crofter Handwoven Harris Tweed Co. v Veitch* (1942), where the TGWU combined with Stornaway dockers to prevent yarn imports from the mainland in order to achieve a closed shop. The House of Lords found this conspiracy to injure justified since the predominant purpose was the promotion of the combiners' legitimate interest, for they wished to secure the elimination of price competition which was holding down wages at the largest spinning mill where their members were employed. (See also *Reynolds v Shipping Federation Ltd* (1924).) Lord Wright said that: 'The true contrast is between the case where the object is the legitimate benefit of the combiners and the case where the object is deliberate damage without any such just cause.'

Courts have also held legitimate: attempts to force an employer to abandon a policy of refusing to employ trade unionists (*D. C. Thomson & Co. Ltd v Deakin* (1952)); a campaign against a colour bar in a club (*Scala Ballroom (Wolverhampton) Ltd v Ratcliffe* (1958)); and the enforcement of a closed shop (*Reynolds v Shipping Federation* (1924)). The case of *Huntley v Thornton* (1957) was an exception since most members of a union district committee who expelled the plaintiff, a fellow member, acted merely out of personal grudge and a desire for vengeance, although two were acquitted of such motivations and thus were not liable for the tort. The bitterness arose because he had not complied with union instructions to stop work some 24 hours before.

15.7.2 Criminal conspiracy

The law of criminal conspiracy was the most potent weapon against the early trade unions, both as in restraint of trade and for strike action. The Conspiracy and Protection of Property Act 1875, s. 3 provided a first small step towards the modern immunities when it excluded criminal liability for acts in contemplation or furtherance of a trade dispute which would not be punishable as a crime if done by an individual. It also removed liability for conspiracy to injure committed without use of unlawful means. This was repeated by the Criminal Law Act 1977, now TULR(C) A 1992, s. 242, which specifically provides that where the acts agreed upon are to be done in contemplation or furtherance of a trade dispute any offence that would be committed shall be disregarded so long as it is a summary offence which is not punishable with imprisonment.

There is, indeed, now little incentive to bring a charge of conspiracy since the maximum sentence is the same as that for the substantive offence. The Criminal Law Act 1977, s. 3 took the sting out of the furore over the Shrewsbury Pickets case where two 'flying pickets' received three years' imprisonment for conspiracy to intimidate even though the substantive offence carried a maximum of only three months' imprisonment. Further, where the substantive crime is triable only summarily, proceedings for conspiracy may be brought only with the approval of the Director of Public Prosecutions. The Criminal Law Act 1977 does, however, enact two offences which might be used against factory work-ins which became an aspect of worker militancy in the 1970s; they consist of threatening violence to persons or property to gain entry to premises (s. 6) and being a trespasser on any premises with a weapon of offence (s. 8).

15.8 Duress

There have occasionally been suggestions by the courts that economic duress can itself amount to a tort (e.g. the House of Lords in *Universe Tankships Inc. of Monrovia* v *ITWF* (1983); see Sterling, (1982) 11 ILJ 156). But the position is not clear (*cf. Dimskal Shipping Co. SA* v *ITWF (The Evia Luck) (No. 2)* (1992)). The problem is that it is difficult to reconcile with *Allen* v *Flood* (1898) and without specific statutory immunity it would make the process of collective bargaining difficult to operate.

15.9 Trade dispute immunity

As we have seen, the tortious liability of trade unions is negated by providing wide immunities. This system of immunities rather than rights is largely present for historical reasons but, for trade unions, it has the unfortunate consequence that it gives the appearance that they are above the law. In fact, the statutory immunities can just as well be seen as delineating the areas of tortious liability. The tort of inducement, after all, was initiated in *Lumley* v *Gye* (1853) which was not an industrial action case. It was found that the basis of liability could cover industrial action but, instead of limiting the area of liability in tort (which would be done by the courts), Parliament stepped in to do so in statutory form. For this and other reasons some have argued that the system of immunities should be replaced by a scheme of positive rights (see e.g. Ewing, (1986) 15 ILJ 143). It is doubtful, however, whether this would now be acceptable to any Labour or Conservative Government.

The immunity is granted by TULR(C)A 1992, s. 219. This states that an act done in contemplation or furtherance of a trade dispute shall not be actionable in tort on the ground only that it induces a breach of contract, that it interferes with contract, that it induces any other person to interfere with its performance, that it constitutes a threat of breach, inducement or interference, or that it constitutes a conspiracy to do any of these things.

It should be noted that s. 219 covers only tortious liability. There is no immunity granted for breaches of contract or crime, for example. Neither does it cover torts other than those specified, for example trespass, harassment, breach of statutory duty, libel and so on. The temptation for the judiciary to find liability in these areas (or in new areas, as in *Thomas v NUM (South Wales Area)* (1985)) has been great.

It should also be noted that the torts are rendered only 'not actionable'. *Prima facie*, torts covered by s. 219 could remain unlawful means for the indirect torts. For this reason, TULRA 1974, s. 13(3)(b) provided that this should not be so. The subsection was, however, repealed by Employment Act 1980, s. 17(8), and the effect of the repeal arose in *Hadmor Productions Ltd v Hamilton* (1983). The company produced a series of programmes called 'Unforgettable' featuring pop musicians. They hired freelance members of the ACTT, rather than direct employees, which was viewed at the time with suspicion by the union. This hostility had led in the past to a complete blacking of programmes made by facility companies (as they were called), but by the time of Hadmor's foundation in August 1979 this stance had softened somewhat, as was confirmed in a letter from the union. As a result, Thames TV informally undertook to purchase the relevant series; but the ACTT shop stewards at Thames were not amused, threatened to black the series and consequently the company withdrew its transmission. Lord Denning MR in the Court of Appeal held that the repeal of the subsection meant that the action was unlawful, as it would have rendered it *not* unlawful. However, the House of Lords disagreed for the reason that that would make all secondary action unlawful, and Employment Act 1980, s. 17 had specifically brought some secondary action within the statutory immunity. This is no longer the case since the repeal of s. 17 by Employment Act 1990, s. 4 (see now TULR(C)A 1992, s. 224), although immunity for secondary picketing remains (see below).

15.9.1 Trade dispute

To be protected by immunity, the individual or trade union must be acting in contemplation or furtherance of a trade dispute, and by TULR(C)A 1992, s. 244(1) this means: 'a dispute between workers and their employer, that is to say, which relates wholly or mainly to one of the following:

(a) terms and conditions of employment, or the physical conditions in which any workers are required to work. (In *P v NASUWT* (2003) school teachers took industrial action on being called to teach disruptive students. The House of Lords refused to draw a distinction between terms and conditions and the application of terms and conditions. The trade dispute immunities could not have been intended to have turned on such fine distinctions);

(b) engagement or non-engagement, or termination or suspension of employment or the duties of employment, of one or more workers;

(c) allocation of work or the duties of employment as between workers or groups of workers;

(d) matters of discipline;

(e) the membership or non-membership of a trade union on the part of a worker;

(f) facilities for officials of trade unions; and

(g) machinery for negotiation or consultation, and other procedures, relating to any of the foregoing matters, including the recognition by employers or employers' associations of the right of a trade union to represent workers in any such negotiation or consultation or in the carrying out of such procedures.'

This is commonly termed the 'golden formula' and dates back to the Conspiracy and Protection of Property Act 1875, although in that statute it dealt with picketing alone. It was extended in the Trade Disputes Act 1906, passed by the Liberal Government to give protection to trade unionists specifically against the decision introducing tortious conspiracy, *Quinn* v *Leathem* (1901), since this case threatened to make most strike action unlawful.

The Industrial Relations Act 1971 altered the nomenclature to 'industrial dispute' and restricted the scope of the immunity to exclude disputes between groups of workers. After this short-lived experiment the substance of the 1906 provisions was re-enacted with some extensions in TULRA 1974, amended by the Trade Union and Labour Relations (Amendment) Act 1976, and then again restricted by the Employment Acts 1980, 1982, 1988, and 1990 and Trade Union Act 1984. It does not add up to a general right to strike. The economic torts reign supreme where the variant of tort committed is not precisely within those granted immunity and where the act is not in contemplation or furtherance of a trade dispute, as defined. This has left the judges much room for manoeuvre.

15.9.2 **Parties**

The freedom to strike afforded by the golden formula used to extend to a dispute between employers and workers or between workers and workers and thus protected demarcation disputes or arguments over union recognition. This was restricted by Employment Act 1982, s. 18(2) (now TULR(C)A 1992, s. 244(1)) to disputes between 'workers and their employer'. The operative word is 'workers' and this used to include those who seek to work, and those reinstated after dismissal. Section 244(5) now excludes a person who has ceased to be employed unless his employment was terminated in connection with the dispute or was one of the circumstances giving rise to it. It is irrelevant that the employer might change his business identity during the course of the conflict. Thus, Lord Denning said 'the words "employers" and "workers" in [TULR(C)A 1992, s. 244] apply to employers whatever the particular hat those particular employers may wear from time to time' (*Examite Ltd* v *Whittaker* (1977), and *The Marabu Porr* (1979)). The corporate veil will not, however, be lifted as between long-established separate companies in respect of secondary action (*Dimbleby & Sons Ltd* v *NUJ* (1984)). Section 224(4) provides that, for the purposes of establishing liability and immunity for secondary action, employees are not to be treated as parties to a dispute between other employers and workers, and where more than one employer is in dispute with his workers, that is to be treated as a separate dispute.

A dispute will only relate to employees' terms and conditions where it concerns their relationship with their *current* employer. This was the Court of Appeal's conclusion in *University College Hospital NHS Trust* v *Unison* (1999), in which an NHS Hospital Trust obtained an injunction preventing Unison calling its members out on strike. The dispute had arisen after the Trust refused the union's demand that it enter into an agreement with a consortium taking over the hospital which bound the consortium, 'its associates, subcontractors and successors', for a period of up to 30 years, to provide terms and conditions equivalent to those applying under the Trust. The court was persuaded that the strike would be unlawful since it related to employers other than the Trust and, in view of the length of the guarantee sought, to employees who would never have worked for the Trust.

15.9.3 The dispute

Lord Denning MR said that a dispute 'exists whenever a difference exists, and a difference can exist long before the parties become locked in combat...It is sufficient that they should be sparring for an opening' (*Beetham* v *Trinidad Cement Ltd* (1960)). There may also be a dispute even if the employers concede to the demands of the union. For TULR(C)A 1992, s. 244(4) provides that 'an act, threat or demand done or made by one person or organisation against another which, if resisted, would have led to a trade dispute with that other, shall, notwithstanding that because that other submits... [and] no dispute arises, be treated as being done...in contemplation of a trade dispute with that other'. This provision reverses the decision in *Cory Lighterage Ltd* v *TGWU* (1973) where the employers were at one with the union in seeking to preserve a closed shop, but could not get permission from the statutory National Dock Labour Board to dismiss the employee whose sacking the union sought. Buckley LJ decided:

If someone threatens me with physical injury unless I hand over my wallet and I hand it over without demur, no one could, in my opinion, sensibly say that there had been any dispute about my handing over my wallet.

A clear illustration of the effect of the statute was provided in *Hadmor Productions Ltd* v *Hamilton* (1983), where Thames TV submitted without a fight to the union's demand not to show a series made by a facility company. There is, however, no immunity from any action taken after a dispute has been settled (*Stewart* v *AUEW* (1973)).

15.9.4 Subject matter

A trade dispute must relate wholly or mainly to one or more of the matters set out in TULR(C)A 1992, s. 244(1). (See p. 413 above.)

This is a list which is intended to separate the sheep of industrial grievances which it is legitimate for trade unions to pursue, from the goats of political or personal grievances with which, according to the policy of statute, they should not concern themselves. The 1906 immunity was restricted to disputes 'connected with the employment or non-employment, terms of employment or conditions of labour of any person'. This has been greatly extended in several directions, although the Employment Act 1982 restricted it again, especially by requiring that the dispute relate wholly or mainly to the listed matters rather than merely being connected therewith, the lesser requirement under TULRA 1974, s. 29(1) (now s. 244(1)) as originally enacted.

The fact of the strike itself cannot be a dispute; it must be the manifestation of a grievance over something comprised within the definition of trade dispute. This was clearly demonstrated in *BBC* v *Hearn* (1977). The BBC sought to enjoin television technicians who were threatening to prevent transmission of the FA Cup Final to South Africa because of the policy of the Association of Broadcasting Staffs (of which the defendant was General Secretary) to oppose racial discrimination in that country. The Court of Appeal rejected the union's claim that this in itself amounted to a dispute about whether there should be a condition that employees should not be compelled to transmit to South Africa while its Government practised apartheid. There had been no such demand made before the strike was called and accordingly no trade dispute existed. Lord Denning described the union's actions as 'coercive interference', and not within s. 244(1), even though he thought the definition included:

not only the contractual terms and conditions but those terms which are understood and applied by the parties in practice, or habitually or by common consent, without ever being incorporated into the contract. If the union had only asked: 'We would like you to consider putting a clause in the contract by which our members are not bound to take part in any broadcast which may he viewed in South Africa', and the BBC had refused, they *would* then have been cloaked with the immunity.

Lord Diplock, however, confirmed in *NWL Ltd* v *Woods* (1979)) that the *ratio* of the *Hearn* case would be strictly construed (*cf.* also *Hadmor Productions Ltd* v *Hamilton* (1983)). There are *dicta* in the *BBC* case that the dispute must be about the current contract and that the claims of a union may be so preposterous as not to be genuine. One of the defendant union's arguments in *Dimbleby & Sons Ltd* v *National Union of Journalists* (1984) was that there was a dispute over terms and conditions in that there was an implied term in the journalists' contracts entitling them to refuse to comply with instructions given to them by the employers to provide copy of the kind they were employed to obtain if the NUJ gave them an instruction to the contrary. Lord Diplock stated that 'it passes beyond the bounds of credibility that any responsible newspaper proprietor would agree to such a term in contracts of employment with his journalists'. (See *Universe Tankships Inc. of Monrovia* v *International Transport Workers' Federation* (1983).)

It may be a matter of some difficulty to identify properly what a strike is actually connected with, especially when it is called for a variety of different reasons. However, in some cases the reasons for action clearly have nothing to do with pursuing a trade dispute. In *Conway* v *Wade* (1909) Lord Loreburn said:

If, however, some meddler sought to use the trade dispute as a cloak beneath which to interfere with impunity in other people's work or business, a jury would be entirely justified in saying that what he did was done in contemplation or in furtherance, not of a trade dispute, but of his own designs, sectarian, political or purely mischievous as the case might be.

Huntley v *Thornton* (1957) was a case which clearly fell outside of protection. As a result of the plaintiff's refusal to take part in a one-day strike, his workmates declined to work with him and the Hartlepool District Committee of his union attempted to ensure that he did not get another job in the area. They threatened to organise strikes to secure the success of this policy. The atmosphere was poisonous and Harman J decided that even if there had been a trade dispute in the first place, the union was now acting merely out of ruffled dignity in a personal vendetta. Similarly, in *Torquay Hotel Co. Ltd* v *Cousins* (1969), the court found that the blacking of the plaintiff's hotel by the defendant union was motivated by a desire to suppress criticism by its manager of their existing dispute; there was no trade dispute between the defendant and plaintiff so that there was no immunity available to the defendant. In *J. T. Stratford & Son Ltd* v *Lindley* (1965) the House of Lords held that there was no trade dispute because the union's contentions were really not about terms and conditions but arose because the WU was annoyed with the employer in the course of rivalry with the TGWU.

15.9.5 Political strikes

The distinguishing features of a political strike are by no means easy to delineate, but there is a danger that a political strike will not amount to a trade dispute. As Roskill LJ commented in *Sherard* v *AUEW* (1973):

it is all too easy for someone to talk of a strike as being a political strike when what that person really means is that the object of the strike is something of which, as an individual, he objectively disapproves.

There is also great force in Kahn-Freund's questions (Davies and Freedland, *Labour and the Law*, 3rd edn (London: Sweet & Maxwell, 1983), p. 317):

Is not every major industrial problem a problem of governmental economic policy? Is it not true that, not only in publicly owned industries, governmental decisions on wages policies—whether statutory or not—on credits and on subsidies, on the distribution of industry and on housing and town planning, and on a thousand other things, affect the terms and conditions of employment at least as much as decisions of individual firms?

The most famous determination of a political dispute was the General Strike of 1926 which was deprived of immunity by Astbury J (*National Sailors' and Firemens' Union of GB and Ireland* v *Reed* (1926)). (See a famous article by Goodhart, (1927) 36 Yale LJ 464.)

Strikes held to protest against Government policies have received the same treatment, whether called, as in *Associated Newspapers Group Ltd* v *Flynn* (1970), to protest against the Industrial Relations Bill, or as in *Beaverbrook Newspapers Ltd* v *Keys* (1978) the unions' collective 'day of action' against the Conservative Government's economic policies. One outstanding characteristic of these disputes is, however, that the employer is in no position to concede the demands of those taking the industrial action. Thus, in *Gouriet* v *UPW* (1978), the Post Office, whose employees threatened to stop mail to South Africa, could have no direct effect on the racialist Government there. Similarly, there is no immunity where employees strike with the aim of bringing about a change in their employer's policy, e.g. objecting to the contribution of the employer to the Conservative Party, local government workers protesting about their employer council's policy of investing in South Africa, or hospital workers rejecting the principle of pay beds. On the other hand, in *Sherard* the Court of Appeal would not enjoin a one-day strike against the Government's wage freeze on the grounds that it was political in nature. The union had some members who were employed by the Government and objected to their pay being restrained in this way, and this was a typical industrial grievance. Further, union members are protected if they are directly affected by the Government policies against which they strike, for example, concerning denationalisation as in *General Aviation Services UK Ltd* v *TGWU* (1974), since this might lead to redundancies (see also *Hadmor Productions Ltd* v *Hamilton* (1983); *Associated British Ports plc* v *TGWU* (1989); and, most recently, *Westminster City Council* v *Unison* (2001) concerning a city council's privatisation plans). In *University College Hospital NHS Trust* v *Unison* (1999), which the union lost on other grounds (see above), the Court of Appeal held that the fact that the union was opposed in principle to hospital privatisa-tion did not mean that industrial action aimed at protecting employees' terms and conditions on the transfer of their employment to a private consortium was unlaw-ful. A particular cause of industrial action, they said, may have broader, political objectives as well as more limited aims, namely to alleviate the anticipated conse-quences of the general policy. The more limited aim can be the reason for taking action and, if so, will satisfy the requirements of s. 244.

It is necessary in this area to distinguish the role of the Government as national guardian and also as employer. The 'golden formula' does not cover the former but in the latter capacity it is no different from any other management. Moreover, a dispute between a Minister and workers may be a trade dispute, even where he is not the employer, if he must approve a settlement s. 244(2)). Examples closer to the line include road workers striking against a decision not to build a motorway, or prison officers against any increase in prison numbers which they fear may lead to violent confrontation. Action designed above all to change the policies of the union's own executive is, however, clearly outside the scope of the immunity (*PBDS National Carriers* v *Filkins* (1979)).

15.9.6 **Territorial considerations**

The TULR(C)A 1992, s. 244(3) states that a trade dispute exists even though it relates to matters occurring outside the UK and requires that the person or persons whose actions in the UK are said to be in contemplation or furtherance of a trade dispute relating to matters outside the UK are likely to be affected in respect of one or more of the matters specified in s. 244(1) by the outcome of that dispute. This sanctions the taking of action in solidarity with colleagues working for the same multinational abroad, but only if their pay is likely to have an effect on that in the UK. The utility of the provision is therefore minimal.

15.9.7 **'Relate wholly or mainly'**

Until 1982 a dispute need only have been 'connected with' the acceptable subjects of the 'golden formula'. The TULR(C)A 1992, s. 244(1) now states that it must 'relate wholly or mainly' to one or more such subjects. This restriction sought to deal with the wide connotation given to 'connected with' in *NWL Ltd* v *Woods* (1979), where the House of Lords considered that there need be only a genuine connection between the dispute and the relevant subject matter. The industrial issue need not be predominant in the minds of the strikers.

The significance of the reform arose first in *Mercury Communications Ltd* v *Scott-Garner* (1984). The union objected to the Government's liberalisation of telecommunications from which the plaintiff as one of the first licensed operators besides British Telecom stood to gain. The plaintiff planned to establish a digital communications network partly using the BT network. The National Executive Committee of the Post Office Engineers Union instructed its members, the vast majority of whom were employed by BT, not to connect Project Mercury to the BT system. The Court of Appeal decided that the dispute was wholly or mainly about Government policy. Although the union honestly and fervently believed that their campaign was in the best interests of the jobs and conditions of service of employees in the industry, it did not follow that industrial action in the course of that campaign constituted a dispute 'wholly or mainly' about the threat of redundancy if the monopoly were not maintained.

Sir John Donaldson MR thought that:

In context the phrase 'wholly or mainly relates to' directs attention to what the dispute is about and, if it is about more than one matter, what it is mainly about. What it does *not* direct attention to is the reason why the parties are in dispute.... A contributory cause of the dispute and possibly the main cause is the belief that redundancy ('termination... of employment' in the words of the section) is just around the corner, but the dispute is not about that or, if it be preferred, relates wholly or mainly to pay...

He added that Parliament 'intended a relatively restricted meaning to be given to the phrase "relates wholly or mainly to"' and that the most obvious way to find out what a particular dispute is wholly or mainly about 'is to inquire what the men concerned... said to management at the time'. Here it was fatal that the union at no stage referred to the job security agreement, which it would have done had the dispute been truly about redundancies. May LJ commended an 'ordinary common sense approach' analogous to that which is adopted when a court has before it a question of causation. He saw the present action as springing from 'a political and ideological campaign seeking to maintain the concept of public monopoly against private competition'. (See further, Ewing and Rees, (1984) 13 ILJ 60.)

15.9.8 **Contemplation or furtherance of a trade dispute**

As we have seen, there must be a starting point to the coverage of the immunity; simply anticipating a fight as a future possibility is not enough. The words meant, according to Lord Loreburn in *Conway* v *Wade* (1909), 'that either a dispute is imminent and the act is done in expectation of and with a view to it, or that the dispute is already existing and the act is done in support of one side to it'. (See also *Bents Brewery Co Ltd* v *Hogan* (1945).) On the other hand, in *Health Computing Ltd* v *Meek* (1980), the union NALGO sought, as a matter of policy, to ensure that its members in the National Health Service had nothing to do with the plaintiff, a private company which sought to supply computer systems. Goulding J upheld the union leaders' contention that a dispute was contemplated as likely to arise between its members and any Health Service employers who engaged the plaintiff's services, notwithstanding that there was apparently no original demand made to management (*cf. J. T Stratford & Son* v *Lindley* (1965), *BBC* v *Hearn* (1977), and *London Borough of Wandsworth* v *National Association of Schoolmasters/Union of Women Teachers* (1993)).

The words 'in contemplation or furtherance' were fashioned by the Court of Appeal into a 'remoteness' test only to be struck down several times by the House of Lords. In several cases the Court of Appeal held that a union could not properly claim immunity for secondary action because it found, objectively reviewing the evidence before it, that it was not furthering their trade dispute but was too remote from it (*Star Sea Transport Co. of Monrovia* v *Slater* (1978), *Express Newspapers Ltd* v *McShane* (1980), and *Associated Newspapers Ltd* v *Wade* (1979). The House of Lords, however, decided that the only proper consideration was whether the defendant honestly and genuinely believed the action he was taking would contribute in the disputes (*NWL Ltd* v *Woods* (1979), *Express Newspapers* v *McShane* (1980), and *Duport Steels Ltd* v *Sirs* (1980)).

In *NWL Ltd* v *Woods* the ITF threatened to black the *Nawala*, a ship owned by the plaintiff company, in pursuance of their longstanding protest against flags of convenience. They wanted to force the owners to pay higher wages in line with the ITF norm, but the Court of Appeal decided that this was not connected with matters listed in TULR(C)A 1992, s. 244(1) because the employers could not accede to the union's demands. The House of Lords overruled this and Lord Diplock stated:

> If a demand on an employer by the union is about terms and conditions of employment the fact that it appears to the court to be unreasonable because compliance with it is so difficult as to be commercially impracticable or will bankrupt the employer or drive him out of business, does not prevent its being a dispute connected with terms and conditions of employment. Immunity under [TULR(C)A 1992, s. 219(1)] is not forfeited by being stubborn or pig-headed.

(See also *Norbrook Laboratories Ltd* v *King* (1984).)

15.10 Statutory control of secondary action

Following some of the wide interpretations of the golden formula by the House of Lords in the late 1970s, as we have seen, the incoming Conservative Government in 1979 determined to restrict the ambit of lawful action as a major part of its industrial relations policy. More particularly, it was concerned with reducing the immunity for tortious acts where employers who suffered were not party to the trade dispute.

Even if the employer were at some commercial distance from the dispute, if the action taken which affected him was believed by the union to further their dispute, he was not able to sue. The Employment Act 1980, s. 17 was therefore enacted to deal with this. It took away immunities for much secondary action, except in three instances. The first was where the employer was the first customer or first supplier with the employer who was the party to the trade dispute, which is to say, a supplier or customer in direct contractual relationship with that employer. Such suppliers or customers were so closely connected to the dispute that the Government felt action against them justified retention of the immunity. However, employers in that position might try to distance themselves by placing another employer between them and the employer who was party to the dispute. If this were done by the use of the corporate veil, the immunity would be retained. The 'associated employer' exception thus recognised the realities of the situation in that the two employers, although different in company law, were in fact the same employer. The second exception to s. 17 was where there was secondary picketing.

However, s. 17 was highly complicated. Lord Denning in the Court of Appeal's decision in *Hadmor Productions Ltd* v *Hamilton* (1981) called it 'the most tortuous section I have ever come across'. The Conservative Government in 1990 therefore repealed it and replaced it with Employment Act 1990, s. 4, now TULR(C)A 1992, s. 244(1). This has the effect of outlawing all secondary industrial action, bar secondary picketing subject to particular conditions. Secondary action is defined as occurring where there would normally be immunity under s. 219, but the employer under the contract of employment in question (where there is inducement to break etc.) is not the party to the trade dispute. A contract of employment for these purposes includes work done by independent contractors who undertake to perform the work personally.

15.11 Strike ballots

The TULR(C)A 1992, ss 226–235 remove the immunity of unions and individual strike organisers from certain actions in tort unless a majority of union members likely to be called out in industrial action have approved that action in a properly held ballot (see generally, Simpson, (1993) 22 ILJ 287; (2005) 34 ILJ 331). This applies, however, only to the torts of inducing an employee to break his contract of employment, inducing an employee to interfere with the performance of his own contract of employment, and indirectly procuring a breach of or interference in a commercial contract by the unlawful means of inducing a breach of a contract of employment. It does not apply to intimidation or conspiracy to injure.

15.11.1 The requirement for a ballot

A ballot is required only in respect of 'an act done by a trade union'; that is, if it is authorised or endorsed by the principal executive committee, the president or general secretary, some other person in accordance with the rules of the union and any other committee of the union or any other official, whether employed or not (TULR(C)A 1992, s. 20(1)). The identity of the person or persons authorised to call the industrial action must be specified on the voting paper. The industrial action will not be supported by the ballot if there has been a call for such action before the date of the ballot (s. 233(3)). However, the Court of Appeal held in *Newham London Borough Council* v *National and Local Government Officers Association* (1993) that s. 233(3) does not require the union to take a neutral stance in dealing with the ballot question. A union can thus indicate its desire for industrial action to be held without that amounting to a call for, or authorisation or endorsement of, such action.

15.11.2 When a ballot must take place

The action must be called within four weeks of the ballot. However, in the docks dispute in 1989 the TGWU were prevented from calling industrial action during this period because of an injunction, granted because the strike was said by the

Court of Appeal to be outside the golden formula, a decision overturned by the House of Lords. If similar circumstances arose again the union may apply for an extension of time, but no application may be made more than eight weeks after the ballot (TULR(C)A 1992, s. 234). If the ballot no longer appears to represent the views of the members, however, the court retains discretion not to grant the extension. This means that the courts may be drawn into the merits of the dispute and into hypothetical areas (see Carty, (1991) 20 ILJ 1). The union and the employer are permitted to extend this period by agreement for up to another four weeks.

15.11.3 **Rights to vote and rights in voting**

The union must give the right to vote to all those members of the trade union who it is reasonable at the time of the ballot for the union to believe will be induced by the union to take part in the strike or other industrial action. This is not restricted to those directly affected by the subject matter of the dispute, according to the High Court in *British Telecommunications plc* v *Communication Workers Union* (2004). Each such person must have one and only one vote. No one else may be permitted to vote, not even those who will be subject to an enforced lay off as a result. The ballot is required even if there are no individual members of the union and the rules do not make any provision for a ballot (*Shipping Company Uniform Inc.* v *ITF* (1985)). It is not reasonable to expect that only those in fact balloted will be induced to take part, according to the Court of Appeal in *National Union of Rail, Maritime and Transport Workers* v *Midland Mainline Ltd* (2001).

There are also provisions protecting the voter which are similar to those relating to the election for the principal executive committee. He must not be interfered with or constrained in exercising his right to vote, nor should he have to bear any direct costs in so doing (s. 230(1)). Ballots must be fully postal.

Inadvertent failure to give a member a ballot paper will not invalidate a ballot (*British Railways Board* v *NUR* (1989); see Simpson, (1989) 18 ILJ 234). This approach is given statutory force by s. 232B which provides that overlooking one or more members during the balloting process will not invalidate the final result, if the omission of these individuals was inadvertent and on a scale unlikely to affect that result.

15.11.4 **Coverage**

The union may call out members who have joined since the date of a ballot, and to do so does not deprive the union of the immunity it otherwise would have (*London Underground Ltd* v *RMT* (1995)). The Court of Appeal decided this important point on the basis that it was the industrial action which was required to be supported by a ballot, not industrial action in which a particular person has been induced to take part. Their Lordships rejected the proposition that the industrial action which had been called was thus different from that on which the ballot had been held. Again, subject to the reasonable practicability defence, the voting must be in secret.

15.11.5 **Counting the vote**

A majority of the voters must be in favour of the action in question for the union to have immunity (*West Midlands Travel Ltd* v *TGWU* (1994)). Thus spoiled votes in effect count against the action. The union must take reasonably practicable steps to inform those entitled to vote of the complete result of the ballot, although here again it can exempt overseas members. Any inaccuracy in counting the votes is to be disregarded if it is accidental and on a scale which could not affect the result of the ballot (TULR(C)A 1992, s. 230(4)). The position under the 1984 Act as originally enacted was that a union might seek to achieve a favourable result in a ballot by manipulating the constituency of each ballot, or by holding only one ballot. Section 228, attempts to deal with this by requiring separate ballots for each place of work, with a majority at each workplace to authorise or endorse action. It operates in respect of members whom it is reasonable at the time of the ballot for the union to believe will be called upon to take part, or continue to take part, in a strike or other industrial action and who have different places of work.

'Place of work' means the premises occupied by the employer at or from which the employee works or, if this does not apply, the premises of his employer with which the employee has the closest connection (s. 246). A broad view should be taken, so that in *Intercity West Coast Ltd* v *RMT* (1996), there was no distinction to be drawn between different buildings at the Manchester Piccadilly rail station. Exclusive occupation is not required.

Provisions contained in the Employment Relations Act 1999 establish important exceptions to the above principles. The TULR(C)A 1992, s. 228A provides that the union need not ballot different workplaces separately because of s. 228 in any of the following situations:

(a) at least one union member in a workplace is directly affected by the dispute in question;

(b) entitlement to vote is restricted to union members who have an occupation (or occupations) of a particular kind and are employed by a particular employer (or any of a number of employers) with whom the union is in dispute;

(c) entitlement to vote is restricted to union members who, according to the union's reasonable belief, have an occupation (or occupations) of a particular kind and are employed by a particular employer (or any of a number of employers) with whom the union is in dispute.

There is an exception, however, intended to apply where employees are in fundamentally the same job for the same employer but working at different places. The High Court has held, in *University of Central England* v *NALGO* (1993), that it is not necessary for entitlement to vote in a ballot to be restricted to employees of one employer. In reaching this decision, Latham J paid particular regard to the fact that it would have been easy for reference to be made to a restriction to one employer in s. 228, but none was made.

15.11.6 **Further requirements**

The TULR(C)A 1992 requires that a statement be made on every voting paper that 'if you take part in a strike or other industrial action, you may be in breach of your contract of employment. However, if you are dismissed for taking part in strike or other industrial action which is called officially and is otherwise lawful, the dismissal will be unfair if it takes place fewer than eight weeks after you started taking part in the action, and depending on the circumstances may be unfair if it takes place later.'

A further important requirement for the validity of a ballot was added by TURERA 1993, s. 18, substituting a new s. 226A into TULR(C)A 1992 as now amended by Employment Relations Act 2004, s. 22. The trade union must 'take such steps as are reasonably necessary to ensure that not less than the seventh day before the opening day of the ballot' there is received, by every person whom it is reasonable for the union to believe will be the employer of those persons who will be entitled to vote in the ballot, a written notice to the effect that the union intends to hold a ballot, specifying the opening date of the ballot and describing the employees who will be entitled to vote. Further, such an employer must be sent not later than the third day before the opening date of the ballot a sample voting paper. The employer must also be informed of the ballot result (TULR(C)A 1992, s. 231A).

The weighing of the balance of convenience in giving an injunction when there has been no valid ballot may be seen in *Solihull Metropolitan Borough* v *National Union of Teachers* (1985). The NUT issued guidelines to its members to refuse to cover for absences of colleagues known in advance and various other tasks. Warner J granted an injunction that the union must rescind its instructions. Whilst he saw detriment to the plaintiff in the harm done to the children in their schools, which could not be remedied in damages, there would be little inconvenience to the union. It was merely a matter for the union of choosing between holding a ballot and accepting arbitration. (See further, Hutton, (1985) 14 ILJ 255.)

15.12 Notice of industrial action

The TULR(C)A 1992, s. 234A requires the union to give advance notice of industrial action to the employer(s) likely to be affected by it. It must now take such steps as are reasonably necessary to ensure that the employer receives a specified notice of industrial action. This notice must describe the numbers of employees affected and their categories.

There is a Code of Practice on Industrial Action Ballots and Notice to Employers published in 2005, which may be taken into account in legal proceedings.

15.13 Consumer actions

In 1993 consumers were given statutory rights to pursue trade unions in respect of unlawful industrial action by TULR(C)A 1992, s. 235A. (See further, Morris, (1993) 22 ILJ 194.) An individual may apply to the High Court where he claims that any trade union or other person has done, or is likely to do, an unlawful act to induce any person to take part, or to continue to take part, in industrial action, and an effect, or a likely effect, of that industrial action is or will be to prevent or delay the supply of goods or services, or reduce the quality of goods or services supplied to that individual. That individual need not actually have an entitlement, however, contractual or otherwise, to be supplied with the particular goods or services in question (s. 235A(3)). The normal remedy will be an interim injunction to restrain such action, and such an application may be considered by the court even if an application is also made by an employer. The union may thus have to fight at very short notice on two separate fronts, defending actions brought by employers and by consumers.

15.14 Liability of trade unions

Both employers' associations and trade unions used to have similar immunity from actions brought against them in tort for acts alleged or threatened, whether in their own names or by way of representative action. This derived from the Trade Disputes Act 1906 passed in response to the *Taff Vale* decision, was enacted as TULRA 1974, s. 14 but was repealed by Employment Act 1982, s. 15. There had for some time been disquiet about the scope of immunity for trade union funds. Indeed, the Donovan Commission had recommended that it should be restricted to acts in contemplation or furtherance of a trade dispute, as is the case with the protection of individual union members (Report of the Royal Commission on Trade Unions and Employers' Associations, Cmnd 3623, para. 909). The effect of the Industrial Relations Act 1971 was to remove protection from unregistered unions and unofficial strikes. The Government indicated in its statement on industrial relations law reform (23 November 1981) that it 'did not accept that the breadth of the immunities is any longer necessary in modern conditions to represent their members effectively' (para. 30). The Government thought there was a lack of incentive for unions to ensure that their officials operate within the law.

A union is now fully liable in tort except where it acts in contemplation or furtherance of a trade dispute, but this immunity, already diminished by the Employment Act 1980, was further reduced by the 1982 Act. There is, however, a maximum level of damages to be awarded under TULR(C)A 1992, s. 22 depending on the membership of the union as follows: £10,000 when the union has fewer than 5,000 members; £50,000 where it has between 5,000 and 25,000; £125,000 between 25,000 and 100,000 members; and £250,000 where more than 100,000 belong. Interest may be added to the figure of damages even if this takes the total figure of damages and interest above the statutory limits according to the High Court in *Boxfoldia Ltd* v *National Graphical Association (1982)* (1988).

For the union to be liable at all the action must be taken to have been authorised or endorsed by it, defined as when the act was done, or was authorised or endorsed:

(a) by any person empowered by the rules to do, authorise or endorse acts of the kind in question, or

(b) by the principal executive committee or the president or general secretary, or

(c) by any other committee or any other official of the union (whether employed by it or not).

(Section 20(2).)

It was held by the Court of Appeal in *Tanks and Drums Ltd* v *TGWU* (1992) that a person empowered to call for industrial action may do so by delegating that function, and that whether this has been done is a matter of fact and degree.

The most significant aspect of the widening of the categories compared to the position prior to 1990 is that now shop stewards are included even if the rules of the union do not empower them to authorise action. This is because the Conservative Government felt it was easier to organise unofficial rather than official action, and that many unions were thereby escaping the liability they deserved (see Green Paper, *Unofficial Action and the Law*, Cmnd 821). A union has the power to repudiate action purportedly done in its name and on its behalf, but there are stringent conditions. Written notice of the repudiation must be given to the committee or official in question, without delay, and the union must do its best so to do with regard to every member of the union whom it has reason to believe is taking part, or might take part, in the action as a consequence, and to every employer of the members (s. 21(2)).

The notice given to members must contain this statement: 'Your union has repudiated the call (or calls) for industrial action to which this notice relates and will give no support to unofficial industrial action taken in response to it (or them). If you are dismissed while taking unofficial industrial action, you will have no right to complain of unfair dismissal' (s. 21(3)). The principal executive committee, president, or general secretary must not thereafter behave in a manner which is inconsistent with the purported repudiation. This will be taken to be the case if, on a request made to them within three months of the purported repudiation by a party to a commercial contract the performance of which has been, or may be, interfered with, they do not confirm it in writing (s. 21(6)). As Hazel Carty has pointed out ((1991) 20 ILJ 1 at p. 13), these extending provisions were unnecessary if the Government's concern was with unions hiding behind the cloak of unofficial action, as it has been clear since *Express and Star Ltd* v *NGA (1982)* (1986) that unions may be held in contempt if they, while complying with the law, at the same time encourage their members to take unlawful action (see too O'Dair, (1986) 15 ILJ 271).

15.15 Statutory restrictions on industrial action

15.15.1 Restrictions on classes of workers

There is nothing in Britain to compare with the wide restrictions on strikes existing in other countries, such as those on industrial action by public servants in Germany. There are, however, several statutory limitations on the right to withdraw labour for various classes of workers, and these generally concern the public sector.

Armed forces

Any member of the armed forces who engages in disruptive activity in order to redress a grievance can be disciplined under the Armed Forces Act 2006 and Incitement to Disaffection Act 1934, s. 1 also makes it an offence 'if any person maliciously and advisedly endeavours to seduce any member of her Majesty's forces from his duty or allegiance to her Majesty'.

Police

The Police Act 1996, s. 91 enacts the offence of causing disaffection or inducing a policeman to withhold his services or commit breaches of discipline.

Postal workers

The Postal Services Act 2000, s. 84 makes it an offence to interfere with mail, and s. 88 does so with regard to obstruction of the business of a universal service provider.

Endangering life

The TULR(C)A 1992, s. 240(1) states, where any person 'wilfully and maliciously breaks a contract of service or of hiring, knowing or having reasonable cause to believe that the probable consequences of his so doing, either alone or in combination with others, will be to endanger human life or cause serious bodily injury, or to expose valuable property whether real or personal to destruction or serious injury', he is guilty of an offence punishable by fine up to level 2 on the standard scale of fines or imprisonment for three months. This includes doctors, firemen, nurses and also lorry drivers, within its scope. There is no record of prosecution under this section, but it may be a ground for an injunction.

15.15.2 **Emergencies**

In the event of a national emergency the Government retains very wide powers under the Civil Contingencies Act 2004. However, by virtue of s. 23(3)(b) any regulations made under that Act may not prohibit industrial action activity. The power to deploy troops, by virtue of the Emergency Powers Act 1964, remains unaffected, however. The Army has been called in to assist in several disputes, including the firefighters' strikes of 2002–03.

15.16 **Injunctions**

15.16.1 **Use of injunctions in strikes**

Most employers are not concerned to claim damages from striking employees. The employer wants them back in order to work to prevent any further losses of production, rather than an ability to claim monetary judgments which would be difficult to enforce. He thus naturally turns to the equitable remedies. As we have seen, it is only in very exceptional circumstances that the courts have countenanced specific performance of a contract of employment in that it is an order which is difficult to supervise in open-ended contracts. The TULR(C)A 1992, s. 236 now provides that no court may by an order for specific performance of a contract of employment or by an injunction to restrain breach thereof compel an employee to work.

The courts have no similar compunction about making injunctions to prevent torts and these have very much the same effect. Injunctions may be sought at any stage of proceedings 'in all cases in which it appears to the court to be just and convenient to do so'. Application may be speedily made by an application notice. Although the claimant must in most circumstances give three days' notice, this may be dispensed with in case of urgency and an application may even predate the issue of a claim form in the action. If an interim injunction without notice to the opposing party is granted the absent defendants will usually be given leave to apply to discharge it on short notice. The actions in trade disputes differ from most (though not all) other areas of law in which injunctions are sought, since they rarely go for trial. The need for special rules here to reflect this fact was confirmed in particular by a change in the principles governing the granting of interim injunctions.

15.16.2 **Principles determining whether injunctions are granted**

Before 1975, the plaintiff had to establish a *prima facie* case before he was entitled to injunctive relief (*J. T. Stratford and Son Ltd* v *Lindley* (1965)), so that the merits of the case were at least partially aired in court at this early stage. What is now the leading case arose in the completely different jurisdiction of patent law. For in *American Cyanamid Co. Ltd* v *Ethicon Ltd* (1975) the House of Lords postulated that it was only necessary that the plaintiff have an arguable case, and that there was a serious issue to be tried. Then the only other consideration was the balance of convenience of giving or refusing the injunction. The court was thus not justified in embarking on anything resembling a trial of the action on conflicting affidavits in order to evaluate the strength of each party's case. This makes it considerably easier for an employer to gain an interim injunction against a strike not covered by immunity. It is balanced only to some degree by the claimant having to give an undertaking in damages, promising to compensate the defendant if he has suffered loss as a result of its issue and the trial court after the hearing determines, on reviewing all the evidence, that the injunction should not in fact have been granted. This is, however, of little use in dispute cases to a union enjoined because, first, full trials are very few and far between and, secondly, because the loss which the union could prove it has suffered by not being able to strike is likely to be nominal in money terms (*cf. Cayne* v *Global Natural Resources plc* (1984)).

For the same reason the balance of convenience frequently sways in favour of preserving the *status quo*, which, in the case of a trade dispute, normally means in the interests of maintaining production. The particular union concern here is that it is easy to portray to the court the fact of the employer losing immediately and irretrievably by a strike, and the union as suffering little tangible hardship in being restrained from striking. The industrial reality is, however, that the impetus of the workers' case is lost when it is restrained; once postponed it is difficult to revive. Further, the employer can organise to defeat a subsequent strike, including making alternative arrangements for supplies or subcontracting his work to other firms. Lord Diplock realised this when he said in *NWL Ltd* v *Woods* (1979):

It is in the nature of industrial action that it can be promoted effectively only so long as it is possible to strike while the iron is hot; once postponed it is unlikely to be revived.

The Labour Government reacted to the judicial developments on the principles in granting injunctions by passing what is now TULR(C)A 1992, s. 221(1), which provides that if there might be a 'trade dispute' defence to an injunction, the court must not grant relief without notice unless all reasonable steps have been taken to notify the other side of the application and to give them an opportunity of putting their side of the story. Further, s. 221(2) states that on an application for an interim injunction the court must 'have regard' to the likelihood that the defendant would succeed at trial with a trade dispute defence. Employers have still raised the argument that the court may consider it, yet find that it was outweighed by the damaging consequences of the dispute in question. The House of Lords in *NWL* v *Woods* (1979), however, indicated that if the defendant had shown that it was more likely than not that he could prove that he was within the terms of the trade dispute definition the injunction should be refused, except where the seriousness of the consequences for the employer, a third party or the general public, demanded a higher degree of probability. Lord Diplock thought the subsection was a reminder to judges that:

they should in exercising their discretion whether or not to grant an interlocutory injunction put into the balance of convenience in favour of the defendant those countervailing practical realities, and in particular that the grant of an injunction is tantamount to giving final judgment against the defendant.

Section 221(2) applies only in relation to the torts specified in s. 219(1). If other torts are committed, the ordinary test will apply. However, since *American Cyanamid*, a number of cases have been decided which have eroded its effect. In *Lansing Linde Ltd* v *Kerr* (1991), not an industrial dispute case, the Court of Appeal held that a factor in the decision may be whether or not the trial (which is virtually never reached in industrial action cases) is likely to occur before a party has achieved the advantage he seeks. As Zuckerman has pointed out ((1991) 107 LQR 196) claimants as a result are in something of a Catch-22 situation. As the new test makes it somewhat harder for claimants to succeed, they may well be tempted to add a claim for damages as well, but this may backfire as one of the considerations in awarding an interim injunction is the fact that monetary compensation is an inadequate alternative. However, it should not be thought that courts will always apply the stricter test, for the House of Lords have made it clear (in *R* v *Secretary of State for Transport ex parte Factortame (No. 2)* (1991)) that a discretion remains to issue an interim injunction even though the claimants' case appears no more than arguable. That case was one involving a question of pure law, which is not usually so in industrial action cases, and may therefore be distinguished on that ground.

Even where s. 221(2) is applicable, where the public interest is involved the granting of an injunction is likely, particularly if there would be immediate threats to health and safety if a strike were to go ahead (*Beaverbrook Newspapers Ltd* v *Keys* (1978)). Lord Scarman applied this to a dispute by journalists in *Express Newspapers Ltd* v *MacShane* (1980). He said:

In a case where action alleged to be in contemplation or furtherance of a trade dispute endangers the nation or puts at risk such fundamental rights as the right of the public to be informed and the freedom of the press, it could well be a proper exercise of the court's discretion to restrain the industrial action pending trial of the action.

This is open to a good deal of subjective judgment and in *Duport Steels Ltd* v *Sirs* (1980), Lord Scarman took the opposite view on the facts in relation to the 1980 national steel strike, commenting:

The economic damage threatened by the extension of the strike to the private sector, though very serious, is not so immediate as to justify intervention by the court granting relief to which it is probable that the plaintiff was not entitled.

The courts are much more likely to grant an injunction when it is prohibitory than when it is mandatory on the basis that the former gives the other party greater bargaining power. However, it is not clear wholly why in principle this should be so (see *Jakeman* v *S. W. Thames Regional Health Authority* (1990)).

15.16.3 Criminal injunctions

Where a strike constitutes a crime it may also be restrained by injunction, but the private citizen does not usually have standing to maintain an action. Instead he must ask the Attorney-General to proceed in a relator action. The House of Lords declared this still to be the law in the case of *Gouriet* v *UPOW* (1978). The Post Office unions were there alleged to be about to commit offences under the Post Office Act 1953 if they implemented plans to boycott mail to South Africa. The Attorney-General's refusal to bring a relator action was upheld by the House of Lords.

15.17 Breach of injunctions: enforcement

The primary methods of enforcement on the breach of injunctive orders are committal for contempt and sequestration of assets.

15.17.1 Committal for contempt

The claimant may apply for committal of the trade union or one or more of its officers for contempt. This may lead to a fine or imprisonment. Not surprisingly, courts insist that all procedural aspects of a committal for contempt are fully complied with. The injunction must be served personally on the defendant save in the most exceptional circumstances (see *Bernstein* v *Bernstein* (1960)). In *Express Newspapers Ltd* v *Mitchell* (1982), however, personal service was dispensed with since it was proved that the injunction had been served on the defendant's wife and had been widely announced in the news media. It was highly unlikely that the defendant had failed to hear of it.

The allegations in the motion to commit must be proved 'with all the strictness that is necessary in such a proceeding as this when you are going to deprive people of their liberty' (*Churchman* v *Joint Shop Stewards Committee* (1972)). A defendant is not, however, excused on the ground that he did as much as he could unless the order merely required this standard to be applied. Sir John Donaldson said in *Howitt Transport* v *TGWU* (1973):

It is not sufficient by way of an answer to an allegation that a court order has not been complied with, for the person concerned to say he 'did his best'. The only exception to that proposition is where the court order itself only orders the person concerned to 'do his best'. But if a court order requires a certain state of affairs to be achieved, the only way in which the order can be complied with is by achieving that state of affairs.

When it is alleged that the respondent failed to take a positive step required by an injunction, the applicant must nevertheless prove that there was something the respondent could reasonably have done but failed to do to secure its enforcement. This was the central issue in *Express Newspapers* v *Mitchell* (1982). The plaintiffs gained an injunction against unlawful secondary action by electricians in Fleet Street in support of the TUC's 'day of action' for the health service workers then on national strike. The order restrained, among others, Sean Geraghty, leader of the Fleet Street electricians, from inducing workers to breach their contracts, and required him to withdraw the strike call. The strike went ahead. Geraghty argued that there was nothing he could do to withdraw the strike call since he had not made it in the first place. Leonard J thought, however, that he could have done more in the time available to encourage compliance with the injunction granted and committed him for contempt.

In *Austin Rover Group Ltd* v *AUEW (TASS)* (1985) the union TASS sought to avoid liability with the argument that the act of calling a strike which the order said should be reversed was that of a larger body of which it was part, namely the staff side of the Joint Negotiating Committee and not the action of the union alone. The union had authorised industrial action without a ballot and the plaintiff obtained an order that the union should 'withdraw and cancel any instruction, direction or decision' to take strike action. Hodgson J said that: 'In a proper case it may be permissible in the face of a mandatory injunction for someone to sit back and do absolutely nothing but it is obviously highly dangerous because by definition, the court has been satisfied by evidence that there is something he can do.' His Lordship thought that it was obvious here what was required and condemned the attitude of the union's general secretary that because he did not consider the order should have been made there was no need to obey it. It was not possible for the union, which had not appeared when the order was made, to claim at this late stage that the injunction should not have been granted.

The union may be in contempt of court if it does not prevent its officials from acting in contempt of court. The code of responsibility for authorising or endorsing industrial action set out in the Employment Act 1982 (then in force) did not apply to contempt proceedings (*Express & Star Ltd* v *NGA (1982)* (1986); see O'Dair, (1986) 15 ILJ 271)) so that one had to go back to the general principles of vicarious liability (*Heaton's Transport (St Helens) Ltd* v *TGWU* (1972)). However, that is no longer the position since under TULR(C)A 1992, s. 20(6) unions are now liable in any proceedings for failure to comply with an injunction.

The court may imprison the contemnor for up to two years (Contempt of Court Act 1981, s. 14), fine or order him to give security for good behaviour. In *Austin Rover Group Ltd* v *AUEW* (1985) the judge did not decree any punishment since the contempt was not serious and the union might have taken sufficiently vigorous steps to dissociate themselves from the industrial action had they taken legal advice at an earlier stage, while in the *Richard Read (Transport) Ltd* v *NUM (South Wales Area)* (1985) case the NUM (South Wales Area) was fined £50,000. The largest fine so far levied was visited upon the NUM in 1984 of £250,000.

15.17.2 **Sequestration**

Sequestration is the remedy of last resort, designed to enforce a judgment requiring a person to do an act within a specified time or to abstain from doing a specified act. It is preceded by a writ and operates by sequestrating all the real and personal property of the union or person subject to the order, and is cumulative to other methods of enforcing an order such as committal. The writ is addressed to not fewer than four commissioners. In more recent strike cases chartered accountants have usually been appointed to fulfil this role. The writ binds all property of the person sequestered from the date of its issue, and the sequestrators enter at once to take possession of his real and personal estate.

The sequestrators act as officers of the court, and may from time to time be given directions by the judge. Any resistance or interference by any person with the sequestrators carrying out their proper duties is in itself a contempt of court. Where there is, however, a dispute about the ownership of property, a party may apply to the court by summons or motion to direct an enquiry as to the precise nature of the respective interests in the property.

The court must be satisfied that disobedience to the order has been more than casual, accidental or unintentional, save in the event that disobedience is repeated (*Worthington* v *Ad-Lib Club Ltd* (1965)). The remedy is in the discretion of the court. In *Richard Read (Transport) Ltd* v *NUM (South Wales Area)* (1985) the judge ordered sequestration of the defendant area union's assets 'because from a report in the *Daily Express* . . . it would appear that the defendant may be seeking to avoid payment of any fines imposed by this court by the device of transferring its funds into the private bank accounts of its leaders'. The funds of the Society of Graphical and Allied Trades 1982 (SOGAT) were sequestrated in 1986 because of the union's defiance of an injunction restraining the blacking of newspapers owned by subsidiaries of News International plc during the 'Wapping dispute'. The Court of Appeal in *News Group Newspapers Ltd* v *SOGAT ex parte the London Branch of Clerical Administrative and Executive Personnel of SOGAT 1982* (1986), determined that this order did not entitle the sequestrators to seize the considerable funds of the unions' branches and chapels. In construing the rules, their Lordships decided that branch funds were to be used solely for the benefit of their members and not for the union as a whole.

A third party is prohibited from knowingly assisting in a breach of the sequestration order (*Eckman* v *Midland Bank Ltd* (1973)) and the defendant union's accountant must give full co-operation. This sensitive issue was explored in *Messenger Newspapers Group Ltd* v *National Graphical Association* (1984). The assets of the NGA were sequestered in order to ensure that the union pay substantial fines imposed on it for contempt in failing to desist from picketing the Warrington premises of the plaintiff. The union's auditors, mindful of their duty of confidentiality, refused to disclose details of the union's assets. The Court of Appeal decided that the accountants must not obstruct the sequestrators' investigations, even though they did not hold any property belonging to the union. Sir John Donaldson MR thought that: 'A sequestration would be quite impossible if it required the consent of, for example, the officers of the company against whom the writ of sequestration is issued.' In *Clarke and others* v *Heathfield and others (No. 2)* (1985) the court went further and removed the trustees of the NUM who had sought to frustrate the efforts of the sequestrators by sending money abroad.

15.18 **Picketing**

Picketing is an ill-defined term which covers various methods of strengthening strike action by employees standing at the factory gate. It has over time subtly changed its function. At the beginning of the 20th century, the picket was mainly concerned to prevent blackleg labour being taken in to replace strikers. Later it became a medium of protest, and the 1970s and 1980s witnessed a growth in 'secondary picketing' broadly aimed at parties extraneous to the actual trade dispute to bring pressure on the employer in dispute. By this means union members sought to prevent goods leaving their employer's factory and to stop him moving his production elsewhere. The target may be fellow workers who have not joined the strike or substitute labour. The modern phenomenon is also a recognition that employers are increasingly organised on a multi-plant, if not multi-national basis, and that such solidarity action by strong unions is of particular value to weakly organised sectors.

The tactic was used to particular effect during the two miners' strikes of the 1970s, when picketing by various groups of workers prevented the delivery of replacement oil to power stations, and made the strike much more effective in bringing almost the whole of industry to a halt. During the bitter Grunwick dispute 300 arrests were made between June 1977 and January 1978. A useful corrective to this scene is to consider the words of the Chief Constable of South Wales giving evidence to the House of Commons Select Committee on Employment, on 27 February 1980:

You must not assume that on every occasion there is a mass picket there is going to be trouble. You sometimes get a very jaundiced picture from the news media who tend to highlight the occasions when things go wrong, but this is by no means the norm because there are many other incidents which pass off day by day without any difficulty whatever.

There was, however, unprecedented picket-line violence during the miners' strike in 1984–85; by March 1985, 10,372 criminal charges were brought (*The Times*, 20 March 1985). There was also violent picketing and many arrests in 1986 outside the News International plc printing plant at Wapping. In recent years, there have been few examples of mass picketing.

The central justification of peaceful picketing lies in the right to freedom of speech and peaceful protest, and in many countries that right is protected by the Constitution. Typically, in Britain what freedom exists is found in the interstices of a narrow immunity from several general and particular prohibitions of common law and statute by way of crimes and torts, although rights to peaceful assembly and freedom of expression under the Human Rights Act 1998 may give some protection—see e.g. *Gate Gourmet London Ltd* v *TGWU* (2005). Much depends on the practice of police on the spot in controlling pickets, with relatively little guidance from the case law which has typically proceeded in a very pragmatic way, little bounded by principle in the search for solutions in order to secure justice in the instant case—an approach which has attracted no small degree of criticism (see e.g. Auerbach, (1987) 16 ILJ 227). The Employment Act 1980, however, restricted the right to picket to the workers' own place of work. There is a Code of Practice on Picketing which supplements this body of law.

15.18.1 Offences

Obstruction of the highway

By Highways Act 1980, s. 137, 'if a person without lawful authority or excuse, in any way wilfully obstructs the free passage along a highway he shall be guilty of an offence...'. This is a charge frequently brought against pickets. The illegality of an obstruction is in all cases a question of fact, and depends on, *inter alia*, 'the length of time the obstruction continues, the place where it occurs, the purpose for which it is done, and of course whether it does in fact cause an actual obstruction as opposed to a potential obstruction' (*Nagy* v *Weston* (1965) per Lord Parker CJ). In *Lowdens* v *Keaveney* (1903) the judge said: 'No body of men has a right to appropriate the highway and exclude citizens from using it. The question whether use is reasonable or not is a question of fact to be determined by common sense with regard to ordinary experience.' The offence is one of strict liability (*Arrowsmith* v *Jenkins* (1963)), committed by anyone freely causing an obstruction; it is irrelevant that he *bona fide* believes he has a right to picket or demonstrate. (See also *Broome* v *DPP* (1974).) There is statutory control of processions and assemblies under Public Order Act 1986, ss 11–16 (see below).

Obstructing a police constable

The Police Act 1996, s. 89 makes it a criminal offence to obstruct a police constable in the execution of his duty and that duty is to prevent trouble where he reasonably apprehends a breach of the peace as a 'real possibility'. Very few magistrates' courts *ex post facto* doubt the policeman's opinion at the time, and this provides an enormous discretion for the police to control picketing. It allows a constable to tell demonstrators to all go home or reduce their number and visit any resistance to these instructions with prosecution for the Police Act offence.

Breach of the peace

One of the most important offences is that of behaving in a manner likely to cause a breach of the peace at common law. In *Kavanagh* v *Hiscock* (1974) a policeman claimed he had reason to believe there would be a breach of the peace if an exit from a hospital was not completely clear of pickets, and he thus proceeded to remove those who were waiting to harangue 'blacklegs' being transported to work by bus. The court held that the offence of breach of the peace had been committed and the pickets had no legal right to stop a vehicle without the consent of the driver.

In *Piddington* v *Bates* (1960) the defendant was prevented from reaching a factory entrance by a constable who told him that two pickets were enough. The report quaintly states that he 'pushed gently past the policeman and was gently arrested'. Although this occurred without obstruction or threats of violence, Lord

Parker held that a policeman was entitled to 'take such steps as he thinks proper', including limiting the number of pickets. He continued:

> ...it is not enough that his contemplation is that there is a remote possibility but there must be a real possibility of a breach of the peace. Accordingly in every case it becomes a question whether on the particular facts there were reasonable grounds on which a constable charged with this duty reasonably anticipated that a breach of the peace might occur.

It is immaterial whether the breach of the peace is likely to be caused by the pickets themselves, the picketed, or bystanders (*Kavanagh* v *Hiscock* (1974)).

In *Moss* v *McLachlan* (1985) the Divisional Court determined that the offence might be committed when pickets ignore police orders some distance from the site to be picketed if the policeman in question honestly and reasonably fears an imminent breach of the peace if the accused continues with his journey. This sanctioned the practice of the police during the miners' strike of 1984–85 of stopping persons on the way to picketing in the Midlands coalfields far away from the scene—including one famous incident at the Dartford Tunnel. (See further Morris, (1985) 14 ILJ 109.)

A constable can arrest without warrant in the case of obstruction if that obstruction was such that it actually caused or was likely to cause a breach of the peace (*Wershof* v *Metropolitan Police Commissioner* (1978)).

By Public Order Act 1986, s. 4A, a person is guilty of an offence if he, with intent, causes another person harassment, alarm or distress by using threatening, abusive or insulting words or behaviour or disorderly conduct, or by displaying any writing, sign or other visible representation which is threatening, abusive or insulting. It is a defence for an accused person to prove that his conduct was reasonable in the circumstances of the case. The offence carries a maximum penalty of six months' imprisonment or a fine not exceeding level 5 on the standard scale, currently £5,000. It is an arrestable offence.

Assaults

While assaults may be committed on a picket-line, there is no such crime or tort unless the capacity to carry into effect the intention to commit a battery is present at the time of the overt act indicating an immediate intention to commit a battery. There was thus no liability in *Thomas* v *NUM (South Wales Area)* (1985) since the threats uttered by the picketing striking miners were made from the side of the road to working miners who were in vehicles which the pickets could not reach, so there could be no immediate intention to batter.

Affray, violent disorder, and riot

Affray, violent disorder, and riot are other possible charges for violent pickets. The former at common law meant unlawful fighting by one or more persons in a public place in such manner that reasonable people might be frightened or intimidated. The Public Order Act 1986, s. 3 codifies this offence, defining it as the use or threat of unlawful violence to another such as would cause a person of reasonable firmness present to fear for his personal safety. A riot can be charged under Public Order Act 1986, s. 1 where 12 or more use or threaten such violence, and violent disorder under s. 2 where there are three or more involved.

Public nuisance

It is an offence at common law to obstruct the public in the exercise or enjoyment of rights common to all, including free passage along the highway. Picketing often falls foul of this prohibition, but picketing in itself probably does not constitute a common law nuisance. In *J. Lyons & Sons* v *Wilkins* (1899) Lindley LJ thought it did, since it constituted an attempt to persuade, regardless of any obstruction. But Lord Denning MR, more recently in *Hubbard* v *Pitt* (1975), considered that this view 'has not stood the test of time...'. He was concerned not to restrict free speech and assembly by restricting picketing, and in a dissenting judgment stated that a group of non-industrial protesters standing on the pavement outside an estate agency, in reasonable numbers and orderly manner, to protest against the 'gentrification' of Islington was quite lawful and not a nuisance. The majority of the Court of Appeal, on the other hand, merely affirmed the use by Forbes J of his discretion in deciding to grant an interlocutory injunction to the plaintiffs. They said little on the general principle. The Master of the Rolls commented:

There was no obstruction, no violence, no intimidation, no molestation, no noise, no smells, nothing except a group of six or seven people standing about with placards and leaflets out-side the plaintiff's premises, all quite orderly and well-behaved. That cannot be said to be a nuisance at common law.

He considered that, in any case, the real grievance of the plaintiff concerned the defendants' placards and leaflets and that to enjoin these would be an interference with free speech: 'These are rights which it is in the public interest that individuals should possess: and indeed that they should exercise without impediment so long as no wrongful act is done... As long as all is done peaceably and in good order, without threats or incitement to violence or obstruction to traffic, it is not prohib-ited.' He saw no reason to distinguish between picketing connected with a strike and other purposes. (See also *Mersey Dock and Harbour Co.* v *Verrinder* (1982); *News Group Newspapers Ltd* v *SOGAT 1982 (No. 2)* (1987).)

In *Tynan* v *Balmer* (1967) the presence of 40 people walking in a circle was held unreasonable and a nuisance: that a passer-by might avoid the obstruction by a detour did not make it lawful. Further, the pickets were held not to be protected by what is now the TULR(C)A 1992 picketing immunity because they were doing more than was absolutely necessary for conveying information about their own cause. In *Thomas* v *NUM (South Wales Area)* (1985) Scott J decided that regular pick-eting of a person's home would in itself be a common law nuisance.

Public nuisance is a tort as well as a crime but civil proceedings may be brought only with the consent of the Attorney-General on a relator action. He has, how-ever, complete discretion (*Gouriet* v *UPOW* (1978)) whether or not to allow it, and a private individual can act only if he can show that he has suffered damage greater than that borne by the general public.

Offences under TULR(C)A 1992

It was originally an offence under the Combination Act 1825 'by threat or intimi-dation or by molesting or in any way obstructing another, to endeavour to force any workman or other person not being employed from accepting employment'. This very general prohibition was abolished by the Conspiracy and Protection of Property Act 1875, but re-enacted therein as specific offences, which are now consolidated in TULR(C)A 1992. Section 241 thus makes it a criminal offence if a person 'wrongfully and without legal authority':

(a) uses violence or intimidates another;

(b) persistently follows another from place to place (see *Smith* v *Thomasson* (1890));

(c) hides any tools, clothes or other property owned or used by such other person, or deprives him of or hinders him in the use thereof;

(d) watches or besets the house or other place where such other person resides, or works, or carries on business or happens to be, or the approach to such house or place;

(e) follows such other person with two or more other persons in a disorderly manner in or through any street or road.

In each case the action must be without legal authority for liability to arise.

J. Lyons and Sons v *Wilkins* (1896) decided that the wrongful action might consist solely of the trespassing of the provisions of s. 241 in itself, whereas *Ward Lock & Co.* v *Operative Printers' Assistants Society* (1906) suggests that it must be independently unlawful. Fletcher Moulton LJ summed up the provision thus; 'It legalises nothing and it renders nothing wrongful that was not so before. Its object is solely to visit certain selected classes of acts which were previously wrongful, i.e. were at least civil torts, with penal consequences.' (See Bercusson, (1977) 40 MLR 268.) Scott J decided in *Thomas* v *NUM (South Wales Area)* (1985) that conduct must first be tortious in order to constitute an offence under s. 241. The purpose of the Act is thus merely to render certain tortious acts unlawful in the criminal sense.

Most of the subsections add little to common law nuisance but subsection (a) is of importance, especially since James LJ in *R* v *Jones* (1974) extended intimidation to include 'putting persons in fear by the exhibition of force or violence or the threat of violence, and there is no limitation restricting the meaning to cases of violence or threats of violence to the person'. Hence violence against buildings was sufficient and even 'harsh words' were enough. (See also *Gibson* v *Lawson* (1891); *Elsey* v *Smith* (1983).) Occupying property as a 'sit-in' may amount to 'watching and besetting'.

The fact that the respondents' actions are protected from civil liability within the meaning of TULR(C)A 1992, s. 219 does not, however, mean that they could not be done 'wrongfully and without legal authority' for the purposes of criminal proceedings. There is nothing in the language of s. 219 which can convert what was a wrongful act into one which is legally innocent (*Galt* v *Philp* (1984); see Miller, (1984) 13 ILJ 111).

Many pickets were charged during the 1984–85 miners' strike with these offences even though they had lain dormant for many years. The TULR(C)A 1992, s. 241(1) makes the maximum sentence six months' imprisonment or a fine not exceeding level 5 (presently £5,000) on the standard scale or both. Further, a police constable may arrest without warrant anyone who he reasonably suspects is committing an offence under the section.

Public processions and assemblies

The Public Order Act 1986 gives the police powers to impose conditions on public processions and assemblies under threat of criminal sanctions for failure to obey these conditions. Since pickets are usually stationary, only the latter powers are considered here. The Public Order Act 1986, s. 14 applies if a senior police officer present at an assembly'...having regard to the time or place at which and the circumstances in which any public assembly is being held or is intended to be held, reasonably believes that it may result in serious public disorder, serious damage to property or serious disruption to the life of the community, or the purpose of the persons organising it is the intimidation of others with a view to compelling them not to do an act they have a right to do, or to do an act they have a right not to do'. He may then give directions imposing on the person organising or taking part in the assembly 'such conditions as to the place at which the assembly may be (or continue to be) held, its maximum duration, or the maximum number of persons who may constitute it as appears to him necessary to prevent such disorder, damage, disruption or intimidation'. Failure to obey such conditions is itself a criminal offence. The intimidation leg of the section was clearly drafted with picketing in mind. The effect has been watered down, however, by the addition of a definition of public assembly, in s. 16, as being an assembly of more than 20 persons in a public place which is wholly or partly open to the air. Section 14 has been labelled 'highly objectionable' in that it shifts the rationale of the previous law from maintaining public order to limiting public inconvenience (see Carty, (1987) 16 ILJ 46), but other offences too have always had this latter aim, so there would appear to be no significant practical consequence in the shift.

Bail conditions

Where there is a likelihood of further offences being committed while the accused is on bail on a charge connected with picketing, magistrates may properly grant bail subject to a condition that the accused shall not participate in picketing in connection with the industrial dispute in the course of which he was arrested (*R v Mansfield Justices ex parte Sharkey* (1984); see Morris, (1985) 14 ILJ 109). The magistrates' court merely had to ask the question: 'Is this condition necessary for the prevention of the commission of an offence by the defendant when on bail?' It is enough if they perceive a real and not a fanciful risk of an offence being committed.

Other offences under the Public Order Act 1986

Under Public Order Act 1986, s. 4, a person is guilty of an offence if he:

(a) uses towards another person threatening, abusive or insulting words or behaviour, or

(b) distributes or displays to another person any writing, sign or other visible representation which is threatening, abusive or insulting with intent to cause that person to believe that immediate unlawful violence will be used against him or another by any person, or to provoke the immediate use of unlawful violence by that person or another or whereby that person is likely to believe that such violence will be used or it is likely that such violence will be 'provoked'.

By s. 5 of the Act a person commits an offence if he:

(a) uses threatening, abusive or insulting words or behaviour, or disorderly behaviour, or

(b) displays any writing, sign or other visible representation which is threatening, abusive or insulting, within the hearing or sight of a person likely to be
caused harassment, alarm or distress thereby.

The requirement that another person must be present is intended as a safeguard,
although it is not necessary for the prosecution to show that that person was actually alarmed, harassed or distressed.

15.18.2 Civil liability

Civil liability is important in relation to picketing, just as in strike cases, not
because damages are often awarded, but due to the availability of injunctive relief
particularly of an interim nature.

Private nuisance

Private nuisance is an unlawful interference with an individual's enjoyment or use
of his land. To sue for the tort, the claimant must have some proprietary interest
in land and this action is thus most likely to arise where pickets block an access
route. Picketing accompanied by violence, or even merely noise, may be a private nuisance. The most thorough recent analysis of nuisance was by Scott J in
Thomas v NUM (South Wales Area) (1985). He held that mass picketing at the gates
of five collieries in South Wales during the miners' strike of 1984–85 was tortious
and could be restrained at the suit of the plaintiffs who were working miners. The
picketing was of a nature and was carried out in such a manner that it represented
an unreasonable harassment of the plaintiffs in the exercise of the right to use the
highway in order to go to work. While picketing of itself is not a nuisance, this was
different since by sheer weight of numbers it blocked the entrance to premises or
prevented the entry of vehicles or people. Where feelings ran high, the presence
of substantial numbers of pickets was almost bound to have an intimidatory effect
on those going to work, especially as here some 50–70 striking miners attended at
the gates each day. Even if nothing was said, the action could not fail to be highly
intimidatory (*cf. News Group Newspapers Ltd v SOGAT 1982* (1986)).

   In *Mersey Dock and Harbour Co. v Verrinder* (1982) the picketing was entirely peaceful. Judge McHugh nevertheless decided that there was a nuisance since the pickets
had mounted 'an attempt...to regulate and control the container traffic to and
from the company's terminals' and so their intention was not merely to obtain or
communicate information. (See also *Messenger Newspaper Group Ltd v NGA* (1984);
British Airports Authority v Ashton (1983); *News Group Newspapers Ltd v SOGAT 1982
(No. 2)* (1987).)

Trespass to the highway

A person commits a tort if he uses the highway 'otherwise than reasonably for
passage and repassage and for any other purpose reasonably incidental thereto'
(*Hickman v Maisey* (1900); see also *Hubbard v Pitt* (1976)), and pickets may trespass even though moving around in a circle (*Tynan v Balmer* (1967)). The proper
claimant is the owner of the soil beneath the relevant highway—usually abut-
ting landowners who may have such rights up to midpoint in the road, or the
local authority. The liability is more apparent than real since few such landowners
would be able to show special damage from the picketing.

page 440 industrial action

Interference with contracts

The existence of a picket-line may be sufficient to induce another person to break his contract of employment and not attend for work. Alternatively, it may be an interference with a commercial contract but it is then necessary that a primary obligation under the contract is interfered with (see *Thomas* v *NUM (South Wales Area)* (1985)).

15.18.3 **Immunity**

The immunity for peaceful picketing is found in TULR(C)A 1992, s. 220 in a similar way to the immunity of strikers. Section 220(1) reads:

It is lawful for a person in contemplation or furtherance of a trade dispute to attend—

  (a) at or near his own place of work, or

  (b) if he is an official of a trade union, at or near the place of work of a member of the union whom he is accompanying and whom he represents,

  for the purpose only of peacefully obtaining or communicating information, or peacefully persuading any person to work or abstain from working.

The provision derives in part from the protection against the watching and besetting offence originally in the Conspiracy and Protection of Property Act 1875. It offered immunity for attendance 'merely to obtain or communicate information', and since the early case of *J. Lyons & Sons* v *Wilkins* (1896), which held that it did not include the persuasion of men not to go into work, it has been narrowly defined. The Trade Disputes Act 1906 added the proviso that picketing be carried on 'peacefully' and restricted it to action 'in contemplation or furtherance of a trade dispute'. It thus does not extend to picketing for non-industrial purposes, e.g. to protest against the practices of a shopkeeper or estate agents (as in *Hubbard* v *Pitt* (1976)), and this fact has led to claims that trade unionists have privileges beyond those open to other members of the community.

The 1980 reforms were radical, the direct effect of widespread public disquiet about 'secondary' or 'flying pickets' who moved about the country from factory to factory. Such pickets were thus made liable for the tortious consequence of their actions, most commonly inducing breach of contract. When the Secretary of State for Employment introduced the reforms into the House of Commons, he said: 'We are proposing to withdraw the present immunity from secondary picketing wherever it takes place, whoever undertakes it and whatever the nature of the dispute' (House of Commons Standing Committee A, 18 March 1980, cols 1314–5). In fact, the law does retain some scope for secondary picketing and such legitimate action is defined in the same way as secondary strike action. The TULR(C)A 1992, s. 224 has the effect that all secondary action is unlawful except in the case of secondary picketing. So long as the workers who are picketing are within TULR(C)A 1992, s. 220 (and therefore picketing their own place of work) they may do so even if the picketing affects secondary employers.

According to the Code of Practice on Picketing, 'place of work' means 'an entrance to or an exit from the factory, site or office at which the picket works' (*News Group Newspapers Ltd* v *SOGAT 1982 (No. 2)* (1987)). There are some statutory elaborations. First, if an employee works at more than one place or it is impossible to attend that place, he can picket the administrative headquarters of his employer (for example, if it is a North Sea oil rig or a pit) (s. 220(2)). Secondly, a person dismissed during an industrial dispute in question may picket his former place of work (s. 220(3)). A union official appointed or elected for a section of union members may lawfully protest at property other than his own place of work but he must be representing members for whom he is responsible (s. 220(4)); thus national officials have 'licence' to picket any place where their members are working, but a regional union officer may only accompany members of a branch within his region. It is not apparently necessary that the member accompanied should himself be a lawful picket. There is, however, no recognition of support by one union of another. The previous location restriction against picketing at an employer's home, which was added by the Industrial Relations Act 1971, remains.

The immunity has also been severely limited by case law. It legalises only the *attendance* of the pickets for peaceful communication and not their criminal or tortious activities while so attending. As Lord Salmon said in *Broome* v *DPP* (1974): 'The section gives no protection in relation to anything the pickets may say or do while they are attending if what they say or do is itself unlawful...The section therefore gives a narrow but nevertheless real immunity to pickets. It clearly does no more.' Lord Reid said:

I see no ground for implying any right to require the person whom it is sought to persuade to submit to any kind of constraint or restriction of his personal freedom...But if a picket has a purpose beyond those set out in the section, then his presence becomes unlawful and in many cases such as I have supposed it would not be difficult to infer as a matter of fact that pickets who assemble in unreasonably large numbers do have the purpose of preventing free passage. If that were the proper inference then their presence on the highway would become unlawful.

The immunity does not prevent a picket being liable in trespass at common law (*Larkin* v *Belfast Harbour Commissioners* (1908); *British Airports Authority* v *Ashton* (1983).

The statute contains no specific restriction on the number of pickets, but clearly large numbers may intimidate more easily than the actions of the few. The Code of Practice describes mass picketing as 'obstruction if not intimidation' and recommends ensuring that 'in general the number of pickets does not exceed six at any entrance to a workplace, frequently a smaller number will be appropriate' (para. 31).

In *Thomas* v *NUM (South Wales Area)* (1985) Scott J decided that the attendance of between 50 and 70 striking miners at colliery gates could not fall within the scope of the immunity. He could not understand the need for so many people to attend if the aim was merely peaceful persuasion: threats of violence and intimidatory language were inconsistent in any event with such peaceful persuasion. Insults were not in themselves against the peace but here the language was carried to extremes and persisted in over a long period. The judge thought that the Code of Practice provided a sensible guide as to the maximum number of pickets who could lawfully attend and beyond which, simply by weight of numbers, pickets will commit intimidation (see too *News Group Newspapers Ltd* v *SOGAT 1982 (No. 2)* (1987)).

Most controversy has surrounded the claim of pickets to stop vehicles in order to convey their message, often somewhat forcefully, to drivers who may be bringing in supplies in order to keep the plant open, and which it is the aim of the pickets to prevent. This was obviously not relevant as an issue when the immunity was substantially formulated in 1875 and 1906. It is now vital, since picketing may otherwise be thought to be wholly ineffective. In *Broome* v *DPP* (1974) the House of Lords put a decisive brake on any flexibility in the current law. The defendant stood with a poster in front of a lorry trying to enter a factory and was convicted for his temerity even though there was no violence, and the whole incident lasted only nine minutes. Lord Reid said he could see:

no ground for implying any right to require the person whom it is sought to persuade to submit to any kind of constraint or restriction of his personal freedom. One is familiar with persons at the side of the road signalling to a driver requesting him to stop. It is then for the driver to decide whether he will stop or not. That, in my view, a picket is entitled to do. If the driver stops, the picket can talk to him but only for as long as the driver is willing to listen.

15.18.4 The Code of Practice on Picketing

Trade unions have accepted that some actions of pickets have not been in the interests of the wider trade union movement. The TUC thus advised that official pickets wear distinctive armbands and consider restriction of numbers. The Department for Business, Innovation and Skills' Code of Practice includes this advice but goes considerably further, including the following 'guidance':

[Mass picketing] . . . is not picketing in its lawful sense of an attempt at peaceful persuasion, and may well result in a breach of the peace or other criminal offences.

Moreover, anyone seeking, to demonstrate support for those in dispute should keep well away from any picket line so as not to create the risk of a breach of the peace or other criminal offence . . .

Large numbers . . . exacerbate disputes and sour relations not only between management and employees but between pickets and their fellow employees. (paras 49–51)

It also suggests that six is the maximum number required at any entrance or exit, and frequently a smaller number is appropriate.

The Code is also concerned to maintain essential services and supplies: this is a direct response to picketing associated with widespread strikes in the public sector and especially among health service manual workers. (See para. 63.)

The Code seeks to influence union discipline by providing that: 'Disciplinary action should not be taken as threatened by a union against a member on the grounds that he has crossed a . . . picket line' (para. 59). Such action will amount to 'unjustifiable discipline' giving rise to a claim against the union in an ET. An exclusion or expulsion is likely to be unlawful.

The Code is 'admissible in evidence' and must be 'taken into account'. These phrases do not, however, indicate the weight to be attached to its provisions nor to what is relevant. Unlike the ACAS Codes, many of its provisions go considerably further than previous legislation and judicial determinations, and there must remain a serious question as to whether it is constitutionally legitimate for sub-delegated legislation which is not extensively debated before Parliament to do so. Scott J in *Thomas* v *NUM (South Wales Area)* (1985) relied on the Code for the proposition that no more than six pickets should be allowed at each entrance to the workplace. He said that: 'This paragraph simply provides a guide as to a sensible number for a picket-line in order that the weight of numbers should not intimidate those who wish to get to work.' But the consequence has been that, due to this decision, six is now considered to be the legally sanctioned maximum.

SELECTED READING

Carty, H. (2008), 'The Economic Torts in the 21st Century', (2008) 124 LQR 641

Carty, H. (2001), *An Analysis of the Economic Torts*, Oxford: Oxford University Press, 2001

Deakin, S. and Randall, J., (2009) 72 MLR 519

Howarth, D. (2005), 'Against *Lumley v. Gye*', (2005) 68 MLR 195

Novitz, T. (2003), *International and European Protection of the Right to Strike*, Oxford: Oxford University Press

Painter, R. W. and Holmes, A. E. (2010), *Cases and Materials on Employment Law*, 8th edn, Oxford: Oxford University Press, chs 11 and 12

Simester, H. and Chan, W. (2004), 'Inducing Breach of Contract: One Tort or Two', (2004) 63 CLJ 132

16

Human rights in employment

SUMMARY

In this chapter the various articles of the European Convention on Human Rights are examined in order to see how, following the passage of the Human Rights Act 1998, the subject of human rights has had, and may have in the future, an impact on UK employment law.

16.1 **Introduction**

The European Convention for the Protection of Human Rights and Fundamental Freedoms (the Convention) was adopted by the Council of Europe in 1950, and came into force in 1953, for the purpose of protecting individuals' rights against infringement by states. (See generally, Palmer, (2000) 59 CLJ 168.)

The Convention has not so far been recognised as a direct source of law by UK courts although, when interpreting ambiguous statutes, courts have sometimes had regard to Convention provisions. It has, however, been used to resolve an ambiguity in a statute, or as a guide in developing the common law when the common law was uncertain. Lord Bridge explained in *R v Secretary of State for the Home Department ex parte Brind* (1991):

> ...it is already well settled that, in construing any provision in domestic legislation which is ambiguous in the sense that it is capable of a meaning which either conforms to or conflicts with the Convention, the courts will presume that Parliament intended to legislate in conformity with the Convention, not in conflict with it.

The Human Rights Act 1998 (HRA 1998) in effect incorporates Convention rights further into UK law and the Equality Act 2006 creates the Commission on Equality and Human Rights to underpin its work. The White Paper, *Rights Brought Home; the Human Rights Bill* (October 1997), gave as the primary aims of this incorporation:

- to enable Convention rights to be enforced in the UK
- to save time and money
- to enable alleged breaches of rights in the UK to be decided by UK courts and tribunals
- to increase the influence of UK judges on European case law
- to ensure closer scrutiny of human rights implications of new legislation.

The aim of the Act is to do all this while maintaining parliamentary sovereignty (White Paper, para. 2.13). This explains the delicate balancing at the core of the statute. The Act, which came into force for most purposes on 2 October 2000, has three main principles:

(a) interpreting legislation in accordance with the Convention;

(b) rendering unlawful acts of public bodies which are not in compliance with the Convention; and

(c) giving courts the right to make declarations on incompatibility.

16.2 Interpreting legislation

Under HRA 1998, s. 3, all courts and tribunals, in determining questions which arise in connection with a Convention right, must take into account judgments of the European Court of Human Rights, so far as relevant and so far as it is possible to do so. (See Sales, (2009) 125 LQR 598.)

This goes beyond using the Convention as a way of resolving ambiguity in legislation; courts will simply not be bound by previous interpretations of existing legislation, even by higher courts (a point made explicitly in the White Paper), if they are incompatible with the Convention. This rule of statutory interpretation applies whenever the legislation was enacted. As Lester and Pannick put it at para. 2.3.2 of *Human Rights Law and Practice*, 2nd edn (London: Lexis Butterworth, 2004), 'the role of the court is not (as in traditional statutory interpretation) to find the true meaning of the provision but to find (if possible) the meaning which best accords with Convention rights'.

However, if domestic primary legislation is unambiguous and simply cannot be interpreted in accordance with the Convention, the domestic statute must be implemented. A statutory instrument will, however, be struck down if inconsistent with Convention rights unless the primary legislation prevents the removal of the incompatibility.

There is nothing in the HRA 1998 about the relation between the Convention and contract, on which see Morris, (2001) 30 ILJ 49.

16.3 Public authorities

Under HRA 1998, ss 6–8, all public authorities must act in compliance with the Convention. Indeed, 'It is unlawful for a public authority to act in a way which is incompatible with a Convention right' (s. 6(1)). It is a defence, however, to show that the public authority was prevented from acting in accordance with the Convention as the result of UK legislation (s. 6(2)).

If a public authority acts in a way which is inconsistent with Convention rights then a claim for a declaration, damages, or an injunction will lie against it. Clearly, central government, executive agencies, and local government are public authorities.

The Home Secretary stated in debate on the Human Rights Bill that he wanted a 'realistic and modern definition of the state so as to provide correspondingly wide protection against an abuse of rights'. The definition does not include, however: the Houses of Parliament, sporting bodies (*R* v *Disciplinary Committee of the Jockey Club ex parte Aga Khan* (1993) or religious bodies (*R* v *Chief Rabbi ex parte Wachmann* (1993)).

Courts and tribunals are deemed by s. 6(3) to be public authorities for the purpose of the Act. Thus courts themselves act unlawfully if they breach Convention rights. This may mean that courts will impose Convention obligations in disputes between private individuals, but the scope of such horizontality will have to be carefully worked out. However, when interpreting legislation or exercising discretion, courts and tribunals must have regard to Convention rights.

There are also bodies with mixed public and private functions (for example Railtrack, which has statutory public functions relating to health and safety and private functions relating to land development). When exercising their public functions, such bodies must apply Convention rights. When exercising private functions, however, no such obligations exist. This creates an anomalous situation since entering into an employment contract is often viewed as excercising a function of a private nature (*Ex parte Walsh* (1984); *McLaren* v *Home Office* (1990); *R* v *Derbyshire CC ex parte Noble* (1990); *R* v *Secretary of State for Education ex parte Prior* (1994)), so that employers who are mixed bodies will argue that the obligation to comply with the Convention does *not* arise in employment disputes. (See further discussion in Lightman and Bowers, [1998] EHRLR 560.)

16.3.1 Claims by victims

A victim of acts by such a public authority which are rendered unlawful by the new statute may:

(a) bring proceedings against the public authority in the appropriate court; or

(b) rely on the Convention right in any legal proceedings (s. 7(1)).

The applicant must, in order to be able to bring a claim himself, be a victim of the act in question (s. 7(3)). 'Victim' is, however, narrowly defined in art. 34 of the Convention, to which express reference is made in HRA 1998, s. 7(7). The court may take into account the importance of the issue and the absence of any other responsible challenger. This is a narrower test than obtains in judicial review applications.

16.3.2 Remedies

A court which finds that an act of a public authority is unlawful, may grant such relief or remedy, or make such order, 'within its powers' as it considers just and appropriate (s. 8(1)), but:

(a) damages may be awarded only by a court which can award damages or order payment of compensation in civil proceedings (s. 8(2));

(b) damages are to be awarded only if it is necessary to afford just satisfaction to the victim (s. 8(3));

(c) the quantum of awards in Strasbourg is relatively low, e.g. £10,000 in *Johnson* v *United Kingdom* (1999) for unlawful detention of a mental patient for over three years.

16.4 **The impact in employment law**

The articles of the Convention which need to be considered in relation to employment law are:

- the right not to be subjected to inhuman or degrading treatment (art. 3)
- the right not to be required to perform forced or compulsory labour (art. 4)
- the right to a fair trial (art. 6)
- the right to respect for private life (art. 8)
- the right to freedom of thought (art. 9)
- the right to freedom of expression (art. 10)
- the right to freedom of peaceful assembly and to freedom of association with others, including the right to form and to join trade unions (art. 11)
- the right to enjoy the substantive rights and freedoms set forth in the Convention without discrimination (art. 14).

Before looking at these articles in detail, it is important to distinguish the different respects in which the Act and Convention make an impact in employment law, and they may be said to be as follows:

(a) as against public authorities, by direct s. 6 claims, provided that the employment relationship has a public element;

(b) as against public authorities and private bodies and individuals, in the interpretation of statutory provisions, in particular the exercise of discretion in unfair dismissal and discrimination claims;

(c) as against public authorities and private bodies and individuals, in the continued development of implied terms in the contract of employment, especially that of mutual trust and confidence.

16.4.1 **Article 3: degrading treatment**

Article 3 of the Convention states that 'No one shall be subjected to torture or to inhuman or degrading treatment or punishment'. This is an absolute right, without any qualification at all. This may be relevant to issues of serious racial or other types of harassment. It is relevant to such cases as *De Souza* v *AA* (1986), where one employee told another not to get typing done 'by that wog', which was held not to be racial discrimination within the meaning of the RRA 1976.

16.4.2 **Article 4: prohibition of slavery and forced labour**

Article 4 of the Convention provides:

1. No one shall be held in slavery or servitude.
2. No one shall be required to perform forced or compulsory labour.

3. For the purpose of this Article the term 'forced or compulsory labour' shall not include:
   (a) any work required to be done in the ordinary course of detention…or during conditional release from such detention;
   (b) any service of a military character…;
   (c) any service exacted in case of an emergency or calamity threatening the life or well-being of the community;
   (d) any work or service which forms part of normal civic obligations.

This article does not have much effect upon domestic employment law. It was itself based on the ILO Convention No. 29 on forced and compulsory labour. The Convention defines such labour as 'all work or service which is exacted from any person under the menace of any penalty and for which the said person has not offered himself voluntarily'.

The European Court of Human Rights has held that the word 'forced' in art. 4 connotes physical or mental constraint. In *van der Mussele* v *Belgium* (1984), from which this test derives, it was held that an obligation on pupil barristers to provide services free to those without legal aid did not amount to forced or compulsory labour. Economic duress will thus not suffice. Further, the services to be rendered by such pupil barristers did not fall outside the ambit of the normal activities of an advocate and the services contributed to the applicant's general training. The burden on the applicants was not in any sense disproportionate, accounting as it did for a small proportion of their time. If, however, 'the service imposed a burden which was so disproportionate to the advantages attached to the future exercise of that profession that the service could not be treated as having been voluntarily accepted beforehand' then it would breach the article.

In *van Droogenberck* (1980), the Commission said that 'in addition to the obligation to provide another with certain services, the concept of servitude includes the obligation on the part of the "serf" to live on another's property and the impossibility of changing his condition'.

16.4.3 Article 6: right to a fair trial

Article 6(1) of the Convention provides (in material part):

1. In the determination of his civil rights and obligations or of any criminal charge against him, everyone is entitled to a fair and public hearing within a reasonable time by an independent and impartial tribunal established by law…

The basic requirements

The basic requirements of art. 6(1) in civil proceedings are:

(a) a fair and public hearing;
(b) an independent and impartial tribunal;
(c) a trial within a reasonable period;
(d) a public judgment (although there are some exceptions to this); and
(e) a reasoned decision to be given.

It may also require in some cases the opportunity to cross-examine witnesses and to give and receive adequate disclosure of documentation. Certain features have been held to be implied in the article, such as the right to be present or at least represented at any determination of the case (*X* v *Sweden* (1959)).

The centrality of this article to the Convention as a whole should be obvious since it sets out the fundamentals of the rule of law itself. The scope of the article in employment issues often turns on the autonomous Convention concept of 'determination of a civil right or obligation' which alone gives rise to claims under art. 6. We will approach the matter, first, in respect of the obligations of the State in relation to publicly provided ETs and, secondly, in respect of those private disciplinary matters which may be subject to art. 6.

Public tribunals

(a) The impartiality of the tribunal It is indeed a curiosity of the tribunal system that it is the Department for Business, Innovation and Skills (BIS) which appoints lay members to the tribunal that may have to adjudicate in disputes involving employees of BIS. The tribunals are paid for and administered by the Employment Tribunal Service of BIS. Whether the ET could be described as an independent and impartial body to adjudicate on matters involving the Secretary of State for Trade and Industry was called into question in *Smith* v *Secretary of State for Trade and Industry* (2000). The applicant sought payment by the Insolvency Fund of BIS of sums arising upon bankruptcy. The EAT did not expressly decide the issue of impartiality, since the Attorney-General had not been notified or given an opportunity to make representations on the point. Further, the EAT said that it felt diffident itself about deciding the matter since its lay members, while being appointed by the Crown, are paid out of monies provided by BIS and their remuneration and allowances are determined by the Secretary of State. Thus, if the tribunal was not impartial, neither was the EAT.

(b) Lengthy delays The European Court of Human Rights has underlined more than once in employment cases 'the importance of rendering justice without delays which might jeopardise its effectiveness and credibility' (*H* v *France* (1990); see too *Somjee* v *United Kingdom* (2002)). In *Obermeier* v *Germany* (1991) the Court said more specifically that 'an employee who considers that he has been wrongly suspended by his employer has an important personal interest in securing the judicial decision of the lawfulness of that measure promptly'. Lengthy delays of the sort which were commonplace in tribunals a decade ago are now happily long forgotten, but a very long time can still elapse where a case goes on to appeal to the Court of Appeal, and is then remitted and after reconsideration by the ET again goes up the judicial hierarchy.

There are also some cases where there are long drawn-out internal procedures before the matter gets into the tribunal system. The most obvious case is in the medical arena, where there are many stages of the process in the case of hospital consultants, and it was from there that the leading case of *Darnell* v *United Kingdom* arose (1994). There was a nine-year delay between dismissal and final disposal of the case. The European Court of Human Rights found the UK to be in default for allowing such a delay to occur.

In *Kwamin* v *Abbey National plc* (2004) the EAT held that an excessive delay between a tribunal hearing and the promulgation of its decision will contravene art. 6.

(c) Equality of arms Another feature inherent in the concept of a fair trial at the heart of art. 6 is the equality of arms between the parties. This may render the inability to gain legal aid in ETs open to challenge. It is no part of Strasbourg jurisprudence that the lack of legal aid in every case is a breach of the principle of a fair trial, but there have been some circumstances in which the unavailability of legal assistance in respect of complicated issues has been held to be a breach of the principles of a fair trial. The leading case is *Airey* v *Ireland* (1979). The applicant complained that she could not enforce her civil right to separate from her alcoholic and violent husband because she could not afford legal representation in the separation proceedings. The Irish Government countered with the proposition that she could represent herself, but this received short shrift in Strasbourg. The Court stated that:

The Convention is intended to guarantee not rights that are theoretical or illusory but rights that are practical and effective. This is particularly so of the right of access to the courts in view of the prominent place held in democratic society by the right to a fair trial. It must therefore be ascertained whether [the applicant's] appearance...without the assistance of a lawyer would be effective in the sense of whether she would be able to present her case properly and satisfactorily.

It was held that this was not so for Mrs Airey because of the legal and factual complexity of the case in which she was involved, and the emotional involvement of the applicant in it. It is true that later cases have resisted the notion that *Airey* can be used to provide a general right to legal aid. For example, an application that the refusal of legal aid in defamation cases was in breach of the Convention failed in *Munro* v *United Kingdom* (1987). It could, however, be argued in accordance with *Airey* that the complexities of some aspects of employment law, such as TUPE and the Working Time Regulations, are such that the principle of equality of arms is breached by the complete absence of legal aid in ETs as a generic group.

It was suggested, *obiter*, by the Court of Appeal in *Kulkarni* v *Milton Keynes Hospital NHS Foundation Trust* (2010) that art. 6 could not be invoked where the loss of a specific job was at stake, but it could be if the employee was at risk of losing the right not to practice in the profession. However, no reasons were given for this distinction, or why the dividing line was placed where it was, which seems to be founded purely on the gravity of the impact on the employee.

(d) Restriction on publicity of hearings The issue here relates to the use in ETs of restricted reporting orders and private hearings. There are exceptions in the Convention itself to the general rule that hearings should be held in public. Those most relevant to the tribunals are where 'the protection of the private life of the parties so require or to the extent strictly necessary in the opinion of the court in special circumstances where publicity would prejudice the interests of justice'. This requires the court to weigh in each case whether restriction on publication is proportionate to the risk involved.

The European Commission on Human Rights has itself sanctioned private hearings in cases involving medical issues in order to protect the private lives of patients (*Guenoun* v *France* (1990)). It is likely that most cases in which restricted reporting orders are made would fall within the exceptions to the rule, but the method of arguing about them must change to one of proportionality of the expense to the degree of harm which may genuinely be anticipated.

(e) Part-time chairmen The use of part-time chairmen and the appointment of lay members was thrown into relief by the decision of the High Court of Justiciary in Scotland (where the HRA 1998 was already in effect for devolved issues) in *Starrs* v *Ruxton* (1999), to the effect that the temporary sheriffs who tried criminal cases were not independent and impartial. This was because they were appointed only for a year and might have their appointments revoked with no reasons being given. Although part-time chairmen and lay members are appointed for rather longer than this, there may be some possibility of challenge to their role.

(f) Other issues A whole host of other issues might arise under this article. The obvious possibilities include the admission of unlawfully obtained evidence and the extent to which that may be inimical to the fairness of the trial; and the lack of assistance for disabled litigants. For a discussion of the issues raised by a claim of State immunity, see *Fogarty* v *United Kingdom* (2002) where the Court held that this fell under art. 6(1).

Private hearings

(a) Professional disciplinary bodies The article may also have scope in disciplinary hearings before professional disciplinary bodies. These have been held to fall within the concept of determining 'civil rights and obligations' within art. 6(1) in several Strasbourg cases (e.g. *Le Compte* (1982); *König* v *Germany* (1978)). The term 'civil rights and obligations' is treated as an autonomous Convention concept, so that it is not appropriate to apply UK notions of what is a civil right to its construction. The lines of distinction between the cases on what are 'civil rights' are not, however, easy to delineate. Thus, it has covered a disciplinary hearing in relation to disqualification of a doctor by the French Medical Association, a private body regulated to some extent by statute (*Diennet* v *France* (1995), or the United Kingdom General Medical Council (*Wickramsinghe* v *United Kingdom* (1998), or the General Dental Council (*Preiss* v *General Dental Council* (2001)). See too the decision of the Outer House of the Court of Session in *Tehrani* v *United Kingdom Central Council for Nursing, Midwifery and Health Visiting* (2001) and a decision to re-admit a barrister to the Ordre des Avocats (*H* v *Belgium* (1987)). On the other hand, the Commission held in *X* v *United Kingdom* (1984) that disciplinary proceedings which resulted only in a reprimand did not fall within art. 6(1).

(b) Recruitment, employment, and dismissal of public officials Generally, disputes relating to the recruitment, employment, and retirement of public servants have been held to fall outside the scope of art. 6(1). There is also some jurisprudence excluding disputes about the recruitment, employment, and dismissal of public officials, although as with much Strasbourg jurisprudence the rationale and precise scope of the doctrine has not been clearly spelt out (e.g. *Neigel* v *France* (1997)). It may be that some have been decided as they were because there was originally a clause in the draft of the Convention providing that 'everyone has the right of equal access to public service in his country' but this was eventually rejected.

There is a civil right within art. 6(1) where the 'claims in issue relate to a "purely economic right" such as payment of a salary or pension' (*Huber* v *France* (1998)). Violation by a public authority of the article has been found where there has been a dismissal or threat of dismissal (*Vogt* v *Germany* (1996)), or a suspension or reprimand (*Morrisens* v *Belgium* (1988)). In *Balfour* v *United Kingdom* (1997), however, a former diplomat was unable to use art. 6 to challenge the use of public interest immunity certificates in an ET case he brought on the termination of his service.

The prospect of an end to the uncertainty of when art. 6 would apply came in *Pellegrin* v *France* (1999) where the Court held that a new functional criterion should be applied based on the nature of the employee's duties and responsibilities. The only disputes excluded from art. 6 were those raised by public servants whose duties typified the specific activities of the public service in so far as the public service was acting as the depository of public authority responsible for protecting the general interests of the State or other public authorities. A clear example would be the armed forces or police. No disputes between administrative authorities and employees who occupied posts involving participation in the exercise of powers conferred by public law could use art. 6(1). On the other hand, disputes concerning pensions all came within the ambit of art. 6(1) because, on retirement, employees broke the special bond existing between themselves and the authorities. The applicant in *Pellegrin* was recruited as a technical adviser to the Minister for the Economy, Planning and Trade, which gave him considerable responsibilities in the field of the State's public finances, which was *par excellence* a sphere in which states exercised sovereign power. Thus art. 6(1) was not relevant.

If a matter is within the scope of civil rights then the sorts of issues which may there arise include the employee being on an equal footing with the employer; the right to representation at the hearing; access to documents and witnesses; the need for a reasoned decision; and the public nature of the hearing. It may be particularly difficult to fit impartiality and independence into disciplinary matters in a small organisation.

16.4.4 Article 8: right to respect for private and family life

Article 8 of the Convention provides:

1. Everyone has the right to respect for his private and family life, his home and his correspondence.
2. There shall be no interference by a public authority with the exercise of this right except such as is in accordance with the law and is necessary in a democratic society in the interests of national security, public safety or the economic well-being of the country, for the prevention of disorder or crime, for the protection of health and morals, or for the protection of the rights and freedom of others.

This right includes respect for personal identity including sexual identity, moral or physical identity, sexual activities (perhaps other than those that take place in public places—*X* v *Y* (2004); but contrast with the ECJ's decision in *Pay* v *UK* (2009); and see Mantouvalou, (2008) 71 MLR 912; (2009) 38 ILJ 133), and personal relations. It is to be noted that the word used is 'respect', so that there is no absolute right to privacy, see e.g. *De Keyser Ltd* v *Wilson* (2001). The right to respect for private life, however, clearly does not stop at the doors of the workplace. This has a number of implications for employers in relation to security measures, dress codes, disclosure, medical checks, and email intrusion. The scope of operation may particularly involve the exercise of discretion in unfair dismissal cases.

Security measures

Security measures at work may fall within the scope of the article; thus a search of a lawyer's office was held to be in breach of art. 8 (*Niemitz* v *Germany* (1993)). The Court said that 'to interpret the words "private life" and "home" as excluding certain professional or business activities or premises would not be consonant with the essential object and purpose of Article 8'. In *Halford* v *United Kingdom* (1997), the absence of domestic legislation dealing with an employer's right (or lack of right) to 'tap' telephone calls at work was found to be a breach of art. 8. In that case, the applicant (who was a senior police officer) had alleged that her office telephone was being tapped by her employers in order to obtain evidence to use in a sex discrimination claim which she had brought. The European Court of Human Rights held that to tap an office telephone was a *prima facie* breach of art. 8, unless the employer warned the employee that it was doing so.

In *Leander* v *Sweden* (1987) the European Court decided that storing information about a job applicant in a secret police register and releasing it to a prospective employer breached the applicant's right to respect for private life. This interference could however be justified as 'necessary in a democratic society' (the defence in art. 8(2)). Whether it was so justified in a particular case would depend on whether the action taken was proportionate to the risk posed. The use of such information for vetting candidates for posts which are not of importance for national security may be harder to justify.

The use of CCTV to monitor employees at work is becoming increasingly common. It may be justified on the grounds that it is necessary for the protection of health (for example, on an assembly-line) or to protect the rights of others (the employer), but it must be a proportionate response, so that its indiscriminate use throughout the workplace may not be justified.

Likewise, employers interfering with e-mails at work may *prima facie* be breaching the right to respect for correspondence under art. 8. In some cases, it may be justified on the basis that it is necessary to protect the rights of others (either the employer—to prevent employees wasting time at work, or to check that employees are not acting against the employer's interests by working for a competitor—or fellow employees, by monitoring to ensure that employees are not sending offensive e-mails which might amount to harassment). Proportionality is the key to resolving this point.

Dress codes

Dress codes may be subject to human rights considerations under art. 8 and under art. 10 (freedom of expression). An employee may seek to 'express her personality' by wearing, for example, a nose-ring which the employer finds offensive and off-putting to customers or clients. She may be able to argue that she has a right to express herself by wearing a nose-ring, and that the employer is failing to respect her right to express herself or her right to a private life. Again, the real issue is proportionality of the response to the harm caused to others. Tribunals will attempt to apply an even-handed approach without requiring identical treatment—see *Department for Work and Pensions* v *Thompson* (2004).

Medical checks

The collection of medical data and the maintenance of medical records fall within the sphere of private life (*Chare née Julien* v *France* (1988)), and there may be interference when the employer collects highly sensitive health-related information about its employees. There was a potential breach in *MS* v *Sweden* (1997), where the applicant injured her back at work and claimed compensation under the Industrial Injury Insurance Act. The clinic which treated her disclosed her medical records in full to the Social Insurance Office without her permission. While this was a potential breach, it was held to be proportionate in the pursuit of the legitimate aim of protecting the economic well-being of the country by ensuring that public funds were allocated only to deserving claimants. The Court said that 'the domestic law must afford appropriate safeguards to prevent any such communication or disclosure of personal health data as may be inconsistent with the guarantees in article 8'.

Surveillance

The EAT held in *McGowan* v *Scottish Water* (2005) that an employer did not infringe art. 8 in covertly videoing an employee's home in order to see if he was falsifying timesheets. The reasons were not 'external or whimsical'.

16.4.5 Article 9: freedom of thought, conscience, religion

Article 9 of the Convention provides:

1. Everyone has the right to freedom of thought, conscience and religion; this right includes freedom to change his religion or belief, and freedom, either alone or in community with others and in public or private, to manifest his religion or belief, in worship, teaching, practice and observance.
2. Freedom to manifest one's religion or beliefs shall be subject only to such limitations as are prescribed by law and are necessary in a democratic society in the interests of public safety, for the protection of public order, health or morals, or for the protection of the rights and freedoms of others.

The article covers a wide scope of religion and conscience, so that in *Arrowsmith* v *United Kingdom* (1980) the Commission accepted that 'the attitude of pacifism may be seen as a belief protected by article 9(1)'. A balance is struck between the needs of the religion and wider societal requirements, including the concerns of employers, which was most clearly articulated in *X* v *United Kingdom* (1984) where the Commission stated that:

Article 9 primarily protects the sphere of personal beliefs and religious creeds...In addition, it protects acts which are intimately linked to these attitudes, such as acts of worship or devotion which are aspects of the practice of a religion or a belief in a generally recognised form. However in protecting this personal sphere, Article 9 of the Convention does not always guarantee the rights to behave in the public sphere in a way which is dictated by such a belief, for instance by refusing to pay certain taxes because part of the revenue so raised may be applied for military expenditure.

The article clearly protects not only ideas which are favourably received but also expression of ideas which would be regarded as offensive to all or a sector of the population. This is another important right, which has the potential to cover a variety of employment situations.

First, and most obviously, it presents employees of public authorities with a general entitlement to practise their religion and, more importantly, not to be disciplined or dismissed for doing so. It provides employees of private bodies with some protection if they are dismissed, since a dismissal on grounds which infringe a Convention right will be unlikely to be found to be fair (since tribunals must interpret the ERA 1996 in a way which is consistent with Convention rights). This has the potential to go further than the protection afforded to employees (and prospective employees) by the RRA 1976, which protects individuals from discrimination on grounds of colour, race, ethnicity or national origin but not merely a religion or set of beliefs. Jews, Sikhs, and gypsies have been held to fall within the RRA 1976, but Rastafarians have been held to be a religious grouping only and not to come within any of the prescribed categories. The same is probably true for Hindus and Muslims. In a claim under art. 9, it is overwhelmingly likely that Rastafarians, as well as various denominations of Christianity and other world religions, will be able to claim protection.

Such guidance as exists from Strasbourg does not, however, suggest that art. 9 is a licence for employees to insist on time off to practice their religion during working time. For example, in *Ahmad* v *United Kingdom* (1982) a Muslim schoolteacher wanted to pray at his mosque for 45 minutes every Friday. The Inner London Education Authority (ILEA) refused permission and relied on the contract of employment which required the teacher to work on Fridays. The European Court of Human Rights held that the ILEA's refusal did not infringe art. 9, since the employee had voluntarily accepted a teaching post which prevented his attendance at prayers (and had not complained, or requested time off, during his first six years at work). The Court identified the issue as being whether, in relying on the contract of employment, the ILEA was arbitrarily disregarding the right to freedom of religion. To some extent this means that employers can contract out of their obligations under the Convention, provided they have good reason for doing so. Further, in *Knudsen* v *Norway* (1985) the Commission said that art. 9 might apply where an individual is already employed but faces dismissal unless he changes his beliefs.

Secondly, art. 9 has implications for working on religious holidays and Sundays. However, in *Stedman* v *United Kingdom* (1997) the applicant was dismissed for refusing to work on Sundays in accordance with her religious belief. The Commission rejected her claim on (it seems) the grounds that she was not dismissed because of her religious beliefs, but because she refused to work contractual hours. It did not consider at any length the point that her refusal to work contractual hours was because of her religious beliefs (*cf. Prais* v *EC Commission* (1976)). The protection in ERA 1996, s.43 currently applies to those who do not wish to work on Sundays, but this might have to be extended under the ambit of this article to those who do not wish to work on other religious days of worship.

The Court has also emphasised that a balance must be struck between the religious views and the essential needs of the job, including the ethos of the organisation in which the applicant works. In *Kalac* v *Turkey* (1999) the application was brought by a judge advocate in the air force with the rank of group captain who was compulsorily retired from that post because his 'conduct and attitude revealed that he had adopted unlawful fundamentalist opinions'. The principle of secularism was inherent in the Turkish armed forces and the Court did not think that his rights were infringed.

It should be noted that HRA 1998, s. 13 makes specific provision for a court or tribunal, in determining any question which 'might affect the exercise by a religious organisation...of the Convention right to freedom of thought, conscience and religion', to have particular regard to the 'importance of that right'. This arose from the concerns felt by some such organisations that their ethos might be challenged by the Act, for example that they would have to allow gay priests or marriages, or engage persons who were hostile to their beliefs.

16.4.6 Article 10: freedom of expression

Article 10 of the Convention provides:

1. Everyone has the right to freedom of expression. This right shall include freedom to hold opinions and to receive and impart information and ideas without interference by public authority and regardless of frontiers. This article shall not prevent states from requiring the licensing of broadcasting, television or cinema enterprises.

2. The exercise of these freedoms, since it carries with it duties and responsibilities, may be subject to such formalities, conditions, restrictions or penalties as are prescribed by law and are necessary in a democratic society in the interests of national security, territorial integrity or public safety, for the prevention of disorder or crime, for the protection of health or morals, for the protection of the reputation or rights of others, for preventing the disclosure of information received in confidence, or for maintaining the authority and impartiality of the judiciary.

In this respect, 'expression' covers not only words, but also pictures, images and actions intended to express an idea or to present information (*Stevens* v *United Kingdom* (1986)). The exceptions to the right should be 'narrowly interpreted' and 'convincingly established'. Crucially, the right applies not only to ideas which are favourably received or regarded as inoffensive, but also to those which 'offend, shock or disturb the state or any sector of the population. Such are the demands of pluralism, tolerance and broadmindedness.' In the employment sphere, the cases may be analysed under the following heads.

The right to political views and to manifest them

The crucial case is now *Vogt* v *Germany* (1996). A teacher was dismissed because of active membership of the German Communist Party. She had already been appointed to a tenured position and this dismissal was held to infringe her art. 10 rights. On the other hand, previous claims to an office have been held not to be protected (*Glasenapp* v *ERG* (1987); *Kosiek* v *ERG* (1987)).

Ahmed v *United Kingdom* (1997) was an important challenge in Strasbourg to the restriction on senior local government officers engaging in political activity set out in the Local Government (Political Restrictions) Regulations 1990, and shows how the Court reasons in such cases. The first issue was that the restriction was prescribed by law (although there was some uncertainty, it was inevitable that such measures were couched in broad terms given that they were laying down rules of general application). It was in pursuance of one or more legitimate aims (to protect the rights of the council members and the electorate to effective political democracy at the highest level); local government has long resided on a bond of trust between elected members and permanent corps of local government officers who both advise them on policy and assume responsibility for implementation of policies adopted, and this was necessary in a democratic society. The test was whether there was a pressing social need, and states have a wide margin of appreciation in assessing whether such need exists. Thus the Regulations passed muster under art. 10.

The nature of particular employment may require some degree of restriction of freedom of speech. Thus in *Morissens* v *Belgium* (1988) the Commission said that 'by entering the civil service [as a teacher] the applicant accepted certain restrictions on the exercise of her freedom of expression, as being inherent in her duties'. On the other hand, in *B* v *United Kingdom* (1990) the discipline of an Aldermaston atomic weapons worker who criticised atomic weapons on a TV programme was found to be justified. In *Rekvenyi* v *Hungary* (1999), the Court considered a provision in the Hungarian constitution whereby members of the armed forces and police could not join any political party or engage in political activity. The Court recognised (especially in the light of Hungary's recent history) the legitimacy of the public being entitled to expect that 'in their dealings with the police they are entitled to be confronted with politically-neutral officers who are detached from the political fray'.

Whistleblowing

There may be challenges to the compatibility of the Public Interest Disclosure Act 1998 with art. 10. Only a limited number of disclosures are protected under the Act, and those disclosures must either be to designated persons or comply with the strict requirements of ERA 1996, ss 43G and 43H. The right to freedom of expression may go further, although its effect might be limited depending on how the courts construe the limitation imposed by art. 10(2) that the right does not extend where the law (for example, the law of contract) prohibits such disclosure on the grounds that it may affect the reputation or rights of others (i.e. the employer). See e.g. *Tucht* v *West Germany* (1982). (See Lewis, [2005] WebJCLI, issue 5.)

Dress codes

The requirement by the employer of a certain dress code may raise issues under art. 10 (*cf. Burrett* v *West Birmingham HA* (1994)). Some restrictions may be justified and proportionate. In *Kara* v *United Kingdom* (1999) for example, the Commission dismissed an application from a bisexual male transvestite employed by the London Borough of Hackney as a careers adviser. He went to work in female clothing such as leggings, tights, halter-neck tops, and a dress. His manager warned him not to do this as it was likely to break the code of conduct on 'appropriate clothing'. The Commission held that this instruction was in accordance with law and a proportionate measure in pursuit of a lawful aim.

16.4.7 Article 11: freedom of assembly and association

Article 11 of the Convention provides:

1. Everyone has the right to freedom of peaceful assembly and to freedom of association with others, including the right to form and to join trade unions for the protection of his interests.

2. No restrictions shall be placed on the exercise of these rights other than such as are prescribed by law and are necessary in a democratic society in the interests of national security

or public safety, for the prevention of disorder or crime, for the protection of health or morals or for the protection of the rights and freedoms of others. This article shall not prevent the imposition of lawful restrictions on the exercise of these rights by members of the armed forces, of the police or of the administration of the State.

There are various respects in which this article may give rights to workers, but also to trade unions—see Hendy and Ewing, (2005) 34 ILJ 197. So, in *ASLEF* v *UK* (2007) the European Court of Human Rights held that trade unions were free under art. 11 to expel a member of the grounds of membership of a political party. This led to Employment Act 2008, s. 19, which made consequential amendments to TULR(C)A 1992, s. 174. (See above, p. 369 above.)

Closed shop

The Court first examined the closed shop in 1980 in *Young, James and Webster* v *United Kingdom* (1982). This case concerned three British Rail employees dismissed pursuant to a closed shop agreement and the closed shop provisions of the TULRA 1974 and the Trade Union and Labour Relations (Amendment) Act 1976. All three had principled—but not religious—objections to belonging to a trade union. It was a strong case because the applicants had joined British Rail before the closed shop agreement was entered into.

The Court unusually sat in plenary session for this case. Eighteen of the 21 judges found for the sacked employees; three against. The necessary foundation of the majority's decision was its finding that the very notion of freedom of association implied 'some measure of freedom of choice as to its exercise'. In other words, the freedom to associate included, to some extent, the freedom not to associate.

On the facts of the case, the majority held the threat of dismissal, involving loss of livelihood, 'a most serious form of compulsion...[which] strikes at the very substance of the freedom guaranteed by Article 11...[rendering that freedom] non-existent or so reduced to be of no practical value'. Because of the three workers' principled objections to trade union membership, the majority also held their treatment to have been in violation of their rights of freedom of thought and expression.

Lastly, the Court examined the UK's submission that the closed shop legislation was nevertheless necessary in a democratic society and proportionate, and hence lawful under the provisions of art. 11(2). The majority concluded that it was not, but emphasised that it had considered only the facts of the case before it. Its judgment did not mean that closed shop arrangements would always be in contravention of the right to freedom of association: indeed, '[a]ssuming that Article 11 does not guarantee the negative aspect of that freedom on the same footing as the positive aspect, compulsion to join a particular trade union may not always be contrary to the Convention.'

Since *Young, James and Webster* the Court has held compulsion to join a particular trade union lawful under the Convention on one occasion. In *Sibson* v *United Kingdom* (1994) a lorry driver objected when he was given the choice of joining the trade union at his existing depot or moving to another depot. This followed his being expelled from the TGWU when he made allegations of dishonesty against a branch official. The Court distinguished the facts of this case from those pertaining in *Young, James and Webster* in two ways. First, in this case there was not the same threat of dismissal leading to loss of livelihood: Mr Sibson had the alternative of moving depots and the employer was contractually entitled to move staff between depots. Secondly, Mr Sibson had no principled objections to trade union membership, unlike Messrs Young, James, and Webster.

The European Court of Human Rights held in *ASLEF* v *United Kingdom* (2007) that it would be in contravention of art. 11 to exclude or expel people from membership of trade unions because of their membership in political organisations. The effect is that the Government will have to amend domestic legislation on exclusion and expulsion in this regard, and will probably do so with regard to these issues in general, without restricting amendments to politically-based decisions. However, it is not clear at the time of writing what the changes will amount to. (See further, Ewing, (2007) 36 ILJ 425.)

Right of union to be heard and to be recognised

Establishing and joining a trade union may be of little practical value if the employer does not recognise the union as its employees' representative in negotiations over pay and conditions. The Court considered the extent to which art. 11(1) protected more than just the right to *join* a trade union in *Swedish Engine Drivers' Union* v *Sweden* (1979–80). This case concerned the refusal of the Swedish National Collective Bargaining Office to enter into a collective agreement with the Engine Drivers' Union. The union asserted that this represented a violation of art. 11(1). The union lost because the Court held that art. 11(1) did not oblige a member state to treat trade unions in any particular way. The right to negotiate through collective bargaining was not inherent in the right to form and join a trade union.

In the *Engine Drivers* case the Court went on to consider the extent to which a member state should assist trade unions and their members to conform with its duties under art. 11. It observed that art. 11(1) obliges public authorities to protect an individual's 'right to form and to join trade unions *for the protection of his interests*' (emphasis added). It refused to 'accept the view expressed by the minority in the Commission who describe the phrase "for the protection of his interests" as redundant'. 'These words', the Court continued, 'clearly denoting purpose, show that the Convention safeguards freedom to protect the occupational interests of trade union members by trade union action, the conduct and development of which the Contracting States must both permit and make possible. In the opinion of the Court, it follows that the members of a trade union have a right, in order to protect their interests, that *the trade union should be heard*' (emphasis added). It was a matter for the State to determine how this right would be provided.

Article 11(1) therefore requires the UK to ensure that trade unions should be heard. This may be argued to mean some form of compulsory consultation by employers, although states have a discretion as to how this should be done. The Court said that 'the article does not secure any particular treatment of trade unions, or their members, by the State, such as the right that the State should conclude any given collective agreement with them'.

However, the Court went further in *Demir* v *Turkey* (2009) when it said that it was taking note of evolution in international law (such as the ILO and the European Social Charter) and domestic legal systems. Although recognising that it should not depart from its precedents without good reason, this was a case when it should. Therefore the right to collective bargaining, contrary to the decisions to the contrary, should be recognised as coming under art. 11. Unfortunately, it did not give clear reasons as to why the evolution of itself was the right trend to follow, and future decisions by the Court on this will be necessary in order to discover where this is likely to lead.

Rules about which unions are appropriate for the worker

Cheall v *United Kingdom* (1986) was an action brought by a worker expelled from his new union (APEX) because, in breach of the Bridlington Principles, it had not checked that his old union was content with the change of his membership. The TUC Disputes Committee thus intervened pursuant to rules set up by agreement. The Commission found against Mr Cheall, explaining that in 'the exercise of their rights under art. 11(1), unions must remain free to decide, in accordance with union rules, questions concerning admission to and expulsion from the union'. The role of the State was limited, in such circumstances, to protecting 'the individual against any abuse of a dominant position by trade unions...[such as] might occur...where exclusion or expulsion was not in accordance with union rules or where the rules were wholly unreasonable or arbitrary or where the consequences of exclusion or expulsion resulted in exceptional hardship such as job loss because of a closed shop'. The Court said that 'the State must protect the individual against any abuse of dominant position by trade unions'.

Restrictions on rights of the unions to organise

The best known challenge to the restrictions on the rights of unions failed. The Thatcher Government famously banned unions recruiting at the Government Communications Headquarters GCHQ. The complaint was rejected by the Commission because of wide discretion in matters of national security (*CCSU* v *United Kingdom* (1988)).

The following points can be drawn from the Commission's decision and art. 11(2) itself:

(a) Whether a worker is a member of the 'administration of the state' may be important when determining if his or her rights under art. 11(1) have been violated. The second sentence in art. 11(2) seems to provide considerably greater scope for bans on trade union membership than the first sentence. The first sentence deals with employees other than members of the 'administration of the state'. The Commission, in its decision in the GCHQ case, declined to define precisely who is, and who is not, involved in the 'administration of the state'.

(b) The first sentence of art. 11(2) is directed towards workers, other than those engaged in the army, the police or the administration of the State, who might endanger others' rights, morals, property or persons by embarking on mass industrial action. Health professionals, members of the emergency services and prison officers are probably to be included in this category. Restrictions on the freedom of these groups to form and join trade unions are thus subject to the requirements that they are (i) lawful, (ii) necessary in a democratic society to serve one of the important social goods set out in art. 11(2), and (iii) proportionate to the seriousness of the mischief that they are designated to prevent.

Requirement to reveal names of strikers

Article 11 was not infringed by the requirement to reveal names of strikers. In *NATFHE* v *United Kingdom* (1998) the Court held that the obligation on the union to disclose the names of union members taking part in a ballot did not infringe the Convention. It was 'not a significant limitation on the right to take collective action' but it might become so if there was evidence that an anti-union employer would use the information to put pressure on employees not to participate in a ballot or to vote in a particular way in the ballot.

Right to take industrial action

There is also no general right to strike guaranteed by the Convention. This was the clear conclusion reached by the Court in *Schmidt and Dahlstrom* v *Sweden* (1979–80). This case concerned collective bargaining practices in Sweden. In the event that national pay negotiations continued beyond the date on which the annual pay increase was due to take effect, the normal practice was to give retroactive effect to the pay increase when it was finally agreed. However, it was a principle of the system that the members of any union which chose to strike during this period would automatically forfeit the right to benefit from this retroactive effect.

The applicants in *Schmidt and Dahlstrom* claimed that this practice violated their rights under art. 11. However, the Court found against them. It reasoned that the right to strike was not inherent in the right to freedom of association, and accordingly the State was free to restrict the right to strike as it saw fit.

Inducement not to belong to a union

The European Court of Human Rights decided in *Wilson and the NUJ; Palmer, Wyeth and the RMT; Doolan and others* v *United Kingdom* (2002) that the failure of the UK to outlaw a practice whereby employers could offer financial inducements to employees not to belong to a union, or members to withdraw their membership, was a breach of art. 11. The consequence of this was Employment Relations Act 2004, s. 29 amending TULR(C)A 1992, s. 145, making such inducements unlawful. (See further on the decision in *Wilson and Palmer*, Ewing, [2003] 32 ILJ 1.)

16.4.8 Article 14: discrimination

Under art. 14 of the Convention:

The enjoyment of the rights and freedoms set forth in this Convention shall be secured without discrimination on any ground such as sex, race, colour, language, religion, political or other opinion, national or social origin, association with a national minority, property, birth or other status.

This article is an unusual provision, narrower in some important respects than might be anticipated but wider than the national law in the variety of statuses which are prohibited as grounds for discrimination. It does not prohibit discrimination by public bodies; rather, it prohibits public bodies from discriminating on the above grounds (which includes the vague ground 'status') when complying with other Convention requirements. In that sense it is dependent on the other rights; there need be no breach of the particular article but the allegation must come within the ambit of one of them. A key example of the operation of this aspect was *Abdulaziz Cabales & Balkandali* v *United Kingdom* (1985). The applicants were lawfully and permanently settled in the UK. They complained that their husbands were refused permission to join them. There was no breach of art. 8 alone but there was breach of art. 14 in conjunction with art. 8. Although it was legitimate to restrict admission of non-national spouses to the UK, it was not legitimate to distinguish between non-national spouses of males (who were permitted entry) and non-national spouses of females (who were not).

The use of the words 'such as' and 'other status' indicates that the categories of prohibited discrimination are not closed; they include sexual orientation, marital status, military status, status as a trade union, and imprisonment.

Further, art. 14 covers a much wider range of subject areas than does domestic law which is restricted to discrimination in employment, education, and the provision of goods and services.

Unlike as a matter of domestic law, discrimination under this article can be justified by an 'objective and reasonable justification' for the different treatment. This depends on the aim and effect of the measure; whether there is a reasonable relationship of proportionality between the means employed and the aims sought to be realised. (See further, Baker, [2006] *Public Law* 476.)

Discrimination on some grounds may be sufficiently serious to be inhuman and degrading treatment under art. 3.

See further, on the potential of art. 14 as an important source of anti-discrimination protection, O'Connell, (2009) 29 OJLS 211.

SELECTED READING

Allen, R., Beale, A. and Crasnow, R. (2007), *Employment Law and Human Rights*, 2nd edn, Oxford: Oxford University Press, 2007

Alston, P. (ed.) (2005), *Labour Rights as Human Rights,* Oxford: Oxford University Press

Fredman, S. (2008), *Human Rights Transformed: Positive Rights and Positive Duties*, Oxford: Oxford University Press, 2008

Hendy, J. and Ewing, K. (2005), 'Trade Unions, Human Rights and the BNP', (2005) 34 ILJ 197

Ovey, C. and White, R. (2006), *Jacobs and White: The European Convention on Human Rights,* 4th edn, Oxford: Oxford University Press

INDEX